Foreign Relations
of the
United States
Diplomatic Papers
1942
(In Seven Volumes)

Volume V
The American Republics

United States
Government Printing Office
Washington : 1962

DEPARTMENT OF STATE PUBLICATION 7373

HISTORICAL OFFICE
BUREAU OF PUBLIC AFFAIRS

For sale by the
Superintendent of Documents, U.S. Government Printing Office
Washington 25, D.C. - Price $3.00 (Buckram)

PREFACE

The principles which guide the compilation and editing of *Foreign Relations* are stated in Department of State Regulation 045 of December 5, 1960, a revision of the order approved on March 26, 1925, by Mr. Frank B. Kellogg, then Secretary of State. The text of the current regulation is printed below:

045 DOCUMENTARY RECORD OF AMERICAN DIPLOMACY

045.1 *Scope of Documentation*

The publication *Foreign Relations of the United States, Diplomatic Papers*, constitutes the official record of the foreign policy of the United States. These volumes include, subject to necessary security considerations, all documents needed to give a comprehensive record of the major foreign policy decisions within the range of the Department of State's responsibilities, together with appropriate materials concerning the facts which contributed to the formulation of policies. When further material is needed to supplement the documentation in the Department's files for a proper understanding of the relevant policies of the United States, such papers should be obtained from other Government agencies.

045.2 *Editorial Preparation*

The basic documentary diplomatic record to be printed in *Foreign Relations of the United States, Diplomatic Papers*, shall be edited by the Historical Office, Bureau of Public Affairs. The editing of the record shall be guided by the principles of historical objectivity. There shall be no alteration of the text, no deletions without indicating where in the text the deletion is made, and no omission of facts which were of major importance in reaching a decision. Nothing shall be omitted for the purpose of concealing or glossing over what might be regarded by some as a defect of policy. However, certain omissions of documents or parts of documents are permissible for the following reasons:

   a. To avoid publication of matters which would tend to impede current diplomatic negotiations or other business.
   b. To condense the record and avoid repetition of needless details.
   c. To preserve the confidence reposed in the Department by individuals and by foreign governments.
   d. To avoid giving needless offense to other nationalities or individuals.
   e. To eliminate personal opinions presented in despatches and not acted upon by the Department. To this consideration there is one qualification—in connection with major decisions it is desirable, where possible, to show the alternatives presented to the Department before the decision was made.

III

045.3 *Clearance*

To obtain appropriate clearances of material to be published in *Foreign Relations of the United States, Diplomatic Papers*, the Historical Office shall:

> *a.* Refer to the appropriate policy offices of the Department and of other agencies of the Government such papers as appear to require policy clearance.
>
> *b.* Refer to the appropriate foreign governments requests for permission to print as part of the diplomatic correspondence of the United States those previously unpublished documents which were originated by the foreign governments.

The responsibilities of the Historical Office, Bureau of Public Affairs for the preparation of this *Foreign Relations* volume were entrusted, under the general supervision of the Director of the Office, G. Bernard Noble, to the Foreign Relations staff under the direction of the Officer in Charge of the Foreign Relations Series (Editor of *Foreign Relations*), E. R. Perkins. *Foreign Relations*, 1942, Volume V, The American Republics was compiled by Almon R. Wright.

The Division of Publishing Services is responsible with respect to *Foreign Relations* for the editing of copy, proofreading, and preparation of indexes. Under the general direction of the Chief of the Division, Norris E. Drew, the editorial functions mentioned above are performed by the Foreign Relations Editing Branch in charge of Elizabeth A. Vary, Chief, and Ouida J. Ward, Assistant Chief.

For 1942, the arrangement of volumes is as follows: Volume I, General, The British Commonwealth, the Far East; Volume II, Europe; Volume III, Europe; Volume IV, The Near East and Africa; Volume V, The American Republics; Volume VI, The American Republics. The *Foreign Relations* series for 1942 also includes the unnumbered volume on 1942, China, previously published.

E. R. Perkins
Editor of Foreign Relations

March 5, 1962.

CONTENTS

ESTABLISHMENT OF THE INTER-AMERICAN COMMISSION FOR TERRITORIAL ADMINISTRATION OF EUROPEAN COLONIES AND POSSESSIONS IN THE AMERICAS [1]

710.Consultation (2)A/47

Memorandum by the Chief of the Division of International Conferences (Kelchner) [2]

[WASHINGTON,] February 17, 1942.

I have had further discussions with the Pan American Union concerning the status of the membership of the Inter-American Commission for Territorial Administration of European Colonies and Possessions in the Americas. The Emergency Committee provided by the Act of Habana [3] was "Constituted" on October 24, 1940, when the fourteenth American republic appointed its representative.

The Convention on the Provisional Administration of European Colonies and Possessions in the Americas [4] became effective on January 8, 1942, when two thirds of the American republics had deposited their respective instruments of ratification. The question arises as to whether the members of the "Emergency Committee" shall constitute the "Inter-American Commission for Territorial Administration" as established by the convention. Neither the convention nor the Act of Habana is clear on this point, although the Act of Habana does state that "as soon as the convention comes into effect, the authority and functions exercised by the committee (Emergency) shall be transferred to the Inter-American Commission for Territorial Administration". The governments appointed their respective members on the Emergency Committee and no appointments have been made specifically to the Commission under the convention. I think there can

---

[1] For previous correspondence, see *Foreign Relations*, 1940, vol. v, pp. 341 ff.

[2] Addressed to the Acting Chief of the Division of the American Republics (Bonsal), to the Adviser on Political Relations (Duggan), and to the Under Secretary of State (Welles).

[3] Provisional Administration of European Colonies and Possessions in the Americas, Act of Habana, contained in the Final Act of the Second Meeting of Ministers of Foreign Affairs of the American Republics, signed at Habana July 30, 1940; Department of State Executive Agreement Series No. 199; 54 Stat. (pt. 2) 2491.

[4] Signed at Habana, July 30, 1940; for text, see Department of State Treaty Series No. 977, or 56 Stat. (pt. 2) 1273.

be no question but that it was the general intention to have the Emergency Committee merge into the Commission when the convention became effective, although no definite provision is made for that transfer.

All of the governments which have ratified, except Argentina and Colombia, have already designated their representatives on the Emergency Committee. Bolivia, Cuba, Mexico, and Nicaragua have designated members on the Emergency Committee but have not yet ratified the convention. (There is attached herewith a list of the members of the Emergency Committee and also a list of the ratifications of the convention.)[5]

Under the circumstances it would seem advisable for the Governing Board of the Pan American Union to take cognizance of this situation and at its meeting next week take action which will make definitive the establishment of the Inter-American Commission for Territorial Administration. Dr. Manger[6] and I have discussed the procedure, and the most feasible solution would seem to be the Governing Board to adopt a resolution calling upon each member government which has ratified the convention to inform the Pan American Union prior to a definite date (in the near future) of its representative in case it wished to designate a representative on the Commission who is other than its representative on the Emergency Committee. This action has the advantage of not endeavoring to interpret the terms of the convention or to commit any government, since it is doubtful whether the Governing Board has the authority to do either of these things. It would have the advantage, however, of establishing definitively the membership of the Commission by placing the responsibility upon each government to take positive action prior to a certain date. I have discussed this procedure with Mr. Barnes[7] of TD, who agrees.

If you agree, Dr. Rowe[8] might request the Cuban Ambassador to present the matter to the Governing Board since the convention and the act were adopted at Habana. I shall be glad to have your views on the proposed solution as soon as possible so that the Pan American Union may be informed accordingly.

WARREN KELCHNER

---

[5] Neither printed.
[6] William Manger, Counselor of the Pan American Union.
[7] Charles M. Barnes, Chief of the Treaty Division.
[8] Leo S. Rowe, Director General of the Pan American Union.

710.Consultation (2)A/47

Memorandum by the Acting Chief of the Division of the American Republics (Bonsal) [9]

[WASHINGTON,] February 19, 1942.

RA [10] concurs in Dr. Kelchner's proposal for establishing the Inter-American Commission for Territorial Administration (under the Convention of Habana) as set forth in his attached memorandum.[11]

It is worth noting that the following republics which have designated members for the Emergency Committee (Under the Act of Habana) have not yet ratified the Convention and therefore are not entitled to designate representatives to sit on the Commission:

> Bolivia
> Cuba
> Nicaragua.

The following republics have neither ratified the Convention nor designated representatives to sit on the Emergency Committee:

> Chile
> Paraguay
> Uruguay.

The passage in the Convention of Habana which provides for the creation of the Commission reads as follows:

"A commission to be known as the 'Inter-American Commission for Territorial Administration' is hereby established, to be composed of a representative from each one of the States which ratifies this convention; it shall be the international organization to which this convention refers. Once this convention has become effective, any country which ratifies it may convoke the first meeting proposing the city in which it is to be held. The Commission shall elect its chairman, complete its organization and fix its definitive seat."

The question of whether it would be desirable to convoke a meeting of the Commission appears to depend largely on the status of relations with the Vichy Government.

NOTE: RA understands that the Mexican Government ratified the Convention last month, though its instrument of ratification has not yet been deposited with the Pan American Union.

PHILIP W. BONSAL

---

[9] Addressed to the Adviser on Political Relations (Duggan) and to the Under Secretary of State (Welles).
[10] Division of the American Republics.
[11] *Supra.*

710.Consultation (2)A/50

Memorandum by the Adviser on Political Relations (Duggan) to the Under Secretary of State (Welles)

[Washington,] April 14, 1942.

Mr. Welles: The Inter-American Commission for Territorial Administration may now be convened at any moment by any country adhering to the Habana Convention, as a result of the approval voted by the Governing Board of the Pan American Union at its last meeting of a resolution interpreting the Convention to provide that the Emergency Committee (Act of Habana) automatically becomes the Commission for Territorial Administration (Convention of Habana).

Laurence Duggan

710.Consultation (2)A/51

The Director General of the Pan American Union (Rowe) to the Secretary of State

Washington, April 15, 1942.

My Dear Mr. Secretary: I beg to send you herewith a copy of the resolution on the Inter-American Commission for Territorial Administration, approved by the Governing Board of the Pan American Union at the session held on April 6, 1942.

The Government of the United States has already ratified the Convention on the Provisional Administration of European Colonies and Possessions in the Americas, and has designated its representative on the Inter-American Commission for Territorial Administration. For your information, however, I am attaching hereto a statement [12] on the present status of the Convention.

I beg to remain [etc.]

L. S. Rowe

[Enclosure]

Resolution on the Inter-American Commission for Territorial Administration Approved by the Governing Board of the Pan American Union at the Session Held on April 6, 1942

The Second Meeting of the Ministers of Foreign Affairs of the American Republics held at Habana in July 1940 adopted the "Act of Habana" concerning the Provisional Administration of European Colonies and Possessions in the Americas. At the same time there was signed the "Convention on the Provisional Administration of European Colonies and Possessions in the Americas", to come into effect when two-thirds of the American Republics should have deposited their respective instruments of ratification.

---

[12] Not printed.

The Act of Havana created an Emergency Committee, composed of one representative of each of the American Republics. It was further stipulated that the powers and functions of this Emergency Committee should be transferred to the "Inter-American Commission for Territorial Administration" as soon as the Convention should come into effect.

The Convention has been ratified and the respective instruments of ratification deposited by fourteen, or two-thirds of the signatory Governments and consequently has become effective. While it is clear that the authority and functions of the Emergency Committee, set up under the Act of Habana, shall be transferred to the Inter-American Commission for Territorial Administration provided for in the Convention, it is not clear whether the members appointed to serve on the Emergency Committee also shall be considered as members of the Commission for Territorial Administration.

With a view to clarifying the question thus presented it is recommended that the following interpretation and resolution be adopted by the Governing Board:

1. That until the respective Governments shall communicate to the Pan American Union the name of another representative, the member designated to serve on the Emergency Committee created by the Act of Habana shall be considered to be a member of the Inter-American Commission for Territorial Administration.

2. That the Governments which have ratified the Convention, but have not named a representative on the Emergency Committee or the Inter-American Commission for Territorial Administration, be urged to designate their member on the latter Commission as soon as possible.

3. That those Governments that have not yet ratified the Convention on the Provisional Administration of European Colonies and Possessions in the Americas be urged to give early consideration to such ratification.

4. That the representatives of those Governments that have not yet ratified the Convention but have appointed members on the Emergency Committee, be considered as eligible to attend any meetings that may be held by the Inter-American Commission for Territorial Administration pending ratification of the Convention by their respective Governments.

5. That the Government which desires to convene the Commission, as provided for in the Convention, shall communicate this desire to the Pan American Union, indicating the city in which the meeting is to be held, and the Union shall notify the members of the Commission and shall inform all the other States, parties to the Convention.

THIRD MEETING OF THE FOREIGN MINISTERS OF THE AMERICAN REPUBLICS, HELD AT RIO DE JANEIRO, JANUARY 15–28, 1942 [1]

710.Consultation (3)/105 : Telegram

The Secretary of State to the Ambassador in Chile (Bowers) [2]

WASHINGTON, December 25, 1941—3 p. m.

633. The Department is advised that the Minister of Foreign Affairs of Argentina [3] expects to have conferences with the Ministers of Foreign Affairs of Chile,[4] Paraguay,[5] Bolivia,[6] and possibly Peru [7] on their way through Buenos Aires to the meeting of Foreign Ministers in Rio [8] with a view to securing their support of the "Argentine position".

Although the Department does not yet have any precise information as to the "Argentine position" recent indications of Argentine policy would appear to leave considerable room for its modification until it comes up to the level toward which the policy of the countries which have not yet declared war or broken off relations seems to be evolving.

Accordingly you are instructed to find some appropriate opening for suggesting to the Foreign Minister that since there are a number of projects, resolutions, and policies now under consideration by the Governments of the American Republics he may wish to defer taking any position with respect to them, at least in a definitive way, prior to the convening of the conference and until an opportunity has been afforded of learning fully there the views of all the other Governments.

HULL

---

[1] Continued from *Foreign Relations*, 1941, vol. VI; see also Pan American Union, Congress and Conference Series No. 36: *Report on the Third Meeting of the Ministers of Foreign Affairs of the American Republics, Rio de Janeiro, January 15–28, 1942* (Washington, 1942). For lists of printed materials on the Conference, see Pan American Union, *Bibliografía de las Conferencias Interamericanas* (Washington, 1954), pp. 221 ff.

[2] Repeated on the same date as telegram No. 553 to the Ambassador in Peru, No. 155 to the Minister in Paraguay, and No. 278 to the Chargé in Bolivia.

[3] Enrique Ruiz Guiñazú.

[4] Juan Rossetti.

[5] Luis A. Argaña.

[6] Eduardo Anze Matienzo.

[7] Alfredo Solf y Muro.

[8] For the membership of the American delegation to the Conference, see Department of State *Bulletin*, January 3, 1942, p. 12.

710.Consultation 3/130 : Telegram

The Ambassador in Chile (Bowers) to the Secretary of State

SANTIAGO, December 29, 1941—1 p. m.
[Received 4 : 20 p. m.]

837. For the Under Secretary. Rossetti asks me to request that you see him before opening session. Am warning him subtly as possible about commitments en route. Mexican Ambassador showed me cable from his Government expressing concern over fact most Foreign Ministers will have 3 or 4 days with element that was not helpful at Lima [9] and Habana.[10]

BOWERS

710.Consultation 3/133 : Telegram

The Ambassador in Brazil (Caffery) to the Secretary of State

RIO DE JANEIRO, December 29, 1941—2 p. m.
[Received 4 : 12 p. m.]

2224. For the Under Secretary. My telegram No. 2223, December 29, 1 p. m.[11] Aranha [12] observed also, "You can tell Welles that I shall be whole heartedly with him at the conference on every question except one; and that is the blacklist.[13] The British handle their blacklist in such a way as not to offend us. Your publication of the blacklists et cetera, has caused me personally no end of trouble".

CAFFERY

710.Consultation (3)/138 : Telegram

The Ambassador in Chile (Bowers) to the Secretary of State

SANTIAGO, December 30, 1941—3 p. m.
[Received December 31—1 : 51 a. m.]

849. For the Under Secretary. . . . He [Rossetti] asked again that you see him before opening session to give him the opportunity to give you the Chilean outlook. He hopes that no resolutions, to which all the American nations cannot agree for reasons peculiar to their own situations, will be introduced since this might indicate to the public a divergence that would be unfortunate. He referred to the Central

---

[9] Eighth International Conference of American States, December 1938. For correspondence, see *Foreign Relations*, 1938, vol. v, pp. 1 ff.

[10] Second Meeting of the Foreign Ministers of the American Republics, July 1940. For correspondence, see *ibid.*, 1940, vol. v, pp. 180 ff.

[11] Not printed.

[12] Oswaldo Aranha, Brazilian Minister for Foreign Affairs.

[13] For correspondence on the Proclaimed List, see pp. 280 ff.

American Declarations of War.[15] I gave him the impression that you are counting heavily on Aranha and himself which pleased him. I think that is what he wants and I hope you will see him and give him time to describe the Chilean situation since I feel positive that he is most eager to please us in every way at Rio.

Your telegram No. 631, December 24, midnight.[16]

2. He says that this is a general policy and that he wants no more Japanese, including diplomats, coming to Chile. The only exception would be should a Japanese diplomat be transferred to the Legation here who has not been declared *persona non grata* by any American country.

3. Your telegram No. 637 [*638*], December 27, 7 p. m.,[17] last paragraph. He says I misunderstood him and that he did not request our reaction as he knew what it must be, and that he delayed his answer to the Japanese Minister pending the restoration to the banks of the money withdrawn by Japanese. Under no circumstances would he think of taking over the interests of the Japanese in any American country. In this connection he says Chile's Minister in Tokyo is practically a prisoner and held incommunicado as are all the American diplomats, and that he is sending for the Japanese Minister to demand an explanation and in the event this is unsatisfactory he is determined to accord similar treatment to him and his staff. He says the relations of Chile with Japan are at the breaking point.

4. He admitted for the first time that there is a possibility that he may not be Minister after the new President [18] comes in and says electoral situation is very confused though he is confident the Lefts will win. He says he is anxious to have Chile's policy as it relates to the war made definite and so written in the record that any successor would find it painfully embarrassing to deviate from it one hair's breadth.

BOWERS

710.Consultation (3)/130 : Telegram

The Secretary of State to the Ambassador in Chile (Bowers)

WASHINGTON, December 30, 1941—7 p. m.

646. From the Under Secretary. Your 837, December 29, 1 p. m. Please tell the Foreign Minister that I deeply appreciate his message.

---

[15] The Dominican delegation sponsored a proposal for a joint declaration of war. The reaction of the Central American nations seemed to be favorable but the South American countries were not inclined to support the proposal.

[16] Not printed; this telegram asked whether it was Chilean policy to invalidate visas of all Japanese, including diplomats (825.111/100a).

[17] Not printed; the Department indicated in this telegram that it deplored the idea that any of the American Republics might take over the interests of an Axis embassy or legation (740.0011 Pacific War/1427).

[18] Juan Antonio Ríos.

Tell him that I expect to reach Rio de Janeiro in the late afternoon of January 12 and that I trust I may have the privilege of conferring with him immediately after my arrival. I hope that his plans contemplate his arrival in Rio de Janeiro in sufficient time in advance of the opening of the Conference to permit me to have this opportunity.

I received today your personal letter of December 23.[19] I shall bear fully in mind the very helpful suggestions you have made.

I am contemplating asking the Chilean Government to adopt as of its own initiative a project of resolution which we are now completing for presentation at the Rio Conference. This proposed resolution provides for the convoying of merchant vessels of the American Republics and for the setting up of inter-American defense machinery. It is in accordance with one of the suggestions advanced by the Chilean Government for inclusion in the agenda for the Conference. I shall cable you the text of it as soon as it is completed and I will likewise give the Chilean Ambassador here a copy thereof. I suggest however that you make no mention of this until receipt of my further cable on this subject.[20] [Welles.]

HULL

710.Consultation (3)/143 : Telegram

The Ambassador in Brazil (Caffery) to the Secretary of State

RIO DE JANEIRO, December 31, 1941—3 p. m.
[Received 3 : 21 p. m.]

2250. Aranha showed me telegrams this morning from his Missions in Peru, Chile, Paraguay and Bolivia replying to telegrams from him instructing them to do their best to keep those countries from lining up with the Argentine in any anti-United States move at the approaching Conference. The telegrams were all in an optimistic vein as to the result of their effort.

CAFFERY

740.0011 European War 1939/18087 : Telegram

The Secretary of State to the Ambassador in Uruguay (Dawson)

WASHINGTON, January 1, 1942—3 p. m.

1. From the Under Secretary. Your 594, December 31, 3 p. m.[21] Please tell Dr. Guani[22] with what great satisfaction I am looking forward to having the privilege of being associated with him at the

---

[19] Not found in Department files.
[20] No further cable on this subject found in Department files.
[21] Not printed.
[22] Alberto Guani, Uruguayan Minister for Foreign Affairs.

Rio meeting. His presence there will be of the greatest value in achieving results beneficial to the cause of inter-American solidarity in these critical times.

Please tell him also that as always this Government desires to work in the closest cooperation with the Government of Uruguay at the approaching meeting. To this Government, the main issue presented to the American Republics in the emergency now existing, and in view of the fact that 10 of the 21 republics have declared war upon the Axis powers and 3 others have severed all relations with those powers, is whether the practical solidarity for which Uruguay and the United States have worked so hard during these past 9 years is to be a reality or not.

In the opinion of this Government the continued functioning of the Axis diplomatic and consular establishments in the Western Hemisphere creates under present conditions the gravest danger to the security of all of the republics and to the ability of the American governments to take necessary and adequate measures of defense. It is well known that Axis consular officials are reporting continuously on the movements of ships and on defense preparations. It is likewise notorious that the Axis diplomatic missions are engaging in every type of subversive activity and are intervening in the most blatant manner in the purely internal and domestic concerns of the countries where they are stationed in order to foment internal discord and to promote the existence of conditions which are in the highest degree prejudicial to the security of us all. With that in mind, this Government has under consideration the urgent need for the adoption of a resolution couched more or less in the following terms:

"WHEREAS: The American Republics in the 'Declaration of Lima' [23] proclaimed their determination to make effective their continental solidarity in case the peace, security, or territorial integrity of any American Republic is threatened;

The Ministers of Foreign Affairs of the American Republics at Habana declared that any attempt on the part of a non-American state against the integrity or inviolability of the territory, the sovereignty or the political independence of an American state would be considered as an act of aggression against the other American states;

The concerted plans for world conquest on the part of the Governments of Germany, Italy, and Japan, members of the Tripartite Pact, have now suddenly been placed in execution against the Western Hemisphere through the treacherous attack committed by Japan upon the United States and by the declaration of war immediately thereafter against the United States by the Governments of Germany and of Italy.

---

[23] Declaration of the Principles of the Solidarity of America, approved December 24, 1938, *Report of the Delegation of the United States of America to the Eighth International Conference of American States, Lima, Peru, December 9–27, 1938* (Washington, Government Printing Office, 1941), p. 189.

The Third Meeting of the Ministers of Foreign Affairs of the American Republics

RESOLVES: First. The American Republics declare that they regard these acts of aggression against one of the American Republics as acts of aggression against all of them and as an immediate threat to the liberty and independence of the Western Hemisphere.

Second. The American Republics reaffirm their complete unity and their determination to cooperate closely for their mutual protection until the existing menace has been totally destroyed.

Third. They have determined that those non-American states at war with nations in the Western Hemisphere have forfeited all right to treatment as nations with which friendly relations can be continued.

Fourth. Consequently, they announce that by reason of their solidarity and for the purpose of protecting and preserving the freedom and integrity of the twenty-one Republics of the Americas, relations, whether political, commercial, or financial, can no longer be maintained by any of them with Germany, Italy, and Japan, and they likewise declare that, with full respect for their respective sovereignty, they will individually or collectively take such further steps for the defense of the New World as may in each instance seem to them desirable and practicable."

Please ask Dr. Guani to regard this draft as confidential and as preliminary and say that I shall be most grateful if he would let me have, through you, as soon as possible his opinion with regard thereto and any suggestions or counter-proposals which he would care to make. It is my present impression that this draft would receive the support of the overwhelming majority of the American governments. [Welles.]

HULL

740.0011 European War 1939/18138: Telegram

The Ambassador in Uruguay (Dawson) to the Secretary of State

MONTEVIDEO, January 2, 1942—4 p. m.
[Received January 2—3:34 p.m.]

1. Department's telegram No. 1 of January 1. Personal for the Under Secretary. Your message and draft were communicated to Guani this morning. He reciprocates your sentiments and authorizes me to inform you that he is in complete agreement with the draft, that he will support the proposal and that if so desired he would even be prepared to present the proposal. He added that the President [24] is also in agreement.

In the same conversation Guani remarked that he would proceed as planned with his proposal for the extension of non-belligerent treatment to British vessels. Referring to our readiness to support the

---

[24] Alfredo Baldomir.

proposal, which I had conveyed to him several days ago in compliance with the Department's telegram 380 of December 7 [*27*],[25] he said that he would appreciate any advance assistance we can give him in marshaling support.

DAWSON

710.Consultation (3)/188 : Telegram

The Ambassador in Argentina (Armour) to the Secretary of State

BUENOS AIRES, January 2, 1942—5 p. m.
[Received 6 : 55 p. m.]

3. Both the British Embassy and ourselves are of the opinion that measures taken by Argentine port authorities to prevent acts of sabotage leave much to be desired due largely to inadequate number of surveillance personnel, the authorities themselves stating that funds appropriated by the Congress for this purpose are insufficient. It is our belief that this situation might be corrected if action could be taken at the Rio de Janeiro Conference to ensure adoption of adequate anti-sabotage measures by all of the American Republics.[26]

ARMOUR

710.Consultation (3)/194 : Telegram

The Ambassador in Uruguay (Dawson) to the Secretary of State

MONTEVIDEO, January 3, 1942—6 p. m.
[Received 7 : 05 p. m.]

6. Guani expressed the opinion to Chapin [27] today that at Rio de Janeiro quite aside from difficulties to be anticipated from Argentina, Chile will hesitate to join in any strong stand against the Axis because of its fear of Japan. He added that according to reliable reports there is in Chile and Peru too great reluctance to take any action which might provoke Axis reprisals.

DAWSON

740.0011 European War 1939/18138 : Telegram

The Secretary of State to the Ambassador in Uruguay (Dawson)

WASHINGTON, January 3, 1942—8 p. m.

5. From the Under Secretary. Your No. 1, January 2, 4 p. m. Please inform the Minister for Foreign Affairs of the deep appreci-

---

[25] Not printed.
[26] In telegram No. 9, January 5, 5 p. m., the Secretary of State indicated to the Ambassador that this suggestion was being incorporated in a resolution to be presented at Rio de Janeiro.
[27] Selden Chapin, Assistant Chief, Division of the American Republics.

ation of this Government and of myself personally for the message he has sent me.

Please state also that this Government will do everything possible to marshal support for the Uruguay proposal to which reference is made in the second paragraph of your telegram under acknowledgment. [Welles.]

HULL

710.Consultation (3)/18 : Telegram

The Secretary of State to the Ambassador in Colombia (Braden)

WASHINGTON, January 4, 1942—2 p. m.

10. From the Under Secretary. Your 9, January 3, 10 p. m.[28] I handed to the Colombian Ambassador [29] 4 days ago a draft resolution providing for the breaking of all relations between all of the American Republics and the Axis powers which this Government hopes will be unanimously adopted at the Rio de Janeiro Conference. The Ambassador has informed me that his Government will of course be wholly in accord with this resolution.

It is my further belief that this resolution will be supported, in addition to the 10 Republics which have declared war and the 3 Republics which have already broken all relations, by the Governments of Brazil, Uruguay, Bolivia, Ecuador, and Peru. It is my further belief that Paraguay will support any position which may be taken by Brazil.

I am as yet uncertain of the position which will be taken by Chile and it is my understanding that the Chilean Government, being fearful of its long and relatively unprotected coastline, may hesitate against taking any action against the Axis powers unless all of the other American Republics insist that such action as that above indicated be unanimously taken.

With regard to the position of Argentina, I am as yet uncertain. As you know, the Argentine people in their vast majority seem to be strongly opposed to the hesitant course so far followed by their Government. I am inclined to believe however that Argentina will not permit herself to be placed in a minority of one at the meeting, even on an issue of this fundamental character.

It may be wiser for you to speak directly with President Santos with regard to the above than with the Foreign Minister.[30] Please state that this Government will appreciate any assistance and support which Colombia can afford prior to the Conference in urging the

---

[28] Not printed; it indicated that Colombia would support the United States at Rio de Janeiro (706.6535/18).
[29] Gabriel Turbay.
[30] Luis Lopez de Mesa.

Chilean and Argentine Governments' support for the steps contemplated in the resolution in question.   [Welles.]

HULL

710.Consultation (3)/209 : Telegram

The Minister in the Dominican Republic (Scotten) to the Secretary of State

CIUDAD TRUJILLO, January 5, 1942—noon.
[Received 5 : 53 p. m.]

3. Referring to the Department's number 4 January 3, 8 [7] p. m.[31] The Minister for Foreign Affairs [32] has asked me to inform the Department that he greatly appreciates its views as expressed in the telegram under reference and that the Dominican delegation at the Conference will act accordingly.   He assured me that the program of the Dominican delegation has been drawn up with a view to flexibility . . .

The Department will be interested in the following declaration given by Trujillo [33] in a press interview last night and published in the papers this morning.

"Our Secretary of State for Foreign Affairs will attend the Conference at Rio de Janeiro; he will take with him among the projects which our Government proposes to submit to the consideration of that meeting, one by which all the nations of the American continent are invited to declare war jointly against the signatory nations of the Tripartite Pact".[34]

SCOTTEN

710.Consultation (3)/212 : Telegram

The Chargé in Bolivia (Dawson) to the Secretary of State

LA PAZ, January 5, 1942—5 p. m.
[Received 9 : 05 p. m.]

7. For the Under Secretary.   Minister of Foreign Affairs tells me that his reports indicate Argentine resistance to strong action at Rio de Janeiro Conference and increasing Chilean uneasiness about going the whole way.   He asserts, however, that he will cooperate with the United States thoroughly at the meeting and will support

---

[31] Not printed; in this telegram the Department expressed its approval of a Dominican-sponsored resolution calling for a joint declaration of war by the American Republics against the Axis (710.Consultation (3)/149).

[32] Arturo Despradel.

[33] Rafael Leonidas Trujillo Molina, President of the Dominican Republic.

[34] Three-Power Pact between Japan, Germany, and Italy, signed at Berlin, September 27, 1940; for text, see League of Nations Treaty Series, vol. CCIV, p. 386.

any decisions which the bulk of the American Republics may reach. While Bolivian cooperation has been so far purely lip service, I feel that if Rio de Janeiro meeting defines situation we can by tactful pressure probably secure action particularly in controlling German interests in Bolivia.

DAWSON

710.Consultation (3)/222 : Telegram

The Ambassador in Colombia (Braden) to the Secretary of State

BOGOTÁ, January 5, 1942—6 p. m.
[Received January 6—12 : 16 a. m.]

16. For the Under Secretary. Your telegram No. 10, January 4, 2 p. m. I know the President will greatly appreciate the information you have sent me and which I will convey to him as soon as possible after his return to town on January 7. On January 2 Santos referring to the draft resolution said that of course Colombia would strongly support it in every way but he felt it would be more effective if boiled down to only a concise resolution by all the Republics to break relations. He added that the Colombian delegation would wish to help us in every way at Rio.

The Secretary General of the Foreign Office when he gave me copy of aforementioned resolution expressed his personal opinion that Argentina had been frightened by it and therefore had accepted the representation of Italy in order to use it at Rio as an estoppel to her agreeing to break relations.

BRADEN

710.Consultation 3/219 : Telegram

The Ambassador in Brazil (Caffery) to the Secretary of State

RIO DE JANEIRO, January 5, 1942—9 p. m.
[Received January 6—2 : 15 a. m.]

46. Department's telegram 27, January 4, 3 p. m.[35] Aranha believes he can handle Chile and Uruguay although Rodrigues Alves [36] is not so optimistic; he says that Chile is fearful of Japanese aggressions; they are much worried over newspaper reports from our Pacific coast regarding blackouts and alleged plans for evacuation, etc. Rodrigues Alves related some conversations he had with Guiñazú who made it plain that he will oppose efforts to break off Axis relations. Rodrigues Alves suggests that in order to attract the Argentine,

---

[35] Not printed.
[36] Brazilian Ambassador in Argentina and General Secretary of the Third Meeting of Foreign Ministers of the American Republics.

the matter might be approached in this way; a resolution be introduced setting out that the following acts shall be considered definite acts of aggression against the American Republics:

1. The sinking of a vessel within a prescribed maritime zone;
2. Any Axis military activity in northwest Africa;
3. Any act on the part of an Axis diplomatic or consular official against the sovereignty or integrity of an American country.

CAFFERY

710.Consultation (3)/435

The Ambassador in Argentina (Armour) to the Secretary of State

No. 3823   BUENOS AIRES, January 5, 1942.
                                           [Received January 21.]

SIR: I have the honor to submit the following observations with regard to the general attitude and position which the Argentine Delegation may be expected to take at the Rio de Janeiro Conference. These observations are based upon conversations with various Argentines, in and out of the Government, as well as officers of the Army and Navy and certain of my diplomatic colleagues.

POLITICAL

Unless some important event should occur in the meantime to change the international situation, it appears virtually certain that the Argentine Government will not agree at Rio de Janeiro to consider declaring war on the Axis Powers. The suggestion to that effect already communicated to the Government here by the Dominican Republic has not been favorably considered and while so far as can be learned no official reply has been given, from talks with the Foreign Minister and other officials it seems clear that the Government is not disposed to go to such lengths. This was made clear to the Brazilian Ambassador, Dr. Rodrigues Alves, in a talk he had with the Foreign Minister just before the former left for Rio de Janeiro to take over his duties as Secretary General of the Conference (see Embassy's telegram No. 1573, of December 28 [*27*], 7 [*8*] p. m.).[38] The same decision would probably apply so far as the breaking off of diplomatic relations with the Axis Powers although being a less drastic step, this is not so certain. The fact that the recall of the German Ambassador [39] by his Government has been definitely announced as well as the withdrawal of the Argentine Ambassador in Berlin,[40] and the efforts which will be made by influential Argentines

---

[38] Not printed.
[39] Baron Edmund von Thermann.
[40] Ricardo Olivera.

to prevent successors to the above being appointed might possibly result in a situation somewhat similar to that in our own relations with Germany prior to the state of war, with Chargés d'Affaires in charge of both missions, but for the present at least, it seems doubtful whether the Government here would permit matters to proceed beyond this point. In considering both the question of declaration of war and severance of diplomatic relations, it is necessary to remember that so far as Argentina is concerned, a distinction must be drawn between the three principal Axis Powers. A declaration of war against Japan would be far easier to envisage than against Germany, and particularly Italy. As the Under Secretary for Foreign Affairs, Dr. Gache, remarked cynically in a burst of frankness, when I expressed some concern that Dr. Ruiz Guiñazú seemed more hesitant in agreeing to the decree declaring the United States would not be regarded as a belligerent following the declaration of war by Germany and Italy than he had been in the case of Japan: "You must remember that there are virtually no Japanese in the country; but there are many Germans and more Italians: that, to a politician, is important."

The clearest and most objective presentation of Argentina's position that I have yet had came from Rear Admiral Gonzalo D. Bustamante, at present in command of the River Squadron, in a recent talk when we discussed the coming conference at Rio de Janeiro. His thesis was roughly as follows:

First and most important of all, it must be remembered that the vital interests of our country call for the closest cooperation with the United States. That is the point from which any discussion of our foreign policy must begin. Aside from commitments formally taken, ideologically, geographically, economically and from the naval and military standpoint, we are bound to the United States. No other position is conceivable. Admitting this, as all serious Argentines must, let us consider our position at Rio de Janeiro. I do not believe that it is to your or to our interest that Argentina should declare war against the Axis Powers. We are not, certainly, at this time, in a position to defend ourselves if attacked. Should Brazil and Argentina declare war, the Axis Powers might well attempt to make an example of us. In such a case, could we count on assistance from the United States and Great Britain? If you attempted to help us, as we feel sure you would, it would mean further extension of your lines. Also do not forget that one fifth of our population is of "Totalitarian" origin, principally Italian. While many of the Italians are at present not Fascists, declared war against the country of their origin or of their parents would present them with a clear cut issue. Sabotage in many industries and fields of production essential to the United States might well take place. Argentina's best role for the present, I feel, is to patrol its coastal waters, to prevent enemy activities from gaining foothold on our coasts or operation within our waters; clean house within the country by putting an end to fifth column and subversive activities and cooperate fully with you in making available all supplies you need, repairing your ships if damaged on convoy or in enemy engagements, etc.

"What about breaking off diplomatic relations," I asked. "This would eliminate the heads of subversive movements and stop communications now made possible through diplomatic immunity?"

"We must weigh the advantages against the disadvantages," he replied. "I still feel that the advantages to be gained by such a step would not compensate for the disadvantages I have mentioned."

I asked him about convoy: whether it was not logical that, with our country making every effort to keep Argentina supplied with necessities, even at a sacrifice to our own people, they should at least assume part of the burden of convoy, should this step be found necessary. He hesitated. "For the moment" he said, "let us use our ships for patrol purposes. Convoy is the first step to war, and again I do not feel we are ready."

Admiral Bustamante, who has spent much time in the United States and is married to an American, represents the element in the navy more favorably disposed to the United States. Our Naval Attaché [41] informs me that he is generally considered to have the best mind among the higher naval officers. With Admirals Guisasola, Stewart, Zar, and certain others, Bustamante can, I feel, be considered to favor cooperation with us within the limits set forth.

On the other hand, Dr. Gancedo,[42] the conservative deputy who recently visited the United States and returned a firm advocate of closest cooperation with us, informs me that he has had frank talks with the Acting President,[43] with General Justo,[44] and with the Foreign Minister, and that the Government is prepared to convoy its own vessels. Furthermore he thinks that, if pressed, they might agree to participate in convoying United States ships carrying Argentine goods as far as Brazilian territorial waters, where Brazilian ships could then take up the escort. While he avoided the question of declaration of war or official severance of diplomatic relations, he believes that in all other matters we can count on Argentina's support at Rio de Janeiro. He assures me that in all his talks he has insisted that at the forthcoming conference at Rio Argentina must take the

---

[41] Capt. William D. Brereton, Jr.
[42] Deputy from the Province of Santiago del Estero in the Argentine Chamber of Deputies.
[43] Ramón S. Castillo.
[44] Gen. Agustín P. Justo, former President and Minister of War.

lead in declaring full solidarity with the United States. He it was who told me he hopes with Justo's support to prevent the appointment of a successor to Olivera, recently recalled from Berlin, and who is slated for another post. He is also working to the end that a successor to von Thermann shall not be accepted by the Argentine Government. Dr. Gancedo also informed me that Candioti [45] is not to proceed to Tokio—in other words that the post of Ambassador in Japan will be left unfilled. He . . . is planning to be in Buenos Aires during the conference and assures me that should the Argentine delegation at Rio not be disposed to cooperate he will be glad to use his influence with the Acting President, which is considerable, and with the Acting Minister for Foreign Affairs, Dr. Rothe, his closest friend in the cabinet.

So far as concerns Argentina's part in continental defense measures, it is presumed that the plan taken to Washington by the Argentine Military-Naval Mission [46] is now known to the Department. While I am not myself familiar with the plan, the Minister for Foreign Affairs intimated that it is very comprehensive and envisages cooperation particularly as regards naval defense, with the east coast republics, particularly Brazil and Uruguay, as well as with Chile in defense of the Straits. (The Argentine plan was drawn up presumably prior to the initiating by Chile of negotiations to amend the treaty of 1881 [47] to provide fortification of the Straits for the duration of the war.) The fact that our delegation does not include Naval or Military experts presumably indicates that we do not envisage at Rio discussions regarding the technical aspects of defense against external aggression.

So far as concerns measures to curb alien activities within the country, this is certainly a point on which a clear understanding with Argentina will have to be reached. Under declarations VI and VII of Habana,[48] Argentina is committed to take the necessary steps to prevent such activities. This, as the Department is aware, the Argentine Chamber of Deputies, through its Investigating Committee, has attempted to do, and so far as the work of the Committee itself was concerned, it performed a very satisfactory and thorough job.

From the outset, however, it received no assistance or cooperation from the Government. On the contrary, the Committee found itself continually blocked and hampered in its efforts, particularly by the Minister for Foreign Affairs. Without discussing the reasons for this, which lie largely in the personality of the Foreign Minister and

---

[45] Alberto Candioti, Argentine Ambassador to Colombia.
[46] See correspondence between the United States and Argentina concerning defense, pp. 371 ff.
[47] For English version of treaty, see *British and Foreign State Papers*, vol. LXXII, p. 1103.
[48] Department of State *Bulletin*, August 24, 1940, p. 132.

the narrow and provincial attitude of the Acting President in viewing the activities of the Chamber Committee merely as Radical attempts to embarrass the Government and encroaching upon the jurisdiction of the Executive, it seems probable that, unless a clear understanding is reached in Rio de Janeiro, the Government here will adopt the same attitude and obstructionist tactics in the future. As the Embassy has reported, the "State of Siege" widely heralded as designed to implement Argentina's commitments taken at Habana, particularly as regards not considering the United States as a belligerent, has thus far had little effect other than to prevent the 95 percent pro-democratic press and public from presenting or making known their viewpoint without, so far as can be seen, seriously hampering the subversive activities and insidious propaganda of the Axis Powers. It would seem clearly indicated that the declarations of Habana dealing with subversive activities [49] should be re-discussed and interpreted so clearly and unequivocally as to leave no possible room for doubt as to what are the duties assumed by each of the Republics in this respect. (The negligent attitude of the Argentine Government in permitting the escape from the country of many officers and men of the *Graf Spee* [50]—a negligence which could only be interpreted as deliberate after repeated warnings given them by the British Embassy—falls within a different category, since regardless of commitments taken at Habana, the Argentine Government's responsibilities under Neutrality required the internment or close supervision of these men.)

It would seem that if we could go further and have a clear distinction drawn between subversive alien activities and anti-democratic propaganda by the Axis Powers on the one hand and the exposition by the democratic belligerents ("democratic belligerents" to include the non-American allies of American belligerents) of their aims in the war, this might be a means of preventing the continuance of the present state of affairs in Argentina by which all the press is muzzled.

ECONOMIC

So far as concerns the questions to be considered under this heading of the agenda proposed for Rio de Janeiro,[51] there would seem to be no reason to envisage particular difficulties raised by the Argentine delegation except possibly on point 5. The Embassy, under date of December 18 last, presented to the Argentine Government a note based upon the Department's circular telegram of December

---

[49] Resolutions VI and VII.

[50] For correspondence concerning the violation of the Security Zone by this vessel, see *Foreign Relations*, 1939, vol. v, pp. 85 ff.

[51] See Department's circular telegram of December 10, 1941, 6 p.m., printed in *Foreign Relations*, 1941, vol. vi, section entitled "Third Meeting of the Foreign Ministers of the American Republics, held at Rio de Janeiro, January 15–28, 1942: Preliminaries."

15 [52] last with regard to the measures to be adopted to curb the economic and financial activities of the Axis countries (as reported in the Embassy's despatch no. 3735 of December 22, 1941 [53]). No reply has yet been received, although an early reply had been promised. On December 26, I handed an *aide-mémoire* [53] to the Under Secretary for Foreign Affairs summarizing measures of this character taken by certain other South American countries, the information having been compiled from the data contained in the Department's telegram No. 1148 of December 24.[53] Copies of the note and of the *aide-mémoire* were also given to Raúl Prebisch, General Manager of the Central Bank.

The only action which the Argentine Government or the Central Bank has thus far taken to curb financial transactions for the benefit of the Axis countries has consisted of two circulars issued by the Central Bank and dated December 11 and 22 (Nos. 262 and 264), respectively. The first of these, which was issued at the direction of the Ministry of Finance, provides for an embargo on transfers of funds to and from Japan and "freezes" accounts of funds and securities in Argentina of persons or firms domiciled in Japan (as well as prohibits deposits in such accounts), although operations may be conducted if expressly authorized by the Central Bank. The circular of December 22 purports to render more difficult the extensive practice of making transfers to certain countries of Europe and the Far East through Switzerland and other third countries.

A factor in this entire situation, of course, is that before the United States entered the war, the Central Bank had already been given a substantial control over transfers of payment to Europe and the Far East. The measures providing such control, as well as the circulars of December 11 and 22, were reported in the Embassy's despatches nos. 3744 of December 24, 1941 and 3752 of December 26, 1941.[54]

How much further the Argentine authorities will be disposed to go in curbing economic and financial activities of the Axis countries is difficult to say. An impression prevails that the Central Bank and perhaps certain persons within the Government would be willing to go at least some distance further in meeting our desiderata but that Dr. Ruiz Guiñazú is the retarding influence. It is to be recognized, however, that the large number of Italian and German nationals in Argentina present real difficulties in the formulation of

---

[52] Not printed; for efforts to control financial transactions involving the Axis, see pp. 453 ff.
[53] Not printed.
[54] Neither printed.

any measures that would pertain to internal transactions of those nationals and their business enterprises.

As to external transactions, the Embassy has continuously emphasized in conversations on the subject with the Argentine authorities that even though the Central Bank already has considerable control over such transactions, a clear-cut measure at this time that would apply specifically to Germany and Italy (as the measure of December 11 refers specifically to Japan) would have a good psychological effect, and has implied that the absence of such a measure is having a correspondingly bad effect.

The Embassy has also emphasized in these conversations that the prompt adoption of a measure of this kind could be calculated to produce a better impression abroad than would be the case if no such steps were taken before the taking of collective action at the conference at Rio de Janeiro.

As of possible interest to the Department, I am enclosing a memorandum [55] based on information given by the Paraguayan Minister to Argentina, Colonel Garay.

Respectfully yours,   NORMAN ARMOUR

710.Consultation (3)/219 : Telegram

The Secretary of State to the Ambassador in Brazil (Caffery)

WASHINGTON, January 6, 1942—10 p. m.

46. Your 46, January 5, 9 p. m. From the Under Secretary. I would appreciate your expressing appreciation to Aranha and to Rodriguez Alves for their kindness in keeping you so well informed with respect to the information they have received concerning the probable attitude at the Rio meeting of Argentina and Chile. I am sending you a separate telegram [56] with respect to the Argentine attitude as it has been conveyed to me by the Argentine Ambassador here [57] on instructions from the Foreign Minister. My information with regard to the Chilean attitude is much the same as that of Aranha and Rodriguez Alves, namely that there is indecision and timidity and some fear.

I was glad to have the suggestions of Rodriguez Alves with regard to the amplification of our proposals in order to attract the Argentines and am looking forward to discussing them with Aranha and Rodriguez Alves immediately upon my arrival in Rio. [Welles.]

HULL

---

[55] Not printed.
[56] Not printed; it was similar to telegram No. 24, January 7, 6 p.m., to the Ambassador in Argentina, p. 24.
[57] Felipe A. Espil.

710.Consultation (3)/254c: Telegram

The Secretary of State to the Ambassador in Argentina (Armour)

WASHINGTON, January 7, 1942—5 p. m.

23. From the Under Secretary. The prime objective of this Government at the Rio Conference would be to obtain a joint declaration of all the American Republics that they feel it necessary to sever all relations with the Axis powers.

It seems inconceivable in view of existing inter-American agreements, in view of the pledges of solidarity recently given and in view of the fact that 10 American Republics are now at war because of acts of aggression committed against one of them, that the territory of other American republics can continue to be used by agents diplomatic and consular of the Axis powers when the prime purpose of these agents is to instigate subversive movements, to report to their governments upon the defense measures and preparations of all of the American republics, to report upon the movements of American or Allied ships so that these may be sunk at sea, and to create a never ending threat to the security of the nations engaged in war. It seems therefore in simple terms that the action proposed would be the minimum required on the part of the Republics which have not broken relations if the term solidarity is to be anything other than an empty phrase.

For your strictly confidential and personal information I have received assurances so far from all of the Republics except Chile and Argentina that they will support the United States in this objective.

I have received word this morning from Aranha that he has come to the conclusion that it would be expedient for this Government to submit the following draft resolution to the Argentine Foreign Minister through you for the latter's information.

[Here follows text of draft resolution which is the same, except for last paragraph, here printed, as that quoted in telegram No. 1, January 1, 3 p.m., to the Ambassador in Uruguay, page 9.]

["] Fourth. Consequently, they announce that by reason of their solidarity and for the purpose of protecting and preserving the freedom and integrity of the twenty-one Republics of the Americas, relations, whether political, commercial, or financial, can no longer be maintained by any of them with Germany, Italy, and Japan, and they likewise declare that they will individually take such further steps for the defense of the New World as may in each instance seem to each of them desirable and practicable."

Please confer with the Minister before his departure and say to him after having made orally the general explanation above outlined that I am anxious that he be informed of this draft in view of the message which he was kind enough to send to me yesterday through

Espil. (This message is being reported to you in a separate telegram.[58]) On account of the very close and friendly relations between our two countries I trust that I may have the opportunity of conferring with the Minister upon this and other problems to be discussed at the Conference immediately after my arrival in Rio de Janeiro. Please report by telegram urgently any comments that may be made to you. [Welles.]

HULL

710.Consultation (3)/254b : Telegram

The Secretary of State to the Ambassador in Argentina (Armour)

WASHINGTON, January 7, 1942—6 p. m.

24. From the Under Secretary. Espil yesterday called upon me by instruction of his Government and gave me the oral message from his Foreign Minister which follows.

"We are preparing our voyage to Rio de Janeiro with the full proposal of collaboration and with the desire to act within the bounds of harmony compatible with the high interests of the nation.

We have learned of the signing in Washington of the pact of alliance of twenty-six countries of all continents to fight against the Axis.[59] Among these are numbered nine American nations who, without previous consultation, had already individually declared war and which now are entering into an alliance with non-continental nations which would not seem to be in accord with existing commitments, in particular the Declaration of Lima of 1938 and other inter-American peace agreements.

This omission exceeds any regional concept and approaches an almost universal position and in fact raises doubts as to the utility of any consultation in Rio de Janeiro. There is a certain contradiction in inviting us to participate in the study and adoption of measures of common defense at the same time that nine countries proceed without prior exchange of views in defining in absolute form their double position, intracontinental and extracontinental, with the consequent risks and responsibilities of a state of war.

The Argentine Foreign Office could not keep silent with regard to this impression since it is its intention to join in loyal application of the consultative system. It believes that a reservation is imperative in view of that decision, all the more because the pact of alliance remains open for the adherence of other countries, [not?] necessarily American. For any nation jealous of its sovereignty, the procedure which has been observed is objectionable in as much as consultation is undertaken subsequent to the resolution adopted. The system of consultation has as its object the seeking of directives

---

[58] *Infra.*
[59] For Declaration by United Nations, signed January 1, 1942, see vol. I, p. 25.

by means of the coordination of wills. In the international order, every state retains its sovereign power and international solidarity can only be admitted through free determination contemplating the gravity of existing facts and their consequences within the unity of views regarding continental defense.

Moreover, this situation is complicated in view of Article 20 of the new Regulations for the Consultative Meeting,[60] which establishes majority decisions among the votes of the countries represented in the respective session. In the situation which we are examining as a practical matter, that majority has already been anticipated in the pact of alliance, thus changing completely the exclusively American concept of solidarity.

Please bring to the knowledge of the Department of State the apprehension with which this Government views this deviation from Pan American norms of procedure according to the stipulations of the original agreements of Buenos Aires.

In taking this step, the Argentine Government desires to insure, free from any erroneous interpretations, the conception with which it will accord the Consultative Meeting at Rio de Janeiro in accordance with the continental commitments which it has undertaken and whose application, through the system of consultation, it desires to see duly discussed and agreed upon in Rio de Janeiro."

I made no official comment merely stating that I would confer with the Foreign Minister as soon as possible after I reach Rio de Janeiro. [Welles.]

HULL

710.Consultation 3/248 : Telegram

The Ambassador in Colombia (Braden) to the Secretary of State

BOGOTÁ, January 7, 1942—7 p. m.
[Received 10 : 19 p. m.]

23. For the Under Secretary. My telegram No. 18 of January 5, 11 p. m.[61] In response to my inquiry Minister of Foreign Relations this morning had no further information except his belief if [is] that resistance to a resolution calling on all American Republics to break relations with the Axis would take as juridical basis, "false though it be," the thesis that the aggression had been committed against islands outside this hemisphere.

BRADEN

---

[60] *Report on the Third Meeting of the Ministers of Foreign Affairs of the American Republics*, p. 24.
[61] Not printed.

710.Consultation (3)/314: Telegram

The American Representative to the Third Meeting of the Foreign Ministers of the American Republics (Welles) to the Secretary of State

RIO DE JANEIRO, January 14, 1942—6 p. m.

[Received 8:20 p. m.]

8. I had interviews yesterday, among others, with the Ministers for Foreign Affairs of Peru, Paraguay and Bolivia. All three delegations will support a declaration for the rupture of relations with the Axis [62] although the Peruvian Foreign Minister is obviously lacking in enthusiasm.

The Foreign Ministers of all of the Caribbean, Central American and northern South American Republics are vehemently of the opinion that the destiny of the hemisphere should not be determined by the veto power which the Argentine Government apparently desires to exercise. This tendency, of which you personally saw so much at the Lima Conference, is stronger today and is I think uncontrollable.

The Chilean, Uruguayan and Argentine Foreign Ministers arrived this morning. Aranha is still of the opinion that Argentina can be brought into line but from the public statements already made by Dr. Ruiz Guiñazú and from the intemperate declarations he has made to the Peruvian and Paraguayan Foreign Ministers, of which they informed me yesterday, I am decidedly less optimistic in this regard than Aranha.

Aranha is making every effort to force an immediate agreement for the settlement of the Peru–Ecuador boundary dispute.[63] At a conference at which he and I met yesterday with the Peruvian Foreign Minister, the latter indicated that his Government was now willing to agree to a far more equitable and generous settlement than Peru had up to now given any indication that she would be willing to accept. The Ecuadoran delegation has informed me that it will not attend the sessions of the conference unless an agreement, at least in principle, is found before the opening session tomorrow.

WELLES

---

[62] In his address at the opening session of the Conference, Under Secretary of State Welles emphasized the danger to the American Republics which lay in the ability of Axis Embassies and Consulates to communicate war information to their home offices. For text of address, see Department of State *Bulletin*, January 17, 1942, p. 55.

[63] Concerning this dispute, see bracketed note, p. 268.

710.Consultation (3)/329 : Telegram

The Ambassador in Argentina (Armour) to the Secretary of State

BUENOS AIRES, January 15, 1942.
[Received January 15—10 : 37 p. m.]

92. Following telegram sent to Rio de Janeiro, January 15, 7 p. m.

For Under Secretary Welles. The Acting Minister for Foreign Affairs has made it clear to me that the Argentine Government will not agree to break relations with any of the Axis Powers, using the same old arguments—their lack of military and naval defense which makes it impossible to take what he described as "any pre-belligerent action" that might subject them to attack by the Axis Powers. (The Acting President made the same statement to my deputy friend, adding confidentially that both army and navy are opposed to a break.) With this exception Rothe insists that they are prepared to follow the United States and other American Republics in all measures of a political and economic nature including prevention of Axis propaganda and subversive activities, furnishing us with essential materials and facilities of their port for our naval vessels, repairs, fueling, et cetera.

I assume it is still our prime objective at the Conference to obtain a joint declaration of all American Republics severing relations. In this case, I believe the strongest argument we could use with Argentina would be that any country which refused to join in the resolution cannot expect the same assistance from United States in essential defense material and other necessary products as those who have broken relations and consequently, according to Argentina's own thesis, subjected themselves to danger of attack.

I am informed that Castillo feels reasonably certain that Argentina can count on one or more countries siding with them in refusing to join in resolution. If they find all other countries support resolution this will have telling effect since, no matter what they say, they genuinely fear isolation and its inevitable consequences for them externally and internally.

Repeated to Department.

ARMOUR

710.Consultation (3)/344 : Telegram

The American Representative (Welles) to the Secretary of State

RIO DE JANEIRO, January 16, 1942— 5 p. m.
[Received January 17—2 : 25 a. m.]

15. The situation remains approximately the same as indicated in my last telegram.

As you know, I completely share your own feeling that every effort should be made to preserve unanimity, but that if the Argentine Government is unwilling to join in a continental declaration for a severance of relations with the Axis Powers, Argentina should be allowed to proceed alone.

I had a very frank talk yesterday morning with Dr. Ruiz Guiñazú. I found him wavering and vacillating, and obviously very much under the impression of the strong line taken by the other delegations and by the general state of public opinion in Brazil. Without making any commitment, he gave me to understand that he was inclined to go along with a declaration for the severance of relations, but he stated he would first have to cable President Castillo and get new instructions.

President Vargas [64] told me yesterday afternoon that the Argentines would come along and that he himself had personally made it absolutely clear to Ruiz Guiñazú that Brazil would support the United States 100%; that the final decision of Brazil in this regard had been reached, and that he, Vargas, had the support of practically every citizen of Brazil in following this policy.

The Foreign Ministers of Mexico [65] and Venezuela [66] and the Chief of the delegation of Colombia, [67] are today jointly presenting to the committee a project for the severance of relations with the Axis Powers. They have been to see Ruiz Guiñazú, and have shown him the project. They have told him that they will not agree to a compromise and that they will under no conditions recede from the position they have taken, and that in this position they have the support of every nation of the hemisphere, except Chile and Argentina.

The speech made yesterday by Dr. Guani was decidedly helpful as an indication to the rest of the Continent that Argentina's assumed control over the smaller republics of South America is nonexistent.

The general atmosphere of the Conference could not be more favorable from our standpoint. I am now beginning to believe that the Argentine Government may decide to come along largely because of the firm attitude taken by President Vargas and Aranha. . . . Aranha feels and I agree, however, that if Argentina is brought into line Chile will be forced without question to adhere to any joint declaration.

WELLES

710.Consultation 3/363 : Telegram

The American Representative (Welles) to the Secretary of State

RIO DE JANEIRO, January 18, 1942—7 p. m.
[Received 10 : 50 p. m.]

22. Department's 24, January 17, 10 p. m.[68] For Secretary Morgenthau [69] from Welles. There is appended a copy of a new draft of

---

[64] Getulio Vargas, President of Brazil.
[65] Ezequiel Padilla.
[66] Caracciolo Parra-Pérez.
[67] Gabriel Turbay.
[68] Not printed; this telegram concerned international monetary stabilization.
[69] Henry Morgenthau, Jr., Secretary of the Treasury.

a resolution which includes I believe such changes in the wording of the earlier draft as may satisfactorily meet the points raised in your cables to me.

You will note that in the appended draft all references to nations other than the American Republics are omitted. Though it is to be hoped that the meeting of Finance Ministers [70] referred to in the appended draft of the resolution would include, when called, representatives of other countries and may so be interpreted by some there is nothing in the resolution which commits the United States Government to a meeting which need necessarily include the Finance Ministers of nations other than the American Republics. There will be of course ample time later for sounding out other governments and their participation in the Conference assured before the calling of the Conference referred to in the resolution.

Since the absolute deadline must be Monday noon Rio time, January 19, I would appreciate it if you could have your reply and possibly suggested changes telephoned instead of cabled. White [71] will remain in his room at Copacabana Palace Monday morning waiting to receive telephone message from Washington. Please note Rio time is about 2 hours earlier than Washington time.

RESOLUTION ON THE STABILIZATION FUND OF THE UNITED AND ASSOCIATED NATIONS

WHEREAS
1. A more effective mobilization and utilization of foreign exchange resources of [apparent omission] would be of assistance in the struggle against aggression and would contribute to the realization of the economic objectives set forth at the First and Second Meetings of the Ministers of Foreign Affairs of the American Republics at Panama and Habana; and
2. The American Republics which are combined in a common effort to maintain their political and economic independence can cooperate in the creation of an organization to promote stability in foreign exchange rates, encourage the international movement of productive capital, facilitate the reduction of artificial and discriminatory barriers to the movement of goods, help correct the maldistribution of gold, strengthen monetary systems, and facilitate the settlement of public and private international debts and the maintenance of monetary policies that avoid serious inflation or deflation;

RESOLVES
1. To recommend that the Governments of the American Republics participate in a special conference of Ministers of Finance or their representatives to be called for the purpose of considering the establishment of an international stabilization fund;
2. To recommend that the conference in considering the establishment of such a fund shall formulate the plan of organization, powers

---

[70] For correspondence on this meeting, see pp. 58 ff.
[71] Harry Dexter White, Assistant to the Secretary of the Treasury and Director of Monetary Research of the Treasury Department.

and resources necessary to the proper functioning of the fund, and shall determine the conditions requisite to participation in the fund, and shall propose principles to guide the fund in its operation.

WELLES

———————————

710.Consultation 3/396 : Telegram

The American Representative (Welles) to the Secretary of State

RIO DE JANEIRO, January 19, 1942—1 p. m.
[Received 9 : 57 p. m.]

27. I have now had three very long conversations with the Argentine Foreign Minister. I have made all of the obvious arguments in favor of unity but I have likewise made it clear that my Government like almost every other government of the American Republics believes that the continued presence of Axis representatives on the territory of the American Republics is a fundamental danger to the security of those republics which are at war and to the capacity of the other American Republics for effective self-defense. I made it very clear that in my judgment the issue is one regarding which no compromise can be found although, of course, I as well as the other chiefs of delegations will make every effort to find some phraseology acceptable to all, provided the necessary principles are maintained intact.

In a conversation which I had with Dr. Ruiz Guiñazú the night before last he maintained that Argentina would be willing to break relations with the Axis Powers in April but that because of the fact that congressional elections are scheduled to take place in Argentina in March the raising of this issue at the present moment in Argentina would create insuperable political difficulties for the Government which intends in any way that may be necessary to see that the outcome of these elections is satisfactory to it from the political standpoint.

He has raised the same issue in his conversations with President Vargas.

Until yesterday he was alleging that Peru, Chile and Paraguay would support the Argentine position of opposition to a joint declaration breaking relations. I had arrangements made, however, to have him informed by a source in which he has confidence that the President of Peru [72] only yesterday gave categorical instructions to his delegation to support our position and that the Paraguayan Foreign Minister had received final instructions to support Brazil and the United States. At the same time the Chilean Foreign Minister came to see me and told me that notwithstanding instructions he

———————————

[72] Manuel Prado Ugarteche.

had originally received against the severance of relations, he was now personally convinced that the step should be taken and he had sent the most urgent messages to Santiago requesting full authority to join in the proposed declaration. At midnight last night he told me that he expected to receive satisfactory instructions today.

All of these facts have created a state of panic in the mind of Dr. Ruiz Guiñazú. He now sees Argentina completely isolated but whether, as he tells me, he has urged Acting President Castillo to change the orders or not, the position taken by the Acting President of Argentina appears to be consistently obstinate with regard to the issue of the severance of relations.

After his interview with President Vargas last night Dr. Ruiz Guiñazú came unannounced to see me to tell me that the Argentine Government was willing to take the following steps:

(a) to request that an additional article to the project for the severance of relations as presented by the Mexican, Colombian and Venezuelan Foreign Ministers (the text of which is practically identical with that drafted in the Department of State) be adopted which would state that any American republics which felt it impossible to take the action contemplated by the proposed joint declaration immediately would be able later to adhere thereto. In this way he said Argentina could take the proposed action in April.

[(b)] Argentina would present a project of which he gave me the text providing for a joint declaration which, after the customary preambles of reference, contains two articles as follows:

"1. The American Republics condemn the attack upon the United States of America and reaffirm their firm decision to lend assistance to the nation which has been the subject of aggression.

2. Each American state will negotiate with the United States of America the form in which such assistance shall be lent and will enter into bilateral or multilateral conventions necessary for the defense of the Continent."

I have told Dr. Ruiz Guiñazú that I responded sincerely to his desire to adopt a course which would promote unity and avoid the tragic impression at this time that the unity of the hemisphere had been broken. I said, however, that I did not see that the steps which he contemplated provided any solution. I said that the mere fact that Argentina would refrain from signing the proposed declaration for the severance of relations with the Axis Powers could only be interpreted as demonstrating Argentina's unwillingness to join in measures believed essential for the defense of the hemisphere by the other 20 American Republics. With regard to the specific project which he had handed me and which he emphasized should be regarded as supplementary to the proposed declaration for the severance of relations I said I would give the matter the most attentive study and discuss it with other chiefs of delegation but that it was my firm belief that it constituted a retrogression and was highly unsatisfactory.

I have studiously avoided in my conversations with him any syllable which could be used by him as a complaint that the United States was bringing economic or financial pressure upon Argentina. I have, however, asked some of the advisers in the delegation in talking with Prebisch and Irgoyen [73] to continue to make it clear as from me that at a time like this the economic and financial assistance which the United States can give the other American Republics will necessarily be given only to those nations which are whole-heartedly and effectively cooperating with us in the defense of the hemisphere. All of the necessary effect in this regard has consequently undoubtedly already been created.

I am seeing President Vargas this evening and I will then learn from him what message he may have received directly from the Acting President of Argentina.

Repeated to Buenos Aires for the strictly confidential information for Ambassador Armour.

WELLES

710.Consultation 3/422 : Telegram

The Ambassador in Chile (Bowers) to the Secretary of State

SANTIAGO, January 21, 1942—11 a. m.
[Received 1 : 31 p. m.]

121. The following telegram has been sent to Rio.

For Welles. Your January 19, 1 p. m. I am reliably informed that the night before last Rossetti [telegraphed?] from Rio for permission to modify Chile's stand against breaking relations, but that Acting Foreign Minister Pedregal told him that he must not only maintain this position but expressed alleged feeling of the Chilean Government that Rossetti was weakening whereas his stand should be more resolute even than that of Argentina. Pedregal is said to have told Rossetti that this instruction was at the behest of the Vice President [74] and represented the views of the majority of the Chilean Senate.

Repeated to the Department.

BOWERS

710.Consultation 3/425 : Telegram

The American Representative (Welles) to the Secretary of State

RIO DE JANEIRO, January 22, 1942—9 a. m.
[Received 10 : 02 a. m.]

39. In a 4-hour meeting between the Argentine, Peruvian and Chilean Foreign Ministers and Aranha and myself I am glad to say

---

[73] Presumably Alonzo Irigoyen, Argentine Under Secretary of Finance.
[74] Gerónimo Mendez.

that a satisfactory agreement was reached upon the text of a joint inter-American declaration for the severance of relations with the Axis Powers.

The text is as follows:

"(1) The American Republics reaffirm their declaration to consider every act of aggression on the part of a non-continental power against one of them as an act of aggression against all of them since such act constitutes an immediate danger to the liberty and independence of America.

(2) The American Republics reaffirm their complete solidarity and their determination to cooperate as one for their mutual protection until the effects of the present aggression upon the Continent shall have disappeared.

(3) The American Republics consequently declare that in the exercise of their sovereignty and in conformity with their constitutional institutions and powers, provided the latter are in agreement, they cannot continue their diplomatic relations with Japan, Germany and Italy since Japan has attacked and the others have declared war upon a nation of the Continent.

(4) Finally, the American Republics declared that before reestablishing the relations mentioned in the preceding paragraph they will consult among themselves in order that their determination may have a collective and solidary character.["]

The Argentine Government has officially accepted this text: the Chilean Minister has accepted likewise but with the proviso that he must obtain official approval from his Government.

WELLES

710.Consultation 3/424 : Telegram

The Ambassador in Peru (Norweb) to the Secretary of State

LIMA, January 22, 1942—9 a. m.
[Received 10 : 05 a. m.]

55. President Prado last night stated to press that Peruvian Foreign Minister at opportune time at Rio meeting would express decision Peru break off relations with Axis Powers and cooperate resolutely in common task defense American Continent without omission any effort or contribution.

NORWEB

710.Consultation 3/436 : Telegram

The American Representative (Welles) to the Secretary of State

RIO DE JANEIRO, January 22, 1942—8 p. m.
[Received 8 : 25 p. m.]

41. As the Department has undoubtedly been informed by Ambassador Armour the Acting President of Argentina this morning refused to approve the agreement reached with his Foreign Minister

last night upon the text of a joint declaration for the breaking of relations.

Dr. Ruiz Guiñazú informed all of us yesterday evening that he was fully authorized to reach this agreement. He is now disauthorized by his own Government.

He has this afternoon communicated by telephone with Buenos Aires urging approval by Castillo of a slightly modified text for article III of the proposed joint declaration.

The Acting President of Chile has informed Aranha that the Chilean Foreign Minister has received precise instructions permitting him to sign the joint declaration.

A decision was reached this afternoon by all of the other Foreign Ministers that a plenary session would be held tomorrow afternoon at which all of the Foreign Ministers would sign the joint declaration for the breaking of relations. If Argentina is not prepared to go along the others at that time will go along without her.

The very definite conclusion has been reached by all of the Foreign Ministers with whom I have spoken that some influence of an extra continental character is responsible for the decision reached by Dr. Castillo. The entire Argentine delegation now without exception is vehemently of the opinion that the Argentine Government should support the joint declaration as agreed upon last night.

WELLES

710.Consultation 3/456 : Telegram

The Ambassador in Chile (Bowers) to the Secretary of State

SANTIAGO, January 23, 1942.
[Received January 23—9 : 13 p. m.]

142. Following telegram has been sent to Rio, January 23, 5 p. m.

For the Under Secretary. Saw Pedregal, Secretary of the Council of Ministers, which accepts the latest Brazilian resolution but wishes to add the phrase from original resolution about legislative approval. Pedregal now trying to reach Rossetti with instructions to seek this addition and to support resolution. This stand is predicated on alleged ground that here foreign relations is an executive function and war is legislation and the resolution is generally considered equal to a declaration of war.

BOWERS

710.Consultation 3/460 : Telegram

The American Representative (Welles) to the Secretary of State

RIO DE JANEIRO, January 23, 1942—11 p. m.
[Received January 24—1 : 42 a. m.]

45. After an all day debate in committee in which feelings ran exceedingly high and in the course of which I stated that I felt that

unless a satisfactory agreement on the rupture of relations could be reached today the meeting of Foreign Ministers must publicly confess its complete incapacity to confront the vital issues of the moment a draft formula was agreed upon late this afternoon.

The text transmitted to the Department in my telegram no. 39, January 22, 9 a. m., is retained insofar as articles 1, 2, and 4 are concerned, except that in article 2 the word "mutual" is replaced with the word "reciprocal" and in article 4 the final phrase reads "may have a solidary character" instead of the explanation "collective and solidary".

Article 3 which, of course, has been the crux of the debate in its present form reads as follows:

"The American Republics consequently, following the procedure established by their own laws within the position and circumstances of each country in the actual continental conflict, recommend the rupture of their diplomatic relations with Japan, Germany, and Italy, since the first of these states has attacked and the other two have declared war upon an American country."

The interpretation to be given to the phrase "within the position and circumstances of each country in the actual continental conflict" refers to whether a country is ready [already] at war or has already broken relations.

Inasmuch as Argentina by means of this official declaration now joins with Chile and the other American Republics recommending that all of them break diplomatic relations with the Axis Powers the concrete effect is exactly the same as that which would have resulted in the text agreed upon on January 21.

At a formal session of the Political Committee this evening all of the 21 Foreign Ministers publicly voted for the project in the form now communicated to the Department.

The Uruguayan Foreign Minister publicly stated at this session of the Committee that he expected to be able to inform the conference tomorrow that Uruguay had already broken relations with the Axis Powers. The Peruvian Foreign Minister has informed me that his Government will likewise take action immediately and so have the Bolivian and Paraguayan Foreign Ministers.

The Chilean Foreign Minister came to see me this afternoon to inform me that he himself would break relations with the Axis Powers before the expiration of the term of office of the present Government. I have already fully reported the attitude of Brazil in this regard.

WELLES

710.Consultation (3)/462: Telegram

The American Representative (*Welles*) *to the Secretary of State*

RIO DE JANEIRO, January 24, 1942—noon.
[Received January 24—10: 28 a. m.]

47. I told the press this morning for guidance that our objectives here were twofold, namely, to obtain the breaking off diplomatic relations and to prevent the breaking of hemisphere unity. I explained that if Argentina and Chile had gone their separate ways, Germany could have called it a great victory. This also would have put Brazil in a difficult position because two of her largest neighbors would have become centers for Axis activities. Obviously, some compromise was necessary. Under the resolution approved yesterday Argentina and Chile have recommended to themselves that relations be broken and they have for the first time admitted that there is a continental conflict. The phraseology of any resolution is meaningless unless its spirit is fulfilled. Several of the countries have already stated that they would immediately break relations including Uruguay, Peru and Brazil. Furthermore, the very strong resolution on the breaking of financial and commercial relations which it is expected will be adopted this morning with a minor reservation by Argentina will be a further practical implementation of yesterday's recommendation to break diplomatic relations.

WELLES

710.Consultation 3/598: Telegram

The American Representative (*Welles*) *to President Roosevelt*

RIO DE JANEIRO, January 24, 1942—3 p. m.

48. I am sure you will understand my feeling of amazement and complete confusion as a result of my conversation with the Secretary of State last night.[75]

In the last conversation which I had with you the night before I left for Rio, we agreed that the two main objectives at the Conference from the standpoint of our own Government should be the breaking of political, commercial, and financial relations between the Axis Powers and the American Republics which had not yet taken such action, and likewise the making of every effort to prevent the breakdown of the unity of the hemisphere for the creation of which your own Administration is solely responsible.

_____

[75] No record of conversation found in Department files. In his *Memoirs* (vol. II, pp. 1148–1149), Secretary Hull described this telephone conversation, indicating his feeling that the Under Secretary had changed the Department's policy without consulting the Secretary, and that the escape clause to which the Under Secretary had agreed was a surrender to Argentina.

During the nearly 2 weeks that I have been here I have worked night and day to attain these objectives. As you remember, an agreement was reached with the Argentine Foreign Minister on January 21 upon the text of a joint declaration for the breaking of relations which contained four articles. The full text as then agreed upon reads as follows:

[Here follows text of draft resolution quoted in telegram No. 39, January 22, 9 a. m., from Mr. Welles, page 32.]

As a result of the unwillingness of the Acting President of Argentina to confirm the agreement previously reached by the Argentine Foreign Minister on January 21 and which agreement the latter had informed us all he was fully authorized to make, the Conference was thrown into a state verging upon chaos on January 22 and 23.

During that period both President Vargas and Aranha told me of their tremendous concern at the possibility of a rupture between Brazil and Argentina in view of the fact that Brazil's traditional friendship with Chile, as a counterpoise to Argentina, had practically vanished as a result of the dubious character of the present Government of Chile. They reaffirmed their decision to go one hundred percent with the United States, but they urged that if possible Brazil should not be forced to take an open attitude of antagonism to Argentina. Exactly the same pleas were made to me by the Uruguayan and Bolivian Foreign Ministers. The joint opinion of all of them was that if Argentina and Chile now broke with the other American Republics, it would be primarily Brazil, Uruguay and Bolivia that would suffer. If a rupture took place in the American family of nations, Argentina and Chile would become the *foci* of Axis agents and of subversive activities directed primarily against neighboring countries with the very great probability that the Brazilian Army would view such a situation with the utmost alarm and probable unrest on account of its belief that the Argentine Army is dominated to a considerable extent by German influence.

It seemed to me, therefore, in the highest interest of our own country, that I should make every effort to preserve unity and yet at the same time achieve the objectives upon which you and I agreed.

In my telegram No. 45, January 23, 11 p. m., I reported to the Secretary of State the events of yesterday and the exact text of the agreement for the rupture of relations as finally approved unanimously by all of the Foreign Ministers. You will see from this telegram that articles 1, 2, and 4 are practically left unchanged except for a slight strengthening of the phraseology employed in article 2.

The only other remaining article, No. 3 reads as follows:

"The American Republics consequently, following the procedure established by their own laws within the position and circumstances of each country in the actual continental conflict, recommend the rupture of their diplomatic relations with Japan, Germany and Italy since the first of these states has attacked and the other two have declared war upon an American country."

In this article for the first time, notwithstanding recent earlier official declarations to the contrary by the Acting President of Argentina and by the Chilean Government, both Argentina and Chile publicly go on record as recommending to all of the American Republics, including themselves, the breaking of diplomatic relations with the Axis Powers. In addition to that, the reason for such action is specifically declared to be the attack upon the United States, and finally, the conflict involving the Americas has now for the first time officially been declared to be "continental." In the considered judgment of Aranha, of the Foreign Minister of Mexico, of the Foreign Minister of Peru, of the Foreign Minister of Venezuela, and of the chiefs of delegation of Colombia, Cuba, and Bolivia, this text is stronger, more satisfactory, and has less reservations and weasel words than the text agreed upon on January 21.

This fundamental issue has consequently been raised: would it have been better for 19 Republics, including the United States, to announce that the American Republics "should not continue" diplomatic relations with the Axis Powers, in the full knowledge that the united American front would thereby be broken and that Argentina and Chile would in all likelihood become hotbeds for Axis activities; or for the United States in conjunction with every other American Republic to agree upon the text set forth above by which all of the American Republics jointly recommend the severance of their diplomatic relations with the Axis Powers.

The Brazilian press, which is not today controlled, has unanimously proclaimed the agreement reached as a triumph. Every delegate and Foreign Minister with whom I have spoken last night and this morning likewise shares this point of view. If the United States had taken the opposite course and Argentina and Chile had finally been forced out of the united line-up, before this Conference had terminated the United States would have been attacked from one end of the continent to the other for having broken the united American front and for having through undue pressure tried to force its own views upon Argentina and Chile in order to save American skins. I think you will likewise agree that nothing would have given greater satisfaction to the Axis Powers themselves than to be able to announce to the rest of the world that they had succeeded in breaking up the solidarity of the American Republics.

I fully share the point of view you yourself expressed to me last night and that is that immediate implementation in the sense of action is required in order to counteract the alleged mistaken press comments which have been reported. Aranha has authorized me specifically to state to you by authorization of President Vargas that at the close of the session of the Conference on the afternoon of Monday, January 26, he will announce in the name of the Government of Brazil the severance of relations between Brazil and the Axis Powers. The Minister for Foreign Affairs of Uruguay who had intended to make that announcement today has decided likewise to withhóld the announcement of Uruguayan rupture of relations until the closing session of the Conference because of the increased effect that such an announcement would have there.

[The representative from] Paraguay has just informed me he has requested similar instructions. Both Ecuador and Bolivia with full authorization have given me assurances to the same effect.

May I say to you again how deeply grateful I am for what you said last night.[76] In full accord with the policy you approved, what we have achieved, in my personal judgment, is a result which is the safest for the interests of our own country. I have kept the Secretary of State fully informed as a review of the telegrams I have sent him since my arrival in Rio will demonstrate. It has been manifestly impossible for me in the kind of constant turmoil and continuous conferences which a meeting of this kind inevitably implies, to request prior authorization for agreeing to every word. I took it for granted that so long as the desired objectives were attained and so long as the policy you and the Secretary of State had approved was carried out, I was entitled to have sufficient confidence from the Secretary of State to make it possible for me within those bounds to agree upon texts.

In conclusion I am glad to add that at this morning's session the text of the resolution for the severance of commercial and financial relations as drafted in Washington was approved *in toto* save for colorless reservations by Argentina and Chile. This unanimous inter-American agreement will make as water-tight as possible [the] cutting off of all commercial and financial relations between the American Republics and the Axis Powers.

WELLES

710.Consultation 3/598 : Telegram

The American Representative (Welles) to the Secretary of State

RIO DE JANEIRO, January 25, 1942—1 p. m.

52. The Chilean Foreign Minister announced at the Plenary Session last night that "without the slightest shadow of a doubt, Japan immediately is going to attack Chile".

---

[76] According to Secretary Hull's account in his *Memoirs*, the President interrupted the conversation between the Secretary and the Under Secretary to state that a decision had been made, and that, with the Conference in the act of adjourning, reconsideration was not feasible.

Early this morning the Minister visited me and urged that I sign with him a document of which the text is the following:

"Meeting together, the Minister for Foreign Affairs of Chile, Don Juan B. Rossetti, and the Under Secretary of State of the United States of America, Mr. Sumner Welles, have considered the situation created by the conflict in the Pacific with regard to continental defense measures and in particular the defense requirements of Chile whose coasts are notoriously open to attack. In view of the circumstances set forth by Minister Rossetti, the Under Secretary of State, Mr. Welles, declared that the United States would take precautionary defense measures in the waters of the Pacific adjacent to South America and that should some emergency occur, Chile could count upon effective military assistance from the United States and that technical details of such assistance would be agreed upon in the immediate future."

The Minister has informed me that he has received word from his Government that Chile is now prepared to break without further delay all relations with the Axis Powers. He alleges that he has requested authorization to make an announcement of an actual rupture of relations at the closing session of the Conference on Tuesday.[77] He states that he has likewise cabled to the presidential candidate Rios, whose election the Minister tells me is assured, asking authorization by Rios for the making of such an announcement.

In as much as the declarations contained in this proposed statement are in accord with our traditional policy and covered by joint staff agreements already reached, I see no objection.

I beg to request an urgent reply from the Department as to whether I am authorized to sign the proposed joint agreement.

WELLES

710.Consultation 3/598 : Telegram

The American Representative (*Welles*) *to the Secretary of State*

RIO DE JANEIRO, January 25, 1942—2 p. m.

53. In addition to recommending the severance of diplomatic relations with the Axis Powers, concerning which I have already reported, the Consultative Meeting has already approved a number of resolutions embodying specific and practical measures, including the following:[78]

1. Severance of commercial and financial relations with the Axis Powers drafted in practically the same terms as those drafted in

---

[77] This rupture of relations took place approximately one year after these assurances were made.
[78] On January 24 Mr. Welles summarized the measures which the Conference had approved in a broadcast from Rio de Janeiro; for text, see Department of State *Bulletin*, January 24, 1942, p. 77. For text of the Final Act of the Conference, see *ibid.*, February 7, 1942, p. 117.

Washington. (While Chile made a reservation of its sovereign rights, and Argentina a reservation applying the measures of control to all non-American belligerents, both countries supported the substance and basic objectives of the resolution);

2. Production of strategic materials for supplying the essential defense needs of the continent;

3. Approval of principles and practices regarding priorities, allocations, and price controls, entirely consistent with our own principles and practices;

4. The improvement of maritime and other communications with emphasis on defense requirements;

5. A resolution regarding the stabilization fund in practically the same form as cleared in Washington;

6. Support for the Inter-American Development Commission;

7. Urging the early establishment of the Inter-American Bank;

8. One major resolution on the control of subversive activities, embodying all points previously agreed to in Washington; and a few other resolutions of a similar character (Smith of Justice is entirely satisfied with the resolution on subversive activities); and

9. A resolution condemning the Japanese aggression, and extending this condemnation to the other Axis powers.

The resolution excluding Axis citizens or companies from civil and commercial aviation has been approved by the subcommittee but not yet reported to the full committee. The same applies to the resolutions on public health, Red Cross, post war problems, and the reorganization of the Inter-American Neutrality Committee. The resolution on telecommunications has been approved in principle but has not yet been approved by the full committee. It is probable that approval will be given these latter resolutions at a session of the full committee scheduled to begin tonight at 8:30.

It will be observed that many of the projects supported by the United States have been given approval along the lines agreed upon prior to the departure of the delegation, and that the remaining ones have progressed favorably so far as the schedule here has permitted.

WELLES

710.Consultation 3/598 : Telegram

The Secretary of State to the American Representative (Welles)

WASHINGTON, January 26, 1942—8 p. m.

79. For the Under Secretary. Your 52, January 25, 1 p. m. You are authorized to sign a document in the following sense:

"Meeting together, the Minister for Foreign Affairs of Chile, Dr. Juan B. Rossetti, and the Under Secretary of State of the United States of America, Mr. Sumner Welles, have considered the requirements of continental defense, and particularly the requirements of Chile to defend its long coastline in view of the situation created by the fact that the United States has been the victim of an aggression by a non-American state, that ten of the American Republics are at war with the Axis powers, and that the Meeting of Foreign Ministers at Rio de Janeiro has agreed to a resolution recommending that all the American Republics sever their relations with the Axis.

In view of the circumstances set forth by Minister Rossetti, the Under Secretary of State, Mr. Welles, declared that, in accord with unequivocal assurances to go to the assistance of any Nation of the Western Hemisphere which has been the victim of non-American aggression, the United States in the event of an attack by a non-American country against Chile will take immediate steps to send naval, air and land forces to repulse this aggression. In the meantime precautionary defense measures have been taken to render as unlikely as possible attack upon the coastline of Chile. The War and Navy Departments would welcome further opportunity to discuss amplification and implementation of the conversations previously held with the appropriate officers of the Chilean Government."

The President, who was consulted with respect to your telegram, thought that you should point out to Rossetti that the United States has undertaken and expects to carry forward with the assistance of the other American Republics concerned the defense of a seaboard on the Pacific of 10,000 miles; that since we do not have enough ships to locate them for patrol duty immediately off the coast of each country, they are being located in such areas as to derive the maximum utility; and that in the execution of our assurances of support, which have been made to all countries on the same basis, due account will of course be given to the special geographical situation, the importance of the country as a source of the production of strategic materials, and any other special factors.

The President has made it very clear, however, that Chile cannot anticipate any preference over any other American Republic in the protection we can afford which as stated above will take into account all pertinent considerations.

The Navy Department suggests that you should also further remind the Chilean Foreign Minister that this Government expects Chile will make all possible military efforts herself to defend her territory and off-shore waters and will protect friendly shipping near the Chilean coast.

As Rossetti undoubtedly understands, until Chile signs a Lend-Lease agreement, no deliveries of war materials can be made.

HULL

740.0011 European War, 1939/19015 : Telegram

The Ambassador in Brazil (Caffery) to the Secretary of State

RIO DE JANEIRO, January 28, 1942—8 p. m.
[Received 8 : 24 p. m.]

270. Aranha announced at the close of his closing speech (7 : 30 p. m.) rupture of relations and also settlement of Peru and Ecuador dispute.

He explained that appropriate communication was being made to Axis representatives here and in Axis capitals.

Delegation will send full details.

CAFFERY

710.Consultation 3/552 : Telegram

The Ambassador in Chile (Bowers) to the Secretary of State

SANTIAGO, January 31, 1942—noon.
[Received 7 : 40 p. m.]

186. Saw Rossetti last night in company with Mendez, Vice President, and the Minister said he will present resolutions of Rio to Congress next week and go before that body to insist on speedy ratification. He is confident he will succeed. This is undoubtedly the program since Mendez has instructed along this line. Rossetti said we may be sure that within a month the Axis Missions will have departed.[79]

BOWERS

825.00/1609

The Ambassador in Chile (Bowers) to the Under Secretary of State (Welles)

SANTIAGO, February 4, 1942.
[Received February 10.]

DEAR MR. WELLES: Rossetti gave a full exposition of the Rio Conference to the Council of Ministers yesterday and was warmly congratulated by his colleagues and by Mendez, who said that he had acted precisely in conformity with the instructions of the Government. I have heard much talk against Rossetti at Rio, and since it is evident that much of this is based on a lack of understanding both of his position and his power, I want to go on record on it.

1) Nine tenths of the public men of all parties in Chile including bitter enemies of Germany and warm friends of the United States,

---

[79] For correspondence on the Chilean breach with the Axis, see vol. VI, section under Chile entitled "Efforts to secure cooperation between the United States and Chile on certain measures for Hemisphere defense."

like Barros Jarpa,[80] were absolutely opposed to breaking off diplomatic relations because of their coast line and vulnerability and their realization that they lacked the facilities to defend themselves against a surprise attack. Rossetti was miles ahead of nine-tenths in favor of complete cooperation with the United States.

2) He went to Rio under iron clad instructions of the Government and Congress backed by the press without exception. He could not violate his instructions.

3) Two days after the meeting began he was telegraphed by Pedregal that he was reported weakening on his instructions and that he should take an advanced stand upon them.

4) He telegraphed the Government asking release from the instructions, strongly urging that he be instructed to go along with sentiment in favor of breaking relations, which was overwhelming in the Conference.

5) As a result of his very strong representations, the Government then agreed to permit him to vote for breaking off relations provided it were stipulated that there should be ratification by Congress. In other words there would have been no agreement on this phase but for the fight Rossetti made.

6) The ratification's hope is in the fight Rossetti will undoubtedly make before Congress. Remember that neither Ortega, Saenz, Mora, Bianchi or Alamos[81] had the courage or enterprize to get a ratification for the agreements of Peru, Panama and Habana, and that Rossetti went to Congress, made the fight, spoke and fought for four hours and got them all ratified. He is a powerful man in debate and very effective and I hope he succeeds in getting the Rio ratification promptly. He thinks he will. As a result of Rio sentiment is changing here; fears are dissipating because of the feeling now that we will help protect the Coast; and there is a general conviction that Chile cannot afford to stand aloof.

Juan Antonio Rios, the new President, attended the cocktail of the Chile-American Society for the visiting American journalists. I talked with him briefly. He is a tall, slender, fine looking man with iron grey hair and a fine eye, looking the President. However, he is not a genius or brilliant but he had good sound sense and is conservative in the better sense. He has not been favorable to breaking relations in the past, but since the Rio Conference he has taken no real position. Were he to intervene in Congress he could do much harm but I have a feeling that since action will be taken before he takes power he will stand aloof. I hope so.

[Here follows a passage of irrelevant characterizations.]

With warmest regards [etc.]   CLAUDE G. BOWERS

[80] Ernesto Barros Jarpa succeeded Rossetti as Chilean Minister for Foreign Affairs in April 1942.
[81] Chilean Ministers for Foreign Affairs in 1939 and 1940.

710.Consultation 3/693

Memorandum by Mr. Emilio G. Collado [82] *to the Under Secretary of State (Welles)*

[WASHINGTON,]February 28, 1942.

PROGRESS IN CARRYING OUT ECONOMIC ARRANGEMENTS DISCUSSED AT THE RIO MEETING

MR. WELLES: Reference is made to my memorandum of February 9, 1942 [83] detailing the economic discussions and agreements at the Rio meeting. The present memorandum is intended to indicate what action has been taken with respect to these matters in the four weeks since the return of the United States Delegation.

Bolivia

1. The Bolivian Government has ratified the arrangement with the Standard Oil companies of Bolivia and New Jersey.

2. The Export-Import Bank and the Department have transmitted suggestions to Mr. Bohan [84] for the charter and by-laws of the proposed development corporation, and discussions are actively taking place at La Paz.

Brazil

1. The visit of the Minister of Finance [84a] will draw to a close next week with the following accomplishments:

a) Broad agreement for a cooperative program for the development of strategic and basic materials involving a $100,000,000 credit agreed to by Mr. Jesse Jones. [85]

b) Arrangement for carrying out the long discussed Itabira iron ore project—this is in its final stages.

c) The rubber project contract has been agreed to by the Minister and Mr. Will Clayton. [86]

d) An organization to stimulate the collection of wild rubber for the United States war effort is being discussed and worked out with the Brazilian mission.

e) A revised lend-lease agreement will be signed with the Ambassador on Tuesday. [87]

Chile

No action pending further developments in Chile.

Costa Rica

The Export-Import Bank has agreed to the extension of a credit of $160,000 for improvements in the San José water supply system.   Mr.

---

[82] Special Assistant to the Under Secretary of State.
[83] Not printed.
[84] Merwin Lee Bohan, Chief, U. S. Economic Mission to Bolivia.
[84a] Arthur de Souza Costa.
[85] Administrator of the Federal Loan Agency; for correspondence on strategic materials, see pp. 674 ff.
[86] Deputy Federal Loan Administrator; for correspondence concerning rubber, see pp. 691 ff.
[87] March 3, 1942; for text, see p. 815.

Wheeler of the Department of Agriculture [88] is arranging for the Agricultural Attaché [89] to proceed to San José to discuss the possibility of increasing production of strategic materials and foodstuffs with Dr. Luis Anderson and the Costa Rican Government.

Ecuador

The four point program entered into at Rio [90] is being rapidly implemented:

a) The waterworks and other improvements in Quito and Guayaquil have been studied by engineer Del Valle who has returned to draft and present his final report.

b) An understanding for the establishment of a development corporation and the extension to it of a credit of $5,000,000 has been reached by Dr. Salazar [91] with the Export-Import Bank.

c) Dr. Salazar has signed with the Secretary of the Treasury a $5,000,000 monetary stabilization agreement.

d) Agreement regarding the $2,000,000 health and sanitation program grant has been worked out with the Office of the Coordinator of Inter-American Affairs and entered into by the Department with Dr. Salazar.

Honduras

The Honduran Minister has presented his Government's interest in a program of highway construction and establishment of a national bank with issue, commercial, and agricultural mortgage functions. The highway program involves completion of the Inter-American Highway (the Honduran third would amount to $1,000,000),[92] a highway from the Pacific to Tegucigalpa (about $1,700,000), a highway from Tegucigalpa to the north (total cost estimated at $5,200,000). Discussions are going forward with the Export-Import Bank on the basis of handling the first two items totaling $2,700,000.

Discussions are going forward with the Treasury looking towards the sending of an expert to study the central bank matter regarding which very few details are available in Washington.

Nicaragua

The Ministers of Foreign Affairs and Finance will arrive in Washington at the end of next week to discuss among other things, presumably, the completion of the Inter-American Highway and other

---

[88] Leslie A. Wheeler, Director, Office of Foreign Agricultural Relations.

[89] Presumably Charles L. Luedtke.

[90] For correspondence on this program, see vol. VI, section under Ecuador entitled "Program for economic cooperation between the United States and Ecuador."

[91] Eduardo Salazar Gómez, Ecuadoran Minister-Counselor.

[92] For text of agreement between the United States and Honduras regarding the construction of the Inter-American Highway, effected by exchange of notes signed September 9 and October 26, 1942, see Department of State Executive Agreement Series No. 296, or 56 Stat. (pt. 2) 1848.

highway matters, and a possible increase in the exchange credit to the National Bank. The Department has recommended that the Export-Import Bank consolidate the present two $2,000,000 loans into one $5,000,000 loan to handle the entire highway program, due regard being given to the priorities situation.

Uruguay

The Uruguayan Government has agreed in principle to the terms proposed by the Maritime Commission for the chartering of the refrigerated vessel *Laura*.

E. G. COLLADO

THE INTER-AMERICAN CONFERENCE OF POLICE AND JUDICIAL AUTHORITIES, MEETING AT BUENOS AIRES, MAY 27–JUNE 9, 1942

710.Consultation 2 (C)/40b : Telegram

The Secretary of State to the Ambassador in Argentina (*Armour*)

WASHINGTON, May 18, 1942.

696. Please inform Foreign Office that the President has approved following Delegation to Conference of Police and Judicial Authorities to convene at Buenos Aires May 27, 1942: Delegate, Carl B. Spaeth, Member, Emergency Advisory Committee for Political Defense, Montevideo; Adviser, William Sanders, Assistant to Mr. Spaeth at Montevideo; Secretary, Clifton P. English, Vice Consul at Buenos Aires.

The Department regrets that limited time precluded consultation with the Embassy concerning designation of Mr. English and trusts that this detail will be satisfactory.

HULL

710.Consultation 2 (C)/44 : Telegram

The Secretary of State to the Ambassador in Uruguay (*Dawson*)

WASHINGTON, May 20, 1942—9 p. m.

284. For Spaeth: Department's 274, May 18.[1] In your capacity as delegate to the Inter-American Conference on Coordination of Police and Judicial Measures you should be guided by the following instructions:

"1. The Department is extremely doubtful of the advisability of entering at this time into any agreement which might be reached at Buenos Aires for the establishment of any system of exchange of information with regard to subversive activities which might entail obligations, real or implied, for this Government to furnish such information on demand of any other American republic. The present attitude of the Argentine Government with respect to full and unreserved cooperation for defense of the continent is too well known to require comment. Moreover, there is serious doubt in the minds of policy officers of this Department whether any information which might be transmitted to a central exchange might not find its way through one means or another into Axis hands.

---

[1] Not printed.

48

2. For this reason, while desirous of strengthening in every way consistent with the broad interests of this Government the general structure of inter-American machinery, the Department's attitude towards the conference in Buenos Aires has necessarily been conditioned by the attendance at the Conference of certain officials harboring doubtful sympathy toward this Government.

3. Accordingly, while the American delegate should take every opportunity to show his willingness to cooperate with the delegates from the other American republics, he should avoid making any commitment for an information center on subversive activities of the type described in numbered paragraph 1 above, as well as any other commitments for the exchange of intelligence information without prior reference to the Department and definite approval of those projects by Washington.

4. The Department feels, however, that the conference at Buenos Aires will afford a useful opportunity for the members of our delegation to get in touch and to establish friendly relations with representatives of the law-enforcement agencies of the other American republics who are concerned with subversive activities and other matters affecting the political defense of the continent.

5. Upon your arrival in Buenos Aires you will doubtless want to discuss the conference and its possible aims and political implications with Ambassador Armour so as to obtain the benefit of any suggestions which he may desire to communicate to you.

6. The Department does not intend to present any draft resolutions for consideration by the conference."

It is requested that you forward immediately a copy of these instructions to the American Ambassador in Buenos Aires for his information, guidance and comment.

HULL

710.Consultation 2 (C)/50 : Telegram

The Ambassador in Argentina (Armour) to the Secretary of State

BUENOS AIRES, June 5, 1942—4 p. m.
[Received 10 p. m.]

1051. (Section 1). For Chapin [2] from Spaeth. Number 13, part I. Reference is made to my telegram number 12, Embassy's telegram number 1026.[3]

The most important resolutions which have been submitted to the Conference, and the resolutions in which the delegates have indicated the greatest interest are the following: The proposal of Honduras for an inter-American registry of police and judicial records, the proposal of Peru for an inter-American police union, the proposal of Argentina for an interchange of information under the police convention of 1920, and the proposal of Bolivia for a uniform system of identification of criminals.

[2] Selden Chapin, Assistant Chief, Division of the American Republics.
[3] Not printed.

(Section 2). In order to avoid the recommendation of more than one new inter-American organization and in order to comply with the spirit of the Department's cable 284 to Montevideo, the American delegates have supported two principal propositions: First, that the several recommendations which propose new inter-American organizations should be included in a single statute of limitation [*or convention?*] which will propose a single organization with several functions. Second, that the single project should be submitted to the Pan American Union as a possible basis for an inter-American convention with the provision that the Union will solicit suggestions from the Governments and from the committee at Montevideo,[4] and that on the basis of the suggestions thus received the Union will prepare a revised draft of convention which may be submitted to a later conference or, in the alternative, may be opened for signature at the Union.

(Section 3). In its present form as described in part II of this cable, the single project leaves much to be desired but because the proposed convention is in fact being submitted to the Pan American Union for study, it is recommended that I be authorized to accept it in its present form.

Part II. The single project of convention which would be submitted to the Pan American Union for study would create an inter-American police union with the following characteristics:

(1) Each participating country would send one police or judicial officer to serve permanently at the capital selected for the seat of the union. The functions of the union would be purely advisory in character.

The police union would compile statutes and regulations dealing with the prevention and prosecution of crimes of an international character, would compile information regarding methods used in crimes against the states and its fundamental institutions, would compile reports and studies relative to nationals of countries at war with an American power, would study the possibility of devising an inter-American system of identification which would be used only in inter-American exchange of information, would sponsor periodic meetings of police authorities for the exchange of technical information, would promote the creation of civilian defense units, and would give advice and assistance in the national defense against subversive activities undertaken by nationals of countries at war with an American Republic and which are directed against the external or internal security of the state, its fundamental institutions or its national economy.

(Section 4). (2) As part of the secretariat of the union there would be an inter-American registry for information received from national courts regarding persons indicted or condemned for international crimes or subversive activities directed against the American Republics individually or collectively. The information would be limited to copies of the sentences and other documents of record.

---

[4] For correspondence concerning the Emergency Advisory Committee for Political Defense, see pp. 74 ff.

Political crimes are excluded from the scope of the convention but crimes which directly or indirectly serve the interest of a non-American state at war with an American Republic are included.

(3) The union would promote the interchange of police information relative to subversive activities undertaken by nationals of a non-American State at war with an American Republic and relative to common crimes in which one of the member countries would be interested. This exchange of information would not be made if any country interested deemed the exchange prejudicial to its national interests, and will be made only when it is deemed that this communication might be useful to other authorities.

(Section 5). Part III. The Conference will undoubtedly approve and it is recommended that the American delegate be authorized to approve the following recommendations.

(1) That the American Republics that have not yet done so adopt measures to prevent and repress during the present war all public exhibitions or other manifestations favorable to any of the countries of the members of the Tripartite Pact [5] and states subservient to them.

(2) That the Governments direct their law-enforcing officers to enforce vigorously existing laws against subversive elements acting in favor of the Axis; that the committee at Montevideo consider the desirability of convoking regional and general inter-American meetings of such officers; that the countries which do not have appropriate special units for the control of subversive activities, organize such units within their existing police organizations.

(3) That the Governments consider the obtaining of the status of native born citizens by fraudulent testimony a crime against the state.

Part IV. (1) With reference to the Argentine draft convention for the unification of criminal law referred to in my number 12, Embassy's number 1026, we will recommend that it be referred for study to the Governments, the Montevideo Committee, and the Inter-American Bar Association.

(2) With reference to the Argentine proposal for the control of the formation of organizations to carry on activities against the state, we will propose that it specify that such activities include appropriate express reference to the Tripartite Pact.

(3) With regard to the Argentine proposal on the expulsion of foreigners described in my number 12, we propose to give our approval provided that there is exclusive reference to the nationals of the Tripartite Pact and provided that it be in the form of a recommendation rather than of a convention.

---

[5] Three-Power Pact between Japan, Germany, and Italy, signed at Berlin, September 27, 1940; for text, see League of Nations Treaty Series, vol. CCIV, p. 386.

(4) With reference to the Argentine proposal recommending adoption of a South American treaty on criminal law, we propose to recommend that the study of this treaty be referred to the Montevideo Committee and the Inter-American Bar Association.

(5) With reference to the Haitian recommendation that the Governments adopt measures for supervision of fishing boats in order to avoid aid to submarines, we propose to give our approval and to recommend the inclusion of proposals for the protection of shipping facilities in line with those covered by the resolution adopted by the Montevideo Committee.

(6) With reference to the Colombian proposal on extradition, we propose to recommend that it be referred for study by the Montevideo Committee, together with the Argentine proposal on Extradition. [Spaeth.]

ARMOUR

710.Consultation 2 (C)/50 : Telegram

The Secretary of State to the Ambassador in Argentina (Armour)

WASHINGTON, June 6, 1942—5 p. m.

820.   Your 1051, June 5, 4 p. m.   For Spaeth.

1. The Department approves your attitude as outlined in sections 1, 2, 3 and 4 and authorizes you to accept the proposed convention in its present form since it is being submitted to the Pan American Union for study.

2. With regard to section 5, the Department authorizes you to approve of items 1 and 2 of part III. With respect to item 3, while this Government has no objection in principle to the proposal it would seem that in view of the differences in practice and theory between Roman law and our own, there is some doubt whether our Congress would be disposed to enact the necessary legislation, although you may point out that fraudulent testimony of that character is already a serious offense punishable by law.

With regard to section 5, part IV, items 1, 2, 3, 4, and 6, the observations just made with regard to the distinction between Roman law and our own apply with equal force even though the Department approves the principles involved. However, as long as these proposals are made in the form of recommendations and are subject to study, the Department sees no objection to your approval of them.

With regard to item 5 under part IV, the Department authorizes you to give your approval.

HULL

710.Consultation 2 (C)/70 : Telegram

The Ambassador in Argentina (Armour) to the Secretary of State

BUENOS AIRES, June 11, 1942—10 p. m.

[Received 10 : 38 p. m.]

1112. Before leaving Spaeth gave the following statement to the Saporiti Agency [6] in response to their request and for background purposes.

"The Police Conference terminated in an atmosphere of open hostility toward the Argentines, even Chile deserting Argentina by abstaining from voting on the resolution that became the determining factor in the conversations of the last 2 days of the Conference. This resolution was number 4 Argentina's proposal for certain amendments in the penal codes of the American countries. As you will recall the first few days of the Conference dragged along without much being accomplished when suddenly on Sunday Dr. Spaeth cleared the air by a few words and extricated the delegates from a morass of technical and philosophical considerations. At once all pretense of continental solidarity, maintained in previous inter-American conferences was abandoned and various delegates (exclusive of our own) 'went after' the Argentine delegation. It was plainly intimated that, had Argentina since Rio shown the slightest indication of being disposed to fulfill the promises made at the Conference of Foreign Ministers by men like Prebisch[7] that short of breaking relations the Government was disposed to take all necessary steps to join in hemisphere defense, the Conference would probably have accepted Argentina's proposal. As it was the lack of any such action could be interpreted only as bad faith and thus the delegates did interpret it. In addition the delegates of Brazil and I believe Mexico said to Frias'[8] face that Argentina should not keep saying its neutrality policy is dictated by realistic and practical considerations because they felt it is dictated by fear—fear of losing a few pesos of foreign trade, fear of attack, et cetera—and frankly in these days something more is expected of a nation that thinks itself important than that fear should govern its foreign policy. The last 2 days of the Conference were spent in this atmosphere with 19 countries against Argentine and its only ally, Chile, abstaining on important questions."

(The Haitian and other delegates not nationals of the country they were representing apparently at times voted with their countries of birth which were Chile and Argentina, but Dr. Spaeth apparently did not consider them worth mentioning when he was discussing the continental attitude toward Argentina).

---

[6] A news agency.
[7] Raúl Prebisch, General Manager, Banco Central de la República Argentina.
[8] Jorge H. Frias, Chairman, Argentine delegation to the Inter-American Conference of Police and Judicial Authorities.

Apparently full unanimity at the Conference found expression only and finally in the motion of solidarity with the United States reported in my telegram No. 1108, June 11, 5 p. m.[9]

ARMOUR

710.Consultation 2 (C)/65

Report of the American Delegate to the Inter-American Conference of Police and Judicial Authorities (Spaeth) [10]

[The first four sections of this report indicate the name of the Conference, a citation to its agenda, a summary of the representation of the participating countries, and an outline of the committee organization of the Conference.]

V

Results of the Conference:

The documents requested under this item are attached.[9] Annex "C" contains the resolutions as submitted to the Conference, and Annex "D" contains the texts of the resolutions as approved in the Final Act.

The resolutions in the Final Act follow the order of the program of the Conference. Resolutions one and two relate to Topic I of the program, namely, control of propaganda. Resolution three relates to Topic II of the program, the control of associations. Resolution four relates to Topic III, espionage and sabotage activities. Resolution five relates to Topic IV, cooperation and coordination of national law-enforcing bodies. Resolutions 6, 7, 8, 9, and 14 relate to Topic V, legislation and judicial procedures for uniform control of subversive activities. Resolutions 10, 11, 12 and 13 relate to the second chapter of the program, namely, inter-American cooperation.

Annex "E" is a copy of the preliminary report of the Delegate [11] and indicates both the important points on which full agreement was not reached because of the position taken by Argentina, and also the position taken by the American delegation.

General Comments:

Four of the proposals were combined in a single instrument of draft convention which is referred for study to the Pan American Union. The "proyectos" thus combined were submitted by Honduras (1), Nicaragua-Bolivia (3), Argentina (6), Peru (10). (See

---

[9] Not printed.
[10] Transmitted to the Secretary of State by Mr. Spaeth in covering letter of July 6, 1942.
[11] Report of June 18 summarizing the position of the American delegation.

Annex "C") The Argentine proposal on the establishment of national records of habitual criminals on the basis of the Vucetich system of identification (resolution 8, Annex "C") was considered indirectly, in the draft convention on the Inter-American Police Union, but no specific mention was made in the text of the resolution for the reason that the question of the use of the Vucetich system had been rejected by implication when the Nicaraguan-Bolivian proposal for the use of that system internationally was modified in the sense that the Conference merely recommended the study of an inter-American system of identification.

The Argentine proposal for the unification of penal law (No. 4 of Annex "C") was rejected completely and was replaced by Resolution No. 6 of the Final Act requesting the Committee at Montevideo to undertake the study of a uniform penal law.

The Argentine proposal relative to associations (No. 5 of Annex "C") was modified so as to include direct reference to the members of the Tripartite Pact and states subservient to them.

The Argentine proposal relative to expulsion of aliens (No. 7 of Annex "C") was referred to the Committee at Montevideo for study.

The Argentine proposal relative to extradition (No. 9 of Annex "C") was rejected and in its place it was recommended that the governments study the Convention of Montevideo of 1940.

The Venezuelan proposal (No. 13 of Annex "C") relative to the vigorous enforcement of existing laws, was combined with the Bolivian proposal (No. 16 of Annex "C") relative to the creation of national police units to combat subversive activities.

Comment with regard to the position taken by the several delegations:

As I have indicated in my preliminary report, it was the almost unanimous view that the Conference should recognize specifically by direct reference to the Axis Powers that its principal purpose was to recommend measures relative to subversive activities arising out of the present emergency; that it was not the function of the Conference to formulate preventive penal legislation which would anticipate criminal action arising from any source whatsoever. The general formula proposed by Argentina (see a reservation of Argentina at Page 15 of Annex "D") was recognized as inadequate because (1) it implied an attitude of antagonism towards Russia, (2) it was so flexible that it could be used by any Government to persecute its own nationals for political reasons.

It is certain that the breach between Argentina and the other republics would have been more serious and more obvious had it not been for the efforts of the Secretary General, Raúl C. Migone, a member of the Argentine Foreign Office, who was successful in persuading the Argentine Government not to raise the Communist issue by specific reference to that party in their resolutions. Dr. Jorge H. Frías, the principal Argentine delegate, strongly urged his own Government, and in conversations outside of the committee meetings, urged delegates from the other republics to include specific reference to the Communist menace. The principal Argentine technical assistant, Dr. Eusebio Gómez, had been described as a staunch democrat, but he took the extreme Argentine position throughout the Conference. . . .

The delegate from Chile took every opportunity to avoid an express commitment on controversial issues. He frequently abstained from voting, and near the end of the Conference advised the American delegate confidentially that he had received instructions from his Government to abstain from voting rather than to vote against the United States.

The best qualified delegates, both from a technical viewpoint and from the viewpoint of the basic political issues, were those from Brazil, Uruguay and Bolivia. This was due to the fact that the countries named had appointed special delegates to the Conference and had not contented themselves, in the manner of so many other countries, with naming their diplomatic representatives in Buenos Aires.

The position taken by the delegate appointed by Haiti deserves special mention and it is possible that the Department may wish to pursue the matter with the Haitian Government. The Haitian delegate, Dr. José Manuel Alvarez Aránguiz, a citizen of Chile, has lived in Argentina for almost 20 years. In several of the subcommittee meetings he voted with Argentina and on no occasion ventured beyond the middle-of-the-road position taken by Chile. He avoided taking a position at the final vote in the plenary session by leaving the meeting immediately before the vote.

Publications:

The minutes of the meetings and other material published by and for the use of the Conference, together with a set of the principal press clippings, is submitted herewith as Annex "F".

VI

Importance of the Conference to the United States:

This topic is treated in my preliminary report, Annex "E". In brief, the Conference clearly accentuated the position of isolation from the rest of the Hemisphere now occupied by Argentina. This accentuation can be attributed principally to the fact that Argentina was required to take the initiative in the presentation of resolutions. In taking this initiative she presented her usual case for non-discrimination among non-American belligerents. Because this position was recognized as antithetical to the program of Rio, the Argentine resolutions were rejected, for all practical purposes, completely.

The other principal result of the Conference is the additional strength given by its resolutions to the Committee for Political Defense at Montevideo.

The resolution which requires careful follow-up consideration by the United States is the measure which recommends that the governments study the project of convention for an Inter-American Police Union, a union which offers the basis for continued cooperation among the police and judicial authorities. The project for the Police Union is to be studied by the Committee for Political Defense and the American citizen member of the committee will submit the results of his study of the union to this Government at an early date.

Annex "G" is a copy of the Final Act as signed by the delegates.

C. B. SPAETH

THE INTER-AMERICAN CONFERENCE ON SYSTEMS OF ECONOMIC AND FINANCIAL CONTROL, MEETING AT WASHINGTON, JUNE 30–JULY 10, 1942

710.Consultation (3)B/109a

The Secretary of State to Diplomatic Representatives in the American Republics

WASHINGTON, August 4, 1942.

SIRS: The Inter-American Conference on Systems of Economic and Financial Control met in Washington, D. C. from June 30, 1942 to July 10, 1942. That Conference, called pursuant to Resolution VI adopted at the Third Meeting of the Ministers of Foreign Affairs held at Rio de Janeiro in January of this year,[1] was attended by representatives of each of the American Republics. All the representatives considered the Conference a most successful one. There was a free and open discussion of economic and financial controls resulting in the passing of eight Resolutions which are to serve as standards for the American Republics in the establishment and administration of their controls.

There are being transmitted under separate cover three copies of the final act [2] of this Conference both in English and in the language of the country to which you are accredited and copies of the speeches made by the Honorable Sumner Welles, Chairman of the Inter-American Economic Advisory Committee, and by the Honorable Edward H. Foley, Jr., the United States delegate to the Conference.[3] It is suggested that the Resolutions which were adopted be examined carefully and that there should be included in your periodical reports on the administration of freezing controls in the country to which you are accredited a full description of the progress which is being made by the government thereof toward effectuating each of those Resolutions.

There are also being transmitted under separate cover three copies of a handbook which was prepared by the Treasury Department out-

---

[1] For correspondence concerning this Meeting, see pp. 6 ff.; for text of Resolution VI, see Department of State *Bulletin*, February 7, 1942, p. 125.

[2] Pan American Union, Congress and Conference Series No. 39: *Final Act of the Inter-American Conference on Systems of Economic and Financial Control* (Washington, 1942).

[3] For texts of speeches, see Pan American Union, Congress and Conference Series No. 40: *Proceedings of the Inter-American Conference on Systems of Economic and Financial Control* (Washington, 1942), pp. 91, 96, and 99.

lining the wartime financial and property controls in the United States.[4] Copies of that document have been given to each of the representatives of the other American Republics at the Conference. It is expected that the officers in each mission who are responsible for the work on freezing, alien property controls, and the Proclaimed List will familiarize themselves with the contents of this document. Each Resolution should be carefully studied in connection with the subject matter on the particular topic in the handbook.

This Government regards the Conference as having been very successful, bearing in mind the limited role which any conference of this nature can play in contributing to the ultimate objectives. The work done both at the formal sessions of the Conference and at the numerous informal meetings with the representatives of the other governments has, it is believed, clarified for all concerned what should be the ultimate objectives of any successful program. The steps which this Government has taken to carry out these objectives have been fully presented, and many of the problems which the other governments are facing have been fully discussed. If the Resolutions which were adopted at the Conference are actually carried out in the same spirit in which they were, at least from all outward appearance, adopted at the Conference, this phase of our program of economic warfare can be regarded as being highly successful. It is fully realized however that the work done at the Conference is, from a broad point of view, only the beginning and that the biggest part of the job lies ahead. The effective carrying out of these Resolutions by the governments of the American Republics is the step which really counts. In this connection the importance of the role which the officers in the field, who are working on these matters in our diplomatic and consular missions, can play cannot be overemphasized. These officers should keep in close contact with the local freezing control authorities of the respective Republic concerned, consulting with them on the various problems which will arise and furnishing them with ideas as to the steps to take. Except where special circumstances dictate otherwise, those phases of the program envisaged by the Resolutions, which the respective Republic concerned has not effectively carried out, should be called to the attention of the local authorities; and the Department should be kept currently informed as to the progress being made in this connection.

There follows a comment on each of the Resolutions for your guidance.

---

[4] For information concerning wartime financial and property controls, see Inter-American Conference on Systems of Economic and Financial Control, *Administration of the Wartime Financial and Property Controls of the United States Government* (Washington, 1942), and *Documents Relating to Wartime Financial and Property Controls of the United States Government* (Washington, 1942).

I

FINANCIAL AND COMMERCIAL TRANSACTIONS WITH AGGRESSOR NATIONS AND NATIONS DOMINATED BY THEM

This Resolution is aimed at completely cutting off all financial and commercial transactions between the nations of the Western Hemisphere and the Axis and Axis dominated countries. The Resolution provides for the effective immobilization of all funds, securities, and any property of any nature whatsoever which is now held or is subsequently acquired in an American Republic for the account of a person or firm residing or situated in the Axis or Axis dominated countries. Provision is made for complete cessation of trade between the American Republics and the Axis and Axis dominated countries.

An individual or firm resident or situated within an American Republic cannot initiate instructions or orders for putting through financial or commercial transactions in Axis or Axis dominated countries. Financial and commercial transactions cannot be effected in one of the American Republics pursuant to instructions given directly or indirectly by a person within the Axis or Axis dominated countries. Thus, instructions or orders given by a person in the Axis or Axis dominated countries relative to use or disposition of his property or funds cannot be carried out in the American Republic where such property or funds are situated. Similarly, the execution of the orders or instructions of a person within an American Republic acting under a power of attorney from a person or firm in the Axis or Axis dominated countries, concerning the use or disposition of any property whatsoever belonging to the donor of the power is contrary to the provisions of Resolution I.

However, for your information this Government has not construed Resolution I in such a way as to prevent attorneys-in-fact from effecting transactions under powers of attorney in accordance with certain general licenses when such powers were received in this country prior to the effective date of blocking of the country of the donor and when no current or future communication directly or indirectly with Axis or Axis dominated countries is involved. For example, pursuant to General License No. 4 [5] a bank acting under such a power of attorney can sell on a national exchange, securities held in a blocked account in the name of the owner provided that the proceeds of such sale are placed in a blocked account in the name of the owner and provided that such transaction does not involve any current or future communication direct or indirect with enemy territory as defined in General Ruling No. 11.[5] Of course the other terms and conditions of that General License would have to be complied with.

---

[5] For text, see *Documents Relating to Wartime Financial and Property Controls.*

The examples appearing on page 8 of the above-mentioned handbook on the "Administration of the Wartime Financial and Property Controls of the United States Government" demonstrate some of the transactions covered by Resolution I.

Two types of remittances are excepted from the prohibitions of the Resolution. The first of the excepted remittances is one by the government of an American Republic to an Axis or Axis dominated country for such purposes as (1) living expenses of the citizens of such American Republic who may be in Axis territory, or (2) the expenses of representing the governmental interests of such American Republic in the Axis or Axis dominated countries, such as the care and safeguarding of the property of the government of the American Republic in the Axis territory. Such remittance must be made directly by the Government of the American Republic involved, or, as in most cases where diplomatic relations have been severed, it may be made through the government representing the interests of the respective American Republic in the Axis or Axis dominated country.

A second type of excepted remittance is one which the governments of each of the American Republics may authorize (1) for living expenses of the citizens of Axis or Axis dominated nations residing within such American Republic or (2) for expenses of representing the governmental interests of the Axis or Axis dominated nations in the American Republic involved, such as the care and safeguarding of property belonging to such government.

Attention is directed to the provision that none of the excepted remittances from the Axis or Axis dominated countries may be made from blocked funds except in those cases where there is an effective reciprocal agreement between the American Republic involved and the Axis or Axis dominated countries. Thus, if the Government of Japan has blocked funds in Peru, (or in any other American Republic), those funds cannot be used for living expenses of Japanese citizens in Peru. However, if Peru has blocked funds in Japan and Japan agrees and does permit the use of such funds for living expenses of Peruvian citizens in Japan, Peru could, consistent with the Resolution, agree to permit the use of a similar amount of the blocked funds of the Japanese Government for necessary living expenses of Japanese citizens in Peru.

That phase of the program concerning the severance of commercial and financial relations with the Axis and Axis dominated countries is one which is very clearly defined both in Resolution V [6] adopted at the Third Meeting of the Ministers of Foreign Affairs at Rio de Janeiro in January of this year, and in the subject Resolution. Accordingly, every transaction engaged in contrary to the purposes and

---

[6] Department of State *Bulletin*, February 7, 1942, p. 124.

provisions of such Resolutions coming to the attention of the missions should promptly be called to the attention of the government involved unless circumstances make such a procedure unfeasible.

II

Financial and Commercial Transactions With Countries Outside the Western Hemisphere

This Resolution relates to financial and commercial transactions with neutral countries outside the Western Hemisphere. The Resolution requires the other American Republics to supervise "adequately" property and funds within their boundaries belonging to countries outside the Western Hemisphere, and their nationals, which have not severed commercial and financial relations with the Axis. The latter of course excludes nations at war with the Axis. Under this provision each of the American Republics should take steps to locate and identify such property and prevent its use in any way that would benefit the Axis. The governments of the other American Republics should take action to assure that persons and firms within their boundaries do not engage in financial and commercial transactions for the benefit of the Axis nations with persons and firms in neutral nations. This prevents all exportations to and importations from the neutral countries as well as remittances to or from such countries if any of these transactions are of benefit directly or indirectly to the Axis or Axis dominated countries.

Furthermore, in fulfillment of the Resolution the governments of the American Republics are to prevent all financial and commercial transactions with persons or firms in the neutral countries who are known to be engaged in activities inimical to the security of the hemisphere. In this connection, you might discreetly point out to the local freezing control authorities that the Proclaimed List for the countries outside the Western Hemisphere is one means of determining those persons known to be engaged in inimical activities. However, in carrying out this provision, the other American Republics should use all other information available to them.

In connection with the requirements of the subject Resolution, you should carefully study the measures which this Government is taking, vis-à-vis, the various areas outside the Western Hemisphere as described in the above-mentioned handbook on page 9 and following.

This Government through freezing control and export control has exercised great caution to determine that the neutral nations outside the Western Hemisphere are not used as channels for Axis trade, financing and communications. In addition to the supervision of trade and commercial transactions with the four European neutral countries through general licenses based upon assurances by those governments that transactions effected pursuant to such general licenses will not benefit the Axis directly or indirectly, this Government has used export control and the Proclaimed List of Certain Blocked Nationals to determine that individuals who are known to be acting for the benefit of the Axis countries have no commercial or financial relations with persons and firms residing or situated in the United States. In general the criteria which this Government has used in determining whether specific export trade transactions will be permitted are the following: (1) that goods or merchandise exported to the neutral involved will not be re-exported to the Axis or Axis dominated countries; (2) that goods or merchandise exported to the neutral involved is not a substitute for goods or merchandise in the neutral country which can be exported to the Axis or Axis dominated countries; (3) that the goods or merchandise exported does not benefit that phase of the economy of the neutral involved which is being used for the benefit of the Axis war effort. While it may be argued that all export trade to the European neutrals benefits the Axis countries, this Government is not prepared to take such a position at this time and does not wish to press that position with the other American Republics in connection with the subject Resolution.

Through freezing control and export control this Government has stopped all trade with unoccupied France, and financial transactions are permitted only when it is clear that the Axis will not benefit in any way. This Government through export control supervises trade transactions with those neutral countries outside Europe and the Western Hemisphere, and freezing control licenses are required for financial and commercial transactions with those countries when there is an interest of a blocked national or a person whose name appears on the Proclaimed List of Certain Blocked Nationals.

The steps which this Government has taken should not necessarily be construed as meaning that such steps are regarded as compliance with Resolution II. It may be that more drastic steps will be required as events develop. It is hoped that as a minimum the other American Republics as soon as possible will take the necessary steps designed to achieve the results which have been achieved by this Government. Some of those governments may be in a position to take more drastic steps even at this time, and as time passes, it is probable that pursuant to the broad scope of the subject Resolution all of the American Republics may have to take more drastic steps to curtail the benefits which the Axis and Axis dominated countries may derive through trade between the neutral countries outside the Western Hemisphere and the American Republics.

Your attention is directed to the phrase "endeavoring not to cause unnecessary damage to neutral nations" appearing in the first paragraph of the recommendation. That phrase was inserted at the suggestion of the delegation from Chile to cover essential transactions with Spain. It is the hope of this Government that the phrase will not be interpreted in such a manner as to prevent effective action being taken.

III

TRANSACTIONS AMONG THE AMERICAN REPUBLICS

Paragraph (a) provides for the establishment of an interchange of information with respect to financial and commercial transactions carried on between two different American Republics and in which persons engaged in activity inimical to the security of the hemisphere are involved, or in which one of the persons involved in the transaction is acting for a person outside the Western Hemisphere, in order that each American Republic can prevent such transactions within its jurisdiction. This provision contemplates that the American Republics will effectuate policies similar to the one followed by this Government in connection with the Proclaimed List and it is hoped that the other American Republics will use our Proclaimed List as one means of preventing such international transactions. Thus the program is made more effective by having an international control to prevent such transactions in addition to local controls and in establishing a means of detecting such transactions where one person within the American Republics is acting as a cloak for an individual or firm outside the Western Hemisphere. As illustrations, if A who is residing in Chile and who is not engaged in any sort of inimical activity seeks to remit funds to B in Brazil who is known to be engaged in inimical activity through a bank in Uruguay, Uruguay in fulfillment of the Resolution, as well as Chile, is obligated to prevent the transaction. Similarly, if A in Chile should seek to remit to B in Brazil who is acting for a person outside the Western Hemisphere and this fact is known to Brazil, Brazil is obligated to prevent the transaction. Of course in either case the local controls of Brazil should be sufficient. However, by the international controls the entire program is strengthened and the laxity of controls in any particular country is guarded against by the international controls.

The efficacy of this Resolution depends upon the extent to which each mission pursues the policy of interchanging information with the local government concerned. The importance of this Resolution and of the interchange of information provisions cannot be overemphasized. Pursuant to this Resolution we may eventually be able through such interchange of information to ascertain the true ownership of assets held in this country by firms in the other American Republics as cloaks for principals outside the Western Hemisphere and the true ownership of the assets of Panamanian holding companies, etc. The Axis Powers in preparing for their attempt at world conquest have cloaked their funds and property in the names of individuals and firms located in the Western Hemisphere and have planned to carry on financial and commercial transactions to further the Axis war effort through these cloaks. They have done their work well and the problem of ascertaining the true ownership of assets is a difficult one. However, if the wholehearted cooperation of the government to which you are accredited can be obtained in the free exchange of information concerning cloaking activities and the ownership of assets, such can be uncovered and stopped. However, if the United States and the other American Republics are left to determine this matter by acting independently, the prevention of cloaking and the discovery of the true ownership of certain assets is most difficult if not impossible in many cases.

If the spirit and provisions of paragraph (b) are carried out, transactions involving the monetary unit of an American Republic undertaken by persons or firms in countries outside the Western Hemisphere which have not severed financial and commercial relations with the Axis can only be effected through the controls of the American Republic whose monetary unit is involved. Thus, the other American Republics are required to prevent transactions in dollars undertaken by persons or firms located in such nations outside the Western Hemisphere unless that transaction is undertaken through a bank in the United States. Effecting such transactions through the branch of a United States bank located in one of the other American Republics is not a compliance with the Resolution.

The following examples show some of the transactions comprehended by the Resolution: (a) An Argentine bank is holding dollars in New York in an account in its name but actually for the account of a firm in Switzerland; (b) A Brazilian bank has a dollar account on its books in Brazil for a firm in France; (c) An Argentine bank has an obligation to a French firm, which although not expressed directly in dollars is linked in one form or the other to the dollar (and probably covered by dollar deposits in a New York bank in the name of the Argentine bank). If the spirit and provisions of Resolution III are carried out, transactions in the dollar accounts in (a) and (b) could only be effected pursuant to the United States freezing control since they would have to be effected through a United States bank and such bank is to be furnished with a report sufficient to establish the nature of the transaction. Example (c) goes a step further and probably should not be pressed with the local authorities at this time. However, such transactions coming to your attention should promptly be reported to the Department.

Paragraph (c) includes the all important category of cases in which a person in an American Republic seeks to avoid the local controls by using the financial and commercial facilities of another American Republic whose controls are not as strict as those of his own country to effect a financial or commercial transaction with a person or firm residing or situated in a country outside the Western Hemisphere which has not severed commercial and financial relations with the Axis. For the purpose of illustration, assume that Argentina has not taken adequate measures to effectuate Resolution II or that the Argentine controls effectuating that Resolution are not as strict as those of Brazil. X, who resides in Brazil, intends to remit funds to Y in Switzerland. Brazil refuses to license the transaction, whereupon X transfers his funds to an Argentine bank and seeks to remit such funds to Y in Switzerland. Notwithstanding that Argentina might permit persons resident in Argentina to effect such a remittance, it is obligated under this Resolution to prevent the remittance unless the Brazilian authorities expressly give their consent. Likewise if A in Switzerland remits to B in Argentina who has instructions to remit to C in Bolivia, notwithstanding the policy of Argentina concerning such transaction, if Resolution III is fulfilled, Argentina is obligated to prevent the transaction unless the Bolivian authorities expressly give their consent. The same is true of trade transactions. Thus paragraph (c) of Resolution III, if fulfilled, prevents persons within the American Republics avoiding their local controls by using the commercial and financial facilities of the American Republic whose controls are weakest.

Another type of case included within the provisions of paragraph (c) is a transaction in which a firm in the United States is involved with a Brazilian concern. With the knowledge of the Brazilian concern and the Brazilian authorities, but without the knowledge of the United States firm, a French firm is also interested in the transaction. Brazil should prevent the transaction unless the United States freezing control authorities, with full knowledge of the facts, give their approval.

IV

CONTROL OF MOVEMENT AND TRANSFER OF SECURITIES

This Resolution is directed toward preventing transactions in securities in the American Republics which may benefit the Axis. As you know, the Nazis obtained considerable quantities of securities from the invaded countries and have attempted to use these looted securities to obtain exchange for the purpose of furthering their war effort. To guard against this, all securities imported into the American Republics from points outside the Western Hemisphere are to be blocked until it is definitely established that the Axis, Axis dominated countries, or individuals or firms within such countries have not had an interest in such securities since the beginning of the present emergency, i. e., September 1, 1939.

Paragraph (*a*) refers to securities which are being imported and the phrase "directly or indirectly" would make the provision applicable to securities imported into Colombia from Venezuela if those securities had been imported into Venezuela from nations outside the Western Hemisphere since September 1, 1939. Except for such situations, the Resolution does not obligate the American Republics to take measures to subject securities which have been imported in the past to precautionary blocking except that non-bearer securities imported after September 1, 1939, may, in the discretion of the government involved, be subjected to such precautionary blocking. The Resolution recommends that necessary supervisory measures be taken in order to prevent transactions of any nature relating to securities located outside the Western Hemisphere, if such transaction will benefit a person within Axis or Axis dominated countries. Unless this provision is rigidly enforced, a way is left open for the Axis to acquire badly needed foreign exchange for its war effort. The Axis could sell looted securities located in Switzerland to a person in Argentina and thus acquire free Argentine pesos which it could convert into whatever currency was most needed at the time to obtain materials for the Axis war machine. It is known that the neutrals are being used in this manner.

Paragraph (*c*) recommends that the American Republics take the measures necessary to determine whether the Axis or Axis dominated countries, or persons resident therein, have any interest in securities issued or payable in any of the American Republics. This paragraph was inserted at the suggestion of the Mexican delegation. As originally drafted the Mexican delegation intended that each American Republic should require a registration with its diplomatic and consular offices of all securities issued or payable in such American Republic, together with the presentation of evidence to prove that no individual or firm within the Axis or Axis dominated countries had any interest in such securities. In view of the enormous amounts of securities issued or payable in the United States, this would have placed an impossible administrative task on this Government. Accordingly, the phrase "or adopt any other appropriate measures" was added and the paragraph otherwise changed to its present form.

As originally drafted this Resolution covered other situations, such as the effective blocking of securities in which individuals or firms in the Axis and Axis dominated countries had an interest; the prevention of transactions effected within the American Republics in securities, such as sale, hypothecation, etc., pursuant to instructions from Axis or Axis dominated territory; and provisions preventing persons within the Axis or Axis dominated countries from exercising any rights in connection with securities issued or payable within any American Republic (including that of voting at meetings). The Resolution was passed in its present form and without certain of the provisions contained in the original draft on the theory that such provisions were covered by Resolutions I, II and VI. Accordingly, you should bear in mind such Resolutions in addition to the subject Resolution in so far as transactions in securities, security interests, dividends, coupons, etc. are concerned.

V

STANDARDS FOR THE APPLICATION OF FINANCIAL AND ECONOMIC CONTROLS WITHIN THE AMERICAN REPUBLICS

The Resolution recommends that the economic and financial controls have as one objective the control of property and transactions of all persons within the American Republics who are known to be engaged in activity inimical to the security of the hemisphere. Many of the American Republics which have adopted controls have applied those controls upon the basis of nationality. It is well known that many of the persons in the Western Hemisphere, who are engaged in activity on behalf of the Axis nations, have acquired the citizenship of one of the American Republics. Furthermore, there are many persons in the American Republics who are citizens of the Axis countries but whose loyalty to the country in which they reside is unquestioned. Accordingly, it is highly desirable that the financial and property controls be directed against the individuals and firms who are known to be engaged in inimical activity rather than to attempt to control the activities of individuals and firms on the basis of nationality when there is nothing to indicate that many of them are engaged in inimical activity.

The Resolution provides that when the controls are directed against those who are known to be engaged in inimical activity, the object of the controls shall be the elimination of the undesirable activity and influence of such individuals and firms from the economic life of the country involved. In this connection, it is pointed out that, while such controls will not have as their express objective the permanent elimination of such individuals and firms from the economic life of these countries, the measures which are required to eliminate their undesirable influence from the economic life of the American Republics during the time of the present emergency will, in many cases, necessarily be such as to eliminate them permanently.

No specific reference was made to the "Proclaimed List of Certain Blocked Nationals" in any of the Resolutions. It was felt that any reference to the Proclaimed List in such Resolutions might open the way for attack on that list and for requests for deletions on the basis that local controls had been instituted. The Department and the Treasury Department were of opinion that any problems relating to the Proclaimed List could best be settled by bilateral rather than multilateral discussion. It is possible, however, that as the other Republics institute controls and subject firms appearing on the Proclaimed List to such controls, requests will be made by the governments involved for the deletion of the controlled firms from the list. Such requests should promptly be transmitted to the Department, together with your recommendation and the facts necessary to make a determination as to the effectiveness of the local control in each particular case. In this connection your attention is directed to the relevant discussion herein concerning Resolution VII.

VI

STANDARDS OF EFFECTIVE BLOCKING

Obviously, control measures are meaningless if they do nothing more than block certain funds and release those funds at the request of the owners or allow the use of such funds to the benefit of the owners. Accordingly, it is most important that this Resolution be carried out in all respects. The blocking measures will necessarily include all cash, securities, income or other assets of any other kind.

Your attention is directed to the fact that the proceeds of sale or liquidation of undesirable firms must be effectively blocked. In the absence of such controls, little if anything will be accomplished in this area.

Under paragraph 3 of such Resolution the American Republics are in agreement that blocked assets may not be disposed of without the authorization of the government involved and any attempt to dispose of them or to transfer them without such authorization is null and void. One of the purposes of this provision is to prevent blocked individuals from selling their blocked assets to a person who is willing to take the chance of their eventually being unblocked and paying free funds to the blocked person for such assets. Also, this provision is an effective measure for the enforcement of financial and property control laws and decrees.

Paragraph 4 provides that all blocked cash or securities are to be deposited in the central bank, approved banks or appropriate organizations designated by the government involved. The purpose of this provision is to tighten the blocking controls and have certain designated institutions carrying the blocked accounts rather than having every individual or firm carrying blocked accounts on its books or otherwise for blocked individuals.

Careful examination should be made to determine the manner in which the government to which you are accredited allows the withdrawal of blocked assets. No withdrawal should be permitted under the terms of the recommendation if it would benefit the Axis either directly or indirectly in any way. Obviously, blocking does not mean that there may be no withdrawals or that individuals subjected to such control measures may not be allowed funds for minimum living expenses. However, pursuant to the recommendation, they may receive for this purpose only such funds as are *essential to the subsistence* of the blocked individual and that of his family. The recommendation contemplates that the governments of each of the American Republics will set maximum periodical amounts and that no authorizations for living expenses will exceed such amounts.

VII

CONTROL OF BUSINESS ENTERPRISES

This Resolution is directed at the business enterprises which are acting against the political and economic independence or security of the American Republics. The business enterprises which fall in this category are to be determined by the government of the American Republic involved. However, as provided in Resolution VIII, it is contemplated that there will be a free exchange of information on this and other matters. Thus, if you have facts that a business enterprise is engaged in inimical activity, such facts should be made available to the appropriate local authorities. Likewise, if this Government through censorship, reports from other missions, etc., obtains information indicating that a firm resident or situated in the country to which you are accredited is engaged in some sort of inimical activity, that information will be forwarded to you in order that you may bring it to the attention of the appropriate authorities. In such cases, you will, of course, follow the situation and keep the Department fully informed.

The Resolution provides that business enterprises which are acting against the political and economic independence or security of the American Republics shall be the object of forced transfer or total liquidation or if, in the opinion of the government concerned, this is not convenient, then the purposes of the Resolution are to be carried out through means of blocking, occupation or intervention. The term "forced transfer" includes vesting, i. e., transfer to the government.

The delegations of the United States and of certain other countries would have preferred a Resolution requiring: (*a*) the vesting of all businesses essential to the economy of the particular country which act in the interests of the Axis; (*b*) the liquidation of all non-essential firms which so act; and (c) the reorganization, through intervention or otherwise, of firms which are only partially bad or which have been subjected to control for trading reasons, etc. However, some of the other delegations took the position that in view of the fact that forced sales of Axis properties are cited in Resolution V adopted at the Third Meeting of the Ministers of Foreign Affairs, as one alternative method of procedure with respect to essential enterprises, the recommendations in the subject Resolution for the handling of such firms must also be stated in the alternative. However, in the actual drafting of the Resolution, it was possible to obtain agreement on emphasizing the methods of liquidation and vesting which are set forth as the general rule to be followed. In deciding upon the desirability of intervening in the management of Axis controlled firms instead of subjecting them to the forced transfer procedure, it should be borne in mind that in cases of firms owned or controlled from enemy territory and firms owned by persons engaged in inimical activity, wherever resident, this Government is not in general prepared to accept intervention as a basis for their deletion from the Proclaimed List. In such cases, the device of forced transfer, including vesting (or liquidation) would therefore be more desirable to all parties concerned.

Paragraph (b) of the subject Resolution provides for the removal of undesirable employees from firms which are engaged in inimical activities. Under the law of some of the American Republics, persons so removed would be entitled to severance payments. Pursuant to the terms of the Resolution, such payments would be blocked. It is possible that there will be cases where undesirable employees cannot be replaced immediately, in which case it will be necessary that they be kept in the employ of the firms subjected to the measures outlined above. However, it is emphasized that such retention should only be of a temporary character. In such cases, salaries and other remuneration of those so *temporarily* employed shall be supervised in such a manner as to comply with the terms of this Resolution. It is felt that such salaries and other remuneration can only be adequately supervised by blocking according to Resolution VI.

Paragraph (c) provides that contracts contrary to the purposes of the Resolution, (such as patent agreements, etc. with German firms like I. G. Farben) entered into by individuals and firms comprehended within the Resolution shall be rescinded and such of those firms holding contracts or concessions for the exploitation of natural resources, public services, such as lands, mines, water rights, transportation and such, may also be rescinded. This provision might be construed so as to require the American Republics to protect firms and individuals who refuse to comply with contracts entered into with firms subsequently found to be engaged in inimical activity and thus subjected to control.

Many of the firms comprehended by the provisions of this Resolution will no doubt be subjected to forced sale. The proceeds accruing from such sale are to be blocked according to Resolution VI, and the same is true in connection with income accruing from intervened or supervised businesses. Of course where a firm is subjected to total liquidation, the proceeds of the liquidation will be subjected to blocking as set forth in Resolution VI.

Paragraph (e) provides that properties comprehended in the terms of this Resolution can only be sold or transferred to nationals of the country involved or to juridical persons formed by them. It is important to note that under the terms of this paragraph a person, real or juridical, whose property is subject to the provisions of this Resolution and the transfer of which is forced, cannot have any direct or indirect participation in the transaction, such as in the selection of buyers, etc. Accordingly, it is important that each mission investigate each such transaction and where it appears that the buyers of the properties comprehended in the terms of the Resolution are such as are likely to be friendly, now or later, with the Axis interests or those individuals whose interests have been taken over, such facts should be brought to the attention of the appropriate local authorities and promptly reported to the Department.

It is probable that some of the other American Republics may need financial assistance in the form of loans from this Government to the government of the American Republic involved in order to carry out an effective program along the lines of the subject Resolution. For your confidential information, it is expected that this Government will be able to render such assistance where necessary.

VIII

RECIPROCAL COOPERATION AMONG THE AMERICAN REPUBLICS

This Resolution provides for reciprocal cooperation among the American Republics in carrying out Resolutions V and VI adopted by the Third Meeting of the Ministers of Foreign Affairs of the American Republics, the recommendations adopted at the Inter-American Conference on Systems of Economic and Financial Control, and measures which have been or may be taken by the governments of the American Republics. Pursuant to this recommendation, it is envisaged that there will be close cooperation between this Government and each of the other American Republics, and among the other American Republics concerning the actions which each has taken to implement its financial and property controls as stated above. If this

Government is in possession of information which indicates that a transaction which is contrary to the purposes and provisions of any of the above Resolutions is being attempted in the country to which you are accredited, such information will be forwarded to you in order that you may bring it to the attention of the appropriate local authorities. You should indicate to the local authorities that, in the event that they are in possession of information which would be of benefit to this Government in enforcing its financial and property controls, such information should be given you for transmission to the Department. Similarly, the local government should be encouraged to exchange information with the governments of the other American Republics.

It is suggested that each mission promptly communicate to the Department any questions concerning any of the provisions of the Resolutions which are not clarified by the subject instruction in order that circular reply may be made.

Very truly yours,   For the Secretary of State:
                                                     DEAN ACHESON

THE EMERGENCY ADVISORY COMMITTEE FOR POLITICAL DEFENSE, MEETING AT MONTEVIDEO, URUGUAY

710. Consultation (3)A/2 : Telegram

The Uruguayan Minister for Foreign Affairs (Guani) to the Secretary of State

[Translation]

MONTEVIDEO, March 23, 1942.
[Received March 23—4 : 20 p. m.]

In accordance resolution approved Board Directors Pan American Union 25 February last [1] I have honor to invite through you the Government of United States of America to participate inaugural session to be held Montevideo 15 April next Emergency Consultative Committee for Defense Policy created by Resolution XVII of the Third Consultative Meeting Ministers Foreign Affairs American Republics.[2] Should appreciate knowing as soon as possible name and rank of person who will represent your Government on said committee.

I salute the Secretary of State [etc.]   ALBERTO GUANI

---

710. Consultation (3)A/2 : Telegram

The Acting Secretary of State to the Uruguayan Minister for Foreign Affairs (Guani)

WASHINGTON, April 8, 1942.

In reply to Your Excellency's courteous telegram of March 23, 1942, I have the honor to inform you that, with the approval of the President, Mr. Carl Spaeth, former Director American Hemisphere Office of the Board of Economic Warfare, and former Assistant Coordinator of Inter-American Affairs, has been designated a member of the Emergency Advisory Committee for Political Defense under the formula approved by the Governing Board of the Pan American Union.

---

[1] For text, see Pan American Union, *Strengthening of Internal Security* (Washington, 1953), p. 113.
[2] For correspondence on this meeting, see pp. 6 ff.; for text of Resolution XVII, see Department of State *Bulletin*, February 7, 1942, p. 128.

74

Mr. Spaeth plans to arrive in Montevideo in advance of the inaugural meeting of the Committee scheduled for April 15.

Please accept [etc.] SUMNER WELLES

---

710. Consultation (3)A/32: Telegram

The Ambassador in Uruguay (Dawson) to the Secretary of State

MONTEVIDEO, April 15, 1942—8 p. m.
[Received 9 : 25 p. m.]

283. From Spaeth. Party arrived from Buenos Aires this morning. Ambassador, Sanders [3] and I met with Guani late morning. Conference indicated Guani's personal interest in work of commission. Inaugural session 5 : 30 this afternoon opened by Guani who was followed by each of the members. All speeches stressed need for unity combating subversive activities. Summaries being sent by air mail. Very little done to date to establish organization and secretariat. My impression is that both in organization [of] the committee and in development of its work chief responsibility will fall on American member which points up need for adequate briefing within Department. Guani elected chairman. Following is official list of the delegates: Argentina: Miguel Angel Chiappe; Brazil: Mario de Pimental Brandão; Chile: Joaquin Fernández Fernández; Mexico: Carlos Darioojeda; Venezuela: Eduardo Arroyo Lameda; Uruguay: Alberto Guani. Ambassador and staff have been most helpful in getting us established. [Spaeth.]

DAWSON

---

710. Consultation (3)A/49: Telegram

The Ambassador in Uruguay (Dawson) to the Secretary of State

MONTEVIDEO, April 29, 1942—7 p. m.
[Received 7 : 15 p. m.]

327. For Chapin [4] from Spaeth. No. 7. Brazilian member has introduced a resolution which recommends that all of the Republics require nationals of the Tripartite Pact [5] and states subservient to them, as well as organizations of all kinds controlled by such nationals, to file periodic reports as a condition precedent to receiving a certificate of good conduct. The required reports would include statements as to whether the Axis national or organization has contributed funds or property in the interest of the Tripartite Pact, participated

---

[3] William Sanders, Assistant to the American representative, Spaeth.
[4] Selden Chapin, Assistant Chief, Division of the American Republics.
[5] Between Japan, Germany, and Italy, signed at Berlin, September 27, 1940; for text, see League of Nations Treaty Series, vol. CCIV, p. 386.

in any manner in any activity on behalf of the Tripartite Pact, or had knowledge of such activity on the part of others. Substantial fines or imprisonment would be imposed for failure to report, for falsification of the reports, and for any repetition of pro-Axis activities actually disclosed. The proposal is not only designed to put additional pressure upon enemy groups, but would afford nationals of the Tripartite Pact who are friendly to the democracies, an opportunity to establish their loyalty and by so doing, to free themselves from prejudice or discrimination under local laws. In addition, the proposal seems to have the merit of hitting directly at a basic problem pending the preparation of more comprehensive recommendations on the subject of registration and identification. Full text of proposal will be sent airmail pouch.[6] [Spaeth.]

DAWSON

710.Consultation (3)A/50 : Telegram

The Ambassador in Uruguay (Dawson) to the Secretary of State

MONTEVIDEO, May 5, 1942—1 p. m.
[Received 2 : 13 p. m.]

341. For Chapin from Spaeth. No. 8. Reference Embassy's No. 327, my No. 7, April 29. The proposal of the Brazilian member for reports by Axis nationals received a full discussion on the merits in Monday's meeting. The Argentine member, who was clearly acting on instructions, declared that he would support the recommendation only if it were submitted to the Conference of Police and Judicial Authorities.[7] Argentina based its argument on the untenable jurisdictional point that the Committee's powers are subordinate to the powers of the Conference. Chilean member who was also acting on instructions said that he would have to abstain from voting because Chile has already adopted registration laws. The registration law of Chile is general in character and of course is not aimed directly at Axis nationals in the manner of the Brazilian proposal.

All of the other members (who are apparently authorized to vote without reference back to their respective Governments) supported the Brazilian proposal on its merits and vigorously opposed the narrow jurisdictional point raised by Argentina. The discussion emphasized that the system of reporting would afford friendly enemy aliens an opportunity to establish their word in addition to inducing disclosure by unfriendly groups.

Because of the sharp fundamental difference of opinion thus developed it is probable that I shall be required to participate in a

---

[6] Text of Brazilian proposal transmitted to Department as Exhibit C of Report No. 2, May 1, by Mr. Spaeth (710. Consultation (3) A/62).
[7] See pp. 48 ff.

[apparent omission] on the matter prior to the Department's receipt of the full text of the Brazilian proposal. Because I believe that the proposal is fundamentally sound, and because it would be extremely unwise to give an impression of doubt with regard to the first serious disagreement on a matter of principle, I intend to vote affirmatively. If it is possible to do so with apparent good cause, I shall try to defer the vote. [Spaeth.]

DAWSON

---

710. Consultation (3) A/50 : Telegram

The Secretary of State to the Ambassador in Uruguay (Dawson)

WASHINGTON, May 7, 1942—9 p. m.

250. Embassy's 341, May 5, 1 p. m. For the Ambassador and Mr. Spaeth. Although it is not entirely clear whether the Chilean and Argentine members stated that their actions with regard to the proposal introduced by the Brazilian member were in response to specific instruction from their Governments, the Department feels that the situation thus created poses a basic issue which if allowed to become a precedent would adversely affect the whole future of the Committee for Political Defense. The Department believes therefore that provided you both perceive no objection the Ambassador acting on behalf of this Government, but accompanied by Mr. Spaeth, in order to indicate the gravity with which we view the situation, should present orally to Guani as President of the Committee the views of this Government somewhat along the following lines:

"The Government of the United States has been informed by its Ambassador in Montevideo that there appears to be some divergence of view on the part of the members of the Committee for Political Defense with respect to the character of their functions and those of the Committee.

It is the understanding of the Government of the United States based upon Article 2 [8] of the regulations for the Committee for Political Defense approved by the Governing Board of the Pan American Union that the idea in creating a committee of 7 rather than 21 members appointed by individual American republics was that the Committee and the members thereof would represent the 21 American republics as a whole and not the individual Governments who appointed the 7 members. This Government considers it not only proper but necessary that individual governments supply such information as may be called for by the Committee as well as any useful background information which may serve as a guide for the individual members of the Committee with respect to the attitudes and policies of the several American republics. It does not, however, believe that it would be either just or conducive to the utility of the Committee were 7 Governments to claim for themselves the

---

[8] *Strengthening of Internal Security*, p. 116.

privilege of attempting to speak for all 21 American republics by controlling the action of the members. It would appear that since the resolutions of the Committee are merely advisory in character, each American government is amply protected in its liberty of action in determining whether part or all of any recommendation which may be submitted to it can be accepted and put into effect. Moreover, it is only to be expected that certain recommendations, however well founded in principle, may not be susceptible of adoption by certain Governments because of constitutional or political impediments. Also the fact that a country may have adopted legislation or taken action along pertinent lines in advance of the receipt of a recommendation from the Committee should not affect the desirability of addressing such recommendations to all of the Governments, nor does it affect the collective responsibility of any member of the Committee in acting for all the Governments."

In discussing the matter with Guani you may suggest that as President of the Committee he might discuss the matter with the individual members, or that he may wish, as Foreign Minister of Uruguay, to take up the matter through appropriate diplomatic channels. Finally, Mr. Spaeth may wish to observe that the record clearly shows that the Committee for Political Defense was organized without any reference to or necessary connection with the forthcoming Police and Judicial Conference in Buenos Aires.

Hull

---

710. Consultation (3)A/46 : Telegram

The Secretary of State to the Ambassador in Uruguay (Dawson)[9]

Washington, May 8, 1942—8 p. m.

253. For Spaeth from Chapin. Your No. 4. Embassy's No. 315, April 27, 6 p. m.[10] Since an informal canvass of the views of the intelligence services indicates that for reasons which appear substantial to the Department this Government is not prepared at this time to enter into any multilateral arrangement for an exchange of intelligence information, the Department suggests that the provision for the exchange of information "with respect to the nationality, identity and loyalties of seamen and other employees of shipping companies and port authorities" be eliminated from your draft resolution.

Our further suggestions and those of Coast Guard, Naval Intelligence, and War Shipping Administration are contained in following proposed redraft of resolution.

"The Emergency Advisory Committee for Political Defense resolves to recommend and respectfully urge the Governments of the American Republics:

---

[9] Notation on file copy, apparently by drafting officer: "This telegram is based on a rough draft prepared by Mr. L. M. C. Smith of the Justice Department and cleared by him with the Navy Department and the Maritime Commission."
[10] Not printed.

(1) To prevent persons from engaging in espionage activities with regard to port and dock facilities, the movement and anchorage of ships, their cargoes, routes, and sailing times, and to redouble their efforts to apprehend and punish persons who engage in such activities or who transmit information with respect to such matters, directly or indirectly, to any nation at war with an American Republic, or to a nation subservient thereto, by any means of communication.

(2) To exercise a greater degree of care in the employment of all personnel of shipping companies, port authorities, and other facilities for or enterprises engaged in shipping, waterfront, or harbor activity, and to exercise strict surveillance and control over all such personnel, and over any other persons permitted to enter waterfront areas or to board ship.

(3) To prevent public knowledge of the movement or anchorage of ships, their identities, destinations, cargoes, routes, or sailing times by:

> (*a*) Prohibiting the publication or disclosure of such information through newspapers, trade circulars, journals, or periodicals, through shipping and other commercial documents and correspondence of exporters, importers, and shipping companies, through radio, or through any other means; and
>
> (*b*) By adopting adequate rules and regulations to prohibit and punish the giving of such information inadvertently, through careless or unguarded talk, by individuals who receive such information in the course of their duties, or otherwise.

(4) To transmit to the Emergency Advisory Committee for Political Defense pertinent information as to the methods now being employed by national, state and local authorities with respect to the matters to which reference is made in this recommendation; such information to be provided on specific request, and subject to normal security considerations."

Revisions in paragraph 4 were proposed by Naval Intelligence.

We are endeavoring to obtain from Naval and Maritime authorities the information you request concerning shipping practices and the statement of methods called for by paragraph 4 of the resolution. This will require some time, but will expedite as much as possible. [Chapin.]

HULL

---

710. Consultation (3)A/86⅔

The American Representative on the Emergency Advisory Committee for Political Defense (Spaeth) to the Under Secretary of State (Welles)

MONTEVIDEO, May 8, 1942.
[Received May 14.]

MY DEAR MR. SECRETARY: I have today transmitted my Report No. 3 to the Department.[11]

---
[11] Not printed.

I particularly wish to draw your attention to the thoughts which I express in the first two or three pages thereof. In essence, those thoughts are a reiteration of what you recognized in your first statement to me about the work of the Committee: that the Committee will be no more than what our Government is able to make of it. You will recall that we also recognized that the task was threefold: first, thorough preparation in Washington; second, negotiation in Montevideo; and, third, follow-through by tactful representations to the several Governments.

As my reports indicate, notwithstanding the difficulties caused by the member from Argentina, I have full confidence in the potentialities of the Committee. I believe, however, that the Committee can be of substantial assistance in working toward our basic objectives only if I am adequately briefed by the Departments in Washington. I wish to emphasize that by "briefing" I do not mean the presentation of formal recommendations from our Government which might be construed as binding upon it once affirmative Committee action is taken. I have in mind, rather, the information about problems and the informal suggestions with regard to their solution which will enable me as a representative of all of the Republics to give effective guidance to Committee discussions.

In the short time that I have been privileged to work with you I have been impressed above all by your desire to strengthen the organizations which have been established on an inter-American basis. I believe, as I am certain you do, that there could be nothing worse for the long term Hemisphere program than failure by inter-American bodies in the realization of the purposes for which they were established. The impact upon international morale of the failure of the League of Nations and some of its subordinate organizations constitutes a warning for those who are endeavoring to strengthen the spirit of cooperation among the American republics. Under the impetus of the emergency we have an extraordinary opportunity to establish the proposition that inter-American bodies such as the Committee for Political Defense can be made to function effectively. The sincerity and strength of my feeling in this matter explain my insistence that persons working on the problems of the Committee in Washington appreciate the seriousness of their responsibility to brief (in the sense expressed above) the Committee thoroughly on all aspects of Resolution XVII.

With best regards,

Sincerely yours,

CARL B. SPAETH

710. Consultation (3)A/86¾

The Under Secretary of State (Welles) to the American
Representative (Spaeth)

WASHINGTON, May 28, 1942.

DEAR CARL: Thank you for your letter of May 8. I hope you will continue to write me in complete frankness with regard to developments in connection with the Committee on Political Defense.

First let me assure you, as I said prior to your departure from Washington, that we in the Department attribute great importance to the Committee and its work. In our opinion the potentialities which lie ahead of the Committee are far reaching, not merely as an instrument for the prosecution of political warfare today, although that alone is considerable, but also as a stabilizing element of the greatest value in the inter-American machinery. It seems probable that either this Committee or some other inter-American instrumentality will have to continue to function in the unsettled post-war period.

We cannot therefore afford to let the Committee fall short of its purpose. For this reason we are building up as rapidly as possible the promised organization within the Department which I feel sure will provide you with the "briefing" which you have requested for your work. As you know, the permanent Departments of the Government do not have the same freedom in budgetary matters as do the emergency agencies, but I am glad to say that the Bureau of the Budget has just approved the establishment of a special section in the Division of the American Republics which is already being recruited.

I have said above that no one can foresee the future of the Committee but I would like to make certain observations with regard to its possible growth. The prestige of the Committee depends, as you have observed, on these first few months of its existence. If it is to be the permanent or semi-permanent organ of inter-American action which we hope it will be, it is important both that it not die of inanition and that it not become so active that it run against opposition which might stunt its growth. In other words, it would be advisable that the Committee, during the first months of its existence, should put roots down and become firmly embedded before attempting to weather the storm that might blow up if a subject of too serious disagreement on the part of the members appointed by Argentina and Chile is broached. Both Argentina and Chile must be continually reminded of their commitments and stimulated to take action, but it would definitely not be desirable to risk a show-down at this juncture, particularly since there are signs that Chile is reconsidering its policy.

I repeat, the CPD should not wreck itself on an issue in international politics which it now lacks power to handle. Meanwhile, the Department's bilateral action bears the brunt of this situation. There are grounds for hope that it will improve.

Once the prestige and semi-permanent character of the Committee is established, particularly if one of the states which has not carried out the recommendations of Resolution I [12] of the Rio Meeting should be brought back into the fold, the Committee would be in a position to expand the field of its action and to make stronger recommendations with good prospects of success. It might even reach the point where its moral influence would have great effect directed at a non-cooperative state.

Although it is probable that this Government, particularly the intelligence agencies thereof, would not have any objection to the establishment of an information center along the lines laid down in Annex B of your report no. 4 of May 15 [13] as modified by your telegram no. 10 of May 23, 1 p. m. to Chapin,[14] we feel very definitely that an exchange of information with regard to persons engaged in subversive activities should be limited to persons either under indictment or who have been convicted. This would seem to be as far as we can go on information with regard to individuals which we "must" transmit to such an organization. It is possible, however, that on a voluntary basis we might wish to make use of such a center for distribution of information with regard to dangerous suspects engaged in espionage, sabotage or dissemination of totalitarian propaganda whom we had reason to believe were at large in the American republics. For obvious reasons, however, we would not wish to be in the position of having to supply this information on demand. As you know the process of tracking down subversive groups must necessarily proceed in its initial stages in complete secrecy lest the individuals concerned become alarmed and take cover.

The preparation of background material with regard to control of aliens and similar related problems is being continued in conjunction with the Department of Justice. Likewise it is my understanding that some work is being done in connection with measures for the protection of shipping and port facilities looking to the submission of tentative suggestions on this subject.

In paragraph II F of Annex B of your report under reference there is a reference to the proposed Inter-American Information Center on Subversive Activities serving as a depository for samples of totalitarian propaganda material of all kinds. We have given

---

[12] For text, see Department of State *Bulletin*, February 7, 1942, p. 118.
[13] Not printed.
[14] Not printed; it was transmitted as No. 411 from Montevideo.

considerable thought to this problem and believe that the Committee on Political Defense could serve a most important role in combatting totalitarian propaganda. While our ideas have not crystallized we have in mind the possibility that the Committee might engage in propaganda analysis with a view to the issuance of regular bulletins to the Governments and the press of the American republics pointing out the major lines followed by Axis propaganda in all media.

With this in mind you may wish to consider as a temporary measure pending consideration of the recommendation for the establishment of the information center, suggesting that the Committee call upon the American Governments to submit samples of totalitarian propaganda circulating in their countries together with any analyses of content and media as may have been undertaken. It would seem necessary that this step be taken not only so that the collection can be complete, but so that this Government could appear to respond to request rather than to force the Committee to undertake the additional burden.

This, I realize, is a very large order and would, at first blush, require a considerable organization to undertake properly in Montevideo. Fortunately we have such an organization now functioning very efficiently under Professor Doob in the Office of the Coordinator of Inter-American Affairs. We therefore propose some arrangement whereby the bulk of the analysis could be done in Doob's office with the results forwarded to you promptly by air mail. These results could be checked in Montevideo with the observations of the Committee. Eventually after the ground work had been laid and propaganda analyzed and typed on a systematic basis it might be possible to speed up the process by weekly cable reports.

It is our feeling that giving widespread publicity to a dispassionate analysis of enemy propaganda would do as much to defeat the value of the campaign as would any amount of counter propaganda which we might produce, since counter propaganda itself is bound to be labeled as prejudiced no matter how true or how striking be the presentation.

I should be glad to have your reactions to the proposal whose broad lines have merely been sketched here. Chapin, who is discussing the matter with Harrison and Doob of the C. I. A. A. will write you further details shortly.

Finally, I am sure you will understand me when I make the suggestion that it might be well in the future to clear with the Department any proposals which you yourself submit to the Committee for discussion as possible recommendations. Although I am sure we are in full agreement that the official attitude of the member appointed by the United States should be that he represents the twenty-one republics and not merely this Government, unavoidably there attaches a certain moral obligation to proposals which may have been submitted by that member. It would be embarrassing both to you and to us were the Committee to transmit officially some recommendation based on one of your proposals which we were not in a position to adopt, unless we could prove that we were arriving at the same result through another way. I believe that on normal occasions it should be possible to clear any proposals by air mail pouch but in cases where urgent action seemed essential, you could cable us the essential points of your proposal.

With all kindest regards and best wishes for your continued success in the Committee, believe me,

Sincerely yours,   SUMNER WELLES

---

710. Consultation (3)A/70a : Telegram

The Secretary of State to the Ambassador in Uruguay (Dawson)

WASHINGTON, June 24, 1942—5 p. m.

382. For Sanders from Spaeth. In another cable [15] we are transmitting the text of a resolution which we hope will be introduced either by you or if he is agreeable by the Mexican member of the Committee, substantially in its present form.

The resolution is intended to open the way for propaganda analysis and regular reports thereon by the Committee to the various governments. A preliminary agreement has been reached with the Coordinator of Inter-American Affairs for the assignment of personnel for this work both in Montevideo and in Washington. We are therefore anxious to secure material from the other American republics as rapidly as possible so that the program may get under way.

It is also requested that you advise by cable of the work undertaken by the Committee since the police conference as well as its projected program for the next few weeks. [Spaeth.]

HULL

---

710. Consultation (3)A/70b : Telegram

The Secretary of State to the Ambassador in Uruguay (Dawson)

WASHINGTON, June 24, 1942—6 p. m.

383. For Sanders from Spaeth. Reference Department's telegram no. 382 of June 23 [*24*], 5 p.m.

WHEREAS:

1. (Cite appropriate portion of Resolution XVII);
2. the fate of the formerly free nations of Europe, now tempo-

---

[15] *Infra.*

rarily under the yoke of the oppressor, shows clearly that the systematic dissemination of subversive propaganda by the member states of the Tripartite Pact is an integral part of their program of total attack;

3. the purpose of such propaganda attack is to misrepresent the truth, to attack the fundamental bases of democracy, and to weaken and divide the American Republics, both within themselves and with each other, and to create and exploit racial, religious, political, social and economic dissension among the peoples of the hemisphere;

4. subversive totalitarian propaganda continues to be disseminated throughout the hemisphere by or on behalf of such states, by means of the press, the mails, the radio, the motion picture, by word of mouth, and by other methods of communication;

5. such subversive propaganda is unable to function effectively or to survive when its sources, methods, themes, and techniques are exposed to those whom the propaganda seeks to influence;

THEREFORE THE EMERGENCY ADVISORY COMMITTEE FOR POLITICAL DEFENSE RESOLVES THAT

1. Each of the American Republics be requested

(a) to transmit to the Committee samples of all such propaganda material circulated in any Republic in any form, whether by means of the press, the mails, the radio, the motion picture, by word of mouth, and by other methods of communication;

(b) to transmit to the Committee any reports, studies, or analyses which have been made of the sources, methods, themes, techniques, and effect of such propaganda;

(c) to advise the Committee as to the methods used and the facilities available for the preparation of such reports, analyses and studies of such propaganda;

(d) to furnish the Committee with copies of all laws, decrees, and information as to other measures which have been taken by the Government for the control, prevention, or punishment for the dissemination of such propaganda;

2. That the Committee will study the above material in order that it may propose and develop such recommendations and programs for combatting such propaganda as may be indicated. [Spaeth.]

HULL

710.Consultation (3)A/71 : Telegram

The Ambassador in Uruguay (Dawson) to the Secretary of State

MONTEVIDEO, June 26, 1942—2 p. m.
[Received 5 : 17 p. m.]

532. Sanders to Carl Spaeth care of Chapin. No. 14. Resolution on propaganda transmitted in Department's 383 will be submitted to Full Committee this afternoon as a project of Subcommittee for

Registration and Internal Control of Persons. I fully expect Committee to approve without reservations as it has already approved recommendation that that Committee undertake this type of work formulated in my note on organization included with my letter to you June 18.[16] I shall urge upon Chouhy Terra [17] the immediate communication of the recommendation to the Governments after its approval by Committee. At the meeting of Tuesday, Committee approved all recommendations formulated in my note above mentioned, with an addition proposed by Mexican Ambassador that Subcommittee on Organization also be authorized to reexamine his original proposal relative to establishment of National Committee of Political Defense.

With reference to recommendations approved by Committee before Buenos Aires Conference,[18] Subcommittee on Registration and Extend [*Internal*] Control of Persons is re-examining recommendation on registration of aliens in light of suggestions of Department. Pimentel considers original draft is preferable in many respects but I do not believe he will oppose its revision. The recommendation on protection of shipping will be resubmitted to Committee this afternoon by special Subcommittee on Protection of Shipping mentioned in my memorandum on organization and it will probably go to Governments next week. The recommendation on the Inter-American office is now discarded in view of Resolution XIII [19] of Buenos Aires Conference. Most members feel that draft uniform penal law is now one of major assignments of Committee for next period. It is important that we be prepared to deal with this problem on your return.

Pimentel, Arroyo and other members of the Committee are determined to put full pressure behind the work of the Committee, particularly in connection with the assignments of the Conference of Buenos Aires. The subcommittees are meeting every day and the full Committee will continue to meet twice a week. Pimentel is talking of holding a public session of the Committee to awaken interest in the right of the Committee. He and Bouza [19a] also are convinced that the Committee should have a special intelligence service at its disposal. I am arguing against both of these suggestions and do not believe anything will come of them. I believe Pimentel's attitude arises in part out of an increasing concern over developments in Africa and about implications for Brazil of complete Axis control in that region.

---

[16] Not found in Department files.

[17] José L. Chouhy Terra, Secretary General of the Committee.

[18] For correspondence concerning the Inter-American Conference of Police and Judicial Authorities, which met at Buenos Aires, May 27–June 9, 1942, see pp. 48 ff.

[19] Pan American Union, Congress and Conference Series No. 38: *Final Act of the Inter-American Conference of Police and Judicial Authorities* (Washington, 1943), p. 15.

[19a] Luis A. Bouza, delegate from Uruguay.

In view of your indication that we may expect personnel in Montevideo to deal with propaganda analysis, I assume you want us to make definite arrangements for securing the apartment next door. Please advise. Guani, Chouhy Terra and I will have a meeting next week to discuss the budget of the Committee. [Sanders.]

DAWSON

710.Consultation (3) A/138

The American Representative (Spaeth) to the Under Secretary of State (Welles)

MONTEVIDEO, August 1, 1942.
[Received August 10.]

MY DEAR MR. SECRETARY: Pursuant to your suggestion, immediately upon my arrival I arranged to see Guani relative to the problems presented by Argentina's membership on the Committee. My interview was arranged for Saturday, and I went to see Guani at his apartment where he has been kept for ten days by illness. I had not been with him more than ten minutes when the President [19b] was announced. After he and Guani had had about a quarter of an hour alone, I had the good fortune to spend well over an hour with the two of them.

I was greatly impressed by Baldomir. He has a direct and simple manner, gets down to the essentials of a problem very quickly, and seems to know the detailed facts of the important questions facing his country. He has a realistic appreciation of the tremendous fight that lies ahead for the United Nations, and is nevertheless not pessimistic about the ultimate outcome. With regard to the most discussed question of the day (both here and in Argentina)—that of a second front—he stated that he did not see how the Allies could possibly be ready to undertake the job until 1943. He is, of course, much concerned about the economic situation of this country, and stated that there were now twenty thousand unemployed, principally in the Montevideo area, and that unemployment will certainly continue to increase. He recognized that we are doing our best to keep Uruguay supplied with essential materials.

After a general discussion of economic and military questions, the President gave me an opportunity to speak to the point about which I had come to see Guani by asking me about the work of the Committee and the attitude of our government toward its future. I told him that it is our opinion that the Committee can make a substantial contribution to the political defense of the Hemisphere, but that it will be handicapped considerably so long as Argentina is represented

---

[19b] Alfredo Baldomir, President of Uruguay.

and pursues its present foreign policy. I stated that this was your view and that you had asked me to discuss the question with Guani. I added that there seemed to be two alternatives, the one less drastic than the other; the appointment by Argentina of a member sympathetic to the cause of the United Nations, or, more drastically, a reorganization of the Committee by the Governing Board of the Union to eliminate Argentina. Without any hesitation, the President stated that the more drastic step seemed necessary, and expressed the opinion that, because of the nature of the subject matter, the membership of the Committee should be limited to republics which have broken relations with the Axis. When I indicated that it is our hope that Chile will soon swing over, the President stated that he held the same opinion, but he maintained that effective Committee work in the control of subversive Axis elements requires a break in relations by the countries which nominate members to the Committee. Guani stated his complete agreement with the President's position, and authorized me to advise you accordingly. As you will recall, Pimentel Brandão of Brazil has on several occasions expressed substantially the same opinion.

It appears that during my absence, Chile has continued to take approximately the same position as Argentina. During the course of the next week I plan to have a frank talk with Fernandez y Fernandez, who has just returned from Santiago, to ascertain whether we can expect a more sympathetic attitude from Chile.

It is my own unqualified opinion that the position taken by President Baldomir is the correct one. The political defense program of nineteen republics is being undermined by two governments which refuse to recognize the danger; and in these times we would be mad, and derelict in our defense responsibilities, were we to permit the situation to continue. The fact is that while Argentina and Chile have accepted that part of Resolution XVII of Rio which creates the Committee, they have repudiated, time and again in the Committee's deliberations, practically all of the substantive provisions of the same Resolution. It is both practically and legally sound to maintain that a republic which has not accepted the substantive recommendations of Resolution XVII should not be privileged to nominate a member of the Committee which is charged with the development of joint programs for the enforcement of the very same recommendations.

I appreciate, of course, that action to eliminate Argentina from the Committee would be instituted only after a full survey of the entire Argentine picture; it would necessarily be integrated with other action similarly designed to challenge the ambiguous position of that government. I shall advise you immediately of any further indication of Guani's attitude, and will explore the question, quite informally and in a general manner, with the members from Mexico, Venezuela and Brazil.

[Here follows paragraph concerning a personnel matter.]

Sincerely yours, CARL B. SPAETH

---

710. Consultation (3)A/138

Memorandum by the Adviser on Political Relations (Duggan) to the Under Secretary of State (Welles)

[WASHINGTON,] August 24, 1942.

MR. WELLES: I have given considerable thought to Mr. Spaeth's proposal that the Montevideo Committee be reorganized so as to omit Argentina.

I have been troubled by the idea of eliminating Argentina from an inter-American committee, it being my belief that we have not wanted to put Argentina beyond the pale.

I share the view expressed by Mr. Bonsal [20] and Mr. Chapin that the elimination of Argentina from this Committee would irritate Argentina considerably but would not be of a sufficient jolt to move Argentina from its present position.

With Brazil in the war and Chile about to break relations it seems to me that the Committee, if there was a real desire on the part of all of the members except Argentina, should have little difficulty in securing the adoption of whatever resolutions seem desirable even though Argentina might object and append dissenting opinions. If Argentina were to continuously oppose the resolutions adopted and this information were to be circulated, I do not think that Argentina would gain thereby or that the Argentine views would affect the thought of the other countries.

LAURENCE DUGGAN

---

710. Consultation (3)A/104a : Telegram

The Acting Secretary of State to the Ambassador in Uruguay (Dawson)

WASHINGTON, August 29, 1942—4 p. m.

519. You are requested to make known to Spaeth and informally to Guani the approval of this Government for the resolution of the Emergency Advisory Committee for Political Defense that the Committee has powers to investigate and make recommendations with respect to the Falange. You are requested to express the opinion that all foreign organizations operating in the American republics

---

[20] Philip W. Bonsal, Chief, Division of the American Republics.

for foreign principals and suspected of acting in the interest of the Axis should be subjected to thorough investigation.

WELLES

---

710. Consultation (3)A/120b

The Under Secretary of State (Welles) to the Chairman of the Emergency Advisory Committee for Political Defense (Guani)

WASHINGTON, September 4, 1942.

EXCELLENCY: I have the honor to address your Excellency concerning the Resolution approved by the Emergency Advisory Committee for Political Defense on May 5 [7], 1942, entitled "Resolution Relative to a Questionnaire for Identifying Friendly Aliens and for the Disclosure of Subversive Elements within the American Nations",[21] and concerning the letter of May 9, 1942 [22] addressed by your Excellency to the Secretary of State of the United States transmitting a copy of that Resolution.

In compliance with the request made in your letter to the Secretary of State and in order to assist the Committee in its compliance with Article 21 of the Regulations, I beg to report herewith on the measures which are being undertaken by this Government to accomplish the objectives set forth in the Resolution.

The following steps have been taken by this Government to secure the identification and reporting of Axis nationals:

In 1940 all aliens were required by a special statute of the United States [23] to register and to make an initial and complete report of their activities.

Under the statute known as the Alien Enemy Act of 1798 [24] all nationals of those States with which this country is at war are subject to summary apprehension, internment and to such other restrictions upon their liberty as may be found necessary in the interest of national security. Upon the declaration of war and pursuant to the authority vested by this statute those nationals of the member States of the Tripartite Pact who were deemed particularly dangerous were immediately apprehended and interned for the duration. In addition, all enemy nationals were required again to register and in that connection to make an immediate and comprehensive report to the authorities as to their activities and affiliations, including information as to the organizational activities set forth in the Annex to the Resolution approved by the Committee. Unfriendly enemy nationals who were not considered sufficiently dangerous to be interned or confined for the duration were temporarily paroled and ordered to report weekly, or less often, to the proper authorities.

---

[21] For text, see Emergency Advisory Committee for Political Defense, *Annual Report*, July 1943 (Montevideo, 1943), p. 51.
[22] Not printed.
[23] The Alien Registration Act of June 28, 1940; 54 Stat. 670.
[24] 1 Stat. 577.

Under the provisions of another statute any alien who desires to work in any private corporation or business which produces any material for the war effort is required to make a special application and report to the Secretary of War or the Secretary of the Navy. The alien is then carefully investigated by the intelligence agencies and if his loyalty to the United States is confirmed a special certificate is issued permitting his employment.

Those who comply with all the laws of the country and with all the special regulations restricting their conduct and liberty have been given assurance by the President that they will be permitted to exercise the usual rights and privileges accorded aliens by the Constitution and laws of this country.

The following steps have been taken with respect to the surveillance and control of organizations:

Those organizations which were deemed dangerous to the national security have been proceeded against, their records seized, and many of their members prosecuted. This and other action has resulted in the effective dissolution of a considerable number of organizations.

In addition, enemy nationals are forbidden to retain any membership in or connections with any organization found to have been subversive in character.

Organizations which still exist for certain purposes or are engaged in certain activities are required under applicable statutes to file with the Department of Justice a complete statement of their membership, finances, purposes and activities, and to report periodically in order to keep current the information thus furnished. Adequate penalties are provided for failure to report fully and accurately.

A total of some sixteen thousand organizations and branches thereof are kept under constant surveillance by the investigative agencies of the Government, even though they do not appear to be subversive in character. In addition, continuous studies and analyses are made of some fifteen hundred publications in English or in various foreign languages, some of which act as organs for suspected organizations.

It is believed that the foregoing described laws and regulations give effect in this country to the substance of proposals contained in said recommendation, except for the suggestion relating to the general issuance of "Certificates of Compliance".

With respect to this subject and in accordance with the statement in the last paragraph of the letter from your Excellency requesting the observations of this Government, I beg to transmit to your Excellency certain inquiries which have been made by officials of this Government who are charged with the control of enemy nationals and of subversive organizations. They would like to know the precise scope of the certificate of compliance and the extent to which it would represent an official verification of the information supplied in the report by the individual or organization concerned. They would appreciate being informed as to whether it is intended that the certificate would be issued mainly upon the basis of an examination of the report furnished by the individual or organization or whether the certificate would be issued only after a complete investigation of all the associations and activities of the individual or organization. The officials further inquire whether such certificates of compliance would be given a permanent validity or would be limited in time, to be renewed at intervals.

In addition, they also seek to inquire as to whether there exists a danger that the certificate might be misinterpreted as an official approval of the individual or organization, of official sanction of its activities, or that the certificate might be used by the unscrupulous to mislead others into believing that it indicated governmental endorsement or sponsorship.

The officials of this Government are continuing to give consideration to this problem and deeply appreciate the opportunity of being able to take advantage of whatever further information or advice the Committee will be disposed to offer with respect thereto.

Please accept [etc.]   SUMNER WELLES

---

710. Consultation (3)A/121 : Telegram

The Secretary of State to the Chairman of the Emergency Advisory Committee for Political Defense (Guani)

WASHINGTON, September 10, 1942.

I have the honor to acknowledge receipt of Your Excellency's telegram of September 2 [25] informing me of the resolution adopted by the Committee to investigate the activities of the Falange.

My Government will endeavor to collect information of the character outlined in the resolution for transmission at an early date to the Committee.

Accept [etc.]   CORDELL HULL

---

710. Consultation (3)A/213

Resolution on Clandestine Radio Communications Approved by the Emergency Advisory Committee for Political Defense on September 11, 1942

[Translation]

WHEREAS:

A. The Third Meeting of Ministers of Foreign Affairs of the American Republics recommended in Resolution XL [26] that the governments adopt immediate measures to eliminate clandestine communication

---

[25] Not printed.
[26] Department of State *Bulletin*, February 7, 1942, p. 140.

stations and that they conclude bilateral or multilateral agreements in order to carry out this purpose;

B. It was recommended in the Annex to Resolution XVII that the governments adopt measures to prevent acts of espionage, to punish the divulgence of defense information, and to surveille all communications to and from member States of the Tripartite Pact of States subservient to them or in contact with them;

C. The security of information relating to the defense and security of any American Republic is of vital importance to all the American Republics, and the lack of effective control over the transmission of said information from any country endangers the security of all countries of the hemisphere;

D. Essential information, including that relating to cargoes and movements of ships, military and naval forces, defense equipment and installations, and production of strategic materials is being transmitted at the present time to the military and naval forces of the Axis countries by means of clandestine transmission stations located on the continent.

E. A coordinated and efficient system of detection and discovery by means of local stations is essential in order to be able to locate, intercept, surveille and eliminate all clandestine communications.

F. There has been instituted in the United States of America, in accordance with Resolution XL a program of training and equipping persons of the American republics in the discovery of clandestine transmission stations.

THE EMERGENCY ADVISORY COMMITTEE FOR POLITICAL DEFENSE RESOLVES:

To recommend to the Governments of the American Republics:

1. That they participate in and lend all possible support to the program of the creation of a coordinated and efficient system for the discovery, interception, and surveillance of clandestine stations and also to the program of locating and equipping personnel, including the supplying of land, buildings, equipment and personnel necessary for the establishment and operation of adequate stations for discovery, interception and surveillance.

2. That the organization charged in each country with the discovery, interception and surveillance of clandestine stations establish direct contact and cooperate fully with similar organizations in the other American republics, or with any other hemisphere headquarters established to integrate the work of these organizations in order that:

(a) there may be immediate communication among the American Republics of information relating to the existence and operation of any clandestine telecommunication station within the boundaries of any country.

(*b*) the findings of the various stations charged with discovering, intercepting and surveilling in the hemisphere will be unified to the end that communication stations—in non-continental countries—may be discovered and located with exactitude.

3. That in order to facilitate the coordination of the systems of detection, interception and surveillance, the Governments make whatever modifications are necessary in the regulations which govern their boundaries and international communications,—so that such regulations will not imperil the success of this work.

4. That each government direct its political and military authorities and other authorized agencies

(*a*) to cooperate in the work of discovering clandestine transmission stations and

(*b*) to seize and close any station which is operating illegally or communicating with military, naval or other agents of member States of the Tripartite Pact or States subservient to them, or which is operating in any manner prejudicial to the defense and security of the hemisphere.

Provided that the continued operation and surveillance of said transmitting station would serve the interests of or defense of the American republics, the closure and capture of said station will not be carried out immediately, but full reports on said station and its activity will be given to all American Republics.

5. That in order to facilitate the punishment of persons guilty of espionage, the unauthorized communication of vital information, or other crimes against the security of the State or the hemisphere, the competent tribunals in each of the American republics be permitted to accept as legal evidence authenticated information concerning clandestine communications obtained by the official operative personnel charged with discovery, interception and surveillance in any American republic.

710.Consultation (3)A/159½

The American Representative (Spaeth) to the Adviser on Political Affairs (Duggan)

MONTEVIDEO, October 5, 1942.
[Received October 12.]

DEAR LARRY: Since the beginning of my work for the Committee, I have been seriously handicapped by the apparent reluctance of the Department to supply me with summaries of intelligence information bearing on problems within the Committee's jurisdiction. I believe that this reluctance on the part of some officials in the Department is based upon a misunderstanding of the type of intelligence information which I need, and the use which I would make of it.

With regard to the type of information which I require, I would stress that I am not interested in, and do not need, names of persons or sources of information. All that I require is a summary statement indicating that intelligence information, which the Department has reason to credit or accept, indicates the existence of specific problems relating to subversive activities in some part of the Hemisphere. I must, of course, have a full statement of the problem, and an indication of the country or place in the Hemisphere where it exists. To illustrate: I was tremendously aided in connection with the Rivera meeting [27] on Entry and Exit of Persons by information from Buenos Aires that Nazi groups in Argentina have been organizing what amounts to an underground railway system to aid Germans seeking to escape from Brazil. This information not only confirmed my opinion with regard to the need for an immediate meeting of border officials, but affected the content of the measures proposed at Rivera. Furthermore, it was not necessary for me to know the source of the information in Argentina, the names of the Germans involved, or anything else of a more specific character; all that I needed to know was that our intelligence information established the existence of a specific problem within the jurisdiction of the Committee. And the same would be true of summaries of intelligence information relative, for example, to Falangist activity in Peru, or propaganda activities in Bolivia.

With regard to the use which I make of such information, I can state without qualification that it will not be made directly available to any member of the Committee. The Committee will benefit by it only as it may induce me, by reason of the indication of urgency or practical importance, to promote certain programs and recommendations more vigorously than others. It should be obvious that with problems as changing, as dynamic, as those with which we are concerned, it is imperative that the American Member of the Committee be supplied with current information which, by reference to specific problems, will indicate apparent weak spots in our political defense structure. Without such information it is difficult for me to assist in making the Committee a useful instrument of political defense, whether by keying its recommendations directly to practical problems, by revealing deficiencies in recommendations or programs already approved, or by laying the groundwork for consultation with the several governments.

In the instructions relative to the C. P. D. as originally drafted there was a direction that the missions forward:

---

[27] See translator's summary of a letter from the Chairman of the Emergency Advisory Committee, October 16, *infra*.

"... [28] by courier direct to the Embassy in Montevideo for transmission to the United States member of the Committee, the bimonthly summaries on activities in the American Republics by the Axis powers or states subservient thereto and any additional material or information dealing with important problems of subversive activities and political defense of the Hemisphere. Such information is for the guidance of the United States member and will be regarded as strictly confidential by him. Individual case reports need not be sent to Montevideo, except as they may be useful in illustrating a particular type of problem or action."

In my opinion this paragraph, which, at the request of FC, [29] was deleted from the instructions as finally sent to the missions, effectively stated my needs, and it is my opinion that the objective of prompt action in these times warrants an instruction which will enable me to receive information directly from the missions.

I understand that, pursuant to my request, FC is reconsidering its decision, and, pending a final disposition, I urge that Toop or Lampson [30] be charged with the preparation of fortnightly reports which summarize the principal "weak spots" as evidenced by our intelligence information. It will be recalled that such an assignment was contemplated when I stated at the time of accepting my present position that it would be necessary to organize a unit which would service me with intelligence summaries bearing on the problems covered by Resolution XVII.

With best regards [etc.]   CARL SPAETH

---

710. Consultation (3)A/197

The Chairman of the Emergency Advisory Committee for Political Defense (Guani) to the Secretary of State [31]

This meeting was held at the instance of Brazil and upon the decision of the Advisory Committee. Five countries—Argentina, Bolivia, Brazil, Paraguay and Uruguay—were represented and two members of the Committee (from Brazil and the United States) attended. Brazil had proposed it because of the problems arising in connection with its entry into the war, particularly the presence of large numbers of people in its territory whose interests were opposed to the defense and security of the continent. The Committee felt it advisable that measures be taken so as not to nullify Brazil's efforts at control by the emigration of such people to adjacent countries.

---

[28] Omission indicated in the original.
[29] Division of Foreign Activity Correlation.
[30] John R. Toop and Edward T. Lampson, Division of the American Republics.
[31] This document is translator's summary of letter dated October 16 from Mr. Guani to the Secretary of State, transmitting a copy of the Final Act and the Secretary General's report of the Regional Meeting at Rivera concerning the entry and departure of individuals and clandestine transit across borders.

The general subject matter recommended by the Committee embraced three matters:

1. Measures for the control of travel between the five Republics in order to adopt the necessary precautions in these times of emergency;
2. Organization of effective patrols on the borders;
3. Cooperative measures between the five Republics.

The meeting opened on September 22 and closed on September 26. Its decisions were approved by the Emergency Advisory Committee's Delegates and their report to the Committee was unanimously approved by the latter.   At present the Committee is studying the recommendations approved at the Rivera meeting to determine which of them may be used and applied by the other American countries not represented thereat. When it reaches a decision on this matter, it will immediately advise the American Government.

The Final Act reports approval of recommendations on the following subjects:

1. A motion proposing the creation of political–social police agencies within the police organizations of the various countries to have charge of matters affecting the internal and external security of the State.
2. A motion proposing that the Governments represented arrange to exchange information concerning certain aliens and measures adopted by the different countries to meet situations involving them.
3. A motion recommending the adoption of regulations governing the entry and departure of nationals and naturalized or legal citizens, including special provisions for those living in "border zones".
4. A motion recommending the adoption of special regulations governing the entry and departure of aliens from non-continental States.
5. A motion recommending that, in agreement with the authorities of a bordering State, each State determine points of entry into and departure from its territory.
6. A motion recommending that international transportation companies be required to demand identifying documents of an individual before furnishing him with transportation.
7. A motion recommending that hotels and lodging houses be required to demand presentation of identifying documents, make a record thereof and transmit the information to the authorities.
8. A motion recommending the adoption of rules concerning the registration of aliens.
9. A motion suggesting general lines to be followed in the guarding of borders between countries.
10. A motion recommending the creation of Rural Police to protect rural frontier zones.
11. A motion recommending the adoption of measures restricting the activities of immigrant farmers and experts in rural industries.
12. A motion submitting to the Emergency Advisory Committee two resolutions, proposed by Brazil, concerning restrictions on the

naturalization of aliens and the fixing of prohibited zones for the residence of Axis nationals.

13. Vote of thanks to the presiding officer.

The second enclosure, the Secretary General's report, lists the different matters submitted for discussion, showing which were amalgamated, which withdrawn, how they compared with the agenda suggested by the Emergency Advisory Committee, etc.

---

710. Consultation (3)A/184

Resolution Concerning Inter-American Protection Against Sabotage, Approved by the Emergency Advisory Committee for Political Defense on October 16, 1942[32]

[Translation]

[The "Exposition of Reasons" which precedes text of the resolution is here omitted.]

WHEREAS:

A. The Third Meeting of Ministers of Foreign Affairs of the American Republics recommended in the memorandum attached to Resolution XVII that the American Republics take comprehensive measures to prevent nationals of States members of the Tripartite Pact and of States subservient to them from possessing, trading in or using instruments of sabotage, "in order to protect and safeguard vital documents, installations and operations" and to "punish all acts of sabotage, injury to or destruction of essential defense materials, factories, buildings, areas and utilities for manufacture and storage, public services, means of transportation and communication, water front areas and facilities";

B. Trustworthy reports prove that agents of States members of the Tripartite Pact or of States subservient to them are in a position to and intend to commit acts of sabotage for the purpose of injuring or destroying indispensable materials and vital services within the American Republics;

C. Such acts of sabotage would endanger and delay the "economic mobilization of the American Republics" which was recommended in Resolution II of the Third Meeting of Ministers of Foreign Affairs,[33] "with a view to assuring to the countries of this hemisphere, and particularly to those which are at war, an adequate supply of basic and strategic materials, in the shortest possible time" and for the purpose of giving practical expression to continental solidarity in the common struggle against political and military aggression of the

---

[32] Transmitted to the Department by the Chairman of the Committee with his communication of November 10, 1942; received November 27.

[33] Department of State *Bulletin*, February 7, 1942, p. 119.

States members of the Tripartite Pact and the States subservient to them;

D. In Resolution XVII, the Third Meeting of Ministers of Foreign Affairs entrusted to the Emergency Advisory Committee for Political Defense the responsibility for studying and coordinating the measures recommended in the said Resolution and attached Memorandum;

E. The Inter-American Defense Board has recognized that grave danger of sabotage exists and has recommended to the American Republics that they cooperate closely with this Committee in fulfilling the responsibility mentioned above, which was entrusted to this Committee by the Third Meeting of Ministers of Foreign Affairs of the American Republics;

F. In view of the importance and urgency of preparing defense against such acts of aggression of a non-military character which threaten the whole continent, the Committee considers that it has the imperative duty of calling attention to the existence of this serious danger and of suggesting certain preliminary measures of precaution pending receipt from the Governments of reports and suggestions which will help it to draw up detailed recommendations and coordinated plans on the individual and collective security of the American Republics against the same;

THE EMERGENCY ADVISORY COMMITTEE FOR POLITICAL DEFENSE RESOLVES:

To recommend to the Governments of the American Republics that they:

1. Immediately repeat to the competent authorities instructions urgently to undertake a strict watch against acts of sabotage.

2. Designate the competent governmental division or agency which is to:

a) Examine and determine which materials and services within their frontiers are important in relation to the war and in defense of the American Republics, such as mines, oil installations, factories, railroads and other means of transportation, bridges, workshops, means of communication and other public services, warehouses and stored material and water front areas and services.

b) Study and adopt adequate measures for the protection of the various classes of material and services which require defense against sabotage.

c) Require that such measures be adopted by the officials of the companies which have the said material and services under their charge.

d) Make periodic investigations for the purpose of seeing to the execution of the said measures.

3. Cooperate closely with one another for the purpose of adopting preventive measures against sabotage which will assure ever further the military and economic defense of the hemisphere.

4. Transmit to the Committee, as promptly as possible, copies of laws and regulations which they have adopted for protection against the sabotage of the material and services mentioned above, and also all information concerning:

a) The measures planned or already put into force by the respective Government or by the owners or managers of factories, mines, oil installations or other vital installations, specifically showing which of the measures mentioned in the enclosure to the present resolution have been taken, either by governmental authorities or by private owners or managers.

b) Agencies of the Government, planned or in existence, intended to take charge of the execution of the measures for protection against sabotage.

5. Transmit to the Emergency Advisory Committee for Political Defense, as soon as possible, reports and suggestions which may be useful in the compilation of a booklet of instructions concerning the protection of plants and public services by the owners and operators thereof, and in the formulation of a resolution concerning minimum legislative and administrative rules to protect against sabotage and in inter-American coordination thereof, documents with which the Committee is at present occupied.

6. Transmit to the said Committee, as soon as possible, their opinion or recommendations concerning the possibility and advisability of the establishment of an inter-American exchange of technical personnel and of information of a technical nature relative to the adoption and operation of control against sabotage.

862.20225/620 : Telegram

The Secretary of State to the Ambassador in Uruguay (Dawson)

WASHINGTON, November 1, 1942—1 p. m.

657. Please call upon Dr. Guani immediately and lay before him the following considerations.

It is becoming increasingly evident that Axis interests and those reactionary elements in Chile who are making every effort to prevent any change in Chilean policy have prevented Chilean public opinion and even the great majority of the members of the Chilean Congress from having the slightest knowledge of the serious nature of the Axis subversive activities which have been going on for so long a time in Chile. Chilean public opinion has no conception of the dangers to Chile's own interests created by these activities nor the vital dangers to the defense interests of the entire Hemisphere which the continuation of these activities constitutes.

It therefore seems essential that the true facts as set forth in the secret memorandum handed to the former Chilean Foreign Minister by the American Ambassador in Santiago on June 30 last be made public.[34]

Owing to present conditions, if the United States Government itself makes this document public, the extreme nationalists and the Axis interests in Chile will undoubtedly attempt to create the impression that this is an effort on the part of the United States Government to bring pressure to bear upon the Government of Chile and for that reason this Government feels it undesirable, at least at this time, for it to release this information to the press.

This Government believes however that the subject matter involved is precisely the kind of problem with which the Committee on Political Defense, under the able and effective chairmanship of Dr. Guani, is called upon to deal. It believes that the danger inherent in the situation which continues in both Chile and Argentina is an increasingly serious danger to all of the other American Republics and that Dr. Guani will coincide with the belief of this Government that the Committee, an Inter-American defense organization created for this purpose, should make it possible for the people of the entire Hemisphere now to have full knowledge of the details involved in Axis activities in all the American Republics and the serious menace resulting therefrom to the security of the Hemisphere.

Please suggest therefore to Dr. Guani the desirability of his making public, in his capacity as Chairman of the Committee on Political Defense, not later than Wednesday, November 4, the full text of the secret memorandum of June 30 which is now in his possession and which Dr. Guani has already undoubtedly read. This Government does not know whether Dr. Guani will consider it necessary to submit this question for the formal consideration of the full membership of the Committee, but it would seem that Dr. Guani, as Chairman of the Committee, would be entirely warranted in taking that action without the necessity of any formal approval by the other members of the Committee.

In either case, you may say to him, and so inform Spaeth, that the latter is authorized to transmit this document to Dr. Guani for the official cognizance of the latter in his capacity as Chairman of the Committee.

You may inform Dr. Guani, for his confidential information, that a similar detailed document covering Axis activities in Argentina [35] is being officially communicated to the Argentine Foreign Minister in the immediate future and that, should Dr. Guani approve, a copy of this document would be later given to Dr. Guani for similar publication.

Please cable as soon as possible what the views of Dr. Guani may be.

HULL

---

[34] For summary, see p. 225.
[35] For a draft of this document, see p. 218.

740.0011 European War 1939/25215 : Telegram

The Ambassador in Uruguay (Dawson) to the Secretary of State

MONTEVIDEO, November 2, 1942—1 p. m.
[Received 2 : 44 p. m.]

949. Department's 657, November 1, 1 p. m. Guani's reaction to the Department's proposal is favorable and he stresses his desire to take any action considered necessary by our Government. He expressed reservations on the following three points :

(1) In conversations with Fernández prior to the latter's departure, Guani discussed with him the course of action outlined in Embassy's telegram 928 of October 26.[36] The proposed publication would, of course, interfere with Fernández declared plans and might alter those plans.
(2) The document delivered to the Government of Chile on the 30th of June should not normally be published without its consent.
(3) Committee procedures required that the publication receive the prior approval of the majority of the Committee.

Guani is prepared to proceed with the following plans for publication notwithstanding the first reservation since he feels that our Government must have convincing information that this course is necessary. In order to meet the second and third reservations, he suggests the following procedure with which Spaeth agrees:

A special meeting of Committee will be called for tomorrow. At the meeting Guani will state that on Monday Spaeth advised him that when our Government transmitted its memorandum of June 30, to Barros Jarpa,[37] it also sent a copy to its member on the Committee. At that time it was not believed that presentation of the document to the Committee would be necessary, but it was believed important that the American member be fully informed in the event that Committee action proved desirable. It is now the position of the American member that the political defense of the hemisphere requires that the Committee have full cognizance of the document and that the document be released for publication by Committee after a reading of the document to the Committee, Guani will state that in his opinion knowledge of the facts by all of the people of the Americas is imperative for hemisphere defense. Upon approval by the Committee, publication will follow immediately.

Guani and Spaeth agree that approval of the publication by the members from Mexico, Brazil and Venezuela should be secured before the special meeting is called, and Guani has authorized Spaeth to discuss the matter today with those members.

DAWSON

---

[36] Not printed.
[37] Chilean Minister for Foreign Affairs. For summary of memorandum, see p. 225.

740.0011 European War 1939/25215 : Telegram

The Secretary of State to the Ambassador in Uruguay (Dawson)

WASHINGTON, November 3, 1942—7 p. m.

661. Your 949, November 2, 1 p. m. Please express to Guani my deep appreciation of his favorable reaction and coöperative attitude to the proposal that the June 30th memorandum delivered by Ambassador Bowers to the Chilean Government be made public through the Committee for Political Defense. With regard to Guani's reservations, the Department has the following comments which you may communicate to Guani if you believe it would be helpful:

(1) It is believed that Fernández has now had ample opportunity to study the Chilean situation and to make his plans accordingly. The Department believes that the publication of the June 30th memorandum by an inter-American body such as the Committee for Political Defense will be of real assistance to those Chileans who favor the carrying out of Chile's inter-American obligations. As you know, this memorandum was disregarded, if not suppressed, by those interested in the maintenance of the *status quo*.

(2) The Department does not feel that prior consent of the Chilean Government is required. (For your own confidential information, various Chilean high officials are familiar with the contents of the June 30 memorandum and intend to make use of it in certain forthcoming events in Chile, so that the document no longer has the same confidential character as when it was handed to the Chilean Government 4 months ago.)

(3) The Department is in full agreement that the question of publication should receive the approval of the majority of the Committee. The procedure proposed by Guani seems entirely satisfactory.

HULL

---

710. Consultation (3)A/165 : Telegram

The Ambassador in Uruguay (Dawson) to the Secretary of State

MONTEVIDEO, November 3, 1942—10 p. m.
[Received 11:45 p. m.]

954. From Spaeth for the Under Secretary. After 4 hours of debate the committee approved the following resolution:

A. The Emergency Advisory Committee for Political Defense was charged by Resolution XVII, as approved unanimously by the Third Meeting of the Ministers of Foreign Affairs of the American Republics at Rio de Janeiro, with the study and coordination of the measures to be taken by the said republics to combat the subversive activities of states members of the Tripartite Pact and of states subservient to them.

B. The member appointed by the United States of America has submitted for consideration to the Committee a copy of a memorandum entitled "German Espionage Agents in Chile", dated June 30, 1942, [which] indicates the existence in the said country of very serious threats to the security of the continent and which demonstrates that the dangers which it reveals are directed not only against one of the republics but against all of the other republics of the continent.

C. In view of the gravity of the charges made in the memorandum, which specifically mentions acts undertaken by agents of the Axis against the security of the hemisphere, it is of vital interest to give publicity to the information set forth in the said document, as well as any other facts of the same character, in view of the great value in the collective defense of America.

The Emergency Advisory Committee for Political Defense;

Resolves: To authorize the President of the Committee to release for general publication through the press and any other means of communication the memorandum dated June 30, 1942 entitled "German Espionage Agents in Chile" prepared by the Government of the United States of America.

The memorandum was released to the press at 6 p. m. this evening under the title "Memorandum Prepared for Ambassador Bowers, German Espionage Agents in Chile" and under the date June 30, 1942.

The title of the referendum and the presentation to the Committee followed the suggestion by Dr. Guani that the document be presented to the Committee as a copy of a memorandum sent by the American Government simultaneously to the American Ambassador in Chile and the American member of the Commission (refer to Embassy's cable No. 949 of November 2, 1 p. m.). This method of presentation proved to be extremely important because of the position taken by the members from Argentina and Chile that the memorandum is a diplomatic document which relates exclusively to a matter in discussion between Chile and the United States and should, therefore, not be released by the Commission. The majority took the position that the Commission had no knowledge of any pending negotiations or discussions between the two Governments concerned in which the memorandum was involved, and that the issue for the Commission was whether or not publication of the memorandum by an inter-American body would serve the general interest of the continent.

The Chilean member voted against the proposal and made a statement for the record to the effect that in view of the fact that the memorandum related to a matter being discussed by the Governments of Chile and the United States, he did not consider it desirable or expedient for the Commission to publish the same without first consulting the two Governments. The Argentine member abstained from voting on substantially the same grounds.

Too much emphasis cannot be placed on the assistance and leadership afforded by Dr. Guani in securing the approval by the Commission, notwithstanding that at one point the Chilean member attempted to embarrass Guani in his position as Foreign Minister by stating that the Chilean Foreign Office could not but look with disfavor upon the publication of the document. The support given to Guani by members from Brazil, Mexico and Venezuela was characterized principally by their support of his position that content of memorandum was a matter of vital concern to defense of all American Republics and that by publishing the document the Commission was not involving itself in a diplomatic situation between two Republics. The majority also shared view of Brazilian member that in consulting Commission regarding publication of memorandum the Government of United States was in a sense curtailing its freedom of action and its sovereign right in order to secure advice of an inter-American body regarding a problem which it felt involved a basic collective interest of the continent, and that Commission could not but respond favorably to this recognition by the most powerful nation on the continent of the validity and efficacy of cooperative method.

The Venezuelan member voted with majority but did not participate in debate because of fact Parra Pérez [38] arrives in Santiago tomorrow morning.

Sent to Department, repeated to Santiago. [Spaeth.]

DAWSON

740.0011 European War 1939/25630 : Telegram

The Ambassador in Uruguay (Dawson) to the Secretary of State

MONTEVIDEO, November 13, 1942—3 p. m.
[Received 7 : 40 p. m.]

996. For the Under Secretary from Spaeth No. 43. Reference is made to the statement in the Department's cable no. 669 of November 7, 7 p. m.,[39] that one objective of the total effort being made in support of the North African campaign is to "immediately consolidate hemisphere solidarity against the Axis by having Chile and Argentina break relations". For the Department's consideration of the contribution which the Committee might make to the realization of this objective I submit the following tentative draft resolution subject to appropriate textual changes including those necessary to protect codes.

"WHEREAS:

(a) The Second Meeting of the Ministers of Foreign Affairs, at Habana, Cuba,[40] found that the political activities of diplomatic agents of certain non-American powers accredited to the American Republics constituted a threat to the defense and security of the continent and

---

[38] Venezuelan Minister for Foreign Affairs.
[39] Not printed.
[40] See *Foreign Relations*, 1940, vol. v, pp. 180 ff.

resolved in Resolution II (quote last paragraph of Resolution II of Habana).[41]

(*b*) The efforts of the American Republics pursuant to Resolution II of Habana failed to prevent propaganda, espionage and other political activities by the diplomatic agents of the States members of the Tripartite Pact, and in recognition of the danger to the security of the hemisphere caused by the continuance of such activities the Third Meeting of the Ministers of Foreign Affairs resolved unanimously to recommend the breaking of diplomatic relations with Japan, Germany and Italy.

(*c*) Eleven of the American Republics are now at war with States members of the Tripartite Pact and nineteen of the American Republics have broken diplomatic relations with said States.

(*d*) The diplomatic representatives of the Tripartite Pact accredited to the Governments of Argentina and Chile continue to disseminate Axis propaganda, to direct and participate in espionage, and to carry on other political activities in violation of Resolution II adopted at the Second Meeting of the Ministers of Foreign Affairs, and in flagrant disregard of international law and the [apparent omission] these two American Republics.

(*e*) The studies of the Emergency Advisory Committee for political defense demonstrate that the political defense of the hemisphere, pursuant to Resolution XVII, adopted unanimously at the Third Meeting of the Ministers of Foreign Affairs, is apt [to] continue to be seriously endangered so long as any American Republic maintains diplomatic relations with the Axis.

(*f*) The studies and reports appended hereto demonstrate conclusively that the presence in any country of the Western Hemisphere of diplomatic representatives of the States members of Tripartite Pact seriously threatens the gigantic war effort of other United Nations, constitutes a source of internal weakness and a grave and constant menace to the peoples of each and every one of the American Republics, and nullifies the principles and spirit of continental solidarity and reciprocal assistance pledged by all the republics at the Third Meeting of the Ministers of Foreign Affairs.

THE EMERGENCY ADVISORY COMMITTEE FOR POLITICAL DEFENSE RESOLVES:

1. To report to the Governments of the American Republics that responsibilities of the Emergency Advisory Committee for Political Defense under Resolution XVII in the struggle against subversive activities cannot be effectively discharged so long as any Axis diplomatic representative continues to be accredited to any American Republic, and that the presence of such diplomatic representatives in the Western Hemisphere constitutes a threat to the security and defense of all of the American Republics.

2. To recommend to the Presidents of the nineteen American Republics which have severed diplomatic relations with the Axis that they present a joint appeal to the Governments of Argentina and Chile urging those Governments to terminate their diplomatic relations with States members of the Tripartite Pact."

---

[41] The Ministers for Foreign Affairs resolved to urge the governments of the American Republics to prevent diplomatic or consular agents from engaging in activities endangering peace. For text, see Department of State *Bulletin*, August 24, 1940, p. 130.

The studies and reports referred to in paragraph F might include a report on subversive activities in Argentina and a report specially prepared to indicate political activities of Axis diplomats in both Argentina and Chile. If, however, the publication of such reports were deemed inexpedient at this time, the resolution could be used without reference to specific reports. [Spaeth.]

DAWSON

EFFORTS TO PREVENT COMMUNICATION WITH THE AXIS COUNTRIES THROUGH COMMERCIAL WIRELESS COMPANIES

810.74/239a : Telegram

The Secretary of State to the Ambassador in the United Kingdom
(Winant)

WASHINGTON, January 21, 1942—2 p. m.

243. In addition to matters discussed in Department's 160, January 13,[1] Harry Hopkins [2] took up with Lord Beaverbrook [3] the desire of this Government to accomplish the total severance of telecommunications circuits between the other American Republics and Berlin, Tokyo, and Rome.

For your information, the telecommunications systems in the other American Republics are operated mainly by two groups: the first, comprised of affiliates of I. T. & T.,[4] and the second, which is known as a consortium, consisting of United States, British, French, and German members. Up to the beginning of the present war, the stock was evenly divided, and, under a trust agreement, each country was represented by two trustees over whom a ninth member with the title of Chairman presided. By mutual agreement, the chairmanship permanently fell to a United States citizen, thereby giving the United States a permanent veto power. The chairmanship remained vacant since the retirement of General Dawes [5] and was not filled until January 19, 1942.

For your information, the consortium stations are located in Argentina, Brazil, and Chile. These stations are organized under local laws, although 60 percent of the stock is owned by the consortium trustees. Department is informed that since Great Britain's involvement in the war, the control of the German stock of this organization has been taken over by the London Government. However, the consortium stations in South America have continued to take traffic to and from the enemy countries. Solely for your information, R. C. A.[6]

---

[1] Not printed; it dealt with direct radiotelegraph circuits between the United States and points in the British Empire (811.7448A/12a).
[2] Special Assistant to the President.
[3] British Minister of Supply.
[4] International Telephone and Telegraph Corporation.
[5] Gen. Charles G. Dawes.
[6] Radio Corporation of America.

has strongly emphasized the necessity of obtaining the unequivocal concurrence and cooperation of the British consortium interests in order effectively to close the circuits in question.

In this connection, Beaverbrook transmitted to Hopkins on January 2 a copy of a telegram from a London official named Layton,[7] who stated that at Beaverbrook's suggestion he had discussed the above question with Wilshaw of Cable and Wireless, who said that he "would be personally delighted to see the traffic stopped and will cooperate in whatever line the Government proposes". This information has been telegraphed to Rio in order that this Government's resolution concerning the elimination of Telecommunications facilities to Axis countries may be presented to the Meeting of Foreign Ministers with some assurance of the concurrence of British consortium representatives.

Will you determine as soon as possible if Cable and Wireless Limited has been instructed by the British authorities to notify its consortium representatives in South America to take every necessary step to cooperate fully with this Government's effort to close communications channels in that area to enemy countries. If this has not been done it may seriously affect outcome of this government's telecommunications Resolution at Rio meeting.

HULL

810.74/264 : Telegram

The Ambassador in Brazil (Caffery) to the Secretary of State

RIO DE JANEIRO, March 3, 1942—4 p. m.
[Received 6 : 51 p. m.]

669. Department's airmail instruction 2243, February 24 and telegram 525 March 2, midnight.[8] The Minister of Communications informed the Embassy that he would issue instructions today closing all radio-telephone and radio-telegraph communication between Brazil and the Axis nations et cetera, in compliance with Resolution XL of the Rio de Janeiro Conference.[9]

CAFFERY

---

[7] Sir Walter Layton of the Advisory Committee on Imperial Communications; copy of telegram not found in Department files.
[8] Neither printed.
[9] For correspondence on the Third Meeting of the Foreign Ministers of the American Republics at Rio de Janeiro, see pp. 6 ff.; for text of Resolution XL, see Department of State *Bulletin*, February 7, 1942, p. 140.

810.74/332

Memorandum by the Assistant Secretary of State (Long) to the Under Secretary of State (Welles)[10]

[WASHINGTON,] April 21, 1942.

MR. WELLES:

RADIO COMMUNICATIONS WITH AXIS POWERS FROM ARGENTINA AND CHILE

For some months we have been engaged in efforts to discontinue radio communication from South American countries to the Axis capitals—Berlin, Rome and Tokyo. We have been successful in some measure. However, communication still continues from stations in Buenos Aires and Santiago, and information is received that service is to be improved by instituting a new telephoto service from Japan to the Argentine.

I

The situation in Argentina and Chile is complicated. In each of those capitals a station is operated by a local company which is a subsidiary of the AEFG[11] trust. This AEFG trust is a British organization with headquarters in London (its address is c/o Cables & Wireless Inc.). The business of the trust is transacted by a committee composed of two representatives each of British, American, French and German interests. The trust was formed in 1921. Under its terms the American member, RCA, may appoint a chairman who shall have no vote except in case of tie but who shall have a veto over any resolution of the Board. There was for a long time a vacancy in the chairmanship formerly filled by General Dawes who resigned. For several years and up to about the first of 1942, there was no chairman. About the first of this year, Retired General Robert C. Davis (Chairman of the New York Red Cross) was named chairman but no meeting of the Board has been held since.

The component companies are RCA, Marconi Wireless of England, the French wireless, and the German wireless. The trust is a pooling of resources. Each member transferred (*a*) all of its concessions, (*b*) all of its licenses to use apparatus devices and systems for communication, and agreed (*c*) to abstain from communicating through competitors, and (*d*) to use its best endeavors to obtain assignments and transfers to the trustees from the South American companies of any patent rights or licenses which might be held by any of the subsidiary companies. The trust further witnesses an agreement for an exclusive traffic control within the membership and between them and its

---

[10] Notation by Sumner Welles: "I agree—S. W."

[11] Consortium Trust Affiliates; presumably these initials stand for "American, English, French, German" trust.

subsidiary companies. This trust and its combined control over its subsidiary organizations in South America expires in 1945, at which time there will be a distribution of the trust property among the parties.

Another contemporaneous trust between the same parties sets up an Argentine national company, a Brazilian national company and other companies. The Chilean national company has grown out of the original arrangement and is a later development.

(a)

The Argentine subsidiary company is called Transradio Internacional Argentina. The voting control of stock in the hands of the trust over the Argentine company is as follows:

A. E. F. G. Trust—(under British laws)............. 60%
R. C. A. Communications—U. S. A................. 6%
Cables & Wireless Ltd.—British.................... 5%
Telefunken Co.—German......................... 5%
Italoradio—Italian.............................. 4%
Compagnie Generale—French...................... 4%
Scattered public holdings, Argentina............... 16%

In addition, Transradio Internacional Argentina has an outstanding issue of Debenture Bonds which are held as follows:

Public holdings in Argentina....................... 65%
Radio Corp. of America (R. C. A. C.).............. 18%
Marconi's W. T. Co. (C. & W.)—British........... 12%
Italoradio—Italian.............................. 5%

(b)

The Chilean subsidiary of the trust is Transradio Chilena of which the voting control of stock is as follows:

A. E. F. G. Trust—(under British law)............. 60%
Telefunken Co.—German......................... 11%
Compagnie Generale—French...................... 10%
Cables & Wireless—British........................ 9%
R. C. A. Communications—U. S. A................. 9%
Scattered public holdings, Chile................... 1%

Transradio Chilena has no outstanding funded indebtedness.

(c)

Since the beginning of the war in 1939, and perhaps for a time before, the German interest on the board of trustees has been represented by Swedish members but since the war England has refused visas for the Swedish trustees to visit England to attend the meetings. The British interests under the protection of their Government have exercised control of the German interest and of a small Italian minority interest and have eliminated the Swedish trustees of the

German interest so that the British presently dominate and control the situation—through Cables and Wireless Ltd. Consequently, Cables & Wireless Ltd. now really dominates the South American field. It is the same company which has assumed control of all communication between England and its dominions and which the Department has found obstructive in its efforts to establish communications with various parts of the British Empire.

II

It is worthwhile to consider briefly the situation of the Argentine company and of the Chilean company.

(a)

Argentina. 16% of the stock of the company is held by the public in Argentina. 65% of the bonds are held in Argentina. There is a small (4%) Italian and (5%) German interest in the Argentine company. Furthermore, there is an Italian as well as a German representative on the committee which operates the Argentine station. There are also on the committee representatives of the French, British and American ownership.

The composition of the committee operating the company and the considerable local financial interest in the company are questions which have to be considered for they present possibilities of internal difficulty for the Argentine Government even if it desired to close the station to Axis communications. It could probably not do so without incurring the enmity of some of its important financial groups. Furthermore, the Italian and German membership on the operating committee lead immediately to the idea of pressure being brought to bear from the German and Italian Governments through their embassies in Argentina.

In Argentina there are three companies operating radio stations:

(1) The Consortium has beams to 21 different cities of which five have been closed. Amongst those still open are Berlin, Rome, Santiago, (Chile), Bern, Tokyo, Barcelona, and two recently opened, one to Stockholm and one to Moscow, each of which was opened on January 2, 1942.

Incidentally, these two last named stations to Moscow and Stockholm have been opened as a direct result of the imposition of censorship in the United States, and through them there is an increasing traffic which up to the time of their opening had been routed through the United States.

(2) The International Radio Company (I. T. & T.—Mackay) of Argentina has only one circuit and operates from B. A. to New York.

(3) The Sociedad Anónima Radio Argentina, (also I. T. & T.), has only one beam to Europe which is to Madrid, its only other European beam to Prague having been closed.

Of the three companies operating in B. A., the Consortium station is the most important for it connects Rome, Berlin, and Tokyo directly, and it has a supplementary route through Santiago for its line to Tokyo and it can collect from Rio, Asunción, La Paz, and Lima messages for relay to Rome, Tokyo, or Berlin.

Under the circumstances which exist in Buenos Aires, it would be more difficult for the Argentine Government to close the station than if there was no public Argentine ownership of either stocks or bonds or if the committee were simply an American or a British or a joint American and British effort.

(b)

Chile. The situation in Santiago is quite different from that in Buenos Aires. There are small German, French, British, American and only 1% Chilean ownership under a 60% Consortium (Trust) stock control. There are no outstanding bonds. Consequently, the selfish interest of gain does not appear in Santiago. There is no financial investment of Chilean money in the enterprise. There is no Italian ownership and no Italian membership on the local operating committee. There is French membership and German membership on that committee. Opposition in Chile would come from the small German stock ownership amounting to 11% and the presence of a German on the operating committee, but opposition would immediately be manifested by Japan also, for Chile sends to and receives from Tokyo. B. A. is the only other radiotelegraph circuit Japan has in South America and the importance of each station to Japan is obvious.

In Chile there are only two stations:

(1) The I. T. & T. subsidiary communicates between New York and Santiago only.

(2) The Consortium station has beams to Berlin, Tokyo, Lima, Rio, and B. A., as well as London and New York. We are now advised a new telephoto service is to be inaugurated between Santiago and Tokyo.

It is quite possible that if the Consortium station at B. A. were shut down that the beams now used by it might be transferred to the Consortium company at Santiago and its less important circuits would thereby be built up into a communicating system which would rival or even surpass that of B. A. The equipment is there and could easily be used, so that in spite of the present comparative unimportance of the Santiago Consortium station, it is just as important that it be closed as that the B. A. Consortium station be closed.

Consequently, threats and pressure from Japan may be expected in Santiago if the closing of the circuit is to be debated. It would be called "an unfriendly act" and various other statements would be made to frighten Chile into maintaining communication.

(*c*)

So it would appear there will be need for intelligent pressure by the United States on the governments at each of these capitals to persuade them to discontinue communication with the Axis. Failure to achieve closure after the exertion of pressure would be unfortunate.

Furthermore, it would seem very important to secure the closing of stations in both countries for the reason that if one were left open there would be (1) constant effort on the part of the other to reopen, and (2) an importance of increasing magnitude in the one remaining open as it would be developed into a single line of communication between the Axis powers and their South American agents and would be treated by the Axis powers as a major matter. The government of the particular country concerned would be the object of Axis attentions to whatever point the Axis powers felt it advisable to go in order to retain the circuit in operation.

III

From our point of view situations differ in each country in that different reasons appear as probable to develop locally as the basis for the objection by each country to closing their respective circuits. In Argentina it is apt to be largely native financial opposition supplemented by German influence. In Chile, international political considerations would seem to be the principal basis upon which opposition to our desires would develop.

However, it ought not be overlooked that, since the closing of the station in Lima, Argentina and Chile remain the only places in this hemisphere in direct communication with Axis powers. The traffic which formerly flowed through other stations is now flowing through those two. Each of them is assuming an importance it did not have before. Largely due to this increasing importance there may develop a hostility nurtured by a sense of growing importance and directed against the movement to close the circuits. It is certain that if only one of the countries remains in communication with the enemy that the combined force of the enemy in the way of propaganda and threats of all kinds will be brought into play against that country and we may have to resort to unusual lengths in giving assurances in order to offset the threats of the Axis.

The gist of our information is that different reasons will appear in each of the two countries for maintaining the circuits open in spite of our desires.

To the same effect apparently is the British judgment for Cables & Wireless Ltd. has recently advised (London's 1812, April 13, 8 p. m.[12]) that there are difficulties in the way of their arranging a discontinuance

---

[12] Not printed.

of radio communication by the Argentine company and by the Chilean company. The difficulties are stated to be local in each country. They suggest that the only way of accomplishing the object in view is for the Government of the United States to ask the South American republics to conform to Resolution XL of the Rio Conference by issuing suitable orders to the companies operating in their respective jurisdictions.

IV

There is no intimation that they (Cables & Wireless) would co-operate to that end—nor is there any assurance that they would not obstruct the movement for financial reasons as they have in so many instances in recent months.

The stations ought to be closed to Axis powers.

The United States should direct its efforts to that end.

Resolution XL of the Rio Conference affords a definite and reasonable base. It is proposed, with that Resolution as a base, to

1. Submit the matter to the Inter American Committee [13] for the purpose of making recommendations to Argentina and Chile to stop communication with the Axis.
2. The United States to support the recommendations through its Ambassadors at B. A. and Santiago.
3. Request the American Chairman of the AEFG Trust to call a meeting of his board in either New York or London (preferably New York) to act on the policy.
4. Request the British Government (through Winant) to adopt as a government policy the closing of these Consortium stations to the Axis.
5. Request the British to direct the English citizens in control of AEFG to apply to the Argentine and Chilean Governments for authority to close the beams to the Axis.
6. The United States Government to support the movement in all reasonable ways.

As a supplemental step or as an alternative in case closure is not achieved—

7. Submit to the Inter American Committee the proposal that each of the American Republics prohibit the sending of any land wire, cable or radio messages to B. A. or to Santiago if the address or the text of the message indicates it is intended to be forwarded to enemy destination.

V

These proposals, with reference to all but the alternative (7) which would be held in abeyance, should be qualified to the extent that a confidential inquiry be made to our Ambassadors at B. A. and Santiago to

[13] Presumably the Emergency Advisory Committee for Political Defense. For correspondence concerning this Committee, see pp. 74 ff.; see also Department of State *Bulletin*, April 11, 1942, p. 322.

instruct them to ascertain discreetly and report as to the extent to which each of those governments might be induced to go. This step seems advisable in view of the fact that those governments have not responded to the more important Rio Resolution about breaking relations [14] and so might be found cool to the less important provisions of Resolution XL.

On receipt of the information from our Ambassadors, the Department would then be in a better position to plan its course.

If you approve, cables will be drafted to B. A. and Santiago and the rest of the program will be reviewed in the light of that information.

B[RECKINRIDGE] L[ONG]

810.74/315b : Telegram

The Secretary of State to the Ambassador in Argentina (Armour)

WASHINGTON, May 2, 1942—9 p. m.

616. In the interest of common hemispheric defense it is essential that communications between this hemisphere and the Axis powers be completely severed. With this end in view Resolution XL of the Rio conference provided that each American Republic should adopt necessary and immediate measures to close all radiotelephone and radiotelegraph communications between the American Republics and the Axis powers.

The other American Republics have for all practical purposes closed channels of communication between their countries and the Axis powers and it is believed that at this time Argentina and Chile remain the only places in this hemisphere with radio stations in direct communication with the Axis powers. The traffic which formerly flowed through other stations is now flowing through stations in these two countries, as a result of which each is assuming an importance it did not have before. The three companies operating radio stations in Argentina are the consortium, the International Radio Company (the I. T. & T.—Mackay) and the Sociedad Anónima Radio Argentina (also I. T. & T.). The closing of the consortium station as far as Axis communications is concerned might present possibilities of internal difficulties for the Argentine Government in view of the fact that 16% of the stock is held by the public in Argentina and that the operating committee includes Italian and German membership which might cause the German and Italian Governments to bring pressure to bear upon the Argentine Government.

---

[14] Resolution I; for text, see Department of State *Bulletin*, February 7, 1942, p. 118.

However, as already stated, it is essential in the interest of the common defense that these Argentine stations, as well as the stations in Chile, be closed to Axis communications. Various ways of bringing this about are at present being studied by the Department but before taking any definite steps in the matter the Department would appreciate your confidential views as soon as possible as to the extent to which the Argentine Government might be induced to go, bearing in mind the fact that it has not responded to the more important Rio resolution about breaking relations with the Axis powers.

HULL

810.74/315a : Telegram

The Secretary of State to the Ambassador in Chile (Bowers)

WASHINGTON, May 2, 1942—9 p. m.

491. In the interest of common hemispheric defense it is essential that communications between this hemisphere and the Axis powers be completely severed. With this end in view Resolution XL of the Rio conference provided that each American Republic should adopt necessary and immediate measures to close all radiotelephone and radiotelegraph communications between the American Republics and the Axis powers.

The other American Republics have for all practical purposes closed channels of communication between their countries and the Axis powers and it is believed that at this time Argentina and Chile remain the only places in this hemisphere with radio stations in direct communication with the Axis powers. The traffic which formerly flowed through other stations is now flowing through stations in these two countries, as a result of which each is assuming an importance it did not have before. There are two companies in Chile operating radio stations:

(1) The I. T. & T. subsidiary communicates between New York and Santiago only.

(2) The consortium station has beams to Berlin, Tokyo, Lima, Rio, and Buenos Aires, as well as London and New York. We are now advised a new telephoto service is to be inaugurated between Santiago and Tokyo.

It is quite possible that if the consortium station at Buenos Aires were shut down the beams now used by it might be transferred to the consortium company at Santiago and its less important circuits would thereby be built up into a communicating system which would rival or even surpass that of Buenos Aires. The equipment is there and could easily be used, so that in spite of the present comparative unimportance of the Santiago consortium station, it is just as important that it be closed as that the Buenos Aires consortium station be closed.

Consequently, threats and pressure from Japan may be expected in Santiago if the closing of the circuit is to be debated. It would be called "an unfriendly act" and various other statements would be made to frighten Chile into maintaining communication.

However, as already stated, it is essential in the interest of the common defense that these Chilean stations, as well as the stations in Argentina, be closed to Axis communications. Various ways of bringing this about are at present being studied by the Department but before taking any definite steps in the matter the Department would appreciate your confidential views as soon as possible as to the extent to which the Chilean Government might be induced to go, bearing in mind the fact that it has not responded to the more important Rio resolution about breaking relations with the Axis powers.

HULL

810.74/318 : Telegram

The Chargé in Bolivia (Dawson) to the Secretary of State

LA PAZ, May 5, 1942—6 p. m.
[Received 8 : 12 p. m.]

294. Department's 233, April 24.[15] Bolivian Government has taken no steps to implement Rio Resolution XL despite efforts of Legation. Communications with Axis powers and territory controlled by them are in every case on the alert through [16] other American Republics whose implementing of the resolution would accordingly have the desired practical effect on messages from Bolivia. All America Cables has received instructions from New York not to accept communications to Axis countries except government messages.

DAWSON

810.74/333 : Telegram

The Ambassador in Argentina (Armour) to the Secretary of State

BUENOS AIRES, May 8, 1942—6 p. m.
[Received 8 : 05 p. m.]

858. Department's telegram 616, May 2. Matter in general has been discussed repeatedly with Foreign Office and although there is certain compliance with sections 2 and 3 of Resolution XV [*XL?*] there is no evidence of intention to cooperate with respect to section 1. Possibly Argentina can eventually be persuaded to comply if it can be shown that all other American Republics have definitely done so.

Local American companies are of opinion that severing Axis communications is very difficult, since messages would be relayed through

---

[15] Not printed.
[16] The apparent meaning of this sentence is indicated by substituting the words "dependent upon" for the words "on the alert through."

Spain, Sweden, Switzerland, Portugal or other so-called neutrals. This excuse probably would be offered by Argentine authorities for not taking such action. Embassy would appreciate any information which would help combat this argument.

Regarding trans-radio consortium, it claims to be under American and British control. It is believed that some progress toward Argentine compliance could be achieved by convincing American affiliates of all three companies mentioned in Department's telegram as to necessity for such action.

ARMOUR

862.20210/1729

Memorandum by the Assistant Secretary of State (Long)[17]

[WASHINGTON,] June 10, 1942.

I addressed to Mr. Welles a rather exhaustive memorandum on this subject.[18] That memorandum is referred to in Mr. Halle's[19] memorandum of April 30 attached.[20]

The telegrams to B. A. and Santiago[21] went out. The reply from B. A.[22] was unsatisfactory and the one from Santiago,[23] after long delay, was more so.

There is no doubt in my mind that if the companies refuse to operate the beams to the Axis capitals that the respective governments will take them under control. Irrespective of this fact, I think, and for months have thought, that the attempt should be made or that the other governments of South America should be requested to withhold telegrams to B. A. and Santiago intended for enemy destination.

Late last fall and early winter I attempted through the intermediation of Harry Hopkins with Beaverbrook to accomplish the closing of these stations. Beaverbrook promised everything and nothing happened. The obstacle is very simple to be identified. It is Cables and Wireless, Limited. They do not want to lose the revenue. They are obdurate and obstructive. Their tactics are directed by Mr. Wilshire[24] and Sir Campbell Stuart.[25] Sir Campbell Stuart has just

---

[17] Addressed to the Under Secretary of State (Welles) and to the Adviser on Political Relations (Duggan).

[18] i. e., "Radio Communications with Axis Powers from Argentina and Chile"; see memorandum of April 21, p. 110.

[19] Louis J. Halle, of the Division of the American Republics.

[20] Not printed.

[21] Telegrams No. 616 and No. 491, respectively, dated May 2, 9 p. m., pp. 116 and 117.

[22] Telegram No. 858, May 8, 6 p. m., p. 118.

[23] Despatch No. 3539, June 9, not printed; it enclosed a report by the Santiago Manager of All America Cables and Radio, Inc., on Transradio Chilena (810.74/341).

[24] Presumably this refers to Sir Edward Wilshaw, Chairman of the Board of Cables and Wireless, Ltd.

[25] Chairman, Commonwealth Communications Council, 1933–1945.

arrived in this country again. He has blocked direct communication between us and South Africa. He is prepared to give lip service to closing the stations down there but will not do so unless his Government directs it. His Government has eliminated the influence of Beaverbrook in communication matters. My recent information is that Cables and Wireless has driven a wedge between Beaverbrook and the Government, due very probably to his favorable attitude to our suggestions. Nevertheless, Beaverbrook is now, temporarily at least, divorced from any authority over communications. Campbell insists that he is not subordinate to Downing Street and that he is the head of a communicating system established by Parliament and co-extensive with the Empire. The British Embassy here will not recognize him, probably for two reasons: (a) he does not want to be subordinate to the Ambassador, and (b) it serves the interests of the British Empire to have Campbell Stuart operating independently. He recently sent word to me that he would like to talk to me during the coming week. I replied that I would be glad to see him but that I hoped that he would come with the authority of the British Embassy. Without authority from the Embassy for him to negotiate it is difficult to secure the cooperation of the British Government.

Because of the independent authority of this particular individual, the efforts that I have made for more than twelve months have been very difficult of successful prosecution and in certain respects frustrated. The frustrated attempts are B. A., Santiago, and Pretoria. In spite of his opposition we have succeeded in establishing telecommunications or permission for telecommunications of various kinds with Cairo, Baghdad, Lagos, Bathurst, Australia—two circuits, Wellington—two circuits, New Delhi (if equipment is furnished—which is not really needed), and Singapore and Rangoon too late.

The principle difficulties remain with Pretoria having just refused and having frankly stated in one paragraph that it was due to Cables and Wireless and their disinclination to lose the revenue because of rerouted traffic. The other two unsolved difficulties are Santiago and B. A.

The only way that I know to stop them is for the British Government itself to control its own creatures, that is, Cables and Wireless, Limited, as presently directed, and to tell them that revenue or no revenue they are to cease communications with the Axis powers out of B. A. and Santiago.

That can be done through the mediation of Halifax [26] with contemporary pressure through Winant.[27]

If that is done, and if thereafter the Governments of Argentina and Chile desire to communicate on their own with the Axis, we will have

---

[26] Viscount Halifax, British Ambassador in the United States.
[27] John G. Winant, Ambassador in the United Kingdom.

more and better reason to request that other South American governments refrain from forwarding to them for transmission communications addressed to the Axis.

B[RECKINRIDGE] L[ONG]

810.74/339a : Telegram

The Secretary of State to the Ambassador in Chile (Bowers)

WASHINGTON, June 13, 1942—4 p. m.

680. Your 881, June 2, 6 p. m.[28] The telecommunication circuits that Chile is maintaining with enemy territory are being used to transmit to the Axis vital information from all parts of the hemisphere regarding movements of ships, individually and in convoy. We have confidential information to bear this out. This may result in a situation in which political considerations will have to be weighed against paramount military considerations.

The Chilean Government should immediately be impressed with the serious view which this Government takes of a situation in which nations that have solemnly agreed to stand together in the joint defense of the hemisphere operate and insist upon maintaining facilities whereby the enemy is enabled to destroy the lives and property of citizens of the American Republics and to interrupt lines of communication indispensable to their common defense. Shipping no less vital to the survival of Chile than to that of the United States is being lost every day because the Chilean Government has failed to cut off the channels through which the Axis is given information without which it could not successfully maintain this attack on the vital communications of all the American republics. The prompt action whereby 19 of the republics have already severed direct communication with Axis territory is in large part nullified by the failure of Chile and Argentina to do likewise.

The Department is now considering the possibility of bringing about action the result of which would be to have the Consortium in which the British and United States interests are dominant and the I. T. & T. subsidiary in Argentina abandon their circuits with the Axis. Were the Chilean circuits to be abandoned, how great do you think the possibility is that the Chilean Government would then proceed to operate the circuits itself or to transfer them for operation to other private interests?

Please telegraph the Department your views both with respect to further action that might be taken to induce the Chilean Government to abandon these telecommunication circuits and with regard to the

---

[28] Not printed.

probable attitude of the Chilean Government should the companies take independent action in order to shut down these circuits.

HULL

740.0011 European War 1939/22389 : Telegram

The Ambassador in Chile (Bowers) to the Secretary of State

SANTIAGO, June 22, 1942—7 p. m.
[Received June 23—3 : 55 a. m.]

1021. For Welles. Barros Jarpa [30] this afternoon at my house set forth a plan he mentioned to me Saturday at lunch that he is prepared to inform the Missions of Germany, Italy and Japan that they no longer can communicate with their Governments in code and he thinks this will lead to a controversy eventuating in the breaking of relations. He wants to know if we will take this as proof that a pretext is being sought and with a certainty of finding it soon with the intention of breaking relations.

It seems a big step forward. Sentiment here is changing so rapidly and is becoming so strong for breaking relations that I dare entertain the expectation that it is certain to come very soon.

In this connection he tells me he has just heard from his Ambassador in Washington that you had told him Chile could expect nothing more from us until relations are broken. He is to make an exposition on foreign affairs before Congress tomorrow and would prefer not to mention this ultimatum at that time since he says it would create an opposition in quarters where it does not exist. I am persuaded that he now knows that relations must be broken and that he is really searching for a pretext on which he can break without imperiling his personal prestige. Since outside this one phase he is strongly pro-American and pro-Ally this would be satisfactory to me. Your plain statement to Michels [31] wipes out any false impressions that may have come from Davila.

Last night 10,000 people attended a homage to Mexico because of the war and with misgivings I agreed to attend on the stipulation that no attacks be made on the Government directly. None were made and I received a great ovation. The leaders of all parties that supported Ríos [32] at the polls spoke in favor of Chile aligning herself vigorously on the side of complete alignment with the Allies. Marcella Mora, leader of the radicals, made a strong speech. It gives an impetus to public opinion forming in our favor.

BOWERS

---

[30] Chilean Minister for Foreign Affairs.
[31] Rodolfo Michels, Chilean Ambassador in the United States.
[32] Juan Antonio Ríos, President of Chile.

810.74/346 : Telegram

The Ambassador in Argentina (Armour) to the Secretary of State

BUENOS AIRES, June 26, 1942—10 p. m.
[Received June 27—2 : 14 a. m.]

1258. Department's 871, June 13, 9 p. m.[33] Counselor of Embassy discussed matter in general with Bunge [34] of Foreign Office, who agreed it was of utmost importance to close circuits between Argentina and Chile and Axis countries. However, he was unable to suggest effective method of actually closing them. In response to inquiry as to Argentine Government attitude in the event companies were forced to take such action through external pressure, Bunge replied he had no information on the subject but would endeavor to see that matter received attention.

Local managers of All America Cables and Radiar [35] doubt Argentine Government would attempt to operate circuits if they were closed by companies. However, managers point out that closing circuits with Germany and Italy would not solve basic problem since messages could easily be relayed through Spain, Switzerland, Sweden or other so-called neutrals. While this relay traffic might be partly controlled through local censorship, Department's opinion is requested as to the general problem.

Embassy has obtained traffic figures showing number of messages November 1941 and May 1942, as suggested Department's instruction 2533, June 12,[33] from Radiar, All America, Transradio and Ital Cable traffic through Transradio. Western Telegraph (British) refused similar data. Compilation of data received shows total 26,800 messages sent from Buenos Aires November and 26,300 May, with 27,700 received November and 24,400 May. Comparing May with previous November, there was substantial decline in messages to and from the United States, and slight total decline both to and from South American countries. Substantial increase in total messages sent Europe in May, but number received about the same. Spain, Germany, Italy, Switzerland, Sweden show largest gains in messages sent from here in May, although this partly ascribed to present inadequate air mail facilities which existed last November. Messages sent to Japan total 510 November, 622 May; received 425 November, 420 May.

Transradio obtains preponderant share of traffic with continental Europe and Japan, partly due to its direct circuits and more complete facilities.

---

[33] Not printed.
[34] Ricardo F. J. Bunge, Director of the Division of American Political Affairs in the Argentine Foreign Office.
[35] Sociedad Anónima "Radio Argentina", said to have been a subsidiary of I. T. & T.

The Transradio situation remains complicated. Embassy's despatch no. 5544, June 25 [38] proposes that duly authorized officials, such as high executive of RCA Communications perhaps accompanied by Government communications expert, be sent to Argentina with complete powers from American and British interests in Transradio. Visit of such officials highly desirable if not essential to effective investigation of Transradio personnel and other company matters, as well as evaluating practical possibilities of severing undesirable circuits.

Apart from considerations expressed my 1238, June 24, midnight, to Under Secretary,[38] Embassy has hesitated to make urgent representations without being better acquainted with practical methods of procedure. Department's opinion would be helpful on the following points:

(a) Should attempts also be made to close questionable circuits with Sweden, Switzerland, Spain, et cetera, and if not, what other control measures are suggested?

(b) Will British communications companies cooperate in bringing pressure to close undesirable circuits?

(c) Does Department believe that American and British interests in Transradio are sufficiently strong to exercise complete control including severance of lucrative European connections?

ARMOUR

810.74/372

Memorandum of Conversation, by the Adviser on Political Relations (Duggan)

[WASHINGTON,] June 29, 1942.

Participants: Colonel David Sarnoff, President of the Radio Corporation of America;
Mr. Breckinridge Long, Assistant Secretary of State;
Mr. Laurence Duggan, Adviser on Political Relations.

Mr. Long told Colonel Sarnoff that he was getting more perturbed every day by the continued operation of the consortium circuits between Argentina and Chile and Berlin and Tokyo. These circuits were being used for the transmission of vital information regarding ship movements, cargoes, and general intelligence. The closing of these circuits required the cooperation of the British interests. Despite conversations between Mr. Hopkins and Lord Beaverbrook, at the time of Mr. Churchill's first visit [39] as a result of which Lord

---

[38] Not printed.
[39] Prime Minister Churchill came to Washington for conferences with President Roosevelt, December 22, 1941–January 14, 1942, interrupted by trips to Ottawa and Palm Beach. Correspondence on these conferences is scheduled for publication in a subsequent volume of *Foreign Relations*.

Beaverbrook promised a cooperative attitude by the British interests, these interests have so far been reluctant to take any affirmative action other than to close the station at Rio. As a result of developments elsewhere, the possibilities of British cooperation seem better. Sir Campbell Stuart, in a recent meeting, expressed ignorance of the discussions last winter regarding the closure of the circuits with Argentina and Chile but stated that he would be glad to go into the matter fully after his return from a trip to Canada. A meeting has been arranged for Monday, July 6 at 3:00 p. m. Mr. Long expressed the hope that Colonel Sarnoff would be able to attend that meeting. General Davis and Mr. Winterbottom [40] of the RCA have also been invited to attend the meeting.

Colonel Sarnoff said that he was prepared to do whatever was necessary. Speaking without having given any previous thought to the matter, he believed that there were various alternatives. The first was for the Argentine and Chilean Governments to take over the stations themselves. The RCA had no objection to this. On the contrary, it had favored such action by the Argentine Government about two years ago. The I. T. & T. blocked the deal.

The second alternative was for the United States and British interests to place in the stations reliable personnel experts in cryptography, et cetera, who could detect whether the circuits were being used for the transmission of intelligence to the enemy. He would be glad to send General Davis on a trip to Argentina to look into the situation if that was desirable. Colonel Sarnoff stated that he, of course, would be glad to attend the meeting on Monday afternoon provided that he could return in time from a detail on which he was being sent to Florida. In his wide experience, Sir Campbell Stuart was the only man whom he had never been able satisfactorily to size up. He was the acme of courtesy but always turned up as the man behind the scenes blocking the extension of the RCA service.

Mr. Long permitted Colonel Sarnoff to look over the list of unsatisfactory personnel as obtained from the Embassy at Buenos Aires. . . . Colonel Sarnoff thought that there was no reason for delaying any further in getting rid of any undesirable employees. He thought that this was a first step which should be taken regardless of action with regard to severance of communications. In fact, he thought that with code experts in the stations it would be possible to ascertain what the Axis was sending back and forth.

Mr. Duggan stated that he had always been informed by the competent authorities of this Government that what was desired was the complete severance of these circuits since it was always possible to arrange the most innocent code for the sending of highly important messages.

---

[40] W. A. Winterbottom, vice president and general manager of R. C. A.

Colonel Sarnoff said that, of course, the Axis could always continue to transmit information via neutral countries. This would be more difficult but nevertheless entirely feasible.

810.74/347 : Telegram

The Ambassador in Chile (Bowers) to the Secretary of State

SANTIAGO, June 30, 1942—4 p. m.
[Received 9 : 42 p. m.]

1069. In reply to the question in the third paragraph of the Department's 680 of June 13, 4 p. m., I am of the opinion that at this moment the Chilean Government would proceed to operate the circuits itself since it is not prepared at present to entirely cut off telecommunications with the Axis Powers. It is, however, apparently prepared to forbid code messages being sent over telecommunication circuits to Axis countries but is awaiting the Department's reply to the tentative proposal to that effect, transmitted in my 1021 of June 22, 7 p. m. May I suggest that I be authorized to say that the Department thinks that the prohibition of code messages to Axis regions would be a decided step in the direction of continental defense.

BOWERS

810.74/355a : Telegram

The Secretary of State to the Ambassador in the United Kingdom (Winant)

WASHINGTON, July 3, 1942—3 p. m.

3046. Meeting is being arranged Monday July 6 with Sir Campbell Stuart and representatives of RCA to discuss the closing of the circuits to Axis countries operated by consortium stations at Buenos Aires and Santiago. As a result of concerted action by the various American Republics, the United States and the American companies concerned, direct telecommunications between the other American Republics and the Axis have been shut down with the exception of the two stations mentioned above and I. T. & T. radio-telephone station in Buenos Aires. It is possible, of course, that should the consortium stations close their Axis circuits the Argentine and Chilean Governments might establish circuits of their own. It is believed, however, that at this time it is psychologically bad, not to say incongruous, for British and American communication companies to allow stations over which they have the control and in which they have a financial interest to facilitate the stream of intelligence between South America and the Axis so detrimental to the best interests of Great Britain, the United States and the other United Nations.

In connection with the meeting referred to above, Department would appreciate receiving at your earliest convenience as full information as possible concerning the trust which operates the consortium station whose seat is in London, the personnel thereof, the exact relation between the trust and Cable and Wireless and the British Government, whether and if so how the German interest in the trust has been taken over by the British, what has been done with the Italian and French interests in the trust, and in general the attitude of British interests involved concerning the closing of the consortium stations' Axis circuits. In all your dealings with British officials and company representatives, you should constantly emphasize the fact that the closing of Axis circuits to Latin America is a vital factor in the campaign to end submarine warfare in the waters of this Hemisphere.

Please give this matter your most urgent and careful attention.

HULL

810.74/356 : Telegram

The Secretary of State to the Ambassador in the United Kingdom
(Winant)

WASHINGTON, July 7, 1942—8 p. m.

3116. Your 3721, July 4, 9 p. m.[41] Conference took place in Department yesterday at which were present the British Chargé d'Affaires, Sir R. I. Campbell, Sir Campbell Stuart, and representatives of RCA, including Colonel Sarnoff and Mr. Winterbottom, and General Davis, Chairman of the Consortium Trust.

In view of the situation in Argentina and Chile and in consideration of the fact that the consortium stations in those countries continue to carry traffic to and from Axis countries, it had become apparent that nothing short of positive joint action by the British and United States consortium trustees under the direction of their respective governments would result in the ultimate closing of these major circuits to enemy countries.

Therefore, the above meeting was called mainly for the purpose of reaching a mutual agreement upon which a unified course of action could be taken with regard to Argentina and Chile.

It was unanimously agreed at the meeting that RCA would request the Secretary of the Consortium Trust, whose office is in London, immediately to call a meeting in New York of the trustees for the purpose of arriving at a formal agreement under the consortium bylaws which would result in the closing of the consortium circuits in Argentina and Chile to outgoing and incoming messages from enemy countries. In addition, it is contemplated that such a de-

---

[41] Not printed.

cision by a majority vote of the consortium would be followed by prompt action to eliminate all pro-Axis sympathizers and agents from the directorates or working personnel of the Argentine and Chilean companies.

In connection with the calling in New York of the above-mentioned meeting the Department is keeping in mind the fact that if the German trustees are represented it would appear likely that Swedish proxies will be used or, if the French trustees accept an invitation to attend the meeting, they may be empowered by the Germans to vote in their behalf.

During the conference mentioned in paragraph 1 it was the consensus that even if Germany and France were represented and voted against the action which we contemplate in Argentina and Chile, the deciding vote could be cast by General Davis, the American Chairman. This procedure would be in line with the consortium bylaws which the Department would prefer to adhere to as closely as possible in order to avoid the claim of illegality which it is reasonable to assume will be raised by the Germans in Santiago and Buenos Aires.

In view of the above you are instructed promptly to discuss the matter with the Foreign Office and strongly to urge that the British Government lend every assistance in the carrying out of the above plan. In order to expedite matters it might be well to suggest that the Department has discussed with Sir Ronald Campbell and Sir Campbell Stuart the possibility that Wilshaw and Inverforth [42] designate to attend the consortium meeting in New York two persons already in this country, possibly from the Embassy, to act as their alternates. Also, you are authorized to suggest that the British Government promptly transmit to its representatives in Buenos Aires and Santiago confidential advice of the above plan. Please keep the Department currently informed of developments.

HULL

810.74/360 : Telegram

The Chargé in Argentina (Reed) to the Secretary of State

BUENOS AIRES, July 10, 1942—10 p. m.
[Received July 10—7 : 42 p. m.]

1359. Embassy's despatch 4338, March 6.[43] The Minister of Interior [44] today addressed a note to the Director General of Posts and Telegraphs [45] quoting Resolution XL of the Rio conference and terminating as follows:

---

[42] Andrew Weir, Lord Inverforth, President of Cables and Wireless, Ltd.
[43] Not printed.
[44] Miguel Culaciati.
[45] Horacio C. Rivarola.

"Consequently, it is necessary that Posts and Telegraphs adopt pertinent measures for the purpose of complying with the provisions of said resolution in such manner that the three points contained therein be amply satisfied.

"The Director General will please advise if his agency finds itself in condition to undertake the respective controls, and suggest measures considered pertinent for such objective."

REED

810.74/363a : Telegram

The Secretary of State to the Ambassador in Chile (Bowers)

WASHINGTON, July 11, 1942—8 p. m.

796. The Argentine Minister of the Interior today issued instructions [46] for the complete implementation of all provisions of Rio Resolution XL. When these instructions are carried out, Chile will be the sole remaining nation of the Western Hemisphere through which intelligence detrimental to continental defense is permitted to flow to the Axis. Consequently, it is more urgent than ever before that Chile take action to sever the telecommunication circuits which it now maintains with Axis territory. By continuing to maintain them it will in large part nullify the effectiveness of the action taken by the other American republics, since it will provide a channel that may be used by Axis agents throughout the hemisphere. Please bring this matter again to the attention of the foreign office and telegraph what measures, if any, have so far been adopted by the Chilean Government in accordance with the aforesaid resolution; and what reasons are advanced by the foreign office for failure to sever telecommunication circuits with the Axis.

In emphasizing to the foreign office the urgency of taking prompt action on this matter, you should avoid reference to the contents of the Department's telegram no. 781 of July 9, 1942, 7 p.m.,[47] regarding the possibility of action being taken by the companies in the same sense.

HULL

810.74/381

The Ambassador in Chile (Bowers) to the Secretary of State

No. 3936   SANTIAGO, July 17, 1942.
                                           [Received July 27.]

SIR: I have the honor to refer to the Department's No. 680 of June 13, 4 p. m., and subsequent instructions and to my telegraphic reply

---

[46] See *supra*.
[47] Not printed.

No. 1170, July 17, 6 p.m.[48] I first presented orally the matter of closing Chilean telecommunication circuits to the Foreign Minister and followed it up on July 13 with a written communication to the Foreign Minister, copy of which is enclosed, to which I received a reply on July 14, a translation of which is also enclosed.

Taking my cue from the statement in the last paragraph of the Minister's letter that if we presented proof of the misuse of the communication circuits the Chilean Government would take prompt action, I went to see the Foreign Minister today and allowed him to see translations of intercepted telegrams from the German Embassy transmitted over authorized Chilean telecommunication circuits, which contained not only information dangerous to hemispheric defense but proof of subversive activities of the German Ambassador and members of his staff as well. A copy of my oral remarks to the Foreign Minister is enclosed.[48] It will be seen therefrom, and from my telegram No. 1170 of July 17, 6 p. m., that he expressed himself as convinced of there having been misuse of the radio circuits and misuse of diplomatic immunities by members of the staff of the Embassy and said that he was considering the matter with the President. He referred to his inquiry whether prohibiting the sending of code messages by Axis Embassies would be regarded in the nature of a solution by us and expressed surprise that he had not received my communication to him of July 13 in which I stated that such action would be helpful in decreasing the dangers to our cause of maintenance of these circuits. I have sent him a replacement copy of this communication.

Respectfully yours,   CLAUDE G. BOWERS

[Enclosure 1]

The American Ambassador (Bowers) to the Chilean Minister for Foreign Affairs (Barros Jarpa)

SANTIAGO, July 13, 1942.

MY DEAR MR. MINISTER: I have the honor to refer to our recent conversation in which, under instructions from my Government, I informed you that the telecommunication connections which Chile maintains with Axis territory were being employed to carry to the Axis Governments information of vital importance from all parts of this hemisphere with respect to the movements of individual ships and ships in convoys, and that we had confidential information bearing this out.

I have now again been instructed by my Government to bring to your attention the serious concern with which my Government views the con-

---

[48] Not printed.

tinued operation of facilities whereby the enemy is able to interrupt the lines of communication indispensable to the common defense of the American Republics and to destroy the lives and property of citizens of these Republics.   My Government feels that shipping, which is just as vital for the survival of Chile as that of the United States, is daily being lost because of Chile's maintenance of the channels through which the Axis is provided information without which it would not be able successfully to maintain its attacks on the vital communications of the various American Republics.

In effect, my government has felt that the prompt action of nineteen of the American Republics in severing direct communications with territory under the control of the Axis is nullified to a large extent by the fact that Chile and Argentina have not taken similar measures.

Since our conversation, I have been informed by my Government that the Argentine Minister of the Interior on July 11th issued instructions that all of the provisions of Resolution No. XL of the Conference at Rio de Janeiro shall be completely implemented.   With the execution of the instructions of the Argentine Minister of the Interior, Chile would therefore be the only nation remaining in the Western Hemisphere through which military intelligence detrimental to hemispheric defense would be permitted to flow to the Axis.

My Government therefore asks me to convey its views that it is more urgent than ever before that Chile undertake action to sever the telecommunications circuits which it now maintains with Axis territory since their continued operation would provide a channel that might be used by Axis agents throughout the hemisphere.

Believe me [etc.]   CLAUDE G. BOWERS

[Enclosure 2—Translation]

The Chilean Minister for Foreign Affairs (Barros Jarpa) to the American Ambassador (Bowers)

SANTIAGO, July 14, 1942.

MY ESTEEMED MR. AMBASSADOR: I have the honor to acknowledge the receipt of the communication of Your Excellency dated the 13th instant in which you refer to our recent conversations concerning the use of telecommunication between this country and those of the Axis.

Because of these conversations this Ministry has concerned itself, with every interest, to consider with the Ministry of the Interior, to which corresponds the taking of the measures referred to, the best form of drafting them and assuring their efficient and satisfactory application.

Careful consideration will be given to the antecedents and points of view which Your Excellency has expressed to me, for following with the same interest the consideration of the matter in order to take adequate measures which I shall shortly have the pleasure of making known to Your Excellency.

I must also express to Your Excellency that, if there are sufficient reasons to assure that, under the regime concerning telecommunications existing up to now—which is not one of absolute and unconditional liberty—it has been possible really to commit the abuses to which Your Excellency refers and should this Ministry have concrete antecedents respecting the matter, the application of the corresponding measures and sanctions will be hastened.

Please accept [etc.]   ERNESTO BARROS JARPA

810.74/376 : Telegram

The Chargé in Argentina (Reed) to the Secretary of State

BUENOS AIRES, July 21, 1942—3 p. m.
[Received 4 : 38 p. m.]

1415. Department's telegram No. 1083, July 20, 2 p. m.[50] Following information obtained confidentially from an Argentine official.

Director of Posts and Telegraphs sending reply today to Minister of Interior stating that severance of telecommunications will depend upon instructions to be received from the Foreign Office, and that establishment of effective control over clandestine stations and similar measures will depend largely on obtaining appropriation of about half million pesos previously requested.

It is expected that matter will be referred to Foreign Office within a day or two and it was suggested that Embassy make casual inquiry at Foreign Office latter part this week, which will be done.

REED

810.74/363a : Telegram

The Secretary of State to the Ambassador in Chile (Bowers)

WASHINGTON, July 22, 1942—7 p. m.

827. The Department would appreciate your answering the two specific questions which it posed in its telegram no. 796 of July 11, 8 p. m. Lest there be any misunderstanding the Department desires to make it clear that it does not consider the denial of the use of codes by Axis missions as an alternative to cutting the circuits with Axis territory. While the Department would be gratified by the denial of

---

[50] Not printed.

the use of codes to the Axis missions it believes that your effort should be directed to bringing about severance of the circuit.

HULL

810.74/378 : Telegram

The Ambassador in Chile (Bowers) to the Secretary of State

SANTIAGO, July 23, 1942—9 p. m.
[Received 10 p. m.]

1202. For Under Secretary. Your telegram No. 827, July 22, 7 p. m. I understand the point absolutely and I have made entirely clear to the Minister.

BOWERS

810.74/383a : Telegram

The Secretary of State to the Ambassador in Argentina (Armour) [51]

WASHINGTON, July 24, 1942—4 p. m.

1103. 1. A meeting was held in Department on July 20 attended by representatives of RCA, Sir Campbell Stuart and General Robert C. Davis, chairman of the consortium trust.

2. It was decided to call a meeting of the trustees at New York City August 24 "to review position of consortium companies in present world situation." Notice of this meeting is being sent to the German trustees through their Swedish representatives at Stockholm by the intermediary of the American Legation at that city and to the French trustees by the intermediary of the American Consul at Lyon.

3. It was further decided that General Davis should proceed to Buenos Aires and Santiago on July 28 accompanied by two Government radio experts to examine the questions of closing the consortium circuits to the Axis and of removing undesirable personnel from the stations. He would return to New York in time for the meeting of August 24 to submit his report.

4. Embassy at London has been instructed to advise appropriate authorities of foregoing and to request that latter forward information to British representatives at Buenos Aires and Santiago, asking them to cooperate fully with you and with General Davis.

5. General Davis will be accompanied by Mr. Philip F. Siling, Chief, International Division, Federal Communications Commission,

---

[51] This telegram was also sent to the Ambassador in Chile as No. 834, with the addition of the following paragraph:

"6. Substance of your 1166, July 17, 1 p. m. [not printed], has been transmitted to London with the statement that the Department trusts that the British Foreign Office will instruct British Ambassador at Santiago to suggest to Chilean Government that it close existing telecommunication circuits with Axis."

and Mr. George Shecklin. They will advise you fully of all discussions in the Department and you are requested to lend them every possible aid and assistance.

HULL

810.74/390 : Telegram

The Ambassador in the United Kingdom (Winant) to the Secretary of State

LONDON, August 3, 1942—5 p. m.
[Received August 3—4 p. m.]

4321. The contents of the Department's telegram No. 3444, July 24, 4 p. m.,[52] were duly conveyed to the Foreign Office. In accordance with our request the latter have instructed their Embassies at Buenos Aires and Santiago to afford all possible assistance to General Davis. In addition they say that they have kept the aforesaid Embassies informed of all developments. They say that while we may rest assured that General Davis will be given the fullest support in dealing with the Chilean authorities, it seems "a little premature" to make formal representations to the Chilean Government in advance of the report which General Davis is expected to make.

In view of the foregoing it would be helpful, if the Department desires that British representations be made at Santiago prior to General Davis' survey of the situation, if the Embassy could be furnished with more detailed background information.

(While the Foreign Office fully shares our views as to the desirability of severing communications between the Axis countries and Argentina and Chile, they are at present inclined to feel that steps to that end through the Consortium Trust Affiliates in the latter countries would only result in their substitution by purely Axis controlled communications companies with the added disadvantage that we would not as at present be able to obtain complete and highly useful knowledge of the messages which are being sent. This is however only a preliminary view and if we can convince the Foreign Office and other interested authorities of the greater advantages of attempting to close down the Corsortium Trust Affiliates they are quite prepared to cooperate).

WINANT

---

[52] Not printed; this telegram gave information regarding developments to be transmitted to the British Foreign Office, and urged that the Foreign Office instruct the British Ambassador in Chile to suggest to the Chilean Government that it close the existing telecommunication circuits with the Axis (810.74/383c).

825.73L/16 : Telegram

The Ambassador in Chile (Bowers) to the Secretary of State

SANTIAGO, August 13, 1942—7 p. m.
[Received August 14—1 : 00 a. m.]

1294. For Under Secretary. My telegram 1258, August 5, 3 p. m.[53] Decree promulgated and published in morning papers. Will be noted it does not prohibit sending of coded messages from Axis Missions. Mysterious feature is that same day of publication head of All-America Cables was instructed officially orally with a promise of a written order not to accept code messages of these Missions and later this order was withdrawn. Shall see Barros Jarpa and get his interpretation. It may be a step by step process. Would appreciate any observations of Department.

BOWERS

810.74/390 : Telegram

The Secretary of State to the Ambassador in the United Kingdom (Winant)

WASHINGTON, August 13, 1942—11 p. m.

3841. Your 4321, August 3, 5 p. m. Department has felt that both in Argentina and Chile action by the governments to cut the circuits with Axis territory would be more definitive and less likely to create confusion and ill will than action by the consortium interests that would have to be taken without the concurrence of the governments and possibly in violation of the concessions under which the companies operate. Preparation for action by the consortium is being made only because of the likelihood that this is the only means of achieving this important objective in the near future. Nevertheless, our Embassies in Buenos Aires and Santiago are continuing, on every appropriate occasion, their representations to the governments, and there appears to be a possibility that these representations will succeed. Our Embassy in Chile feels that this possibility would be definitely increased, with regard to the Chilean Government, if the British Embassy in Santiago should likewise inform the Foreign Office there that it has evidence that the existing telecommunication circuits with the Axis are being wrongly used. It feels that otherwise the non-rupture element in the Chilean Cabinet will argue against cutting the circuit, pointing out that the British have made no objection to its continuation.

[53] Not printed.

Should the circuits be closed by action of the consortium, it is possible though far from certain that the local governments would continue them under other auspices. This would, however, represent positive action by them in opposition to recommendations of the Rio Meeting which they would probably be reluctant to take. In any case, there are no "purely Axis-controlled communications companies" in either Argentina or Chile.

HULL

810.74/445

Memorandum of Conversation, by the Assistant Secretary of State (Long)

[WASHINGTON,] August 26, 1942.

Sir Ronald [55] came in this afternoon and I advised him of the report made at yesterday's meeting by General Davis concerning his activities on his trip to Rio, B. A., and Santiago, and said that the report seemed to indicate that there was a satisfactory condition now existing in those three capitals and that the communication facilities of the Consortium group in each of those capitals was now in friendly hands. I related to him in some detail the report made by General Davis in connection with each of the three stations.

I further told Sir Ronald that General Davis had not been able to determine whether the British Ambassador in Santiago had received instructions to cooperate with him and with the American Ambassador although General Davis assumed he had received instructions and that his manner was that of an astute diplomat who could carry on a conversation without making any commitment. I added that I thought it would be helpful, in case he had not received instructions, for him to receive them. Sir Ronald said he would check up and see that that was done if the Ambassador had not already been instructed.

B[RECKINRIDGE] L[ONG]

810.74/441 : Telegram

The Ambassador in the United Kingdom (Winant) to the Secretary of State

LONDON, August 28, 1942—7 p. m.
[Received August 28—6 : 50 p. m.]

4817. Department's 3841, August 13, 11 p. m. Foreign Office informs us that the British Ambassador at Santiago has been instructed to consult with our Ambassador there with a view to bringing jointly

---

[55] Sir Ronald I. Campbell.

to the attention of the Chilean Foreign Office that evidence was in their possession that the circuits with the Axis were being improperly used.

Foreign Office assures us that British authorities are concerned solely in cooperating with us and that such specific instructions as have now been sent to the British Ambassador were not sent previously because British authorities thought that we were awaiting report of General Davis before deciding definitely on a course of action.

It would be helpful to us to receive from the Department as soon as possible information regarding any decisions that may have been reached at the meeting of the trustees of the consortium trust which was to take place in New York City on August 24.

WINANT

810.74/442a : Telegram

The Acting Secretary of State to the Ambassador in Chile (Bowers)

WASHINGTON, August 29, 1942—6 p. m.

982. This Government is deeply disturbed at the fact that the Government of Chile continues to maintain telecommunication circuits with the Axis. By doing so, it upholds the hands of the Axis in its struggle to overcome the free peoples of the American continent. The information that is supplied to the Axis by the channels which Chile keeps open makes as material a contribution to the Axis cause as if Chile were supplying the Axis armed forces with the actual materials of war. It may be measured in terms of the torpedoes that are sinking the ships and thereby disrupting the vital communications of the American republics.

The Department, taking cognizance of frequent verbal assurances of complete solidarity and cooperation on the part of the Chilean Government, feels sure that President Ríos and the Foreign Minister would not continue to countenance this extension of aid to the Axis if they were fully aware of the wounds being inflicted on the entire American community of nations as a result of it. The Department's assurance is reinforced by the Foreign Minister's statement that, if we presented proof (as we have done) of the misuse of the Axis circuits, the Chilean Government would take prompt action to remedy the situation. The Department feels that time is of the essence in remedying it.

You should find an immediate opportunity to impress this situation anew upon President Ríos, reporting to the Department the results of your representations.

WELLES

810.74/411½

*The Chairman of the Trustees of the Transradio Consortium Trust
(Davis) to the Assistant Secretary of State (Long)*

NEW YORK, August 31, 1942.
[Received September 1.]

MY DEAR MR. SECRETARY: I wish to advise you that at the meeting of the Consortium Trustees held this date they approved the action taken by the Brazilian Company in closing its Axis circuits.

On motion of General Harbord [56] the Trustees approved the following policy for the guidance of the Argentine and Chilean Companies:

It is in the interest of all parties concerned that each National Company promptly comply with the wishes of its Government relating to the operation of its international circuits and not hesitate to close any circuit whenever such closure shall be suggested, recommended or ordered by the Government under which it is operating.

Sincerely yours,   ROBERT C. DAVIS

810.74/448 : Telegram

The Ambassador in Chile (Bowers) to the Secretary of State

SANTIAGO, September 3, 1942—7 p. m.
[Received September 4—12 : 52 a. m.]

1421. For Secretary and Under Secretary. Your telegram 982, August 29, 6 p. m. finally reached the President. It was evident that he has been confused and through the failure of Barros Jarpa to inform him. He reiterated his readiness to do whatever we think necessary for the protection of the Americas and his determination that Chile shall not be used against them. When I told him the German Embassy's wires have increased 216% since 1941 he was astonished and said that since none could deal with commercial matters it seemed very strange. I then showed him a selected number of intercepts showing what is going out on war matters from German Embassy. He asked if I had ever called them to the attention of Barros Jarpa. When I replied that I had he seemed more than ever astonished. I asked if he would like to see more and he said he would.

He then amazed me by asking if I had seen the decree cutting off communications with the Axis and when I said it applied to all but the Axis Embassies he took issue, insisting that it did. I told him it was not so interpreted. I then asked what the attitude of the Government would be if the messages of these Missions were refused.

---

[56] Gen. James G. Harbord, Chairman of the Board, Radio Corporation of America.

He suggested that they be refused and we would see what would happen. They would complain to the Government which would not interfere.

It was all so clearly new to him that I finally asked if he would shut down telecommunication circuits with Axis countries if we could prove to him that they were being used to serve the enemy and the submarines and he reiterated that he would do anything necessary to prevent Chile from being used as a base of operations against the American nations. I shall see him again and furnish additional proof.

To me the most depressing revelation was the evident fact that his Minister has not passed on to him vital information.

The Brazilian Ambassador has not yet received instructions.[57]

BOWERS

810.74/592

The American Ambassador in Chile (Bowers) to the Chilean Minister for Foreign Affairs (Barros Jarpa) [58]

No. 1353 SANTIAGO, September 5, 1942.

EXCELLENCY: I have the honor to refer to our several previous conversations upon the subject and to inform Your Excellency that my Government is deeply disturbed by the continuance of telecommunication circuits between Chile and the Axis countries. The information which is being supplied to the Axis by the channels which Chile permits to remain open makes as substantial a contribution to the Axis cause as if Chile were supplying the Axis armed forces with actual war material. Its effect can be measured in terms of the torpedoes that are sinking American and other vessels and thereby disrupting the vital communications of the American Republics. Human lives and ships of the American Republics are paying for the fact that the Axis nations can send vital military and shipping information freely in secret codes over the circuits maintained by the Transradio Chilena.

My Government, in view of the frequent and appreciated demonstrations of Chile's position of complete solidarity and cooperation with our cause, feels certain that Your Excellency's Government will not continue to countenance this extension of aid to the Axis powers when it realizes the wounds which are being inflicted on the entire American community of nations as a result of it. I am accordingly, under instructions from my Government, taking this occasion again to

---

[57] In telegram No. 2635, September 8, 7 p. m., the Department informed the Ambassador in Brazil that "the Brazilian Embassy in Santiago has not yet received instructions to make representations regarding severance of the telecommunication circuits between Chile and the Axis." (810.74/448)

[58] Copy transmitted to the Department by the Ambassador in his despatch No. 4755, October 23; received November 2.

bring this situation urgently to Your Excellency's attention and to express our confidence that, in accordance with Resolution XL of the Conference at Río de Janeiro, Your Excellency's Government will at this time close the telecommunication circuits existing between Chile and the Axis powers.

Accept [etc.] CLAUDE G. BOWERS

810.74/471

Memorandum of Conversation, by Mr. Louis J. Halle of the Division of the American Republics

[WASHINGTON,] September 9, 1942.

Participants: The Secretary (later) ; Assistant Secretary Long; Mr. Hackworth, Legal Adviser (later) ; Mr. Bonsal, RA ; [62] Mr. Daniels, RA; Mr. Halle, RA; Mr. Reinstein, A–A ; [63] Mr. Tannenwald, FF ; [64] Mr. deWolf, IN.[65]

Mr. Long pointed out that after months of conversation the American interests in the Consortium Trust (Radio Corporation of America) had done nothing actually to bring about a closure of the circuits maintained with the Axis by the Consortium companies in Argentina and Chile.   He said they had proved what degree of control they could exercise over these companies by what had been accomplished in the course of General Davis' visit to Buenos Aires and Santiago, and that consequently he had no doubt but what they could order the companies to suspend the operation of the undesirable circuits.   He said that the RCA representatives were coming to see him at 3 p. m. today, and that he had in mind telling them to do what was necessary in order to shut down the circuits by midnight tomorrow (September 10).

Mr. Bonsal suggested the advisability of informing the Argentine and Chilean Governments in advance of the contemplated action, pointing out that the political consequences of doing otherwise might have wide ramifications involving the basic policy governing our relations with the two republics. Specifically, he said, action taken by the companies in response to an initiative from this Government to close the circuits might raise the whole question of control by national governments over public utilities operating within their own

---

[62] Division of the American Republics.
[63] Office of the Assistant Secretary of State, Acheson.
[64] Foreign Funds Control Division.
[65] Division of International Communications.

jurisdiction. He felt that one of the consequences might be that nationalistic interests would point out that the public services in these countries were controlled by Washington, rather than by the national governments which should properly have jurisdiction.

Mr. Long expressed the view that, should the Governments be notified of the proposed action in advance, they would immediately call in the Axis representatives and that then we would have a fight on our hands. Mr. Bonsal felt that, in any case, we should be much better informed than we were of what the legal and political consequences of such action would be before we embarked on it.

The suggestion was advanced by Messrs. Daniels and Halle that it might be sufficient to have the RCA representatives be prepared to issue the necessary orders immediately when the Department gives them word to go ahead. This suggestion was based especially on the possibility that the Chilean Government might cut the circuits in the near future on its own initiative, and that since such initiative would lead the country nearer to a complete diplomatic break with the Axis, it would be preferable to company initiative.

The meeting thereupon adjourned to the Secretary's Office, where Mr. Long placed the problem and various considerations that had been advanced before the Secretary. The Secretary, citing the vital economic assistance that we were extending to Argentina, especially in the way of iron and steel shipments, said that we had a right to expect a good deal more cooperation in return than we were getting. He said that, while he had not been in close touch with the situation in Argentina over the past few months, he felt the time had come when we should deal more severely with the Argentine Government. Consequently, he favored Mr. Long's proposal to ask RCA to have the circuits abandoned by midnight tomorrow. Mr. Bonsal expressed his view that we should have more information on the provisions of the franchises under which the companies were operating before proceeding further. The Secretary said that he felt the question of what the franchises provided concerned the Consortium and the Consortium companies rather than this Government. It was agreed that, because of indications that the Chilean Government would not oppose company initiative in this matter, the Chilean authorities should be notified in advance. In the case of Argentina, the Secretary expressed no objection to our having the company take the action forthwith.

810.74/470

Memorandum of Conversation, by Mr. Louis J. Halle of the Division of the American Republics

[WASHINGTON,] September 9, 1942.

Participants: General Davis, Chairman of the Consortium Trust; Colonel Sarnoff, President of the Radio Corporation of America; Mr. Winterbottom, Acting President of RCA; Mr. Long, Assistant Secretary; Mr. Hackworth, Legal Adviser; Mr. deWolf, IN; Mr. Bonsal, RA (first part of meeting only); Mr. Halle, RA.

Mr. Long gave the substance of a telegram just received from Buenos Aires (1720, September 7),[66] indicating that the Argentine Government might insist on the appointment of an Argentine as Manager of Transradio Internacional,[67] rather than the American, George Hayes, who was about to be appointed by the Board of Directors in accordance with a decision taken at the meeting of Consortium trustees in New York. In the course of the meeting it was decided that RCA would immediately instruct its representatives on the Board of Directors to insist on Hayes' appointment.

Mr. Long then requested that RCA take action to discontinue the Consortium circuits with the Axis, saying that company initiative in this matter would be preferable to action by the Argentine and Chilean Governments as it would avoid the political issues involved. He cited the recent order of the Argentine Minister of the Interior to the Director of Posts and Telegraphs to implement Resolution XL of Rio, an order that has not been carried out.

General Davis said the impression he had gathered on his recent trip was that our Embassies in Argentina and Chile were in accord that if the companies close the circuits on their own initiative, the governments might take them over. He thus explained the wording of the minutes of the recent trustees meeting in which the trustees had gone on record as approving any action the companies might take in accordance with any "suggestion" from the governments that they abandon any international circuits they were operating.

Mr. Bonsal raised the question of whether the franchises under which the companies were operating their Axis circuits actually did not allow them to abandon those circuits without permission of the governments. Neither General Davis nor Colonel Sarnoff could give a categorical answer, but the General expressed his belief that reason had to be given to the governments for taking such action.

---

[66] Not printed.
[67] The former resident manager, a French citizen, resigned in August.

Colonel Sarnoff said that, speaking for RCA, he would gladly waive consideration of the commercial interests at stake. He said the only question was whether RCA had it in its power to achieve the desired end. He pointed out that first the British Consortium interests would have to concur in the proposed action. If they did so, the question would arise as to whether the trustees had the requisite authority. If they did, would their order be obeyed by the local management in each case? If so, what action would the Argentine Government, in particular, take? He was fearful that the Argentine Government would then take over the company and he wished to know what support this Government would then give to RCA. Mr. Long indicated that this Government would do all it appropriately could to protect RCA from the consequences of any action it might take to close the circuits.

Mr. Long indicated confidentially that IT&T was prepared to discontinue immediately its telephone circuit between Buenos Aires and Berlin. Colonel Sarnoff stated that, if IT&T could do this, there was no reason why the Consortium company could not also do it. He then went on to say that, if we wished RCA to go ahead with this after we had considered all the consequences, RCA would show no hesitation.

The question was raised of whether there were any physical means, such as inadequate machinery, by which the circuits might be abandoned. Colonel Sarnoff and Mr. Winterbottom indicated they did not believe there were any such means, since the machinery required was for the most part interchangeable.

Mr. Winterbottom expressed the belief that if the Argentine company closed the Axis circuits, the Argentine Government would the next day open and operate them by itself, and he indicated that it had the facilities with which to do this. It was pointed out that such action by the Government would not interfere with the continued operation of its other circuits by the company. The following course of action was then agreed upon:

(1) RCA would immediately issue instructions to its representatives on the Board of Directors of the two companies to have the companies discontinue the Axis circuits immediately on their own initiative, the action to be taken by a Directors' meeting in each case. RCA would also instruct its representatives to insist on the appointment of Hayes.

(2) The Department would approach the British Foreign Office immediately with a request that it do what was necessary to have identical instructions issued forthwith to the respective Directors of the two companies who represent Cable and Wireless, Limited.

It was agreed that this would be a more practical approach to the matter than would be an attempt to achieve the same results through another meeting of the Consortium, which would require 30 days notice to the trustees in any case.

———

Mr. Winterbottom complained at the fact that the Department, in its own communications with its missions in South America, gave preference to All America Cables over the RCA Radio Companies. Colonel Sarnoff stated that the common view that cable traffic was more secret than radio traffic was erroneous, and that in point of fact the reverse was true. He also complained bitterly that IT&T had spread the report in Government circles that RCA was preventing the establishment of additional circuits with Europe and the Near East needed by the War Department by invoking a consent decree. He said that he had been called to Mr. Thurman Arnold's [68] office in the Department of Justice and that Mr. Arnold was preparing to have the consent decree abandoned on the basis of misinformation that he had received from IT&T.

———

810.74/454 : Telegram

The Ambassador in Chile (Bowers) to the Secretary of State

SANTIAGO, September 9, 1942—noon.
[Received 8 : 53 p. m.]

1449. For Secretary and Under Secretary. Your telegram 1017, September 8, 7 p. m.[69] As stated in my telegram 1421, September 3, 7 p. m., I saw President Ríos and submitted proof which to my astonishment had not been called to his attention. I again saw Barros Jarpa yesterday (Tuesday) on his return to city and after reiterating all that had been said before and giving him additional proof of the damage being done through the Axis communications, I left with him a stiff note saying, among other things, that these constitute as much a contribution against the defence of the continent as though Chile sent war material. I then wrote personally to President Ríos using as pretext an acknowledgment of an inscribed photograph reminding him of our conversation of a few days ago and enclosing a copy of the note to Barros Jarpa as of possible interest.

Barros Jarpa always seems impressed and distressed when proof of these Axis activities are submitted and this time he said he would go into the matter with the President. He said just one significant thing, that "until we break relations it looks like we must forbid the Axis Missions the use of their code in communicating with their Governments". Thus in circular fashion he gets back to the proposi-

[68] An Assistant Attorney General.
[69] Not printed.

tion he had made me many weeks ago. I suspect that in conformity with his strategy of yielding only inch by inch this will be his proposal. I told him that Washington is gravely concerned and asked him to let me know immediately when a decision has been reached and he promised to send for me very soon. I shall follow this up closely.

At reception at Brazilian Embassy I talked with Alvarez [70] and asked him if Barros Jarpa had actually told him he had proposed cutting off use of codes to Axis Embassies and that I had not favored it and he said it is true. I expressed astonishment and told him the opposite was true. He did not appear surprised (see my telegram 1442, September 7, 2 p. m., point 2.[71])

BOWERS

810.74/464c : Telegram

The Secretary of State to the Ambassador in Chile (Bowers)

WASHINGTON, September 10, 1942—7 p. m.

1031. At a meeting on September 9 in the Department with representatives of the Radio Corporation of America, the following decisions were taken:

(1) RCA will immediately instruct its representatives on the Board of Directors of Transradio Chilena to take action immediately at a meeting of the Board to have the company discontinue its circuits with the Axis on its own initiative.

(2) The Department is communicating immediately with the British Government with a view to having the representatives of Cable and Wireless on the Board of Directors receive identical instructions.

Similar action will be taken immediately with regard to the Axis circuits maintained by the Consortium Company in Argentina.

While the action outlined above will not be taken in the name of this Government or ostensibly on its initiative, you should inform the President that it is contemplated and that you assume, in view of the conversation with him reported in your 1421, September 3, 7 p. m., that he will have no objection to it. If, however, it appears to you that informing the President in this sense may prejudice a good prospect that the Chilean Government will cut the circuits promptly of its own accord, you should so inform the Department immediately and await further instructions before approaching the President in the sense indicated above.

HULL

---

[70] Pedro Alvarez Suárez, Chilean Minister of Commerce and Supplies.

[71] Not printed; point 2 gives the same information contained in this paragraph concerning Barros Jarpa's reported action (740.0011 European War 1939/24079).

810.74/471 : Telegram

The Secretary of State to the Ambassador in the United Kingdom
(Winant)

WASHINGTON, September 10, 1942—8 p. m.

4357. At a meeting on September 9 in the Department with representatives of the Radio Corporation of America, it was decided that the following action would be taken to bring about a closure of the circuits with the Axis maintained by the Consortium companies in Argentina and Chile.

RCA will immediately instruct its representatives on the Boards of Directors of the two companies to have the companies discontinue the Axis circuits immediately on their own initiative, the action to be taken by a Directors' Meeting in each case. It will further instruct its representatives in Argentina to insist on the appointment of George Hayes as General Manager, in accordance with the decision of the Consortium Trustees Meeting in New York last month.

The Department agreed to approach the British Foreign Office immediately with a request that it do what is necessary to have identical instructions issued forthwith to the respective Directors of the two companies who represent Cable and Wireless Limited.

It is believed that the American and British interests together command a majority on each of the Boards of Directors. The success of the procedure depends on joint action by the American and British interests. Its purpose is to eliminate one flagrant means by which the Axis is enabled to sink ships of the United Nations.

The Department has reason to believe that, while it is possible that the Argentine Government would undertake to operate these circuits itself if the companies abandoned them, it is unlikely that either the Argentine or Chilean Governments would take any more drastic action.

Please bring the foregoing to the confidential attention of the Foreign Office, making the indicated request and emphasizing the urgency of the matter, and report to the Department.

We are keeping the British Embassy here informed.

HULL

810.74/460 : Telegram

The Ambassador in Chile (Bowers) to the Secretary of State

SANTIAGO, September 11, 1942—6 p. m.
[Received 8 : 43 p. m.]

1469. For Secretary and Under Secretary. Your 1031, September 10, 7 p. m. When Davis was here and I asked Barros Jarpa if Chile would raise objections if the RCA itself cut off telecommunications with Axis countries, he immediately replied in the negative, expressing a certain satisfaction. He then qualified by saying he could conceive of nothing like opposition from Chile, but if it came up he would have to study the question to see but thought it would not be opposed here. This information I gave General Davis the same day.

In my telegram 1421, September 3, 7 p. m., I reported statement of President Ríos to effect he would shut down telecommunications with the Axis if being used against the safety of American nations; and his suggestion that the Transradio Chilena refuse messages for Axis countries and see what would happen; the implication being that the Axis Missions would protest and the Government do nothing about it.

My note asking the closing of telecommunication with Axis countries was handed Barros Jarpa at 5 o'clock, September 8. He promised an early reply. He was busy all day Thursday with Senate. Suggest that I inquire tomorrow if answer is ready, and if not ready Monday that I inform him that RCA will act and remind him that he had expressed some satisfaction with this procedure. Assume British Government will issue similar instructions to its representatives on board of directors but should we not first know if such are being sent.

Since only 2 or 3 days should determine whether Chile will close telecommunications on its own with the Axis countries, am persuaded nothing as an alternative should be suggested before it has time to act.

BOWERS

810.74/462 : Telegram

The Ambassador in Chile (Bowers) to the Secretary of State

SANTIAGO, September 12, 1942—4 p. m.
[Received 10 : 37 p. m.]

1474. For Under Secretary. Brazilian Ambassador received instructions to ask observance of article number XZ [*XL*] Rio Conference yesterday and is seeking audience with Minister this morning. Heard nothing to indicate British has yet acted. Think it well to test effect of Brazilian request before informing Government here of decision in your 1031 and plan to ask appointment for Monday.

BOWERS

810.74/471a : Telegram

The Secretary of State to the Ambassador in the United Kingdom (Winant)

WASHINGTON, September 16, 1942—7 p. m.

4493. A representative of the British Embassy, came in this afternoon to suggest, on instructions from his Government, that Wilshaw is anxious to be of assistance in closing the circuits but thought that the trustees of the Consortium ought to express some agreement with the action indicated and suggested that Ginman, who represented the British members of the Consortium at their recent meeting, should be consulted by General Davis.

It was explained that that was at variance with the theory upon which we were operating to close the beams of the two stations concerned. General Davis was the Chairman of the Consortium which was composed of German and French as well as British and American members. The business could not be considered at a Consortium meeting except after 30 days notice. It was not considered either necessary or advisable to bring the Consortium into it. Consequently, it was inadvisable to have Davis consult Ginman as both were operating in connection with the Consortium group. As distinguished from that, the present movement is to have the American member, which happens to be R. C. A., communicate directly with its representatives on the Boards of Directors of the two local companies and instruct them to take action looking to the immediate closing of the two stations. It was hoped, and is still expected, that the British member, Cables and Wireless, will take the same action in regard to its own representatives on the Boards of each of these companies. The British and American members control a majority on each Board.

Consequently, it is hoped that Cables and Wireless will send instructions direct to its own representatives in the sense of the instructions which they have been advised are being sent to the American representatives.

While it would be contrary to the theory of our operation to have Davis confer with Ginman and the suggestion that Ginman should report to London, it would be quite in keeping with the spirit if Cables and Wireless should communicate directly with Ginman if they so desired, but the effort is being made for definite political reasons to have the initiative taken and the action consummated by act of the local companies acting at the instigation of their respective superiors who are the owners of the American and British interests.

The texts of the telegrams to be forwarded on behalf of R. C. A. are in the Department but are being held until after a meeting of the Board of Directors in B. A. scheduled for the 25th of September at which Hayes is expected to be elected manager. As soon as that has transpired, the telegrams both to B. A. and Santiago will be dispatched simultaneously. Of course, you will appreciate the confidential nature of this information which you may in your discretion communicate to the British. It was not divulged to the representative of the British Embassy this afternoon.

You are requested to continue your contacts with the Foreign Office in this particular matter and bend your efforts to secure the influence of the British Government upon Cables and Wireless to have instructions sent along the lines indicated. If the action develops as we anticipate, it may be necessary for the American and British Governments to act simultaneously and along similar lines in supporting the action of the British and American members of the local Boards of Directors. That contingency is assumed to have been taken care of in the instructions which we understand have been sent by the British Embassy to its Ambassadors and which we have sent to our Ambassadors at those respective capitals.

HULL

810.74/476a : Airgram

The Secretary of State to the Ambassador in Chile (Bowers) [72]

WASHINGTON, September 18, 1942—6 : 20 p. m.

A–139. There are quoted hereunder instructions to the representative of RCA on the board of Transradio Internacional for the purpose of bringing about an immediate closing of the Axis radio circuits operated by that company. You should hold these instructions until it transpires that similar instructions have been received by the representative of Cable and Wireless on the board of Transradio Internacional, when you should immediately transmit them to Señor Jory [73] with the injunction that they are to be regarded as secret :

"Our Board of Directors desires that the radio circuits operated by your company with Axis countries be closed immediately for reasons of continental security and in accordance with obligations undertaken at the Rio conference. Our Board of Directors has directed the dispatch of this message to you as our representative on Transradio Chilena Board of Directors strongly requesting you to use every effort to bring about this closure of Axis circuits. We are informed that your colleague on the Board representing Cable and Wireless Limited should receive immediately instructions from London similar to these after which we trust your combined efforts will bring about the desired result. J. G. Harbord, Chairman of Board, RCA Communications, Inc."

HULL

---

[72] Sent, *mutatis mutandis*, as airgram No. A–170 to the Ambassador in Argentina for Beccar Varela, director for American interests of Transradio Internacional.

[73] R. C. A. representative in Santiago, Chile.

810.74/480½ : Telegram

The Ambassador in Brazil (Caffery) to the Secretary of State

Rio de Janeiro, September 21, 1942—7 p. m.

[Received 11 p. m.]

3736. My 3525, September 10, 4 p. m.[74] I have just received the following informal notes from Aranha [75] dated September 18 and 19, respectively:

(1) "With reference to Your Excellency's note of September 8, regarding radiotelegraphic communications with the Axis countries, I telegraphed the Embassies of Brazil in Santiago and Buenos Aires on this subject. The latter informs me that the Acting Minister for Foreign Affairs [76] said that Argentine technicians are studying the matter. He suggested that when the study is concluded, there should be an exchange of ideas among Brazilian, Argentine, and Chilean technicians with a view of possibly taking appropriate uniform measures.

It was further stated to Ambassador Rodriguez [77] that the Argentine Government had requested the Government of the United States of America to furnish an apparatus of American invention capable of identifying clandestine radio telegraph stations but that thus far it had not received a reply which leads it to suppose that the apparatus is secret.

(2) With reference to my letter of the 18th instant, the Brazilian Embassy in Santiago advises me that the Chilean Government continues to study with great interest the matter of prohibiting the use of codes by the diplomatic representatives of the Axis countries. The Chilean Government, however, calls attention to the recommendation of the Inter-American Neutrality Committee of June 22, 1940, favorable to the use of codes.[78]

On the other hand the Government of Chile believes that the application of a prohibitive measure in the case of the Axis diplomatic missions would remove a motive which might be involved in case it has to justify the breaking off of relations at some future date".

CAFFERY

810.74/492 : Telegram

The Secretary of State to the Ambassador in Chile (Bowers)

Washington, September 28, 1942—11 p. m.

1139. Reference your 1575, September 28, 2 p. m.[74] You should not disclose to the Chileans that the company itself will act.

HULL

---

[74] Not printed.
[75] Oswaldo Aranha, Brazilian Minister for Foreign Affairs.
[76] Guillermo Rothe.
[77] José de Paula Rodrigues Alves, Brazilian Ambassador in Argentina.
[78] For correspondence concerning the activity of this Committee, see *Foreign Relations*, 1940, vol. v, pp. 257 ff.

810.74/493 : Telegram

The Ambassador in Chile (Bowers) to the Secretary of State

SANTIAGO, September 29, 1942—noon.
[Received 2 : 38 p. m.]

1585. Reference your airgram A–139, September 18, 6 : 20 p. m. The following are the instructions sent to the Chilean representative of Cable and Wireless:

"You are probably aware of resolution passed by trustees of C. R. I. C. at meeting held in New York on August 31 in which trustees approved that following policy should be recommended to each national companies.

It is in the interests of all concerned that each of national companies in this country comply with wishes of its government relating to operation of its international circuits and not hesitate to close any circuit whenever suggested, recommended or ordered by government under which it is operative [*operating*]."

It has been stated that the Cable and Wireless representative is accordingly being asked to press for the closure of these companies' circuits with Germany, Italy and Japan. He is asked to concert with his United States colleagues who will have received similar instructions and to act accordingly.

BOWERS

810.74/495 : Telegram

The Ambassador in Chile (Bowers) to the Secretary of State

SANTIAGO, September 29, 1942—4 p. m.
[Received 9 : 05 p. m.]

1587. Jory, RCA representative, points out that with his vote and those of British representative and manager they are at present only sure of 3 out of 7 votes on Board of Directors. Reference Department's telegram 1138, September 28, 10 p. m.[79] It will be necessary to get vote of one of the Chilean directors both of whom are pro-Allied but Valenzuela [80] more daringly so. Jory is seeing him late today. Jory points out that Chilean directors may be hesitant to vote for closure for fear the Government may take action against the company so that some indication from the Government that it would not act against the company would be desirable.

Next meeting of board of Transradio Chilena is scheduled for October 6 but could be advanced. Jory points out that for complete protection it would be necessary to prevent Axis Embassies from sending over other circuits which could be listened to from Berlin or

---

[79] Not printed.
[80] Enrique Valenzuela, a director of Transradio Chilena.

sending to Argent[ina;] also states that favorable action by local board might be accelerated if it could be informed that the Board of Directors of Transradio Internacional in Argentina will vote to close its Axis circuits. Am accordingly repeating foregoing to Buenos Aires with a request for information as to local situation.

BOWERS

810.74/496 : Telegram

The Ambassador in Chile (Bowers) to the Secretary of State

SANTIAGO, September 30, 1942—7 p. m.
[Received 10:42 p. m.]

1599. In continuation my 1587, September 29, 4 p. m. Jory has discussed, in strict confidence, closure of Axis circuits with Valenzuela, Chilean director of Transradio Chilena, who has expressed himself as personally in favor closing not only circuits to Axis territories but all European circuits on grounds Transradio services must be reserved for American countries. The crux of situation now appears to be votes [of] Valenzuela and another Chilean director, Balmaceda, both representing C. R. I. C.

Valenzuela inclines toward using pretext that vital supplies for Transradio might be cut off if they continued to accept traffic for enemy countries rather than Rio Resolutions on grounds that this would be more easily accepted by Government. This line has been adopted by this and British Embassies in all other questions of enemy commerce in Chile and has not been seriously resisted by Chilean Government. Alternatively Valenzuela suggests that he might take line that in order to conserve existing apparatus and material it is essential to close the circuits to the heavy traffic now existing with enemy countries.

Valenzuela believes that his co-director, Balmaceda, might hesitate to vote for closure merely on grounds of compliance with Rio Resolutions but probably would go along on basis of first mentioned procedure. In this connection he observed that of a total of 7 votes 4 against 3 would not be very satisfactory and that every effort should be made to get at least 5 votes. This point has been discussed with British Embassy which is telegraphing its Foreign Office suggesting that it be arranged with C. R. I. C. to telegraph immediately to Valenzuela and Balmaceda instructions in the sense that supplies for Transradio will be cut off if they continue accept traffic for enemy countries.

Request that Department take the matter up urgently with C. R. I. C. in the same sense. C. R. I. C.'s instructions must reach

Chilean directors prior to next meeting of Transradio Chilena board on October 6.

Please telegraph urgently instructive comment on foregoing.

BOWERS

810.74/506a : Telegram

The Secretary of State to the Ambassador in Argentina (Armour)

WASHINGTON, October 1, 1942—9 p. m.

1473.   Your 1891, September 30, 4 p. m.[82]

1. The Department had understood that at the time of General Davis' visit, general agreement had been reached that Hayes should be appointed manager.   Consequently, it does not understand what difficulties have apparently arisen or why his appointment should in any way be contingent on the issuance of the decree providing for official observers.   Please clarify this point.

2. Department advised by Winterbottom, Vice President, RCA, that in a telephone conversation with Dr. Becu [83] on September 30 latter who at that time was in Los Angeles stated that he could not understand why Hayes had not already been appointed manager on Friday. He added that he would send a personal telegram to the president of Transradio to the effect that he was entirely satisfied with Hayes, was in favor of his appointment and that he saw no reason for the delay of such appointment pending his return to Buenos Aires.

3. The Department feels that the objective of cutting the circuits would be jeopardized by informing the Argentine authorities in advance.   There appears to be no reason to believe that the permission of the Argentine Government, which Roberts [84] suggests be requested in advance, would be forthcoming.   The Department feels that the objective should now be pursued without delay and consequently does not favor any postponement of consideration of this matter by the board, unless it is certain that a majority of the board in favor of closure can not be secured.

4. All communication companies in Buenos Aires maintaining direct circuits with the Axis have received the necessary instructions. There are only two such companies, namely, Transradio and CIDRA, the I. T. & T. subsidiary.   The instructions referred to are contained in the Department's airgrams A–169 [82] and A–170 of September 18 [85] which should have reached you by now.

---

[82] Not printed.
[83] Teodoro Becu, official of Transradio Internacional.
[84] British representative on the Board of Transradio Internacional.
[85] See footnote 72, p. 149.

5. The Department believes it essential to treat this entire matter on a strictly confidential basis, so that interests in Argentina opposed to closure of the circuits will not be informed in advance of these plans.

Please repeat to Santiago as No. 1155.

HULL

810.74/504 : Telegram

The Acting Secretary of State to the Ambassador in Chile (*Bowers*)

WASHINGTON, October 2, 1942—9 p. m.

1163.   Your 1599, September 30, 7 p. m., and 1607, October 1, 7 p. m.[87]   This Government is prepared to cut off all supplies for Transradio Chilena if it continues to maintain its circuits with the Axis. This is a decision that can be taken only by governmental authority, not by C. R. I. C. You may inform Jory of the foregoing.

No objection is seen to Valenzuela's alternative suggestion regarding conservation of existing material. In fact, any or all of the several valid objections to continuance of the circuits may be used to achieve the objective of their prompt closure.

WELLES

810.74/497

Memorandum by the Chief of the Division of the American Republics (*Bonsal*)[88]

[WASHINGTON,] October 2, 1942.

I did not sign the Department's 1473, October 1, 9 p. m., addressed to Buenos Aires because I disagree with the third paragraph thereof, to the effect that "the Department feels that the objective of cutting the circuits would be jeopardized by informing the Argentine authorities in advance". Since there is every probability that no action will be taken by the companies for some days or weeks at least, it may be worthwhile for me to set forth reasons for my opposition.

1. These companies are operating under Argentine jurisdiction and in accordance with Argentine law. That law does not, I am confident, permit them to either establish or cut off circuits without permission of the Government. Our instruction, therefore, states that we believe that these United States companies should break the law.

2. I understand that the theory behind our action is that since the Argentine Government has failed to comply with the Rio Resolutions regarding the telecommunications, the companies are justified in going ahead. I understand that we further believe that if the Argentine Government is confronted with a *fait accompli* it will find

---

[87] Latter not printed.
[88] Addressed to the Adviser on Political Relations (Duggan) and the Assistant Secretary of State (Long).

it difficult to order the circuits restored. In my judgment nothing could be further from the probabilities of the case. In fact, the Argentine Government together with a great many Argentines, many of them good friends of ours will be highly indignant that a foreign company operating in Argentina should presume to dictate to the Argentine Government what it should do in carrying out its international commitment. The nationalization of utilities, perhaps a desirable end in itself, will have been given a highly undesirable boost.

3. The correct procedure in my opinion is for the company to notify the Argentine Government that as of a set date they will no longer be able to give service to the Axis countries. They can allege a variety of reasons including lack of material, faulty transmission, failure of their German connections to observe proper operating practices, et cetera, et cetera. The Government will then be placed in a rather uncomfortable position with relation to the carrying out of a commitment which it entered into at Rio.

These circuits will not be cut off unless the Argentine Government wants them cut off, or at least is willing to acquiesce in their being cut off. The only possible alternative is some form of direct action which would render the circuits unusable (interference, or jamming). I assume that IN has explored this possibility from the technical angle.

PHILIP W. BONSAL

810.74/497

Memorandum by the Adviser on Political Relations (Duggan) to the Assistant Secretary of State (Long)

[WASHINGTON,] October 3, 1942.

MR. LONG: With regard to Mr. Bonsal's memorandum attached,[89] it is my understanding that the Secretary, with full knowledge of the consequences, decided that the Department should press ahead to bring about the severance of the circuits between Argentina and Chile and the Axis countries.

LAURENCE DUGGAN

810.74/567

Memorandum of Telephone Conversations, by Mr. Louis J. Halle of the Division of the American Republics

[WASHINGTON,] October 4, 1942.

Section One:

I telephoned General Harbord on the evening of October 3 to read him a paraphrase of the message addressed to him by Mr. Beccar Varela of Transradio Internacional, which was contained in telegram

---

[89] *Supra.*

no. 1908, October 2, 5 p. m.,[90] from Buenos Aires. He wrote the message down as I gave it to him, then inquired as to the Department's wishes with regard to the reply he should make. In accordance with Mr. Long's instructions, I told General Harbord that it was the hope of the Department that he would find it advisable to indicate to Mr. Beccar Varela the desirability of not informing the Argentine officials in advance of the plans afoot for closing the Axis circuits maintained by Transradio. General Harbord said that Beccar Varela's message more or less confirmed the view that R. C. A. had held right along that the contemplated action would result in the taking over of the company by the Argentine Government. He added that, however, it had been felt R. C. A. had no choice but to go along in view of the Department's wishes. I assured him that the cooperative attitude of R. C. A. in this matter was very much appreciated by the Department, and added that while there was no absolute assurance of the reaction of the Argentine Government, it was to be hoped that, if it did take counter measures, these would be confined to ordering the immediate reopening of the circuits. He replied that this, of course, depended upon the political problem of how anxious the Argentine authorities might be to take over full control of the company. I reminded him of the assurance he had received, at a meeting in Mr. Long's office, that the Department would do everything that it appropriately could to back them up in case they ran into serious difficulties as a result of the contemplated action. He said he understood and appreciated this.

General Harbord said he would consult with General Davis and Mr. Winterbottom and telephone me at 9:30 the following morning (October 4) to give me his message in reply to the one from Beccar Varela.

Section Two:

General Harbord telephoned this morning to say that it had been decided to defer sending a reply to Beccar Varela pending the opportunity of having another meeting with Mr. Long to discuss the matter. His opinion, and that of his associates, he said, was that the situation had now changed to one in which they were being asked to tell the Argentine directors of Transradio not to let their own Government know what was going on. He asked me to arrange for General Davis and Colonel Sarnoff to call on Mr. Long at 3 o'clock tomorrow. I replied that I would endeavor to make the arrangements. He said he would send General Davis down to Washington tonight, on the chance that the meeting would be arranged for tomorrow. He said that there would be no need for him to attend the meeting, even though the reply to Beccar Varela would go in his name.

---

[90] Not printed.

810.74/562

Memorandum of Conversation, by Mr. Louis J. Halle of the Division of the American Republics

[WASHINGTON,] October 5, 1942.

Participants: General Davis, Chairman of the Consortium; Colonel Sarnoff, President of RCA; Mr. Winterbottom, Acting President of RCA; Mr. Long, Assistant Secretary; Mr. Duggan, Political Adviser; Mr. deWolf, IN; Mr. Halle, RA.

Mr. Long expressed the view that the prospective election of Mr. George Hayes as manager of Transradio Internacional in Buenos Aires should precede any action by the Company to close its circuits with the Axis.   Everyone present agreed.

General Davis read a message he had received from Aguirre, President of Transradio Internacional, in which he indicated that the meeting to elect Hayes would take place this week and that he expected there would be a majority in favor.   Mr. Duggan raised the question of whether it was necessary or would be possible to get Dr. Becu, now in Mexico, to send his proxy to Buenos Aires in favor of Hayes. Mr. Winterbottom said that the customary procedure was for the substitute director to attend meetings in a director's absence, upon the invitation of the President.   Since it was not certain how Becu's substitute, Cardenas, might vote, it was decided that the Department ask the Embassy in Buenos Aires immediately to obtain Hayes' estimate of whether Cardenas was going to attend the meeting, how he would vote, and how the other directors would line up.

It was decided that General Harbord should acknowledge the message from Beccar Varela (contained in the Embassy's 1908 of October 2, 5 p. m.[91]), in which the latter suggested consultation with the Argentine Government prior to action by the Company to cut the circuits, with a message urging that Hayes' election be expedited and stating that he would give his reaction to Beccar Varela's suggestion after it had taken place.   General Davis said he would send a reply to the message he had received from Aguirre, in which he would again express the hope that everything would be done to expedite the election of Hayes.

General Davis and Colonel Sarnoff advanced the view that it would not be practical to ask Beccar Varela, an Argentine, to withhold from his Government information which his loyalty to it might prompt him to make available.   Colonel Sarnoff felt that, should the Chilean Company take action tomorrow to sever its Axis circuits, the directors of Transradio Internacional could use this as a supple-

---

[91] Not printed.

mentary argument for the action they were proposing to take. Mr. Duggan pointed out that should it be decided that the Company would notify the Argentine Government in advance, it would be advisable to defer such notification for as long as possible in order to leave as little time as possible for counter-action. However, it was agreed that no decision would be taken in this regard until after the election of Hayes.

Mr. Long stated that we had word from Chile to the effect that a valuable pretext for breaking the Chilean circuits would be supplied if it could be shown that otherwise necessary supplies of material for the Chilean Company would be cut off. He read the draft of a telegram to our Embassy in Santiago, containing a message to this effect from General Davis to Mr. Jory, RCA representative on the Board of the Company. General Davis agreed to having the message go.

Colonel Sarnoff referred to the "Cicero's Oration" he had delivered in Mr. Long's office on September 9 with regard to the possibility that the enemy was tapping our undersea cables. He said he had been called in to see General Strong, the Chief of G2 about this matter, and that as a consequence of the interview an experiment was being made to find out just how difficult it might be to tap our cables. A Navy craft was being sent out in the Atlantic to make the attempt, and Colonel Sarnoff offered to inform Mr. Long of the results of this experiment.

Colonel Sarnoff suggested that a study be made of all cable messages on ship movements that were transmitted during a recent period of some three months with a view to determining whether any correlation is evident between such messages and the actual sinking of ships. Mr. Long accepted the suggestion and said the Department would act upon it. He asked Mr. deWolf to see that this was done.

810.74/504 : Telegram

The Acting Secretary of State to the Ambassador in Chile (Bowers)

WASHINGTON, October 5, 1942—5 p. m.

1174. The Department does not wish the information contained in its 1163 of October 2, 9 p. m. regarding the cutting off of supplies for Transradio to be used in such a way as to be subject to the interpretation that it contains a direct threat from this Government.

General Davis requests that the Embassy transmit the following from him to Jory immediately, for Jory to use, in his discretion, in his conversations with the other directors of Transradio: "I understand that all supplies for Transradio Chilena will be cut off if it continues to maintain its circuits with the Axis."

Please make sure that, in any use that Jory makes of this information, he refers to it as emanating from the Chairman of C. R. I. C. rather than from this Government or your Embassy directly.

WELLES

810.74/513 : Telegram

The Ambassador in Chile (Bowers) to the Secretary of State

SANTIAGO, October 5, 1942—7 p. m.
[Received 10 : 15 p. m.]

1633. 1. Saw Barros Jarpa this evening about closing telecommunications. He said he had been discussing the matter with one of the men of the company which had proposed what he, the Minister, had suggested to me long ago, to refuse the use of the code to the missions of all countries sending outside this hemisphere. He said the German Ambassador would promptly protest and there would be a battle but that he would take the position that this Government cannot insist on a company controlled mostly by the people of the United Nations to put their property to the use of the enemies of these nations and that the Government could not interfere. He said then the Axis would probably plan to use the national telegraph to get their code messages to Argentina for transmission but that he could not conceive that Argentina would care to be put in the position of carrying forward this work against continental defense.

He said the President cannot break relations just now on the eve of his departure since he should be here in the event of any sabotage trouble and that on his return all these problems would solve themselves thus implying that on his return the President proposes to break relations. He said he does not want the President to go away with the telecommunication matter hanging fire because of the unpleasant feeling that would result.

2. Valenzuela, Chilean director who proposed the compromise solution of the Company's refusing to accept for transmittal or delivery code messages, claims this would be a better solution than merely closing circuits with Axis territories, which would allow Axis Embassies to transmit over other circuits which could be listened into from their capitals. Jory asks that RCA instruct him how to note [*vote*] on this proposition.

3. Since writing the foregoing Valenzuela says he has just received a personal request from President Ríos asking him to postpone the scheduled directors' meeting from tomorrow until October 8.

Reference Department's 1163, October 2, 9 p. m.

BOWERS

810.74/529a : Telegram

The Secretary of State to the Ambassador in Chile (Bowers)

WASHINGTON, October 7, 1942—8 p. m.

1189.   Reference Heath's [92] telephone conversation with Duggan.[93]

1.   Department approves plan to deny the use of code on circuits going out of the hemisphere, subject to the provision of adequate safeguards for maintaining the code privileges of the British Embassy.

2.   In approving this plan, the Department understands that it is without prejudice to the carrying out of the plan to discontinue the Axis circuits. Please continue your endeavors to promote this objective. If it is necessary to postpone the meeting of the board for a few days in order to accomplish this, you may arrange for such postponement, informing the Department immediately of such action and enumerating any unforeseen difficulties that may have arisen to prejudice the attainment of this objective.

Your reply to the Department's 1174, October 5, 5 p. m., has not been received.

HULL

810.74/518 : Telegram

The Ambassador in Chile (Bowers) to the Secretary of State

SANTIAGO, October 7, 1942—10 p. m.
[Received October 8—2 a. m.]

1652.   For Welles and Duggan. Heath's telephone conversation and my 1633, of October 5, 7 p. m. In tomorrow morning's directors' meeting Transradio Chilena will probably decide to refuse to transmit or receive for delivery any messages in secret code destined for or originating in any non-American country. It would continue, however, to accept clear and registered commercial code messages on non-American circuits. This will not prevent Axis Embassies here from transmitting in their codes to Axis Embassies in Buenos Aires for retransmittal to Axis capitals or perhaps arranging for Axis radio authorities to listen in on the Santiago–Buenos Aires radio circuits. This decision would, however, prevent the Swiss, Spanish, Portuguese, Swedish, and British diplomatic representatives from being able to communicate over Transradio in confidential code directly with their capitals but missions of these countries can still continue communicate directly or indirectly in code over All America and West Coast cables via routes crossing Allied censorship lines.

This is as far as the two Chilean directors who, after having been in touch with Barros Jarpa and President Ríos, will go at this meeting.

---

[92] Donald R. Heath, Counselor of Embassy in Chile.
[93] Transcript of conversation not printed.

Jory confirmed this and asks to communicate to Radio Corporation of America his conviction that it will be impossible at this time to secure a vote to completely close the Axis circuits.

The directors assert, however, their proposal will accomplish more than merely closing Axis circuits. They also say that this is to be regarded as a first step toward the possible closure of circuits to the transmission of all messages to non-American countries.

The British Commercial Counselor who has handled the matter for his Embassy at first feared that his Government might object to a prohibition on code messages to Britain but after talking with the directors said he was convinced that no obstacles should be placed in the way of the proposed action at this moment, and would advise London. He observed that an exception could later be made in Britain's favor if desired. If insisted on now the Spanish and other European missions would claim equal treatment and thus provide further loopholes for Axis communications.

The British Embassy does not use Transradio.

BOWERS

810.74/523 : Telegram

The Ambassador in Chile (Bowers) to the Secretary of State

SANTIAGO, October 8, 1942—8 p. m.
[Received October 9—2 : 33 a. m.]

1659. For Welles and Duggan.

1. Trans Board of Directors without record vote approved following motion:

"I desire submit for the approval of directors a measure to bring to an end the rumor which has circulated for some time that our company is serving for the transmission of messages relating to war operations. Since several days these charges have been published in press articles which without specifically referring to us have placed us in a disagreeable situation. In conformity with instruction received from the shareholders I propose that beginning today the company not accept communications in secret cipher or code directed to or received from any non-American country".

Department's 1189, October 7, 8 p. m.

2. Prior to the meeting directors Ricci, Jory, Blood[?] and the President of the company, Valenzuela, orally informed the Embassy that this decision of the Board was to be regarded as a "first step" directed toward the entire possible closure of the Axis communications. They also expressed the sincere belief that it would be a mistake to postpone the meeting and the decision until the problematical date when the Chilean Government would be willing to indicate to the two Chilean members of the Board it desired them to vote for outright discontinuance of Axis circuits. Without such indication the two Chilean di-

rectors, while friendly disposed, feel they could not vote since it would be taking political action beyond that approved by the Chilean Government itself and would also endanger the concession of the company.

3. The following new complication has, however, arisen: despite the tentative approval of his Commercial Attaché, the British Ambassador [94] today endeavored to get the Board to postpone applying the decision until he received instructions that London had no objections. He was told the decision could not be modified until another meeting was called. I trust that the British Government will not object at this time since it would give useful grounds for the Axis Embassies and the Spanish and other European neutral missions to make similar protests, devitalize the whole decision of the Board and provide additional loopholes for German communications.

In my opinion the British Embassy needs to take no notice of a purely company decision at this moment. The British Embassy is not sending code messages over Transradio and has no intention of doing so since it is not a means of confidential communication. At some later date or if and when it becomes necessary for the British Embassy to send a cipher telegram over Transradio then, if it should be refused, the matter would become a practical issue and could be settled at once.

What the British Government might do if it feels it necessary to oppose any prohibition of its code communications over Transradio is to take it up later leisurely with CRIC asking it to instruct the directors here to accept the suggestion of the British that exceptions be made to the board's decision as regards code communications to Britain. However, the British Ambassador should be instructed immediately not to use his influence to set aside or postpone the actual application of the board's decision since in so doing he would be following the lead of the German director, the only one actively to oppose the decision. British Embassy intervention at this time would make a diplomatic issue of a commercial company decision and place the Chilean Government in a position which it could with difficulty refuse sympathetically to entertain protests from the other European countries with which confidential communication has been cut off by the decision of Transradios' board.

I have no doubt that if we continue our representations to the Chilean Government particularly in view of the recent German spy exposures that we can within a not too distant date proceed to direct closure of the Axis radio circuits restoring at a later time, if the Department thinks best, the privilege of code communication over Transradio circuits to England alone.

Jory asks RCA be informed.   Bowers

---

[94] Charles W. Orde.

810.74/523 : Telegram

The Acting Secretary of State to the Ambassador in Chile (Bowers)

WASHINGTON, October 9, 1942—7 p. m.

1198. The Department is communicating urgently with the British Embassy here and our Embassy in London, outlining the circumstances related in your 1659 of October 8, 8 p. m., and stating its opinion that it would be most unfortunate if the British Government should express to the Chilean Government any objections at this time to the action taken by Transradio, since this action impairs the official communications of the Axis without having any practical effect on those of the British.

WELLES

810.74/527 : Telegram

The Ambassador in Chile (Bowers) to the Secretary of State

SANTIAGO, October 9, 1942—7 p. m.
[Received 9 : 40 p. m.]

1671. Reference Embassy's 1659, October 8, 8 p. m. Yesterday afternoon the Post and Telegraph asked the manager of Transradio to suspend enforcement of the directors decision not to accept code messages from or to non-American territory. This afternoon the director of Post and Telegraph gave tacit approval to Transradio directors decision and at 3 : 45 refused to accept a code message for Berlin from the German Embassy. The German Ambassador protested to the Foreign Office but, we are told, without effect.

BOWERS

810.74/528 : Telegram

The Ambassador in Argentina (Armour) to the Secretary of State

BUENOS AIRES, October 9, 1942—8 p. m.
[Received 8 : 14 p. m.]

1959. Embassy's 1908, October 2, 5 p. m.[95] Hayes elected general manager of Transradio this afternoon by vote of 4 to 3 to serve until next annual stockholders meeting in March 1943.

My 1952, October 8, 10 p. m.[95] Foreign Office last night announced Government intervention in all telecommunications companies and lines functioning in Argentina, saying strict measures essential to avoid transmission of information prejudicing security of nation, and adding that war status of various American countries and obli-

---

[95] Not printed.

gations in Pan-American agreements subscribed to by Argentina counseled adoption of necessary provisions to avoid use of telecommunications in Argentina to the detriment of military interests of those countries.

However, exact significance and scope of such action cannot be judged until actual decree and regulations are made public, which is expected shortly. It is not yet known whether measure is designed to forestall closing of circuits on companies' initiative or whether it is a first step toward compliance with Resolution XL Rio conference.

ARMOUR

810.74/592

The Chilean Minister for Foreign Affairs (Barros Jarpa) to the American Ambassador in Chile (Bowers)[97]

No. 06529   SANTIAGO, October 16, 1942.

MR. AMBASSADOR: Upon reviewing the correspondence exchanged with Your Excellency regarding the matter of telecommunications in cipher between Axis countries and their diplomatic missions in Santiago, I notice that your Note No. 1353 dated September 5th and your personal letter of the 25th of the same month [98] have not been answered. Although Your Excellency was informed verbally of the developments in the matter, and was in accord that my answer to said communications could be deferred, I believe that the moment has arrived to inform you about the present state of the problem.

The decision of the 9th instant of the Board of Directors of the Chilean Transradio Company, Ltd. not to transmit more code messages to non-American countries, evoked immediate protests of the German and Italian Embassies, and the Japanese Legation, to which I answered stating that, in order to adopt the appropriate solutions, reports had been requested from the Directorates General of Electrical Services and Mail and Telegraphs, and the consultative legal bodies. As such reports will have to be the object of careful consideration by the competent authorities, and in the meantime the Axis Missions are deprived of communicating in code with their Governments, we have instructed our diplomatic agents in those countries to also refrain from sending their messages in code to this Ministry.

Due to the existing situation, they have renewed their protests to which I have replied that my Government must await the reports requested from the competent authorities. Such is the present state of the affair.

I avail myself [etc.]   ERNESTO BARROS

---

[97] Transmitted to the Department by the Ambassador in his despatch No. 4755, October 23; received November 2.
[98] Latter not printed.

810.74/572

Memorandum of Conversation, by the Assistant Secretary of State (Long)

[WASHINGTON,] October 19, 1942.

Sir Ronald Campbell came in this afternoon at his request. We discussed the situation in B. A. and Santiago and further steps to be taken in B. A. I told him that we were proposing to take the next logical step which was either to go through with the movement to sever the beams to the Axis or to repeat in B. A. the step which Santiago had taken and stop all communications by cipher or code to powers outside of the American hemisphere. That would be decided late this afternoon or tomorrow, and I would keep him advised.

Sir Ronald said that the British Embassy would probably take the same attitude about its denial of cipher privileges from B. A. that it took in Santiago. He had received from his Government information that instructions had been sent to the British Ambassador in Santiago that he do not protest the denial of cipher privileges there for the reason that they did not use the radio. The same situation existing in B. A., he thought his Government would take the same position but he could not speak for his Government without consulting them.

I called Sir Ronald's attention to the fact that we had heard unofficially that the British Western Telegraph Company which operates cable lines up and down the west coast of South America, and which had either land lines or radio from Santiago to B. A., were transmitting messages, intended for the Axis, to B. A. which messages would be forwarded from B. A. direct to the Axis capitals. I told him that we had not been officially advised of that fact but in case we should be officially advised I would be glad to bring it to his attention in the thought that his Government might care to take the same attitude to those communications as it had to the Consortium station. He said he thought his Government would do so if it was brought to their attention and if it was a fact, and that he assumed that the proper step would be to communicate with the Board of Directors there as had been done in the case of the Consortium.

B[RECKINRIDGE] L[ONG]

810.74/540 : Telegram

The Ambassador in the United Kingdom (Winant) to the Secretary of State

LONDON, October 19, 1942—5 p. m.
[Received October 19—2 : 30 p. m.]

5840. Foreign Office informs us with reference to the action of the Board of Directors of Transradio Chilena dealt with in Embassy's

5649 of October 10, 3 p. m.[99] that the British Ambassador at Santiago has been instructed to advise the Government of Chile that the British Government does not propose to lodge any overt protest against the company's decision as this decision does not actually affect British convenience or interests. Foreign Office adds, however, that British Government would resent strongly and immediately any extension of the ban on the use of secret ciphers to cables that are utilized by the British.

WINANT

810.74/548a : Telegram

The Secretary of State to the Ambassador in Argentina (*Armour*)

WASHINGTON, October 23, 1942—4 p. m.

1592. The Department has received the following message from Harbord of RCA to Hayes of Transradio:

"Transradio Chilena has suspended the use of code and cipher telegrams to and from all countries outside the American continent. This action greatly safeguarded that country's security and incidentally benefited the company. Strongly recommend you take similar action notifying Bern accordingly. This action is authorized by Article 27, Madrid Convention [1] to which Argentine Government is signatory and is not likely to be opposed by your authorities as it will greatly simplify the work of the Government intervenor. Give copy of this message to President Aguirre as alternative action to my previous suggestion regarding closing of Axis circuits." (The country referred to is, of course, Chile.)

The Department feels that the action proposed in the above message would be more effective than action to close the Axis circuits only, since it would prevent the Axis missions in Chile and Argentina from communicating with their Governments in confidential code by way of neutral countries. Such action by Transradio would not have any practical effect on communications between your British colleague and London, since the British Government does not use the facilities of Transradio for confidential messages in any case. However, the question has been raised as to whether the Argentine Government, in response to the contemplated action of Transradio, might forbid the use of confidential code on all telecommunication circuits extending out of the hemisphere, in which case the British would be denied the use of the cable operated by the Western Telegraph Company from Buenos Aires to Ascension and thence indirectly to London for messages in confidential code. In view of this possibility, the Department is requesting the concurrence of the British Government in

[99] Not printed.
[1] International Telecommunication Convention signed December 9, 1932, at Madrid, *Foreign Relations*, 1932, vol. I, p. 873.

the proposed action of Transradio, and you should await word that this concurrence has been received before delivering General Harbord's message.

Please telegraph your comment.

HULL

810.74/549 : Telegram

The Ambassador in Argentina (Armour) to the Secretary of State

BUENOS AIRES, October 24, 1942—noon.
[Received 2 : 18 p. m.]

2081. Department's 1592, October 23, 4 p. m.   The Embassy agrees that refusal of coded and cipher telegrams to and from all countries outside of American continent is more effective than closing Axis circuits, provided there is proper surveillance by Argentine authorities over messages sent *en clair*.

With regard to Transradio, it is not believed that local board will undertake such action on own initiative.   German, Italian and French directors certainly will oppose.   The three Argentine directors Aguirre, Becu and Huergo would hesitate to approve not because they necessarily oppose such action but because they are extremely reluctant to move without prior approval of Argentine Government. Despite remote foreign control Transradio has been regarded here as essentially Argentine, and the recent election of American manager was not received enthusiastically by some government officials.   Consequently Transradio feels that it is particularly vulnerable.

Also it is extremely doubtful whether Transradio directors would vote such action without being assured that competitive companies will act concurrently.   While Transradio now obtains large bulk of traffic with Continental Europe and Japan, code messages at least with Europe would be diverted to other companies unless they acted likewise.

Posts and Telegraphs Department apparently planning accounting inspectors in each communications company in endeavor to prevent messages to Axis countries regarding shipping movements.   We do not see how this would be effective unless code and cipher facilities are refused to local Axis Embassies, but it is not yet known if Argentina will go this far.

ARMOUR

810.74/547 : Telegram

The Ambassador in Chile (Bowers) to the Secretary of State

SANTIAGO, October 24, 1942—noon.
[Received 7 : 30 p. m.]

1808. Your 1245, October 16, 9 p. m.[2] West Coast Cables claims no such messages have been accepted. Company is cooperating but as manager in Chile apparently is without instruction from his home office British Commercial Counselor has telegraphed London that all West Coast Cable offices in this country be specifically instructed to follow in every respect the same policy as All-America Cables. I believe it would be desirable to also take up this matter with British officials in Washington to assure prompt action.

As there now is reason to believe Chilean authorities would interpose no objection to British and American companies even refusing plain language messages from Axis Government representatives in Chile to similar representatives in this country, and if offered to their representatives in Argentina, I am suggesting to All-America Cables and the British Embassy to the West Coast Cables that they refuse such messages.

I understand Axis Embassies are sending practically all their messages encoded by Transradio to Buenos Aires from where they presumably are being retransmitted to their Governments. I shall endeavor to persuade Transradio to refrain from accepting this traffic. To date Chilean Government has not denied Axis Government representative use of state lines in Chile or to Buenos Aires. However, Ríos told Gajardo [3] last week that he now favors a complete closing of all facilities to Axis Missions.

BOWERS

810.74/556 : Telegram

The Ambassador in Argentina (Armour) to the Secretary of State

BUENOS AIRES, October 26, 1942—6 p. m.
[Received 7 : 52 p. m.]

2088. Department's 1592, October 23, 4 p. m.; and Embassy's 2081, October 24, noon. Proceeding on the assumption that Transradio by itself will not follow the action of its Chilean affiliate, it is likely that such a plan could be made effective only by action of Argentine Government, in which case it is probable that the British also would be affected. British Embassy here says its experts feel

---

[2] Not printed; this communication called attention to reports that the West Coast Cables Company was transmitting messages to Axis countries (810.74/534).
[3] Oscar Gajardo, Chilean Minister of Justice.

that inability to use code or cipher would cause great inconvenience, although it would abide by whatever decision is reached in Washington and London.

Another plan has been suggested to me by Gache, Under Secretary for Foreign Affairs, which would prohibit international messages by radiotelegraph thus limiting them to cable.   While prohibition of code or cipher was not mentioned, his plan has considerable merit in that it would force the Axis to send their messages by the cable facilities of either All America Cables or Western Telegraph, thus enabling messages to be held up and scrutinized in the United States or England.

I do not believe that Gache would propose such a plan without knowledge of the Cabinet, which may wish to answer the Under Secretary's Boston speech in this manner.[4]   At the same time there may be considerable difficulty in achieving the plan due to opposition which would come from the radio communications companies such as Transradio and Radiar, which would stand to lose most if not all of their traffic depending on the scope of the proposal.

Gache asked my opinion of the plan and I told him I thought it offered distinct possibilities.   He also mentioned it to the British who also feel that it deserves full consideration and are so advising their Government.

If the Department thinks well of the idea, which has the advantage of coming from the Argentine Government itself, then even if the British Government concurs in the former plan of restricting coded and cipher messages to the American Hemisphere, it may be advisable to hold up delivery of the Harbord message to Hayes pending further developments on the Gache plan.

The Department's comments would be appreciated.

ARMOUR

810.74/556 : Telegram

The Secretary of State to the Ambassador in Argentina (Armour)

WASHINGTON, October 28, 1942—1 p. m.

1622. Your 2081, October 24, noon, and 2088, October 26, 6 p. m. It appears that Gache's suggestion goes beyond what is necessary in order to prevent the Axis from using Argentine communications to the detriment of the American republics, in that it would close down international radio telegraph circuits within the hemisphere. The Department feels that the objective would be achieved by pro-

---

[4] Speech at the World Trade dinner of the Twenty-ninth National Foreign Trade Convention, October 8, 1942.   For text, see Department of State *Bulletin,* October 10, 1942, p. 808; for correspondence concerning the accusations made by Mr. Welles, see *post,* pp. 210 ff. *passim.*

hibiting the transmission or acceptance of messages merely on those radio telegraph and radio telephone circuits that extend directly out of the hemisphere. It is, furthermore, persuaded that this would be acceptable both to Transradio and Radiar. You will recall that at the meeting of the Consortium Trust in New York last August the trustees recommended that each national company should promptly comply with the wishes of its government relating to the closing of any circuit. The attitude of IT&T has been consistently cooperative.

You may wish to suggest to Gache the possibility of putting his plan into effect in the modified form indicated above. This would contribute effectively to isolating the Axis agents in Argentina and Chile from their bases.

Having regard for the likelihood that a satisfactory plan along the lines of Gache's proposal may be put into effect in the near future, you should use your discretion as to whether or when to deliver Harbord's message keeping the Department currently informed.

HULL

810.74/547 : Telegram

The Secretary of State to the Ambassador in Chile (Bowers)

WASHINGTON, October 29, 1942—11 p. m.

1302. Your 1808, October 24, noon. Please seek an early interview with President Ríos for the purpose of bringing the following to his attention:

Since the Axis missions in Santiago have been denied the use of secret code or cipher on circuits extending directly out of the hemisphere, they have continued to communicate in secret code or cipher with their Governments by way of the Axis missions in Buenos Aires, resorting to the commercial circuits that connect the two capitals. They are, consequently, still free to transmit to their Governments by secret rapid communication, as they have in the past, information that may lead to the loss of ships and lives of the American republics. This Government is most anxious that means may be found for bringing under control this last channel of secret rapid communication by Axis agents in Chile with their Governments, and it feels that it can count on the sympathy and friendly cooperation of the Chilean Government in achieving this objective.

Having made the foregoing clear to President Ríos, you should ask for any suggestions that he may have for remedying this situation, saying that you feel free to make this request in view of the cordial relations that exist between our two Governments and previous assurances that the Chilean Government will do whatever is necessary to prevent Axis agents in Chilean territory from taking any action detrimental to the American republics.   You should point out to the President that, even if the private companies were to refuse all messages in secret code or cipher over the lines to Buenos Aires, the Axis missions would still be free to communicate secretly over the national telegraph system to Argentina.

You should indicate clearly that, in our view, the telecommunication situation will not have been completely remedied while it is still possible for Axis agents in Chile to make any use of Chile's external telecommunication facilities, whether for plain messages or code.   You may say, however, that a complete denial of secret code facilities to the Axis missions would be an important step in this direction.

Of course, if the Axis missions in Chile are denied the use of telecommunication facilities, they will still be free to send confidential communications to Buenos Aires by overland or air mail.   However, the delay involved would have an important effect in limiting the means by which Axis agents in Chile can do damage to us and to the other American republics.

You should, of course, be alert to guard against any action by the Chilean Government that would impair our communications or those of your British colleague.

HULL

810.74/592a : Telegram

The Secretary of State to the Ambassador in the United Kingdom
(Winant)

WASHINGTON, October 29, 1942—midnight.

5407. If we eventually succeed in closing radio circuits to Axis countries operated by the consortium radio stations in Buenos Aires and Santiago, it is of course imperative that the traffic carried by such circuits should not be diverted to cables.   It is therefore desired to know as soon as possible whether all cable traffic between Buenos Aires and continental European points (which is believed to be handled by the Western Telegraph Company, a British concern) is diverted via London and does not go directly to Portugal.   It is also desired to know whether the British authorities are prepared to stop and not reforward any messages intended for Axis countries including all diplomatic messages except those of the Argentine Government, whether in code or not.   Please endeavor to obtain as much information as possible concerning the cable situation between Argentina and Europe and assure British authorities that it will be kept in strictest confidence.

HULL

810.74/611 : Telegram

The Ambassador in the United Kingdom (Winant) to the Secretary of State

LONDON, November 12, 1942—9 p. m.
[Received 10 : 25 p. m.]

6368. Reference Department's 5240, [5] 5241, 5242, October 23, 4 p. m. [6] 5407 October 29, midnight, and 5528 November 5, 3 p. m.[7] Foreign Office states that if all wireless messages in code were prohibited and attempts were then made by the Axis to send telegrams in code by cable the British authorities would be able to control these telegrams. Foreign Office points out in this connection that British cable communications between Buenos Aires and the Axis go by way of Portugal and London and that telegrams of the Axis could be stopped in London.

With reference to telegrams from one neutral to another neutral Foreign Office says that it assumes that we would not wish the British authorities to attempt to stop them. British authorities of course would, Foreign Office adds, exercise control over telegrams to the Axis *en clair*. Foreign Office also assumes we would be able to stop any Axis messages if the attempt were made to send them over cables on the West Coast.

Foreign Office sums up British view as follows: British authorities would be glad to see all code messages by radio prohibited or, in case this is not found to be feasible, they would be glad to see all radio code messages sent to or received from non-American countries, as in the case of Chile, prohibited.

Under no circumstances the Foreign Office emphasizes would the British authorities agree to the prohibition of their cable code message. If this were attempted by the Argentinians the British authorities, according to the Foreign Office would throughout the British Empire take retaliatory measures against Argentina.

No part of the foregoing has been repeated to Buenos Aires.

WINANT

810.74/611 : Telegram

The Secretary of State to the Ambassador in the United Kingdom (Winant)

WASHINGTON, November 16, 1942—9 p. m.

5738. Your 6368, November 12, 9 p. m. Our Embassy in Buenos Aires informs us that the Argentine decree regarding telecommuni-

---

[5] Not printed.
[6] Telegrams Nos. 5241 and 5242 not found in Department files, and there is no record of telegrams with these numbers being sent to London.
[7] Telegram No. 5528 not printed.

cations of October 8 [8] will prohibit the use of code or cipher by radio for messages outside of the continent.   This will apply also to all diplomatic missions.   It was further asserted that code and cipher messages would be permitted by cable.

In view of foregoing, the only authorized channels of rapid secret communication between the Axis missions in Santiago and Buenos Aires and their Governments will be via cables controlled by London, and it is assumed that the British authorities will take the necessary steps to prevent such communication.

HULL

810.74/618 : Telegram

The Ambassador in Chile (Bowers) to the Secretary of State

SANTIAGO, November 16, 1942—midnight.
[Received November 17—2 : 33 a. m.]

1996.   All America Cables Company today refused traffic from the Vichy Legation here to Vichy and immediately cabled West Coast Cables asking them to verify that they would also refuse.   The manager and later the Commercial Counselor of the British Embassy confirmed that West Coast could not refuse to accept the message since they are still without instructions from London.   Can't London be moved to stop all traffic to Axis-controlled territory or is this British loop-hole of espionage transmission to continue to be made available?   Reference is my 1981, November 14, 6 p. m.[9]

BOWERS

810.74/622 : Telegram

The Ambassador in the United Kingdom (Winant) to the Secretary of State

LONDON, November 21, 1942—1 p. m.
[Received November 21—11 : 43 a. m.]

6562.   Foreign Office was glad to receive the information in Department's 5738, November 16 regarding the Argentine decree concerning telecommunications.   The British authorities, Foreign Office emphasizes, have every intention of controlling Axis cipher messages transmitted by cable, and they are now investigating the best means of putting the control into operation.   Foreign Office has promised to inform Embassy as soon as the arrangements are completed.

WINANT

---

[8] See Embassy's telegram No. 1959, October 9, 8 p. m., p. 163.
[9] Not printed.

740.0011 European War 1939/26005 : Telegram

The Ambassador in Argentina (Armour) to the Secretary of State

BUENOS AIRES, November 24, 1942—9 p. m.
[Received 10 : 39 p. m.]

2362. I called by appointment on the President this afternoon. It was the first opportunity I had had to speak to him other than on formal occasions. He received me with his customary cordiality and as usual seemed to be in agreement on various points raised. Regarding the war he made the categorical statement that he feels Germans are already beaten. He congratulated me on our success Pacific and also on North African expedition which he fully realized had resulted not only in effective defense of American continent against attack, but had as one of its prime motives freeing France from Nazi domination. In response to my suggestion he said he would take favorable opportunity to make clear this was his feeling. In the meantime he felt Foreign Minister's message to Secretary of State had made Government's position clear.

He told me the Government was proceeding vigorously to complete investigation of Axis activities brought to their notice in our memoranda and assured me results would be fully published just as soon as opportunity had been afforded to complete examination of voluminous documents seized, most of them in German. In the meantime he agreed with my suggestion that his Government should proceed promptly to issue communications decree prohibiting use of cipher messages by radio outside of continent.

While previous experience has warned me against accepting such assurances too literally it seems possible that war news has had salutary effect even in these high quarters as it undoubtedly has on certain others hitherto in opposite camp and that we may expect more cooperation on matters mentioned. However, I shall remain skeptical until words have been transformed into action.

ARMOUR

810.74/625 : Telegram

The Ambassador in Argentina (Armour) to the Secretary of State

BUENOS AIRES, November 26, 1942—noon.
[Received 3 : 20 p. m.]

2384. Embassy's telegram No. 2362, November 24, 9 p. m. I have been working closely with British Embassy to persuade Government to put through the original decree on telecommunications which would prohibit transmission of cipher messages by radio outside of the continent including messages by diplomatic missions. The real value of the decree would, in fact, be that it would prevent transmission of such messages by Axis missions here.

I am now informed that in conversation yesterday with Under Secretary of Foreign Affairs the Counselor or [of] the British Embassy was informed that as now framed decree would not deny to Embassies the use of radio for cipher messages. It seems quite evident that this change has been due to pressure from Axis missions. Gache indicated that final decision was in hands of the President alone and agreed to facilitate interview for British Ambassador with him in last minute effort to obtain publication of decree as originally drafted.

ARMOUR

810.74/628 : Telegram

The Ambassador in Argentina (Armour) to the Secretary of State

BUENOS AIRES, November 26, 1942—8 p. m.
[Received 10 : 55 p. m.]

2389. In a very outspoken talk with Gache this evening I told him that I was amazed to learn, in spite of the assurance given me by the Minister for Foreign Affairs and by the Minister of the Interior to the effect that the use of cipher and code will be prohibited for radio messages outside of the continent, that the Government was now considering permitting these. Gache very much on the defensive said that the plan was that such messages would be restricted as to number of words permitted but that the Minister felt to forbid them completely would run counter to the international policy hitherto followed by the Government. To this justification point of view I replied by asking what interpretation my Government could be expected to place upon their having agreed to forbid cipher messages prior to having full knowledge of the extent of Axis espionage activities and now having through Napp's confession [10] learned, if they had not known it before, of the full complicity of the German Embassy, decided to permit them. The Minister had, I said, himself shown me the figures of numbers of cipher groups sent by the three Axis Embassies and told me that on the basis of these alone the decree as originally drafted was necessary. The Minister of the Interior had volunteered to me that with the extensive use made of the code by Axis Missions there was no need for them operating clandestine stations. I asked to see Guiñazú but was told he would prefer to discuss the decree with me after it has been signed and he had it in

---

[10] See telegram No. 2339, November 21, 5 p. m., from the Ambassador in Argentina, p. 253.

definite form. On my insistence that the main reason for seeing him was to make my Government's position clearly known to him before the decree was issued in final form he promised to try to arrange a meeting for tomorrow.

ARMOUR

810.74/629 : Telegram

The Ambassador in Argentina (Armour) to the Secretary of State

BUENOS AIRES, November 27, 1942—7 p. m.
[Received 8 : 35 p. m.]

2394. My 2389, November 26, 8 p. m. I saw the Foreign Minister today and the results were most discouraging. He confirmed in detail what Gache told me yesterday. He tried to defend the Government's position on the ground that under international law the rights [to] use the cipher was a privilege of which Axis Missions could not be completely deprived without risking a break in diplomatic relations. To my question whether he did not feel that Axis representatives had forfeited any rights that they might have even under international law by their actions now clearly disclosed he insisted that these have not yet been proved but that if it should later develop that German or any other Axis Embassies were actually implicated in subversive or espionage activities Government would then be prepared to take further action. In the meantime they proposed to limit the three Embassies to a maximum of probably not more than 100 code groups each per day. I told him that in my opinion this was entirely unsatisfactory and that the only solution that could accomplish purpose desired would be to forbid the use of [cable?] and radio outside of the continent to all Embassies for all cipher messages. He gave no indication, however, that the Government would be disposed to withdraw from its position unless some unexpected development arises. Therefore, I am afraid Government is determined to issue decree with above modifications.

The Minister of the Interior and another official with whom I have spoken made the confidential suggestion that our Government might consider having Transradio close some circuit to Axis countries. I intimated this had always been considered but that we would naturally have preferred to see such action taken by Argentine Government itself. In this connection I understand that proposed decree contains clause which would forbid private companies from closing any of Italian circuits without Government approval. If this is true it may present a serious difficulty for the companies particularly Transradio to take such action even if a majority of the directors be disposed to approve it.

The British Ambassador saw the President this evening in last attempt to persuade him to adhere to the original terms [of] the decree. He left with the impression that something would be done but what, exactly, he did not gather.

ARMOUR

810.74/629 : Telegram

The Secretary of State to the Ambassador in Argentina (Armour)

WASHINGTON, December 1, 1942—8 p. m.

1858. Your 2394, November 27, 7 p. m. In your discretion, you are authorized to make vigorous representations in the premises to the President, who appeared to agree with you (your 2362, November 24, 9 p. m.) that the decree should prohibit use of cipher messages by radio outside of continent.

HULL

810.74/628 : Telegram

The Secretary of State to the Ambassador in Argentina (Armour)

WASHINGTON, December 1, 1942—9 p. m.

1859. Your 2389, November 26, 8 p. m. I am glad that you clearly indicated to Gache your amazement at the Argentine Government's apparent yielding to the Axis. If you have not already done so, you might point out in your future interviews that even if the Argentine Government should prohibit the transmission of messages in code and cipher by radio it falls short of the terms of Resolution 40 of the Rio Conference which was signed by Argentina and provides for the closing of all radiotelephone and radiotelegraph communications between the American republics and the aggressor nations. You might also point out that denying the right to Axis missions to transmit messages in code may be an inconvenience to them but that failure to prohibit the transmission of such code messages results in the loss of life and property belonging to the United Nations, a most one-sided interpretation of neutrality.

In the last war, during the period of our neutrality, the only means of communication between this country and Germany was by radio. We controlled the radio stations and refused to send any messages in code for the diplomatic missions of the Central Powers unless a copy of such code was furnished to the Navy personnel in charge of the radio stations. You might bring this information to the attention of the Argentine officials. The pertinent provisions of the Regulations relative to the operation of the Tuckerton radio station, which provisions were brought to the attention of the diplomatic representatives of foreign governments in Washington, are as follows:

The stations shall be used only for transmitting to or receiving from shore stations in Europe and the United Kingdom.

Naval officials at this station must assure themselves that the messages handled are strictly neutral in character. No unneutral message will be permitted to be handled.

No messages in cipher or code shall be transmitted or received for delivery unless the United States officials are furnished with a key to such messages.

No messages will be transmitted or delivered until they have been first paraphrased by the censors as may be necessary to ensure their neutral character, whether they are received or are to be sent in plain language or in code, cipher, or foreign language.

No messages shall be sent or delivered until countersigned by the censor.

You have our fullest support in continuing to press most strongly for the prohibition of the transmission of any confidential code or cipher radio messages from Argentina to points outside of this continent.

HULL

835.741/16 : Telegram

The Ambassador in Argentina (Armour) to the Secretary of State

BUENOS AIRES, December 4, 1942—11 a. m.
[Received 8 : 32 p. m.]

2453. Embassy's despatch 7343, November 16; [11] and telegram 2394, November 27, 7 p. m. Decree controlling telecommunications published last night. [12] It suspends international exchange of radiograms in code excepting 100 code words per day which may be sent by Embassies or Consulates. No such restrictions are placed on cables nor on radio messages in clear. Messages in clear are limited to Spanish, Portuguese, French, English, German and Italian. All telecommunications are prohibited which might prejudice security or defense of American states. Radiotelephone messages infringing on foregoing will be interrupted. International telecommunications messages of private parties will be controlled through license and registration. Facsimile service is suspended.

Other sections of decree refer to functions of official interventors to be placed in communications companies and the installation of ten monitoring stations with special reference to clandestine stations.

Text of decree being forwarded by air mail.

---

[11] Not printed; it transmitted a translation of the decree of October 8.
[12] The Ambassador transmitted a copy in Spanish of the decree of December 2 with his despatch No. 7605 of December 4; received December 12.

Today being a holiday most of Foreign Office officials were absent. However, a memorandum was prepared embodying information in section 2 and section 3 of Department's 1859, December 1, 9 p. m.[13] Original was sent Under Secretary for Foreign Affairs at his house and duplicate was delivered by member of the staff to a Foreign Office official familiar with the matter. The latter said memorandum was very interesting and promised full study. As to decree itself he made following informal comments.

While recognizing that we were not satisfied with the scope of decree as finally issued, he claimed that, nevertheless, it would accomplish a great deal. Previously some of the local Axis Missions had been sending as high as 1500 to 2,000 code words daily, and reduction to a 100 would seriously curtail their activities. Also he said perhaps we were placing too much emphasis on Embassy messages, since formerly any private citizen could transmit subversive messages freely and henceforth this would be strictly controlled. He said there was a definite possibility of imposing further restrictions on Axis communications, and intimated we could make much stronger demands along these lines if we were able to show concrete evidence of subversive information being transmitted by Axis Embassies here.

ARMOUR

835.741/20

The American Embassy in Argentina to the Argentine Ministry for Foreign Affairs [14]

MEMORANDUM

The Embassy of the United States of America acknowledges the receipt of the memorandum dated December 4, 1942, from the Ministry of Foreign Affairs and Worship,[15] relating to the control measures affecting telecommunications as contained in the Argentine Government's decree of December 2, and desires to make the following observations on the subject:

Article 1 of Resolution XL adopted at the Third Meeting of Ministers of Foreign Affairs of the American Republics at Rio de Janeiro refers to the closing of "all radiotelephone and radiotelegraph communications between the American Republics and the aggressor States

---

[13] Sections 2 and 3 apparently consist of the entire telegram except first and last paragraphs.
[14] Copy transmitted to the Department by the Ambassador in Argentina in his despatch No. 7779, December 17; received December 26.
[15] Not printed. A copy of this memorandum was transmitted to the Department by the Ambassador in Argentina in his despatch No. 7644, December 7. It noted that the decree allowed the foreign embassies a daily minimum of code words for transmission and justified this provision as a privilege that had always been "the essence of diplomatic status". (835.741/18)

and all territories subservient to them, except in so far as official communications of the American Governments are concerned."

The Argentine Government would have gone a long way in complying with Resolution XL by prohibiting the exchange of all coded messages between Argentina and the aggressor states and their satellites. In fact, it was the understanding of this Embassy that such a prohibition was planned by the Argentine Government when the December 2 decree was being drafted.

However, the effectiveness of such a prohibition will be largely vitiated if all diplomatic missions are to have the privilege of sending 100 coded words daily, bearing in mind that this privilege apparently is accorded not only to the diplomatic representations of the Tripartite Pact but also to the representations of other countries temporarily under the domination of the Axis powers.

When it is considered that all of the other American Republics have prohibited the transmission of coded messages to these aggressor states, and that virtually all of the American Republics have severed such telecommunications altogether, the 100-word privilege for code and the apparent lack of restriction on plain language messages still leaves ample opportunity for the transmission of communications which "impair or endanger, directly or indirectly, the security of the American nations, or which may be contrary to the defense thereof", notwithstanding Article 5 paragraph 3 of the Argentine Government's December 2 decree.

This Embassy is in complete agreement with the desirability of establishing efficient control over the transmission of private international messages, by whatever system of telecommunication, but wishes to point out that it remains possible for Axis banking institutions, mercantile establishments, and even private individuals to transmit subversive information by disguising it in the form of innocuous messages.

The memorandum of December 4 from the Ministry for Foreign Affairs and Worship envisages the "total suppression of secret language if in the use of such privilege there is evidence of abuses or transgressions affecting the security", but adds that the Argentine Government has no proof of such transgressions. In the meantime, however, the charges made by the judicial authorities of the Argentine Government against Axis agents, in which at least one member of the German diplomatic mission appears to be definitely implicated, would seem to indicate that there are additional and sufficient reasons for further implementing Argentine telecommunications control in still closer adherence to Resolution XL adopted at Rio de Janeiro.

BUENOS AIRES, December 11, 1942.

835.741/14 : Telegram

The Secretary of State to the Ambassador in Argentina (Armour)

WASHINGTON, December 17, 1942—7 p. m.

1966. Your 2467, December 5, noon.[16] With reference to the Department's 1592, October 23, 4 p. m., the British Foreign Office is agreeable to the prohibition of code messages to or from non-American countries by radio, although it would under no circumstances agree to the prohibition of code messages on cables used by the British.

Please consult your British colleague and, unless you feel definitely that it would be inadvisable, transmit Harbord's message to Hayes with a view to having Transradio take the proposed action immediately.

You may tell Hayes, if you believe it desirable, that there is no objection to informing the Argentine authorities of the contemplated action. It would appear desirable, however, to allow the least possible time to elapse between notification of the Argentine authorities and the contemplated action.

HULL

810.74/663 : Telegram

The Ambassador in Argentina (Armour) to the Secretary of State

BUENOS AIRES, December 18, 1942—2 p. m.
[Received 10 : 02 p. m.]

2588. Department's 1966, December 17, 7 p. m. After consulting with British Chargé d'Affaires it was decided to read Harbord's message to Hayes and obtain latter's opinion on desirability of transmitting it to Aguirre. Hayes flatly stated that it would not have desired effect. He said local directors would question Harbord's authority to make such request and that it would have to come from Hallauer[17] addressed to the company for Aguirre's attention before it would receive proper consideration. Even then he doubted if Board would take such action without previous approval from Argentine Government as otherwise there would be certainty of further official intervention. With regard to Transradio Chilena action he pointed out that it was Chilean Government which took initiative. His general remarks confirmed observations made in Embassy's 2081, October 24, noon, and he added that Aguirre might resign rather than attempt to carry out such action on company's initiative.

As mentioned in Embassy's despatch 7779, December 17,[18] now en route both this and British Embassies made representations to the

---

[16] Not printed.
[17] Secretary of the Consortium.
[18] See footnote 14, p. 179.

Argentine Government on December 11 regarding the 700 code words weekly by radio accorded to each diplomatic mission. Yesterday the German, Italian and Japanese diplomatic representatives separately visited Foreign Minister to complain that decree placed them at disadvantage. Foreign Minister replied that although it was intention to maintain existing regulation their claims would be brought to the attention of the President.

It now appears that December 2 decree will be interpreted broadly to allow transmission of coded radio messages by unofficial entities also provided code is in common use and other provisions of decree complied with.

Referring to Department's airgram A–369, November 16,[19] we would be in much stronger position to press for total elimination of coded messages by radio if we could show Argentine Government copies of any subversive messages sent by local Axis missions.

ARMOUR

810.74/863a : Telegram

The Secretary of State to the American Delegate on the Emergency Advisory Committee for Political Defense (Spaeth)

WASHINGTON, December 24, 1942—7 p. m.

796. From Chapin.[20] The following is a paraphrase of telegram No. 2219 of December 23, 3 [2] p. m., received from Ambassador Bowers:

"The Chilean Foreign Office, disturbed over the reported introduction of a motion calling for strong control of communications from and to those nations which as yet have not severed diplomatic relations with the Axis powers, has instructed its Ambassador in Montevideo to ask that consideration of this motion be delayed. Since the breaking of relations by Chile is imminent, Ambassador Bowers feels that it would be well to forget the motion until some time after the first of the year, particularly since the Foreign Office has no objection to the motion once Chile has broken, but fears that the motion itself may be interpreted by opponents in Chile as undue pressure and an attack on the national dignity of Chile. Ambassador Bowers adds that he understands that this motion was introduced by the American delegate."

The Department concurs in the Ambassador's opinion and therefore requests that you delay action on the motion until further notice from the Department.   [Chapin.]

HULL

---

[19] Not printed.
[20] Assistant Chief, Division of the American Republics.

810.74/663a Suppl. : Telegram

The Secretary of State to the Ambassador in Argentina (Armour)

WASHINGTON, December 26, 1942—4 p. m.

2017. Hallauer, as Secretary of the Consortium could presumably not instruct Transradio in the sense indicated in your 2588, December 18, 2 p. m., without an explicit directive to that effect from the trustees themselves. This would necessitate another trustees' meeting, which hardly seems practicable. However, Harbord has consented to having his message addressed to Beccar Varela, who represents RCA, instead of to Hayes. There appears to be no reason why Beccar Varela, acting on this recommendation from the interests which he represents, could not ask for a directors' meeting for the purpose of considering the recommendation. It is understood that the representative of the British interests would cooperate. See your 1883, September 29, 7 p. m.[21]

The Department is agreeable to having the Argentine authorities notified in advance that such a meeting was going to be held to consider such a proposal. It recognizes that the Argentine authorities may forbid the contemplated action, but feels that nothing would be lost thereby and that something might be gained. The Argentine Government would be placed in the position of taking a positive action in opposition to a measure designed to strengthen hemisphere defense in the spirit of the Rio Resolutions. Since the Board would presumably not take action contrary to the expressed instructions of the Argentine Government, the company would presumably not expose itself to punitive measures.

The Chilean Government did not take the initiative in the action of Transradio Chilena. It refrained from opposing that action, and after it had been taken, Chilean authorities indirectly indicated their approval in public statements relating to the Under Secretary's Boston address.

The Department is not at present in a position to make a positive reply to the suggestion contained in the last paragraph of your telegram under reference.

Please deliver Harbord's message to Beccar Varela, indicating if it seems appropriate that the American company has reason to be embarrassed by its participation in an enterprise that renders such service to the Axis as enables it to destroy ships and personnel of the United Nations. If you feel there are decided objections to such a course, you should defer action, informing the Department and awaiting further instructions.

HULL

---

[21] Not printed.

810.74/675 : Telegram

The Ambassador in Argentina (Armour) to the Secretary of State

BUENOS AIRES, December 30, 1942—7 p. m.
[Received 11 : 10 p. m.]

2669. Department's 2017, December 26, 4 p. m. Harbord's message delivered to Beccar Varela who after discussing it with Roberts, British representative on Local Board, has furnished Embassy memorandum along following lines.

"Today I spoke with Roberts who said that for some time he has held opinion that no approach should be made by the Company and still less by any of the directors. Such approach should be of an official or diplomatic character exclusively. From another viewpoint it is not believed that step suggested would produce any practical result.

Roberts' viewpoint is also mine, and I add that the nature of our concession and the attitude of the authorities who have drastically regulated everything pertaining to communications to the exterior make it impossible for a company to adopt resolutions without first submitting them officially to the Government.

Private consultation with the authorities by Roberts and myself probably would not give any practical result. Anyway this should not be done without intervention of Aguirre and, furthermore, to do it without the previous assent of the Board itself would be improper. Roberts believes that matter should not be discussed even with Aguirre and consequently does not believe it should be submitted to the Board, which probably would not approve it in any event.

As can be seen our personal desire to cooperate with ideas of Harbord collides with Company's position before the Government, the presumable attitude of the latter, and the difficulties which would arise among the directors."

Hayes insists that Transradio Chilena was first approached informally by a Chilean official before its board agreed to take action.

It is apparent that Argentine directors will be much more stubborn, even in unlikely event that Argentine Government gives informal assent to proposed action.

Position assumed by local company as represented in above memorandum would appear to present us with impasse so far as carrying out procedure suggested by Department. I am entirely in agreement with Department that if in some way Company could take action suggested this would place Argentine Government in position of taking positive action in opposition to measure carrying out spirit of Rio resolutions.

Only suggestion Embassy has to make would be to present question squarely to Foreign Office along following lines: that it is incredible to expect company half owned by American and British interests to continue to send messages to Axis countries enabling them to sink our ships and conveying information of value to enemy. In view of this, our Government proposes to instruct American representative in Company (presumably British Government would do likewise) to propose to Board that no messages in code be sent to non-American countries, a measure originally envisaged in Argentine Government's own decree but later modified. If Foreign Minister as seems probable, were to give negative answer this would at least have accomplished purpose mentioned in Department's telegram. However, if such action could be timed to follow closely upon break in relations by Chile, this might make Argentine Government more hesitant to take such a position.

ARMOUR

EFFORTS TO COUNTERACT THE WORK OF AXIS ESPIONAGE AGENTS

811.248/258 : Telegram

The Secretary of State to the Ambassador in Brazil (Caffery)

WASHINGTON, January 22, 1942—7 p. m.

175. Your 2222, December 28, 6 p. m.[1] War Department increasingly concerned for safety of trans-Atlantic ferrying operations,[2] particularly because of continued operation of clandestine stations. Department desires you if you deem it advisable to approach Brazilian authorities to ascertain extent to which Brazil has facilities available for locating such stations.

War Department also states that since former Axis-hired employees are still operating stations, particularly those of Lati [3] and Condor,[4] it feels only remedy is to dismantle stations. In view of your 2222, do you consider such steps necessary? Department desires your comment in this connection.[5]

HULL

862.20210/1098½

The Assistant Secretary of State (Berle) to the Ambassador in Brazil (Caffery)

WASHINGTON, March 9, 1942.

DEAR JEFF: I have your letter of March 4.[6]

As you probably realize, there is only one kind of information which could be called "absolutely reliable" in this situation. This is information which comes from enemy sources. Unhappily, they have been getting and sending information which, in many instances, has been accurate. They insist that it comes out of the Embassy. The assertion by itself would mean nothing; and the information by itself would not prove anything. The combination of the two, however,

---

[1] Not printed; it reported the Brazilian prohibitions on code messages.
[2] For correspondence regarding Brazilian-United States defense measures, see pp. 632 ff.
[3] Lineas Aéreas Transcontinentales Italianas.
[4] Sindicato Condor, Ltda.; for correspondence on the denazification of this line, see pp. 766 ff.
[5] The Ambassador reported in telegram No. 227, January 24, noon, that dismantling was unnecessary (811.248/309).
[6] Not printed; in this letter the Ambassador discounted the possibility of an information leak within the Embassy.

does give cause for very grave concern. The information is principally military in character.

I regret that I cannot give you excerpts of the various data. The proprietors of the information seem to feel that they can't do so lest the source be compromised; and very regretfully I am forced to agree with them.

I wish I could be more definite at this stage, but I do not see how I can be until I find someone who is traveling to Rio, who can talk to you directly.

With kind regards, I am

Faithfully yours,   A. A. BERLE, JR.

862.20210/1110 : Telegram

The Ambassador in Brazil (Caffery) to the Secretary of State

RIO DE JANEIRO, March 19, 1942—11 a. m.
[Received 11 : 52 a. m.]

935. Rio police last night arrested several important Germans among whom were Albrecht Gustav Engels (Alfredo of CEL group) and Herbert von Heyer (Humberto of CEL group). Police is expected to round up the remaining individuals in the radio rings within next 24 hours with our guidance. It will be necessary to furnish police confidentially some little of the evidence contained in intercepted messages if these men are to be held in permanent custody. The Brazilian authorities themselves have no evidence against them. I repeat that these individuals are the principal agents who have been telegraphing the movement of planes, ships, et cetera to Germany. If we can hold them we can probably cripple the whole German espionage setup here.

Please inform FBI immediately.

CAFFERY

862.20210/1110 : Telegram

The Acting Secretary of State to the Ambassador in Brazil (Caffery)

WASHINGTON, March 19, 1942—9 p. m.

696. Your 935, March 19, 11 a. m. The Department is in entire agreement that you furnish the police confidentially such evidence as you and West [7] may consider necessary; FBI shares this view. We confidently leave to your discretion any measures with respect to guiding the police in the round up of the remaining individuals of the radio rings. You will appreciate the necessity of avoiding disclosure

---

[7] Intelligence Officer attached to the Embassy in Brazil.

450858—62——13

of the source of our information since in that case our present source of information would be jeopardized if not cut off. Please cable further developments.

WELLES

862.20210/1119 : Telegram

The Ambassador in Brazil (Caffery) to the Secretary of State

RIO DE JANEIRO, March 20, 1942—7 p. m.
[Received 8 : 36 p. m.]

966. Department's 696, March 19. Under our guidance the police have so far today arrested 26 of the 30 persons we have indicated to them as connected with the four espionage rings operating Rio and sending clandestine wireless messages. This should paralyze their operations.

The police hope to have the other 6 [4?] by tomorrow.

All of the evidence necessary to hold them is contained in the intercepted messages. I do not perceive how the authorities can be furnished with this evidence without discreetly letting them know that it comes from intercepted messages.

Inform FBI immediately.

CAFFERY

862.20210/1119 : Telegram

The Acting Secretary of State to the Ambassador in Brazil (Caffery)

WASHINGTON, March 21, 1942—9 p. m.

725. Your 966 March 20, 7 p. m. Department highly commends the result of your efforts and trusts that the remaining members of the ring may be apprehended as anticipated. We are anxious that the source and method by which knowledge was obtained of the activities of the ring shall not become public, or fall into enemy hands. Can you not say that we have secret information as to the activities of these men, supplying such detailed information as may be necessary, without indicating the source of the information?

WELLES

862.20210/1125 : Telegram

The Ambassador in Brazil (Caffery) to the Secretary of State

RIO DE JANEIRO, March 21, 1942—9 p. m.
[Received March 22—12 : 44 a. m.]

987. My 966, March 20, 7 p. m. Following members of LIR espionage ring now in custody: Friedrich Kempter, Herbert Muller, Karl

Haering, Hans Muth, Doctor Heinrich Niemeyer, Hans Dives, Josef Pessek, Fritz Haering, Karl Sandberg. Following members being sought: Edgar Brombergard, Hans Muller.

Following members of CEL espionage ring now in custody: Albrecht Engels, Herbert Von Heyer, Fritz Kohler, Wolfgang Klee, Antonio Gamepinto, Otto Meier, Otto Linhart, Arno Von Muhlon, Stanislau Golak. Following members being sought: JPED Schluchtmann, Eduardo Schmidt, Eugenio Muhler.

Following members of CIT espionage ring now in custody: Karl Muegge in Rio, N. Christian Christensen and Hans Ulrich Uebele in São Paulo. Following members being sought here: Leo V Hus, Antonio Lucas, Herbert Spencer and Albert O. Schwab.

Fritz Noack of LFS espionage ring now in custody and Herbert Winterstein, his co-agent, is being sought.

[Here follows a list of Post Office boxes covered.]

A grill type Hallicrafter radio transmitter located in Kempters residence was seized, photographs by next air mail.

Please inform FBI immediately.

CAFFERY

862.20210/1126 : Telegram

The Ambassador in Brazil (Caffery) to the Secretary of State

RIO DE JANEIRO, March 22, 1942—7 p. m.
[Received March 23—12 : 50 a. m.]

992. Department's 725, March 21, 9 p. m. When we give the police some of the evidence we have they will probably know how we got it.

If we do not give them any evidence they will not be disposed to hold the spies because they have no evidence against them other than the captured radio transmitter; they did not capture them operating it.

CAFFERY

862.20210/1127 : Telegram

The Ambassador in Brazil (Caffery) to the Secretary of State

RIO DE JANEIRO, March 22, 1942—11 p. m.
[Received March 23—12 : 48 a. m.]

994. My 987, March 21, 9 p. m. All 30 members of the espionage rings are now under arrest and being questioned. They managed to destroy much documentary evidence before apprehension but a good deal has been seized and is being examined and translated by the police.

Please inform F. B. I. immediately.

CAFFERY

862.20210/1147 : Telegram

The Ambassador in Brazil (Caffery) to the Secretary of State

RIO DE JANEIRO, March 23, 1942—4 p. m.
[Received 9 : 15 p. m.]

1000. My 992, March 22, 7 p. m. In connection with the arrests made during the past 3 days, I respectfully submit the following thoughts to the Department:

1. It seems reasonable to assume that the Germans will strongly suspect that the 30 arrests were made on evidence intercepted in radiograms as specifically these 30 implicated in the messages were arrested and no others: We have no evidence to arrest others.

2. With these arrests more than 70 per cent of the agents in South America connected with these radio rings are at least temporarily out of the way. This includes many carefully trained men whom it will take at least one or two years to replace.

3. The police have arrested these men at our request and are holding them on the definite promise that we would furnish evidence for their prosecution. By evidence I mean more than our statement that we have secret information.

4. These arrests have dealt a paralyzing blow to the German communications system but if we cannot furnish the local police with real evidence, they must release them and they will without doubt reorganize somehow, somewhere, their communications which will result in further sinking of ships and may impede operations of our bomber ferry service.

CAFFERY

862.20210/1144 : Telegram

The Acting Secretary of State to the Ambassador in Brazil (Caffery)

WASHINGTON, March 23, 1942—10 p. m.

738. Your 992, March 22, 7 p. m., and 993, March 22, 8 p. m.[8] The Department appreciates that it will be necessary to supply such evidence as in your discretion will be essential to deal with the situation, but in view of the importance of the source of information we are extremely anxious that everything possible be done to prevent its being jeopardized or destroyed. In view of the fact that it is at least uncertain on which side the sympathies of the Rio de Janeiro Chief of Police lie, could you go direct to President Vargas or Aranha [9] with the evidence which it may be necessary to supply? This might have the double advantage of decreasing the danger of the spies being released and also diminish the chances of publicity concerning the arrests and the method of the accomplishment thereof.

---

[8] Latter not printed.
[9] Oswaldo Aranha, Brazilian Minister for Foreign Affairs.

As to the messages accruing since Department's instruction 2286 of March 5,[10] Department is forwarding them (Supplement 13) by courier reaching Rio de Janeiro on Friday, March 27. Will that be in sufficient time for your purposes?

[Here follow two sentences on decoding and paraphrasing.]

WELLES

862.20210/1147 : Telegram

The Acting Secretary of State to the Ambassador in Brazil (Caffery)

WASHINGTON, March 25, 1942—noon.

759. The Department agrees with the views set forth in your 1000, March 23, 4 p. m. and trusts that the suggestion as to the manner of handling the evidence made in Department's 738, March 23, 10 p. m., which crossed your cable under reference, may fit in with these views. The Department of course is desirous that nothing shall jeopardize the complete breaking up of this ring by the Brazilian police or other authorities.

Of the messages now en route by courier, the latest is only dated March 15. Messages from March 19 onwards, as requested in your 993, March 22, 8 p. m.,[10] are still being processed; any interesting results will be cabled you as soon as obtained.

WELLES

862.20210/1185 : Telegram

The Ambassador in Brazil (Caffery) to the Secretary of State

RIO DE JANEIRO, March 27, 1942—1 p. m.
[Received 2 : 16 p. m.]

1049. My 1000 March 23, 4 p. m. The police of the Federal District have now in custody nearly 200 Axis suspects which number includes the four espionage rings. The Rio police told me that the premature release of these arrests to the press was brought about by their desire to beat the São Paulo police to the press.

Please inform Federal Bureau of Investigation immediately.

CAFFERY

862.20210/1186 : Telegram

The Ambassador in Brazil (Caffery) to the Secretary of State

RIO DE JANEIRO, March 27, 1942—5 p. m.
[Received 8 : 12 p. m.]

1059. My 1049, March 27, 1 p. m. In addition to the arrests already mentioned the police have now arrested Elemer José Nagy and

---

[10] Not printed.

Mariana Fischer, co-agents of Salomon Jaios who left Brazil for Lisbon on February 17. Nagy was the sender of the recently decoded "Toni" messages dated in November and December 1941 and transmitted with Department's instruction 2286 March 5.[13] A dismantled transmitter was seized in the house of Nagy. Dismantled transmitters were likewise apprehended in the houses of Herbert von Heyer and Niel Christian Christensen. The seized radio transmitter which belonged to Friedrich Kempter was in a condition for immediate use when it was located. Other evidence accumulated through the raids consists of chemicals used in the preparation and developing of letters in secret ink, documents, photographs of Hitler, photographic equipment et cetera.

Please inform Federal Bureau of Investigation immediately.

CAFFERY

862.20210/1197 : Telegram

The Ambassador in Brazil (Caffery) to the Secretary of State

RIO DE JANEIRO, March 31, 1942—6 p. m.
[Received 8 : 25 p. m.]

1104. Department's 808, March 28, noon.[13] Since the São Paulo police have seized the code used by N. C. Christensen (Lucas) they are of course able to decode some of the intercepted messages. The Brazilian Government intercepted a great many messages but was formerly unable to read them.

CAFFERY

---

862 20210/1221 : Telegram

The Ambassador in Brazil (Caffery) to the Secretary of State

RIO DE JANEIRO, April 2, 1942—8 p. m.
[Received 10 : 30 p. m.]

1139. Aranha says that the Director of Posts and Telegraph has ascertained that certain Axis agents here are carrying on secret communications with Axis agents in Argentina and that he is taking steps to check communications. He said that the Brazilian Government would cut the Italcable (Italian Government owned) between Rio de Janeiro, Buenos Aires, because the Brazilian Government suspects that the company is cooperating with the agents in transmitting clandestine messages.

CAFFERY

---

[13] Not printed.

862.20210/1220 : Telegram

The Ambassador in Brazil (Caffery) to the Secretary of State

RIO DE JANEIRO, April 2, 1942—11 p. m.
[Received April 3—7:15 a. m.]

1141. Nils C. Christensen who signed in intercepted messages as Lucas, last night under heavy questioning made the following admissions:

1. That he at no time had any informant in or connected with the American Embassy at Rio. That he stated so in messages to enhance his value in the eyes of his superiors and because he felt he was losing the confidence of his associates. That he also lied to his principals in Germany regarding information obtained from the third officer of the SS *Sabor*. That he spent on himself the 20 contos authorized by Germany in its message of October 25, 1941 for use in the Green matter.

2. That his true name is Josef Starziczny and that his signature is on file at Hazelwood and Tarney, patent attorneys, New York.

3. That he was in contact with a member of the crew of the SS *Uruguay* named Boettscher whose cover name was Fass and who was in contact in New York or Hoboken with a German named Vogel. That Vogel also was in contact with Otto Uebele, ex-German Consul in Santos who was arrested again today and from whom efforts are being made to secure the addresses of Boettscher and Vogel.

4. That there is a German agent in Curaçao named Mueller, a brewmaster, who is in contact with one Weber, an official of the VASP [14] Airline through PAA [15] personnel. Weber was arrested today.

5. That Albert K. Schwab has been referred to in the messages as Herbert Spencer.

6. That Karl Muegge, who had a station and was working for him as radio operator, had the cover name Moss; and that he met Karl Muegge through Albert K. Schwab in May 1941.

7. That Ulrich Uebele who has been under arrest since March 6, son of Consul Otto Uebele used the cover name Mendes. That Otto Uebele's cover name was Kuntzet.

8. That Ulrich and Otto Uebele furnished all fuel oil destined for Axis vessels at Santos and it was they he placed himself in touch with in connection with the supplying of submarines.

9. That an employee of the British Consulate at Santos named Esilvac Mosilveira or Silvio was to produce routing orders of British vessels through an intermediary named Giesele located at Santos whose cover name was Green.

10. That he met Engels in April 1941 through German Naval Attaché Bohny, the master of the SS *Hermes* and Albert O. Schwab of the firm Theodor Wille.

11. That his agent in Recife and Natal was von Densteinen, son of the German Consul at Recife.

12. That Engels principal agents were Herbert von Heyer in custody here and one Backhaus who is supposed to be in Recife.

---

[14] Viação Aerea São Paulo.
[15] Pan American Airways.

13. That his and Engels cover address in Lisbon was Simon Simon, Travessa Rio de Janeiro 73.

14. That one Bukhoff connected with Standard Oil Company in Rio was one of Engels agents who furnished information on ship movements.

Please inform FBI immediately.

CAFFERY

862.20210/1277 : Telegram

The Ambassador in Brazil (Caffery) to the Secretary of State

São Paulo, April 10, 1942—11 a. m.
[Received April 13—1 : 08 p. m.]

Yesterday the São Paulo Political Police seized medium power radio transmitter at Fazenda Tesouro, Buri, São Paulo, believed to have had daily communication with Germany, and to have been integrating with the existing German system of espionage communications. The proprietor of the Fazenda Tesouro, Carl Heinz Bohne, has been arrested together with Hans Rudolph August Bohn, Teodor Bohl and Francisco Winkler all of them together with a [all?] seized material are en route to São Paulo for questioning. More details will be transmitted when available.

Also arrested yesterday was Iundi Yoshikawa, Lieutenant Colonel of the Japanese Army. When apprehended he was writing a letter to Japan, which he attempted to destroy. His case will be investigated.

Also apprehended as the result of a letter addressed to the Italian Ambassador in Rio de Janeiro was Oswaldo Scognamillo who, it is satisfactorily established is an Italian espionage agent in São Paulo. He appears to have been acting also as a private agent of General Lucio Esteves. Scognamillo's companion, Fernando Martini is being sought for arrest. Please inform immediately FBI.

CAFFERY

862.20210/1262 : Telegram

The Ambassador in Brazil (Caffery) to the Secretary of State

Rio de Janeiro, April 10, 1942—10 p. m.
[Received April 11—3 : 27 a. m.]

1224. In view of the Department's insistence on caution in connection with the intercepted messages the Embassy has not given copies of these messages to the local police: In other words although the local police are still holding the spies they have no evidence against them other than intimations and insinuations that we have given them; and they would like to release them.

In the meantime a report has been brought to my attention by the British Embassy from their agent at Recife containing the following statement:

"I have since received through my police contact copies of radio intercepts handed to the Army General Staff by the American Naval Observer, Recife. Intercept of January 18, from Worto, Germany, states (extract) 'star (Fink) reports are held back on account of personal supervision' which seems to be about this contention."

In view of this does the Department still desire me to continue to withhold the messages from the police. As the Department is aware the police are holding the 30 principal spies whom we asked them to arrest; as the Department is also aware, since these men have been in jail German spy communications with this country have been practically interrupted.

CAFFERY

862.20210/1262 : Telegram

The Acting Secretary of State to the Ambassador in Brazil (Caffery)

WASHINGTON, April 11, 1942—noon.

937. Your 1224, April 10, 10 p. m. In its 759, March 25, noon, the Department agreed with the views set forth in your 1000, March 23, 4 p.m., which meant that the Department agreed with the necessity of your supplying such evidence as you feel it essential to give the Police to insure the detention and successful prosecution of the espionage radio ring. As indicated in its 759, the Department feels that it is of the first importance that nothing shall jeopardize the complete breaking up of this ring by the Brazilian authorities and the Department's alternative suggestion in its 738, March 23, 10 p. m., made with a view to protecting the source of information as far as possible, was and is subordinate to the primary consideration of putting this ring completely out of business.

WELLES

862.20210/1307 : Telegram

The Ambassador in Brazil (Caffery) to the Secretary of State

RIO DE JANEIRO, April 20, 1942—10 p. m.
[Received April 21—4 a. m.]

1351. From statement made by Friedrich Kempter, OLIR group, it appears that Otis, Berko and Tannin of Buenos Aires are respectively Ottomar Mueller, Walter Napp and Walter Freiwald; that Hiag of São Paulo is Joseph Karl Eisenhammer; and that Kempter contacted Elvezio Ortelli, a Swiss citizen, in Buenos Aires in September 1940. Please inform F. B. I. immediately.

CAFFERY

862.20210/1344 : Telegram

The Ambassador in Brazil (Caffery) to the Secretary of State

RIO DE JANEIRO, April 25, 1942—6 p. m.
[Received 7 : 30 p. m.]

1413. Department's 1069, April 24, 8 p. m.[16]   These spies were arrested because we asked the police to do so.

They are being held in custody and will continue to be held because we have requested the Brazilian Government to do so.

No charges have been made against these individuals nor are any charges likely to be brought against them for the reason that their espionage activities do not constitute crime while Brazil is not at war.

CAFFERY

862.20210/1344 : Telegram

The Secretary of State to the Ambassador in Brazil (Caffery)

WASHINGTON, April 27, 1942—10 p. m.

1098. Your 1413, April 25, 6 p. m., and Department's 1069, April 24, 8 p. m.[17]   Your despatch 7021 of April 11 [16] states that the police are badly handicapped in view of the fact that you have not been allowed to furnish them evidence of the nature described in the following line of your despatch. Department's 759, March 25, noon, by agreeing with the views set forth in your 1000, March 23, 4 p. m., authorized you to give the police such evidence of the nature above referred to as you considered necessary. As your 1224, April 10, 10 p. m. indicated that you had not understood that such authorization had been given you, Department's 937, April 11, noon, made it clear (in reply to the question in the first sentence of the last paragraph of your 1224) that it did not desire you to continue to withhold the evidence in question from the police. This telegram crossed your despatch of April 11, but on receipt of the latter to make assurance doubly sure Department sent you its 1069 containing its assumption that you had supplied the evidence in question. Your 1413, however, is not directly responsive to the Department's assumption and leaves us in uncertainty as to whether the police activities are still being handicapped because you feel that you should not furnish them with the evidence in question. To dispel any possible uncertainty, the Department hereby explicitly states that you are authorized to give

---

[16] Not printed.
[17] Latter not printed.

the Brazilian police such messages when and as you deem necessary for their activities against the espionage radio rings and Department desires to be informed if and when you have furnished the police with such evidence.

HULL

862.20210/1360 : Telegram

The Ambassador in Brazil (Caffery) to the Secretary of State

RIO DE JANEIRO, April 28, 1942—4 p. m.
[Received 7 : 08 p. m.]

1435. Department's 759, referred to its 738 which while it gave some discretion in handling the source nevertheless made it clear that everything possible should be done to prevent the source of the messages from being jeopardized or destroyed.

Department's 937, April 11, clarified the question of giving this evidence to the police here.

The police as you know have arrested and have held these at our request. It was necessary, the more so because as indicated in my 1413 April 25 their espionage activities did not constitute a crime while Brazil is not at war, to show the authorities here that we did in fact have "the goods" on them. The police have therefore been given some of the messages in strict confidence, with the request that they be used only to assist in questioning the prisoners, and under no condition, to be published. The form in which the messages have been given to the police to use has been either as a straight translation into Portuguese of these messages when as in the case of the HTT group, they presented an understandable record of the activities of the Hungarian ring, or as quotations in interrogatories prepared for them by the Embassy as was necessary in order to question Engels, von Heyer and Kempter. A selected group of Alfredo's messages was furnished to the President, to Aranha and to the police. Another group of Alfredo messages dealing with leaks from the Air Ministry was given to Aranha to show to General Eduardo Gomes.[18] As an example of the difficulty in holding these spies, Dr. Edmundo De Miranda Jordao, head of the Brazilian Bar Association, today made energetic representations both to me and to the police concerning the case of Rosa Debalas who is implicated in the HTT ring and is under arrest.

CAFFERY

[18] General Gomes represented Brazilian interests in the construction by United States interests of air bases in northeast Brazil,

862.20210/1384 : Telegram

The Ambassador in Brazil (Caffery) to the Secretary of State

RIO DE JANEIRO, April 30, 1942—8 p. m.
[Received 9 : 30 p. m.]

1447. My 1458 April 29, 6 p. m.[20] Karl Teelen, one of the operators of Schlegel and Engels, has been arrested and is now on his way to the Fazenda Coregodofeijao, 80 kilometers from Bello Horizonte where he will show police escorting him the exact present location of station CEL which was operating until last night. Operator Trautman and Caretaker Paul Rabe, both now on the Fazenda will also be arrested. Schlegel's arrest was brought about by the confession of Erwin Backhaus who is known as an agent of Albrecht Gustav Engels. Please inform FBI immediately.

CAFFERY

862.20210/1390 : Telegram

The Ambassador in Chile (Bowers) to the Secretary of State

SANTIAGO, May 2, 1942—1 p. m.
[Received 8 : 20 p. m.]

666. Berle from Ambassador. De Bardeleben's[21] equipment reached him only first week in April. In view of our doubts as to the discretion of Chilean officials, it seemed better for him to work alone until PYL was finally located. Unfortunate extreme difficulties of terrain, surveillance activities of Nazi organization and sudden irregularities in transmission so far rendered impossible final exact location of station. There is now also the question of locating Noispagzces circuit. Further work held up pending receipt of replacement material requested in my 664, of May 2, 11 a. m.[20] De Bardeleben, excellent technician, and with good fortune should succeed in exact location of both stations within a fortnight or 3 weeks after receipt of replacement equipment.

We feel it advisable to wait to obtain exact location of stations and agents operating out of them before asking the Chilean Government to proceed to arrests. I believe that on that occasion with insistent instructions from the Department authorizing me to carry the matter if necessary to the President, the Chilean Government will proceed to arrests, but it probably will be necessary to disclose pertinent intercepts at least to Ministers of the Interior[22] and Foreign Affairs[23] for which authorization is requested.

BOWERS

---

[20] Not printed.
[21] Assigned by the Federal Communications Commission to radio monitoring in Chile.
[22] Raúl Morales Beltrami.
[23] Ernesto Barros Jarpa.

862.20210/1430 : Telegram

The Ambassador in Chile (Bowers) to the Secretary of State

SANTIAGO, May 5, 1942—7 p. m.
[Received 9 : 50 p. m.]

682.   De Bardeleben had an interview with Minister of Interior and Chief of the Department of Electrical Services of that Ministry and both promised complete cooperation and secrecy in the first stage of his work which is location of active stations.   As stated in my 670 of May 2,[25] the replacement material requested in my 664, May 2, 11 a. m.,[25] and mentioned in my 666, May 2, 1 p. m., is now found not to be necessary.

BOWERS

862.20210/1456 : Telegram

The Ambassador in Brazil (Caffery) to the Secretary of State

RIO DE JANEIRO, May 15, 1942—5 p. m.
[Received 7 : 45 p. m.]

1650.   My 1246, April 13, 1 p. m.[25]   Local police last night apprehended a second transmitter belonging to Nagy of the HTT group. Inform FBI immediately.

CAFFERY

862.20210/1390 : Telegram

The Secretary of State to the Ambassador in Chile (Bowers)

WASHINGTON, May 19, 1942—4 p. m.

550.   Your 666, May 2, 1 p. m.   As soon as you notify us that you feel the moment has arrived to ask the Chilean Government to proceed to arrests the Department will send you instructions of the nature mentioned in your telegram and in case you should have to act at once without awaiting such exchange of telegrams you are hereby authorized to take the action mentioned in the last sentence of your telegram and to give the officials concerned such evidence as may be essential to effect the arrest and prolonged detention of the Axis agents in question.

HULL

---

[25] Not printed.

862.20210/1468 : Telegram

The Ambassador in Chile (Bowers) to the Secretary of State

SANTIAGO, May 20, 1942—7 p. m.
[Received May 20—6 : 45 p. m.]

774. For Berle. Have now made contact with Chilean official in charge of radio monitoring and have received his approval and cooperation in permitting De Bardeleben to work exclusively on locating PYL and the Noiges circuit. When these are definitely located instructions in your telegram 550, May 19, 7 [4] p. m. will be carried out.

BOWERS

862.20210/1533 : Telegram

The Ambassador in Brazil (Caffery) to the Secretary of State

RIO DE JANEIRO, June 9, 1942—8 p. m.
[Received 10 : 40 p. m.]

1948. My 1178, April 7, 7 p. m.[29] Acting on clues furnished by Othmar Gamillshegg and Adalbert Vamszer police of Federal District last night seized another clandestine transmitter on a farm owned by Kurt Weingartner. Weingartner was recently arrested by police of the State of Rio and is connected with Engels and Ramus. His mistress Helen Lohse who is said to have been very active is in custody here.

Please inform F. B. I. immediately.

CAFFERY

862.20210/1653

The Ambassador in Chile (Bowers) to the Secretary of State

No. 3781   SANTIAGO, July 6, 1942.
[Received July 18.]

SIR: I have the honor to acknowledge receipt of the Department's strictly confidential instruction No. 1626, dated June 16, 1942,[29] relative to secret radio transmission by the German Embassy in Buenos Aires and to report that this Embassy is in receipt of as yet unverified information that the German Embassy in Santiago has recently installed a transmitter to contact the one in Buenos Aires. The information is to the effect that during its installation the German Embassy in Santiago used a transmitter belonging to one Arnold Siemson for the first contact.

Respectfully yours,   CLAUDE G. BOWERS

[29] Not printed.

710. Consultation (3)/812

English Text of Informal Memorandum in Spanish Left by the American Ambassador in Argentina (Armour) With the Argentine Minister for Foreign Affairs (Ruiz-Guiñazú) on July 6, 1942 [30]

Five months have now elapsed since the closure of the Meeting of American Foreign Ministers at Río de Janeiro.[31] Week after week the crisis of war deepens and the criminal attacks of the Axis aggressors approach ever closer to the shores of America, without regard for the civilized laws of human conduct and without distinction among the victims. The lives and property of more and more citizens of the American Republics are daily sacrificed to preserve their integrity and independence and the integrity and solidarity of the American continent.

The effective implementation of the resolutions subscribed at the Río de Janeiro Meeting by all of the American Republics is essential in order to nullify and prevent these criminal acts of aggression.

The delay of the Argentine Government in implementing the provisions of Resolutions I, XVII, XXXI, and XL [32] in particular, has permitted the continuance by Axis agents in Argentina of espionage and other activities designed to defeat the war effort of the United States and of the other American Republics now at war, and to undermine the collective integrity and solidarity of the continent.

Information regarding a number of particularly dangerous Axis agents has been communicated to the Argentine Government by the Embassy of the United States. Recently a number of Axis agents whose subversive character had been signalized by other American Republics with a view to their deportation and repatriation had entered Argentina on visas issued by Argentine consuls. So far as is known, no measures have been taken to prevent Axis agents and other foreigners inimical to the principles of the Declaration of Lima [33] from traveling freely on Argentine air lines, in contradiction of the recommendations contained in Resolution XXXI of the Río de Janeiro meeting.

Certain newspaper offices, radio broadcasting stations and publishing houses which are centers for the dissemination of totalitarian propaganda, are openly continuing their activities in Argentina.

---

[30] Transmitted to the Department by the Ambassador in his despatch No. 5694, July 10; received July 16.

[31] For correspondence concerning the Third Meeting of the Foreign Ministers of the American Republics at Rio de Janeiro, January 15–28, 1942, see pp. 6 ff.

[32] Department of State *Bulletin*, February 7, 1942, pp. 118, 128, 137, and 140.

[33] Declaration of the Principles of the Solidarity of America, approved December 24, 1938, *Report of the Delegation of the United States of America to the Eighth International Conference of American States, Lima, Peru, December 9–27, 1938* (Washington, Government Printing Office, 1941), p. 189.

Some of this propaganda finds its way to the other American Republics, often by clandestine means.

The Argentine Government thus far has taken no action, in accordance with Resolution XL of the Río de Janeiro Meeting, to close all radio telephone and radio telegraph communications between Argentina and the aggressor states and all territories subservient to them, with the exception of official communications of the American Governments. Nor have effective steps been taken by the Argentine Government to control, through licensing, the transmission and reception of messages over any telecommunication system which might endanger the security of each American state and the continent in general.

There appears to be no doubt that subsequent to the severance of telecommunications by the majority of the American Republics, Argentina has been used as a center for the reception of information from Axis agents throughout the Continent, and that such information is transmitted to Axis nations directly or indirectly by telecommunications. Any message so transmitted to Axis nations, either directly or indirectly, may endanger the lives of citizens of the American Republics, threaten the safety of their ships, lead to the loss of valuable materials, and imperil the individual and collective security and integrity of the American Republics.

During the past five months the Government of the United States has awaited with serenity and confidence the positive action which it has felt sure would be taken by the Government of Argentina to implement the resolutions subscribed at Río de Janeiro. The Government of the United States does not doubt that this confidence is justified.

BUENOS AIRES, July 6, 1942.

710.Consultation (3)/812

The Argentine Ministry for Foreign Affairs to the American Embassy in Argentina [34]

[Translation]

MEMORANDUM

The Ministry of Foreign Affairs has considered the memorandum presented by the Ambassador of the United States on the 6th instant, regarding the application, on the part of the Argentine Government, of certain resolutions approved at the Meeting of Río de Janeiro. The Ministry believes that only through erroneous information can it be affirmed that the delay in the application of those resolutions "has

---

[34] Transmitted to the Department by the Ambassador in his despatch No. 5694, July 10; received July 16.

permitted the continuance by Axis agents in Argentina of espionage and other activities designed to defeat the war effort of the United States and of the other American Republics now at war, and to undermine the collective integrity and solidarity of the continent". The energetic official intervention in the few concrete cases thus far known makes it possible to affirm, indeed, that on the part of the Argentine Government there has been no lack of diligence or of interest in the suppression of that kind of situation, which the memorandum, morever, limits itself to indicating in general terms. The Government of the United States may be assured that the Argentine Government will not disregard any concrete denunciation that may be brought to its attention regarding the existence of centers of espionage or of activities dangerous to continental defense.

In this sense, it is fitting to point out that in accordance with Resolutions II, VI and VII of the Meeting of Habana,[35] the Chancellery, on June 27, 1941, issued instructions to the Embassies and Legations in America to the effect that, in the event that passport visas should be requested for foreign consuls and employees who had been serving in the offices that were closed in the American countries by reason of the severance of relations with the Axis countries, any decision should be reserved, subjecting it to previous consultation with this Ministry which, moreover, has in no case authorized the admission of that personnel.

With the exception of the diplomatic mission of the United States, no other American diplomatic mission has pointed out the activities of undesirable persons traveling to Argentina. In the only cases formally denounced by the diplomatic mission of the United States, appropriate action has been taken immediately. It is thus that decrees of expulsion have been issued against four German citizens: Carlos Arnold, Walter Giese, Fred von Kockritz Fryland and Enrique Volberg. All have been carried out, excepting that relative to Enrique Volberg, by reason of his being involved in proceedings instituted against him before the Criminal Court of the Capital. By reason of the same denunciations residence in the Republic has been prohibited to Rudolph Borgolte and Augusto Elsner.

The Executive Power has just sent to the National Congress a bill to regulate the right of assembly whereby, in accordance with the spirit of Resolution XVII of Río de Janeiro, there are prohibited assemblies intended to divulge ideas contrary to the system of the National Constitution, of democratic institutions and of the fundamental laws, or tending to supplant that system with any other based

---

[35] Department of State *Bulletin*, August 24, 1940, pp. 130 and 132; for correspondence concerning the Second Meeting of the Foreign Ministers of the American Republics at Habana, July 21–30, 1940, see *Foreign Relations*, 1940, vol. v, pp. 180 ff.

on force or despotism. By the same bill the use of emblems, symbols or printed matter inspired by the same tendencies is suppressed. It is to be noted that the Edict relative to Public Assemblies adopted by the Police of the Capital on June 25, 1941, which is in full force, contains provisions in the same sense. Furthermore, the decree of May 15, 1939 requires all associations functioning in the country to comply with democratic principles and prohibits their depending in any way on foreign governments and entities, provisions which at that time led to the closure of various German institutions.

In the Ministry of the Interior there functions a special organization of "Vigilance and Repression of Anti-Argentine Activities" which acts as a centralizing and coordinating organ of police activities intended to control, watch and suppress any activity contrary to the democratic system and the institutions of the country.

The Direction General of Posts and Telegraphs, from the point of view of radiocommunications, has adopted effective measures to eliminate, in so far as possible, the clandestine stations as well as transmissions contrary to Resolution XL of the Third Meeting of Foreign Ministers of Río de Janeiro. To this end, by a progressive action of control, the Direction General of Posts and Telegraphs has thus far adopted the following measures: a) Intensification of the services of radioelectric control for the location and closure of clandestine stations; b) Suspension of the communications of station LVA (Air France) with foreign stations, limiting its activities to exclusive communications relating to the flights of Aeroposta Argentina; c) Suspension of the radioelectric services of the stations of the Sindicato Condor located at Quilmes (LVW) and at Las Heras (Mendoza) LVJ; d) Suspension of the functioning of radioelectric stations belonging to amateurs throughout the territory of the Nation; e) Stricter control of messages exchanged between private enterprises of public telecommunications services.

Although there exist radiocommunication companies that maintain direct circuits of public service with the Axis countries and countries occupied by the Axis, they are subject to the control provided for by the laws and regulations which, of course, excludes any activity that may affect continental security.

Moreover, the strict measures of control adopted by the Argentine Government to watch internal and external movements of funds, for the protection of continental security and solidarity, within a general action to avoid possible future activities on the part of the agents to whom reference is made in the Embassy's memorandum, are well known. Related to them are the decrees issued by the Executive Power on June 15 last, it being possible to state confidentially that in accordance with their provisions the following companies have already been intervened by placing observers therein: Merk Química

Argentina, La Química "Bayer" S. A., A. J. Roemmers y Cía., Química Schering S. A., Instituto Behring de Terapéutica Experimental, Thyssen Ltda., "Thyssen-Lametal", Sociedad Tubos Mannesmann Ltda., Cía. Platense de Construcciones Siemens Baunion, Cía. Platense de Electricidad Siemens Schuckert, "Inag" Fábricas Reunidas de Utiles Sanitarios, Siemens y Halske, G. E. O. P. E. Compañía General de Obras Públicas, and Hugo Stinnes Ltda.

This summary of background information, the clear significance of which admits of no doubt, permits the assertion that the Argentine Government has instituted, in defense of the security of the continent, a plan of control in keeping with the resolutions of the Meeting of Río de Janeiro, which will be gradually completed in the methodical and progressive manner which the organization and the administrative requirements of the country may permit.

BUENOS AIRES, July 8, 1942.

710.Consultation 3/816

The Chargé in Argentina (Reed) to the Secretary of State

No. 5769   BUENOS AIRES, July 17, 1942.
                                                [Received July 27.]

SIR: Referring to my despatch No. 5694 of July 10,[36] I have the honor to submit the following observations on the Foreign Office memorandum of July 8 in reply to the points raised in the informal memorandum left by the Ambassador with the Foreign Minister on July 6 regarding the implementation of the Resolutions adopted at the Río de Janeiro Meeting of American Foreign Ministers:

1. The Foreign Office memorandum does not deny that the Argentine Government has delayed implementation of the provisions of Resolutions I, XVII, XXXI and XL, specifically mentioned in the Ambassador's informal memorandum, but asserts that "only through erroneous information can it be affirmed that the delay in the application of those resolutions 'has permitted the continuance by Axis agents in Argentina of espionage and other activities designed to defeat the war effort of the United States and of the other American Republics now at war, and to undermine the collective integrity and solidarity of the continent' ".

2. With reference to the activities of Axis agents in Argentina, the Foreign Office memorandum states that the Government has just sent to the Congress a bill to regulate the right of assembly "in accordance with the spirit of Resolution XVII of Río de Janeiro". In response to my request, Dr. Bunge of the Foreign Office furnished

---

[36] Not printed.

me with a mimeographed copy of this bill, on which the original date appeared as June 26, 1941. This date had been crossed out and the date July 4, 1941 superimposed with a rubber stamp. Dr. Bunge's attention was called to the fact that this copy was dated a year ago, although the Foreign Office memorandum stated that the bill had just been submitted to the Congress. He appeared a bit disconcerted and undertook to investigate this apparent discrepancy. He has since informed me that the bill in question was in fact submitted a year ago, but since no action was taken on it before adjournment, it has now been resubmitted with slight alterations. The Embassy has been promised an accurate copy of the bill as now submitted to Congress but has not as yet received it.

The Foreign Office memorandum also refers to the existence of a special organization in the Ministry of the Interior to centralize and coordinate police activities for the suppression of "any activity contrary to the democratic system and the institutions of the country". The organization in question is under the direct control of the Under Secretary of the Interior, Dr. Castells, who has on several occasions stated to members of the Embassy that the organization has been unable to function because no funds have been made available. To date there has been very little indication of any disposition on the part of this organization or any other agency of the national Government to take any effective steps to suppress activities of the kind described on the part of Axis elements in Argentina; the energies of the police authorities have been devoted rather to the suppression of "Communist activities" and to restricting the activities of pro-democratic organizations under the provisions of the existing State of Siege.

3. The Foreign Office memorandum gives assurance that "the Argentine Government will not disregard any concrete denunciation that may be brought to its attention regarding the existence of centers of espionage or of activities dangerous to continental defense," and adds that in the only cases brought to its attention by this Embassy, appropriate action has been taken immediately. The foregoing statement is correct so far as is known with reference to four cases, those of Carlos Arnold, Walter Giese, Fred von Kockritz Frydland, and Enrique Volberg. With reference to the cases of Rudolph Borgolte and Augusto Elsner, however, the Embassy has only now been informed verbally that the police authorities have been asked to take steps to expel them from the country. In this connection, reference may also be made to the case of the Spanish Falangist agent Joaquin Miquelarena, who came to Argentina from Spain several months ago as a representative of the Spanish news agency EFE. As reported in the Embassy's telegram No. 625,

April 8, 3 p. m.,[37] the Foreign Office explained that although it had originally instructed the Argentine Embassy in Madrid not to grant a visa to Miquelarena, it had subsequently authorized the issuance of a diplomatic visa to him in view of the fact that the Spanish Government had granted him a diplomatic passport and had manifested particular interest in the case. Dr. Bunge himself referred to this case in my conversation with him early this week, citing it as the only instance in which the Argentine Government had made an exception to permit the admission of a person signalized by this Embassy as being an Axis agent.

4. With reference to the admission of Axis agents from other American countries into Argentina, the Foreign Office memorandum states that, in accordance with Resolutions II, VI and VII of the Meeting of Habana, the Ministry of Foreign Relations on June 27, 1941 instructed Argentine diplomatic missions in America to refer to the Ministry all requests for passport visas for consuls and employees who had been serving in offices closed by reason of the severance of relations with the Axis countries, adding that in no case has the admission of such personnel been authorized. It is noted that the foregoing statement makes no reference to Axis agents not directly employed in consular offices. Although the Embassy has received no detailed information in this regard from other American republics, reference may be had to the reports submitted by the Embassy at La Paz (despatches Nos. 2066 and 2075 of May 4 and May 7, 1942,[38] transmitted to this Embassy with the Department's strictly confidential instruction No. 2549 of June 16, 1942 [37]) which refer to the "general exodus to Argentina of Axis nationals who have been designated by the Bolivian Government for expulsion".

In this same connection it may be pertinent to observe that the entry of Axis agents into Argentina is not, of course, confined to persons coming from other American Republics. For some time all indications have pointed to the fact that a large number of Axis agents have been entering Argentina from Europe on Spanish vessels (Reference: Embassy's despatch No. 4071 of February 5, 1942 [37]).

5. With reference to telecommunications with Axis countries and territories subservient to them, the Foreign Office memorandum states that "the Direction General of Posts and Telegraphs, from the point of view of radiocommunications, has adopted effective measures to eliminate in so far as possible the clandestine stations as well as transmissions contrary to Resolution XL of the Third Meeting of

[37] Not printed.
[38] Neither printed.

Foreign Ministers of Río de Janeiro". This assertion is directly contradicted by the action of the Argentine Minister of the Interior who on July 10, two days later, addressed a note to the Director General of Posts and Telegraphs inquiring whether his agency was in a position to undertake the pertinent measures of control in accordance with the provisions of Resolution XL. The Embassy is of the opinion that the situation remains as stated in its despatch No. 5431 of June 12, 1942,[41] namely, that although the Argentine authorities appear disposed to cooperate in the detection and elimination of clandestine radio stations, they have taken no action to close telecommunications between Argentina and the Axis countries.

6. The Foreign Office memorandum makes no reference to the point raised in the Ambassador's informal memorandum of July 6 regarding travel by Axis agents on Argentine air lines in contravention of the provisions of Resolution XXXI of the Río de Janeiro Conference.

7. The Foreign Office memorandum makes no reference to the point raised in the Ambassador's informal memorandum regarding the continued dissemination of pro-Axis propaganda by certain newspapers, radio broadcasting stations and publishing houses in Argentina.

8. The Foreign Office memorandum makes a point of mentioning the "strict measures of control adopted by the Argentine Government to watch internal and external movements of funds, for the protection of continental security and solidarity". The financial measures adopted by the Central Bank for the avowed purpose of implementing Resolution V of Río de Janeiro have been the subject of numerous reports by this Embassy within the past few weeks. In view of the fact that at least certain preliminary steps had been taken to this end, no mention of Resolution V was made by the Embassy in its informal memorandum of July 6. The extent and significance of the measures taken in this connection by the Argentine Government will be made the subject of subsequent reports.

In conclusion it may be said that the statements contained in the Foreign Office memorandum of July 8 do not, in the opinion of the Embassy, justify the assertion in the last paragraph thereof that "the Argentine Government has instituted, in defense of the security of the continent, a plan of control in keeping with the resolutions of the Meeting of Río de Janeiro". On the contrary, the Embassy is of the opinion that the action that has been taken in this regard is negligible, and that the true intentions of the Argentine Government are best revealed by its recent actions in connection with the sinking of the *Río Tercero* and the attitude of intransigent isolationism re-

---

[41] Not printed.

vealed in the address of President Castillo on July 6, reported in the Embassy's despatch No. 5652 of July 7, 1942.[42]

Respectfully yours,   EDWARD L. REED

862.20225/715 : Telegram

The Ambassador in Chile (Bowers) to the Secretary of State

SANTIAGO, October 8, 1942—10 p. m.
[Received October 9—5 : 28 a. m.]

1662. Yesterday the Minister of the Interior announced with great publicity the discovery of a Nazi spy ring which was directing and working with Lun[ing] [43] in Cuba and engaged in maritime espionage, using a fishing fleet operating in Chilean waters. He announced the expulsion of three German citizens Kleiber, President of the Banco Germánico and prominent in Santiago, and Ludwig Russbenzinger and Guillermo Dorbachbunge, the latter "engaged in fishing business" in San Antonio. The Government announcement states that the information was sent to Cuba over "a short wave station" avoiding direct mention of Trans-radio Chilena. A Chilean, Carlos Robinson, was detained temporarily but it is understood cannot be sentenced since Chilean legislation punishes only espionage against Chile and not espionage activities directed against other nations.

Referring to the Foreign Minister's request for legal action against Subercaseaux, journalist, for having allegedly made "false" statements regarding Nazi activity in Chile and false accusations of Chilean governmental complacency with regard to such activities, the Communist *Siglo* accused Barros Jarpa of having protected the spy ring during the recent 8 day period in which he held the portfolio of the Interior during the absence of the Minister. Barros Jarpa today issued another declaration asserting that the more important information regarding the discovery of a spy ring was brought to the attention of the Government "after my stay in that Ministry". Questioned by the press as to whether in view of the exposure of Nazi activities the Government case against Subercaseaux would be dropped Barros Jarpa is quoted as saying that "any rumor of the withdrawal of the Government charges is unfounded since the matter of the arrest of spies was entirely separate from the former dispute", adding that Subercaseaux had made assertions which referred to activities of officials of the Ministry of Foreign Affairs and it was in this particular the charges were made. He added however "I have nothing more to do with this case which is in the hands of the judges".

BOWERS

---

[42] Not printed.
[43] German spy in Cuba.

862.20210/2035

The Argentine Embassy to the Department of State

[Translation]

MEMORANDUM

Reference is made to the speech delivered by Under Secretary of State Sumner Welles, on the 8th of this month, before the National Foreign Trade Council.

In that speech Mr. Sumner Welles made the following statements: [44]

"Nor can we here in the United States ever fail to remember with profound gratitude and renewed encouragement that eleven of the other republics of the Americas are joined with us, side by side, in the war and that seven other republics have severed all relations with the Axis and are rendering their neighbors who are at war every form of cooperation and assistance. It is true that the remaining two republics of the twenty-one have still refrained from carrying out the unanimous recommendations of the Inter-American Conference of Rio de Janeiro, in which they themselves joined, that all of the Americas sever all relations with the Axis, and are still permitting their territory to be utilized by the officials and the subversive agents of the Axis as a base for hostile activities against their neighbors. As a result of the reports on Allied ship movements sent by these agents, Brazilian, Cuban, Mexican, Colombian, Dominican, Uruguayan, Argentine, Chilean, Panamanian, and United States ships have been sunk without warning while plying between the American republics, and as a result many nationals of these countries have lost their lives within the waters of the Western Hemisphere. But I cannot believe that these two republics will continue long to permit their brothers and neighbors of the Americas, engaged as they are in a life-and-death struggle to preserve the liberties and the integrity of the New World, to be stabbed in the back by Axis emissaries operating in the territory and under the free institutions of these two republics of the Western Hemisphere."

The Argentine Government, having been informed of the foregoing statements, has instructed its Ambassador in Washington to call on Mr. Welles for the following purposes:

(1) To state that the Argentine Government has learned with extreme displeasure of the statements made before the National Foreign Trade Council, which statements, because of their being in open contradiction to reality in the present state of our relations with the United States and other American countries, we cannot accept.

(2) To point out that such charges, which militate against the frank and definitive understanding that the Argentine Government would like to see established with the United States, are all the more regrettable in that they do not specify cases and merely involve affirmations made lightly in unprecise and general terms, which the Argentine

---

[44] For complete text of address, see Department of State *Bulletin*, October 10, 1942, p. 808.

Government must answer precisely in defense of its friendly sentiments and of the position which, in harmony with such sentiments, it intends to maintain.

(3) To declare that the matter of alleged espionage activities, denounced by Ambassador Armour in July in equally unprecise terms, was fully answered in the memorandum of July 8 to the Ambassador, which stated to him at the time, just as it is now repeated, that "the United States Government may be sure that the Argentine Government will not ignore any concrete denouncement made against it concerning the existence of centers of espionage or activity dangerous to hemispheric defense." On that occasion a full account was given of the control measures adopted and of the expulsions carried out in the few concrete cases duly reported.

(4) To point out that it is inconceivable that Mr. Welles should thus have made a charge the inconsistency of which is evident from the most casual observation of the events in our country. As regards the sinking of merchant ships, it is sufficient to point out that those being sunk are either leaving our ports or arriving from foreign ports, and that the sinkings always occur at great distances from Argentine waters. Hence, it is difficult to understand how they can necessarily be attributed to the reports sent from Argentina.

(5) To point out that the statements in question are particularly inopportune at a time when the Argentine Government, gradually broadening the measures called for by the Rio de Janeiro recommendations in so far as Argentina's position and needs permit, has declared under State control all telecommunication enterprises, companies, and lines operating in the territory of the Republic, a measure adopted in a Ministers' Resolution prior to Mr. Welles' speech, considering "that the state of war in which various American countries find themselves and the commitments resulting from Pan American agreements signed by the Republic render it advisable to adopt the necessary measures to prevent the telecommunication system operating in national territory from being used to the detriment of the military interests of those countries."

WASHINGTON, October 10, 1942.

862.20210/1982 : Airgram

The Ambassador in Argentina (Armour) to the Secretary of State

BUENOS AIRES, October 15, 1942—3 : 15 p. m.
[Received October 22—3 : 25 p. m.]

A–276. This airgram is a confirmation and amplification of the Embassy's telegram 1989 of October 13, 11 p. m.[45]

Following observations are made for the Department's consideration in studying the advisability of turning information regarding clandestine radio groups over to the Argentine Government for appropriate action.

---

[45] Not printed.

There is reasonable certainty that the Germans are aware that we are acquainted with some aspects of their local military espionage set-up. Local press despatches have carried in part details of confessions in Brazil of Friedrich Kempter (LIR–MAX), Gustav Albrecht Engels (CEL–ALD) and Nils Christensen (CIT). In such despatches there was included information that Americans were responsible for the arrests of agents in Brazil, that codes had been captured when arrests were made (i. e., *La Razón* stated that one code was based on *All This and Heaven Too*), that information regarding Allied plane, ship, and troop movements had been sent by them to Germany via clandestine radio.

On the few occasions that we have requested action on the part of the Argentine authorities in deporting Axis agents Argentina has complied, although slowly. Examples are Walter Giese (Greif of LIR–MAX), and Hubert Kemper. On another occasion Immigration Department had granted immigration permits to Hans Emil Andress, Ewald Koch and Kurt Bruening, suspected Axis agents in Peru. Upon representations this Embassy, Ministry Foreign Affairs canceled their permits within 24 hours. However, we have been careful to request action in only the most flagrant cases, and not the cases of clandestine radio groups. Also the Argentines have been extremely slow to take action, even when evidence overwhelming. It was 3 months before Giese was deported and some 8 months before Kemper was interned, an internment which is not yet thought to be satisfactory. In addition, Special Investigating Committee of Chamber of Deputies has presented Government with much more detailed and convincing evidence regarding other local Axis agents. Government has almost completely ignored Committee's findings. This has been main factor dictating Embassy's policy of caution in recommending withholding of information regarding local radio groups from Government.

However, much can be gained by presenting this information to the Foreign Office, signalizing that Argentina's neutrality has been compromised by these agents, and requesting that appropriate steps be taken to apprehend and punish the persons involved. This would serve purpose of illustrating that neutrality is not enough and that there does exist in Argentina subversive organizations which are using the country as a base for carrying out operations against Argentina's interests as well as the interests of the other American nations. The effect it would have on the Argentine people and Congress would be tremendous. At the same time it would constitute a direct answer to the Argentine Government's request for specific instances of local German espionage. Also Germany's reaction to possible Argentine punitive measures probably would be of interest.

Although it is very likely that due to developments in Brazil and

Chile the Germans have dismissed some of their most exposed agents and have changed their systems somewhat, it is practically certain that the arrest or exposure of their leaders here would entail a complete reorganization of their local set-up with a consequent 6 months or more interruption in their reporting services.

It is thought that to submit as convincing an argument as possible it would be necessary to attach to the list of agents a general history of their activities. Of inestimable benefit in this direction would be the inclusion of a few copies of some of the translations of the intercepted clandestine telegrams. These would preferably include a few illustrating the transmission of reports regarding ship movements (including Argentine ships), the ones regarding the bribery (or attempt at bribery) of an Argentine army officer by Ottomar Müller (Otis) of the LIR–MAX group, the one about Walter Freiwald and the plan to attach time bombs to the bottom of ships in Buenos Aires harbor, the one regarding the establishment of a clandestine radio transmitter in Buenos Aires by Müller, of his dismissal and replacement by Hans Napp (Berko), of Napp's visit to the German Naval Attaché for instructions, how the clandestine transmitter was obtained from Siemens, of the post office cover boxes local agents used, and other messages of similar character. Of course, no mention would be made of the persons or messages connected with the CES–NOI group, RDN group, PYL–REW group, or the German diplomatic messages. Only those persons and telegrams connected with the CIT, CEL–ALD, HTT and LIR–MAX groups would be mentioned. It is taken for granted that the Germans have continued operations on the basis that the Americans have obtained copies of the codes and confessions of the persons connected with the last mentioned groups.

The Embassy would appreciate the opportunity of drawing up into practical form a draft of the representations (with all supporting memoranda and documents) to be made to the Ministry of Foreign Affairs; this draft to be submitted to the Department for its approval before action being taken.

In summary it is pointed out that this draft would contain no information which the Germans presumably do not already realize we have in our possession. It is possible, of course, that the Germans do not realize the Embassy is acquainted with the names, identities and locations of the persons implicated as being agents.

In this connection it would be appreciated if the Department could have the Embassies at Santiago and Rio de Janeiro and the FBI in Washington furnish all pertinent information which they think would be helpful for inclusion in the draft. For example, two Integralistas were recently arrested in Brazil. These two men confessed that they had been in contact with Thilo Martens in Buenos Aires.

Thilo Martens has long been suspected by this Embassy as being identical with the Thilo mentioned in the CEL–ALD group. If for no other reason, copies of these two confessions would be of great benefit for the carrying out of local investigations.

ARMOUR

725.00/34

Memorandum of Conversation, by the Acting Secretary of State

[WASHINGTON,] October 16, 1942.

The Ambassador of Chile called to see me this afternoon at his urgent request.

The Ambassador told me that President Ríos had called him on the telephone that afternoon at three p. m. and that the Ambassador's conversation with the President had been rendered almost impossible through the interruptions of the censorship officials, who had prevented the Ambassador from speaking on any of the important and urgent subjects which it was necessary for him to discuss with President Ríos. I expressed to the Ambassador my profound regret and told him that I would have an immediate investigation made since there was not the slightest justification for any official of this Government to interfere with the conversation between the Chief Executive of an American Republic and his diplomatic representative.

The Ambassador said that, owing to the attacks made upon him in Chile under the instigation of Dr. Barros Jarpa, his Foreign Minister, he, the Ambassador, had yesterday cabled his resignation to President Ríos and had informed the President that he felt that the office of Ambassador in Washington should be placed at the disposal of the President. He said that President Ríos had telephoned him in order to let him know that he was not accepting his resignation, that he had his entire confidence and he desired him to remain in Washington.

The Ambassador expressed the belief that Dr. Barros Jarpa would be forced to resign in the immediate future and that, presumably, a full Cabinet reorganization would take place. He said that President Ríos had made it clear to him on the telephone that he desired to break relations with the Axis powers.

The Ambassador then inquired whether I did not believe that President Ríos intended to break relations with the Axis, had he undertaken his trip to the United States, upon his return to Santiago. I replied that I had no doubt that this was the desire of President Ríos but that of course the Ambassador would remember that upon very many occasions in the past this Government had been advised to the same effect and that, nevertheless, regrettably enough, no action had been taken. I said furthermore that it had generally been understood in Santiago in the early days of this month that the Chilean Government believed that it would be very difficult for any action of the nature of breaking relations with the Axis to be taken immediately after the return to Santiago of President Ríos due to the fact that if it were taken immediately after his return it would be interpreted as action taken under pressure from the United States. To this, the Ambassador made no reply.

I then stated that I had noted with considerable surprise during the past few days official allegations on the part of the Chilean Government that the statements which I had publicly made in my address in Boston [47] should have been conveyed to the Chilean Government through diplomatic channels, and also that this Government had never advanced to the Chilean Government any concrete evidence that Axis activities in Chile were being carried on which were detrimental to the defense interests of the United States and the other Republics of the Hemisphere. I said that these statements seemed to me inexplicable in view of the fact that as far back as the 30th of last June the Government of the United States, through Ambassador Bowers, had furnished Dr. Barros Jarpa in writing a very lengthy and complete relation of the information in the possession of this Government concerning Axis activities in Chile,[48] pointing out that these activities involved the sending of the most dangerous information regarding ship movements from South America to the United States. I stated that again in August supplementary evidence had been presented and that this action had been repeated even later. I said the facts therefore were that upon three occasions this Government had informed the Chilean Government precisely and in detail of these facts through the diplomatic channels, and that consequently, the Chilean Government not only had the facts four months ago but that the diplomatic approach had been used three times without any results forthcoming until exactly the time my address was delivered.

The Ambassador expressed great surprise and said that he had never known this before. He asked why I had not informed him. I said that I was frank to confess that I had assumed, when he was in Santiago in August, that these facts had been brought to his personal attention by his own Government inasmuch as this was one of the most serious problems under consideration by our two Governments, and that I had also assumed that Ambassador Bowers had discussed this question with him. I said that I believed that these assumptions were valid assumptions on my part but that I of course regretted now that the question had not been raised in conversations between the

---

[47] Department of State *Bulletin*, October 10, 1942, p. 808.
[48] For a summary of this document, see p. 225.

Ambassador and myself. In any event, I said, his Government had been in possession of these concrete facts and it was all the more regrettable for that reason that Dr. Barros Jarpa should publicly and officially state that no concrete evidence had been presented to the Chilean Government.

The Ambassador talked for the better part of an hour and he concluded by expressing his belief that the whole problem would soon be satisfactorily solved and that the foreign policy of Chile would be modified as soon as the Cabinet change took place. He expressed great chagrin over the attitude taken by the press in the United States and I merely remarked that I felt the Ambassador knew this country so well that he must realize that when the people of the United States were engaged in a desperate war such as this, they could not take lightly the threat to the safety of the whole Hemisphere which resulted from the situation I had set forth in my address in Boston. I expressed the earnest hope that the difficulties of the moment would soon be past and that the relations between our two countries would continue to be as close and understanding and cooperative as it had always been the desire of this Government and of myself personally that they should remain.

S[UMNER] W[ELLES]

862.20225/620

The Secretary of State to the Ambassador in Brazil (Caffery)

No. 3567   WASHINGTON, October 22, 1942.

SIR: With reference to the Department's telegram of October 17, 5 p. m.,[49] there are enclosed two copies of a memorandum entitled *German Espionage Agents in Chile.*[50] This memorandum, the culmination of previous presentation of evidence to the Chilean authorities, is based on unquestionable evidence obtained by officers of this Government. It was handed personally by Ambassador Bowers to Dr. Barros Jarpa, Minister for Foreign Affairs of Chile, on June 30, 1942. After that date, for two months, the Government of Chile took no significant action to restrain the activities set forth in this memorandum, and a period of two months elapsed before any reference was made to this memorandum by the Chilean authorities to the Ambassador.

During September and October, and after the contents of the memorandum had been brought by Ambassador Bowers to the personal attention of the President of Chile, the Chilean Government has

---

[49] No record of telegram dated October 17, 5 p. m., found in Department files.
[50] Not printed; for summary, see p. 225.

made a few arrests and seized one clandestine transmitter. In general, however, no vigorous or adequate action has been taken on the basis of the information contained in this memorandum or with regard to subversive persons and conditions well known both to this Government and to certain Chilean authorities.

Over a period of months, this Government has loyally and patiently drawn the attention of the Chilean Foreign Minister to these matters, all this time making no other use of this material, since although it was aware of the unusual conditions confronting the Chilean Government, it was confident that Axis activities in Chile would be adequately and promptly dealt with.

You are requested personally to present to the Foreign Minister of Brazil one of the enclosed copies of the memorandum presented on June 30 to the Foreign Minister of Chile. In so doing, you are requested to take the opportunity to explain orally and in full the circumstances set forth above. You will wish to bear in mind, during this conversation, the importance of stressing the fact that Mr. Welles' recent public remarks concerning the tolerance of Axis activities by the Government of Chile [51] were made only after this Government had sought to avail itself of all other means of obtaining the cooperation of the Chilean Government. In addition, you may find it appropriate to point out that the danger arising from the conditions referred to in this memorandum has to do primarily not with shipping to and from Chilean ports, but with the use of Chilean soil as a relay point for the transmission of enemy espionage messages leading to the sinking in distant waters of vessels of this and other American republics, and to the furnishing of information prejudicial to the defense of the Americas.

The Department will advise you by cable when the action contemplated in the foregoing paragraphs of this instruction should be carried out. *It is important that no action should be taken until receipt of that confirmatory cable.*

Very truly yours,   For the Secretary of State:
                                         A. A. BERLE, JR.

862.20210/1996

The Ambassador in Argentina (Armour) to the Secretary of State

No. 7065   BUENOS AIRES, October 22, 1942.
                              [Received October 28.]

SIR: With reference to the Embassy's telegram no. 1989 of October 13, 11 p. m., the Department's answer no. 1549 of October 15, 6 p. m., and the Embassy's telegram no. 2059 of October 21, 8 p. m.,[52]

---

[51] Department of State *Bulletin*, October 10, 1942, p. 808.
[52] None printed.

I have the honor to enclose herewith the drafts of the memoranda proposed to be given to the Argentine Ministry of Foreign Affairs regarding the activities of German agents connected with the clandestine radio groups in Argentina. The documents are attached to the memoranda.

It will be noticed that the memoranda contain information regarding the individuals suspected of having connection with these espionage groups which has not been reported to the Department. This information, as well as names of additional suspects, has only recently been received. In spite of the fact that Friedrich Kempter (Koenig) refused to identify a photograph of Hans Napp, additional information recently obtained identifies him more clearly as being identical with Berko of the LIR–MAX group, and the Embassy believes more strongly than ever that Hans Napp is the person involved. For example, it has been definitely established that Hans Napp is an agronomist by profession and that in this capacity he has been manager of several *estancias* in Argentina and Uruguay.

From newspaper articles the impression has been gathered that the information concerning the PYL–REW group has been presented to the Chilean Government. If this is the case, the Department may desire to consider the possibility of enclosing with the memorandum on Group IV a few of the telegrams sent over station PYL–REW. This would strengthen the cases against Herman Bauer (who is closely connected with Heriberto Schwartau Eskildsen (Enrique) and Friedrich Tadeo von Schulz-Hausmann.

The contents of the enclosed memoranda have been compiled from the files of this Embassy and from local sources. It is realized of course that this information may be subject to revision or addition upon the receipt of further reports on the same subject from the Federal Bureau of Investigation and from the Embassies in Rio de Janeiro and Santiago, but the opportunity is taken of submitting the available material at this time in order to save as much time as possible.

Respectfully yours,

For the Ambassador:
RICHARD FORD
First Secretary of Embassy

[Enclosure]

Drafts of Memoranda on German Military Espionage in Argentina

The German military espionage service in South America, operating under the orders and instruction of the German High Command, is known to be using at least four groups of espionage agents in Argentina. These four groups are not isolated entities; they work in connection and in collaboration with similar groups which have been established in varying degrees of importance in almost all the other American Republics. Formerly Brazil was the most important scene of operations of these groups, but due to recent restrictive measures in that country, they lost most, if not all, of their agents and equipment. Those few agents who escaped arrest went into hiding or fled to neighboring countries. It is known that at least two of them are in Argentina at present. Since the punitive measures taken by the Brazilian Government, the German High Command has come to look upon Argentina and one other American country as the new headquarters for its espionage organizations.

Through information regarding the activities of these agents which has come to the attention of the Government of the United States it has been possible to learn that the Germans have used couriers on Spanish and other neutral ships, the diplomatic pouches, and the facilities of ordinary mail for transmittal of their information between the United States and South America. The information sent by mail is usually forwarded in secret ink or in cleverly worded business or social letters. This information, is then transmitted from the South American countries by clandestine radio to the German High Command in Germany.

In carrying out their espionage work the Germans endeavored to secure, and in some instances actually secured, the services of the citizens of South American countries. The Germans have also resorted to bribery of police and other government officials in their espionage activities. They have attempted to place friendly officials in military and other delegations which have gone from the Latin American countries to visit the United States. These German agents also use secret post office boxes, which are usually secured under Spanish names and changed frequently. They also utilize the post office boxes of Nazi party members and of German commercial companies for the purpose of transmitting espionage reports.

A number of the main espionage agents have diplomatic status and are actually attached to the German Embassies as attachés. Particularly is this true of the Naval and Military Attachés. It is also noted that some of the principal espionage agents are Nazi party leaders and are known as such.

The Germans made extensive use of the Italian Lati Trans-Atlantic air line for the transmission of espionage mail and for travel of espionage agents until the Lati Line was suspended on December 18, 1941.[53] The German Embassies have not hesitated to utilize the services of these clandestine radio stations in emergencies and it is

---

[53] See *Foreign Relations*, 1941, vol. VI, section under Argentina entitled "Measures taken by the United States to eliminate Axis-controlled airlines in Argentina."

definitely known that the German Embassy in Rio de Janeiro used the station belonging to Group I for sending messages to the Foreign Office in Berlin.

The chief types of information transmitted by these clandestine radios are: ship arrivals and departures; movement of warships of the fleets of the United States and England; information on imports and exports of the countries covered; information on United States armament and industries; political information on the area covered; weather reports; movements of airplanes of the United States, especially those being ferried to Africa via Natal; information concerning the operations of the Pan American Airways; information transmitted on behalf of the German Embassies; information on war preparation of the United States; information on the Panama Canal; information on the activities of the United States in connection with military and other aid furnished to the countries of the west coast of South America; information on the defense measures taken by the Latin American countries; details of information concerning the British base at Trinidad; information concerning maritime regulations and instructions of the United States; information regarding sabotage on English ships; military information concerning the United States, particularly concerning torpedo nets and naval installations; and information on convoys of merchant vessels.

The work done by these agents has been extremely accurate and especially harmful to the Allied powers as well as to the neutral American Republics. Millions of dollars worth of ships, merchandise, petroleum, munitions and foodstuffs have been sent to the bottom of the sea due to the efforts of these agents. Much of this property belonged to countries still on friendly relations with the Axis powers. These agents are also directly responsible for the loss of the lives of hundreds of men, women and children who died when their ships were destroyed by German torpedoes.

There are attached four memoranda setting forth in detail information concerning the identities and activities of the individuals guilty of participation in the foregoing activities which took place in Argentina. Each memorandum covers a separate group of German espionage agents operating under orders of the German High Command. For want of a better name, these groups are referred to as Group I, Group II, Group III and Group IV. It is pointed out that not all of the guilty persons have been located or identified and only the names of those are included regarding whom there is a reasonable certainty that they are to some degree guilty. These groups include the names of the following persons, many if not all of whom used code or cover names to disguise their activities:

GROUP I

Hans Napp
Ottomar Müller
Dietrich Niebuhr
Jose Mella Alfageme
Walter Freiwald
Elvezio Ortelli
Georg Hohenstein von Lug
Jorge Enrique Richter
Gustav Utzinger
Walter Giese
Martin Schneider
Martin Schwartz
Felipe David Humber
Enrique (Willy) Haupt
Domingo Sozzani
Victor Amilcare Testoni
Otto Hein
Egon Bunze
Ricardo Hoffmann
Compañia Din

GROUP II

Dietrich Niebuhr
Thilo Martens
Hans Bieben
Albert Wassmann
Viktor Mann

GROUP III

Rolf Edmund Stickforth
Rodolfo Hepe
Dr. Heinz Treutler

GROUP IV

Herman Bauer
Friedrich Tadeo von Schulz-Hausmann von Szymonsky
Ludwig Buchwald
Wilhelm von Pochhammer

As evidence of the activities of these agents, there are also enclosed copies of some of the messages which these groups sent to Germany via illegal radio transmitters.[54] These messages are sorted according to the group which transmitted them. Inasmuch as the Germans probably are not aware that copies of these messages are in the possession of the Government of the United States, it is requested that they be regarded as strictly confidential and be treated with the greatest of care.

It is regretted that due to military exigencies it is not possible to enclose copies of the messages sent by Group IV, but it is hoped that copies can be supplied in the near future.

In addition, since the ramifications of the espionage groups in Argentina are directly connected with the success of the war effort of the United States and directly affect the security of the bases which the Allied powers have in various sections of this hemisphere, it is respectfully requested that the Argentine Government keep the Government of the United States informed as to the progress and findings of the action that Argentine Government takes regarding the matter.

ESPIONAGE GROUP I

This group of espionage agents operates in Argentina under the direction of the German High Command and in close cooperation with Captain Dietrich Niebuhr, German Naval Attaché in Buenos Aires. Although Group II is believed to be the most important espionage group as regards the whole of South America, Group I

---

[54] None printed.

appears to have been the most active in Argentina. Its present chief appears to be one Hans (Juan Jacobo) Napp, who uses the code name of Berko to disguise his activities. He appears to have centered the headquarters of his activities in the Compañia Din, Calle Reconquista 331. Guillermo Scheckenbach and Osvaldo Hirner may be operating with Napp. Scheckenbach is owner of the Viena Hotel, Calle Lavalle 368, where the chief agents of Groups I and II of Argentina and Brazil met for several conferences in 1941. Napp once resided at the Hotel Viena. Osvaldo Hirner is reported to work under the orders of Scheckenbach and is located in La Plata where he obtains information regarding the arrivals and departures of refrigerator ships of the Allied nations. He was formerly an employee of the police department in La Plata. He is reported to have been responsible for the sinking of the *Andalucia Star* by a German submarine soon after it departed from La Plata a few weeks ago. Scheckenbach is reported to be one of the chiefs of port espionage in Buenos Aires.

Group I, which is believed to have an illegal radio transmitter in or near Buenos Aires, concerns itself with transmitting information of a strategic nature to the German High Command, this information including reports on boat arrivals and departures; movement of warships of the fleets of England and the United States; imports and exports of the countries covered; United States armament and industries; political information; weather reports; the military and naval activity of Brazil; movements of airplanes of the United States, especially those flown to Africa; and all important matters of interest to the German Government.

Attached is a résumé [56] of the activities of some of the individuals believed to be involved in the affairs of Group I.

ESPIONAGE GROUP II

Group II, as well as the other three espionage groups known to be operating in Argentina, had its headquarters formerly in Brazil, but with the recent widescale measures of the Brazilian Government most of its agents in that country were arrested and the seat of its activities were transferred to Argentina. This same thing is true of Groups I and III.

The local chief of Group II is believed to be Captain Dietrich Niebuhr, German Naval Attaché in Buenos Aires. He uses the code name of Diego to cover his activities in this group. Although Group II is believed to be practically as large in its ramifications as Group I, it has not been possible to date to uncover as many of its agents. However, it was very active and has sent much information of a

---

[56] Not printed.

strategic and harmful (to the Allies) nature to the German High Command. It is believed to have a clandestine radio transmitting station at its disposal in or near Buenos Aires.

The information Group II transmitted to its superiors in Germany included: Boat arrivals and departures (but not as much as Group I); movements of United States war planes; exports and imports; movements of warships of the United States and England; military activities and preparations of the Brazilian Government; operations of Pan American Airways; political information; and information on war preparations in the United States.

Attached is a résumé [57] of the activities of some of the individuals believed to be involved in the affairs of Group II.

Group III

Group III of the German espionage agents acting in Argentina under the orders of the German High Command is not indicated as having been as active as either of Groups I, II and IV. However, very little is known about this group or its leaders, and it may be for this reason that its activities appear to be less than the activities of the other groups. Suffice it to say, however, that the arrests of the principal characters of the Brazilian branch of this group have revealed that it did have an important organization in Argentina, transmitting information regarding ship movements and other Allied military activities in the hemisphere to the German High Command in Germany. At least one of the members of the Brazilian branch of Group III escaped arrest and fled to Argentina where he is now in hiding. It is possible that either Rodolfo Hepe or Rolf Edmund Stickforth may be able to clear up the mystery of his whereabouts. His name is Dr. Heinz Treutler.

The principal information transmitted by Group III concerns boat arrivals and departures; information on the British base at Trinidad; movements of British and American warships; maritime regulations and instructions of the United States; movements of American aircraft; sabotage on British boats; military information concerning the United States and particularly torpedo nets and naval installations; and information on convoys of merchant ships.

Espionage Group IV

Chief of this group in Argentina, and acting in close cooperation with the German Embassy in Buenos Aires and the other local espionage groups, is Friedrich Tadeo von Schulz-Hausmann von Szymonsky. The principal information transmitted by this group consists of data on boat arrivals and departures; information on the activities of the United States in connection with military and other aid fur-

---

[57] Not printed.

nished to the countries of the west coast of South America; information relating to the exports of the United States; information on the defense measures taken by the Latin American countries; general information from the United States; and political information, chiefly relating to Chile.

862.20210/1982

Memorandum by the Assistant Chief of the Division of the American Republics (Chapin) to the Chief of the Division (Bonsal)

[WASHINGTON,] October 23, 1942.

MR. BONSAL: I have discussed BA's Airgram A–26 [*276*], October 15, 3:15 p. m. with Mr. Lyon [58] of FC. As the situation stands, the Embassy in Buenos Aires has been authorized, as you recall, to prepare a memorandum for presentation to the Argentine Government, after first clearing the text with us. Not only are Santiago and Rio sending such supplementary data on subversive activities as may hook up with those in the Argentine, but a very comprehensive memorandum prepared by the F. B. I.[59] was sent down by courier yesterday to the Embassy in Buenos Aires. This memorandum was produced at the last moment just in time to get the outgoing mail and at FC's request I initialed the instruction without reading the enclosure, with the promise that they will make a photostat available to us later on.

The question of releasing the material to the Argentine Government seems primarily a political one, as the Germans undoubtedly know that we have a good deal of this material and they have probably already discounted it in advance. I fear the Embassy is over-sanguine in its belief that German espionage operations might be completely disrupted for six months. In any case, I have told him that any general publicity should of course be postponed until we see whether the Argentine Government is going to act on the information tendered to it.

SELDEN CHAPIN

862.20210/1992 : Telegram

The Ambassador in Chile (Bowers) to the Secretary of State

SANTIAGO, October 26, 1942—3 p. m.
[Received 7:25 p. m.]

1813. For Under Secretary and Mr. Berle. Chilean Government apprehended six subjects PYL organization and seized transmitter

---

[58] Frederick B. Lyon, Assistant Chief, Division of Foreign Activity Correlation.
[59] Not printed.

used by this clandestine station for past year and a half. Heinrich Reimers Chief of organization at present in Argentina. Hans Blume formerly connected with Transradio Chilena now serving as code clerk for German Embassy is being protected by German Embassy. However, it is believed a formal request will be made by Chilean Government to German Embassy for his deliverance to Chilean authorities. Confessions have been obtained from Hans Hoffbauer and Arnold Barcham.

Service of investigations is prosecuting the investigations vigorously but we must reckon with the possibility that the Chilean Government through fear offending Axis Embassies may try to retard an extension of the investigations. The results so far accomplished are largely due to the leads furnished through Mr. Wall [60] and efficient assistance rendered by his organization.

The Government has so far given no publicity to the matter, presumably because investigation is not complete.

BOWERS

862.20210/1993 : Telegram

The Ambassador in Chile (Bowers) to the Secretary of State

SANTIAGO, October 27, 1942—4 p. m.
[Received 5 : 55 p. m.]

1824. My 1813, October 26, 3 p. m. The Minister of Interior has issued strong orders that the investigation of the PYL espionage group be pursued with utmost vigor.

BOWERS

862.20225/620

Summary of Memorandum on German Espionage Agents in Chile [61]

[WASHINGTON,] October 28, 1942.

This memorandum presents detailed and irrefutable evidence concerning the activities of 18 Nazi espionage agents in Chile and other persons associated with them in various ways in their activities.

Information was given the Chilean Foreign Minister as to the manner of operation of these agents on Chilean soil, as to their identity, associations, whereabouts, means of concealment, and other pertinent details.

---

[60] Intelligence Officer connected with the Embassy.
[61] Summary by J. R. Toop, Division of the American Republics, of the memorandum handed to the Chilean Minister for Foreign Affairs by the American Ambassador on June 30. Copy of memorandum was transmitted to the Department by the Ambassador in his despatch No. 3931 of July 17; received July 27.

Especially, detailed information was given to the Foreign Minister in this memorandum concerning the types of information which these agents send from Chile to Germany clearly showing the danger which their transmission constitutes to the security and shipping of many of the other American republics, including the United States. To quote from the memorandum itself, "the following types of information have been transmitted to Germany:

(1) Boat arrivals and departures from ports on the West Coast of South America;

(2) Information on the activities of the United States Government in connection with military and other aid furnished to the countries on the West Coast of South America;

(3) Information relating to the exports of the United States;

(4) Information on defense measures taken by Latin-American countries;

(5) General information from the United States;

(6) Political information, chiefly pertaining to Chile."

The memorandum clearly shows that these agents in Chile relayed to Germany information received from other Axis agents operating in Argentina, Chile, Colombia, Ecuador, Guatemala, Mexico, Nicaragua, Peru, Venezuela, and the United States.

Evidence is contained in this memorandum that this ring of agents in Chile transmitted to Nazi spies in the United States instructions for their activities against the security of this country and the hemisphere, and helped to arrange for the development of communications and the obtaining of secret materials used by agents within the United States.

Certain members of this ring of agents operating on and from Chilean soil are shown in this memorandum to have made frequent journeys to other American republics in order to assist in the organization and maintenance of espionage activities.

Clear evidence was presented to the Foreign Minister that this ring of agents had received from Germany instructions to undertake the employment as spies and traitors to their own countries of nationals of American republics, including Chile itself.

Specific information was given to the Chilean Foreign Minister concerning the use of the Chilean mails by such agents, especially in their contacts with agents in other American republics, including the United States. Even post-office box numbers in Chile were given.

It was shown that this espionage group had well-established contacts with Nazi agents operating in the Far East, contacts carried on with the assistance of the Japanese. The names of persons who carried on this activity were given, along with much detail.

Information was given in detail concerning relations of this Nazi espionage ring, including Chilean citizens, to Japanese espionage agents in South America.

Information was given concerning the person who had been charged with developing a system of agents in the coastal towns of Chile for reporting on ship movements in those ports to be transmitted to Germany.

Information was given to the Foreign Minister of Chile concerning the organization on Chilean soil of a unit directed by a secret section of the High Command of the German army, charged with sabotage. This activity, organized on and directed from Chilean soil, affects not only Chile, but also the republics of southern South America and the West Coast.

There follow some details as to personalities and the working of the system.

As is well known, a principal interest of German espionage is the collection of information with regard to the movements of United Nations and neutral shipping. In Chile, the pattern was very similar to that established by German intelligence in many parts of the world. An important espionage center was the Chilean branch of the North German Lloyd, Compañía Transportes Marítimos. The Chilean company has legally severed its relationship with the Norddeutscher Lloyd, but the espionage activities continued. The system was developed by a North German Lloyd official, manager of the Compañía Transportes Marítimos, Friedrich von Schulz-Hausmann. Schulz-Hausmann has since moved to Buenos Aires, where he is active as a Nazi espionage agent.

The German manager succeeding Schulz-Hausmann was Bruno Dittmann, who was arrested last week in Chile, along with certain other employees of the Compañía Transportes Marítimos. Numerous other spies, some of them in key positions, have had contact with this office. Although there was no German shipping business in Chile, a large staff was maintained.

The pattern of this kind of activity has now become well-known. German commercial firms acting as blinds for espionage activities maintain contact with some member of the German diplomatic mission in the country in question. Such was the case in Chile, the officer of the Embassy being Ludwig von Bohlen, Air Attaché. Also concerned was Walter Boettger, the German Commercial Attaché. Boettger is also a high official of the Nazi Party in Chile, having at one time been Landeskreisleiter.

Bohlen cooperated closely with Japanese agents, maintaining close contact with the Japanese Military Attaché in Santiago, an important figure in Japanese espionage. Bohlen also made use of the diplomatic pouch of an ostensibly neutral nation. Also deeply implicated was the German Consul General at Valparaiso, von Pochhammer.

Thus, the participation of German diplomatic and consular personnel was completely demonstrated.

This group in Chile had contact with the German spy Luning, now under sentence of death in Cuba, also with other known German agents in Cuba, as well as in a number of the American republics, including the United States.

Thoroughly linked with elements of German espionage throughout the hemisphere, and having extraordinary facilities for communication with Germany, the Nazi spy ring in Chile was set up to act as a transmitting agency for espionage information going from the Western Hemisphere to Germany. It was not concerned primarily with reporting to Germany on matters Chilean, but with ship movements in many parts of the world and with the development of the world potential and military, naval and industrial activities of the United States. However, in numerous instances, information which was specifically damaging to Chilean national interest was conveyed by the spies to Germany.

In order better to cover up its activities, this ring drew in a number of Chilean citizens of German extraction, notably from the solid German districts of south central Chile.

Not only in Cuba have agents connected with this ring been apprehended, but also in the United States, Brazil, and elsewhere.

It should be noted that all this time, owing to the fact that Chile maintained diplomatic relations with the Reich, it was possible to transmit such espionage material to Germany through the Embassy.

This group in Chile was in contact with Walter Giese, in Ecuador, who was expelled by that country some time ago, fled to Argentina and has returned to Europe. The ring was also connected with an agent arrested and expelled by the government of Peru.

The financing of operations was carried out through the firm of O. Osterloh in Valparaiso, which maintained an account in the Banco Alemán in Buenos Aires. Money was actually distributed by various means. On one occasion, funds were transported for this ring by a Japanese diplomat.

From time to time, especially since June 30 (when this memorandum was handed to the Chilean Foreign Minister), further detailed information has been given to the government of Chile on the activities of enemy agents.

862.20210/1996 : Telegram

The Secretary of State to the Ambassador in Argentina (*Armour*)

WASHINGTON, October 30, 1942—3 p. m.

1633. Your despatch no. 7065, October 22. Memoranda as drafted is approved, except that on page one of "Enclosure to Espionage

Group I",[62] bottom of paragraph 1, Department suggests omission of words "at the request of the Government of the United States".

Santiago being requested to notify you whether information concerning H. B. Reiner, the known German espionage leader of Chile now taking refuge at Hotel Jousten, Buenos Aires, has been made public. If it has, you may wish to add the information or use it as you deem advisable.

The time of presentation of memoranda to appropriate Argentine authorities is left to your discretion.

Please notify Department promptly when it is presented by sending a telegram in clear "memoranda presented" giving the date and hour; if possible, telegraph several hours in advance of appointed hour for delivery so that copy may be delivered to Argentine Ambassador here at approximately the same hour.

This memorandum should be delivered by you to the Argentine Foreign Office under cover of an *aide-mémoire* stating that the underlying memorandum is in reply to the memorandum presented to the Acting Secretary on October 10 by Ambassador Espil. The *aide-mémoire* should include a statement to the effect that in view of the terms of the Argentine memorandum, the text of which was made public in Buenos Aires by the Argentine Foreign Office, the Department feels free to give publicity to its reply.

With respect to the suggestion in the penultimate paragraph of your despatch as to enclosing in group IV a few of the PYL messages, the Department sees no objection thereto.

HULL

862.20210/2007 : Telegram

The Ambassador in Argentina (Armour) to the Secretary of State

BUENOS AIRES, November 2, 1942—10 p. m.
[Received November 2—9 : 50 p. m.]

2157. Department's 1633, October 30, 3 p. m., reference penultimate paragraph. Does "give publicity to its reply" refer to *aide-mémoire* only or include memorandum. If the latter, while Department undoubtedly has good reason for doing this, consideration should perhaps be given to notice which such publicity would give Axis agents involved. Even public knowledge of fact our Government has communicated to Argentine Government detailed information on this subject might result in causing agents and others involved to take cover. Furthermore, if information communicated to Argentine authorities not effectively used by them they might offer excuse their efforts frustrated by premature publicity. If Argentine author-

---

[62] Not printed.

ities were given sufficient time to act prior to giving publicity to memorandum above considerations would not, of course, apply.

These points presented for consideration with full realization that Department may feel political advantages accruing from full publicity at present time outweigh other factors.

ARMOUR

862.20210/2007 : Telegram

The Secretary of State to the Ambassador in Argentina (Armour)

WASHINGTON, November 3, 1942—7 p. m.

1648. Your 2157, November 2, 10 p. m. In view of the fact that the Argentine protest against the Under Secretary's speech of October 8 [63] was given publicity by the Argentine Foreign Office and the statement was made by the Argentine Foreign Office that the Under Secretary's statement was vague and unspecific, the Department reserves the right to give publicity to all or any part of its reply. The final decision as to the timing and the method of such publicity has not yet been reached. It will take into consideration the factors set forth by you.

For your information, it is probable that when publicity is given to the documents, it will be through the Committee for Political Defense in approximately the same manner as is being done today with respect to the memorandum of June 30 presented by Ambassador Bowers to Barros Jarpa.[64]

HULL

862.20210/2009 : Telegram

The Ambassador in Argentina (Armour) to the Secretary of State

BUENOS AIRES, November 3, 1942—9 p. m.
[Received November 3—8 : 50 p. m.]

2169. Our 2149, November 2, 1 p. m.[65] and 2157, November 2, 10 p. m. Confirming Ford's [66] telephone call to Berle this evening, Embassy is sending *aide-mémoire* with accompanying memorandum [67] to Foreign Office at 9 p. m. tonight. As suggested no publicity will be given this material locally pending flash from Department. If and when publicity is given it is suggested it might be preferable for stories to be

---

[63] See memorandum from the Argentine Embassy, October 10, p. 210.
[64] For correspondence concerning the publicity of this document, see pp. 100–107.
[65] Not printed.
[66] Richard Ford, First Secretary of Embassy.
[67] See drafts of memoranda on German Military Espionage in Argentina, p. 218.

written in Washington and cabled here under Washington dateline, we to supply full text of *aide-mémoire* and memorandum to local offices of Associated Press, United Press, and Reuters.

ARMOUR

862.20210/2035

The Department of State to the Argentine Embassy

MEMORANDUM

Reference is made to the Memorandum left by the Ambassador of Argentina with the Acting Secretary of State on October 10, 1942 with regard to certain statements made by the Acting Secretary of State in an address before the National Foreign Trade Convention on October 8, 1942.

The Memorandum in question states, among other things, that the Argentine Ambassador has been instructed to indicate that the Argentine Government has learned of the aforesaid statements with profound displeasure since they are not consonant with the state of relations between the two countries and because they do not specify concrete cases and therefore only constitute unfounded assertions.

In reply, it may be recalled that the Foreign Ministers of the Twenty-one American Republics at Rio de Janeiro in January 1942 [68] took certain decisions because they recognized that, in view of the aggression committed against the hemisphere by the Axis powers, there should be a rupture of all relations, diplomatic, financial and economic, and a severance of all telecommunications between the American republics and those powers.[69] That decision was taken because the American republics realized from the experience of the European neutrals overrun by the Axis and from the perfidious activities of the Japanese in Asia and in Pacific areas that the mere existence of the aforesaid relations and communications was a guarantee that they would be used and abused, under the direction of the diplomatic representatives of the Axis powers in complete disregard of the norms governing the conduct of such representatives in international law, to further sabotage, espionage and other activities directed against the lives and properties of the nationals and governments fighting for a cause which the American republics have embraced, by their official acts, as their own cause.

In view of the fact that the Argentine Government, simultaneously with the delivery of the Memorandum of October 10 by Ambassador

---

[68] For correspondence concerning this meeting, see pp. 6 ff.
[69] For resolutions of the Foreign Ministers, see Department of State *Bulletin*, February 7, 1942, pp. 117 ff.

Espil, made a public statement setting forth most of the considerations contained in the Memorandum, and specifically questioning the existence of widespread Axis espionage groups in Argentina, the American Ambassador in Buenos Aires has delivered to the Argentine Foreign Minister a statement, a copy of which is attached,[70] summarizing certain information which has come to the attention of the Ambassador regarding Axis espionage rings operating in Argentina.

The information contained in this statement describes in some detail the activities of four groups of German espionage agents, all of which now appear to have their headquarters in Argentina. Approximately thirty agents have been identified. There is no doubt from the messages which have been intercepted, a number of which are included with the statement, that these groups are intimately connected with the German High Command from whom they receive their instructions. In addition their connections with the German Embassy in Buenos Aires through the offices of the Military and Naval Attachés, who took an active part in the direction of these groups, have been well established.

The activities of these groups consist principally in the gathering of information either locally or from agents in other American republics and the transmission of this information to Germany. Among the subjects treated in radio messages which have been intercepted are the following: arrivals and departures of United Nations' and neutral shipping, including war vessels of the United Nations; reports on United States armament and industries and on the military and naval activity of the United States and Brazil; weather reports; movements of United States aircraft, both military and commercial; information on United Nations' bases in the Caribbean. Of particular significance were intercepted messages disclosing discussions as to possible methods of sabotage of United Nations' shipping through activities in the port of Buenos Aires, with obvious peril to the port itself.

The attached statement describes activities undertaken by Axis agents in Argentina prejudicial to the security of the American republics as a whole. Since it is of vital interest that information concerning such activities be made available to the governments and peoples of the American republics, the Government of the United States feels free to make such distribution of the present memorandum and its attachment as it may deem desirable.

WASHINGTON, November 4, 1942.

---

[70] Drafts of memoranda, p. 218.

862.2021.0/2056

Memorandum of Conversation, by the Under Secretary of State (Welles)

[WASHINGTON,] November 4, 1942.

The Argentine Ambassador called to see me this evening at my request. I handed the Ambassador the *aide-mémoire* [71] to which was attached the memorandum [72] covering Axis subversive activities in Argentina. I asked the Ambassador to read the covering *aide-mémoire*, which I told him was similar to the *aide-mémoire* transmitting the same memorandum as that now handed the Ambassador which Ambassador Armour had last night, in Buenos Aires, delivered to the Argentine Foreign Minister.

The Ambassador read the covering *aide-mémoire* and said he would immediately study the enclosure.

Dr. Espil stated that he felt the step taken by this Government was in the highest degree desirable. He said he was only sorry that this step had not been taken a long time ago.

I reminded the Ambassador that during the first days of July Ambassador Armour had informed the Argentine Foreign Minister that this Government was aware in the most detailed manner of Axis activities detrimental to the vital defense interests of the other American Republics which were going on within Argentina and that at that time the Argentine Government had taken practically no steps whatever to do anything to correct this situation. I said that if, under similar conditions, the Argentine Government had communicated a message of that importance to this Government, I did not believe the Ambassador could conceive of this Government refusing to take any action whatever.

I said there was no use of mincing words with regard to the position of the present Argentine Government. It was constantly giving lip service to the principles of the Good Neighbor Policy and to the ideal of inter-American solidarity, and yet, at the same time, it was not only permitting a desperately serious situation of the kind now complained of to continue, but it had also, to all intents and purposes, refrained from any practical implementation of the definite commitments which the Argentine Government made at the Rio de Janeiro conference. I said that so long as the Argentine Government refused to comply with this official obligation to eliminate all means of telecommunication between the Axis agents in Argentina and the outside world, just so long would this most serious aspect of danger to which this Government was referring continue to exist in Argentine territory.

---

[71] *Supra.*
[72] *Ante*, p. 218.

The Ambassador spoke for a while with regard to domestic developments in Argentina. He asked if the Department had any particular information concerning recent political developments and I said that all of the information which we had was covered very fully in newspaper articles which had appeared during the past few days.

The Ambassador stated at the conclusion of our talk that his own position had become almost intolerable and that he hoped earnestly that the document now communicated to the Argentine Government would not be made public if the Argentine Government took effective and prompt steps to correct the situation complained of. He said that publication of a document of this character could only increase bad feeling against Argentina within the United States and within the other American Republics. I replied that I could make no commitment of any kind on that point. I said that as the Ambassador and I both must frankly admit, the situation was not one created by the United States or by any other American Republic, but was solely a result of the failure of the Argentine Government to live up to its inter-American agreements and that the question of publication or non-publication of this document must therefore be left open.

S[umner] W[elles]

862.20210/2011 : Telegram

The Ambassador in Argentina (Armour) to the Secretary of State

Buenos Aires, November 4, 1942—9 p. m.
[Received 9 : 55 p. m.]

2178. Embassy's 2169, November 3, 9 p. m. Minister of Foreign Affairs informed me tonight memorandum handed to Ministry of the Interior 11 o'clock last night. Chief of Police [73] who has taken entire charge has already found very interesting confirmation in first investigations made. Minister expressed hope that every opportunity may be given him without publicity to complete investigations which they promise will be prosecuted vigorously and effectively.

Armour

862.20210/2009 : Telegram

The Secretary of State to the Ambassador in Argentina (Armour)

Washington, November 4, 1942—10 p. m.

1656. Your 2169, November 3, 9 p. m. The Department contemplates no immediate publicity relative to the Memorandum left by you at the Argentine Foreign Office last night. It is probable that if such publicity is found to be desirable, it will be arranged through

---

[73] Lorenzo J. Galatto.

the Committee on Political Defense at Montevideo following the precedent established in the case of the Memorandum delivered by Ambassador Bowers to the Chilean Government on June 30. You are, therefore, requested to forward urgently a copy of your *Aide-Mémoire* and Memorandum to Ambassador Dawson [74] with the request, however, that he await further instructions from the Department before taking any action in regard thereto.

HULL

862.20210/2013 : Telegram

The Ambassador in Argentina (*Armour*) to the Secretary of State

BUENOS AIRES, November 5, 1942—3 p. m.
[Received 5 : 55 p. m.]

2182. I am disturbed by AP despatch originating Montevideo and published in local press last night and this morning to effect that source close to Committee on Political Defense announced memorandum similar to Chilean disclosure but dealing with Axis agents and activities in Argentina would be released to press within next few days. Because of prompt and effective cooperation being extended by Argentine authorities, as explained in my 2178, November 4, 9 p. m. I strongly urge that no publicity be given out or material at least for time being. I understand that several arrests have already been made and that first raids brought out copies of telegrams on ship movements and other important evidence. I am seeing Minister of Interior [75] later today and expect to hear from him more details of results to date and plans for future action.

As instructed copy being furnished by Todadt [*today's?*] courier to Ambassador Dawson with same recommendation regarding no publicity.

ARMOUR

862.20210/2018 : Telegram

The Ambassador in Argentina (*Armour*) to the Secretary of State

BUENOS AIRES, November 5, 1942—4 p. m.
[Received 6 : 13 p. m.]

2183. Department's 1633, October 30, 3 p. m. Following is translation of *note verbale* from the Foreign Office, dated November 4, in reply to the *aide-mémoire* that I left with the Under Secretary at the Foreign Office on November 3.

---

[74] American Ambassador in Uruguay.
[75] Miguel Culaciati.

"The Ministry of Foreign Affairs has the honor to address the Embassy of the United States of America to acknowledge the receipt of the *aide-mémoire* of the 3d instant transmitting the memorandum which as is explained, 'The Government of the United States of America presents to the Argentine Government regarding the activities of Axis agents in Argentine territory.'

The Ministry of Foreign Affairs appreciates the receipt of this information which answers the request which by instruction from the Chancellery was made by Ambassador Espil to the Acting Secretary of State, Mr. Sumner Welles, in view of the statements made by the latter in his Boston speech, in revealing in general terms the existence of such activities.

At this moment and with reference to the last paragraph of the *aide-mémoire* under acknowledgment, the Ministry of Foreign Affairs desires to make clear that in giving publicity in Buenos Aires to the instructions given in this connection to Ambassador Espil, the intention was solely to reply to statements that had already been made public in the United States on the same subject, which naturally does not prevent the information now furnished, specifying the facts in question, from being maintained and examined with the secrecy appropriate to the purpose in mind.

In view of this information the Ministry of Foreign Affairs is called upon to repeat the statements made to the Embassy in its memorandum of July 8 last, to the effect that the Government of the United States may be assured that the Argentine Government will not disregard any concrete denunciation that may be brought to its attention regarding the existence of centers of espionage or of activities dangerous to continental defense. In accordance with this criterion, the Ministry of Foreign Affairs has immediately made known to the Ministry of the Interior the memorandum under reference, the police authorities through it having been called upon this very day to take appropriate action".

Text of memorandum of July 8 mentioned in foregoing note and comment thereon was submitted to the Department with the Embassy's despatch[es] nos. 5694 and 5769 of July 10 and 17.[76]

ARMOUR

862.20225/759 : Telegram

The Secretary of State to the Ambassador in Argentina (Armour)

WASHINGTON, November 5, 1942—5 p. m.

1659. From the Under Secretary. Your 2173, November 4, 4 p. m.[77] I delivered the duplicate memorandum to Espil yesterday, telling him that you had already the previous evening delivered the copy thereof to Ruiz-Guiñazú.

Espil urged that no publication be given to this document, alleging that publication thereof would intensify ill-will against Argentina,

---

[76] Despatch No. 5694 of July 10 not printed.
[77] Not printed.

not only in the United States but in the other American republics as well. I told him that the Argentine Government itself was solely responsible for the present situation and that I could make no commitment whatever with regard to withholding publicity.

I wish you would telegraph me your views as to the most desirable time for the presentation of the document to the Inter-American Defense Committee. It had been my thought that approximately November 12 would be an expedient date. It would seem to be unwarranted from every standpoint for this Government to make public the facts concerning Axis activities in Chile and not to make public documentation covering similar activities in Argentina.

I wish you would also telegraph me your opinion as to the public reaction in Argentina if this document is published. My own judgment would be that it would decidedly strengthen the hands of all of the elements who are opposed to the present course in foreign policy pursued by the Argentine Government. But I realize, of course, that you are a far better judge of this question. [Welles.]

HULL

862.20225/761 : Telegram

The Ambassador in Chile (Bowers) to the Secretary of State

SANTIAGO, November 5, 1942—8 p. m.
[Received November 6—12 : 47 a. m.]

1892. Supplementing seemingly extempore statement published yesterday accompanying news reports from Montevideo and extensive extracts from memorandum handed Chilean Government June 30 concerning Axis espionage activities in Chile, whose text was made public by the Emergency Advisory Committee on Continental Defense, Minister of Interior Morales Beltrami furnished to the press last night an official statement published in full today. Principal points follow:

Given memorandum obliges Chilean Government to make a statement on the subject and to take steps which would otherwise have been postponed until a more appropriate time. The memorandum transmitted to Ministry of Interior by Foreign Minister July 8 but steps had already been taken to locate clandestine radio transmitter in Valparaiso and certain other data were already known to Chilean Government. During July the Minister of Interior by express authority of President was engaged in organizing investigation service competent to handle such matters and memorandum served to accelerate organization so that in August the chief of the service received instructions to exhaust all means to obtain proof of the allegations; in October the efforts were successful and a powerful illicit radio transmitter was seized and complicity of numerous aliens established; these were detained at the disposition of the Court of Appeals of Valparaiso. The Government's investigations are not yet finished since it is desired to establish all the connections and ramifications of the espionage web; at the same time the Government wished to have the courts establish certain facts beyond a doubt in order to avoid criticism that steps had been taken without adequate proof; for this reason the Government has taken steps to ascertain what officials gave out information prematurely to the Valparaiso press about a week ago concerning the measures taken there; the publication of the memorandum has precipitated events in a way that the Minister of Interior had attempted to avoid and for this reason he is compelled to make known to the public steps taken by the Government which it might have been better to conceal for a few days more; the expulsion decrees prepared by the Government on November 2 when the complete data concerning the trial in Valparaiso were at hand will be carried out now that no further reason for secrecy exists in view of the wide publicity given the matter; consequently the Government has issued decrees expelling from the country the following German nationals for the reasons given reserving the right to adopt additional measures when the pending investigations are terminated: (1) Hans Friederich Hostenberger, proprietor of the farm where transmitter was operated; he is port captain of the Compañía de Transportes Marítimos. As he has been found guilty his expulsion will not take effect until final sentence is pronounced. (2) Johannes Abries Peter Szeraws, technician in charge of transmission. He is an ex-member of the crew of a ship interned upon the outbreak of the war. He is residing illegally in Chile. Is at present a fugitive and his whereabouts unknown. (3) Hans Blume Neumann, the person who ordered transmission. Former manager of the Compañía Transradio in Valparaiso. At present code clerk of the German Embassy in Chile. (4) Heinrich Reiners Mahnken, directive head of the espionage organization functioning in connection with the transmitter. Is at present in Argentina. (5) Bruno Dittmann Schluter, manager of the Compañía de Transportes Marítimos, center of espionage in Valparaiso. Is this successor of Friedrich von Schulz von Hausmann considered as the chief of espionage in Chile. (6) Walter Irritier Adler, intimate friend of Reiners with whom he shares a post office box. His close friendship with preceding and his complicity in the illicit radio transmission has been established. (7) Otto Buchholz Hunold, in whose place of business the condensers and transformers of the transmitter were discovered. Former employee of the Compañía Transportes Marítimos. (8) Horst Kettler Schuke, employee of the code section of the German Consulate in Valparaiso gave orders for the transmission. (9) Jorge Hasseldeck Schwerdfeger, assistant manager and agent of the Compañía de Transportes Marítimos and intimately connected with Dittmann. (10) Emilio Simonsen Wiese, who by order of Hofbauer was in charge of hiding the transmitter in various places. He is also warehouseman of the Compañía de Transportes Marítimos. (11) Juan Cuneo Foppiano, Italian in whose house the transmitter was found hidden. (12) Catalina Berg Hartmann, stenographer in the Compañía de Transportes Marítimos who sent and received Dittmann's correspondence concerning transmissions.

Repeated to Buenos Aires.

BOWERS

862.20210/2017 : Telegram

The Ambassador in Argentina (Armour) to the Secretary of State

BUENOS AIRES, November 5, 1942—10 p. m.
[Received 11 : 09 p. m.]

2189. Embassy's 2182, November 5, 3 p. m. Police have arrested Martin Schneider, Osvaldo Hirner, Victor Amil Caritestoni, Otto Hein and Egon Bunze. Homes of Schneider, Hans Napp, Ricardo Hoffmann, Martin Schwartz, José Mella Alfageme and Compañía Din, have been searched. No results except with Schneider and Hoffmann. Many documents found in possession of former, including voluminous material on ship arrivals and departures, cargoes, armament et cetera. Additional documents written in German now being translated. Documents in possession of Hoffmann look suspicious but police say they must be translated first.

Schneider claims documents found in his possession not his, but entrusted to his safekeeping by a friend named William Hans. Claims not to know where Hans lives. Minister of Interior says obvious Schneider is lying and that he intends to hold him under arrest for "few more days" and to try to "squeeze" him into confession. José Mella is not in Buenos Aires at present. Is in Córdoba on vacation. Documents in possession Schwartz prove relationship with Napp.

In addition telephones Ludwig Buchwald, Rodolfo Hepe, von Schulz-Hausmann and Rolf Edmund Stickforth have been tapped by police. Post office boxes nos. 1081 and 386 have also been covered. Minister Interior stated he will order immediate arrest of Ottomar Müller, Hans Napp, Walter Freiwald, Georg Hohenstein and Hermann Bauer.

It is thought that publication in Montevideo of memo on espionage in Chile and published announcement that similar report may be forthcoming regarding Argentina may have given local agents warning to do away with incriminating evidence.

ARMOUR

862.20210/2013 : Telegram

The Secretary of State to the Ambassador in Argentina (Armour)

WASHINGTON, November 6, 1942—6 p. m.

1667. From the Under Secretary. Your telegram 2182, November 5, 3 p. m., crossed my personal telegram to you on the same subject. No publicity will be given to the memorandum except by instruction of the Department. I will appreciate your keeping me very closely posted with regard to the action taken by the Argentine Government on the basis of our memorandum as well as with respect to action taken generally to clean up Axis activities in Argentina. The responsibility for ferreting out Axis subversive activities and vigorously prosecuting them must rest with the Argentine Government. Our memorandum was intended to demonstrate to the Argentine Government the various types of activities which are taking place. Even though the Argentine Government takes steps now to clean up all of the activities described in our memorandum, the situation will still be totally unsatisfactory unless the Argentine Government, utilizing all of the information which it has, undertakes on its own initiative to stamp out all of the Axis activities today going on in Argentina, many of which, of course, we have no knowledge of. I think it important that the Argentine authorities be made aware of our point of view in the premises. [Welles.]

HULL

862.20225/770 : Telegram

The Ambassador in Argentina (Armour) to the Secretary of State

BUENOS AIRES, November 6, 1942—7 p. m.
[Received 10:15 p. m.]

2194. For Under Secretary. Your 1659, November 5, 5 p. m. My first impression is that November 12th would be too early a date for publication and suggest at least another week. As reported in my 2189, November 5, 10 p. m., authorities here acted promptly and made several arrests and raids, but the sincerity, extent, and effectiveness of their further action remains to be seen. Minister of Interior outlined to me yesterday steps he has taken, stated that incriminating documents were seized in connection with arrests made, and promised to keep Embassy informed of developments of investigation. In view of this I should like to have more time to gauge how far Government really proposes to go in arresting, confining, or expelling Axis agents and putting into effect measures to stop communications with Axis countries and further to implement other Rio commitments. In my opinion Argentine public reaction in general would be favorable to publication, particularly if full opportunity had been given authorities to act on information conveyed in our memorandum. Premature publication might be interpreted even by our friends here as indicating we were more interested in showing up Government than in having Axis agents apprehended and activities stopped.

Virtually all influential papers would probably receive such disclosures enthusiastically although under state of siege they might not be able to give full expression to their feelings.

ARMOUR

862.20210/2020 : Telegram

The Ambassador in Argentina (Armour) to the Secretary of State

BUENOS AIRES, November 6, 1942—8 p. m.
[Received 10 : 25 p. m.]

2195. Embassy's 2189, November 5, 10 p. m. Information from reliable unofficial source that Walter Freiwald arrested today and in addition to other incriminating evidence several sawed-off shotguns, many rounds of ammunition and three machineguns found in his home. Osvaldo Hirner arrested yesterday. According to press many incriminating documents and radio set found in his house. Not yet known if receiving or transmitting set.

ARMOUR

862.20210/2023 : Telegram

The Ambassador in Argentina (Armour) to the Secretary of State

BUENOS AIRES, November 7, 1942—4 p. m.
[Received November 7—2 : 31 p. m.]

2206. Embassy's 2195, November 6, 8 p. m. Press states radio in Hirner's possession both receiving and transmitting type. Also states documents in his possession include lists of stations in Chile and southern Argentina, lists of ship movements, cargoes carried, destination, crew, et cetera, documents indicating espionage activities against investigating committee of Chamber of Deputies and propaganda material. Hirner's arrest is the only one to receive publicity thus far.

ARMOUR

862.20210/2019 : Telegram

The Secretary of State to the Ambassador in Argentina (Armour)

WASHINGTON, November 7, 1942—9 p. m.

1681. In view of the fact that various news sources have knowledge that a memorandum regarding Axis subversive activities has been delivered to the Argentine Government, I believe it would be desirable, unless you see objection, for you to authorize the representatives of the associations and newspapers mentioned in your telegram 2196 of November 6, 7 p. m.[78] to carry a story to the simple effect that, in view of the request of the Argentine Government for details of Axis activity in Argentina, a statement has been furnished the Argentine Government. No details need be given as to the content of the memorandum. Such a simple statement would not only put an end to all sorts of speculation but would also let the Argentine public know that the requested proofs have been furnished and that responsibility for action rests with the Argentine Government.

Please inform the Department as soon as you take action.

HULL

862.20210/2032¾

Memorandum of Conversation, by the Under Secretary of State (Welles)

[WASHINGTON,] November 7, 1942.

The Argentine Ambassador called to see me this morning at his request. The Ambassador told me that he understood from Mr. Duggan [79] that the *aide-mémoire* I had given him on November 4 covering the document containing the detailed statement of Axis activities in Argentina had not been communicated to the Argentine Government and that he had consequently cabled down the full text of this memorandum. I told him that I had already made it clear to the Ambassador that while the *aide-mémoire* of November 4 which I had given him was not identical with the *aide-mémoire* transmitted by Ambassador Armour to the Argentine Foreign Minister on November 3, it was similar and contained precisely the same general presentation of views of this Government. I gave the Ambassador to read telegram 2183, November 5, 4 p. m., from Ambassador Armour which communicated the text of the reply of the Argentine Foreign Minister to the *aide-mémoire* of November 3 presented by Ambassador Armour and in which the Argentine Government expresses the desire that the memorandum covering Axis activities in Argentina be kept secret.

The Ambassador then handed me a memorandum,[80] attached herewith, in which the Argentine Government stated that it "understands that secrecy is essential for the purposes of the investigation being

---

[78] Not printed.
[79] Laurence Duggan, Adviser on Political Relations.
[80] *Infra.*

conducted and that those purposes, by reason of their importance and because of their interest for continental security and for the security of the country, should outweigh the reasons set forth in the United States Government's memorandum for giving publicity to the memorandum, the diligent consideration of which has not been delayed in the slightest degree by the Argentine Government."

The Argentine Government in this memorandum continues by stating that "once the investigation already commenced is terminated, the Argentine Government would consider the desirability of publishing by common accord the results obtained which would give rise to rigorous measures and to the proper punishments."

In conclusion, the Argentine Government states "The results of the proceedings now initiated as a result of the information which has just been furnished to the Argentine Government is of interest, as stated above, not only to the continent, but also especially to Argentina because of reasons of her own security."

The Ambassador inquired what reply he should make to his Government.

I stated textually that in the view of the Government of the United States it is a cause of great gratification that the Argentine Government has now appreciated the importance to the security of the entire continent that Axis activities of this nature be "rigorously suppressed". I continued by stating that I was informed by Ambassador Armour that the Federal police authorities in Argentina had already undertaken action against the individuals whose names were set forth in the memorandum communicated to the Argentine Government and that in certain cases a very considerable mass of incriminating evidence had already been obtained. I said I hoped that the most rigorous steps possible would be taken by the Argentine Government to bring those guilty to trial so that they might be appropriately dealt with.

The Ambassador then asked if I would not give the assurances requested by his Government, namely that the memorandum transmitted to his Government should not be made public. I stated that I regretted that this Government could not make any commitment in that sense at this time.

The Ambassador insisted that such a commitment should be made. I again reiterated that I was unable to give such a commitment since the fundamental question involved was one of the utmost gravity to the security of the entire hemisphere and not only to the security of the United States itself.

The Ambassador then said that he wished to see Secretary Hull about the matter in order to see if the Secretary of State would not give him the commitment sought.

I said that I was sure the Secretary would be very glad to see him but that I believed that he would receive the same reply from Secretary Hull that he had received from me.

862.20210/2142

The Argentine Embassy to the Department of State

Reference is made to the memorandum handed to the Argentine Ambassador by the Undersecretary of State, Mr. Sumner Welles, on November 4, 1942.

Apprised of the text of the said memorandum, the Argentine Government has instructed the Argentine Ambassador in Washington to formulate the following considerations to the Department of State:

In conformance with the assurances given at the proper time to Ambassador Armour by the Argentine Ministry of Foreign Affairs, and to which reference was made subsequently in paragraph 3 of the memorandum of October 10, 1942, the information handed on November 3rd by Ambassador Armour specifying for the first time the facts pointed out by the Undersecretary of State in his Boston address, was passed immediately to the Police authorities, who some hours later initiated the necessary investigations. Ambassador Armour is aware of this, as well as of the first impressions derived from these steps.

As expressed to Ambassador Armour when acknowledging receipt of his memorandum, on which occasion the assurances mentioned above were reiterated, the Argentine Government deems highly advisable that the information furnished to them be maintained and closely examined in strict confidence as being conducive to the objectives in view.

The Argentine Government holds that this is essential to the aims of the investigations and that these aims, both in view of their importance and significance as regards the security of the Continent and of the country itself, should prevail over the reasons adduced to circulate and publish a memorandum the diligent consideration of which by the Argentine Government has not been delayed a single moment.

On completion of the investigations already commenced, the Argentine Government would consider the publication, in mutual agreement, of the results thereof, results which may necessitate the adoption of the measures and the enforcement of the penalties deemed fitting.

The success of the proceedings undertaken as a result of the information just furnished to the Argentine Government interests, as already stated, not the Continent alone but specially Argentina by reason of its own security.

In these circumstances, any premature publicity might bring about results concerning which the Argentine Government deems it a duty to state that it declines all responsibility.

WASHINGTON, November 7, 1942.

862.20210/2032¾

Memorandum by the Under Secretary of State (Welles) to the Secretary of State

[WASHINGTON,] November 7, 1942.

MR. SECRETARY: With reference to our conversation of this afternoon I have now received from Ambassador Armour the reply to the inquiry which I sent him on November 5 [81] and which I attach herewith for your reference, particularly the part which I have marked.[82]

I feel we should not only avoid making any commitments at this time with regard to nonpublication of the memorandum, but that we should also emphasize at every opportunity that the facts brought to the attention of the Argentine Government affect the security of all of the other American republics as well as our own security and that the basic question involved is one which has already appropriately been placed in the hands of the Inter-American Defense Committee in Montevideo.

I know that you will bear in mind in talking with the Argentine Ambassador that the Inter-American Defense Committee has already made public the memorandum covering Axis activities in Chile, and that we could therefore hardly in principle agree to take a more favorable position with regard to Argentina than we have with regard to Chile.

862.20210/2024 : Telegram

The Ambassador in Argentina (Armour) to the Secretary of State

BUENOS AIRES, November 7, 1942—10 p. m.
[Received November 8—6 : 42 a. m.]

2207. Embassy's 2206, November 7, 4 p. m. Following are results of conversation between Minister Interior and Vice Consul English this afternoon.

---

[81] For inquiry, see telegram No. 1659, November 5, 5 p. m., to the Ambassador in Argentina, p. 236.
[82] The marking referred to does not appear on file copy of reply, telegram No. 2194 of November 6, 7 p. m., printed on p. 240.

George Hohenstein von Lug confessed his and Ottomar Müller's guilt probably implicating others. Walter Riewald [*Freiwald*] owns yacht anchored hundred yards from shore in River Plate. From his statements police believe radio transmitter to be aboard but low water precludes their boarding it now; it is under vigilance of guards on shore until water rises. Ottomar Müller arrested. Hans Napp escaped.

It is strange that police raided Napp's home and office November 4th but waited until 6th before trying to make arrest. Embassy had Napp under surveillance all this time and until evening of 6th Napp frequented usual haunts, showed no sign of alarm. Müller and Freiwald also under Embassy surveillance but police finally arrested them.

Culaciati [83] claims radio in possession Hirner not a transmitter.

Culaciati has refused two offers of Embassy to loan Embassy official to cooperate with police. He stated frankly that reason was he did not wish police to know Americans had anything to do with the matter. This implies that memorandum not given to police and that police consequently unable judge importance of matter or intelligently question agents after arresting them. Culaciati exhibits considerable lack of knowledge regarding progress being made. When asked if von Schulz-Hausmann or Thilo Martens arrested answered "many agents have been detained". Hausmann and Martens have much influence in official and social circles.

Several letters obtained from Hausmann P. O. Box not very interesting. One is from P. Lock and Cía. Casilla 1286 Santiago Chile. Buchwald's safe deposit box in National City Bank opened; nothing of interest. Buchwald still at large.

ARMOUR

862.20210/2037 : Telegram

The Ambassador in Argentina (Armour) to the Secretary of State

BUENOS AIRES, November 10, 1942—7 p. m.
[Received 11 : 53 p. m.]

2231. My 2222, November 9, 9 p. m.[84] In a talk with the Minister [85] this evening he informed me (1) that at Cabinet meeting Thursday they propose to discuss prohibition of all code messages by radio for countries without American continent. This would permit messages in clear by radio. Free use of cable by Missions for cipher messages would be permitted, but presumably Axis Governments would not wish to use this medium. Minister felt one of advantages is [*of*]

---

[83] Argentine Minister of the Interior.
[84] Not printed.
[85] The Minister for Foreign Affairs, Enrique Ruiz Guiñazú.

forbidding cipher by radio would be assistance in locating clandestine station.

(2) Minister assured me Minister of Interior and Chief of Police are working vigorously on information furnished our memorandum and hoped we would give them sufficient time to complete investigation before insisting on full publicity. He stated they have 11 men under arrest and incommunicado and are working on 20 other cases. He has urged speed and hopes investigation will be completed within week or 10 days when they propose full publication.

In the meantime he will discuss at Cabinet meeting Thursday statement referred to in Department's 1681 November 7, 9 p. m. announcing fact that reply has been submitted by our Government. I am to see him again Friday afternoon.

ARMOUR

862.20210/2048

Memorandum by the Chief of the Division of the American Republics (Bonsal) [86]

[WASHINGTON,] November 11, 1942.

At lunch yesterday, Dr. García Arias [87] argued eloquently and at length against any further publication of material gathered by this Government concerning espionage and subversive activities in the other American republics. He said that the Argentine authorities are now taking these matters very seriously, but that any publication, directly or indirectly, of data which we had gathered would merely furnish ammunition to extreme nationalist elements to say that, apparently, our own counterespionage activities were carried on with as little regard for Argentine sovereignty as the alleged Axis activities.

I am personally of the opinion that there would be nothing to be gained at this time by having the Committee for Political Defense publish the memorandum we furnished the Argentine Government recently.

PHILIP W. BONSAL

862.20210/2042 : Telegram

The Ambassador in Argentina (Armour) to the Secretary of State

BUENOS AIRES, November 13, 1942—7 p. m.
[Received 7 : 58 p. m.]

2264. Department's 1681, November 7, 9 p. m. I saw Foreign Minister this afternoon and he informed me that he was releasing for

---

[86] Addressed to the Adviser on Political Relations (Duggan) and the Under Secretary of State (Welles).
[87] Argentine Minister in Washington.

publication locally tomorrow morning's papers brief statement regarding memoranda of which following is translation:

"As a result of the request made by our Embassy in Washington, following the public declaration of Under Secretary of State Welles, the Ambassador of the United States has presented to the Foreign Office, in the name of his Government, three confidential memoranda dated November 3,[88] 4 and 10,[89] relating to espionage activities in Argentine territory by agents of the countries of the Axis. The Argentine Government has received this concrete collaboration with satisfaction and has ordered immediate study of this information, which at this moment is the object of active investigation on the part of the police authorities and other appropriate agencies. Buenos Aires, November 13, 1942."

The third memorandum dated November 10 is merely a brief amplification of data included in first two memoranda plus data on Antonio Lopez local cover of Heinz Luning of Cuba.

ARMOUR

862.20210/2045 : Telegram

The Ambassador in Argentina (Armour) to the Secretary of State

BUENOS AIRES, November 14, 1942—3 p. m.
[Received November 14—2 p. m.]

2271. Embassy's 2264, November 13, 7 p. m. In conversation with Foreign Minister last evening he indicated that while he expected that investigation would be completed by the middle of next week, some time would probably be required to examine evidence secured before publication of a summary of this would be possible.

He insisted that eventually, and he hopes as soon as possible, there would be full publicity made of the findings. He seemed to think that Government would appoint a special tribunal (junta) to go over evidence and decide procedure to be used against those incriminated. He said that 18 suspects have thus far been arrested and are being held incommunicado.

Now that a statement has been made public by the Government that our memoranda have been presented the Department may wish to give thought to date for submission of these memoranda to the Defense Committee in Montevideo provided this procedure still being considered. Once Government here informs us that their investigation has been completed there would seem no longer any reason to defer publication unless Argentine Government has some valid

---

[88] See telegram No. 2169, November 3, 9 p. m., from the Ambassador in Argentina, p. 230.
[89] Memorandum of November 4 presumably the memorandum to the Argentine Embassy, p. 231; memorandum of November 10 not found in Department files.

reason why further delay would seem indicated. It might be that if the Government could expedite publication of their findings these could be made simultaneously with publication of our memoranda.

ARMOUR

862.20210/2050 : Telegram

The Ambassador in Argentina (Armour) to the Secretary of State

BUENOS AIRES, November 16, 1942—8 p. m.
[Received 8 : 45 p. m.]

2286. Our 2271, November 14, 3 p. m. Minister of Interior informs me that Foreign Minister has apparently secured President's approval for appointment of military tribunal under the President to investigate Axis activities in Argentina including evidence brought out in our memoranda. Ruiz Guiñazú told Culaciati that he felt such a move would make a good impression in United States.

Culaciati told Ruiz Guiñazú that he was against such a committee as this was a matter falling within the jurisdiction of his Ministry. He hopes to have suggestion quashed. He said move was undoubtedly aimed at Chamber Investigating Committee. Furthermore, he feared officers charged with such duties might be unfavorable to our cause.

I said it seemed to me this made it even more imperative that he should terminate investigation as soon as possible and publish findings even though they might not be in final and complete form, adding I thought it probable my Government would shortly have our memo published. I am to see him again tomorrow morning.

In the meantime report has come to me that Cabinet is this afternoon to discuss question of publication of information contained in our memo and findings resulting therefrom.

ARMOUR

862.20210/2053 : Telegram

The Ambassador in Argentina (Armour) to the Secretary of State

BUENOS AIRES, November 18, 1942—5 p. m.
[Received 8 : 32 p. m.]

2302. Our 2286, November 16, 8 p. m. Napp arrested last night. This due efforts provincial police, not capital police. Happened as follows: provincial police assigned Napp case November 12 after local police failed. Two officers provincial police who have cooperated with us for several months called on Embassy yesterday for advice. We supplied all our information on possible whereabouts Napp and made suggestion as to how search should be conducted.

The officers followed our advice to letter and 6 hours later took Napp into custody at his home.

Provincial police plan to keep Napp's arrest secret for few days until they have secured confession from him. They must deliver him to local police as soon as it is known he is arrested. So far he has admitted connection with Friedrich Kempter and Ottomar Müller and Informadora Rápida but denies knowledge of Rata, Berko, Otis, Koenig. He states he knows Müller attempted to purchase bomb sight from Argentine official. Disclaims knowledge of Walter Freiwald's activities, but knows him. Admits he is agronomist by profession and knows nothing of business matters, stating has lost his shirt on various attempted business deals. Admits he was on propaganda program with Müller over Radio Callao.

ARMOUR

862.20210/2050 : Telegram

The Secretary of State to the Ambassador in Argentina (*Armour*)

WASHINGTON, November 19, 1942—9 p. m.

1762. Your 2286, November 16, 8 p. m., and 2271, November 14, 3 p. m. The Department will continue to give careful consideration to the advisability of publishing the memorandum delivered by you to the Argentine Government regarding Axis activities. However, under present circumstances, it appears that publication in the immediate future by the Montevideo Committee would not be necessary. If the Argentine Government publishes the essential information contained in these memoranda and take effective steps to stop the activities disclosed therein, there would seem to be nothing to be gained by the proposed publication. The attitude of the Department is, therefore contingent upon the steps which the Argentine Government may take and concerning which the Department is confident you will report fully.

HULL

862.20210/2070

The Ambassador in Argentina (*Armour*) *to the Secretary of State*

No. 7408   BUENOS AIRES, November 20, 1942.
                                           [Received November 27 (?)]

SIR: With reference to the Embassy's telegram no. 2302 of November 18, 5 p. m., I have the honor to enclose herewith two memoranda [90] regarding the results of conversations between officers of the Embassy, the Minister of the Interior and the chief of the Argentine secret police.

[90] One of the memoranda not printed.

The memoranda also include additional information regarding the progress made to date by the Argentines in the detention of Axis agents.

It should be mentioned that in spite of the explanation of the Minister of the Interior that he did not desire the Embassy to cooperate with the police because it was not desired that even the police know the Americans were involved in the matter, the Ministry of Foreign Affairs gave a statement to the public explaining that the American Embassy had delivered three memoranda regarding the activities of Axis agents in Argentina and that arrests were being carried out based on the information contained in the memoranda. This would indicate that there is either (1) a serious divergence of opinion among the government leaders as to the action which should be taken against these agents, and that as a consequence some sort of compromise was made, implying that a middle course is being pursued in these investigations whereby it is hoped to arouse neither the ire of Germany or the United States, or (2) it was not desired that the Embassy be in a position to know the intimate details of the investigations being carried out and thus see the inefficiency or lack of sincerity of the Argentine Government. It is possible that a little of both conclusions apply, but the fact that in spite of repeated requests we have not yet received any information of value from the Argentines would indicate that they [at] least wish to cover up some phases of the investigations.

Respectfully yours,

For the Ambassador:
RICHARD FORD
First Secretary of Embassy

[Enclosure]

Memorandum of Conversation, by the Ambassador in Argentina (Armour)

[BUENOS AIRES,] November 9, 1942.

I called on the Minister of the Interior by appointment this afternoon at 3:30. I first handed Dr. Culaciati a list of questions which Mr. English had prepared for use by the police in questioning certain of the Nazi agents mentioned in the memorandum handed to the Government. I also gave him a list of the leading figures mentioned in the memorandum showing that out of 44, only 14 had actually been arrested or detained for questioning. Thirdly, I handed him a list of seven leading firms, only one of which—DIN—had been, to our knowledge, investigated thus far.

I then went on to discuss with Dr. Culaciati the great importance of having the Government proceed vigorously and rapidly in making arrests, searching premises, and in general bringing the case to a head as soon as possible. I told him that my Government was considering publishing the memorandum and that while I was prepared to recommend a delay sufficient for them to make a thorough investigation on the basis of facts presented, it was asking a good deal of my Government to refrain from publication unless they had concrete evidence presented of results to date.

In my presence he called up Galatto, Chief of the Secret Police, and Morano, and told them both that he wished to have as soon as possible a report on the results to date. This he promised me he would send to the Foreign Minister in time for him to give it to me when I called on the latter at 6 p. m. tomorrow.

The Minister told me that the evidence secured to date had been very voluminous and many of the documents in German would require some time for translation. I asked him whether their investigations had been carried into the Province of Buenos Aires, and he replied somewhat evasively to the effect that this was somewhat difficult but pointed to the La Plata raid on Hirner as evidence of some action in the Province.

I asked the Minister whether our memorandum had been shown to the police. He said that it had not, as he did not feel it advisable to let the police know at this time that our Embassy had come into the case. I said that I thought it must be difficult for the police to carry on an intelligent and coordinated investigation without having read the memorandum, and having an opportunity to know how the various elements were co-related.

I was impressed by a total lack of any system in the methods employed by Culaciati, and his whole approach to the question seemed to be superficial and extremely "hit or miss".

N[ORMAN] A[RMOUR]

862.20210/2060 : Telegram

The Ambassador in Brazil (Caffery) to the Secretary of State

RIO DE JANEIRO, November 20, 1942—3 p. m.
[Received 7 : 32 p. m.]

4872. My despatch 8826 of October 22, 1942.[91] Tribunal de Segurança Nacional has imposed the following prison sentences on members of the Schlegel espionage ring: Theodore Friedrich Schlegel 14 years; Gustav Eduard Utzinger, Erwin Backhaus, Nicolau von Dellingshausen, Karl Thielen and Rolf Trautmann, 8 years each.

CAFFERY

---

[91] Not printed.

862.20210/2058 : Telegram

The Ambassador in Argentina (Armour) to the Secretary of State

BUENOS AIRES, November 21, 1942—5 p. m.
[Received 8 : 35 p. m.]

2339. Our 2302, November 18, 5 p. m. Provincial police state that Napp has made one eight-page confession, which has been delivered Minister Interior. Napp admitted practically everything known or suspected of him but steadfastly claimed knew nothing of radio transmitters. Seriously implicates Niebuhr and German Embassy. He said he had not expected arrest, since arrangement had been made with police of Capital through Morano, Chief of Orden Social, to secure his immunity. Was extremely surprised when provincial police showed they were determined to secure confession. We consider it extremely fortunate that provincial police had opportunity to intervene in this matter.

Report on Napp's confession will be sent by next courier.

ARMOUR

862.20210/2061 : Telegram

The Ambassador in Argentina (Armour) to the Secretary of State

[Extracts]

BUENOS AIRES, November 23, 1942—10 p. m.
[Received November 23—9 : 38 p. m.]

2356. Embassy's 2339, November 21, 5 p. m. Minister of the Interior yesterday loaned Embassy copy of police report regarding results up to November 20 of its investigations based on our third memoranda. Practically nothing of value is contained in this 35 page report. As examples it is mentioned that report completely "whitewashes" Thilo Martens and Frederick von Schulz-Hausmann, two of the persons against whom we had large amount of evidence. It appears that the report completely ignored information contained in our third memorandum which gave detailed confessions of two Nazi agents in Brazil who had liaison locally with Martens. Report does mention that Schneider, Müller and Freiwald may be to some extent involved and that they are being held for additional questioning.

. . . .

Schneider, Müller, Schwartz, Freiwald and Hoffmann are still under arrest. Others released except Napp who was delivered to local police only yesterday. Complete report by next courier.

Minister of the Interior informed me November 21 he intended publishing above report either November 23 or November 24. However Napp's confession appears to have completely upset Government's plans, since Minister, when informed by member of Embassy staff yesterday that report of local police extremely disappointing, agreed and stated it would be wise to postpone publication few more days until Napp's surprising confession could be incorporated into the report.

It is believed Argentine Government may have had intention of a permanent first report to show lack of Axis espionage activities and discredit our memoranda, but that unexpected action of provincial police in obtaining confession from Napp called for reorientation of policy.   ARMOUR

862.20210/2066 : Telegram

The Ambassador in Argentina (Armour) to the Secretary of State

BUENOS AIRES, November 25, 1942—6 p. m.
[Received 8 p. m.]

2376.   Our 2356, November 23, 10 p. m.   Minister Interior has loaned Embassy copy Napp's confession to local police.   Provincial police have given us verbal résumé Napp's confession to them.

They differ only in minor items.   They will be forwarded as soon as photographed and translated.   Minister stated today that due Napp's practically complete confession Martin Schneider has begun to confess and has implicated other agents, and that police are now searching for them.

Minister also said Federal Judge would be allowed to decide method of prosecuting those guilty.   He stated they would be deported or interned at the least.

Since Napp's confession authorities appear to be cooperating more closely with Embassy as well as taking more active interest in matter. It appears we have benefitted by withholding publication of memoranda and therefore influencing Argentines to act through threat of publication.   At least we have obtained copies of all pertinent police reports which might not have been obtainable otherwise.

Press has given considerable space to Napp's confession details of which have leaked out gradually, and some papers are clamoring for Niebuhrs and other German diplomat's head.

ARMOUR

862.20210/2071 : Telegram

The Ambassador in Argentina (Armour) to the Secretary of State

BUENOS AIRES, November 28, 1942—6 p. m.
[Received November 29—2 : 23 a. m.]

2401.   Our 2376, November 25, 6 p. m.   Embassy has received several reports Germans preparing counter memorandum exposing activities so-called American agents Argentina. When subject broached to Minister Interior, he did not deny it. Nationalist press has stated that mere fact Americans able uncover German espionage activities is proof that Americans have even larger and more dangerous organization in Argentina. While Germans can have no information of value regarding us or be in a position do material harm; it is possible they could fabricate plausible story which would at the least give local Axis controlled press considerable ammunition with which further to attack us. There is no doubt that Foreign Office would welcome such a memorandum.

In view this possibility it is suggested we consider advisability maintaining in readiness for use some statement based on following: Information contained in memoranda obtained from study of clandestine messages intercepted in United States; statements of German spies arrested Brazil and Chile; statements German spies detained Trinidad; national censorship intercepts; use of monitoring services stationed in United States; commercial credit reports received from legally organized commercial investigating agencies in Buenos Aires. Also may be advisable stress fact that stupidity of German agents themselves in working openly as though they feared no local reprisals proved of considerable help.

ARMOUR

862.20210/2084 : Telegram

The Ambassador in Argentina (Armour) to the Secretary of State

BUENOS AIRES, December 4, 1942—1 p. m.
[Received 3 : 43 p. m.]

2455. Embassy's telegram No. 2414, November 30, 9 [7] p. m.[93] The press announces that the police have terminated their investigations and that accusations of espionage and violation of article 219 of the penal code against eight persons have been made in the court of Federal Judge Jantus. This article provides a penalty of from 1 to 6 years imprisonment for engaging activities which may tend to alter the friendly relations existing between the Argentine Government and any foreign power. The press mentions that such accusations resulted from the three memoranda submitted by our Government and states that since yesterday afternoon Judge Jantus has been conducting cross examinations of the individuals accused.

It is believed that no official announcement will be made before the Minister of the Interior returns from his vacation on December 8.

ARMOUR

---

[93] Not printed.

862.20210/2086 : Telegram

The Ambassador in Argentina (Armour) to the Secretary of State

BUENOS AIRES, December 4, 1942—9 p. m.
[Received December 4—7 : 37 p. m.]

2464. Embassy's 2455, December 4, 1 p. m.   Although this morning's press stated 38 Axis agents had been named in accusations placed before Federal Court, press releases this afternoon named only Hans Napp, Ottomar Müller, Elvezio Ortelli, Martin Schneider, Walter Freiwald and Lothar von Reichenbach as having been indicated in this regard.   Also stated that the Federal Judge had placed them under preventive custody and incommunicado.   In addition the press said that the findings of the court seriously implicated several officials of the German Embassy and that the Federal Attorney had requested that the case of these diplomats be placed before the Supreme Court in accordance with the Argentine code of procedure governing the "trial of diplomatic representatives".   The foregoing indicates that only the agents of Group I have been affected so far.

ARMOUR

862.20210/2071 : Telegram

The Secretary of State to the Ambassador in Argentina (Armour)

WASHINGTON, December 4, 1942—9 p. m.

1894. Your 2401, November 28, 6 p. m.   The Department approves in principle the suggestion contained in the second paragraph of your telegram under reference but believes that any statement which you might have to use in case the counter-memorandum allegedly being prepared by the Germans is presented, should be brief and couched in most general terms and should avoid any expressions or affirmations, however well founded in fact, which might lead to undignified open controversy with the German Embassy or to any protracted airing of charges and countercharges for the edification of the Argentine Foreign Office and public press.   Specifically the Department desires that any reference to monitoring in the United States, to breakdowns of radio intercepts or to censorship intercepts be eliminated.

While in advance of precise knowledge as to what might be the text of the rumored counter-memorandum, it is, of course, impossible to give any final indication as to what the Embassy's statement might contain, it is believed that it might well include one or two paragraphs along the following lines:

"The Government of the United States has both before and after the outbreak of hostilities following the treacherous attack on December 7, 1941, been cooperating loyally and openly with the Governments of the other American Republics with a view to combating the Axis subversive penetration of this Hemisphere which has been aimed at the security of the American peoples equally. The extent and the nature of this poisonous threat has been common knowledge to all of the American governments and was proclaimed in resolutions VI and VII of meeting of Ministers of Foreign Affairs at Havana. That common knowledge moreover formed the basis of the agreements freely entered into by the Ministers of Foreign Affairs of all the American Republics at Rio de Janeiro. In the words of Resolution XVII of that meeting, it was resolved that:

'2. Acts of aggression of a non-military character, including systematic espionage, sabotage and subversive propaganda are being committed on this Continent, inspired by and under the direction of member states of the Tripartite Pact [94] and states subservient to them, and the fate of numbers of the formerly free nations of Europe has shown them to be both preliminary to and an integral part of a program of military aggression;

'3. The American Republics are determined to maintain their integrity and solidarity, in the emergency created by aggression by non-American States, and to give the fullest cooperation in the establishment and enforcement of extraordinary measures of continental defense.'

The activities thus to be combated have been hemisphere-wide in their organization, so that it was deemed necessary at the Rio meeting to establish, as a semi-permanent body, an Emergency Advisory Committee for Political Defense at Montevideo. The choice of a capital in the southern quarter of the Hemisphere is not without significance.

The Government of the United States, conscious of its own responsibilities and in collaboration with the governments of the other American Republics has used its full facilities to inquire into activities, now notorious, of the hemisphere-wide network of Axis subversive organizations, and in so doing has uncovered many traces of enemy activities which have crossed and recrossed national frontiers. For obvious reasons, particularly since the activities of non-American governments directed against the security of the hemisphere still continue, it is impossible for the Government of the United States to make known its sources of information. Moreover, the incredibly brazen methods employed by Axis agents have been a chief contributing factor to their identification. Finally, the Government of the United States takes this occasion to express its profound gratitude for the valuable information with regard to Axis activities and political interventions in this Hemisphere which it has received from all those governments and from numerous private individuals in the other American Republics who recognize the serious Axis threat to their institutions and sovereignty."

Please cable urgently any developments.

HULL

---

[94] Three-Power Pact between Japan, Germany, and Italy, signed at Berlin, September 27, 1940; for text, see League of Nations Treaty Series, vol. cciv, p. 386.

862.20210/2089 : Telegram

The Ambassador in Argentina (Armour) to the Secretary of State

BUENOS AIRES, December 7, 1942—5 p. m.
[Received 9 : 25 p. m.]

2480. Our 2469, December 5th, 2 p. m.[95] Yesterday Minister Interior returned from vacation. He was in very cooperative mood and gave impression anxious continue investigation espionage activities and take vigorous measures against those involved. Federal Attorney Gachepiran has caused very favorable impression. He is young and without professional reputation and appears anxious to use this opportunity to make a name for himself.

Minister Interior said the six spies who have already confessed will certainly receive prison sentences and when asked about the others named in our memoranda but who had not confessed he stated categorically he would expel all of those against whom there was reasonable evidence. He explained that by this he meant that the evidence should be sufficient only to satisfy his own conscience. He said there was no question regarding the expulsion of those so highly involved as von Schulz Hausmann. He stated he could not predict what action the Supreme Court would take regarding the German diplomats but that in any case he would recommend to Foreign Office to declare them *persona non grata*. As a consequence we are gathering data for Minister's confidential information which was not included in our memoranda and otherwise cooperating closely. This would include items such as those mentioned in Department's 844, June 11, 3 p. m. and 890, June 17, 6 p. m.[96] It appears we are at last beginning to obtain to a certain degree the kind of cooperation we have wanted on this particular subject and it is felt we should postpone publication our memoranda at least until Minister has had ample opportunity to make decision regarding those who have not confessed. ARMOUR

862.20210/2102½

Memorandum by the Assistant Chief of the Division of the American Republics (Chapin) [97]

[WASHINGTON,] December 16, 1942.

With regard to current discussion as to the advisability of releasing for publication through the C. P. D.[98] (or otherwise) copies of memo-

[95] Not printed.
[96] Neither printed.
[97] Addressed to Messrs. Bacon, Daniels, and Bonsal of the Division of the American Republics, to Mr. Duggan, Adviser on Political Relations, Mr. Berle, Assistant Secretary of State, and Mr. Welles, Under Secretary of State.
[98] Committee for Political Defense.

randa handed to the Argentine Foreign Office concerning the activities of Nazi spies in Argentina, the following points from the attached Buenos Aires despatch of December 2 [99] are brought to your attention:

(a) Mr. English [1] feels that "there is much more to local espionage organization of the LIR-MAX group than either Napp or the local police would like us to believe";

(b) "It is considered of interest that in the enclosed document no mention is made of Napp's arrangement with the local authorities to avoid arrest, although in his confession to the Provincial Police he outlined this agreement in detail";

(c) With regard to the confessions of four other prominent agents known to the Embassy, "an officer of the Embassy has seen these confessions although he was not permitted to read them through";

(d) Mr. English concludes that the attitude of the authorities creates the impression that the police do not wish to get the truth, but "any kind of explanation", and that it might well not be completely cleared up, and that "several of the more guilty ones would be allowed to go free".

In view of this state of affairs, and of that outlined in the summary of a previous despatch (underlying) [2] and despite subsequent telegrams indicating more intensive action on the part of the authorities, the question is raised now whether it might not be considered desirable to draw a definite deadline for effective action, after which these memoranda will be released to the press and radio. If Chile should break off diplomatic relations with the Axis, a most favorable opportunity may arise to place these alternatives squarely before the Argentine Government, with an expression of the intention to achieve the utmost possible publicity in case these memoranda are released.

SELDEN CHAPIN

862.20210/2106 : Telegram

The Ambassador in Argentina (Armour) to the Secretary of State

BUENOS AIRES, December 17, 1942—9 p. m.
[Received 9 : 45 p. m.]

2579. Department's 1920, December 10, 5 p. m.[3] Lothar Von Reichenbach has been released on 2,000 pesos bail. Press reports arrangements have been made whereby the other five confessed agents will be released upon deposit of same amount, but that Freiwald probably will be unable to meet the requirements. Embassy informed

---

[99] Despatch No. 7551, not printed.
[1] Clifton Paul English, American Vice Consul in Argentina.
[2] Not attached to file copy of this document.
[3] Not printed.

that with the exception of these five all agents who were detained have been set free with admonition that they are subject to recall since investigations are still under way.

ARMOUR

862.20210/2111

The Ambassador in Brazil (Caffery) to the Secretary of State

No. 9468   RIO DE JANEIRO, December 17, 1942.
                                        [Received December 21.]

SIR: With reference to my telegram No. 4872 of November 20, 3 p. m., regarding the sentences imposed on Theodor Friedrich Schlegel, Erwin Backhaus, Nicolau von Dellingshausen, Karl Thielen, Rolf Trautmann and Gustav Utzinger on charges of espionage activities, I have the honor to report that the Tribunal de Segurança Nacional has denied the appeal and reaffirmed the sentences imposed.

Respectfully yours,   For the Ambassador:
                                             JOHN F. SIMMONS
                                             Counselor of Embassy

---

862.20210/2175

Memorandum of Conversation, by the Adviser on Political Relations (Duggan)

[WASHINGTON,] December 22, 1942.

Señor García Arias stated that the Ambassador had requested him to review with me the position of Argentina with respect to publication of the memorandum handed the Minister of Foreign Affairs by Ambassador Armour regarding the presence of Axis activities in Argentina. Señor García Arias added nothing new to the statement of Argentine views. I informed Señor García Arias that this Government did not present the memorandum with publication the prime consideration. Our first interest was in eliminating Axis activity. Although the Argentine Government had gone into certain phases of the activities rather carefully, it had failed to do anything whatsoever regarding other phases. Its record was definitely spotty. We were prepared to give the Argentine Government a fair interval to clean up the situation, just as we had the Chilean Government. No indication could be given now when action might be taken.

Señor García Arias expressed the hope that the Ambassador would be informed before a final decision was taken.

862.20210/2133 : Telegram

The Ambassador in Argentina (Armour) to the Secretary of State

BUENOS AIRES, December 31, 1942—4 p. m.

[Received 9 : 55 p. m.]

2678. Embassy's 2615, December 22, 5 p. m.[4] Minister for Foreign Affairs informs me necessary documents based on Supreme Court request regarding Niebuhr were handed German Chargé d'Affaires on December 24. December 29 Minister called in German Chargé d'Affaires and asked him to hasten his Government's reply as to whether Niebuhr will submit to courts jurisdiction since court begins its summer recess December 31. German Chargé d'Affaires indicated that it might require several days more. The Minister informed me that if German Government consents to Niebuhr waiving immunities Supreme Court is prepared to postpone its vacation to deal with case. If as seems likely German Government refuses Supreme Court then fades out of picture and Government will then decide next step. I said that I presumed this would be to declare Niebuhr *persona non grata* but Minister refused to commit himself.

ARMOUR

---

[4] Not printed; the Ambassador indicated in this telegram the request of the Supreme Court that the Ministry of Foreign Affairs obtain a waiver of diplomatic immunity from Germany with respect to the Naval Attaché, and also the President's refusal to intern those arrested as an infringement of the Court's jurisdiction.

GOOD OFFICES OF THE UNITED STATES TO URUGUAY IN THE RESUMPTION OF DIPLOMATIC RELATIONS WITH THE SOVIET UNION

733.61/58

The Ambassador in Uruguay (Dawson) to the Secretary of State

No. 1183

MONTEVIDEO, June 23, 1942.

[Received July 2.]

SIR: I have the honor to refer to my despatches No. 479 of January 12 and No. 760 of March 23, 1942,[1] concerning the question of the possible resumption of diplomatic relations between Uruguay and Soviet Russia. In the first despatch, I referred to newspaper reports to the effect that the Uruguayan Government was studying the possibility of resuming relations with Russia and I quoted Dr. Guani [2] as stating that personally he thought the question should be given consideration in due course and that he had so informed the President. In my despatch No. 760 of March 23, I reported a conversation in which Dr. Guani told me that he had been urged to take steps looking to the re-establishment of diplomatic relations with Russia and that he was in favor of such action but needed a suitable opportunity or pretext.

Labor organizations have for some time been strongly in favor of the resumption of relations with Russia and there is a growing demand for action in this direction on their part and on the part of Leftist groups. The movement is gathering momentum and on June 18 one of the leading opposition candidates for the Presidency, Dr. Eduardo Blanco Acevedo, came out in *La Razón* with a statement advocating resumption, expressing his admiration and sympathy for Russia, and asserting that he had been opposed to the breaking off of relations. *La Razón* has subsequently published interviews with several prominent citizens who take a similar stand.

As reported in my despatch No. 1181 of June 23,[3] there was held last evening in the Ateneo of Montevideo a meeting to observe the anniversary of Germany's aggression against Russia. The gathering was organized under the auspices of the "Comité Ruso pro-Patria", made up principally of White Russians. In response to an invitation

---

[1] Neither printed.
[2] Alberto Guani, Uruguayan Minister for Foreign Affairs.
[3] Not printed.

from the Committee, the British Minister [4] and I had agreed to attend and to make brief remarks, it being understood that no attempt would be made by the organizers or the speakers to raise the question of the resumption of relations, since this might put us in an embarrassing position with the Uruguayan Government. At the time it was not anticipated that Dr. Guani would attend the gathering. He decided to attend at the last moment and obviously his presence gave the meeting quite a different aspect in so far as any embarrassment to the British Minister and me was concerned.

Dr. Guani received an ovation and as he took his place on the platform the crowd called vociferously for the resumption of relations. Subsequently, yielding to the demands of the audience, he made a very brief speech in which he referred appropriately to Russia's magnificent resistance and stressed Uruguay's consistent condemnation of aggression. Speaking very deliberately, he then remarked that he knew that the audience wished to hear from him on the subject of the resumption of relations. He stated that, while it is true that diplomatic relations are severed, his presence proved that there is no severance but rather a close union of ideals between Uruguay and the Russian people, as well as all other Democratic peoples. In order to bring out the full dramatic effect of his words, I find it necessary to give the Spanish text, which was substantially as follows:

> "Si bien es cierto que hay ruptura de relaciones diplomáticas con Rusia, mi presencia aquí esta noche prueba que no hay ruptura"—

at these words, the audience interpreting them as meaning the resumption of relations, rose to its feet and applauded for several minutes. Dr. Guani then continued—

> "mi presencia aquí esta noche prueba que no hay ruptura sino unión de ideales con el pueblo ruso y todos los pueblos democráticos."

This morning I had occasion to see Dr. Guani and we naturally discussed last evening's meeting. He said that, while he appreciates Russia's role in the war and has every sympathy with the country in its present stand, he still has some misgivings on the score of communism and some apprehension as to Russia's role after the war. He said, however, that the movement in favor of resumption is gaining in strength and that the question is of considerable political importance. Dr. Blanco Acevedo's advocacy of resumption he attributes to vote-catching motives. Dr. Guani obviously considers resumption a distinct possibility, not to say a probability, and he remarked that, when the time came for action along these lines, Uruguay might request the good offices of the United States or of Great Britain as an intermediary. He intimated that Great Britain

---

[4] Ralph Clarmont S. Stevenson.

might perhaps be rather more indicated. From his remarks I did not gather that he has any personal preference for Great Britain but rather that he may feel that if the United States were to act as intermediary the impression might arise that Uruguay's action in resuming relations was being taken at our suggestion. (Reference is made in this connection to my telegram No. 527 of June 23, 7 p.m.[5])

Respectfully yours,   WILLIAM DAWSON

733.61/57 : Telegram

The Secretary of State to the Ambassador in Uruguay (Dawson)

WASHINGTON, June 25, 1942—4 p. m.

385. From the Under Secretary.[6] Your 527, June 23, 7 p.m.[5] The question you raise is one of far reaching importance. It is the hope of this Government, and from present indications it is likewise the belief of this Government, that through continuing and more intimate contacts between the Soviet Government and the Governments of the United Nations, the former will be inclined to abandon its former policies and to join with the governments of the United Nations and those sympathetic thereto in all forms of desirable international cooperation. I assume that the Government of Uruguay will bear fully in mind the desirability before a resumption of relations is agreed upon of having a clearcut and explicit understanding with the Soviet Government regarding nonintervention in the domestic affairs of other nations similar to that concluded with the Soviet Government by this Government in 1933 [7] and similar to the provision included in the recent treaty between Great Britain and the Soviet Union.[8] Should the Uruguayan Government so desire, this Government, of course, would be glad to cooperate in any way desired. [Welles.]

HULL

733.61/59

The Ambassador in Uruguay (Dawson) to the Secretary of State

No. 1209   MONTEVIDEO, June 30, 1942.
[Received July 9.]

SIR: I have the honor to refer to my despatch No. 1183 of June 23, 1942, concerning the movement in Uruguay in favor of the resumption of relations with Russia and a conversation which I had with Dr. Guani on June 23.

---

[5] Not printed; in this telegram the Ambassador asked for instructions to cover a request from Uruguay to act as intermediary (733.61/57).
[6] Sumner Welles.
[7] For the exchange of notes, November 16, 1933, between President Roosevelt and Maxim Litvinov, Soviet Commissar for Foreign Affairs, see *Foreign Relations, 1933*, vol. II, pp. 805–806.
[8] *British and Foreign State Papers*, vol. CXLIV, p. 1038.

Reference is made also to my confidential telegram No. 527 of June 23 for the Under Secretary and to the Under Secretary's reply (Department's telegram No. 385 of June 25).

Yesterday, I conveyed the Under Secretary's views verbally to Dr. Guani. He expressed his appreciation.

He stated that he was of course aware of the desirability of having a very definite understanding regarding non-intervention in the domestic affairs of other countries; that the question was fundamental; and that such an understanding with the Soviet Government must be an essential condition of an eventual resumption of relations.

Dr. Guani said further that he did not intend to precipitate matters and that, before taking any steps looking towards the resumption of relations with Russia, he would consult with the Governments of other American republics. He mentioned in particular in this connection the United States, Brazil, and Chile. He intimated that he would not want Uruguay to be the only South American country to resume relations.

In the course of our conversation, Dr. Guani remarked that the principal, if not the only, reason for considering the resumption of relations with Russia at this time was that country's magnificent military resistance.

On the whole, his remarks yesterday were of a nature to convey the impression that he might be less inclined to take early action than his statements quoted in my earlier despatches would indicate. I believe that the change or apparent change in his attitude is to be attributed to the circumstance that he had in the meantime given the matter more serious thought and was weighing his words more carefully than on former occasions.

Respectfully yours,   WILLIAM DAWSON

733.61/60

The Ambassador in Uruguay (Dawson) to the Secretary of State

No. 1619   MONTEVIDEO, September 22, 1942.
                                        [Received October 1.]

SIR: I have the honor to refer to my despatch no. 1209 of June 30, 1942, and to previous reports concerning the movement in Uruguay in favor of the resumption of relations with Russia.

As reported in my despatch no. 1183 of June 23, the question was brought prominently to the fore in connection with the meeting, attended by Dr. Guani, held in the Ateneo of Montevideo on June 22 to observe the anniversary of Germany's aggression against Russia.

Early in July, a delegation of the organization "Acción Antinazi de Ayuda a los Pueblos Libres" delivered to President Baldomir several albums containing petitions for the resumption of relations with Russia said to bear over twenty thousand signatures. The President was quoted in *La Razón* as having told the delegation that resumption was a measure which was "on its way" (*en marcha*) and that Dr. Guani's statements at the Ateneo on June 22 (my despatch no. 1183) "reflected the Government's sentiments".

While the movement has continued, there were no further developments of any particular interest until early in September when a meeting was held in the Ateneo for the purpose of organizing a "Comité pro-Relaciones con Rusia". According to press reports, the committee has been set up with Dr. Pedro Diaz as Chairman, Dr. Héctor Paysse Reyes as Secretary, and Thomas Richardson Arrieta as Pro-Secretary. Among its members is Dr. Raúl Baethgen who is chairman of the non-partisan committee which has launched the presidential candidacy of Dr. Eugenio J. Lagarmilla.

The "Comité pro-Relaciones con Rusia" plans, it is reported, to issue a manifesto and to conduct a vigorous campaign. Its membership includes in particular persons active in the Ateneo and leaders of the Batllista and Independent Blanco political groups.

Respectfully yours,   WILLIAM DAWSON

733.61/61 : Telegram

The Ambassador in Uruguay (Dawson) to the Secretary of State

MONTEVIDEO, October 20, 1942—4 p. m.
[Received 4 : 45 p. m.]

902. For the Under Secretary. Guani tells me that he telegraphed yesterday to the Uruguayan Ambassador in Washington instructing him to explore with you the question of resuming diplomatic relations with Russia.[10]

On October 13 the committee [11] referred to in my despatch 1619 of September 22 handed him a petition urging resumption.

DAWSON

733.61/64

Memorandum of Conversation, by the Under Secretary of State (Welles)

[WASHINGTON,] October 26, 1942.

The Soviet Ambassador [12] called to see me this afternoon at my request.

---

[10] Pursuant to this request the Uruguayan Ambassador, Juan Carlos Blanco, conferred with the Under Secretary and requested that he approach the Soviet Embassy on the matter. Mr. Welles agreed to do so.

[11] Comité pro-Relaciones con Rusia.

[12] Maxim Litvinov.

I told Mr. Litvinov that I had been requested by the Uruguayan Government, in an entirely unofficial and personal way, to sound out the Soviet Government as to whether the latter would be desirous of renewing diplomatic relations with the Government of Uruguay. I said that I had told the Uruguayan Government that I would be very glad to make this inquiry, and requested Mr. Litvinov to let me know what the feeling of his Government might be.

The Ambassador replied that, while in ordinary circumstances he was already authorized to agree with representatives of the other American Republics upon the establishment of diplomatic relations, he would in this particular case have to inquire of his Government. He reminded me of the ruptured relations between the Government of Uruguay and the Soviet Union in 1935, and said that his Government felt that it had been very badly treated in that instance. He went on immediately to state, however, that he himself felt that incidents of this kind should not be remembered and that diplomatic relations should be resumed. He expressed the highest regard for Dr. Guani, the Uruguayan Foreign Minister, whom he said he had seen much of in Geneva.

S[UMNER] W[ELLES]

733.61/66

Memorandum of Conversation, by the Under Secretary of State
(Welles)

[WASHINGTON,] November 6, 1942.

The Soviet Ambassador called to see me this afternoon at his request. Mr. Litvinov told me that he had received instructions from his Government to inform me that the Soviet Government would be glad to renew diplomatic relations with the Government of Uruguay. He suggested that the Uruguayan Ambassador address a letter to him as by instruction of his Government stating that the Government of Uruguay would be glad to renew diplomatic relations with the Soviet Union. He stated that as soon as he received such a letter he would immediately send a letter in reply stating that the Soviet Union would be very glad to undertake a renewal of diplomatic relations with Uruguay.

I told Mr. Litvinov that I would be very glad to transmit this information immediately to the Ambassador of Uruguay and to the Uruguayan Government.[13]

S[UMNER] W[ELLES]

---

[13] The resumption of relations was effected by an exchange of notes at Washington on January 27, 1943, between the Soviet Ambassador in the United States and the Uruguayan Minister for Foreign Affairs.

BOUNDARY DISPUTE BETWEEN ECUADOR AND PERU

[For previous correspondence on this subject, see *Foreign Relations*, 1941, volume VI. For protocol between Ecuador and Peru regarding peace, friendship, and boundaries (signed also by representatives of the United States, Argentina, Brazil, and Chile), signed at Rio de Janeiro January 29, 1942, see Department of State Executive Agreement Series No. 288, or 56 Stat. (pt. 2) 1818. Correspondence for 1942 regarding the conclusion of this agreement and regarding problems with respect to actual demarcation of the boundary line is not published.]

268

NEGOTIATION OF AGREEMENTS REGARDING A CARIBBEAN LAND-SEA ROUTE THROUGH HAITI AND THE DOMINICAN REPUBLIC

838.154/47a : Telegram

The Secretary of State to the Minister in Haiti (White)[1]

WASHINGTON, June 4, 1942—8 p. m.

170. This Government would like to study, in collaboration with the Haitian Government, the possibility of developing an overland supply route to the eastern Caribbean via Cuba, Haiti, and the Dominican Republic to Puerto Rico and the Virgin Islands, thus reducing shipping to the short hauls connecting the islands. In view of the reduced shipping available within the Caribbean area, such a route might have strategic importance in the conduct of the war. As far as can be foreseen at the present time, such a route would only involve the improvement of existing roadways.

In informing the Foreign Minister of the foregoing would you please ascertain whether his Government would be disposed to collaborate in making this survey, and, if the survey indicates practicability of the idea in improving the existing roadways. You may state that this Government would be prepared to pay all the expenses involved in any improvement work undertaken.

If the reply is in the affirmative, one or more Army engineers will immediately proceed to Haiti to discuss the matter with the Haitian Government.

HULL

838.154/50

The Minister in Haiti (White) to the Secretary of State

No. 1130

PORT-AU-PRINCE, June 6, 1942.
[Received June 9.]

SIR: I have the honor to refer to the Department's urgent telegraphic instruction No. 170 of June 4, 11:00 [*8:00*] p. m., 1942, directing me to enquire whether the Haitian Government was disposed to cooperate in an investigation to be made by American Army

---

[1] The same, *mutatis mutandis*, as No. 164, on the same date, to the Minister in the Dominican Republic.

engineers to ascertain the feasibility of an overland supply route to the Eastern Caribbean.

I mentioned this project to President Lescot yesterday and, in expressing his entire approval, he claimed it practically as his own, since he said that for some time he had contemplated a road from the Môle via Cap-Haïtien to the Dominican frontier at Ouanaminthe, whence it would go presumably to Samaná Bay via Ciudad Trujillo itself. He thought there would only be one short piece of new construction on this road in the neighborhood of Le Borgne.

Subsequent consideration of the problems involved, however, made me think that very possibly the Haitian section of the road should start at Port-au-Prince. There have so far been no submarine attacks within the waters of Port-au-Prince inside of the island of La Gonâve, or, for that matter, between Capes Tiburon and the Môle. The approach of submarines into the waters this side of La Gonâve would be fraught with great additional risks, including the protective artillery now installed in the neighborhood of Port-au-Prince. The additional time of this passage could possibly be used during night travel.

At the Môle there are no kind of installations,—piers, warehouses, etc. Everything would have to be created there.

This morning I spoke to Mr. Walker of the J. G. White Corporation to ask his opinion in regard to road possibilities. He thought that the completion and perfection of the northern road considered by the President would take over a year. He also agreed about the comparative installations at the Môle where there are none and Port-au-Prince where everything is ready to receive traffic. He also pointed out that there is a very tolerable and used road from Port-au-Prince into the Dominican Republic and on the Dominican side the road is better than on the Haitian side.

Asked as to the desirability of constructing a road from Port-au-Prince due east via Barahona, he said that this would be only some twenty kilometers shorter, but would be a saving in grades. On the other hand, in view of the sandy nature of the country through which it would have to pass in Western Barahona, it might be difficult to find an adequate base for the road and that it would take some time to build.

Mr. Walker stated that his company did not have any detailed data in regard to the costs of road building, etc., which I thought might be useful to the Army engineers in case they came here.

Respectfully yours,   J. C. WHITE

839.154/96 : Telegram

The Chargé in the Dominican Republic (Lawton) to the Secretary of State

CIUDAD TRUJILLO, June 9, 1942—2 p. m.
[Received 8 : 18 p. m.]

233. Department's 164, June 4, 8 p. m.[2] The Foreign Minister[3] has just informed me that his Government is deeply interested in project and will gladly cooperate in making survey. The Dominican Government would like to have some of its engineers accompany the American engineers who make the survey and would like copies of the survey report upon completion. In case the result of the survey is favorable the Dominican Government would wish to be consulted beforehand regarding improvement work and also at appropriate time regarding details of supply route.

In discussing this with Despradel I considered it opportune to emphasize great advantages which the overland route would have for the Dominican Republic especially in view of shipping shortage. I feel that the prompt carrying out of this project would be extremely beneficial to our relations with the Dominican Republic in view of the increasing economic depression observable here and the prevailing feeling that the United States has not done very much to relieve the situation.

LAWTON

839.154/96 : Airgram

The Secretary of State to the Minister in the Dominican Republic (Warren)[4]

WASHINGTON, August 7, 1942—1 p. m.

A–22. The Department's telegram no. 164, June 4, 1942[2] and the Legation's telegram no. 233 of June 9, 1942 regarding the projected overland supply route to the eastern Caribbean. Precise details of this project have yet to be worked out but the Army Engineers' survey recommends the route from Port-au-Prince over the existing road system through Azua and Ciudad Trujillo to San Pedro de Macorís as the most desirable one. The Department, therefore, wishes to obtain the approval and cooperation of the governments concerned in the first and most important of the steps to be taken in this joint war effort in the hope that work may commence on the highway in the near future.

[2] See footnote 1, p. 269.
[3] Arturo Despradel.
[4] The same, *mutatis mutandis*, as No. A–25, on the same date, to the Minister in Haiti.

A good many details of the plan remain to be worked out. However, it is desired that you discuss the project with President Trujillo along general lines at an early opportunity pointing out that its realization will not only facilitate the moving of supplies to the eastern Caribbean area but will also be of great value in furnishing a supplementary route for Dominican exports and possibly for imports. The Department is confident, in view of the highly cooperative attitude which President Trujillo has demonstrated that he will wholeheartedly assist in the successful carrying out of this project. The lines along which such assistance might be rendered by the Dominican Government include (*a*) the simplification of formalities covering the storage of through shipments, (*b*) cooperation in permitting the acquisition of available trucks, (*c*) assistance to representatives of the Public Roads Administration or other agency of this Government who may proceed to the Dominican Republic in order to make detailed arrangements for road work. You may indicate that this Government will make provision for extraordinary repairs and maintenance costs resulting from truck movements over Dominican roads under the project.

In discussing this matter with President Trujillo you should state that the Department is not unmindful of the very serious restrictions which have been placed upon the movement of automobiles and trucks in the Dominican Republic due to the shortage of petroleum and petroleum products. Careful consideration is being given to this situation.

HULL

839.154/102 : Airgram

The Minister in the Dominican Republic (Warren) to the Secretary of State

CIUDAD TRUJILLO, August 11, 1942—4 p. m.
[Received August 13—11 : 47 a. m.]

A–35. Reference Department's airgram No. A–22. In a conversation with me this morning President Trujillo gave assurances of his enthusiastic support of the project. With respect to the particular points mentioned by the Department, the President said that he would be glad at any time to issue a decree establishing free ports of entry for transit goods, and that he would guarantee that such goods would not be subjected to any taxes or charges whatsover by the Dominican Government. The President also places the entire rolling stock of the Dominican Republic at our disposal for this project, and assured me that all of the other resources and facilities of his Government would be available to us.

WARREN

839.154/127 : Airgram

The Minister in the Dominican Republic (Warren) to the Secretary of State

CIUDAD TRUJILLO, October 20, 1942—11 a. m.
[Received October 22—3 : 25 p. m.]

A–136. Department's instruction No. 158 October 10.[6] The Foreign Minister told me today that he had given consideration to the draft agreement proposed by our Government [7] and that the Dominican Government would be glad to enter into the agreement except that it will be impossible to assume any expenses which might arise under 4 (a) either this year or in 1943. He said that the Government's financial situation was such that it would be unable to provide raw materials for these projects, and that the road building equipment was so limited that it would not be able to make available any equipment for this work.

Despradel said that if our Government would modify the agreement with respect to these two points the Dominican Government would be glad to accept the text proposed by the Department.

WARREN

839.154/127 : Airgram

The Secretary of State to the Minister in the Dominican Republic (Warren)

WASHINGTON, October 29, 1942—7 : 25 p. m.

A–109. Your airgram A–136, October 20. The plan for highway rehabilitation and construction avoids financial outlay on the part of the Dominican Treasury.

(1) Paragraph 4 (a) of the draft agreement, referring to raw materials such as clay, sand, gravel, stone and timber involves no expenditure but merely the granting of the free use of these materials which are to be found in the river beds and in the terrain along the route of the highway, and likely to be a part of the public domain. Any labor and transportation costs involved in handling these materials would be part of the cost of the project borne by the United States.

The Dominican Government would be expected to make such materials freely available when found on the public domain and to lend its assistance in making them available if found on private property.

---

[6] Not printed.
[7] The draft is almost identical with the signed agreement, printed on p. 276, with the following exceptions: In the signed agreement the amount of money to be provided for the Project is indicated, and in paragraph 4(a) the phrase "from the public domain" is inserted.

The Governments of the other American Republics that have participated in cooperative highway projects have been quite willing to enter into such agreements.

(2) With regard to the clause in Paragraph 4 (*b*) regarding the use of equipment, reference is made to the Legation's despatch no. 1015 of April 9, 1942 [8] and other correspondence concerning the credit of $300,000 granted by the Export-Import Bank of Washington for the purchase of rolling stock and equipment for the Dominican Department of Public Works. Another credit of $100,000 was created for the purchasing of tractors and farm equipment for the Dominican Department of Agriculture. The Department is informed that approximately $200,000 was drawn by the Dominican Government on these two credits during June and July, 1942. Please inform the Department of the amount of machinery and equipment which has now reached the Dominican Republic or which is expected to arrive in the immediate future.

You may already have noted that Paragraph 4 (*b*) is reasonably flexible as it stipulates that there should be supplied for use on the project "such of the equipment owned by the Government of the Dominican Republic as it may be possible to make available for this work." The contribution of the Dominican Government would be to allow the use of equipment already owned by it. Part of this project is the improvement and maintenance of an existing highway from San Pedro de Macorís to Elías Piña. Since in any case, it is assumed that a budgetary allowance is made by the Dominican Government for that work, it appears that this sum could be applied to any expenses incurred under Paragraph 4 and that no undue dislocation of the Dominican budget would result. In view of manufacturing and shipping difficulties the Public Roads Administration has indicated its intention to use as little heavy equipment and machinery as possible.

Will you please discuss these points with the appropriate Government officials and inform the Department by airgram of the results of your conversations?

HULL

839.154/127 : Telegram

The Secretary of State to the Minister in the Dominican Republic
(*Warren*)

WASHINGTON, November 2, 1942—6 p. m.

346. Department's airgram A–109, and your A–136 regarding highway rehabilitation agreement. The Department feels that the two

---

[8] Not printed.

governments are in substantial agreement on all material points and that the draft, as presented, should be signed at once.

Immediately upon its acceptance an engineer from the Public Roads Administration will go forward and funds will be made available. It is desired to put a large number of men at work on the Morne a Cabrit road at the earliest possible moment.

HULL

839.154/132 : Telegram

The Minister in the Dominican Republic (Warren) to the Secretary of State

CIUDAD TRUJILLO, November 3, 1942—1 p. m.
[Received 4 : 33 p. m.]

480. Department's 346, November 2, 6 p. m., and A–109 and my A–136. Immediately after receipt of Department's 346 this morning I had an entirely informal conversation with the Secretary of State for the Presidency. He agreed that the Dominican Government will supply all procurable raw materials from the public domain and will make available any public roads or Department of Agriculture equipment possible. He told me that two purchases were made against the credit of $200,000 drawn by the Dominican Government in June and July 1942 comprising two Loraine excavators. They have not arrived and there is no indication when they may arrive. No other purchases of equipment for Public Works or the Department of Agriculture have been completed under the two credits noted in the Department's A–109.

Following this conversation I called this morning also on the Foreign Minister about the same matter. He told me his Government will sign the draft subject to the following change of language in B–4a "all needed raw materials locally procurable from the public domain such as clay, sand, gravel, stone and timber."

If the Department will authorize this change in language, I shall deliver him the revised draft immediately thereafter.

WARREN

839.154/132 : Telegram

The Secretary of State to the Minister in the Dominican Republic (Warren)

WASHINGTON, November 5, 1942—10 p. m.

348. Your telegram 480, November 3, 1 p. m. You are authorized to close road agreement including Clause B–4a as stated in penultimate paragraph your telegram. Insert $200,000 in blank in para-

graph A 1 page 2. Forward signed original. Please telegraph best estimate of number of kilometers of unbuilt portion of Lago Enriquillo route which will be on public domain.

HULL

839.154/133 : Telegram

The Minister in the Dominican Republic (Warren) to the Secretary of State

CIUDAD TRUJILLO, November 9, 1942—6 p. m.
[Received 9 : 42 p. m.]

492. Department's telegram No. 348, November 5, 10 p. m. Road agreement concluded today. In accordance with the request of Despradel it was signed by him and by me. Original being forwarded by air mail pouch tomorrow.

Estimate of unbuilt portion on public domain cannot be obtained except through extensive research requiring at least several weeks but it is believed to be considerable.

WARREN

839.154/126

Memorandum of Understanding Between the Dirección General de Obras Públicas and the Public Roads Administration Concerning the Rehabilitation of Certain Dominican Roads, Signed at Ciudad Trujillo, November 9, 1942 [9]

AGREEMENT made this 9th day of November 1942, by and between the Dirección General de Obras Públicas of the Dominican Republic, represented by H. E. Arturo Despradel, Secretary of State for Foreign Affairs, and the United States Public Roads Administration, represented by H. E. Avra M. Warren American Minister at Ciudad Trujillo,

WITNESSETH THAT:

WHEREAS, the Governments of the Dominican Republic and of the United States are desirous of cooperating in maintaining and reconstructing certain roads and highways that are of importance for the transportation of supplies during the existing emergency and other purposes in facilitating the joint war effort, and

---

[9] The Memorandum of Understanding between the United States and Haiti, signed at Port-au-Prince November 30, 1942, is, *mutatis mutandis*, substantially the same as the one with the Dominican Republic, except in the case of Haiti the Public Roads Administration agreed to provide funds not exceeding $150,000 for expenditure on the project rather than $200,000 as in the case of the Dominican Republic.

WHEREAS, the hauling of supplies will involve the use of certain city streets en route and the road and route from San Pedro de Macorís to the frontier of the Haitian Republic via Ciudad Trujillo, Azua, Cabral and southward of Lago Enriquillo to the terminal of the road from Fond Parisien at the Haitian-Dominican frontier; and of the road from Azua to the frontier via San Juan and Elías Piña, and

WHEREAS, economy in hauling as well as the conservation of tires and gasoline will require construction and some rehabilitation of these roads and the general improvement of their surfaces with some betterment of stream crossings, cross drainage, ditches, such rehabilitation, improvement and betterment being sometimes hereinafter referred to as the "Project";

Now THEREFORE, the following terms and conditions of cooperation are agreed to by the Public Roads Administration of the United States of America and by the Dominican Dirección General de Obras Públicas.

(A) the Public Roads Administration undertakes as follows:

(1) to provide from funds which have been or may hereafter be made available to it for this purpose the sum necessary not exceeding two hundred thousand dollars ($200,000.00) which will be available for expenditure as may be required on the Project including for such construction, rehabilitation and improvement of the above mentioned roads as will serve to facilitate heavy hauling over them, and to maintain them in satisfactory condition.

(2) To exercise the general authority conferred on it to administer the funds allotted to the Project by the approval of the quality and integrity of the work performed.

(3) To provide a Resident Engineer and an Auditor who shall act under the direction of the Public Roads Administration, and whose compensation and expenses shall be charged to an allotment for engineering supervision and administration set aside for this purpose. The Resident Engineer will render engineering services and at all times will cooperate fully to maintain rapid and economical construction of the Project and to obtain its early completion.

(4) To act for the Government of the Dominican Republic without charge as Purchasing Agent in the United States if so requested in the purchase of all supplies, materials and equipment required for use on this work in order that the Dominican Republic may have the benefit, so far as practicable, of all discounts, special rates, priority classifications, and any and all of the advantages that may accrue from such action.

(5) To approve and certify claim vouchers submitted by the Dirección General de Obras Públicas of the Dominican Republic periodically for work satisfactorily accomplished subsequent to the date of

the execution of this Agreement. Claim vouchers for payment shall be on Standard Form PR 20 (Revised) approved by the Comptroller General of the United States, which will be furnished the Government of the Dominican Republic for its use. Said vouchers shall be executed by the Dirección General de Obras Públicas of the Dominican Republic, and certified by the Resident Engineer of the Public Roads Administration.

(B) The Dominican Republic, represented by the Dirección General de Obras Públicas undertakes, on its part, as follows:

(1) To rehabilitate the roads hereinabove mentioned in accordance with plans, cross sections, and other information to be provided by the Resident Engineer.

(2) To maintain accounts which shall be open at all times to inspection, examination, or audit by the representatives of the Public Roads Administration, and to accept audit on the basis of all pertinent laws, applicable regulations, and any other agreements pertinent to this work.

(3) To permit and facilitate inspection and examination by any authorized representative of the Public Roads Administration of all records, construction work in progress or completed, and the checking of all claims as shown on certificates or vouchers submitted as the basis for payment.

(4) To permit the supply for use on the Project without cost to the United States (a) all needed raw materials locally procurable from the public domain such as clay, sand, gravel, stone and timber; and (b) such of the equipment owned by the Government of the Dominican Republic as the Dirección General de Obras Públicas finds it may be possible to make available for this work.

(5) To hold the United States and its employees harmless and protect them against claims of third parties for personal injuries or property damage which may occur in connection with any operations deemed necessary or desirable in respect of the Project.

(6) To waive all duties, import taxes, or any other special or ordinary assessments applicable to the importation of any materials, supplies or equipment brought into the Republic as a result of purchases made by the Public Roads Administration, as outlined in this agreement or applicable to the importation of necessary supplies and equipment for conducting the surveys and for the maintenance of an administrative office by the Public Roads Administration.

(7) To provide all rights of way that may be required in connection with the necessary rehabilitation of these roads, or in constructing approved relocations mutually agreed to be required to improve hauling conditions, or for the purpose of obtaining materials to be used on the Projects, without expense to the United States.

(8) To accept payment for the work on an agreed schedule of prices per kilometer, arranged in advance with the Resident Engineer. In establishing the price per kilometer it is agreed that it will be based on the estimated cost of labor, materials (except as provided in (*b* 4)) above, supervision and project engineering actually employed or used on the work, but not including any of the cost of operating the Dirección General de Obras Públicas.

IN WITNESS WHEREOF the Dirección General de Obras Públicas of the Dominican Republic and the Public Roads Administration have caused this Memorandum of Understanding to be duly executed as evidenced by their signatures below.

Dirección General de Obras Públicas
By: A. DESPRADEL
Secretary of State for Foreign Affairs

The Public Roads Administration
By: AVRA M. WARREN
Commissioner
American Minister at Ciudad Trujillo DR

Signed this 9th day of November, 1942.

ANGLO-AMERICAN COOPERATION ON POLICIES AND PROBLEMS CONNECTED WITH THE PROCLAIMED AND STATUTORY LISTS IN THE EASTERN AND WESTERN HEMISPHERES [1]

740.00112A European War 1939/5876

Memorandum by the Office of the Assistant Secretary of State

[WASHINGTON,] January 5, 1942.

PROPOSED POSITION ON PROCLAIMED LIST FOR OTHER AMERICAN REPUBLICS

The question has been under consideration as to what modifications, if any, should be adopted in our Proclaimed List policies and procedures in respect to the American republics which declare war against or break off all relations with the Axis.

With a view to formulating an agreed position on the question for the present, it is proposed:

1.) That our objective continue to be the sterilization, or, wherever feasible, the elimination of Axis financial and economic influences in the hemisphere.

2.) That we recognize the necessity of receiving the cooperation of the American republics in order to realize this objective fully by encouraging them to adopt local control measures against pro-Axis elements.

3.) That to this end we should be prepared to consult with these governments on additions to and deletions from the Proclaimed List on a basis which will enlist the full cooperation of these countries without surrendering our freedom to act independently whenever the local measures may prove ineffective.

4.) That such joint consultations on proposed additions to the Proclaimed List should be confined to those nations which declare war on or break off all relations with the Axis and that with respect to such nations the consultations may include a joint review of cases now on the list with a view to making deletions on the basis of specific control or clean-up measures instituted by the local government.

Governments not declaring war on or breaking off all relations with the Axis will not be consulted generally on either additions or deletions, but may be consulted on specific cases proposed for deletion

---

[1] For additional correspondence with particular reference to the Proclaimed List program in the Western Hemisphere, see page citations under "Proclaimed List" in Index of this volume and also in that of volume VI. See also W. N. Medlicott, *The Economic Blockade*, vol. II (London, Her Majesty's Stationery Office, 1959), especially pp. 124–152, for an official British account.

if a satisfactory solution is dependent upon or would be facilitated by cooperation of the local government.

5.) That within the scope of such joint consultations the Proclaimed List should be maintained for the present in all the American republics.

6.) That the standards which have been applied heretofore on making additions to the Proclaimed List, i.e.; identification, directly or indirectly, with Axis activities or interests, regardless of nationality, shall continue to be applied in proposing additions to the Proclaimed List.

7.) That we be prepared to forego the addition of many cases to the list where the government consulted requests that such action not be taken and itself takes prompt and positive steps to control or remedy the condition which would otherwise have resulted in listing.

8.) That with respect to countries eligible for consultation we recognize the probable necessity of relaxing our present standards on deletions somewhat in order to permit a fair trial of the cooperative formula and in the case of *certain nationals* of those countries to permit greater experimentation with a "parole" policy, i.e., of making the deletion conditioned upon satisfactory future conduct.

9.) That we reserve the explicit right to list any firm or person which fails to meet or to comply with specified conditions agreed upon by the governments.

10.) That the foregoing statement of position be communicated privately, without publicity, to the interested governments as circumstances may dictate.[2]

11.) That the British and Canadian governments be consulted and their agreement to this position be sought.[3]

740.00112A European War 1939/4979 : Telegram

The Secretary of State to the Ambassador in the United Kingdom
(*Winant*)

WASHINGTON, January 7, 1942—10 p. m.

74. Please telegraph following instruction to American missions Sweden, Switzerland, Spain, Portugal, Turkey.

"Strictly confidential circular from Department.

1. Reference Department's strictly confidential circular telegram of December 15, 1941 and your reply thereto. After careful consideration Department has decided to proceed with publication of Proclaimed List for Sweden, Switzerland, Spain, Portugal and Turkey as proposed. The list for these countries will probably be published in about two weeks and the list will include all cases then on British statutory list for these countries and possessions. British Embassy here is supplying Department with cases which have been or will be deleted from British list. These will be omitted from Proclaimed List.

---

[2] See circular telegram of January 28, 11 p.m., p. 285.
[3] See Medlicott, *The Economic Blockade*, vol. II, p. 144.

2. For present American Embassy London through our observer on M.E.W.[5] Black List committee will act as primary coordination point for our lists on European cases. You are requested to consult closely with your British colleague on all future additions to and deletions from list. He has been instructed to include your views on each case in forwarding his recommendations to London. You are also requested to forward your views and information on such cases to the Department and to send a copy of all such reports to American Embassy London. On any cases on which you disagree with your British colleague you should telegraph your views to the American Embassy at London.

3. Department desires to make future changes in our list for European cases on basis of additions to and deletions from British statutory list. It is expected that close cooperation between the respective missions and between M.E.W. and American Embassy in London will avoid many disagreements on particular cases. Any such disagreements will for present be referred by American Embassy London to Washington for decision.

4. Unless you specifically recommend otherwise on particular cases we will not require independent undertakings from firms on deletion from list but will rely on undertakings received by British. You may suggest terms for inclusion in such undertakings to your British colleague and to American Embassy at London.

5. We contemplate using British Black as distinguished from Statutory List as basis for our confidential list on European cases and you are requested also to consult with your British colleague on cases proposed for such confidential lists. When recommended by you we may include cases on our confidential list which are not on the British black list but as stated above we desire to keep the two published lists entirely harmonious."

Please advise Department if foregoing instruction requires any change in your opinion. You may from time to time communicate directly with the interested American missions to clarify these matters.

HULL

740.00112A European War 1939/6205 : Telegram

The Ambassador in the United Kingdom (Winant) to the Secretary of State

LONDON, January 16, 1942—6 p. m.
[Received January 16—12 : 35 p. m.]

239. 1. Ministry Economic Warfare has asked the Embassy if it could ascertain within the next few days the Department's policy, since Japan's entry into the war, in considering firms of Japanese

---

[5] British Ministry of Economic Warfare.

nationality or race for inclusion in the Proclaimed List. MEW tends to consider the question of race more important in the cases of Japanese than in the cases of Germans or Italians. However, it recognizes the impracticability of carrying every small Japanese trader in the American Republics on the Statutory List. MEW seems to feel that its policy on the nationality factor may not be entirely appropriate for Japanese if adhered to strictly as in the case of Germans and Italians.

2. MEW proposes to accede to the request of the Netherlands Government to send an observer to the Blacklist committee meetings.

WINANT

740.00112A European War 1939/5342½ : Telegram

The Secretary of State to the Ambassador in the United Kingdom
(Winant)

WASHINGTON, January 20, 1942—5 p. m.

232. Reference Department's no. 93 of January 8, 1942.[6]

1. We have discussed with Noel Hall [7] of British Embassy here our desire to have the coordination of British and American listing policies and procedures divided between London and Washington on the basis of having the European cases handled in London and the Western Hemisphere cases handled in Washington. We are satisfied that desired expedition and unity of action can best be secured in this manner.

2. We have already authorized you to represent us with the Black List committee for the purpose of coordinating our lists on European cases and we are prepared to follow the decisions on such cases which you reach in your deliberations with that committee, subject to your reference to Washington for the present of any cases on which you and the committee are unable to reach agreement with the views of the American mission concerned. Whenever necessary you are authorized to communicate directly with our missions in Europe in order to reach agreement on particular cases.

3. We understand from Noel Hall that the general question of having MEW give the British Embassy here more autonomous authority on Western Hemisphere cases will probably be considered at the meeting of the Black List Committee on Thursday, January 22. Before this meeting the Department desires you, if possible, to discuss the matter with the appropriate responsible officials and to inform such officials that you are now authorized to extend an invitation to

---

[6] Not printed; it dealt with various aspects of Anglo-American cooperation on Proclaimed List procedures.
[7] Noel F. Hall, in charge of economic warfare matters at the British Embassy with rank of Minister.

have representatives of the British Embassy here participate fully in the regular bi-weekly meetings of the Proclaimed List Committee. You are authorized to suggest and in your discretion to urge strongly that such participation will only result in the desired increase in expedition and unity of action if the British participant on the committee is generally given the same broad authority on Western Hemisphere cases as you have on European cases as stated in paragraph 2 above. Please report fully.[8]

HULL

740.00112A European War 1939/6205 : Telegram

The Secretary of State to the Ambassador in the United Kingdom (Winant)

WASHINGTON, January 20, 1942—9 p. m.

236. Your 239 of January 16. Since entry into the war we have also considered question of nationality more important in case of Japanese than in cases of Germans and Italians proposed for Proclaimed List. Our present policy is generally to list all Japanese nationals who are engaged in business in American republics and who are recommended for inclusion on list by our missions. In cases involving Germans and Italians the Proclaimed List Committee continues to require information indicating direct or indirect identification with pro-Axis activities. Although many Japanese cases involve small traders we have not so far had an excessively large number of cases to consider and for the present the recommendations of our missions on Japanese cases are being followed without any instructions from the Department with respect to selection according to size of business.

HULL

740.00112A European War 1939/7039

Memorandum of Conversation, by the Assistant Secretary of State (Acheson)

[WASHINGTON,] January 27, 1942.

The Swedish Minister, Mr. Boström, called at his request. He told me that he had been instructed by his Government to protest against the extension of the Proclaimed List to include Swedish firms. He

---

[8] In telegram No. 336, January 23, 1942, 8 p.m., Ambassador Winant reported that the Ministry of Economic Warfare agreed to all points raised in this telegram (740.00112A EW 1939/6499).

On January 29, British and Canadian representatives began participating in the work of the Proclaimed List Committee.

said that upon receipt of this instruction, he had reminded his Government that he had made a similar oral protest last summer at the time of the President's proclamation creating the Proclaimed List and also reminded his Government that names upon our Proclaimed List did not go beyond the British list and included only firms which were subsidiaries of or agents for German companies. He had asked for permission to make an oral protest rather than a written one.

We discussed the matter briefly. The Minister said that he was sure each Government understood the position of the other; that he did not wish to inaugurate any controversy, but merely requested that I make a minute of his call for purposes of the record. He asked that no written reply be made.

DEAN ACHESON

740.00112A European War 1939/6749b : Circular telegram

The Secretary of State to Diplomatic Representatives in the American Republics

WASHINGTON, January 28, 1942—11 p. m.

1. Department postponed publication of forthcoming revision of Proclaimed List and further supplements pending current developments and clarifications.

2. Revision one of Proclaimed List consolidating original list and seven supplements to date will be published about February 7. All new deletions approved since Supplement No. 7 will be reflected in the Revision. No new additions will be made in this Revision. However, numerous changes in firm titles, form of listings, spelling, addresses and other corrections are made. The listing arrangement is changed to use of mail address form for most firm titles. Cross references previously contained in parentheses are eliminated and given separate alphabetical listings. Cross indexing generally eliminated except for few special situations. These changes may cause some erroneous impressions that new additions, and deletions other than those specified, have been made but close comparison with superseded original list and supplements will show changes merely reflect new arrangement, or correction of names of firms or persons previously included on list. A few apparently meaningless firm titles have been eliminated entirely.

3. Magnitude of revision task may result in some new errors or inaccuracies and continuance of others, but after careful study Department is satisfied changes made will provide more satisfactory list for future operations. It is essential that in the future all firm titles should be reported in full mail address form.

4. New deletions to be reflected in Revision will be telegraphed shortly. Revision is now in proof.

5. Air mail instructions are being sent covering names approved by Committee for addition to Proclaimed List in next supplement, which will be Supplement No. 1 to Revision one.

6. Beginning with this supplement if the government to which you are accredited has broken all Axis ties you are authorized, if you consider it desirable and feasible, to consult with appropriate officials concerning cases being proposed for addition to list. In your discretion you may explain that although it is necessary to continue Proclaimed List control policies in order to assure hemispheric defense interests and in order to facilitate channeling of available essential goods to friendly persons and firms in American republics we desire to consult and cooperate closely on these matters with interested governments which are committed to positive cooperation against Axis aggressions.

7. Where consultation on proposed additions results in government's request that specific cases not be listed we are prepared to consider foregoing listing provided prompt and effective measures are taken by government to eliminate inimical elements from firm and to assure future satisfactory supervision of firm's activities. On all such cases full reports should be promptly forwarded to Department. Similarly we may in appropriate cases delete certain firms on basis of satisfactory corrective action being taken by government or the firm. Consultation procedure is particularly applicable to native citizens of American republics. Further instructions will be air mailed shortly. Please telegraph your views regarding consultations on these matters with government to which you are accredited before undertaking such consultations.

8. Supplement No. 1 will not be published until missions have had opportunity for such local consultations on pending additions as seems feasible and desirable. Since this will require several weeks delay all cases recommended for addition to Proclaimed List are placed temporarily on confidential list until supplement is published.

9. British and Canadian representatives are now participating regularly on Proclaimed List Committee. Arrangements are being developed for having coordination of lists for Western Hemisphere handled in Washington and lists for other areas coordinated in London through MEW Blacklist Committee on which we are now represented. Effective coordination of lists here requires closest coordination and cooperation with British in field.

HULL

740.00112A European War 1939/7065a : Telegram

The Secretary of State to the Ambassador in the United Kingdom (Winant)

WASHINGTON, February 5, 1942—1 p. m.

431. In reply to inquiry of British Embassy here concerning Department's position on the listing of French firms situated outside occupied and unoccupied France, we have orally advised the Embassy as follows:

1. We are prepared to include on the Proclaimed List for European countries all cases of French firms which the British include on the Statutory List after consultation with our local mission and with you. We understand that the British policy is generally to list such firms which refuse to give undertakings not to accept direction or control from France; not to remit money to France; and not to trade with or on behalf of the enemy. We have expressed the hope that this policy would not result in the indiscriminate listing of French firms which decline to give such undertakings if the firm was not actually engaged in inimical activities. The case of Orosdi-Back in Turkey was discussed with us and while we doubted the apparent necessity for listing this firm in Turkey we stated that we would not object if MEW considered it necessary.

2. We advised the Embassy that we had no objection to the British continuing to request such undertakings from French firms since this was a matter for their decision but that we could not associate ourselves with such undertakings.

3. We informed the Embassy that we did not consider it advisable for the British to request undertakings from French firms located in this country and that we would exercise such control of these firms as seemed necessary.

HULL

740.00112A European War, 1939/8383

The Minister in Ireland (Gray) to the Secretary of State

No. 275

DUBLIN, February 9, 1942.

[Received March 10.]

SIR: I have the honor to refer to the Department's strictly confidential mimeographed instruction of October 17, 1941, File No. 740.00112A European War 1939/2776A, concerning the proposed extension of the proclaimed list of certain blocked nationals to countries outside the other American republics and, in reply thereto, to submit the following:

1. At the present time, so far as can be learned, there is no German-, Italian- or Japanese-owned firm importing goods from the United

States, exporting goods to the United States, or acting as an agent for American firms; and the only firms in Eire known to be pro-Axis are either German, Belgian, Irish or of undetermined nationality.

2. All imports into Eire, except those from the British Empire, are required to be covered by British navicerts.

3. All exports from Eire, except those to the United States or the British Empire are required to be covered by British navicerts. Although vessels of Irish registry ply between ports in Eire and ports in Spain and Portugal, on their outward-bound voyages from Eire they invariably proceed to a port in South Wales where they are subjected to examination by the British authorities and take on cargoes of coal for Lisbon and Gibraltar; as a general rule they sail from Eire in ballast, although on occasion they have been known to carry luggage belonging to officials of foreign governments. Thus, it is practically impossible at the present time for any item exported from Eire to find its way to an Axis country, or be utilized for the benefit of an Axis country. Vessels of Irish registry proceeding to the United States and vessels of other registry departing from Eire are, of course, subject to British control and frequently sail under British convoy.

4. A careful investigation has been made here with a view to ascertaining the names of all firms which might, under the terms of the Department's instruction under reference, be included in an extension of the proclaimed list of blocked nationals or a confidential blacklist. The results of this investigation are embodied in the enclosed list of firms,[11] in the preparation of which careful consideration has been given to the strictly confidential instruction to offices in the American Republics, dated August 28, 1941, and the chart appended thereto, which were received as enclosures to the Department's circular instruction under reply. While all firms named in the enclosure are listed in current British Statutory Rules and Orders, sources other than local British officials have been consulted in the preparation of the list.

5. No American-controlled enterprise in Eire is known to have any affiliations, connections or ideological sympathies with Axis powers, firms or agencies. A list of firms in which American capital is known to be invested will be found in the following reports from the American Consulate General, Dublin: Report No. 76, dated August 6, 1941, entitled "United States Investments in Eire" and despatch No. 620, dated August 12, 1941, bearing the same title.[12]

6. The inclusion in an extension of the proclaimed list or in a confidential black list of the names appearing in the enclosure hereto would not have any serious adverse effects upon Eire's national economy, since the firms in question are already included in the British list and consequently barred from participation in foreign trade transactions.

7. I do not believe any serious political consequences in respect of Irish-American relations would result from the publication of the names of such firms in a proclaimed list or confidential black list.

The factual information for this despatch and the enclosure hereto have been furnished by Mr. Francis H. Styles, who is assigned to

---

[11] Not printed.
[12] Neither printed.

Dublin as Second Secretary of Legation and Consul in Charge of the Consulate General. The American Consul at Cork has, of course, been consulted.

As further data become available, the Department will be informed. For completeness of reference, I have the honor to cite in this connection the Department's circular telegraphic instruction of July 24, 5 p. m.,[13] and the Legation's telegraphic reply thereto, No. 79 of July 29, 1 p. m.[14]

Respectfully yours,

DAVID GRAY

740.00112A European War, 1939/10509 : Telegram

The Chargé in the United Kingdom (Matthews) to the Secretary of State

LONDON, April 23, 1942—10 a. m.
[Received April 23—5 : 30 a. m.]

2088. Department's 93, January 8,[14] stating Department considering extension of Proclaimed List to Iran and Iraq in near future and last paragraph Embassy's despatch 3053, March 10.[14] Of the other territories where the Statutory List but not the Proclaimed List is applicable (Afghanistan, Andorra, Eire, Liberia, Liechtenstein, Spanish Morocco and Tangier) Embassy believes that Liechtenstein, Spanish Morocco and Tangier are the most important insofar as the immediate extension of the Proclaimed List is concerned. Numbers of cases from those areas have been recently considered by the Black List Committee which in deciding them has expressed a desire for the concurrence of the American representatives in the field. Will the Department, therefore, kindly telegraph list of territories to which the Proclaimed List will be extended in the near future?[15] There have also been some cases from Spanish and Portuguese possessions in Africa—particularly Angola—where although the Proclaimed List applies the United States does not maintain Foreign Service establishments.

MATTHEWS

---

[13] Not printed; this circular telegram to certain missions and consular offices instructed offices to prepare and forward a list of the names of all German, Italian, and Japanese firms which were acting in the capacity of agents for United States concerns or which were relatively large importers of American goods or exporters to the United States (740.00112A EW 1939/188a).

[14] Not printed.

[15] Telegram No. 2197, May 15, 1942, midnight, to the Ambassador in the United Kingdom, stated that the Department was considering extension of the Proclaimed List to certain of these countries but was not yet prepared to take such action.

740.00112A European War, 1939/11961f : Circular telegram

The Secretary of State to Diplomatic Representatives in the American Republics

WASHINGTON, May 25, 1942—10 p. m.

There are increasing indications that Falange members and pro-Vichy French are serving Axis interests in American republics. Accordingly these groups should be considered for inclusion Proclaimed List in appropriate cases.

In Falange cases consideration should be given to local circumstances and recommendations generally confined to leaders and active members who are believed to be pro-Axis.

In Vichy French cases recommendations should be confined generally to (1) firms controlled from occupied France; (2) persons or firms supporting Vichy–Axis collaboration policies and (3) any firm currently remitting funds to or trading with Vichy except under circumstances believed exceptional and not calculated to aid Axis.

Please forward air mail reports covering current status of Falange and Vichy French situations with respect to pro-Axis activities and need for Proclaimed List action.

HULL

740.00112A European War, 1939/10509 : Telegram

The Secretary of State to the Ambassador in the United Kingdom (Winant)

WASHINGTON, June 19, 1942—4 p. m.

2818. Reference Department's telegram no. 2197, May 15, 1942.[17] All cases on Statutory List for Iran and Iraq will be included on Proclaimed List in supplement about June 20. Department has telegraphed these missions concerning standard procedures on these matters.

We will also include in this supplement Statutory List cases for Andorra and Liechtenstein. Please make such arrangements with American missions in Spain and Switzerland as seem advisable to you for handling the few future cases which may be involved for these areas.

HULL

---

[17] Not printed, but see footnote 15, p. 289.

740.00112A European War, 1939/11961f Suppl. : Circular airgram

The Secretary of State to Diplomatic Representatives in the American Republics [18]

WASHINGTON, July 16, 1942—6 p. m.

Reference Department's circular telegram of May 25, 1942 relating to Proclaimed List policy with respect to Vichy French firms. The following is a recapitulation and clarification of the Department's position at the present time on the listing of French firms operating in neutral countries:

1. Firms presently controlled from occupied France should be recommended for the Proclaimed List.

2. In the absence of positive evidence of pro-democratic sympathies, firms controlled from unoccupied France should be recommended for the confidential list but upon any evidence of pro-Axis sympathies or activities should be recommended for the Proclaimed List. Firms controlled from unoccupied France which furnish an undertaking to the British in the form prescribed by M.E.W. for French controlled firms should not be recommended for inclusion or if presently included should be recommended for deletion.

3. Any firm of any nationality supporting Vichy–Axis collaboration policies should be recommended for inclusion in the Proclaimed List.

4. Any firm of any nationality currently remitting funds to or trading with occupied or unoccupied continental France or holding active agencies of firms located in that territory should be recommended for inclusion in the Proclaimed List unless, with respect to unoccupied France, the circumstances are believed to be exceptional and not calculated to aid the Axis. Transactions with French colonies should not result in inclusion in the Proclaimed List unless the trade involved in particular transactions with such colonies appears to our Missions to be designed to aid the Axis or to involve indirect remittances or trade with Vichy France itself.

Please notify consular officers in your area.

HULL

---

[18] Substantially the same message sent to the Ambassador in the United Kingdom as telegram No. 3286, July 16, 1942, 7 p. m., with instructions to repeat those portions which were of general application to Missions in the London Coordination area. The London Coordination area embraced the territory of Sweden, Switzerland, Turkey, Spain, and Portugal, including all African territories of such countries.

740.00112A European War, 1939/14948 : Telegram

The Ambassador in the United Kingdom (Winant) to the Secretary of State

LONDON, July 27, 1942—midnight.
[Received July 28—5 a. m.]

4191. 1. Department's statement of policy in regard to Proclaimed Listing French controlled firms and firms dealing with France, given in telegram 3286, July 16,[19] has been very helpful and British have accepted it as basis instructions their missions. Following, in paraphrase of minute of meeting which considered matter, is only major point requiring clarification:

"Meeting noted fact that according to United States instructions persons at present controlled from occupied France must necessarily be listed and these persons were to be offered no opportunity to give undertakings to Ministry of Economic Warfare to sever their connections with occupied France. In opinion of Ministry of Economic Warfare there were possible advantages to be gained from allowing such persons to give undertakings 'neither to seek nor accept direction from' their head offices where they were in a position to give such undertakings."

2. Department is requested kindly to telegraph as soon as possible regarding foregoing and to instruct Embassy also as to whether applications to make remittances for support of relatives in occupied France are granted by Treasury (British permit such remittances).

3. British will interpret "controlled from occupied France" to mean effective rather than nominal control. They have noted many French firms asserting their head offices have been set up in small towns in unoccupied France, whereas businesses are in reality controlled from headquarters in Paris.

4. British do not intend to send the instructions arising from this coordination of policy to their missions in American Republics until they have consulted British Embassy, Washington.

WINANT

———

740.00112A European War, 1939/966a Suppl.

The Secretary of State to Diplomatic Representatives in the American Republics

WASHINGTON, August 7, 1942.

SIRS: Reference is made to the Department's circular instruction of August 28, 1941 relating to the Proclaimed List.

Although no general effort has been made up to the present time to include in the List Axis organizations which were not engaged in

———

[19] See footnote 18, p. 291.

commerce, in a number of isolated cases non-commercial Axis organizations have been included and the successful results attending such inclusion indicate the desirability of a wider consideration of such organizations with respect to possible inclusion.

You are, therefore, requested to forward reports concerning Axis-inspired political organizations, Chambers of Commerce, schools, or other non-commercial groups with recommendations concerning the desirability of their inclusion in the Proclaimed List. In connection with such recommendations please bear in mind that inclusion may have desirable results through the stigma that will be attached to the organizations in the minds of the local public, through the possible inclusion of such names in local black lists, through the probable desire to resign on the part of persons who are not strongly pro-Axis in their sympathies but who may have joined for business or social reasons, and through the assuring that the sanctions dependent upon the Proclaimed List, including the denial of goods and the interception of communications, will be applied.

Very truly yours,   For the Secretary of State:
                                        DEAN ACHESON

740.00112A European War, 1939/14948 : Airgram

The Secretary of State to the Ambassador in the United Kingdom
(Winant)

WASHINGTON, August 12, 1942—12 : 35 p. m.

A–15. Reference your telegram 4191 of July 27.

1. We have no objection to the taking of undertakings from firms "controlled" from occupied France provided that the undertaking is based on the complete and effective severance of such control. In those circumstances we would no longer consider the firm controlled from occupied France for listing purposes.

2. We do not contemplate seeking such undertakings generally ourselves but we would not ordinarily list a firm from which the British had accepted an undertaking. Although we cannot associate ourselves with their undertakings from French firms we believe it is advisable that our missions be kept informed by the British of all cases where they contemplate accepting undertakings in order that divergent actions may not be taken. In all important cases we believe it would also be desirable for MEW or ourselves to be informed beforehand so that any adverse information available in London or Washington could be considered before undertaking is accepted.

3. Our general views on these undertakings are that an undertaking should only be considered where the mission is satisfied that the firm is genuinely anti-Axis in political sympathy and that caution

should be exercised not to give undue weight to a technical severance of control from French territory as there is evidence that many French firms have taken steps to grant powers of attorney with respect to the operation of their branches, and it is felt that this procedure leads to the possibility of a technical compliance with the requirements of a severance of control without any real change in the influence over the firm's operations.

Any arrangement between a head office in France and a branch in a neutral country whereby control is shifted from the head office to the branch should be scrutinized with particular care where the head office is in occupied France.

4. It is the policy of the Treasury not to license any remittances to enemy or enemy-occupied territory. This includes occupied France. Subsistence remittances to American citizens in occupied territories are handled by State Department through the Swiss Government.

HULL

740.00112A European War, 1939/16880 : Telegram

The Ambassador in the United Kingdom (Winant) to the Secretary of State

LONDON, September 5, 1942—midnight.
[Received September 5—10 : 50 p. m.]

4991. Reference final sentence Madrid's despatch 149, July 15 and second paragraph page 7 Bern's despatch 2857, July 17.[21] British considering advisability retention of war trade lists for some time after end of the war. Purpose would be now to secure greater fear of listing on the part of neutral firms who, largely invulnerable to United Nations' sanctions at present, are not hesitant about indulging in lucrative trade with the enemy as they feel that war trade lists will be abolished at the end of the war and they will be able to resume trade with United Nations on the same basis as firms which have scrupulously foregone enemy business. Proponents of retention recognize that in the American Republics it might be less desirable than elsewhere, but think that an announcement that the lists "will not be abolished" (not necessarily that "the lists will be continued") upon the termination of the war, would be most desirable as an extremely effective way of removing the contempt in which the lists are now held by many business men in neutral countries, especially on the continent.

The British assure us that they will not act on this matter nor give any publicity to its consideration without fully consulting the

---

[21] Neither printed.

Department. The matter is now at the interdepartmental stage, with Ministry of Economic Warfare expecting to induce the Foreign Office to concur in the proposal.

WINANT

740.00112A European War, 1939/16880 : Airgram

The Acting Secretary of State to the Ambassador in the United Kingdom (*Winant*)

WASHINGTON, October 10, 1942—2 : 45 p. m.

A–138. Your 4991, September 5, 1942, concerning MEW proposal that some announcement be made that the War Trade Lists will remain in effect for some time after termination of the war. The following represent our tentative views on this matter.

We believe that any formal announcement by the British Government or this Government along these lines would receive primary attention both in neutral and belligerent countries as representing one of the first concrete statements of post-war policies on the part of our governments. It would probably be given more importance and broader interpretation than would be warranted and in this connection we believe such an announcement would inevitably result in charges that the continuation of our War Trade Lists after the war would involve punitive measures against neutrals and that such a policy would be contrary to and make impossible the establishment of normal and non-discriminatory international commercial relations between peaceful nations. The announcement of such a policy might be distorted to represent policies more in accord with the "new order" of the Axis than the type of post-war settlement for which the United Nations are fighting. Moreover, an announcement now that we proposed to continue the war trade lists after the war would be accepted by persons who are critical of the lists as confirming the charge that the lists are motivated by national trade rivalries and selfish commercial considerations rather than the exigencies of war and national defense. We fear that such charges might discredit seriously the post-war policies of the United Nations and in particular the present economic warfare justification for the War Trade Lists in the eyes of the countries affected and in the eyes of the business community generally. Against these manifest and serious objections to such an announcement at present we find it difficult to see clearly the compensating advantages which would be realized. We believe it is very important in this connection to distinguish sharply between the question of whether it will be necessary to retain the War Trade Lists in operation for a period following the termination of the war and the question of whether it is advisable presently to announce such a policy.

We can imagine that it may well be necessary to retain the lists for a period after the war, but we believe it is impossible at present to foresee with any accuracy what will be the nature of the conditions which might make such a policy necessary. It is quite probable that the immediate post-war conditions would be such that any such policy would have to take into account the situation in particular countries. On the other hand, we cannot at present imagine any useful purpose which would be served by an announcement which suggested that a distinction would be drawn between different countries. In fact, there would be obvious dangers in any such suggestion. Since the principal, if not the only, advantage for making such an announcement of policy now would be the deterrent effect which it would have on otherwise invulnerable firms it would be necessary, in our opinion, to make the announcement absolutely applicable to specified countries or to all countries if its deterrent purpose was to be realized.

If we are correct in believing that the principal or sole purpose of such an announcement would be its deterrent effect in assisting the current enforcement of the War Trade Lists policy we can see very little, if any, need for invoking such an additional sanction with respect to the American Republics since nearly all firms in these countries which are dependent upon international trade are today either subject to the effective threat of inclusion on the War Trade Lists, or are subject to local internal controls which restrict or prevent pro-Axis activities on their part. Accordingly, today we can see no advantage which could outweigh the obvious disadvantages of announcing such a policy with respect to the American Republics. Although we are not in a position at present to say that there would not be important deterrent advantages in announcing such a policy for certain European countries, we are very doubtful, as stated above, that it would be advisable politically or otherwise to single out the European neutrals in any such announcement.

The foregoing represent our preliminary views on this matter and we believe it would be advisable for you to bring these considerations promptly to the attention of responsible officials in the British Government in order that a hasty and ill-advised position may not be taken on this extremely important matter. In this connection you may state that we would now be opposed to making any such announcement with respect to the American Republics and that we would not be prepared to associate ourselves with such an announcement with respect to the European countries without much more careful consideration and a clearer appreciation of the advantages from and necessity for such a move. We, of course, recognize that future developments might be such as to require an entirely different view of this matter.

It is possible that the objective which MEW has in mind might be substantially achieved in particular cases in Europe if informally and unofficially the local Black List authorities found appropriate occasions for replying to inquiries on this subject to the effect that it was not impossible that our Governments would find it necessary to maintain their War Trade List policies with respect to certain persons and firms who had proven unfriendly to our war interests. We should want to give further consideration to even this possibility before anything were done along these lines by our representatives.

WELLES

740.00112A European War, 1939/19800 : Telegram

The Ambassador in the United Kingdom (Winant) to the Secretary of State

LONDON, November 2, 1942—5 p. m.
[Received 10 p. m.]

6128. Reference to the Department's telegram No. A–138, October 10, respecting continuance of war trade lists after the war. The Department's comment on the British proposal has been presented to Ministry of Economic Warfare and exhaustively discussed with its officials. The cogency of the Department's views is realized and we are assured that no hasty action will be taken here or indeed any announcement made of this character without American concurrence. The Ministry of Economic Warfare, however, attaches such importance to this proposal that it requests a renewed examination of the problem in the light of the following observations:

(1) The proposed policy would not be directed against any neutral country in particular but against listed firms and individuals in neutral countries who continue to trade with or otherwise assist the enemy. In executing this policy consideration can continue to be given to the economic interests of neutral countries. Consequently it is believed that we could combat any contention that this policy would represent punitive or discriminatory measures against neutral countries as such inasmuch as any announcement would refer solely to listed firms or persons.

(2) Compensating advantages of such an announcement particularly with respect to European neutrals are in London believed to outweigh the disadvantages cited in Department's A–138. We discussed at some length with Ministry of Economic Warfare the alternative suggestion set forth in the final paragraph of this airgram but the opinion here is that such a method would not be an effective deterrent. Furthermore, the British contend that present developments are such as to warrant action of the nature proposed. They are strongly of the opinion that the moment has come to sharpen this weapon of economic warfare and that the proposed action would

have a salutary effect in Switzerland, Sweden and Portugal. The British missions in Bern and Lisbon are strongly in favor of a public announcement and have stressed that the same effect could not be achieved by informal or unofficial warnings. In Switzerland the Ministry of Economic Warfare believes that the listing policy is at the moment effective in reducing the exportation of fuses to Germany and has indications that the Germans in their effort to obtain as large as possible quantity of fuses from Switzerland have agreed to permit certain additional Swiss exports to us if a relaxation of the listing policy against firms working on Axis orders can be obtained. It has furthermore been brought out in the current negotiations with the Swiss [22] that many firms are anxious to avoid listing even when not particularly vulnerable. Consequently an increased effectiveness of the threat of listing in the next few moments [months] is considered to be of great value.

(3) In respect of Latin America the British argue that as the proposal is directed principally against firms and individuals who assist the enemy and not against any particular countries an announcement would not, therefore, be confined to any country or group of countries. It is immaterial to the Ministry what publicity would be given in that region and it would agree to confine local publicity to European neutrals. It is believed here, however, that it would not be possible to make public this distinction in any official announcement.

(4) Ministry of Economic Warfare cabled its Embassy in Washington under date of October 16 a proposed statement on this matter which has doubtless been communicated to the Department. The Ministry emphasizes that it is not wedded to this particular phraseology and it would welcome any suggestions on our part. For example, it was suggested that the statement might be amplified by the addition of a phrase making it clear that we are merely reserving the right to take such action. We would thereby not be committed to enforcing it fully.

(5) Reverting to the question of the relative merit of a public announcement versus informal and unofficial statements by listing authorities the Ministry believes that if the latter method were adopted it is inevitable once rumors commenced to circulate in neutral countries that a question would be ask[ed] in the House which would have to be answered. Such question would place the whole matter on a publicly defensive plane and would thereby weaken the whole plan.

(6) Ministry of Economic Warfare is informing the British Embassy in Washington.

WINANT

---

[22] See *Foreign Relations*, 1942, vol. III, pp. 376 ff. For the official British account, see Medlicott, *The Economic Blockade*, vol. II, pp. 219–235.

740.00112A European War, 1939/19800 : Telegram

The Secretary of State to the Ambassador in the United Kingdom (Winant)

WASHINGTON, November 21, 1942—10 p. m.

5871. Reference your telegram no. 6128 of November 2, 1942 and Department's airgram no. A–138 of October 10, 1942 regarding continuance of War Trade Lists after the war. We have reviewed this question with the British here but we can not see any satisfactory reason for presently changing our position.

We continue to believe that any such public announcement at this time would be most unwise, particularly in view of the current military operations in the Mediterranean area and the efforts of both governments to reassure Portugal and Spain.[23] Furthermore, in line with the considerations already stated by us, we believe any such announcement would be utilized by the Axis propaganda agencies not only to discredit our post-war aims, but also to create in the minds of their peoples both at home and abroad the impression that they, the people, had no alternative but to fight and resist us to the bitter end. This would be, we believe, contrary to the current propaganda policies of our two governments and not in our best interests at the present juncture. In this connection please emphasize with MEW that the announcement of a post-war policy now regarding continuation of the War Trade Lists with respect to Axis firms abroad inevitably involves implications that Axis firms within the Axis countries will also be subjected to retaliatory international trade restrictions. Manifestly, we cannot risk backing into even an implied suggestion of post-war policies on such a basic question through a statement of policy on the War Trade Lists.

In addition to the foregoing basic considerations and the points made in our previous airgram, we find it difficult to reconcile such a proposed announcement with the current European listing policies which are not themselves as rigorous as they could be made.

If a listed firm is vulnerable to our controls, no further deterrent pressure is needed against it unless we ourselves are dealing with

---

[23] The Allied invasion of northwest Africa (TORCH), begun on November 8, 1942, was under way. For the official narrative on the military operations, see George F. Howe, *Northwest Africa: Seizing the Initiative in the West*, in the series *United States Army in World War II: The Mediterranean Theater of Operations* (Washington, Government Printing Office, 1957), pp. 97–344.

In connection with the military operations, President Roosevelt sent messages to Gen. Antonio Oscar de Fragoso Carmona, President of Portugal, and to Gen. Francisco Franco y Bahamonde, head of the Spanish State. For texts of the messages, see Department of State *Bulletin*, November 14, 1942, pp. 905–907.

For diplomatic correspondence on the invasion and occupation of French North Africa, see *Foreign Relations*, 1942, vol. II, pp. 429 ff.

the firm for supply or pre-emptive reasons or have been compelled to permit our firms to deal with it for similar reasons. If a firm would be vulnerable to our controls but is not presently listed, the answer would seem to be to list it. Such a firm would certainly not be deterred greatly by the announcement of such a policy if it had reason to believe, as it has had up to now, that the list would not be applied to it. In this connection we are aware that there are many circumstances, including the purchasing and pre-emptive buying programs and political problems, which make a more rigorous listing and licensing policy difficult. If a firm is not presently vulnerable because not dependent upon international commerce, we see no reason to believe it would be greatly deterred by a loose threat of continuing a control against it which, even under war conditions, was admittedly ineffective. Under post-war circumstances the control would probably be even less effective.

With respect to the observation in your no. 6128 of November 2, paragraph no. 2, that an increased effectiveness of the threat of listing would be of great value in Switzerland during the next few months, we believe that this purpose can best be achieved by both applying our listing and licensing policies more vigorously in Switzerland and perhaps by letting it be known locally, either informally or by public announcement, that this was being done. We consider such steps, wherever necessary and advisable, much more likely to be effective and less dangerous than any present public announcement with respect to a general post-war policy concerning the War Trade Lists.

The Canadian Legation here has informed us that the Canadian Government is not presently sympathetic to the MEW proposed announcement.

Please keep us fully informed on this matter.

HULL

740.00112A European War, 1939/21360e : Telegram

The Secretary of State to the Ambassador in the United Kingdom (Winant)

WASHINGTON, November 30, 1942—midnight.

6043. British Embassy here has advised Department that Netherlands Government proposes to publish a blacklist of its own in the near future and that the Netherland authorities may shortly suggest their being represented on Proclaimed List Committee. Department has had no word of these developments from other sources and requests any information on it available to you. Tentatively we can see no need for the publication of another list and we believe it would be impossible, for various reasons, to extend further representation on the Proclaimed List Committee.

Please telegraph your and MEW's views and whether British authorities have considered attempting to dissuade Dutch from this step.

HULL

740.00112A European War 1939/21405 : Telegram

The Ambassador in the United Kingdom (Winant) to the Secretary of State

LONDON, December 3, 1942—11 p. m.
[Received December 4—6 a. m.]

6854. 1. Embassy has been informed orally, with reference to Department's 6043, November 30, by Netherlands Ministry of Justice as follows:

(a) Under a Dutch decree of October 22, 1942, a Black List Committee and Black List will be established. Black List Committee will meet under chairmanship of official of Ministry of Justice and will have representatives of Foreign Office, Ministry of Colonies, Ministry of Trade, Industry and Shipping. The Committee will meet in London and will make recommendations to the Minister of Justice who will promulgate list. Although there have been no meetings of Committee as yet it is believed that it will convene before Christmas and that first Dutch Black List will be published at approximately the same time as revision to Statutory List in January.

(b) Prohibition of intercourse with any persons appearing on Dutch list will be binding on all Dutch subjects and Dutch nationals residing in United Nations or neutral territory. The Dutch intend to follow statutory listings in Eastern Hemisphere and Proclaimed listings in Western Hemisphere. Dutch officials believe that creation of their list will stop previously existing breach in blockade for there is at present no sanction against Dutch nationals trading with persons on Proclaimed and Statutory Lists other than threat of listing.

(c) Netherlands Ministry of Justice believes that no concurrence other than that described in paragraph 2 will be necessitated by establishment of Dutch list. In Eastern Hemisphere Dutch Consuls who make independent investigations will report to the Netherlands Minister and he in turn will unofficially consult his British colleague. It is the Dutch desire that a somewhat similar procedure be followed in Western Hemisphere. However, Dutch feel that they would like to have the opportunity of listing Dutch nationals or firms with large Dutch interests in their own list previous to their publication either in the Statutory or Proclaimed List. Further, they believe that if they are to follow the Proclaimed List they would be somewhat loath to do so if they were given no voice whatsoever in the listings.

2. The Dutch attend the Black List Committee here as observers. A formal request was made by them for access to Ministry of Eco-

nomic Warfare's records. In acquiescing in this Ministry of Economic Warfare invited them to attend the Black List Committee and observe its work. Although Ministry of Economic Warfare maintains and [*sic*] that they are only observers a Dutch representative attends every meeting of the Black List Committee. Experience of Ministry officials and American member is that this Dutch representative does not intervene in cases other than those in which there is a Dutch interest.

3. No other United Nations Governments have requested representatives on Black List Committee. Black List Section Ministry of Economic Warfare believes that case of Dutch can be distinguished from others because of control of territory and large overseas interests. Belgian Congo, only other large United Nations territory under administration of government in exile, is adequately controlled by other than Black List means.

4. Dutch state that they have received invitation to attend Lisbon Status Committee. Neither Ministry of Economic Warfare nor this Embassy have any information in this regard.

5. Ministry of Economic Warfare states that far from dissuading Dutch from the establishment of Black List of their own they pressed them to institute one previous to invasion of Dutch East Indies by Japanese. The officials of Ministry believe that as Dutch territory is reoccupied the value of the Dutch Black List may increase. In fact they believe that such a list may well have another advantage in that it may open up additional sources of intelligence. This was emphasized in regard to Sweden where they state the Dutch representative is good intelligence officer. They also believe that existence of a Dutch list would not detract from Proclaimed and Statutory Lists but might even give them added strength. It is added by them that Black List Section of Ministry consults with United Nations Governments when question of listing Allied nationals or firms with large Allied interests arises. This procedure would have to be followed regarding Dutch interests even if the Netherlands Government did not have an observer on the Black List Committee.

6. Embassy hear Netherlands Government concurs in our view that in the circumstances it would not be practicable to cause Dutch withdrawal and suggests that unless there is a compelling reason it would be psychologically undesirable to attempt to dissuade them from establishing list.

WINANT

740.00112A European War, 1939/10035a Suppl. : Circular airgram

The Secretary of State to Diplomatic Representatives in the American Republics

WASHINGTON, December 7, 1942—9 : 15 a. m.

Reference Department's previous instructions regarding status of French firms for Proclaimed List purposes. The Department believes that the recent military and political developments in both continental France and the French African territories have now produced a situation which permits and requires a definite determination of the status of all French enterprises in the American republics with respect to our Proclaimed List and related policies. Accordingly you are requested to review the status of all French enterprises which have been under observation and to report promptly any such persons or firms who maintain any commercial or financial relations with continental France, or who currently are "collaborationist" or "pro-Axis" in political sympathies, or who maintain any corporate or other business connections with enterprises in continental France. We are now prepared to place any such persons or firms on the Proclaimed List and recommendations for such action should be forwarded to the Department promptly.

In this connection it is suggested you consult your British colleague with particular regard to reviewing the status of any French enterprises which may be presently classified as "starred black list" cases on the MEW War Trade Lists.

The Department's circular instruction of October 9, 1942 [24] regarding use of undertakings in connection with French firms remains in effect except that all continental France is now to be treated as occupied France was previously treated for this purpose.

In particular a prompt reply is requested with respect to the status of any Havas Telemundial or Teleradio agency operations in your country. Havas Teleradio has been denied Treasury licenses for funds for further operations in the United States and its operations have ceased here. If the Havas agency is continuing to operate in your country a recommendation for its inclusion in the Proclaimed List should be forwarded to the Department. For your confidential information the Office of War Information here is endeavoring to establish or contact a French news service to Algiers and this service for special purposes may use the name Havas but will in fact have no connection with the old Havas agencies except that they may use certain of the former Havas personnel in New York.

HULL

---

[24] Not printed.

740.00112A European War, 1939/17843 : Airgram

The Secretary of State to the Ambassador in the United Kingdom
(Winant)

WASHINGTON, December 17, 1942—5 :10 p. m.

A–290. Reference BEW 326 dated September 10, 1942 from Bern and Department's A 259 of December 3 and Bern's telegram no. 4574 dated October 8 [25] on Confidential List. The Department believes that it is probably not possible or desirable to fix as exact rules and criteria for listing firms in neutral countries of Europe as are applied with respect to firms in South America. In general, the purpose of the Proclaimed and Statutory Lists is to bring to bear all of the sanctions available to the British and this government against firms and individuals whose operations, activities or known sympathies are favorable to the Axis cause. Such sanctions should be regarded as including the stoppage of transactions between such firms and persons subject to the control of the British and American Governments, the blocking of funds of such firms in the United States, Great Britain or Canada, and such effect as the stigmatizing of the firm may have on local transactions and on transactions with other neutral countries in Europe and South America.

In general, firms which should be considered for inclusion are:

1. Those that are controlled by persons in Axis territory or by Axis nationals known to be sympathetic to the Axis cause.
2. Firms maintaining trade with enemy territory or substantially connected by trade or otherwise with firms on the published lists.
3. Firms whose activities in any way aid the Axis.

Considerations against the strict application of these general rules would be:

1. If the firm had available for export to the United States strategic materials.
2. If the number of firms to be included under the criteria mentioned was so large as to weaken the effectiveness of the list. This consideration should be balanced against the results to be obtained from listing and the mere size of the list would not constitute an objection if any salutary results were to be expected as a result of the listing.
3. Political considerations, including the essentiality of the operations of the firm in the local economy.

In general, in the absence of considerations with respect to strategic materials the fact that a firm has been an agent for or has engaged in trade with the United States or Great Britain should not affect its inclusion in the published lists. In rare cases where the Consul be-

---

[25] None printed.

lieves that considerations of this nature should be taken into account, the case should be reported in full to the Embassy at London and to the Department with a statement of the reasons why the reporting office believes that special considerations are applicable.

With respect to the question raised in your despatch no. 5311 dated September 3, 1942 [26] enclosing communications relating to the application of listing policies to firms in Sweden, the Department believes that the absence of vulnerability may be taken into account in connection with other factors such as the unimportance of the firm and the unduly large number of firms in a given country which might otherwise be eligible for listing. In the absence of such other factors, however, the Department believes that the absence of vulnerability to American or British controls should not usually be a controlling factor as the stigmatizing of a firm which is controlled from enemy territory or which is pro-Nazi in its activities is of itself useful in most cases and may result in indirect sanctions through the unwillingness of other firms in the same country or other countries to transact business with it following its listing.

HULL

---

[26] Not printed.

ARGENTINA

NEGOTIATIONS FOR THE PURCHASE OF EXPORTABLE SURPLUSES OF STRATEGIC MATERIALS FROM ARGENTINA [1]

811.20 Defense (M) Argentina/109 : Telegram

The Secretary of State to the American Delegation to the Third Meeting of the Foreign Ministers of the American Republics at Rio de Janeiro [2]

WASHINGTON, January 15, 1942—7 p. m.

10. For the Under Secretary of State [3] from Acheson.[4] As you know, negotiations have been under way for some time between the Federal Loan Agency,[5] assisted by Ambassador Armour, and the Argentine Government looking to the purchase by the Loan Agency of the exportable surpluses of a long list of Argentine commodities. Of these, the most interesting from the point of view of Argentina is unquestionably linseed. The negotiations up to the present with regard to linseed have been held up because of the failure to agree on price. Today the Federal Loan Agency has agreed, contingent on the satisfactory conclusion of the entire agreement as to the rest of the commodities, to underwrite the purchase of 30,000,000 bushels of linseed, partly from the old and partly from the new crop, at $1.10 per bushel, f.o.b. Buenos Aires. This price we are informed by the representative of the Loan Agency [6] who has been conducting the negotiations in Buenos Aires, will be regarded as entirely satisfactory by the Argentine authorities. I am sending you this information because I believe that you may want to communicate it to the Argentine authorities. [Acheson.]

HULL

---

[1] Continued from *Foreign Relations*, 1941, vol. VI, section under Argentina entitled "Negotiations for an agreement on the purchase of exportable surpluses of strategic materials from Argentina."

[2] For correspondence concerning this meeting, see pp. 6 ff.

[3] Sumner Welles, at this time representing the United States at the Foreign Ministers' meeting at Rio de Janeiro.

[4] Dean Acheson, Assistant Secretary of State.

[5] The Federal Loan Agency operated through instrumentalities such as the Metals Reserve Company and the United States Commercial Company.

[6] Thomas J. Williams.

811.20 Defense (M) Argentina/110 : Telegram

The Secretary of State to the Ambassador in Argentina (Armour)

WASHINGTON, January 16, 1942—5 p. m.

69. From Williams. The Federal Loan Agency has offered a satisfactory basis which should enable the immediate conclusion of the over-all purchase agreement. I am leaving Washington Saturday and should arrive at Rio January 20. I shall explain all details to Sumner Welles. [Williams.]

HULL

835.24/300a : Telegram

The Secretary of State to the Ambassador in Argentina (Armour)

WASHINGTON, February 10, 1942—9 p. m.

192. From the Under Secretary. The Argentine Ambassador [7] called to see me yesterday evening. He told me that he had received several telegrams from his Government since my return to Washington urging that he obtain a statement from me of the general views and policies of this Government with regard to Argentina since the conclusion of the conference at Rio de Janeiro.

The Ambassador, who is laboring under very considerable personal resentment because of the increasingly severe trend of press comment in the United States with regard to Argentina's present policies and attitude, said that he feared that the United States was embarking upon a policy of pressure upon Argentina and a policy of reprisal because of the refusal of Argentina to follow the course taken by 19 other American republics.

I stated to the Ambassador that he could inform his Government that the United States was following neither a policy of pressure nor a policy of reprisal. I said that I was surprised, in view of the relations which had existed between Argentina and the United States during the past 9 years and the well-known and proven policy of the Government of the United States, that such a question could even be raised.

I stated that this Government was pursuing a policy which was completely realistic. I said that at the present time demands were being made upon the United States by all of the united nations in all parts of the world for urgently-needed naval and military material. I continued that adequate defense of the Western Hemisphere was a matter of cardinal concern to this Government. During the past few weeks, moreover, six American republics, in addition to those which had already taken action, had broken relations with

---

[7] Felipe A. Espil.

the Axis powers and had openly sided with the United States. These nations had consequently incurred the dangers inherent in the position which they had assumed. For that reason, I said, it was imperative for this Government to give immediate and prompt consideration to their defense requirements. By reason of the fact that Argentina had not adopted a similar attitude, it should be obvious that the requirements of these other nations were more urgent than those of Argentina and would consequently be given preferential attention by the United States. I concluded by saying that this position would be made clear to the military and naval representatives of Argentina now in Washington by the War and Navy Departments as well as by the Department of State.

In your conversations with the Acting Foreign Minister you may inform him accordingly.

For your personal information, the policies which you and I discussed, and which have been recently referred to in telegrams exchanged between you and the Department, will be followed in detail. As a result of a meeting I had this morning with appropriate officials here in the Department, certain studies will be promptly undertaken of the actual need by the United States of so-called strategic materials in Argentina in order to determine whether the pending contract for the purchase by us of strategic materials in Argentina should be consummated in whole or in part. I feel very strongly that the announcement of a contract of this kind would be politically inexpedient owing to present conditions in Argentina and in the neighboring countries. It seems to me that this Government can purchase in the open market in Argentina the quantities it requires of hides, wool, and linseed and that there is no need to enter into the contract which has been under discussion. I would appreciate having your own views with regard to this question. [Welles.]

HULL

811.20 Defense (M) Argentina/123 : Telegram

The Ambassador in Argentina (Armour) to the Secretary of State

BUENOS AIRES, February 13, 1942—10 p. m.
[Received February 13—9 : 33 p. m.]

271. For the Under Secretary. Your telegram 192, February 10, 9 p.m., reference last paragraph. I agree with you that our Government should be able to purchase in the open market quantities it requires of products mentioned and that there is no need to enter into a contract at this time. However, I should like to discuss this matter with Williams who has been handling negotiations on his return to Buenos Aires next week.

I have heard reports that Government here is contemplating securing control of products mentioned with a view to forcing our hand but in the absence of more definite information I am inclined to think they would only proceed to such length as a last resort.

ARMOUR

811.20 Defense (M) Argentina/142 : Telegram

The Ambassador in Argentina (Armour) to the Secretary of State

BUENOS AIRES, March 3, 1942—4 p. m.
[Received 9 : 20 p. m.]

403. For the Under Secretary. My 271, February 13, 10 p. m., was explained to Williams on his return and he is in entire agreement.

On February 25, Williams called on Alonso Irigoyen[8] and informed him that due to the changed international situation it would be necessary to reconsider proposals included in the over-all purchase program and therefore negotiations would be suspended for the present. Irigoyen was greatly disturbed and urged that the agreement be concluded without delay stating that whatever might be said to the contrary every one would consider suspension as reprisal for not following our Government's international policy. Williams explained that shortage of shipping, the possibility of having to take delivery of commodities here and to advance substantial sums, combined with possible local storage difficulties, were well founded reasons for reconsideration of the program. He emphasized that such reconsideration was in no sense a reprisal: that such action was necessitated by a situation now existing which did not exist when the original offer was made; and furthermore that the commitment to supply essential materials would now be more difficult to fulfill because of increased demands for our own and our Allies' requirements. He also pointed out that export control was less important now than previously.

Williams also spoke to Coll Benegas[9] along similar lines. Latter also was disturbed and appeared pessimistic regarding the Argentine economic outlook. He considered it unfair that the negotiations be suspended claiming that the possible motives mentioned had previously been contemplated.

On February 27, Williams made similar statement to Torriani[10] and also discussed export control clause since Torriani was previously opposed to our wording. Torriani while stating that he felt an

---

[8] Argentine Under Secretary of Finance.
[9] Presumably Carlos A. Coll Benegas, Argentine economic consultant.
[10] Carlos L. Torriani, Director of the Division of Economic and Consular Affairs of the Argentine Foreign Office.

acceptable formula could be agreed upon still maintained previous viewpoint. A detailed report will be airmailed.

Williams requests Federal Loan Agency to advise what commodities they desire to purchase independently. Beryllium oxide contract will be signed March 3. It contains clause making effect dependent on conclusion of over-all agreement. If over-all purchase negotiations should be suspended indefinitely, would Metals Reserve Company be disposed to ratify beryllium contract independently of over-all agreement?

Without any indications that negotiations of over-all agreement are being resumed, it may be found advisable to effect separate agreements for the purchase of certain other specific products, such as linseed, as better terms probably would be offered than obtained in open market. For example it is probable that a separate agreement could be concluded for linseed purchases on the same basis as proposed in over-all agreement.

ARMOUR

811.20 Defense (M) Argentina/142 : Telegram

The Acting Secretary of State to the Ambassador in Argentina
(Armour)

WASHINGTON, March 11, 1942—4 p. m.

338. Your 403 March 3 and particularly last paragraph. The beryllium oxide contract and the possible separate agreements for the purchase of other products are being studied with the Reconstruction Finance Corporation but no decision has as yet been reached.

WELLES

811.20 Defense (M) Argentina/157 : Telegram

The Acting Secretary of State to the Ambassador in Argentina
(Armour)

WASHINGTON, April 13, 1942—5 p. m.

509. William Baum Company of New York has asked Department for an expression of opinion concerning proposed sale of 360,000 tons of Argentine scrap to Bethlehem Steel in exchange for 60,000 tons of manufactured steel. Baum states that Crespo [12] is associated with this offer. Department will inform Baum that maximum available

---

[12] Eduardo Crespo, President of the Banco Municipal de Préstamos.

quantities of manufactured steel are established by quarterly allocations. Whether or not Crespo is in a position to arrange export of scrap, the fact that this offer has been made is an indication that there are probably substantial quantities of scrap in Argentina which cannot be used there.

Reference your 623 [523] of March 20.[13] Survey of available scrap will undoubtedly take a long time and need is increasing here. Department would therefore prefer not to let this matter drop unless you are convinced that to press negotiations now would prejudice our chances of eventually obtaining scrap from Argentina. Please explain in further detail why you recommend deferment of negotiations.

WELLES

811.20 Defense (M) Argentina/163 : Telegram

The Secretary of State to the Ambassador in Argentina (Armour)

WASHINGTON, April 20, 1942—8 p. m.

552. Your 565, March 27, 6 p. m.[13] Department and Metals Reserve Company desire to break present deadlock on beryl ore which is urgently needed by defense industries in this country. You are accordingly requested to approach the appropriate official of the Argentine Government and request that the embargo on exports be lifted in order that a purchase contract for the ore may be negotiated here with Hochschild.[14]

As you know, Metals Reserve Company greatly prefers to purchase ore rather than the oxide, which is an expensive and inefficient method of acquiring beryl. If necessary, however, Metals Reserve might consider making effective the contract already signed for beryllium oxide with Saba[15] provided the Argentine Government grants export licenses for accumulated stocks of beryl ore and a minimum of say 1,000 tons of beryl ore is made available annually. In discussing this matter with the Argentine authorities, you are requested to stress the fact that any oxide carbonate taken will be a sacrifice undergone only because of the great need for beryl ore.

HULL

---

[13] Not printed.
[14] Mauricio Hochschild, S. A. M. I., dealers in lead, zinc, tungsten, and other ores in a number of Latin American countries.
[15] Sociedad Anónima Berilo Argentina ; its Board of Directors appears to have been under the control of the head of the Argentine Government's Military Factories, Col. Manuel N. Savio.

811.20 Defense (M) Argentina/190 : Telegram

The Ambassador in Argentina (Armour) to the Secretary of State

BUENOS AIRES, April 28, 1942—5 p. m.
[Received 7:20 p. m.]

781. Your 552, April 20. Williams advises:

"Consulted Torriani of Foreign Office on April 23 relative to lifting embargo on exports of beryl ore. Torriani informed me that Ministry of War considered it important and desirable to conserve beryl ore supplies which indeed probable Argentine needs. Torriani agreed to consult colleagues but expressed opinion that present attitude would be maintained. Since that date have received no communication from Torriani. Also on April 23 discussed matter with Susini [16] of Saba who agreed in order to make beryllium oxide contract effective to include in said contract 100 tons beryl ore monthly less any quantity sold by others. Susini also agrees obtain export license for accumulated beryl ore stock up to 500 tons. All licenses to be made available when equipment which Saba has purchased in United States and urgently requires is made available for export. Susini advises that Argentine Government willing to agree to his proposal. Accordingly, please advise price and terms covering purchase of beryl ore."

ARMOUR

811.20 Defense (M) Argentina/195 : Telegram

The Ambassador in Argentina (Armour) to the Secretary of State

BUENOS AIRES, May 2, 1942—6 p. m.
[Received 8:07 p. m.]

815. The question of scrap iron has again been discussed with the Director of the Argentine Military Factory of the Ministry of War,[17] as requested in Department's 509, April 13, 5 p. m. While Colonel Savio was very sympathetic regarding United States' needs for scrap, he reiterated his previous position to the effect that most complete data they have been able to obtain indicates that not more than 400,-000 tons of scrap can be said to be in any way readily available in Argentina and that no quantity of this has been collected in any one place. He stated that the most liberal estimate, including much that is practically inaccessible or unobtainable for other reasons, would not increase the total beyond 700,000 tons. He feels that Argentina must increase its own iron and steel production as a matter of defense and

---

[16] Enrique Telemaco Pedro Susini, President of Sociedad Anónima Berilo Argentina.
[17] Col. Manuel N. Savio.

that therefore, it must conserve what scrap is available for that purpose. He further stated that scrap is now being sold at speculative prices, as high as 52 pesos, approximately $12.30 per metric ton, placed Buenos Aires, and that any prospect of export would so increase the speculative price as to make it practically prohibitive. He indicated no interest in a matter of exchange of scrap for finished steel. . . .

While this discussion was entirely informal, it is the Embassy's belief that Colonel Savio's position represents the official viewpoint and that it would be useless to present the matter formally through the Foreign Office unless the Department feels otherwise.

ARMOUR

811.20 Defense (M) Argentina/197: Telegram

The Ambassador in Argentina (Armour) to the Secretary of State

BUENOS AIRES, May 5, 1942—11 p. m.
[Received May 5—10 : 18 p. m.]

825. Reference Williams' letter to Metals Reserve April 23, Department's cable 552, April 20, 8 p.m., and Embassy's cable 781, April 28, 5 p. m., relative beryl ore exports. Following is translation of communication received by the Embassy from the Foreign Office May 1 :

"Saba on March 4 last signed a contract with Metals Reserve Company, an official institution of the Government of the United States agreeing to sell for the period of 2 years with option of a third all beryllium oxide it is able to produce to a maximum of 100 tons yearly.

A condition of this contract was that it would become effective at the conclusion of the over-all purchase agreement being negotiated between Argentina and the United States.

For this reason and in compliance with a request formulated by the Ministry of Agriculture, the Ministry of Foreign Relations takes pleasure in informing the Embassy of the United States of the interest that exists that the clause which subjects the entering into effect of the contract for the sale of beryllium oxide to the conclusion of the over-all purchase agreement be nullified."

In Embassy's opinion beryl ore export permits will not be granted until beryllium oxide contract with Saba is made effective, therefore it is suggested that authorization be granted to make Saba contract effective with paragraph 4 of special conditions eliminated and a clause substituted making the effectiveness of contract contingent upon the Argentine Government granting export licenses for export to the United States for an accumulated 568 tons beryl ore and agreeing to grant export licenses for approximately 100 tons per month with a minimum total of 1200 metric tons per year. Agreement would probably be along lines outlined in last paragraph of Embassy's telegram No. 781 of April 28, 5 p. m.

ARMOUR

811.20 Defense (M) Argentina/197 : Telegram

The Secretary of State to the Ambassador in Argentina (Armour)

WASHINGTON, May 12, 1942—1 p. m.

656. From Metals Reserve. Your 825, May 5, 11 p. m.

"Metals Reserve is prepared to make the Saba contract effective contingent upon the Argentine Government granting export licenses for export to the United States of the accumulated stocks of beryl ore and a further agreement to grant licenses at the rate of a minimum of 100 tons of ore monthly out of current production. Since the consumption of the Saba plant will be only about 1,000 tons of ore per year, export licenses should be granted for any quantity in excess of this requirement of Saba but not less than 1,200 tons annually."

HULL

811.20 Defense (M) Argentina/332

The American Ambassador in Argentina (Armour) to the Argentine Minister for Foreign Affairs (Ruiz Guiñazú) [19]

No. 749   BUENOS AIRES, May 14, 1942.

EXCELLENCY: With reference to the communication of the Ministry of Foreign Affairs and Worship of April 28, 1942,[20] relative to the contract concluded between the Metals Reserve Company and the Sociedad Anónima Comercial e Industrial Berilo Argentina, dated March 4, 1942 and according to clause 4 of special conditions of that contract to become effective upon the execution of the proposed overall agreement between the Government of the United States of America and the Argentine Government for the purchase by the United States Government (or agencies thereof) of certain Argentine products, I have the honor to inform Your Excellency that the Metals Reserve Company, an agency of the United States Government is now prepared to waive the clause mentioned and in lieu thereof to make the contract effective contingent upon the Argentine Government granting export licenses for export to the United States of the stocks of beryl

---

[19] Copy transmitted to the Department by the Ambassador in Argentina in his despatch No. 6697, September 23; received September 30.

[20] Presumably note quoted in telegram No. 825, May 5, 11 p. m., from the Ambassador in Argentina, p. 313.

ore now accumulated in Argentina, and further agreeing to grant licenses for a minimum of 100 tons of beryl ore monthly out of current production and for any quantity produced in excess of that figure after requirements of Sociedad Anónima Comercial e Industrial Berilo Argentina are fulfilled, the total export licenses to be for not less than 1,200 tons annually.

I avail myself [etc.]   [NORMAN ARMOUR]

811.20 Defense (M) Argentina/244

The Ambassador in Argentina (Armour) to the Secretary of State

No. 5593   BUENOS AIRES, July 1, 1942.
[Received July 9.]

SIR: I have the honor to refer to the Department's circular telegram of May 18, midnight, 1942,[21] in which the position of our Government was explained regarding rubber contracts in other Latin American countries, as well as the policy to be followed in making available to the other American republics their essential needs of rubber and rubber products.

The substance of this telegram, as instructed, was communicated to the Argentine Government by Embassy note No. 750, dated May 21, 1942. By note signed by the Minister of Foreign Relations and Worship, dated June 18, 1942, but which was not despatched from the Ministry until June 25, 1942, the Argentine Government acknowledges receipt of the Embassy's note No. 750 and advises that the Argentine Government is anxious to immediately initiate conversations with this Embassy for the purpose of arriving at a "modus vivendi" with respect to the future supply of crude rubber for Argentina. For that purpose they have designated Dr. Raúl E. Arrarás Vergara delegate of the Ministry of Agriculture on the Rubber Distribution Committee (see voluntary report No. 940 of March 31, 1942 [22]) as the person who is authorized to treat with the Embassy on the subject of crude rubber. The announced purpose is to reach an agreement, satisfactory to the essential needs of the Argentine for rubber during the present emergency, including those which contribute to the provision of foodstuffs and supplies to the United States.

Informally the Embassy has, on several occasions, discussed rubber in general with Dr. Vergara and other members of the Rubber Distribution Committee. This information has been supplied the Department by despatches Nos. 4339 of March 6, 1942 and 4935 of May 4, 1942.[23] Dr. Vergara has consistently intimated that the United

[21] Printed in vol. VI, section under Colombia entitled "Negotiation of agreement between the Rubber Reserve Company and Colombia . . ."
[22] Not printed.
[23] Neither printed.

States should advise Argentina of the amount of rubber that it can guarantee for this market. The Embassy's position, lacking further instructions, has been that until Argentina is willing to present a complete picture, including rubber stocks, consumption by articles produced, restrictions now in effect, and those definitely provided for the future, with the dates on which they will be made effective, that there would be little use in our proposal to our Government in Washington that a fixed amount of rubber be set aside. The Embassy has frankly expressed to Dr. Vergara and others of the Rubber Distribution Commission that they cannot expect any rubber whatsoever from the United States or from the countries with whom the United States has purchase contracts until Argentina has actually placed into effect restrictions proportionately equal in their importance to those already in force in the United States.

Early instructions from the Department as to any further position the Embassy should take would be greatly appreciated.

Copies of the original Spanish and of the English translation of the note received are enclosed.[27]

Respectfully yours,

For the Ambassador:
Thomas L. Hughes
Commercial Attaché

811.20 Defense (M) Argentina/212 : Telegram

The Acting Secretary of State to the Chargé in Argentina (*Reed*)

Washington, July 13, 1942—9 p. m.

1042. Department's 784 of June 1.[27] Metals Reserve and Hochschild have now reached an agreement in principle on beryl ore under terms of which Metals Reserve will purchase 1200 tons, of which 600 tons are on hand and balance will be delivered prior to December 31. Price is $8.25 per short ton unit, c & f New York, any increase in ocean freight above prevailing rate of $15 per long ton to be for the account of Metals Reserve. Ore to have minimum content of 9½% BeO.[28] Payment to be made after arrival New York and inspection of goods there. Metals Reserve is prepared to extend same terms to other producers. In addition, in the case of experienced and reputable ore sellers, it would consider paying say, 80% upon shipment, balance after arrival and inspection in New York. This fact should not be communicated in this form to the Argentine Government.

In view of the foregoing will you as soon as possible communicate with the appropriate Argentine authorities and attempt to obtain at once an arrangement of the kind referred to in the last paragraph of

---

[27] Not printed.
[28] Beryllium oxide.

your 825 of May 5 except that the figure for the accumulated stocks should be appropriately increased.

This is a very important matter because of the urgent need, at the earliest possible moment, of the accumulated stocks and of all sources of supply which may be obtained for the balance of this year, and you are requested to do everything possible to expedite a prompt and satisfactory conclusion.

WELLES

811.20 Defense (M) Argentina/254

The Chargé in Argentina (Reed) to the Secretary of State

No. 5742   BUENOS AIRES, July 15, 1942.
                                           [Received July 23.]

SIR: I have the honor to refer to this Embassy's despatch No. 5622 of July 2, 1942,[29] forwarding a copy of an informal unofficial proposal of the Argentine Government to the effect that the United States agree to supply Argentina with a minimum amount of rubber and at the same time to allow Argentina to purchase the entire Bolivian output.

The proposal is self-explanatory and copies both of the original Spanish and the English translation [29] are forwarded for the information of the Department. Reference is also made to Embassy's despatch No. 4935 of May 4, 1942.[29]

After briefly studying the present proposal, it is difficult to see where the Argentine Government has made any headway in the past two months. The situation is basically the same as described in the above despatch. In brief, Argentina has really put in little or no actual restriction on the use of rubber. It will be noted, for example, in the first table, under paragraph 2, that the presumed consumption of rubber in all branches is greater in 1942 than it was in 1941. This is accounted for, presumably, by reason of a reduction in imports of rubber manufacturers. It is true that they suggest sharp reductions in the use of crude rubber, ranging from 40% for shoe manufacture to 55% for industrial, medicinal and miscellaneous, with 45% reduction planned for tires, tubes and repair materials. If these restrictions were actually in effect, the case would be considerably more convincing. Dr. Raúl E. Arrarás Vergara, who signs the present informal proposal, is the representative of the Ministry of Agriculture on the Argentine Rubber Rationing Commission and has also been officially designated to discuss a rubber modus vivendi with

---

[29] Not printed.

the United States. The position of our Government, as set forth in Department's circular telegram of May 18 midnight,[31] which was transmitted by Embassy note No. 750 of May 21, 1942, to the Foreign Minister, has been explained. Further discussions have been very frank to the effect that the Argentine stock position is comparatively better than that of the United States considering demand, and that in view of this, it is quite improbable that our Government would be able to set aside further quantities of rubber for uses now prohibited in the United States.

It is believed that Dr. Arrarás Vergara understands thoroughly this point of view, but as he explains it, his problem is that of facing the different Argentine manufacturers, who are demanding that the Government provide ways and means of obtaining rubber from other American republics. Consequently, while he personally agrees that it would be better for Argentina to reach a modus vivendi with the United States, and withdraw from attempts to make purchase contracts with the other republics, it is thought that he personally fears the political pressure that would be brought by domestic manufacturers, should they be forced to drastically curtail their crude rubber consumption.

With this in mind, the discussion outlined under paragraph 4 was drafted. Likewise, Dr. Arrarás Vergara is now in Bolivia and when he left Buenos Aires, planned to go on to Peru. The proposal to be made to Peru is that, although the United States has a purchase contract with that country, Argentina could still supply rubber manufacturers, provided some Peruvian crude rubber could be diverted to Argentina.

The Embassy would appreciate instructions as to whether or not the United States is prepared to entertain a formal proposal of the Argentine Government to negotiate a rubber modus vivendi. At the same time it is presumed that with the conclusion of purchase contracts by the United States with Bolivia and Ecuador, the Argentine Government will realize that no substantial quantities of crude rubber can be obtained from those sources. It may then be willing to treat Argentine crude rubber requirements the same as those of other critically important materials. The Department will recall that rubber was made a special exception by reason of the sudden appearance of the decree providing for the Rubber Commission and giving to the Ministry of Agriculture the control over acquisition and importation of that product. (See voluntary report No. 870, March 6, 1942, and Embassy's despatch No. 4339, March 6, 1942.)[32] The

[31] See footnote 21, p. 315.
[32] Neither printed.

accomplishments to date of the Commission have not been substantial, probably for the same political reasons mentioned above which have hindered the adoption of any forthright restrictions on consumption.

There is one further point meriting attention, although only indirectly connected with the Argentine proposal. This has to do with the American companies—Goodyear and Firestone. Actually, their branches are Argentine companies and the local managers are interested in maintaining their plants at a level of production that will at least in some way be economical. Consequently, while they would prefer to look to the United States for rubber, they do not feel that it would be advisable to give the impression to the Argentine authorities that they do not wish to cooperate with any program devised for the purpose of obtaining more crude rubber for Argentine manufacturers, regardless of the source from whence it comes. Again, presumably, the contracts with Ecuador and Bolivia should automatically solve this problem, but the Department's opinion, especially as regards the position of the American companies, would also be appreciated.

Respectfully yours,　　　　　　　　　For the Chargé d'Affaires, a.i.
　　　　　　　　　　　　　　　　　　THOMAS L. HUGHES
　　　　　　　　　　　　　　　　　　Commercial Attaché

811.20 Defense (M) Argentina/310c : Telegram

The Secretary of State to the Chargé in Argentina (*Reed*)

WASHINGTON, September 11, 1942—8 p. m.

1358. Following from U. S. Commercial Company:

"1. We are advised there are immediately available in Buenos Aires approximately 50 kilos of platinum which can be purchased on a COD Buenos Aires basis.

2. You are authorized and requested to purchase these (approximately) 50 kilos of platinum COD Buenos Aires at a sum to be expended for this purchase not to exceed $400,000. U. S. C. C. will cable funds when required for payment.

3. This is a preclusive item; therefore, if at any time this authorization does not serve its purpose please cable immediately.

4. It should be emphasized that no transfer of funds should be made until the platinum is actually in your possession and has been appraised by competent platinum experts. It might even be suggested to the principals that the metal be deposited in escrow, subject to assays which might be secured from reputable firms either in Rio de Janeiro or in Buenos Aires. If neither of these places is acceptable for purpose of assays, proper samples should be sent to the United

States for final analysis at Ledoux and Company. If it is refined crude platinum, it should run not less than 975 fine. If it is represented as crude platinum, and if it originates in Colombia, it should not run less than 925 to 950 fine. If the metal is crude, assays should be made for iridium and rhodium as well, although it is possible that the seller may wish the palladium determination.

5. T. J. Williams, Metals Reserve representative in Buenos Aires, is fully informed regarding this matter and should be consulted in the execution of this authorization."

HULL

811.20 Defense (M) Argentina/311a

The Department of State to the Argentine Embassy [33]

MEMORANDUM

There exists in the Argentine an embargo on the export of beryl ore. There is great need of beryl ore in the United States, and our Embassy in Buenos Aires has repeatedly pointed this out to the appropriate authorities. Six months ago the Argentine Government gave as its reason for the maintenance of the embargo its desire to assure sufficient beryl ore for the Saba Plant which manufactures beryl oxide. The Saba Plant is anxious to find a market for this oxide.

In May 1942 our Embassy in Buenos Aires was informed that the Metals Reserve Company was prepared to make a proposed contract with the Saba Plant effective contingent upon the granting by the Argentine Government of export licenses for export to the United States of the accumulated stocks of beryl ore and contingent upon an agreement to grant licenses at the rate of a minimum of 100 tons of ore monthly out of current production. The request was also made that since consumption of the Saba Plant will be only about 1,000 tons of ore per year, export licenses should be granted for any quantity in excess of this requirement of Saba, but no less than 1,200 tons annually.

Our Embassy reported in August that the matter had been submitted to the Inter-Ministerial Commission. In September our Embassy reported that no reply had been received and that the Foreign Office had been informed that on about September 15 freight space would be available for the shipment of the accumulated stocks of beryl ore estimated at 800 tons and that, therefore, an early reply would be appreciated. The Foreign Office stated that the question would be submitted to the Inter-Ministerial Commission shortly.

[33] Handed to the Argentine Chargé by the Acting Chief of the Division of Defense Materials (Finletter) on September 11, 1942.

Since it now appears that the requirements of the Saba Plant have been taken care of and that the Metals Reserve Company is prepared to put into effect the proposed contract with Saba contingent upon an agreement to assure export licenses for beryl ore as described above, it would be greatly appreciated if the Argentine Government would take action to permit the freight space available in the immediate future to be used for the export of beryl ore to the United States, and would agree to the future export of beryl ore in the amounts described above.

WASHINGTON [undated].

811.20 Defense (M) Argentina/197 : Telegram

The Secretary of State to the Ambassador in Argentina (Armour)

WASHINGTON, September 18, 1942—5 p. m.

1397. 1. In view of protracted delay in effecting arrangements for the procurement of beryl, it was suggested at a meeting of representatives of interested agencies that you call together Messrs. Hughes, Jahns, Singewald, and Bates [34] for the purpose of reviewing the question of beryl procurement in Argentina and making such recommendations as, in your opinion, will best facilitate immediate procurement and dispose of existing vexatious questions.

2. In substitution of the proposal made in the Department's no. 656 of May 12, 1 p. m., it has been suggested that Metals Reserve might make a blanket offer to buy the entire Argentine production of beryllium products whether in the form of ore or of oxide leaving it entirely to the Argentine Government to control the amount of the productions of each material. Such proposal would contemplate no stipulation regarding maximum or minimum quantities but would of course call for removal of existing embargo on ore.

3. With respect to the question of our extending assistance in plant expansion to stimulate production of oxide, we believe it would be most difficult to provide necessary equipment during the course of the war. There is also the question whether supplies of beryl or oxide may be going forward to the Axis from Argentina through submarine shipment or other means. Do you believe such to be the case? We naturally should not wish plant expansion promoted by us to result in augmenting any such shipments.

4. Is it your opinion that delay hitherto affecting arrangements springs from obstructive purposes designed to induce us to believe that we can eventually obtain Argentine beryl without there being any bona fide intention to supply it?

---

[34] Thomas L. Hughes, Commercial Attaché in Argentina; William F. Jahns, Joseph T. Singewald, Jr., and Bennett R. Bates, members of a mission sent to Argentina by the Board of Economic Warfare.

5. Your full comment will be appreciated on the foregoing items together with such other suggestions and comment as you may have to offer. If the foregoing proposal is not satisfactory can you make a concrete proposal?

6. In connection with the foregoing care should be exercised that nothing should be said or done to prejudice anticipated favorable replies to the representations already made as set forth in the Department's no. 1314 of September 3, 5 p. m. and no. 1366 of September 12, 10 p. m.[35] Satisfactory replies to such representations would of course be preferred to the adoption of other measures.

HULL

811.20 Defense (M) Argentina/321 : Telegram

The Chargé in Argentina (Reed) to the Secretary of State

BUENOS AIRES, September 22, 1942—10 p. m.
[Received September 22—8 : 30 p. m.]

1840. Embassy's [*Department's*] 656, May 12, 1 p. m., and Metals Reserve contract of March 4, 1942.[36] The Embassy has received a communication from the Argentine Foreign Office today replying in substance as follows:

1. The Argentine Government is disposed to authorize once the requirements of Argentine industry are covered and the maintenance of a permanent stock of 200 tons is assured the exportation of up to 100 tons per month of beryl ore destined to the United States, total export permits not to amount to more than 1200 tons per annum. Prices paid for beryl ore will not be lower than those which the United States may agree upon in similar transactions with other countries.

2. It is likewise disposed to authorize the immediate shipment of up to 500 tons of the exportable surplus of beryl ore destined to the United States.

3. It will adopt the measures necessary for the proper fulfillment of paragraphs [1] and 2 as soon as the Embassy makes known that the Metals Reserve Company makes effective with the exclusion of clause 4 the contract for the purchase of beryl oxide concluded on March 4, 1942, with Saba.

If terms [are agreeable?] please cable authorization acceptance.

REED

---

[35] Neither printed.
[36] Contract not found in Department files; for Foreign Office note concerning its provisions. see telegram No. 825, May 5, 11 p. m., from the Ambassador in Argentina, p. 313.

811.20 Defense (M) Argentina/321 : Telegram

The Acting Secretary of State to the Ambassador in Argentina
(Armour)

WASHINGTON, October 3, 1942—2 p. m.

1483. From Metals Reserve. Your 1860 [*1840*] of September 22. You are hereby authorized to inform the Argentine government that the Metals Reserve Company considers the contract of March 3 [*4*], with the Sociedad Anónima Berilo Argentina for 200 metric tons of beryllium oxide to be in effect and that clause 4 under "Special Conditions" on the third page of the contract has been stricken out. This is the clause that refers to the agreement between the United States and Argentine Governments.

This action has been taken with the understanding that the Argentine government will issue export licenses immediately for the export of 500 metric tons of beryl ore now available in Argentina and that it will make additional export licenses available at a rate of 100 metric tons of beryl ore monthly hereafter, if available. Metals Reserve Company further agrees that the prices paid for Argentine beryl ore will conform to those paid for ores imported by it in similar transactions with other countries.

The attention of the Embassy is called to the fact that it would be extremely undesirable to have the entire 500 tons for which export license is to be issued shipped to this country on a single steamer. It is desired that the material be shipped in several lots with, preferably, not more than 200 tons in any single shipment. This fact has been communicated to Watson Geach & Co., agents for South American Mining Co., which has sold beryllium ore to Metals Reserve Company, but is being repeated to the Embassy to insure that the policy is carried out. Please advise Williams. [Metals Reserve.]

WELLES

811.20 Defense (M) Argentina/396 : Telegram

The Secretary of State to the Ambassador in Argentina (Armour)

WASHINGTON, November 18, 1942—10 p. m.

1754. From U. S. Commercial Company. Embassy's 2282, November 16, 4 p. m.[37] As it was not possible to give you a telegraphic reply in time, we telephoned T. J. Williams to purchase the lot of platinum at the price indicated, on the understanding, which he assured us was correct, that if we did not purchase same it would fall into unfriendly hands.

---

[37] Not printed; it indicated that 2½ kilos of platinum were available.

Please continue to cable us for instructions when further lots of this nature are available on the market. [U. S. Commercial Company.]

Hull

811.20 Defense (M) Argentina/435 : Telegram

The Ambassador in Argentina (Armour) to the Secretary of State

BUENOS AIRES, December 14, 1942—6 p. m.
[Received 7 p. m.]

2547. For Ducas,[38] USCCo, from Albarracin.[39] Embassy reliably informed that small quantities platinum intended for Axis are now being purchased in Colombia through Argentine channels. Informant who entirely trustworthy assures Embassy he can purchase 5 kilos now on hand and arrange purchase 2 kilos monthly thereafter payment against delivery Embassy Bogotá or designee. Price about 18 Argentine pesos gram including informant's travel expenses here to Colombia as his presence there essential.

This would stop at source part supply now coming here for Axis. Please cable if you wish us arrange. [Albarracin.]

ARMOUR

811.20 Defense (M) Argentina/435 : Telegram

The Secretary of State to the Ambassador in Argentina (Armour)

WASHINGTON, December 24, 1942—10 p. m.

2016. Reference Embassy's 2547.[40]

1. Supplementing Department's 2015 [41] in which you have been advised that the United States Commercial Company cannot accept this proposal and that Metals Reserve Company has a contract for and the United States Government an agreement with the Colombian Government for all of that country's platinum.

2. The existence of conditions reflected in your telegram would seem to be evidence that some platinum which should go to Metals Reserve is not being obtained by it in spite of the cooperative attitude of the Colombian Government.

3. In order that this diversion or smuggling operation in Colombian platinum may be halted, the Department suggests you advise

---

[38] Robert N. Ducas, Executive Vice President of the United States Commercial Company.
[39] Louis A. Albarracin, field representative of the United States Commercial Company.
[40] Supra.
[41] Not printed.

American Embassy at Bogotá of all the facts relative to this case for such appropriate action as that Embassy may be able to take.

HULL

EFFORTS TO CONTROL THE DISTRIBUTION OF AMERICAN EXPORTS TO ARGENTINA

740.00112A European War 1939/4700a : Circular telegram

The Secretary of State to All Diplomatic Representatives in the American Republics Except Central America

WASHINGTON, December 6, 1941—9 p. m.

The Department is giving consideration to a plan submitted by Treasury to control transactions undertaken by cloaks with respect to articles exported from the United States. Exporters in the United States would file an extra copy of export declaration, which would be dispatched immediately by airmail to the appropriate American mission. The American mission would then examine these declarations to determine whether cloaks or Proclaimed List nationals were involved. With respect to shipments in which such a person has an interest, the information would immediately be transmitted to the Department with a view to stopping the shipment or preventing delivery to the consignee through the cooperation of Canal Zone authorities, the British and the shipping lines concerned.

Please advise the Department whether such a plan would be practical from an administrative angle in so far as your mission and the consulates subject to your jurisdiction are concerned. In addition the Department would appreciate an expression of your views in general.

HULL

740.00112A European War, 1939/6000 : Telegram

The Ambassador in Argentina (Armour) to the Secretary of State

BUENOS AIRES, January 10, 1942—2 p. m.
[Received January 10—1:48 p. m.]

64. Department's circular telegram December 6, 9 p. m. Control of importations from the United States by cloaks was carefully discussed with the Ravndal Mission [42] and this Embassy is also of the opinion that only by careful control both here and in Washington may ship-

---

[42] Christian M. Ravndal, Assistant Chief of the Division of the American Republics, was instructed on November 19, 1941, to discuss with the American Missions in South America policies and procedures relating to export control, priorities, the freezing of foreign funds, and the Proclaimed List.

ment be prevented from reaching undesirable hands. For example, Armco International was recently advised that several firms not their customers are arbitrarily using Armco's name as supplier and enlisting support of Argentine Embassy to obtain high priority rating.

As it would be exceedingly difficult if not impossible to prevent delivery to consignee of shipments which may have already left the United States it would appear that a thorough check made prior to the embarkation would be more practicable. If the Department were to reinstate the system of individual license and were to forward daily to the Embassy an airmail list of all requests for export license for Argentina, listing the firm making the request, the consignee and the material concerned, it would be possible for this Embassy to determine each doubtful case and to advise by cable or airmail whether or not in our opinion the transaction is bona fide and whether the license should be issued. This system would supplant that now in effect of sending a special cable on each suspicious case and it is believed that it would provide a thorough control such as is not now possible under general license and occasional cables.

ARMOUR

835.24/273

The Ambassador in Argentina (Armour) to the Secretary of State

No. 4000   BUENOS AIRES, January 28, 1942.
                                        [Received February 3.]

SIR: I have the honor to refer to the Department's instruction of December 12, 1941, file No. 810.20, Defense/1791a,[43] concerning the proposed procedure to be followed in the distribution of any product allocated by the United States.

This Embassy is concerned with the procedure providing for issuance of the certificate of necessity by the foreign country, in this case Argentina.

In the case of tinplate, for example, the Argentine Government recently made a partial distribution involving 16,194 metric tons of the approximately 27,000 tons allocated to this country for the first quarter of 1942. Further, the Central Bank immediately advised the individual firms as to the quota pertaining to each. The Bank has also shown us a copy of the cable from the Argentine Embassy in Washington to the effect that the State Department approved of the allocation made by the Bank.

With one exception, that distribution was made on the basis of 1940 consumption. For the first quarter of 1942, however, the semi fiscal

---

[43] Not printed.

Corporación Argentina de Productores de Carnes (CAP) was granted a total of 200% of the tinplate used by the Company throughout the year 1940, whereas in other cases the distribution consistently approximated 25% of 1940 performance. This matter was called to the attention of the Central Bank, which entity insists that not only did they have the State Department's approval, but that the allocation was justified by reason of purchase by the CAP of a small *frigorífico* [44] in Concordia. It was further stated by the Central Bank that they have subsequently received advice from their Embassy in Washington to the effect that the State Department has asked them to immediately distribute 54,000 tons of the total allocation of 77,500 tons granted Argentina for all of 1942, and that in said distribution each *frigorífico* would be guaranteed as much tinplate as it needs up to a maximum production capacity. This has since been done by decree of January 27, 1942.

While this distribution would appear to be fair, it would be regrettable if the Argentine Government were to understand that the United States approved of an 800% increase in the quota for the CAP, while at the same time other producing units were held at their 1940 production levels. Consequently, it is respectfully suggested that the Argentine Embassy be advised that any approval given by the Department was only for the purpose of expediting the deliveries of tinplate and could not be construed as an approval of the actual distribution. Otherwise, should a greater shortage arise in the future, the Argentine Government may plead that the precedent has already been established whereby the CAP is justified to a share equal to or in some cases larger than the other *frigoríficos* who have been heavy producers for years. The basic features governing production capacity include first, the number of animals available and, second, the amount of machinery of each establishment.

This same situation is anticipated for the Yacimientos Petrolíferos Fiscales (YPF—Government Oil Fields) and, possibly, for some private concerns of considerable influence. In order to avoid such a difficulty, it would seem preferable that the power of redress which the Board of Economic Warfare retains, could better be exercised before the firms here are advised by the Argentine Government as to their particular quotas. It is believed that the full cooperation of the Central Bank can be obtained to the end that the Embassy confer with them before each individual firm is advised of its quota. The critical analyses of the Central Bank requirements studies which the Embassy is now preparing and forwarding to Washington contain complete recommendations as to distribution by firms. Hence, in

---

[44] Packing house or cold storage plant.

each case where these analyses have been prepared, the Embassy could immediately make its recommendations to the Central Bank. In those cases where no agreement is reached, an explanatory despatch would be prepared by the Embassy for the Board of Economic Warfare for its guidance. By this method, both embarrassment and unjust discrimination should be avoided.

This matter has been discussed informally with the Central Bank. Unfortunately the Director and his immediate subordinates in charge of this office are now absent from Buenos Aires, but those left temporarily in charge see no objection to that procedure. It is felt that Dr. Prebisch [45] will also approve.

Respectfully yours,

For the Ambassador
THOMAS L. HUGHES
Commercial Attaché

835.24/294 : Telegram

The Ambassador in Argentina (Armour) to the Secretary of State

BUENOS AIRES, February 9, 1942—3 p. m.
[Received 5 : 03 p. m.]

239. In analyzing the import requirements studies of the Central Bank it is noted that several Government departments are requesting large amounts of various materials heretofore not imported by them direct. Likewise the practice whereby Proclaimed List construction companies obtain government contracts at exceedingly low bids is of increasing concern, as this Embassy is convinced that these contracts are let in most if not all cases on the supposition if not tacit understanding that the Government itself will obtain from the United States the necessary raw materials delivering them in turn to the construction firms successful in obtaining government contracts.

In view of the policy expressed in the Department's 151, February 4, 9 p. m.[46] I believe the Argentine Government should be informed to the effect that no material can be allocated direct to government departments for work let or to be let on a contract basis but that rather it will be the responsibility of the individual contractor to obtain this material in his own name. In as much as the Argentine Central Bank is authorized to make both the import requirements studies and the recommendations of the Argentine Government as to the local distribution of materials allocated by the United States, I believe the Department may wish this point of view

[45] Raúl Prebisch, manager of the Banco Central de la República Argentina.
[46] *Post*, p. 377.

expressed to the Bank's manager Prebisch rather than through formal channels.

I would appreciate early instructions on this point.

ARMOUR

835.24/368

Memorandum by the Acting Chief of the Division of the American Republics (Bonsal) to the Under Secretary of State (Welles)

[WASHINGTON,] March 10, 1942.

MR. WELLES: It is my understanding that we have adopted a definitively negative policy toward Argentina in regard to: (*a*) the shipment to that country of war material and (*b*) the conclusion of an over-all purchase agreement covering strategic materials.

The question which now arises in acute form is the policy to be adopted regarding the export to Argentina of scarce materials. These materials are vitally important to the economic activities of the country. No policy of restriction below the extremely low levels made necessary in the case of the American republics as a whole could be effective in the case of Argentina without British cooperation. I do not think that we would wish to ask for such cooperation or that any specific discrimination against Argentina in this matter would be a contribution to the war effort.

I therefore recommend that our allocations, priorities, and export license policies toward Argentina be handled on the same basis as toward the other American republics. It seems to me that to proceed otherwise would be to fail to take a realistic view of Argentina's importance to us and to the British at this time.

PHILIP W. BONSAL

835.24/352 : Telegram

The Ambassador in Argentina (Armour) to the Secretary of State

BUENOS AIRES, March 12, 1942—midnight.
[Received March 12—11:50 p. m.]

477. (Section 1)   Department's 330, March 10, 2 p. m.[47]   The continued approval of export license applications without respect to the merit of the shipper or consignee is the cause of constant embarrassment to the Embassy.   It tends to render nil the work being done both by and with the Central Bank and if it is allowed to continue, will greatly endanger our hope of retaining the cooperation of that insti-

---

[47] Not printed.

tution. It is useless for us to work with the bank and to insist to individual importers that they do not qualify for quotas under allocation when at the same time they are able to see by the manifests of incoming ships that large quantities of iron and steel and other products subject to allocation are constantly arriving, consigned either to order or to firms which would not normally be entitled to any quota whatsoever. Please refer to Department's instruction 1879, February 29 [21], 1942, and to Embassy's 417, March 4, 7 p. m.,[49] the company also the steamship *Penelope*, referred to in cable under reply, brought a total of 178 consignments covering 5269 long tons of iron and steel. Of these, 97 consignments, covering 2400 tons, came to firms who would either not merit any quota, or to order, or to other entities which in numerous cases the Embassy has reason to believe are instrumental in providing materials for Proclaimed List firms. It is difficult to understand why export licenses are granted in such questionable cases without referring the matter to this Embassy, while at the same time a transaction involving the International General Electric Company, Incorporated, and the Compañía Argentina de Electricidad is made the subject of a special inquiry, even though it involved only 475 pounds of mica tape and strips (Department's 342, March 11, 6 p. m.[50]).

A further result of the present practice is the following: The German chemical and pharmaceutical firms, whose monthly sales turnover is 5 million pesos and whose profits are sufficiently large to enable them to be the most effective contributors to the German propaganda machine, are still obtaining all their requirements through a series of small intermediaries in the United States and here. Química Merck, one of the leading German firms, is now advertising recently received American drugs as made in the United States but bottled by Merck here as propaganda to their clients that the Proclaimed List and the export control system of the United States is ineffectual as far as the Axis is concerned. This is but one of many examples.

As the Department feels that the recommendation of Embassy's 372 [322], February 22 [20],[50] to the effect that no further export licenses be granted for products subject to allocation unless accompanied by the corresponding certificate of necessity or in lieu thereof special recommendation of this Embassy, would result in delays in shipping and in upsetting of production schedules, it is suggested that effective control could still be maintained through application of the recommendation contained in Embassy's 64, January 10, 2 p. m. This suggested that Department forward daily to this Embassy an air mail list of all re-

---

[49] Neither printed.
[50] Not printed.

quests for export licenses for Argentina, listing the firm making the request, the consignee, the material concerned, its volume and value.

(Section 2) This system should be employed for all merchandise until such time as final decision on allocations procedure is taken. Thereafter it should still be applied to all merchandise not subject to allocation. There would be relatively little delay if the Department were to follow this suggestion, since the Embassy's recommendation on each application for export license could be in Washington within 1 week from the time the application was made. This would eliminate a term of shipping delays and the upsetting of production schedules, but it would at the same time effectively stop both speculation, which is everywhere in evidence at present, and the shipment of merchandise which we are confident now finds its way into the hands of Axis firms.

I feel sure Department will appreciate the difficult position in which Embassy finds itself as regards work with the Argentine Government in the mutual attempt properly to control destination and distribution of the limited critical and strategic materials which we are in a position to provide for Argentina's most imperative needs. Furthermore, the practice which now allows indiscriminate shipments to reach Argentina does not appear consistent with the policy which I understand was adopted following the Rio Conference.[51]

ARMOUR

835.24/352 : Telegram

The Acting Secretary of State to the Ambassador in Argentina
(Armour)

WASHINGTON, March 18, 1942—7 p. m.

380. The Department is recommending to the Board of Economic Warfare that it follow temporarily the suggestion made in the last sentence of section 1 of your 477 of March 12, midnight.

WELLES

835.24/390⅔

Memorandum by the Assistant Secretary of State (Acheson) to
the Under Secretary of State (Welles)

[WASHINGTON,] March 21, 1942.

MR. WELLES: I agree that the attached *aide-mémoire* [52] raises the point which you wish to take up with Lord Halifax.[53] In the applica-

---

[51] Third Meeting of the Foreign Ministers of the American Republics, held at Rio de Janeiro January 15–28, 1942; for correspondence concerning this meeting, see pp. 6 ff.
[52] Memorandum of March 23 to the British Embassy, *infra*.
[53] British Ambassador in the United States.

450858—62——22

tion of this principle, the British may raise questions which you may wish to have in mind. Yesterday in a conversation with Sir Frederick Phillips [54] he stressed the growing concern of the British Treasury on the increasing British sterling obligations, mentioning specifically obligations arising out of essential purchases in South America, chiefly in Argentina and Brazil. The British will probably be apprehensive if our proposal to them meant reducing the total amount of exports which they could make at this time and which were meant to reduce their sterling obligations. This does not mean that they cannot shift exports from one commodity to another; but even here there may be some difficulty since, for instance, recent cables indicate that they are reducing textile production in order to transfer workers to other industries.

I do not raise these considerations to suggest that the point that we are raising is not sound but merely to anticipate observations that Lord Halifax may make, the answer to which is that obviously in the application of principle considerable study and flexibility will be necessary.

I suggest also that the attached cable might be held up [55] until a start has been made with the British in the discussion of their cooperative program in South America.

Dean Acheson

835.24/390⅔

The Department of State to the British Embassy

Memorandum

In the light of the acute shortage in the joint supply of certain strategic materials available to the Governments of the United States and Great Britain, and of the increasing demands of the United Nations for such materials, it is desired to bring to the attention of the British Government certain aspects of the problem of supplying restricted commodities to Argentina.

The appropriate export agencies of the United States Government have endeavored primarily to meet the material needs of the United Nations and, secondarily, to strengthen so far as possible the national economies of those nations which have associated themselves with the objectives of the United Nations by severing relations with the Axis powers. This course of action has been dictated as much by necessity

---

[54] British Treasury Representative in the United States.
[55] A marginal note indicates that this cable was not sent.

as by choice, since the available supplies of many essential materials have been extremely limited.

In the implementation of this twofold policy, this Government has been forced to reject an increasing portion of the export license applications covering proposed shipments of scarce commodities to Argentina and to make certain reductions in the allocations of such commodities which would normally be made to that country. The effect of this policy, therefore, is to make certain strategic materials available for distribution among those nations which are assisting directly or indirectly in the war effort.

It would clearly not redound to the benefit of the United Nations or their sympathizers if the deficiencies thus suffered by Argentina were fully compensated by the shipment of offsetting amounts of certain strategic materials from British sources. The cooperation of the British Government is therefore desired in the task of assuring that in this connection the limited supplies available will be conserved for purposes of the united war effort.

In the event that the British Government concurs in principle with the considerations set forth above, this Government will welcome a discussion relative to specific commodities, the shortage of which has necessitated the proposed course of action.

WASHINGTON, March 23, 1942.

835.24/389½

Memorandum by the Adviser on Political Relations (Duggan) to the Under Secretary of State (Welles)

[WASHINGTON,] March 25, 1942.

MR. WELLES: It would be consistent with the policy you and Ambassador Armour agreed upon at Rio de Janeiro, and which has since been followed by the Department, the BEW [56] and the WPB,[57] to give Argentina the reduced set of figures for second quarter allocations. These have been worked out, in consultation with our Embassy at Buenos Aires, on the basis of a policy of continuing to furnish those products necessary to maintain public health, essential transportation, et cetera, and of such other products which should not more appropriately be given to those countries which are collaborating more effectively in the war effort. The application of this policy has re-

---

[56] Board of Economic Warfare.
[57] War Production Board.

sulted in a curtailment of the amounts of tight commodities to be made available to Argentina during the second quarter.

I feel that if the policy which has been laid down is to be effective this new set of figures for second allocations should be approved.

Does this have your agreement? [58]

LAURENCE DUGGAN

835.24/386

Memorandum by the Chief of the Division of the American Republics (Bonsal) to the Under Secretary of State (Welles)

[WASHINGTON,] March 28, 1942.

MR. WELLES: Dr. García Arias, of the Argentine Embassy, came in this morning and drew my attention to the attached article headed "Ban on shipments to Argentina is on" in the *New York Times* of this morning. The article emphasizes the fact that there is discrimination between Argentina and Chile, with the latter being favored.

Dr. García Arias expressed the opinion that articles of this nature produce a most unfortunate effect in Argentina, particularly at this time when Admiral Sueyro and General Lapez [59] are explaining to Argentine officials and others the attitude of the United States. It was Dr. García Arias' suggestion that at one of your press conferences you refer to this article and state that the isolated examples therein described could in no sense be considered representative of United States policy.

Dr. García Arias and I then discussed the entire situation of Argentine-United States relations in a general way without arriving at any very novel conclusions.

I am aware that our policy toward Argentina has been given the most careful consideration. It is therefore with some diffidence that I express the view that there are only two effective policies open to us: (*a*) economic cooperation on the same basis as with other American republics, and (*b*) economic warfare. A policy which merely places Argentina in a somewhat less favorable position than the other republics in the distribution of the limited amount of export materials which we can spare is one which will merely cause irritation without, in my opinion, producing any favorable effect upon Argentina's foreign policy. On the other hand, the attitude which we have taken regarding military matériel is perfectly sound and

---

[58] Notation on memorandum by Mr. Welles: "O.K."
[59] Rear Adm. Sabá Sueyro and Brig. Gen. Eduardo T. Lapez headed an Argentine military purchasing mission to the United States; for correspondence on this mission, see pp. 371 ff.

realistic; it places Argentina at a real disadvantage in relation to Brazil and should exert a considerable leverage on military, naval, and political circles.

PHILIP W. BONSAL

835.24/386

Memorandum by the Under Secretary of State (Welles) to the Chief of the Division of the American Republics (Bonsal)

[WASHINGTON,] March 30, 1942.

MR. BONSAL: I still feel that the policy which we are pursuing is the most expedient under present circumstances, and the one best calculated to produce satisfactory results. For the time being, at least, I do not propose making any statement in the press conference for public consumption. I am, however, having a conference tomorrow with the press during which I will speak quite frankly off the record and for background.

S[UMNER] W[ELLES]

835.24/397

The Executive Director of the Board of Economic Warfare (Perkins) to the Secretary of State

WASHINGTON, March 31, 1942.

MY DEAR MR. SECRETARY: I have your letter of March eighteenth [60] in which you state that the Department of State concurs in our view that full British cooperation is necessary in the implementation of the policy of this Government toward Argentina.

I am enclosing, herewith, the second report [60] of the special committee working on licenses and allocations for Argentina. You will note that the action has been quite severe. I cannot emphasize too strongly, however, that in the opinion of the Board of Economic Warfare unilateral economic pressure of this type cannot be made completely effective, and, moreover, may lead to serious misunderstanding with resulting harm to the best interests of the United States.

I shall be glad to discuss these matters with you at your early convenience.

Sincerely yours,

MILO PERKINS

---

[60] Not printed.

835.24/670

Mr. Bernard D. Meltzer [62] to the Assistant Secretary of State
(Acheson)

BUENOS AIRES, April 3, 1942.
[Received April 10.]

DEAR DEAN: The Embassy at Buenos Aires is so exercised about the ineffectiveness of export controls that I thought it desirable to report to you. I understand that Mr. Armour may supplement the Embassy's strong telegram on this subject (No. 477, March 12, 2 p. m. [*midnight*]) with a personal letter to Mr. Welles.

In addition to the points made in the Embassy's telegram, the staff has told me the following: Many new shoestring operators have mushroomed into the import field in Argentina. They are prepared to act as cloaks for blacklisted concerns in return for the high prices which the latter are willing to pay. Established importers are more reluctant to run the risks involved in cloaking.

These new importers have their counterparts in the States where many new exporters have recently sprung up. These exporters appear to be working with the cloaks down here because the latter will pay more than the established importing units in Argentina. OPA's [63] price ceilings are often circumvented by concealed arrangements for extra compensation.

Export controls, in the States, have apparently been ineffective as a means of stopping shipments to questionable consignees in Argentina. The Embassy states that this is true even of those commodities subject to specific licensing requirements. In fact, the Embassy states—this appears to be an exaggeration—that export controls have operated in reverse, permitting shipments to new and doubtful consignees while blocking them to old reliable concerns. The administration of the controls has, according to the Embassy, been so capricious and perverse that local importers and officials grin slyly, put it all down to grafting by the authorities in the States, and consider it a first-class scandal.

I believe that *some* of the Embassy's indignation results from inadequate information regarding the time when the requirement of a specific export license is imposed on particular commodities, and from inadequate information in general concerning the operation of export controls, allocations, etc. As a result of lacking adequate information, 1) The Embassy often suspects that shipments have arrived because of stupid or irregular issuance of export licenses when, in fact, the

---

[62] Mr. Meltzer, Assistant to Assistant Secretary of State Acheson, was on a visit to Argentina.
[63] Office of Price Administration.

difficulty lies in the absence of any requirement of an export license. 2) The Embassy is not in position to explain away to the Central Bank, or to reliable concerns which have been denied licenses, shipments of commodities which left the States a few days before the requirement of a specific license was imposed. 3) The Embassy lacks an adequate framework of reference for its investigations, often seeking to determine the method by which a license was secured by an undesirable when the commodity involved was not subject to the requirement of a specific license at the time it left the States.

I have discussed the whole question of information with appropriate members of the Embassy staff, all of whom say that Washington has kept them very poorly informed. Mr. Lankenau,[64] who is assigned to export control matters, has prepared a despatch to Mr. Ravndal, urgently requesting certain specified information, and proposing a procedure whereby he may be kept informed in the future.

I have not been able to check the merit of the Embassy's objections with respect to specific cases, and I recognize the possibility of another Pennzoil dud.[65] I have, however, suggested that a full report on all questionable shipments, giving the names of ships, days of departure and arrival, names of consignees and shippers and quantities consigned, be transmitted to the Department so that specific cases can be checked by B.E.W., and flaws of [or] irregularities in control system be discovered.

I have also suggested that the Embassy quickly report to Washington any evidence that price ceilings in the States are being violated by exporters there. In this connection, OPA may, with respect to price-controlled commodities, be of some assistance in reducing questionable shipments. Exporters in the States may be encouraging or winking at such shipments because they can be made at prices well in excess of price ceilings. A vigorous enforcement of those ceilings as they relate to exports may remove economic incentive for dealing with questionable customers and thereby cut down such dealings.

As you know, several measures have been suggested for tightening up export controls down here:

1) The requirement of specific licenses for all commodities.
2) Clearance of all applications for licenses with the Embassy.
3) Clearance by the Embassy of applications covering shipments to consignees deemed "questionable" by B.E.W.
4) Furnishing copies of the confidential list to the collectors of custom, with instructions to stop shipments to unsatisfactory consignees. (Collectors may be already doing this, or may be precluded

---

[64] Richard F. Lankenau, junior economic analyst in the Embassy in Argentina.
[65] This is a reference to an unsupported surmise that the Pennzoil firm shipped oil to a Proclaimed List national.

from doing this by administrative or shipping difficulties. I have previously written Donnie [66] on this subject.)

The Embassy favors the first two measures, and particularly the second. If, as seems to be the case, difficulties here result from the repeated issuance of licenses to questionable consignees or for suspiciously large amounts, a trial of the second measure is warranted—unless administrative or shipping difficulties make it unfeasible. In connection with measure 3, a greater degree of skepticism in Washington, particularly in relation to shipments of unusual quantities, would seem to be in order.

Some skulduggery may be taking place in the form of forging of certificates of necessity which are issued by the Central Bank. As you know, the Bank issues a numbered certificate to appropriate importers, and forwards a copy to the Embassy. Since the Embassy does not forward copies to Washington, there appears to be no basis for an adequate check of the authenticity of the certificate of necessity in Washington. Although there is no indication that forgery has occurred, it would seem desirable to have summaries of the certificates transmitted to Washington so that they can be checked against export applications. The Embassy is of the opinion that such a procedure would be desirable and would involve only a negligible administrative burden. I have asked the Embassy to submit its views to the Department.

We have had a most pleasant stay in Buenos Aires, and are leaving for Montevideo tonight.

With best wishes [etc.]   BERNIE

835.24/395 : Telegram

The Acting Secretary of State to the Ambassador in Argentina (Armour)

WASHINGTON, April 8, 1942—3 p. m.

508. Your 604, April 2.[67] The Board of Economic Warfare maintains that it is not practicable to forward a list of all applications as requested. An alternative procedure is being inaugurated immediately, whereby the report of the Special Committee reviewing Argentine applications will be airmailed daily. This report is a descriptive list of the majority of cases considered. The applications listed as approved should be immediately reviewed and the Department telegraphed if rejection is recommended.

The procedure is explained more fully in airmail instruction.

                                                            WELLES

---

[66] Presumably Walter J. Donnelly, Commercial Attaché in Brazil.
[67] Not printed.

835.24/352 : Telegram

The Acting Secretary of State to the Ambassador in Argentina (Armour)

WASHINGTON, April 13, 1942—9 p. m.

513. Embassy's 477, March 12, midnight. The Department is convinced that the only way in which the situation described can be rectified is to call in all outstanding Argentine licenses issued between October 10 and March 1 and refer them to the Embassy for recommendation; and the Department is prepared to request the Board of Economic Warfare to do this. (By *Current Controls Bulletin* No. 11 of March 14,[68] all individual export licenses dated prior to October 10 were revoked effective midnight April 10 and all outstanding licenses issued on or after October 10 will be valid for 6 months only).

As similar action is not at present contemplated with regard to any other American Republic, and since the Department is most anxious that no action should be taken which might give the Argentine Government grounds for alleging pressure or discrimination, the Department is, however, unwilling to make the request without the knowledge and consent of the Argentine Government.

Please take this matter up with the Foreign Office making it clear that the proposed course is the only practicable way in which speculators and other undesirable consignees can be eliminated.

You may add that the Argentine Embassy has informally suggested that licenses be recalled as outlined in order to permit its Government to regularize its own internal procedure.

WELLES

835.24/595d

The Secretary of State to the Ambassador in Argentina (Armour)

No. 2161   WASHINGTON, April 14, 1942.

SIR: I refer to your telegram No. 477 of March 12, 1942 in which it is stated that the distribution in Argentina of materials imported from the United States is most unsatisfactory, owing to the fact that export licenses are issued without due respect to the merits of the consignee or purchaser. The suggestion was made that all applications for licenses be sent to the Embassy for recommendation before action is taken upon them.

---

[68] The *Current Controls Bulletin* was issued periodically by the Office of Export Control of the Board of Economic Warfare.

I have been advised by the Office of Export Control of the Board of Economic Warfare that it is not practicable to delay consideration of all applications for license to export materials to Argentina until the Embassy has given its recommendations with respect to such applications. An alternative procedure, however, has been suggested which appears to be fairly satisfactory in that it will give the Embassy an opportunity to review a majority of the applications approved. This procedure, which is being inaugurated with the forwarding of this instruction, is to transmit daily to the Embassy copies of the reports of the Special Committee which passes on applications for license to export to Argentina. These reports which embody the decisions of the Committee on all applications reviewed by it will be forwarded henceforth by airmail without covering instructions. This Committee takes action on all applications which have a value of $500 or more, and it is understood that the volume of applications considered by it represents over eighty per cent of all applications for license to export to Argentina and includes all items of significance. The Department is represented on this Committee which was established on February 16, 1942 and which has been implementing the Department's policy with respect to Argentina.

It will be noted that these daily reports of the Committee's decisions include the name of the applicant, description of the material, including the volume and value, the names of the consignee and purchaser, and, in the case of a rejection, the reason for the action taken. The Embassy should review these decisions promptly and telegraph the Department immediately if it disapproves the granting of a license in any instance. The Embassy should not, except in exceptional cases, advise the Department regarding the decisions of the Committee to reject applications, as due consideration has been given to the supply situation in each instance before this decision was made. As soon as the Department is informed by the Embassy that it disapproves the granting of a particular license, the Office of Export Control will be notified, and that agency has agreed to immediately revoke the license in question. If the Embassy acts promptly in forwarding recommendations, revocation of licenses can be made before shipment of the goods has been made. This procedure should give the Embassy the means of preventing the shipment of all significant items.

With respect to the statement in the telegram under reference that license applications are approved without due consideration to the merits of the consignee, I should like to point out that, under present procedure, all applications must indicate the names of the consignee and purchaser, and these names are checked by the Office of Export Control against the Proclaimed List and the Confidential List. Apparently, these lists are incomplete and unsatisfactory, and, if the above-outlined procedure does not work out satisfactorily, it would appear advisable for the Embassy to prepare a White List against which all applications could be checked.

In connection with the statement in your telegram under reference that goods are arriving consigned "to order", the Office of Export Control advises that applications are only granted when the names of the consignee and purchaser are given and that if a shipment is indicated as being consigned "to order", the application is rejected. It is believed that your impression that licenses are granted for the exportation of goods consigned "to order" may be owing to the fact that ships' manifests often indicate consignments as being "to order", although the goods in question are covered by a license on which the consignee and purchaser are shown. Licenses are granted, however, to an applicant who indicates that its own subsidiary is the consignee and purchaser. For example, licenses are granted to the United States Steel Corporation for material consigned to the United States Steel Corporation in Argentina. It is assumed that the Embassy can, in a large part, supervise the distribution of materials consigned in this fashion. However, should the Embassy disapprove of the granting of licenses in this manner, you should inform the Department accordingly and the problem will be taken up with the Office of Export Control.

I should like to point out that some of the goods arriving in Argentina were undoubtedly licensed prior to the implementation of the present policy which started with the functioning of the Special Committee on February 16. As licenses are valid for six months, consideration is being given to requesting that outstanding licenses be called in for revalidation, at which time these licenses could be revoked in light of the existing policy. However, if this action were taken with respect to Argentine licenses only, such a step might well be called discriminatory and thus not in accord with our announced policy. I should appreciate your views on such a proposal, as well as those on this entire problem.

Very truly yours,   For the Secretary of State:
                                    DEAN ACHESON

835.24/670

The Ambassador in Argentina (Armour) to the Acting Secretary of State

BUENOS AIRES, April 16, 1942.

DEAR SUMNER: I am glad to acknowledge your letter of March 27,[69] advising me of the manner in which our export control authorities

---

[69] Not printed.

have already started to implement our policy of sharing supplies of scarce commodities with countries siding with us. You ask my further comment on the manner in which we may distribute whatever we find it advisable to supply Argentina in such a way that "the friendly majority of the Argentine people would be strengthened at the expense of the unfriendly but influential minority".

First let me reiterate that not only do we in the Embassy and other Americans here, leaders in our business community with whom I have spoken, heartily approve of this policy, but I further believe that a large bulk of the thinking Argentine people are of the same feeling. In this connection you will recall the views expressed by Alexander Shaw [70] in his memorandum, a copy of which I sent you with my letter of April 11.[71] Consequently, it is gratifying to note the emphasis given to make this policy thoroughly effective.

I have discussed at length with members of the Embassy staff the suggestions contained in your letter, covering diversion of materials through operation on:

(a) The basis of a confidential white list; or,
(b) The basis of reference of questionable license applications to the Embassy for recommendation; or,
(c) The institution of a general requirement that Certificates of Necessity accompany all applications for licenses to export merchandise to Argentina.

It is our opinion that the third method should be the one employed. It is true that the adoption of the combined white list and reference to the Embassy of questionable license applications would provide excellent export control, but this system could not be applied to products under allocation. The Central Bank would also be left in the same position as now, namely, with no voice in approving the prospective Argentine consignee or consumer. I emphasize this point because of the cooperation which the Embassy has enjoyed with the Central Bank and which I feel should be maintained to the end that unnecessary irritation on the part of the Argentine Government be avoided. At the same time, with the Central Bank we are in a position to be quite frank in all of our discussions, both of policy and procedure.

The maintenance of a white list also offers practical difficulties in that many firms of excellent reputation would nevertheless not be acceptable for products which they now desire to import, simply because those products are outside their normal business.

---

[70] Alejandro E. Shaw, Argentine economist.
[71] Letter of April 11 to Mr. Welles not found in Department files; a copy of Mr. Shaw's memorandum was transmitted also by the Ambassador to Mr. Philip Bonsal in letter of the same date, not printed.

Regarding the probable attitude of the Argentine Government, you will be interested to know that only recently Central Bank officials themselves have broached this subject and, in substance, have indicated the hope that a system employing Certificates of Necessity for all imports be adopted. This encourages me even more to recommend that it be placed in effect as soon as is possible.

I believe that some of the essential features of the plan would be:

1. Two series of Certificates of Necessity: one for allocated products and another for those not subject to allocation.

2. A copy of each Certificate issued by the Central Bank to be supplied to the Embassy immediately.

3. The Embassy will recommend to the Department action to be taken on each Certificate; these recommendations would be in numerical order on a special form. The form would include the Certificate number, date, to whom issued, volume and value of product and recommendation of Embassy, with explanation of reason. These sheets would be forwarded with each air mail pouch or preferably by courier.

4. The Department should advise the Embassy immediately of all rejections.

Neither the Argentine importing firms nor the Central Bank should know the extent of Embassy authority in decisions concerning export licenses, but I believe that the latter should be advised of the general procedure so that its officials will consult freely with the Embassy before issuing Certificates. There is still a tendency on their part to issue certain Certificates and advise us afterwards, a practice which we hope will soon be discontinued.

To be successful, this control would require the rejection in Washington of all but very exceptional cases where Certificates of Necessity have not been issued. It will be equally imperative that export licenses be granted for Certificates approved by the Embassy except in those cases where scarcity of the material concerned requires rejection. Probably it will be necessary for the Argentine Government to agree to issue limitation orders in keeping with those issued in the United States. The application of the system will also require a full understanding on our part of general policy as regards use of materials, the issuance of Certificates of Necessity to re-selling firms, relative importance of effect upon the economy of the country and of activities which might be considered as contributing in some way to the war effort. I mention these points in the belief that, while the system could probably be placed in effect through correspondence, the Department may feel that it could be more effectively worked out and subsequent confusion avoided if some officer of the Embassy were to spend a short time in Washington for that purpose. It is also difficult to estimate how much additional work would accrue to the Embassy and, of course, it might be found necessary to request some additional personnel, but it is doubtful if any more would be required under this system than under that utilizing the white list and the reference of questionable applications to the Embassy.

I shall await with interest your decision in this matter and in the meantime we shall do everything possible to expedite our replies to the lists you now plan to forward for checking.

With my best personal regards, I am

Very sincerely yours,   NORMAN ARMOUR

835.24/595e

The Secretary of State to the Ambassador in Argentina (Armour)

No. 2171   WASHINGTON, April 16, 1942.

SIR: There is enclosed a list of the commodities allocated to Argentina for the second quarter of 1942.[72] Iron and steel products, and some other additional items, will be announced shortly.

The allocations, as shown, are based largely on the recommendations of your Mission; and in this connection the Department wishes to express to you and your staff its great appreciation of the reports on essential requirements which have been submitted by your office. It is hoped that the reporting officers will continue to spare no effort to supply the Department with this vitally important information. A questionnaire is being prepared for your guidance in collecting and analyzing the type of information of most value to the agencies in Washington.

The Department is aware that our Missions have been handicapped by lack of information as to the exact procedure followed in the War Production Board and the Office of Export Control with regard to allocations and the licensing for export of allocated commodities. The following is designed to explain the background of the allocations system and to give the Missions a picture of the situation as it exists today.

Last January, it was necessary to announce allocations before the machinery to administer them was set up. Following their announcement, the War Production Board began trying to fit allocations into production schedules. This proved to be so complicated, in view of the rapid conversion of industries to war production, that in effect there was no fixed allocations procedure during the first quarter of the year. The War Production Board, conscious of the necessity of providing for the other American republics, proceeded on the basis of priority

---

[72] Not attached to file copy.

ratings, and it is gratifying to record that very substantial quantities of exports moved forward during a most difficult period.

During the first quarter, at the suggestion of this Government, the other American republics set up Certifying Agencies, most of which are now functioning. It has developed rather logically that in many countries the Certificates have become corollary to systems organized to supervise or control the equitable distribution and the price of the commodities upon arrival. Thus, as is evident from despatches received by the Department, the foreign governments are concerned as to the treatment accorded the Certificates by the Office of Export Control.

In the first quarter the Office of Export Control approved thousands of applications with and without accompanying Certificates of Necessity. The flow of production and export is a continuous process and could not be held up pending receipt of Certificates. The latter are only now beginning to arrive in substantial numbers. Many of the commodities so licensed have been shipped, others are at seaboard awaiting bottoms, while others are still awaiting their turn for manufacture. Statistics are in preparation to show how much of each allocated commodity was licensed or shipped to each country during the first quarter of 1942.

The large number of outstanding licenses not covered by Certificates presents a most complicated problem particularly in the matter of coordinating these licenses with the efforts of the Certifying Agencies and control systems in the other American republics. There must be a transition period during which, concurrent with the approval of licenses covered by Certificates, the noncertified outstanding licenses can be worked off. The extent of this transition period cannot be determined at this time, but it may extend as long as through the second quarter, or until September 1, 1942. Attempt to recall or invalidate all outstanding licenses not covered by Certificates might result in interruption to the flow of manufacture and export. In this connection, however, and with special reference to Argentina, the Department refers to the strictly confidential telegram no. 513 of April 13, stating that the Department is willing, under certain stipulated conditions, to suggest to the Board of Economic Warfare that outstanding licenses for Argentina be recalled and submitted to the Embassy for recommendation.

These problems, and the questions they involve, have actively concerned the several interested agencies of the Government for several months; and the Department, the War Production Board and the Board of Economic Warfare are still trying to work out a practicable allocations and licensing procedure for the second and subsequent quarters of the year. The successful merging of the existing unsatisfactory procedure and a new improved procedure constitutes an administrative problem of the first magnitude; the readjustment must be made while administrative processes carry on.

The Department is pleased to be able to inform you that the production phase of the allocations system is being worked out rapidly and satisfactorily by the War Production Board. An announcement will shortly be made of a procedure which will (1) require manufacturers of an allocated commodity to reserve a definite portion of their production facilities to accommodate foreign orders within the overall total of the allocation for the industry; (2) require manufacturers to accept foreign orders that have been licensed for export; and (3) help the agents in the United States of foreign customers to find a manufacturer in the event difficulty is experienced in placing the order. Owing to the complexity of modern industrial organization, the implementing of orders issued by the War Production Board may be slightly different as regards different commodities, and announcements will be made in the near future with respect to fixed booking dates, etc., for orders to fit into production schedules for certain forward periods.

As for the licensing procedure, and the relation of the Certificate of Necessity thereto, the administrative problem is especially difficult. It is nevertheless hoped that an announcement will soon be made of a procedure which will provide the following: (1) During the transition period of working off the outstanding un-certified licenses, and in order to give certain of the other American republics more time to organize their Certifying Agencies, the Office of Export Control will give definite preference to those license applications covered by Certificates; (2) After a certain date the Office of Export Control will approve only those new applications for license to export which are covered by Certificates of Necessity (Confidential: this is the position being urged by the Department but there is no definite assurance as yet that the Board of Economic Warfare will agree). Thus it is hoped that during the third quarter and thereafter there will be a close coordination between the issuance of licenses and the issuance of Certificates of Necessity so as to enable the other governments to plan effectively the most advantageous distribution of scarce commodities within their economic systems.

With regard to other aspects of the allocations and licensing system the Department desires to give the following information in answer to specific questions presented by the Missions:

1. The Certificate of Necessity is to be used only for allocated commodities. However, the Board of Economic Warfare has by *Current Controls Bulletin* No. 10 of March 5, 1942, authorized its use in connection with rubber and rubber products. To date this is the only exception authorized. Use may be authorized in connection with

other very tight unallocated commodities, but only when specific instructions, as in the case of rubber, have been issued. In the latter case, instances of which will be very few, the Certifying Agencies should issue certificates with the greatest care and only for essential purposes. Such certificates will be considered in relation to the limitation orders affecting identical use in the United States.

2. The Certificate of Necessity will serve in lieu of a PD–1a form with regard to an allocated commodity. In this connection, however, the Certificate should contain full answers to the questions thereon, particularly as regards the end use of the commodity, existing inventories, and availability of substitutes. It is recognized that the Certifying Agencies in some of the other republics are still in process of organization and that all are not yet fully equipped to make the detailed investigations necessary to determine end use of allocated commodities for presentation on the Certificate form. Nevertheless, if such agencies, or any other agencies within the foreign governments, are to supervise the distribution of commodities after arrival they will eventually need to know such details. Thus the Missions are urged to encourage the agencies to persist in obtaining and recording such information, not only to comply with our requirements but also for their own future control purposes.

There are certain vitally important questions regarding allocations procedure which cannot be answered at this time. The first is whether the unused portion of a quarterly allocation will carry forward into subsequent quarters of the year. The problem is so involved that the Requirements Committee has not yet been able to work out a solution. The heavy industries of the United States are working against a strict forward time-table to satisfy the demands of the armed forces of the United Nations, and to attempt to telescope the unused portion of a quarterly allocation into production schedules for following quarters presents serious technical difficulties.

The second concerns the determination of what outstanding licenses shall be charged against first quarter allocations. For example, in many cases commodities licensed prior to January 1, 1942 are only now moving forward, while at the same time there are outstanding thousands of first quarter licenses for commodities that have moved forward only in part, and some not at all. The administrative problem of determining the exact status of the commodities that have been licensed, and checking them against factory production schedules and export shipments, is an extremely complicated one. However, the whole problem is receiving urgent attention and it is hoped that a solution will soon be arrived at.

During the transitional period the Department appreciates that the position of the Missions in this matter will be a difficult one. However, the Missions should continue to cooperate as fully as possible with the Certifying Agencies and encourage the careful issuance of the Certificates, endeavoring to see that there is no cloaking, and that established trade channels, and in particular American firms, receive a proportionately fair share of the trade based on past performance.

The Department believes it inevitable that as the issuance of Certificates progresses the responsibility of the Missions will increase. It is understood that practically all of the Missions have made informal arrangements with the Certifying Agencies to receive a copy of each Certificate as issued. Needless to say, should the Mission feel that any Certificate issued is not in the best interest of the United States, the Certifying Agency should be approached tactfully with a view to rectification. If the case is judged sufficiently serious to warrant intervention, as a last resort, the Mission can effectively nullify the Certificate by advising the Department in the premises.

There is evident a tendency in the other American republics to adopt forms of economic control that are perhaps more comprehensive than the situation warrants. The Department realizes, of course, the sovereign right of the other American republics to institute such controls as they deem necessary to maintain order in their economic systems. In this connection, the Missions should lend their friendly and informal counsel to prevent, if possible, the establishment of controls which appear unnecessarily extensive or impractical. The Missions should be prompt in reporting controls which adversely affect the treaty rights of the United States and its citizens abroad.

Very truly yours,   For the Secretary of State:
                                        DEAN ACHESON

835.24/533

The Ambassador in Argentina (Armour) to the Secretary of State

No. 4808   BUENOS AIRES, April 21, 1942.
                                        [Received May 2.]

SIR: I have the honor to refer to the Department's strictly confidential telegram No. 513, April 13, 9 p. m., in which the Embassy was advised that the Department is prepared to ask the Department of Economic Warfare to reject all outstanding export licenses issued between October 10, 1941 and March 1, 1942, referring them to the Embassy for recommendations. Inasmuch as the same action was not contemplated at this time with regard to any other of the American republics, and since the Department was very anxious that no action be taken which might give the Government of Argentina grounds for alleging discrimination or pressure, the Department was not willing to make the request without the consent and knowledge of the Argentine Government.

In line with the instructions to take this matter up with the Ministry of Foreign Affairs, the subject was discussed with Dr. Carlos L. Torriani, Director of the Division of Economic and Consular Affairs, and Dr. Alberto A. Bonfante, Subdirector of the same division. Both emphasized that they were not in a position to give an official opinion, either formally or informally, as the matter must of necessity be referred to the Ministries of Agriculture and Treasury and to the Argentine Central Bank. This they agreed to do by memorandum and give the Embassy a definite statement later on. Neither was of the opinion that it would be necessary to make the matter the subject of a formal note to the Minister.

In the course of the conversation, both officials raised certain positive objections. They fear that the revocation of all outstanding export licenses would result in harmful delay. Further, they drew the distinction, from the Argentine point of view, as between controlling the imports of merchandise through firms normally engaged in the business and the question of obtaining necessary import requirements regardless of through what channels. In other words, while they agree that it would be much better to have the merchandise allowed export licenses from the United States come direct to the proper firms and entities, they felt that it would be definitely better for the merchandise to reach Argentina through any channel than to run the risk of losing any of the limited supplies which Argentina hopes to receive. It was suggested that a more satisfactory solution would be for the Department to submit to the Embassy in Buenos Aires a list of the doubtful cases of the licenses now outstanding and to revoke only those recommended for that action by the Embassy.

It was explained that the Embassy was in no position to judge whether such a procedure would be feasible or not from the standpoint of the Department.

While definite advice as to the action preferred by the Argentine Government must await further advice from the Foreign Office, it would be appreciated if the Department could, in the meantime, advise as to the practicability of the above suggestion. In the course of the conversation it was emphasized that the United States wishes to follow the course most acceptable to the Argentine.

Respectfully yours,

For the Ambassador:
THOMAS L. HUGHES
Commercial Attaché

835.24/522 : Telegram

The Ambassador in Argentina (Armour) to the Secretary of State

BUENOS AIRES, April 25, 1942—4 p. m.
[Received 6 : 03 p. m.]

767. With regard to Department's willingness to ask the Board of Economic Warfare to revoke all outstanding Argentine licenses issued between October 10 and March 1, mentioned in Department's cable 513, April 13, 9 p. m., it is quite doubtful if Argentina will approve. Officials both of the Foreign Office (see strictly confidential despatch No. 4808, April 21) and of the Central Bank have strictly informally advised that they would be afraid to make such a recommendation, first, because of criticism that might ensue and second, because they fear some much needed merchandise now consigned to unsatisfactory parties might, through cancellation, not reach the country. They wish to know if it would not be possible for the Department to supply a list of the licenses outstanding, giving type of merchandise, quantity, and the name of the Argentine importer. With this list they could recommend those to be rejected. While the above is strictly unofficial, it is apparent that this will undoubtedly be the official position taken later. Consequently the Embassy would like advice as to the possibility of meeting their request.

ARMOUR

835.24/522 : Telegram

The Secretary of State to the Ambassador in Argentina (Armour)

WASHINGTON, May 5, 1942—7 p. m.

632. Your 767, April 25, 4 p. m. In view of indicated reluctance on part of Foreign Office and Central Bank to recommend revocation and reconsideration of outstanding licenses issued prior to March 1st, this proposal may well be abandoned. As regards possibility of supplying statistical record of such licenses, the Board of Economic Warfare estimates that compilation could not be completed in less than a month.

Since the abuses described in your 477 March 12 midnight have been largely eliminated by the checking procedure effective March 24, and since many of the uncertified licenses will have been consummated by delivery or will have expired in the interim, it would not appear practicable to attempt to furnish the data requisite for their re-examination.

The appropriate Argentinian import agencies may be assured that under present procedure the closest possible co-ordination between licensing and certificate of necessity is being achieved, and that their continued cooperation, despite inevitable early difficulties, is fully appreciated.

HULL

835.24/543

The Ambassador in Argentina (*Armour*) *to the Secretary of State*

No. 4954 BUENOS AIRES, May 5, 1942.
[Received May 14.]

SIR:

I. CERTIFICATES OF NECESSITY—ISSUANCE AND APPROVAL

I have the honor to refer to this Embassy's confidential despatch No. 4000 of January 28, 1942, discussing allocation procedure, especially as regards the insistence on the part of the Embassy to Central Bank officials that proper control can only be exercised if the Embassy approves the issuance of each Certificate, both as regards the firm or entity to which it is issued and the amount of the product involved.

This system has worked with relatively complete success from the beginning until recently. We now find that the Central Bank is prone to issue an increasing number of Certificates without prior approval of the Embassy. In some cases they subsequently ask our approval and explain the case and in others no mention is made at all. In order that our control might be complete, every Certificate has been carefully studied and the Department has been advised as to our recommendation on every Certificate issued. These recommendations have gone forward in the form of despatches or reports, for example, see voluntary report No. 982 of April 17, 1942,[73] reviewing Argentine Certificates of Necessity—first quarter allocation—iron and steel, reports Nos. 980 and 981, also of April 17, 1942,[74] and strictly confidential despatch No. 4438 of March 16, 1942, prepared by Mr. J. L. Camp, Senior Economic Analyst.[73] By this procedure, the Embassy has made a specific recommendation for every Certificate of Necessity issued by the Argentine Central Bank. The bulk of the Certificates were covered in the revised estimates of the Central Bank studies and in the Embassy's original recommendation for distribution of quotas. In those cases where the Certificates issued have been to firms and for amounts approved in those reports, no special mention of the Certificate has been made, but in every other case a special reference has been provided to the Department.

---

[73] Not printed.
[74] Neither printed.

As the Department will realize, this offers a means of providing a thorough and complete check, covering the distribution of every allocation. At the same time, it requires a great deal of careful work, as it is not the intent of the Embassy to refuse any request simply because the Argentine Central Bank may have issued the Certificate without prior Embassy approval. This means that each case must be discussed and studied carefully, and while the Embassy prefers to continue with this system, it would very much appreciate the Department's viewpoint as to the extent to which it is utilized by the Board of Economic Warfare in approving or disapproving export license applications. Likewise, except from the standpoint of scarcity, it would be helpful for the Embassy to know the degree to which its recommendations are accepted by the Board. If, except for scarcity of a product, the Embassy recommendations are generally accepted in making final decisions, unless later additional information is available in Washington, the system will be continued. If the Board of Economic Warfare does not utilize these reports or find them sufficiently useful to warrant their continuance, the system will be dropped.

The Embassy feels that it would be much more practicable to apply the greatest element of control possible here in Argentina and thus relieve the Board of Economic Warfare in Washington of the necessity of passing on the relative merits of each individual case. Always, the exception must be made as regards scarcity of the product concerned, as only the Board can be in a position to determine that point. However, the Embassy has certain advantages. It is limited in its work to the requirements of only one country. Staff members engaged in this work, with few exceptions, range from four to twelve years experience in Argentina. The advice and assistance of business men, whose knowledge of this market is still greater, is also utilized. This makes possible the relatively rapid separation of the desirable from the undesirable consignees or purchasers.

This is one of the primary reasons why it is believed that a system requiring the issuance of a Certificate of Necessity for all products, whether allocated or not, would be preferable.

II. Embassy Review of Special Committee Recommendations— WT [76] Reports

The Embassy believes that the combined system of reviewing Special Committee export license recommendations established by Department's instruction No. 2161 of April 14, 1942, and the WT reports initiated by the Department's strictly confidential telegram No. 586 of April 27, 3 p. m.,[77] will do much to eliminate the speculator and cloak

---

[76] Division of World Trade Intelligence.
[77] Not printed.

from future trade with the United States. It is regretted, however, that in the first case, approvals cannot be withheld pending Embassy advices. It is also hoped that the Board of Economic Warfare has been able to revoke the licenses in the 247 cases recommended by the Embassy covering the lists of applications reviewed by the Special Committee from March 24 through April 16, 1942. The efficacy of this system is apparent when it will be noted that these 247 cases represent approximately 17% of the total number recommended by the Committee for approval.

The difficulty anticipated by the Embassy on the WT inquiries is that seldom will we be able to make the "three" recommendation, simply because it is common practice for nearly all firms to attempt entering fields where they have not heretofore been engaged. In any case, this combined procedure should do much to eliminate numerous cloaks and to retain trade in normal channels, at least during the transition period prior to the establishment of the system requiring the Certificate of Necessity for all products, provided always that the Department and the Board of Economic Warfare decide to adopt such a system.

The viewpoint of the Department on the points mentioned above would be greatly appreciated.

Respectfully yours, NORMAN ARMOUR

835.24/533

Memorandum by Mr. John E. Peurifoy of the American Hemisphere Exports Office [78]

[WASHINGTON,] May 6, 1942.

I have transmitted a copy of Mr. Armour's letter [79] to Colonel Lord [80] with the request that he furnish me with his comments.

With reference to despatch no. 4808,[81] concerning the proposed revocation of outstanding export licenses, it does not appear feasible to submit a list of doubtful licenses now outstanding to our missions in Argentina. Such a step would involve reviewing thousands of outstanding licenses. The Department has been furnishing the Embassy with lists of all applications granted subsequent to March 24, and upon the mission's request, all licenses to which they objected have been revoked. I believe we are faced with the necessity of letting

---

[78] Addressed to the Chief of the Office (Ravndal) and the Assistant Chief (Doyle).
[79] Dated April 16, p. 341.
[80] Col. Royal B. Lord, Assistant Director of the Board of Economic Warfare.
[81] Dated April 21, p. 348.

those licenses go which are outstanding, hoping that the new procedure which is now in effect will prove satisfactory.

I should think that in reply to Mr. Armour's letter, it will be desirable to point out the procedure now followed by the Board and the Department, i.e. transmitting abstracts of the licenses issued in order that the Embassy's approval may be obtained. I realize that this action is taken after a license has been issued, but I do not believe that there is any other method which could be instituted which would meet the present situation unless, of course, there is a white list established, and from Mr. Armour's letter I take it he is opposed to such a list.

I will send you Colonel Lord's comments on Mr. Armour's letter when they have been received.

JOHN E. PEURIFOY

835.24/627

The Ambassador in Argentina (Armour) to the Under Secretary of State (Welles)

BUENOS AIRES, May 15, 1942.

DEAR SUMNER: I am increasingly concerned regarding the extent to which the Department and the B.E.W. find it possible to consider and follow Embassy recommendations on allocations and export licenses. This was recently covered in part by Confidential Despatch No. 4954 of May 5, 1942. However, the list of the export applications reviewed by the Special Committee, the WT inquiries, and information received by local firms of rejections in Washington of Certificates of Necessity, lead me to believe that the condition discussed in Embassy cable 477 [82] still exists. I feel that I should emphasize that this practice is having an increasingly detrimental effect and has reached the point at which not only local business men but actually Argentine Government officials openly express the feeling that the Certificate of Necessity is of little if any value. At the same time, from the lists of export license applications reviewed by the Special Committee, approvals are noted of license applications which this Embassy recommends should be revoked for reasons ranging from the fact that the merchandise is outside the normal business of the Argentine importer to that in which the importer has actually been recommended for the Proclaimed List. I know you appreciate fully how this limits the effectiveness of the Embassy in the exercise of its control. A case which I believe to be of vital importance is found in the informal approach yesterday made by officials of the Central Bank regarding the distri-

---

[82] Dated March 12, midnight, p. 329.

bution of the second quarter allocations of iron and steel and of plastics. Their position is that owing to the limited amount of the quotas, they feel that it will all have to be given to Government entities, as they are of first consideration. Obviously, this would produce the exact opposite of the desirable results commented upon in your personal letter of March 27,[83] and the position now taken may be of definite political significance, as up to now, Central Bank officials have agreed completely with members of the Embassy staff to the effect that the maintenance of operations on any kind of an economic basis by Argentine private industry, both small and large, was of greater collective importance to the economy of the country than most Government construction or similar projects. I feel that under present conditions the Embassy is handicapped in combatting effectively the proposed distribution to Government entities. Were it possible to employ our recommendations, especially as regards Certificates of Necessity, we could logically take the position that allocations could not be made to Government departments, but only to the individual firms holding Government contracts for essential works. However, Certificates of Necessity for at least some of the few cases we have recommended of that nature have been rejected.

I note that *Current Controls Bulletin* No. 20, forwarded with the Department's instruction No. 2308, of May 7, 1942,[83] states that Certificates of Necessity will be followed except when interests of national defense dictate the contrary and further, that applications for export licenses of allocated materials unaccompanied by the Certificate of Necessity will be returned without action other than in exceptional cases. Perhaps it has not yet been possible to place this procedure in practice, as on some occasions licenses are granted for allocated materials in quantities greater than the total allocation made to Argentina, and for uses for which both the Argentine Government and this Embassy understood would be unacceptable. As an example, I refer to the case of cellulose acetate, discussed under application No. 2376, reviewed by the Special Committee April 13 and reported on fully and recommended for revocation by Embassy cable 804, May 1, 12 noon.[83] Another case was No. 3633, for bakelite molding powder reviewed on April 30. This company is believed to have stocks for more than two years of normal operations. They would not be eligible for any quota allocation. The amount of the powder for which export license was approved would also be sufficient for another two years normal operations. Similar cases seem to have occurred in

---

[83] Not printed.

formaldehyde, other plastic materials, iron and steel, caustic soda and tanning materials. I particularly refer, for example, to pipe for YPF [86] mentioned in Embassy cable 871, May 9, 2 p. m.[87]

I feel that I must also report the increasing expression on the part of local business people of the belief that so many inconsistencies can hardly be explained by other reasons than plain graft and I regret to state that this accusation is being increasingly made as regards obtaining export licenses. One man who has recently returned from Washington admits that he obtained numerous licenses using fictitious Argentine consignees, subsequently shipping the merchandise to order and receiving it here himself for sale to other people. On at least one other occasion, one person has advised us that he has duplicated his application for export license on the theory that probably one would be granted. Both were. Five cases have been called to our attention where the firms in the United States requested export licenses for materials which have never been ordered by the reported consignee. The duplicate applications appearing in the lists reviewed by the Special Committee suggests that this practice may be rather common.

I fully realize that the magnitude of the problem in Washington makes some confusion inevitable. Also, we appreciate that the WT inquiries now in effect should help considerably. However, I feel that many mistakes could be avoided by adopting the system outlined in my letter to you of April 16, 1942. The Central Bank has recently informed us that they would not only approve this system but that in its application they would use a Committee upon which the Ministries of Agriculture, Treasury and Foreign Relations are represented. They are already preparing "use" priority schedules for certain products and would, I feel, be inclined to accept the major part of our recommendations in that regard. To require Embassy recommendation for all export license, both for allocated and unallocated products, with the further understanding that these recommendations would be considered and under ordinary circumstances accepted in Washington for other than questions of supply and use, would, I realize, require the Embassy to accept some of the responsibility now assumed by the BEW. However, I feel that the Embassy staff, being on the ground, is in a good position to perform that duty effectively for the BEW, and I hope that early action will be possible which will embody this or some other more satisfactory system.

Sincerely yours,

NORMAN ARMOUR

---

[86] Yacimientos Petrolíferos Fiscales.
[87] Not printed.

835.24/672

Memorandum by Mr. Harold W. Moseley, American Hemisphere Exports Office [88]

[WASHINGTON,] May 19, 1942.

PRESENT EXPORT CONTROL PROCEDURE WHICH HAS BEEN ESTABLISHED
TO MEET THE OBJECTIONS OF THE EMBASSY IN BUENOS AIRES THAT
PRESENT CONTROLS ARE UNSATISFACTORY

Reference is made to Mr. Meltzer's letter of April 3 to Mr. Acheson and Mr. Armour's letter to Mr. Welles of April 16 regarding what appears to be an unsatisfactory control procedure on the part of the export control authorities in that imported commodities are still reaching undesirable firms. Several suggestions are made whereby this situation can be met. In this connection I should like to set forth the steps that have been taken to remedy the situation, and to give my views on the matter.

The following are the forms of control procedure which were placed in effect in March and April and which, it is believed, will in part meet the situation:

1. A list of all applications approved and rejected by the Reviews–Appeals Committee giving full information as to the material involved, consignee, and purchaser, and action taken on the particular applications is daily airmailed to the Embassy. The Embassy has been advised to notify the Department immediately if it disapproves the granting of any of the licenses. When the Department receives word to this effect from the Embassy it informs the BEW, which has agreed to revoke the licenses.

The Reviews–Appeals Committee considers all Argentine applications with a value of $500 or over and all applications to export chemical products with a value of $100. I am advised that this amounts to about eighty per cent of all applications received. Although this only gives the Embassy a check after the licenses have been issued, the shipment can be prevented by the ready revocation of the license. (This procedure was worked out as a compromise after the BEW refused to hold all applications pending clearance with the Embassy).

2. In order to check cloaking operations on shipments to Argentina, the World Trade Intelligence Division, in cooperation with the BEW, has arranged to regularly telegraph to the Embassy lists of export license applications on which action has been suspended by the BEW because the consignee is unknown here or the transaction appears questionable.

---

[88] Addressed to the Chief of the American Hemisphere Exports Office (Ravndal), the Executive Secretary of the Board of Economic Operations (Collado), the Acting Chief of the Division of World Trade Intelligence (Dickey), and Mr. Jacques J. Reinstein, Assistant to the Assistant Secretary of State (Acheson).

This form of control should in a large part affect cloaking operations which exist as the result of new firms being established in Argentina. In this way, the Embassy is given an opportunity to check on all cases in which the name of the consignee is unknown to the BEW or WT.

3. Embassy review of Certificates of Necessity in effect provides control by the mission of the issuance of licenses for the export of allocated materials.

A copy of all Certificates of Necessity issued by the Central Bank are sent to the Embassy. If the Embassy disapproves an order, it can either get the Bank to revoke it or notify the Department that the license should not be issued.

These new measures of control plus the implementation of the Argentine policy in general should in large part meet the objections of the Embassy. A means of complete control over every single shipment has not yet been found practicable. For example, the Embassy first requested that it be allowed to advise on all applications. The BEW pointed out that it was impossible to hold up shipments until the Embassy had investigated and approved each application, but agreed to the procedure outlined above. The BEW recommended that the Embassy make up a White List but this proposal was turned down by the Embassy.

The Embassy was further consulted on the question of calling in for revalidation all outstanding licenses issued to Argentina with a view to revoking those which the Embassy disapproved of; however, the Embassy turned down this suggestion as it would obviously be a discriminatory act.

Referring to the suggested measures of control set forth on page 2 of Mr. Meltzer's letter to Mr. Acheson, these have all been considered and are either being carried out or have been found impracticable. As to suggestion (1) that specific licenses be required for all articles, it should be pointed out that general licenses are rapidly being cancelled and that it would be most discriminatory to require individual licenses for Argentina when not requiring them for the other republics. Proposal (2) that all applications be cleared with the Embassy was found to be impracticable by the BEW. Suggestion (3) that cases involving consignees considered questionable be checked with the Embassy is now in effect. Proposal (4) to furnish copies of the confidential list to collectors is not in effect but if it were it would only have the value of stopping the small amount of material such as foodstuffs going out under general license. All individual applications are checked by the BEW against the confidential list.

Mr. Armour's proposal that all orders for imports be covered by Certificates of Necessity bears merit in that it could indeed give the Embassy control at its end. Possibly this is the only means available of obtaining the complete control desired by the Embassy. Before it is attempted the present means of control now functioning should be fully explained to the Embassy, and a further report from it should be received as to whether it is satisfactory.

Difficulties to be considered in the functioning of Mr. Armour's proposal are:

(1) Exporters in this country and importers and certifying agencies in all of the other republics have been advised repeatedly that certificates should be used only with allocated materials. Confusion would arise which might spread to other countries. Furthermore, the charge of discrimination might be made. Undoubtedly these would be procedural difficulties at the BEW.

(2) Certificates cannot readily be used for materials going out under general license unless a new procedure involving the customs is worked out.

HAROLD W. MOSELEY

835.24/602 : Telegram

The Ambassador in Argentina (Armour) to the Secretary of State

BUENOS AIRES, June 12, 1942—midnight.
[Received June 12—10 p. m.]

1115. Department's instruction of May 15 [89] calling for reports on Argentine essential requirements for 1943 of 173 products or groups of products. Iron and steel report is required by July 18 and others by September 1st. The Department is aware that the Argentine Government, through the Central Bank, has cooperated in the preparation of all requirements reports and its further cooperation is essential in this undertaking. However, I feel that this is not an appropriate time to ask the Argentine Government to collaborate in the preparation of the number and type of reports called for by these instructions. For several months the Argentine Central Bank has employed a minimum of 30 to 40 people, on requirements studies requested by our Government. To date they have prepared 46 reports. Unfortunately, export licenses for Argentina have not been granted on the basis, either of their recommendation or of those of the Embassy nor have their certificates of necessity brought anticipated results. Consequently to ask the Argentine Government for these additional reports could not be other than embarrassing. Moreover, I feel that the entire problem is complicated by reason of the necessity of considering the ultimate use as of primary importance. I realize that this cannot be avoided. However, the principal criteria for end-use of any given material seem to be (1) contribution to the

---

[89] Not printed.

war effort and, (2) effect upon the national economy of the importing country. For practical purposes I feel that with very few exceptions, for example tungsten mining and possibly some of the work of the *frigoríficos*, Argentina makes no contribution to the war effort. This leaves national economy as the basic consideration. While realizing that to allow the exportation of material from the United States to Argentina for a use prohibited in the United States carries both substantial political and economic considerations, I feel that the fundamental differences, particularly now, of the economies of the two countries must not be disregarded.

If it were possible for the United States to let the Argentine Government exercise that control, subject only to general limitations, which I feel it would be glad to meet, the import requirements studies would be simple, accurate and practicable. Once the requirements were estimated and allocation made, control of allocation would still be exercised both as regards the Proclaimed List or suspect consignees, and as regards any preference which might be given to local entities such as Caporypf.

I realize that this suggestion requires a determination of policy, but I feel very strongly that this should be taken now rather than to continue as at present. Our further insistence upon detailed statistical studies, followed by unsatisfactory results, is increasingly irritating to the Argentine Government and, I might add, to the Argentine people. In fact I believe that if the Department feels that no consideration can now be given to making the Argentine Government primarily responsible for use-distribution of allocated materials, it would be better if the entire allocation system were abandoned for Argentina and if every order were simply made subject to individual export license, with the understanding that Embassy's approval would be obtained for other than supply and use factors. While this system would not be entirely unsatisfactory, it should at least serve a dual purpose. Argentina would be made to realize that hers is a particular case as compared with other hemisphere countries, and the United States could not be accused of not attempting to fulfill implied obligations.

ARMOUR

835.24/543

The Secretary of State to the Ambassador in Argentina (Armour)

No. 2554   WASHINGTON, June 16, 1942.

The Secretary of State refers to the Ambassador's confidential despatch no. 4954 of May 5, 1942 concerning procedure under Certificates of Necessity issued by the Central Bank, particularly as regards the extent to which the Embassy's recommendations are followed at the Board of Economic Warfare in approving or disapproving export license applications supported by such certificates, and informs the Ambassador that his recommendations are followed in practically every case. There have been some very few exceptions, but the Embassy's observations are of such definite value that the Department desires the Embassy to continue to make recommendations with regard to export license applications forwarded by the World Trade Division of the Department, and decisions of the Argentine section of the Reviews and Appeals Committee of the Office of Exports.

The Secretary of State further desires to inform the Ambassador that orders were duly issued by the competent authority of the Board to revoke the licenses referred to in the Embassy's telegrams concerning cases acted on by the Special Argentine Committee between March 24 and April 16.

The Committee has raised a special point in connection with those cases in which the Embassy recommended disapproval on the grounds that the import is outside of the normal activities of the consignee. In certain of such cases it has developed that the World Trade Intelligence Division has very favorable reports concerning the consignees and the feeling of the Argentine Committee is that the single fact of the import not being "usual" is not a very substantial reason for denying such firm the small amounts of material requested. In this connection, the Committee feels that it is rather logical to assume that many reputable firms, owing to the difficulty of importing customary lines, are branching out into new lines. The Department is inclined to be of the same opinion as the Committee, although the comment of the Embassy is urgently desired in this respect. If the Embassy insists that the fact of a firm importing new lines is sufficient to warrant disapproval of the application, the Department will again inform the Committee in this regard.

835.24/602 : Telegram

The Secretary of State to the Ambassador in Argentina (Armour)

WASHINGTON, June 19, 1942—midnight.

914. Your 1115, June 12, midnight. The Department agrees that it would be embarrassing to the Embassy to ask the Argentine Government at this time to collaborate in the preparation of the essential requirements reports for 1943. However, the Department requires the data requested, and it is hoped that the Embassy will obtain the effective cooperation of the American business community in preparing the desired reports.

Copies of memoranda discussing decentralization of export control have been sent the Embassy for its comment, and it is hoped that it will be possible during the visit of Lord, Peurifoy and Ravndal to work out an administrative routine within your recommendations.

HULL

835.24/633a : Telegram

The Secretary of State to the Ambassador in Argentina (Armour)

WASHINGTON, June 30, 1942—7 p. m.

974. For Ravndal from Ravndal.[90] It seems apparent that existing export control procedure cannot be effectively integrated having regard to supply and shipping problems, and consideration must be given to alternates. Recent telegrams from missions reporting requirements for shipping purposes indicate a definite pattern of import requirements within broad categories leaving only 15 to 20 percent undetermined. The implementation of these expressed needs is complicated by the inability of Export Control to furnish data by commodity on approved licenses and even if this information were available it is improbable that the approved licenses would correspond with the desired pattern and our best efforts would prove futile. The difficulty with present procedure is that applications are filed at unrelated times by individual exporters and not according to a preconceived program. If each of the American republics in cooperation with missions would present a total import requirement for say one full quarter, such total being the composite of all individual applications for the quarter, Export Control could consider each application as a component part of this global requirement and thus minimize present confusion. Would you consider and discuss the following alternative plan:

1. Importers would submit to a control entity minimum requirements for the next quarter. For example, by July 1 the importers would have made known their individual total import requirements for the period October 1 to December 31.

2. These requirements would be checked and certified by the control entity.

3. Present form certificates of necessity would be issued for allocated commodities and, so as to avoid confusion, a different form certificate for unallocated commodities. Importer would send certificate to exporter for attachment to export license application as at present. However, copies of all certificates would be sent in one batch by the Embassy through the Department to the Office of Exports of the

---

[90] Olaf Ravndal and Christian M. Ravndal, Assistant Chief and Chief, respectively, of the American Hemisphere Exports Office.

BEW, thereby with a total known requirement enabling BEW and WPB to determine in advance the quantities by commodity for which production and shipping must be provided.

4. The Embassy would check the importer's requirements, and screen for desirability of consignee, end use, et cetera.

5. The control entity and the Embassy would indicate the shipping priority desired on each certificate for guidance in the distribution of available cargo space.

6. Projects would not be included under this plan. Allocations would continue to be used for the guidance of foreign control entity and missions and by means of these allocations BEW and WPB could retain overall control on the distribution of materials in short supply. This alternate program appears to present a more realistic approach to positive economic warfare, since it contemplates the establishment of a quarterly import requirement that would be known in advance and against which positive production and shipping programs could be worked out. Would appreciate your reaction using Argentina as an example. To what extent would additional staff be required? [Christian Ravndal.]

HULL

835.24/633 : Telegram

The Ambassador in Argentina (Armour) to the Secretary of State

BUENOS AIRES, July 4, 1942—3 p. m.
[Received 5 : 25 p. m.]

1318. For Ravndal from Ravndal. Department's 974, June 30, 7 p. m. I have discussed your alternative plan with officials of the Central Bank, Colonel Lord, the Embassy and representative American businessmen and there is unanimous agreement that it offers a practical solution.

The only modification suggested is that the period should be one of 6 months rather than 3. It is felt here that production and shipping could be more readily coordinated over the longer period.

The Central Bank is prepared to ascertain and advise us before October 1 what will be Argentina's import requirements for the first allocation period of 1943. The estimate will be based upon a monthly United States shipping allocation of 14,000 tons of cargo space plus whatever additional tonnage may be expected from Argentine vessels. If this should not be regarded as a reasonable basis the bank should be promptly informed.

As soon as the United States Government receives Argentina's estimated import requirements it will communicate to the Central Bank the quantities of allocated products and the probable quantities of unallocated commodities in short supply which could be supplied to Argentina. (The Argentine Government would not wish to reserve shipping space for a commodity which cannot be furnished by the United States.) On this basis the bank will undertake to issue certificates covering all import requirements from the United States for the first 6 months of 1943. Every effort will be made to issue all such certificates during the month of October. Copies will be furnished to the Embassy for the information of Washington. The date upon which the certificate can be issued, however, depends in part upon the date when the above advice regarding quantities of products available is received.

The Central Bank agrees that the United States Government cannot and will not tolerate any distribution which would permit our merchandise to reach the enemy. It will in all cases consult with the Embassy before issuing a Certificate of Necessity. When it cannot escape issuing a certificate to a firm on the Proclaimed or Confidential List it will advise the Embassy in the expectation that the certificate will be dishonored.

In view of the need for elasticity in shipping priority from the United States due to possible sinkings of counted goods from Great Britain the Central Bank would prefer not to indicate shipping priority on each certificate. It has prepared a breakdown by commodities of Argentina's import requirements under various tonnages of shipping space and requests that this breakdown plus the advice of its representative in Washington be followed by Port Cargo Clearance Committee in loading vessels for this country.

During July and August merchandise should be allowed despatch to Argentina under existing regulations. Effective September 1, however, no United States goods of any description whether allocated or unallocated should be permitted export to Argentina unless covered by a new certificate showing clearly that the shipment has been reviewed and has the support of the Central Bank. The purpose of waiting until September 1 to institute the new system is to give the Central Bank time to obtain from importers in Argentina full information as to the nature, whereabouts, and condition of manufacture of the goods that have been ordered whether or not covered by an export license and or Certificate of Necessity. Since the factor of merchandise supply of Argentina is in many cases more important than the question of acceptable consignee the Central Bank would like as much as possible of the goods which are now in ports to come forward. By September 1, however, the Central Bank will have examined all outstanding orders and will be able to designate which commodities both allocated and unallocated should be loaded so as most efficiently to make use of available shipping space.

In case it should be desirable from the supply standpoint to let merchandise come forward which is now at the ports in the hands of firms not eligible to receive corresponding certificates the Argentine Government will name an acceptable consignee or will requisition the goods upon arrival for further distribution. In this latter case the Argentine Government will take into consideration the wishes of the United States Government to the effect that the distribution be made only to firms and entities who have access to the United States market.

The foregoing represents the opinion of officials of the Central Bank with whom the problem has been discussed and should not be construed as already having been formally approved by the Argentine Government.

The personnel needs will be discussed in a separate telegram. [Olaf Ravndal.]

ARMOUR

835.24/763½

Memorandum by the Executive Secretary, Board of Economic Operations (Collado)[91]

[WASHINGTON,] September 10, 1942.

CRITICAL MATERIALS SUPPLY OF ARGENTINA

With reference to the questions raised by the Secretary yesterday afternoon as to the supply of critical materials to Argentina the following observations are submitted:

1. *Allocations to Argentina Arbitrarily Reduced.* The allocations to Argentina since last February have arbitrarily been cut substantially. In the case of iron and steel, for example, the allocations in long tons approved by the Requirements Committee of the War Production Board have been cut as follows:

	Allocations Based on Bare Bones Requirements	Allocations Made by the Department
2nd Quarter	78, 000	41, 574
3rd Quarter	42, 304	40, 599
October	17, 854	8, 928
4th Quarter	66, 441	outstanding

2. *Licensing Restricted.* The commodity licensing officers at BEW are under instructions not to license for export to Argentina any article or material which can be construed to be of military use, except such as are clearly intended for the maintenance of existing facilities. They are also under instructions not to license for Argentina any oil

---

[91] Addressed to the Secretary of State and the Assistant Secretary of State (Acheson).

well drilling equipment or maintenance supplies for the oil companies of Argentina. And they have been directed to support subsidiaries or affiliates of American firms and Argentine industries such as the meat packers which contribute to the United Nations' war effort, but not to an extent of jeopardizing our own supply. As a result licenses approved for Argentina have decreased from $11,332,652 in January to $5,975,876 in July.

3. *Shipments Smaller than Reduced Allocations.* Actual shipments of critical materials have been less than the reduced allocations. This has been effected not only through restrictions on licensing but also through restrictions on priority ratings at WPB. In the case of iron and steel, for example, Argentina's half rations for July were 13,533 tons, but according to preliminary reports obtained by the Maritime Commission from various sources at the ports, only 1,486 tons were shipped in that month. For August the allocation was also 13,533 tons; shipments to August 20, 1,883 tons.

4. *Character of Argentina's Imports from the United States.* From the same sources it is apparent that Argentina is at present obtaining from the United States principally coal and newsprint:

U. S. Exports to Argentina in Tons

Commodity	July	August 1-20
Coal	20, 121	12, 100
Newsprint	486	7, 754
Iron and Steel	1, 486	1, 883
Others	23, 660	4, 307
Total	45, 753	26, 044

5. *Argentina's Imports from Other Sources.* Our Embassy at Buenos Aires advises that Argentina's imports from other sources have been chiefly:

(*a*) *Germany*

Powder factory equipment consigned to the Argentine Ministry of War under a British export permit and drugs shipped via Japan and Chile. Ratio increase over 1941—2 : 1.

(*b*) *Spain*

In order of value, foodstuffs, beverages, paper and manufactures thereof, chemicals, pharmaceuticals and related products, wood and manufactures thereof, machinery, and iron and steel. Ratio increase—3 : 1.

(*c*) *Portugal*

Cork and some foodstuffs, beverages and herbs. Ratio increase—2 : 1.

(*d*) *Sweden*

Woodpulp, paper, newsprint, hardware, cutlery and small iron and steel manufactures in general; also some electrical equipment and motors. Ratio of increase—8 : 1. (See **separate** memorandum).

(e) *Brazil*

Textiles and lesser amounts of iron and steel and manufactures, coal, industrial chemicals and drugs, wood, fresh fruits, vegetables and tobacco. Ratio of increase—2 : 1.

(f) *Colombia*

Petroleum and petroleum derivatives with a few herbal products. Ratio of increase—2 : 1.

(g) *Chile*

Copper, nitrates and less important articles. Ratio of increase—2 : 1.

(h) *Mexico*

Relatively small, but ratio of increase—4 : 1.

(i) *Venezuela*

Fuel oil and lesser quantities of coffee and plywood. Ratio of increase 6 : 1.

(j) *United Kingdom*

Coal, soda ash, caustic soda, copper sulphate, naphthalene, cresylic acid, rayon yarn and textiles. Slight increase.

(k) *Canada*

Newsprint. Slight decrease.

(l) *India*

Jute, burlap and manufactures, tea, spices and other colonial products. Ratio of increase—2 : 1.

6. *Possibility of Reducing Iron and Steel Supply.* Iron and steel supply is Argentina's vital weakness in the absence of any source other than the United States which might ship in sizable quantities.

Since the beginning of this year there has been a marked increase in Argentina's imports of these products from Spain and it appears that Spain has undertaken specifically, as one of the conditions of the Spanish-Argentine trade agreement to furnish 30,000 tons of iron and steel in the first year.

Argentina's requests for iron and steel in 1943 total 385,000 tons. Our Embassy regards 93,000 tons as the indispensable minimum requirement. Argentine expects to get 30,000 tons from Spain and small quantities from Sweden and Brazil. Presumably, then, we could cut our share in Argentina's supply to 60,000 tons, or to 5,000 tons a month as against 13,000 tons a month in the present quarter.

7. *Effect on our Shipping Negotiations.* We have been negotiating with the Argentines for the provision of a monthly northbound tonnage to us of 40,000 tons. We might make up the southbound tonnage on a breakdown somewhat as follows:

Commodity	Tons
Coal	16,000
Newsprint	7,500
Paper and manufactures	5,000
Iron and steel	5,000
Tinplate	4,000
Wood and manufactures	1,500
Chemicals	1,000
Total	40,000

With such a breakdown we would fill the southbound tonnage with materials we can spare plus those materials which we would want our war industries in Argentina to obtain.

E. G. COLLADO

835.24/794 : Telegram

The Secretary of State to the Ambassador in Argentina (Armour)

WASHINGTON, October 19, 1942—10 p. m.

1575. Your 1991 of October 14, 4 p. m.[93] The Department will take no action until it receives the report you mention. It is constrained, however, to point out that the issuance of all these certificates of necessity is largely useless. As you are well aware, our program of actual exports and shipping to Argentina for the fourth quarter for successive periods is very reduced, and material covered by the certificates will under no circumstances all be made available.

Rather than permit this type of situation to continue, with the Central Bank doing much unnecessary work, you are requested, unless you perceive strong objection, fully to inform the Argentine Government and the Central Bank of the program for exports which is set forth in the memorandum of September 23,[94] of which you have a copy. (i.e. paragraphs 2. a and b.)

HULL

835.24/825½

Memorandum by the Chief of the American Hemisphere Exports Office (Ravndal) to the Executive Secretary, Board of Economic Operations (Collado)

[WASHINGTON,] October 29, 1942.

MR. COLLADO: With reference to the question raised in your memorandum of October 27 [94] regarding the implementation of our policy towards Argentina, it may be explained that allocations for Argentina are determined on the basis of parity with other American republics. After approval of the proposed allocations by the American Requirements Committee in the past AE,[95] in consultation with a member of the Requirements Branch of BEW, has arbitrarily reduced Argentine allocations by 50 percent. However, as you will recall, beginning with the fourth quarter the iron and steel allocation for Argentina was

---

[93] Not printed; it requested that the Department delay action until the Embassy had reviewed the Central Bank's Certificates of Necessity (835.24/794).
[94] Not printed.
[95] American Hemisphere Exports Office.

sharply reduced to approximately 5,000 tons monthly. Because of the very small tonnage involved (1,427 tons) and the fact that a 50 percent reduction would seriously cripple industries employing a relatively large number of workers, the Embassy was instructed to use its judgment in making any reductions in allocations of commodities other than iron and steel and report to the Department the action taken.

For example, in determining the acetone allocation, supplies were almost restricted to the rayon industry and an arbitrary cut of 50 percent would be reflected in a corresponding curtailment of the operations of the industry. It was therefore felt that Mr. Armour would be in a better position to evaluate the implications of any reduction that might be made. Likewise, a reduction in the allocation of chromium chemicals which are used largely for tanning leather would bring about a curtailment of activities in that industry and it was felt that the Embassy would be better qualified to determine the extent to which such a curtailment would be advisable.

C. M. RAVNDAL

835.24/850½ : Telegram

The Ambassador in Argentina (Armour) to the Secretary of State

BUENOS AIRES, December 11, 1942—9 p. m.
[Received 9:45 p. m.]

2526. Department's A–434, December 3, 7:15 p. m.[96] Embassy agrees to 14,088 short tons as allotment of estimated supply iron and steel and no objection is offered to advising the Central Bank of this allocation.

Entire matter was discussed with Liaudat and Pina of the Central Bank and the following points will be of interest to the Department.

It is recommended that no formal announcement be made to Argentine Government of restriction of Certificate of Necessity issued to Government departments and [as] such announcement might be considered discriminatory. The Central Bank could issue Certificates of Necessity to Government department, Embassy would recommend rejection to Board of Economic Warfare who would refuse to issue export license, Embassy would be advised of such action by cable and the Central Bank, on receiving such advice from Embassy would redistribute material to commercial entities. Government departments thus would be gradually reconciled to their inability to obtain materials.

2. Representatives of American steel mills continually advise the Embassy that orders for less than carload lots of iron and steel are

---

[96] Missing from Department files.

impractical both from standpoint of manufacturing and inland shipping in the United States. Central Bank's present method of distributing Certificates of Necessity provides for all consumers and importers receiving proportion of 1941 consumption or imports. With an allocation of 14,088 short tons thousands of firms will be issued Certificates of Necessity for insignificant amounts of material. Central Bank requires formal statement from Embassy as to steel mill representatives contention above in order to change distribution system. Certificates of Necessity for carload lots would allow Embassy to control more effectively both ultimate use and destination of materials. It would be appreciated if the Department would instruct the Embassy to advise Argentine Government that less than carload lots are impractical.

3. The Central Bank will print new Certificates of Necessity in color different from those of 1942. Embassy requested three copies with the idea of instituting the Randall–Robbins plan immediately this is approved in Washington. It is understood that under this plan two copies of certificates would be forwarded to Washington with Embassy's recommendation, one copy to be returned for delivery to the Central Bank with notation of Board of Economic Warfare's final action.[97] It would be most practical to start this consignee control plan with the first 1943 Certificates of Necessity issued by the Central Bank.

4. Small consumers necessarily have to depend on established reselling firms for their requirements. In the distribution first quarter Certificates of Necessity both the Central Bank and the Embassy consider it highly desirable that part of allocation be given to reliable resellers approved by the Embassy. It would be much more effective from a Proclaimed List standpoint to control the activities of these firms than those of thousands small importing manufacturers. Please advise by cable if export licenses will be issued for steel to reselling firms when the ultimate consignee and end-use is not given.

5. End-use control will be exercised by the Embassy under the Randall–Robbins plan. This can effectively be accomplished with the assistance of the Central Bank and the Argentine iron and steel rationing commission once the material is in the country but it is [impossible?] to obtain a true end-use picture at the time the Certificate of Necessity is issued.

6. Name and address of supplier in the United States will appear on all Certificates of Necessity. The Central Bank inquires if space

---

[97] A notation appears in the margin as follows: "No but lists will be sent."

provided on certificate form for previous orders placed is still necessary.

In connection with this cable refer voluntary report No. 1549, December 4, 1942.[98]

If distribution resolution is to be changed and if the Central Bank is to issue Certificates of Necessity before first of the year I suggest that an immediate cable reply be made.

ARMOUR

DISCUSSIONS BETWEEN THE UNITED STATES AND ARGENTINA REGARDING LEND-LEASE ARRANGEMENTS AND DEFENSE PLANS [99]

835.24/217½

Memorandum by the Chief of Naval Operations (Stark) to the Under Secretary of State (Welles)

WASHINGTON, December 6, 1941.

1. Despatch [*telegram*] No. 1341 from the American Embassy, Buenos Aires, dated November 27, 1941,[1] referring to the composition of the Argentine Mission enroute to the United States contains the following:

"Owing to the work assigned to this Mission, the Ambassador of Argentina or the Chargé d'Affaires in Washington will likewise be included in this Mission, in order to take up matters having a political interest."

2. From various despatches received from the American Embassy in Buenos Aires, it is understood that the Argentine Mission desires to accomplish the following:

(*a*) To discuss by means of staff conversations certain plans for Hemisphere Defense elaborated by the Argentine Army and Navy.

(*b*) To prepare a program for the acquisition of armaments based upon the plans for defense agreed upon in the staff conversations.

(*c*) To negotiate a basic agreement with the State Department for the procurement of the armaments agreed upon, as required by the Lend-Lease procedure.[2]

3. The proposed agenda for staff conversations, forwarded to the State Department for transmission to the Argentine Government,

---

[98] Not printed.
[99] For previous correspondence, see *Foreign Relations*, 1941, vol. VI.
[1] *Ibid.*
[2] Under the Act of March 11, 1941 ; 55 Stat. 31.

emphasized the idea that staff conversations should take place between Military and Naval representatives of the two Governments qualified to make military decisions, and that any agreements arrived at should be first approved by the Chiefs of the Military and Naval Staffs of the two Governments, and afterwards presented to the Argentine Foreign Office and the State Department for final approval. It is, therefore, considered most undesirable that a representative of the Argentine Embassy in Washington should take part in the purely technical discussions of the staff conversations.

4. The participation of the Argentine Ambassador or Chargé d'Affaires should be restricted to the question of the procurement of armaments, after staff conversations have been completed, and the activities necessary in negotiating the basic agreement.

5. It is suggested that this matter be discussed in the next Liaison Committee [3] meeting, with a view to reaching an understanding before the arrival of the Argentine Mission.

H. R. STARK

835.24/255

Memorandum by the Adviser on Political Relations (Duggan)[4]

[WASHINGTON,] December 15, 1941.

Sr. García Arias, Minister of the Argentine Embassy, called to state that his Government desired either the Ambassador or, in the Ambassador's absence, his representative to participate in the discussions which will take place between the Argentine Military and Naval Commission[5] and the military and naval authorities of this Government. Sr. García Arias requested that his Government's desire be brought to the attention of the proper authorities in our War and Navy Departments so that they would not be surprised by the participation of the Ambassador or his representative in the discussions.

I said this would be done.

LAURENCE DUGGAN

---

[3] The Liaison Committee was a high-level policy body consisting of representatives from the War, Navy, and State Departments.
[4] Addressed to the Liaison Officer (Wilson) and the Under Secretary of State (Welles).
[5] The Commission consisted of five military officers headed by Brig. Gen. Eduardo T. Lapez and six naval officers under Rear Adm. Sabá Sueyro.

835.24/298

Memorandum of Conversation, by the Adviser on Political Relations (Duggan)

[WASHINGTON,] January 26, 1942.

The Argentine Ambassador [6] left with me the attached copy of a telegram received from the Ministry of Foreign Affairs with regard to the acquisition of military and naval matériel by Argentina in the United States. The Ambassador stated that so far neither the War nor Navy Department had given the Argentine delegation any idea of delivery dates. The Argentine Military and Naval Commission here, of course, appreciates the heavy demands for military and naval matériel and, in order that the Government in Buenos Aires may understand, is sending two officers by plane to Buenos Aires.

[Annex—Translation]

Telegram Received by the Argentine Ambassador (Espil) From the Argentine Acting Minister for Foreign Affairs (Rothe)

[BUENOS AIRES, undated.]

The Minister, Dr. Ruiz Guiñazú,[7] reported from Rio de Janeiro that he has talked with Mr. Sumner Welles concerning the necessity of providing our country with munitions of war, equipment, and essential materials for our military factories and shipyards and for the development of heavy industries. For this purpose, I request Your Excellency to expedite the conversations of our military mission and to obtain exact information concerning the possibility of obtaining assurances that within a specified period our primary necessities in munitions, equipment and essential materials for military factories and shipyards will be filled.

ROTHE

740.0011 European War 1939/19261

The Ambassador in Argentina (Armour) to the Secretary of State

No. 4035   BUENOS AIRES, January 30, 1942.
                                                [Received February 6.]

SIR: I have the honor to inform the Department that I called this morning on the Acting Minister for Foreign Affairs, Dr. Rothe.

---

[6] Felipe A. Espil.
[7] Argentine Minister for Foreign Affairs.

This was the first occasion I have had to see Dr. Rothe since my two day visit to Rio de Janeiro, and we naturally discussed the conference.[8]

I was disappointed, if not surprised, to find that the events that had transpired at Rio de Janeiro since I had last seen him did not appear to have changed his position or sentiments. He continued to put forth the argument that Argentina in not having broken diplomatic relations with the Axis Powers was in a better position to assist the United States through the exporting of essential materials to us without the attendant risk of having their ships sunk. I pointed out that although relations between the United States and the Axis Powers had not been broken prior to December, this had not prevented Germany from sinking United States vessels. Dr. Rothe admitted this, but insisted that if any attacks were made against Argentine vessels, this would of course lead immediately to a break in relations or declaration of war on their part. He then went on to develop his time-worn argument that Argentina was not in a position to defend itself against attack: that a break in relations would inevitably lead to war and that his Government felt a sense of responsibility to the people not to put themselves in this vulnerable position until they had material to defend themselves. These he said they hoped to obtain from the United States.

I told Dr. Rothe that he must of course realize that the situation had changed materially since the Rio de Janeiro Conference: that as I had pointed out to him in previous conversations, following their own line of argument that if ruptured relations submitted a nation to the danger of attack, those nations which had taken the step must be the ones first served and that we would make every effort to see that they received such materials as they required. I expressed the opinion that this argument applied not only to war materials, but also to other strategic materials, of which there was a growing scarcity in the United States; that where the people of the United States were making great sacrifices to go without such articles but were willing to see such materials supplied to countries which had taken a definite stand with the United States and the democracies, public opinion would certainly not favor having such materials sent to countries which had not made clear their position of solidarity with us. He appeared to admit the logic of these arguments but again reverted to the position in which Argentina found itself and insisted that aside from other considerations, owing to the internal situation it would be impossible for the Government to break relations

---

[8] The Third Meeting of the Foreign Ministers of the American Republics held at Rio de Janeiro, January 15–28, 1942; for correspondence, see pp. 6 ff.

with the Axis Powers at the present time. In any case, they would have to await the regular session of Congress in May, but in the meantime they would of course carry out scrupulously the commitments taken at Rio de Janeiro.

I pointed out to the Minister that nineteen countries having already severed relations, with the probability that Chile would take similar action following the elections next Sunday, this would, I felt, put his country in a very difficult position. As the only country maintaining relations with the Axis it was obvious that the latter countries would concentrate their activities in Argentina, using it as a focal point from which to conduct their subversive activities not only within the country itself but throughout Latin America. While I had no doubt that Argentina would endeavor scrupulously to carry out the commitments taken at Rio de Janeiro with regard to suppressing Axis propaganda, subversive activities, etc., I felt sure he would agree that this would be far more difficult for them than for those countries which had already severed relations with the Axis.

I also called Dr. Rothe's attention to the interview published in *Noticias Gráficas* some days ago attributing to the Acting President [9] statements to the effect that Argentina's position had not changed and that the Government would take no pre-belligerent action such as breaking relations with the Axis Powers. I said that if the Acting President was correctly reported, his statement would seem to be inconsistent with the formula which they themselves had submitted and which had been approved by the twenty-one governments at Rio de Janeiro recommending a rupture of relations with the Axis.

Dr. Rothe parried by saying that the Acting President had perhaps been incorrectly reported.

I shall take the first opportunity to see the Argentine Foreign Minister, Dr. Ruiz Guiñazú, after his return, but in the meantime it seemed advisable to lose no time in bringing home to the Acting Foreign Minister certain salient truths which I was happy to find during my visit to Rio de Janeiro in conversations with the Under Secretary and other members of our delegation represented their views and which, after their return to the Department, will, I presume, be issued in the form of definite instructions as to the policy to be followed here until such time as the Argentine Government may decide to alter its present course.

Respectfully yours,   NORMAN ARMOUR

---

[9] Ramón Castillo.

835.24/277 : Telegram

The Ambassador in Argentina (Armour) to the Secretary of State

BUENOS AIRES, February 3, 1942—6 p. m.
[Received 6 : 25 p. m.]

201. For Under Secretary. Minister of Marine [10] informed me yesterday he is much encouraged with progress of negotiations of Argentine Military Naval Commission now in United States. Minister of War [11] also informed me that two officers of the mission are now here discussing question and intend to return shortly to Washington.

In view of policy outlined by you in conversations at Rio with which as you know I am heartily in accord—in fact my visit to Rio was for the purpose of recommending such policy—I hope the occasion will be taken to implement it as soon as possible. In my talk with Minister of War and Acting Minister for Foreign Affairs I have already made it clear that American countries which have already declared war against or broken relations with Axis Powers will be first to receive available war material but I think you will agree this would have more effect if coming from Washington either through Argentine Ambassador or General Lapez and Admiral Sueyro. (Of course you have already made this clear in your talks with Ruiz Guiñazú of [at] Rio.

My understanding is that any loan to Argentina is out of the question for the present; also that requests for priority on essential materials will not receive support of State Department.

So far as over-all purchasing program is concerned I feel that for the present at least no further steps should be taken to consummate agreement (announcement would presumably be misinterpreted in United States and also weaken our position here). This would not necessarily mean that private buying here of products we require would not continue although I gathered from conversations in Rio that efforts would be made to increase purchases in Brazil, Uruguay and other countries of such products as are available there. Williams [12] left Rio de Janeiro with impression that negotiations on purchase program for which he had secured favorable terms in Washington should be continued but on my advice he has held negotiations in abeyance pending further instructions.

At your convenience I should appreciate word as to whether my understanding as set forth above represents policy we intend to pursue.

ARMOUR

---

[10] Adm. Mario Fincati.
[11] Gen. Juan N. Tonazzi.
[12] Thomas J. Williams acted as agent for the Metals Reserve Company, a buying agency of the Federal Loan Agency.

835.24/277 : Telegram

The Secretary of State to the Ambassador in Argentina (Armour)

WASHINGTON, February 4, 1942—9 p. m.

151. From the Under Secretary. Your 201, February 3, 6 p. m. The outline of policy contained in your telegram is entirely accurate and completely in accord with the policy which this Government will pursue until and unless the position assumed by the Argentine Government changes.

I have consulted General Marshall [13] and Admiral Stark. They will tomorrow inform Admiral Sueyro and General Lapez that inasmuch as the Argentine Government has determined to maintain at least for the time being a position which is tantamount to neutrality and inasmuch as all but one of the other American Republics have either declared war or broken relations with the Axis powers and have thereby incurred the dangers inherent in such action through their support of the United States, the military and naval matériel which can be spared by the United States can logically only be allotted to the latter American nations.

I have already had a preliminary conference with Espil to whom I have given preliminary notification that this would be the policy pursued by this Government. [Welles.]

HULL

835.24/277

Memorandum by the Adviser on Political Relations (Duggan) to the Under Secretary of State (Welles)

[WASHINGTON,] February 5, 1942.

MR. WELLES: With regard to Mr. Armour's telegram no. 201, the following information is of some interest. Early in January, Captain Spears [14] sent me the attached extracts from the Argentine Naval Plan [15] which was submitted by the Argentine Delegation to the United States Delegation. The plan itself goes far beyond any indication heretofore received from the Argentine Government of its willingness to cooperate. The Argentine Delegation, however, has made it abundantly clear that the plan cannot be put into effect until we furnish them with the necessary matériel to make it effective. The matériel stipulated as necessary is far beyond any possibilities of delivery in the foreseeable future.

---

[13] Gen. George C. Marshall, Chief of Staff, United States Army.
[14] Capt. W. O. Spears of the War Plans Division, Navy Department.
[15] Not attached to file copy.

Captain Spears advises that the Argentines have been given a drastically curtailed list of matériel that could be made available. I understand that practically nothing could be made available if, indeed, anything could be made immediately available. Upon presentation of this list the Argentine Commission put on an act to the effect that it was not being taken seriously. Later the Commission calmed down as its members began to realize that the demands for matériel on the United States were extremely heavy.

Several days ago Ambassador Espil told me that two members of the Commission were flying back to Buenos Aires to explain the results of the conversations thus far.

It would therefore seem desirable for the United States members negotiating with the Argentine Delegation to be appropriately advised of our policy with regard to the delivery to Argentina of military equipment.

Ambassador Espil also permitted me to read hastily a joint statement of policy. It concerned the cooperation which each country was to extend to the other in the event that both of them entered the war. The Ambassador had obtained his copy with great difficulty. He found himself in a very embarrassing position since he had been given the responsibility, in the Executive Decree authorizing the trip of the Argentine members to the United States, of handling any questions of international policy. The draft certainly has to do with many important questions of Argentina's political relations with the United States. Nevertheless, the Argentine members of the Commission state that they only deal with military matters. I do not know what action if any the Argentine Ambassador has taken to inform his Government.

I endeavored, through Orme Wilson,[16] to get a copy of this project. Captain Spears told Orme Wilson that the project was in a formative stage and would be presented to the United States and Argentine Governments for approval when ready. He was, therefore, unwilling to furnish a copy.

I suggest that this matter be the subject of a discussion by you at the next meeting of the Liaison Committee. I think it highly important that this Department have an opportunity to advise on this project while it is in a formative stage just as I think that the Argentine Ambassador should be advising his Commission on the international political aspects.

LAURENCE DUGGAN

---

[16] Liaison Officer with the War and Navy Departments.

835.24/331

Memorandum by the Adviser on Political Relations (Duggan) to the Under Secretary of State (Welles)

[WASHINGTON,] February 14, 1942.

MR. WELLES: Captain Spears, while entirely courteous, firmly informed me that he and his associates were under written instructions to sign *ad referendum* an agreement with the Argentine Commission. Unless new instructions are issued he and his colleagues must comply with existing instructions.

Captain Spears, moreover, made it abundantly clear that he and the other military and naval officers making up the United States delegation are most anxious to carry through as originally planned with the Argentine delegation and sign a written document as to what each Government would undertake to do under certain conditions. One of these conditions would be the facilities offered by Argentina in the event of stoppage of communications through the Panama Canal. Moreover, the Argentine Naval authorities have been on good terms with the United States Naval authorities for many years so that the Navy Department would prefer to have the onus for the failure of the agreement to be approved rest upon either the Department or the President.

The War Department concurs in these views.

Both Departments advise me that they have canvassed this whole question apart from the Liaison meeting and feel very strongly that the rather friendly relationships which have been built up and which may prove useful in the future should not be jeopardized as a result of action taken by them. They would like, therefore, to carry through, sign the agreement, present it to higher authorities including the higher authorities in their own departments who would then inform the Argentine Government of our inability to furnish the armament agreed upon.

If, therefore, there is to be any change in the lines along which the War and Navy Departments are working I think it will have to come in the form of instructions issued by General Marshall and Admiral Stark, particularly since the line now being followed was confirmed at the last meeting of the Liaison Committee.

LAURENCE DUGGAN

835.24/331

Memorandum by the Under Secretary of State (Welles) to the Adviser on Political Relations (Duggan)

[WASHINGTON,] February 17, 1942.

MR. DUGGAN: I have spoken personally with Admiral Stark. He is instructing Captain Spears not to sign any written agreement and not to have the Argentines sign any written agreement. Their recommendations will consequently be merely regarded as having been formulated for submission to the Chief of Naval Operations. I think you better make sure that the War Department follows the lead of the Navy Department in this matter.

S[umner] W[elles]

835.24/331

Memorandum by the Adviser on Political Relations (Duggan)

[Washington,] February 17, 1942.

I telephoned Colonel Barber [17] and informed him of the result of Mr. Welles' conversation with Admiral Stark. He said that he would put himself immediately in touch with Captain Spears and suggest to General Marshall, as soon as Captain Spears receives his instructions, that the Army representatives follow this same line.

Laurence Duggan

835.24/343

Memorandum by the Adviser on Political Relations (Duggan) to the Under Secretary of State (Welles) [18]

[Washington,] March 4, 1942.

Mr. Welles: I understand that in the last two days you have discussed with the Argentine Ambassador and with Captain Spears of the Navy Department the results of the conversations between Argentine military and naval authorities and those of this Government. The Ambassador has also spoken with me and Captain Spears has permitted me to review hastily the documents which have been drawn up for signature.

I am impressed by the nonpolitical and cordial atmosphere in which these discussions have taken place. The Argentine Commission made a point in starting the conversations that it was their desire to exclude political conversations in an attempt to arrive at an understanding on a purely technical level of the mutual assistance that each country might lend to the other in the event that it became involved in the war. I am also impressed by the importance of the Argentine fleet which, under the arrangements worked out and in the event Argentina were to enter the war, would prove useful.

---

[17] Col. Henry A. Barber, War Plans Division, War Department General Staff.
[18] Mr. Welles made the following notation on this memorandum: "I have spoken with you about this—S. W."

In order to maintain as a basis of future operation the plans worked out jointly as well as the cordiality apparently existing particularly between the Navies of the two countries, the following recommendation is submitted:

(1) That the American Commission be permitted to sign the report.

(2) That the President, or if he cannot afford the time, yourself explain to the Argentine Ambassador, Admiral Saba Sueyro, and General Lapez jointly the considerations which make it impossible for the United States Government to give its assent to the technical recommendation. It seems to me that the President could point out that the joint recommendation is premised upon the assumption that Argentina is going to enter the war as an ally of the United States. That assumption appears totally unwarranted. Argentina not only has not broken off diplomatic relations but the President of Argentina has disclaimed any intention of doing so. Under the circumstances it would be illogical for the United States to approve an agreement that is based on a premise which the Argentine Government has not shown the slightest intention of fulfilling. Therefore, the signature by the technical commission must not be taken to mean that this country is prepared to go ahead with the Lend-Lease Agreement and provide armament.

I believe that in this way the Argentine military and naval authorities would not feel rebuffed. They came here at our invitation and in good faith entered into discussions on the basis of broad directives which subsequent events have shown the political arm of the Argentine Government had no intention of living up to. Were such a course to be followed as that suggested, I believe that our displeasure would be understood, that the Argentine military and naval officers would not feel personally let down, and that they might, at least with respect to certain persons in Argentina, use this influence in favor of a change in Argentine policy.

LAURENCE DUGGAN

835.34/575a : Telegram

The Acting Secretary of State to the Ambassador in Argentina
(Armour)

WASHINGTON, March 4, 1942—midnight.

305. The tentative agreement which has been worked out by the Navy Department with the Argentine naval mission comprises a contingent agreement providing for cooperation between our two navies in the event that Argentina enters the war against the Axis. It also provides for the furnishing of matériel to the Argentine Navy over a period of years commencing with the year 1942. The furnishing of such matériel, of course, would be premised upon the signing of a Lend Lease Agreement.

Our Navy Department is very anxious to avoid any breach of friendly relations with the Argentine Navy. It fears that if the contingent agreement depending upon the entrance of Argentina into the war is not signed the reaction would be so bad within the Argentine Navy as to create serious difficulties for our Navy. It is of course clearly understood that no agreement providing for the furnishing of matériel would be signed and obviously no Lend Lease agreement will be entered into so long as the present policy of the Argentine Government continues.

I am inclined to think that the point of view of the Navy Department deserves very careful consideration unless in your judgment the signing of any agreement by the Argentine mission in Washington with our Navy Department would be utilized in such a way by the Argentine Government as to discourage completely the opponents of its present policy.

The War Department is not in a position to furnish any material to the Argentine Army and that aspect of the question consequently is purely academic.

Please telegraph me your views and recommendations. Some decision will have to be reached next week.

For your personal and confidential information I have requested Caffery [19] to talk this matter over with Aranha [20] so that whatever decision we may make will be fully known beforehand by the Brazilian Government. I shall also inform the Uruguayan Foreign Minister [21] before any action is taken.

WELLES

835.24/364

Memorandum by the Chief of the Division of the American Republics (Bonsal) to the Under Secretary of State (Welles) [22]

[WASHINGTON,] March 6, 1942.

MR. WELLES: While I was talking with Dr. García Arias of the Argentine Embassy this afternoon, Ambassador Espil dropped in. They then both expressed in emphatic terms their great concern at the current development of relations between Argentina and the United States. They referred specifically to the current negotiations with the Argentine military and naval missions. These negotiations, according to them, will be meaningless unless, in addition to the sign-

---

[19] Jefferson Caffery, Ambassador in Brazil.
[20] Oswaldo Aranha, Brazilian Minister for Foreign Affairs.
[21] Alberto Guani.
[22] Mr. Welles made the following notations on this memorandum: "Talk all you think desirable—S. W."; "I am seeing Sueyro this week—S. W."

ing of military accords, they culminate in the signature and implementation of a lend lease agreement between Argentina and the United States.

It appears that the Argentine officials are really concerned at the possibility of an axis attack in Patagonia as well as of developments in Uruguay which might make necessary the rendering of Argentine assistance to that country. They stated that our action in furnishing large amounts of lend lease equipment to Brazil, while Argentina gets nothing, was of real concern to them. They said that the continuance of our present attitude would weaken the hands of our friends in Argentina and would strengthen our enemies.

Ambassador Espil said that he was afraid that you had not been able to give adequate consideration to this matter because of the many other questions pressing upon you.

I will be glad to make a further opportunity to converse with the Ambassador on this subject if you think it desirable; he himself suggested that he "could talk for two hours about it".

(It will shortly become known in Argentina that although Chile has neither broken off relations with the axis or signed a lend lease agreement, certain war matériel is being made available to Chile. I think we should consider, following the signature of the agreements with the Argentine military and naval missions, and without signing a lend lease agreement, the possibility of furnishing a very limited amount of war matériel to Argentina on a Hemisphere defense basis.[23] This would at least weaken the position of the Argentines who are talking about our policy of reprisals, et cetera.)

PHILIP W. BONSAL

835.34/577 : Telegram

The Ambassador in Argentina (Armour) to the Secretary of State

BUENOS AIRES, March 7, 1942—5 p. m.
[Received 6 : 18 p. m.]

446. For the Under Secretary. Department's telegram 305, March 4, midnight. I can well understand our Navy Department's desire to maintain friendly relations with the Argentine Navy and I recognize the value inherent in an agreement providing for cooperation between our Navies "in the event that Argentina enters the war against the Axis." The implication conveyed by such a clause, namely, the admission in writing of the possibility of Argentina entering the war against the Axis would in itself be of prime importance.

[23] In the margin, in Sumner Welles' handwriting, appears the word "No".

On the other hand there is little doubt that the Government here would attempt to use the signing of any agreement to create the impression that the position taken by the Argentine Government had not affected our policy so far as the furnishing of war material is concerned. We would have to anticipate I fear the impression for a time at least that we had receded somewhat from our original position.

Referring to penultimate paragraph of your telegram effort should be made to avoid creation of impression that we are making a distinction between the Argentine Army and Navy, having in mind the existing jealousies between these services. If this aspect is not carefully handled it might have serious repercussions.

Not knowing the contents of the agreement, I am not in a position to comment on whether the undoubted advantages would be compensation for the aforementioned disadvantages. If the agreement is signed I would suggest that a carefully worded statement be issued at the time of signing to the effect that the actual furnishing of material is premised upon the signing of a lend-lease agreement.

Regarding such a statement, the inclusion in the agreement of a specific date 1942 when the furnishing of material is to commence would appear to present a difficulty. This might be interpreted here as a commitment to enter into a lease-lend agreement during the current year even though no change in the present policy of the Argentine Government had occurred in the meantime. If this point, provided it is well taken, could be cleared up and the suggested explanatory statement issued, it would make it more difficult for the Argentine Government to make capital out of the signing of the agreement.

I do not know whether it would be the intention to publish the text or summary of the agreement if and when signed. If this could be done, the publication accompanied by the statement suggested should indicate that there has been no fundamental change in our policy.

ARMOUR

835.34/575a Suppl. : Telegram

The Acting Secretary of State to the Ambassador in Argentina
(Armour)

WASHINGTON, March 20, 1942—noon.

387. Since my telegram no. 305 of March 4, midnight, there have been several developments of which I think you should know in the event that during the next 2 or 3 days you are engaged by the Argentine authorities in conversations on this subject.

The plan of military and naval cooperation between the United States and Argentina as developed by the military and naval authorities of the two Governments was premised upon Argentine entry into the war on the side of the United Nations. This premise, although wholly acceptable for the purposes of developing a plan of military and naval collaboration, is wholly unrealistic from the standpoint of political actualities, since the Argentine Government does not have the slightest present intention of entering the war. The Argentine naval authorities and Espil have shown an intense desire that the agreement be signed and approved by the two Governments. In addition to the reason they give for signature, namely, the desirability of maintaining cordial technical relations between the military and naval arms of the two Governments, in my judgment there are two important advantages which would accrue to Argentina without any corresponding benefit to this country. In the first place, Argentina would soon maintain before this Government that the agreement contained a moral commitment on our part to provide armament so that Argentina could be in a position to fulfill its obligations in the event that it were to enter the war. It would request the negotiation of a Lend-Lease agreement and the immediate delivery of the armament set forth in the report to be delivered provided Argentina enters the war. In the second place, Argentina would make it appear to Argentine public opinion that signature of the agreement was positive proof that Argentine policy at the Meeting of Foreign Ministers in Rio was not out of harmony with the policy of the United States and the other American republics.

In order to remove this one-sided aspect of the agreement and to secure from Argentina some positive contribution to the maintenance of the security of the Hemisphere, the Argentine Delegation was informed of the desire of the United States Delegation to add certain paragraphs to the agreement reading as follows:

"3. The Argentine Government recognizes the necessity of maintaining uninterrupted sea communications between the United States and Argentina. The United States Committee and the Argentine Delegation agree that the provisions of Annex 4—the Control and Protection of Shipping—should become effective immediately. The High Command of the two navies will immediately make necessary agreements for the control and protection of shipping. The principles and instructions necessary for the control and protection of shipping are attached hereto.

4. In case the Argentine Government agrees to the above cooperative measures while remaining in a non-belligerent status, the Government of the United States will immediately enter into negotiations with the Argentine Government for the purpose of making a Lend Lease contract. This contract will provide for the procurement of the materials and facilities listed in Annex 5—Section 3 which have been recommended to be undertaken in the year 1942."

Annex 4 mentioned in paragraph 3 reads as follows:

"*Annex IV, Control and Protection of Shipping.*

1. United States authorities will issue directions for the control and protection of shipping of the Associated Powers within the areas in which United States authorities assume responsibility for the strategic direction of Military forces. Argentine authorities will issue directions for the control and protection of shipping of the Associated Powers within the areas in which Argentine authorities assume responsibility for the strategic direction of Military forces.

2. United States and Argentine shipping scheduled to pass from an area assigned to one Power into an area assigned to another Power, will be controlled and protected by agreement between the respective Naval authorities. The United States Navy Department is the highest authority in the control of shipping in the South Atlantic bound to and from the United States. It is understood that, in this case, control means the coordination of the shipping routes.

3. The United States Naval Control Service Organization will arrange for the control and protection of shipping of the United States registry or charter within United States areas. Requests from the United States Naval Control Service for protection by Argentine forces within the Argentine zone of Responsibility will be made to the Chief of Staff Argentine Navy."

The Argentine Delegation replied in writing that this proposal "is a political matter, therefore it is outside the orbit and attributes of this Delegation for consideration. It is to be regretted that this Delegation is unable to enter in discussions regarding this added plan of cooperation".

I thereupon made the proposal to Espil who has now informed me that his Government cannot accept it since it would involve his country in the war. He has been instructed to present to the President his Government's views in the premises. As a first step, he is preparing a memorandum setting forth these views which he expects to give me tomorrow afternoon.

I will keep you fully posted of developments.

WELLES

835.34/575a : Telegram

The Acting Secretary of State to the Ambassador in Argentina
(*Armour*)

WASHINGTON, March 21, 1942—9 p. m.

399. My telegram no. 387, March 20, noon. The Argentine and United States Delegations had a final meeting this morning at which Admiral Richardson made the following statement:

"The United States Delegation has welcomed the discussions with the Argentine Delegation regarding certain military questions and has appreciated the spirit of understanding and comradeship of the

Argentine Delegation which is traditional between the Navies of the two countries. It is understood that the arrangements discussed between the two Delegations are to be held in abeyance pending their further consideration by our respective Governments."

The Argentine Delegation is leaving Washington tomorrow and has reservations to leave on Wednesday's plane for Buenos Aires.

WELLES

835.24/534

The Argentine Ambassador (Espil) to the Secretary of State

[Translation]

D. E. No. 61 WASHINGTON, March 24, 1942.

MR. SECRETARY OF STATE: In connection with the suspension of the conversations which recently took place between the naval-military commissions of the two countries and in order to make clear the position of the Argentine Government in this matter, I take pleasure in enclosing a memorandum recapitulating the antecedents and the progress of the said conversations.

I take the opportunity [etc.] FELIPE A. ESPIL

[Enclosure—Translation]

MEMORANDUM FROM THE ARGENTINE EMBASSY WITH REGARD TO THE NEGOTIATIONS ON COOPERATION IN THE CONTINENTAL DEFENSE PLAN

With the departure of our Naval-Military Delegation, the Argentine Embassy considers it opportune to outline below the progress of the recent negotiations for the furnishing of armaments.

1. Under date of July 30 last, the Embassy of the United States in Buenos Aires presented a memorandum to our Foreign Office [25] inviting the Argentine Government to renew the conversations of General Staffs initiated during the visits to Buenos Aires in 1940 of Captain Spears and Colonel Christian. To this end the Department of State expressed the opinion that it would be mutually advantageous for the Argentine Government to appoint a Military-Naval Commission, which should visit the United States not only with authority to continue those conversations, but also to present the needs of the Argentine Army and Navy with respect to military and naval equipment which, according to the same memorandum, could only be obtained within the near future, under the Lend-Lease

---

[25] See telegram No. 810, August 8, 1941, 3 p. m., from the Ambassador in Argentina, printed in *Foreign Relations*, 1941, vol. VI, section under Argentina entitled "Discussions between the United States and Argentina regarding a Lend-Lease Agreement . . ."

Act. As a result of this invitation, the Argentine Government appointed the Naval and Military Commission which, in execution of its task, was in Washington for the last three months.

2. Simultaneously with the departure of our Delegation on December 1 last, Mr. Laurence Duggan, Political Adviser of the Department, delivered to this Mission the text of a proposed basic agreement between the two Governments [26] for the furnishing of armament under the terms of the Lend-Lease Act. The same offer was repeated in a note from the Department of State to this Embassy dated December 9 last.[27]

3. The conversations between the Naval-Military Delegations of the two Governments developed in the spirit they had anticipated and in an atmosphere of mutual understanding. Points of view and data for cooperation in continental defense were exchanged, the value of which, in view of possible eventualities, cannot be denied. The Argentine Delegation offered a plan of defense which, in revealing its war preparations, signifies a great demonstration of friendship towards the United States. And lastly, the imminent conclusion of the plan of collaboration which was to have been signed on the 14th instant constitutes, in the Argentine Government's opinion, noteworthy expressions of its firm desire to cooperate in the common defense.

4. Coincident with the above proposals, as the Department has already been orally advised, the Argentine Government, in a Ministerial Resolution, recently decided to accept the proposed basic agreement for the furnishing of armaments under the Lend-Lease Act, suggesting certain modifications as to the amount and dates of delivery of the materials.

In fact, this Embassy has received a communication from our Ministry of Foreign Affairs, according to which the amounts offered in the proposed basic agreement which the Department submitted to it last December, would be insufficient to assure the adequate organization of the effectives which our Government considers indispensable to guarantee execution of the defense in the zones subject to our responsibility, which were contemplated in the joint, basic, "United States–Argentine Republic" war plan which has just been discussed in Washington.

As the Department must know, the urgent needs of our Army and our Navy were carefully studied during the conversations between the Naval-Military Delegations of the two Governments. From these studies, at least from the technical point of view, there has evolved an

---

[26] Enclosure 2 to Department's instruction No. 1493, December 4, 1941, printed in *Foreign Relations*, 1941, vol. VI, section under Argentina entitled "Discussions between the United States and Argentina regarding a Lend-Lease Agreement . . ."

[27] Not printed.

agreement in opinion between the Delegations which exhibits a discrepancy, as regards figures, with the plans originally contemplated.

5. Always in the same spirit of cooperation in the plan of continental defense, it is to be pointed out that the Argentine Government, without waiting for the signing of the pertinent agreements, has already taken important measures to forward defensive preparation and has expended large amounts in our country for such purposes. A brief list of such preparatory measures is given below :

a) Increase in the Army's peace-time effectives
The figure of 45,000 men which the Army's peace-time effectives reached in 1941 has been increased in the current year to that of 100,000 men. For that purpose, a large part of the class of 1920 has been kept in service and that of 1921 called up.

The cadres of commissioned and non-commissioned officers have been increased in a corresponding proportion by calling up reserve personnel.

b) Possible calling up of reserves
The calling up of other reserve classes to reinforce the effectives mentioned above, if necessary, has been provided for.

c) Defense of Patagonia and Tierra del Fuego
The installation of large nuclei of Army troops—including aviation—has been ordered at the following points on the South Atlantic coast :

1. Rio Gallegos
2. Rio Grande

In addition to these troops, the present garrison units, suitably reinforced, are maintained at Comodoro Rivadavia and Esquel (in the Chubut Territory) at Bariloche (Rio Negro Territory) and in the Neuquen Territory.

d) Defense of the Atlantic coast in the sector corresponding to the Province of Buenos Aires
Measures have been taken for the defense of this sector of the Atlantic coast through the employment of a number of Divisions, with the corresponding intervention of the air forces.

e) Installation of air bases in Patagonia
The installation of air bases has been ordered to the end that aviation may be able to cooperate effectively with the Army forces entrusted with the defense.

6. Taking into account the emergencies with which the United States is faced by reason of the war, it is the Argentine Government's intention not to request transfer of completed armaments, aviation or materials, except in the most moderate amount, compatible with the agreements provided for, and only of those elements which it is practically impossible to manufacture in the country within a short period.

The area of Argentine Patagonia and the importance of its vital and vulnerable points demand special measures with a view to strategic mobility. It most urgently requires that automotive, armored and air units be supplied. It is on such equipment, and on anti-aircraft artillery, that the efficiency with which our troops—already well instructed and reinforced with effectives—will be able to fulfill their protective or defensive mission will rest.

One of the most valuable contributions to continental defense in the southern hemisphere is, in the opinion of the Argentine Government, constituted by the efficient military and naval preparations of commanding officers, officer staffs and other cadres in its Army and Navy and by the ample proportion of instructed reserves which are the product of more than 40 years of compulsory military service.

7. From the foregoing, it is obvious that the effectiveness of our cooperation in continental defense is closely bound to the equipment and materials which the Argentine Republic has a probability of receiving in due time to complete the operative value of its Army and Navy.

WASHINGTON, March 24, 1942.

835.34/575a (Suppl) : Telegram

The Acting Secretary of State to the Ambassador in Argentina (Armour)

WASHINGTON, March 25, 1942—5 p. m.

415. My telegrams nos. 387, March 20, noon, and 399, March 21, 9 p. m. Espil has informed me that his telegraphic exchange with his Government took the following sequence.

Since the Argentine Delegation did not transmit to the Ministries of War and Marine the text of our counterproposal, he sent the text to the Foreign Office for its information. The Foreign Office then telegraphed him in the sense indicated in the penultimate paragraph of my telegram no. 387 (i.e., instructing him to discuss this question with the President). Espil telegraphed that in accordance with the regular procedure it was necessary for him to advise the President, through the Department, of the purpose of his visit. To this end he was drafting a memorandum. The Foreign Office next telegraphed that he should hold up any further action until the Argentine Government had an opportunity of going over the matter with Admiral Sueyro and General Lapez. Espil wired asking whether this meant that he should not even present the memorandum. Today Espil received a reply to the effect that while it was all right to present the memorandum the memorandum should not refer to our counterproposal regarding convoying since that had not been taken up officially by the Department with him. Espil was further advised by Dr. Ruiz Guiñazú that, after his return from the Chilean inauguration about April 6 to 8, he would consider the matter further but that in the meantime he was not to request an audience to receive [*sic*] the President.

In accordance with these instructions Espil presented a memorandum [28] which is merely a recapitulation of the origin of the invitation to hold military and naval discussions in Washington, the preliminaries of the negotiations for a basic Lend-Lease agreement, and a statement of the steps already taken by the Government to place Argentina in a position to repel aggression. A copy of his memorandum will be sent to you by air mail.

I do not agree that the United States counterproposal was not officially taken up with Espil. Although I did not hand him a copy of the proposal, since he already had it through the courtesy of the Argentine Delegation, I did present the proposition to him with the request that he ascertain the views of his Government. In order, however, to make it impossible for Dr. Ruiz Guiñazú to say that our counterproposal was never formally presented to the Argentine Government, in acknowledging receipt of Espil's memorandum which was sent under a covering note, I am transmitting formally to Espil a copy of our counterproposal.

WELLES

835.24/595a

The Acting Secretary of State to the Argentine Ambassador (Espil)

WASHINGTON, April 3, 1942.

EXCELLENCY: I have the honor to acknowledge the receipt of Your Excellency's note of March 24, 1942 enclosing a memorandum recapitulating the antecedents and the progress of the conversations that have recently taken place in Washington between the Naval and Military authorities of Argentina and the United States.

With respect to the proposed agreement under discussion between the military and naval authorities of our two Governments, it will be recalled that the Argentine Delegation informed the United States Delegation that it was not authorized to consider a proposal advanced by the United States Delegation with respect to the control and protection of shipping by Argentina within certain stipulated areas off the coast of Argentina for the reason that the Argentine Delegation considered this proposal of a political character and consequently of a character appropriate for discussion by the proper political authorities of the two Governments. Although I subsequently discussed this proposal with you orally, and you later expressed to me under instructions certain views of your Government, I believe it desirable

---

[28] *Supra.*

to send you formally the exact text of the proposal with the request that you ask that it be given the further consideration of your Government.

May I reiterate that if your Government finds acceptable this proposal regarding the control and protection of shipping and is ready to put into effect immediately the provisions of Annex IV of the proposed agreement this Government will immediately enter into negotiations with the Argentine Government for the purpose of signing a Lend-Lease agreement. Under this agreement, procurement would be effected of the materials and facilities listed in Annex V—Section 3 of the proposed agreement relating to 1942 in accordance with the recommendation of the United States Delegation.

Accept [etc.] SUMNER WELLES

835.24/592a

The Liaison Officer With the War and Navy Departments (Wilson) to the Assistant Chief of Staff, War Plans Division, War Department (Eisenhower)

WASHINGTON, April 9, 1942.

MY DEAR GENERAL EISENHOWER: On March 19 I sent you, at the request of the Acting Secretary, a memorandum [30] enclosing the text in translation of a note from the Argentine Ambassador indicating his Government's desire to obtain certain motorized equipment. You referred this memorandum to Colonel Barber who on March 31 kindly sent me a communication [30] showing various items of the above-mentioned motorized equipment which it would be possible to release promptly.

In this connection you may be interested to learn that, owing to the unwillingness of Argentina to sever diplomatic relations with the Axis Powers and to contribute to hemisphere defense in the same manner as other countries which have taken this step, a decision has been reached to refrain from facilitating to the Argentine Government the same kind of assistance that is being made available to many other American republics. As this decision will prevent the delivery of the motorized equipment desired by the Argentine Government, the Ambassador was informed that, in view of existing conditions, the Government of the United States regretted that it was unable to make available to the Argentine authorities the material in question.

Sincerely yours, ORME WILSON

---

[30] Not printed.

835.34/600 : Telegram

The Ambassador in Argentina (Armour) to the Secretary of State

BUENOS AIRES, April 24, 1942—midnight.
[Received April 25—1 : 04 a. m.]

760. For the Under Secretary. Reference Department's air mail instruction 2103 April 3.[31] Following is translation of note received today from Minister for Foreign Affairs.

"As Your Excellency knows, the Argentine Government, duly appreciative of the plan of collaboration proffered by the Lease-Lend Act, in due course took pertinent steps in Washington, after obtaining the necessary opinions thereon with a view to carrying out insofar as this country is concerned, the program of military aid and supply authorized by that act.

In so doing, in accordance with the communications received and with the explanations made personally by Your Excellency in this chancellery, the Argentine Government understood that the loan to be obtained under the Lend-Lease Act did not necessarily depend on the conversations previously suggested by Your Excellency's Government for the study of a common defense plan. Nevertheless, the military-naval delegation which was sent to the United States for the study of a plan of purchases, was given instructions which, with the collaboration of the Ambassador in Washington made possible the simultaneous discussion of the agreement for the application of the Lease-Lend Act and for the plan of continental defense cooperation, or military agreement, as it was called in the course of the negotiations, thereby admitting the connection logically existing between the purchase plan and the political circumstances to which the plan must apply.

The text of the plan of cooperation having been agreed upon in March last by the technical delegations of both countries, the Argentine representatives—this Government concurring—understood that the agreement for the supply of armaments which was implicitly related to the other, would be considered at the same time. However, such was not the opinion of the Department of State, even though the value of the plan of cooperation could be only relative and its fulfillment would certainly be insufficient without the simultaneous application of the supplies agreement which was to assure the material required.

This Government however being desirous of promoting with Your Excellency's Government every possible understanding in keeping with the needs of cooperation called for by present circumstances, authorized its delegation in Washington to sign the plan of defensive cooperation independently, insofar as it implies the recognition of a policy of collaboration adopted in accordance with the obligations assumed by the country, which it is disposed to fulfill in the measure that its resources may permit.

Your Excellency is aware of the circumstances which also prevented, even in that insufficient form, the conclusion of the agreement negotiated in Washington. Once the terms were modified on which both

---

[31] Not printed.

delegations, Argentine and American, had apparently agreed in the first place with a view to establishing the scope of the plan of defensive cooperation, the Department of State submitted to our Embassy in Washington a new proposal subordinating in our case the benefits of the Lend-Lease Act to certain obligations relating to the control and protection of shipping on the Atlantic Coast.

This condition which in practice could not apply to the other nations of the continent, thus appears to become an exclusively Argentine obligation which this Government did not deem it possible to accept inasmuch as it implies the creation of a situation of belligerency which the country does not desire and for which it is not prepared.

On this occasion, I wish to state to Your Excellency that the Argentine Government, without disregarding the special circumstances that must be borne in mind by the Government of the United States in regulating the delivery of armaments to the various countries which availed themselves of the Lend-Lease Act, hopes at the same time that the difficulties arising in the present negotiations may finally be settled in the spirit of cooperation which at present animates the policy of American countries faced, notwithstanding the diversity of their situations, with similar problems of security and supply.

In that same spirit the Argentine Government will facilitate any solution which, within its own possibilities, may signify a useful contribution in the present situation of the continent. In this sense I take pleasure in informing Your Excellency that, after having obtained from the Government of the United States the facilities requested for the incorporation of the tankers *Victoria* and *Ulysses* under the national flag the Argentine Government has just facilitated in the same manner the transfer of the Argentine tanker *Esso Formosa* to the flag of your country which, as Your Excellency has pointed out, needs its services and has been using the tanker for some time."

Reference paragraph 2 of note regarding Argentine Government's understanding that loan not dependent on outcome defense conversations apparently refers to statements made by you to Espil and by me to Foreign Office based upon Department's 511, August 6, 7 p. m., 1941.[32] See also my 854 August 19, 6 p. m., 1941.[33]

In conversation with the Minister for Foreign Affairs yesterday he raised the point referred to in paragraphs 5 and 6 of note. I took the position that we had if anything favored Argentina since other nations of continent receiving material under "Lease-Lend" had either declared war or broken with Axis Powers. Minister for Foreign Affairs used same arguments set forth in note as reasons why he felt Government could not accept our proposals. To my question whether German submarine attack on *Victoria* might not alter their attitude, he replied he would have to await further reports on this matter before venturing opinion. However, his subsequent remarks on general situation did not hold out much encouragement.

Armour

---

[32] Printed in *Foreign Relations*, 1941, vol. vi, section under Argentina entitled "Discussions between the United States and Argentina regarding a Lend-Lease Agreement . . ."

[33] *Ibid.*

835.34/606

The Ambassador in Argentina (Armour) to the Secretary of State

No. 4920   BUENOS AIRES, May 1, 1942.
                                                 [Received May 8.]

SIR: With reference to the Embassy's telegram no. 760, of April 24, 12 midnight, forwarding the translation of a note received from the Minister for Foreign Affairs on that date with regard to certain proposals of our Government in connection with the furnishing of material for the Argentine Navy under the Lease-Lend Act, I have the honor to transmit herewith a copy, together with translation, of the note in question.[34]

As stated in my telegram under reference, in a conversation with the Minister for Foreign Affairs on the day previous to the receipt of the note, Dr. Ruiz Guiñazú made the point that in exacting certain obligations relating to the control and protection of shipping as a condition precedent to the supplying of materials under the Lease-Lend Act, our Government was discriminating against Argentina, since a similar condition was not stipulated in the case of the other American Republics which had received or been promised assistance under the Act. I took the position that, far from discriminating against Argentina, I felt that our Government had made an exception in their favor in that the other nations of the continent which had been promised material under the Lease-Lend Act had either declared war against or broken relations with the Axis Powers.

To be sure, agreements with certain of these Governments may have been made prior to the decisions taken at Rio; nevertheless it seemed to me that the principle is clear and that our Government's proposal to make available certain material to the Argentine Navy under the conditions stipulated cannot be interpreted as discrimination against this country.

In a conversation with the Under Secretary for Foreign Affairs last evening I took this same position with Dr. Gache. To my surprise Dr. Gache stated that his Government felt that our proposals for convoy constituted a more drastic step towards war against the Axis even than the breaking of relations, since use of Argentine war ships for this purpose would inevitably lead to a clash with the Axis. I pointed out to Dr. Gache that the action of the Germans in sinking United States and other vessels carrying much-needed materials for Argentina virtually constituted a blockade of this country and it would seem only logical—aside from this country's commitments in continental defense—that they should take the necessary steps to

---

[34] For translation of note, see telegram No. 760, *supra*.

assure the safe delivery of materials essential to this country's economy. He did not give any indication, however, that the Government was considering any change in its position from that indicated in the note under reference.

I understand, from other sources, that Admiral Sueyro and the naval officers who accompanied him to Washington are very bitter at what they consider to have been the arbitrary action of the State Department in imposing these further conditions at the last moment after they had come to a complete agreement and understanding with our naval authorities on other points which would have made possible the supply of materials required.

Respectfully yours,   NORMAN ARMOUR

835.34/600

The Secretary of State to the Ambassador in Argentina (*Armour*)

No. 2353   WASHINGTON, May 13, 1942.

SIR: Reference is made to your telegram no. 760, April 24, midnight, for the Under Secretary, transmitting a translation of a note you received on April 24, 1942, from the Argentine Minister of Foreign Affairs concerning the desire of the Argentine Government to obtain war matériel from the United States despite the reluctance of the Argentine Government to enter into any systematic arrangements for the protection of shipping between Argentina and the United States.

There is now enclosed a draft of a note which you are requested to deliver in appropriate form to the Argentine Minister of Foreign Affairs in reply to the note you received from him on April 24, 1942, provided you agree with the wording. The Department would appreciate your telegraphing any suggestions you may have concerning possible modifications in the enclosed draft.

Very truly yours,   For the Secretary of State:
                                                      SUMNER WELLES

[Enclosure]

DRAFT OF NOTE TO HIS EXCELLENCY DR. ENRIQUE RUIZ-GUIÑAZÚ, MINISTER FOR FOREIGN AFFAIRS AND WORSHIP OF THE REPUBLIC OF ARGENTINA

EXCELLENCY: I have the honor to acknowledge the receipt of Your Excellency's note of April 24, 1942 with respect to discussions between representatives of our two Governments concerning collaboration in hemisphere defense and the provision of matériel under lend-lease arrangements. Immediately upon receiving this communication from

Your Excellency, I transmitted it to my Government, which has now instructed me to reply to you as follows:

My Government is impressed by the desire of Your Excellency's Government to make its contribution toward the solution of the problems of security and supply which confront the Argentine Republic and the United States as well as the other American republics. My Government hopes that, on account of this attitude, it will be possible for the two Governments to arrive at an identical appraisal of the situation which confronts them so that the difficulties which have arisen in these negotiations may be immediately resolved to their mutual benefit. Indeed, it is precisely the nature of that situation which has dictated the current policy of the Government of the United States.

Following the drastic reversal in the international situation caused by the fall of France, the American republics, fully aware of the extreme peril and having declared that any attempt on the part of a non-American state against the integrity or the inviolability of the territory, the sovereignty, or the political independence of an American state should be considered as an aggression against all of them, actively engaged in strengthening their defenses and their armed forces against all eventualities and in organizing cooperation for defense among them. During this period, the Government of the United States offered to enter into both lend-lease arrangements and military conversations with the Government of Argentina.

As a result of the aggression of Japan upon the United States on December 7, 1941 and the immediately following declarations of war by Italy and Germany, a very different situation has existed. The United States and nine of the other American republics are at war with the Axis. In addition, nine of the remaining republics have broken off diplomatic and economic relations with the Axis. All nineteen of these republics have, to a greater or lesser degree, each according to its means, taken active, even drastic, measures to eliminate Axis activity within their frontiers.

In accordance with its intention to render assistance to the utmost of its ability to the American republics which have thus placed themselves in the forefront of hemispheric defense, the Government of the United States has made available to these American republics all of the military and naval matériel which it could possibly spare in order that by so doing it might make the utmost possible contribution to the cause of hemispheric solidarity and to the practical defense of the New World. Because of the imperative demand for matériel at the fighting fronts in Europe, in Asia, in Africa, and in the South Seas, and the training requirements of the United Nations, it has unfortunately not been possible for the Government of the United

States to make available to these other American republics all of the military and naval matériel which is required by them in the common interest of all.

It is of course obvious, in view of the situation above indicated, that the Government of the United States could not conceivably divert vitally needed naval or military matériel to the Governments of the American republics which have made no effective contribution to the cause of hemispheric defense.

It was because of this consideration of indisputable validity that my Government offered Argentina a proposal to collaborate in keeping open the sea lanes between Argentina and the United States over which flows the trade which is so important to the well-being and protection of our two countries. My Government has felt that were the Argentine Republic to undertake this responsibility, it would be contributing in a practical and effective measure to the cause of hemispheric solidarity and to the cause of hemispheric defense and that under such conditions all of the nineteen American republics, of which the United States is one and to which reference is above made, would have jointly felt that under such circumstances the Argentine Republic should legitimately share in the supplies of armament available to my Government for distribution among the other American republics.

My Government considers the proposal made to Argentina for protection of shipping in waters adjacent to Argentina eminently fair and reasonable. The United States today is utilizing such of its naval forces as are available for the protection of shipping in the north and even south Atlantic, including shipping to and from Argentina. The least that Argentina should be willing to do is to give protection to such shipping off Argentine shores.

My Government, therefore, sincerely regrets to learn the indication of your Government in its note of April 24, 1942 that Argentina is not disposed to collaborate effectively in the manner proposed in order to further the cause in which nineteen of the American republics are actively cooperating. Candor requires my Government to state that it finds itself in disagreement with the conclusion that the proposal implies the creation of a state of belligerency. The history of the last few years offers many instances of naval action taken by a neutral country in protection of its shipping that did not result in a state of belligerency. The example of my own country might be cited which, for many months prior to the declaration of war upon it by Germany and Italy, was taking daily naval action to assure that its ships arrived safely in the ports of many distant lands. The United States did not become a belligerent as a result of that action.

If the proposal appears like an exclusively Argentine obligation, it is because the nineteen other American republics have already taken steps of far greater consequence and risk. Ten of them are at war with the Axis countries, and another nine have broken off diplomatic relations. In the absence of either action by Argentina, my Government hoped for some positive measures by Argentina that would persuade the other eighteen countries that Argentina was making its contribution to the maintenance of hemisphere solidarity and therefore was entitled to share in the distribution of the armament available for the other American republics.

In view of the position of your Government, my Government regrets to find itself unable to proceed with the signature of the agreement which has been under consideration by the appropriate authorities of our two Governments and with the negotiation of a Lend-Lease agreement which is, of course, in itself only incidental to the actual provision of matériel.

Accept, Excellency, the assurances of my most distinguished consideration.

835.34/607 : Telegram

The Ambassador in Argentina (Armour) to the Secretary of State

BUENOS AIRES, May 26, 1942—5 p. m.
[Received 7 p. m.]

978. Department's strictly confidential air mail instruction 2353, May 13, enclosing draft of note for delivery to Minister of Foreign Affairs in reply to latter's note of April 24 regarding protection of shipping between Argentina and the United States. In my recent conversation with the Acting President I discussed question of their undertaking to protect ships from southern point of Brazil to Argentine ports along the lines of my conversation with Minister for Foreign Affairs (Embassy's despatch No. 5068, May 13,[35] pages 3 and 4). Acting President appeared interested in proposal and promised to study the matter further with the Minister of Foreign Affairs.

I have since learned from the Minister of the Interior that Castillo mentioned the matter to him, from which I judge that he is giving serious consideration to it.

In view of this I think it would be wise to postpone addressing note to Foreign Office along the lines suggested until we have had time to see whether Government intends to do something.

ARMOUR

---

[35] Not printed.

835.34/607 : Telegram

The Secretary of State to the Ambassador in Argentina (Armour)

WASHINGTON, June 1, 1942—11 p. m.

785. Your 978, May 26, 5 p. m.   Please present the Department's note.

HULL

DISCUSSIONS BETWEEN THE UNITED STATES AND ARGENTINA CONCERNING SHIPPING PROBLEMS

800.8830/1382 : Telegram

The Ambassador in Argentina (Armour) to the Secretary of State

BUENOS AIRES, February 9, 1942—6 p. m.
[Received 9 : 27 p. m.]

240. For Duggan.[36]   In my recent cables I have emphasized the difficult problem faced by friendly newspapers by reason of lack of shipping space for newsprint.   Unfortunately it does not appear that any of the shipments mentioned in Department's 54, January 13, 4 p. m.[37] are scheduled for Argentina.   Neither could the total mentioned 4,500 tons, do much to alleviate the situation as Argentina normally imports over 125,000 tons annually.   I understand that the Argentine Government has been asked to assign space on its vessels and that the Acting President [38] has agreed in principle.   There have also been rumors to the effect that the Government might consider assigning an entire ship to newsprint and some publishers fear that should such a decision be taken, it might mean the allocation by the Government here of this newsprint or some other equally effective government control, making it more difficult for those publications critical of administration policy to obtain paper.   Consequently, I feel it essential that our Government make possible sufficient space on American ships to assure, first, immediate delivery of paper now on docks in New York to replenish stocks now almost exhausted for such papers as *La Prensa*, *La Nación*, *Noticias Gráficas*, *La Razón*, *El Día*, *Buenos Aires Herald*, et cetera, and second, to provide a program for the future whereby deliveries of minimum needs can be made as secure as is practicable.   Likewise, it is hoped that our export control will be so exercised as to provide that this paper will continue to be shipped to the ultimate consignee and not to any central organization which might be empowered to make the distribution here.   The Central Bank might be construed as having that authority now.   (See Embassy's report 790, dated January 22, 1942.)[37]   As long as shipments are made to consignee only, a

[36] Laurence Duggan, Adviser on Political Relations.
[37] Not printed.
[38] Ramón S. Castillo.

complete control can be exercised both to the end that prodemocratic press may be assured of stocks sufficient to continue publication and that none reach the hands of firms or publications on the Proclaimed List.

I should appreciate being informed of any decisions taken so that we may be in a position to answer numerous inquiries which we are receiving, especially as regards *La Prensa*, which seems particularly pressing.

ARMOUR

800.8830/1390 : Telegram

The Ambassador in Argentina (*Armour*) *to the Secretary of State*

BUENOS AIRES, February 14, 1942—3 p. m.
[Received February 14—2 : 26 p. m.]

275. Embassy's telegram 240, February 9, 6 p. m., and 263, February 12, 8 p. m.[39] In an interview given representatives of the local newspapers last night the Acting President stated that he had ordered one of the Argentine merchant ships which had left recently for the United States to load a cargo of newsprint instead of coal. He added that this first shipment would satisfy the immediate needs and that future requirements would also be met by the Government according to a plan to carry newsprint in Government vessels. According to *La Nación's* account the Acting President stated that the newsprint will be distributed proportionally permitting the continued operation of all newspapers, and that within a few days an organization would be set up to allocate the newsprint. Newspapers will have representation in the organization.

Many newsprint importers have already wired their principals in the United States informing regarding the above and urging them to oppose such action, since such a system would destroy their business.

ARMOUR

800.8830/1390 : Telegram

The Secretary of State to the Ambassador in Argentina (*Armour*)

WASHINGTON, February 16, 1942—7 p. m.

229. Your 275, February 14, 3 p. m. Is it the intention of the Government to distribute newsprint among all papers, desirable and undesirable? If not, what papers will receive newsprint? Do you believe that the Government will attempt to control the distribution of that newsprint which comes on United States or United States-controlled vessels? Do you foresee an attempt by the Government to control editorial policies of the papers involved to the detriment of

---

[39] Latter not printed.

our interests? Do you advise approval, at least for the time being, of export licenses for newsprint consigned to the Argentine Government? In this connection preliminary information indicates that the 2,000 tons of newsprint on the *Rio Tercero* is for the use of the Argentine Government.

Any suggestions you may have on this problem would be appreciated. A telegraphic reply is desired.

HULL

800.6363/566a : Telegram

The Acting Secretary of State to the Ambassador in Argentina (*Armour*)

WASHINGTON, March 18, 1942—4 p. m.

376. As you have been previously informed, there is an impending shortage of tankers for petroleum deliveries both to the east coast of the United States and to Latin America. It is not desired to apply whatever reduction is necessary in deliveries against industries producing materials for our war effort. These should continue to be supplied with their full requirements. In Argentina the following companies have been tentatively selected: Armour, Swift, LaBlanca, Wilson, Bovril, Frigorífico Anglo, Smithfield and government-owned packing houses.

The Department would appreciate any suggestions you may have for additions to this list. Among these may be certain mining establishments and utilities directly related to such activities.

Please determine the tanker-borne petroleum requirements of these for the year beginning April 1942. Ships bunkers, British Ministry of War Transport, and Navy needs will be determined here. Please cable this information urgently.

You are also requested to commence preparation of studies by uses of all other petroleum requirements for the same period. The studies should give estimates of the reductions possible in the uses of tanker-borne petroleum products, bearing in mind that only the most essential requirements may be met.

WELLES

800.8830/1493 : Telegram

The Ambassador in Argentina (*Armour*) *to the Secretary of State*

BUENOS AIRES, April 14, 1942—5 p. m.
[Received 5 : 30 p. m.]

664. The Advisory Committee on the distribution of newsprint met April 8 and unanimously agreed that newsprint distribution in Argen-

tina should remain in the hands of the present importers. The Embassy understands that the Minister of Agriculture agreed with the opinion of the Committee. It is understood that the Argentine Government has cabled its Embassy in Washington, asking it to ascertain from our Government the amount of shipping space which can be allotted for newsprint to Argentina on our vessels and is also planning to address a similar communication to this Embassy. After receipt of this data the Argentine Government will allot space on its own vessels. Refer to my telegram No. 665, April 14, 6 p. m.[41]

ARMOUR

800.857/662 : Telegram

The Ambassador in Argentina (Armour) to the Secretary of State

BUENOS AIRES, April 22, 1942—6 p. m.
[Received 9:20 p. m.]

728. By decree promulgated April 20 published by yesterday's press merchant vessels of foreign registry may not be repaired in Argentina without prior authorization from the Ministry of Marine. In determining whether or not authorization shall be granted the Ministry will take into consideration the need for the repairs and their cost.

The decree provides that repairs will be authorized on the express condition that the owners of the vessels import into Argentina within a period of 6 months materials of the same quantity and quality as those employed. As a guarantee of the importation of the new materials the owners will be obliged to deposit in the Central Bank to the order of the Ministry of Marine an amount equal to the total value of the materials used. If the owners fail to comply with this undertaking the deposit will be forfeited to the Government.

It is also provided that the contracts for the repairs to foreign vessels must be submitted to the Ministry of Marine and that work may not be commenced until the corresponding permit has been issued.

The official justification for this measure is that many foreign ships have been repaired locally utilizing materials which under present conditions are exceedingly difficult if not impossible to replace owing to the fact that all countries have restricted their exportation.

The British Embassy here is desirous of acting jointly with us in the event our respective governments should decide to take action in this manner and I should therefore appreciate receiving the views of the Department.

ARMOUR

---

[41] Not printed.

800.857/662 : Telegram

The Secretary of State to the Ambassador in Argentina (Armour)

WASHINGTON, April 30, 1942—8 p. m.

605.   Your 728, April 22, 6 p. m.   The materials which this Government has allocated to Argentine shipyards are for the purpose of repairing ships of friendly nations—i.e. those of the United Nations and the American republics.   The allocation of steel plates to Mihanovich,[42] for example, was made on the basis of the size of the yard and the probable amount of business.

Many, if not all, of the countries referred to above are unable to replace materials which are utilized in the repair of their boats.   The United States has recognized this fact and has acted accordingly in the matter of supplying Argentina.

If this new measure taken by Argentina hampers or restricts in any way the repair of ships which are working directly or indirectly in the United Nation war effort, this Government will be forced to divert repair materials and ships to other ports where such restrictions do not exist.

The Department recently took extraordinary action to obtain an allocation, a priority and an export license on 800 tons of steel plates for Mihanovich.   The 800 tons have not yet been shipped and will not be released until appropriate assurances have been obtained from Argentina that the materials we supply will be made available to all ships of friendly nations without the obligation of replacement. Furthermore, it is not desirable to have Argentina force ships in need of repairs to proceed to other ports where repair facilities might be less adequate, solely for the purpose of maintaining in Argentina a hoard of materials.

You should obtain promptly these assurances in any form you deem appropriate, either jointly with the British Embassy or separately.

HULL

800.857/662 : Telegram

The Secretary of State to the Ambassador in Argentina (Armour)

WASHINGTON, May 5, 1942— 6 p. m.

631.   Contrary to the last sentence in the Department's 605, April 30, 8 p. m., you should not take joint action with the British Embassy in this matter but you should request the assurances for the Government of the United States.

HULL

---

[42] Cía. Argentina de Navegación Mihanovich, Ltda.

800.857/675

The American Embassy in Argentina to the Argentine Ministry for Foreign Affairs [43]

MEMORANDUM

The Embassy of the United States of America makes reference to Decree No. 116279 promulgated by the Argentine Government on March 26, 1942, concerning repairs to ships under foreign flags which are to be made in the shipyards within the territory of the Argentine Republic and respectfully invites the attention of the Ministry of Foreign Affairs and Worship to the following observations of the Department of State relative to the provisions of this measure:

The Government of the United States has allocated to the Argentine shipyards certain quantities of materials for the purpose of repairing ships of friendly nations, that is, those of the United Nations and of the American Republics. Many of such countries are unable to replace materials utilized in the repair of their ships as required by Decree No. 116279, and the Government of the United States recognizing this situation has acted accordingly in making allocations of steel plates and other repair materials for use in Argentina.

It is believed that the measures proposed in the decree above referred to would seriously delay the repair of ships which are working directly or indirectly in the United Nations' war effort, since the decree provides that estimates or contracts covering the work to be undertaken for the repair of ships in Argentine shipyards must be submitted to the Ministry of Marine and authorization granted before repairs to ships can be undertaken. Furthermore, ships under the registry of the United States Government are now operated by the War Shipping Administration, an agency of the United States Government, and it would not seem consistent for the Argentine Government to require a deposit by the United States Government as a guarantee for the replacement of materials utilized in the repair of its ships, since such materials in most cases would have been previously allocated to Argentine shipyards by the United States.

Therefore the Government of the United States ventures to express the hope that the Argentine Government will modify the terms of Decree No. 116279 with a view to permitting the materials that are supplied from the United States to be made available to all ships of friendly nations without the obligation of replacement and thus not render it necessary for ships in need of repairs to proceed to other ports where facilities might be less adequate than those in Argentine shipyards.

BUENOS AIRES, May 8, 1942.

---

[43] Copy transmitted to the Department by the Ambassador in Argentina in his despatch No. 5171, May 21; received May 28.

800.857/670 : Telegram

The Ambassador in Argentina (Armour) to the Secretary of State

BUENOS AIRES, May 16, 1942—4 p. m.
[Received 4 : 40 p. m.]

921. Department's telegram number 676, May 14, midnight.[44] Argentine Government's reaction may best be described as one of injured innocence. Admiral Stewart[45] called on me last evening and explained that measure was adopted at his suggestion in order to conserve stocks of steel plates to insure adequate supplies for repair of state merchant marine vessels and more especially to prevent what he described as illegal exports to certain countries, notably Spain, of considerable quantities of plates and materials ordered for repairs to foreign ships here in excess of materials actually required for them.

He insisted that there was no other or hidden reason for the measure and asserted most categorically that it was not the intention of his Government to delay in any way the servicing of foreign ships in Argentine ports. He added that the decree in question had been suspended until May 25 in order to allow for general discussion of the matter with a view to reaching a solution satisfactory to the British and ourselves. After conferring with British the Department will be advised of any conclusions reached.

ARMOUR

800.857/670 : Telegram

The Secretary of State to the Ambassador in Argentina (Armour)

WASHINGTON, May 19, 1942—midnight.

703. Your 921, May 16, 4 p. m. Admiral Stewart's remarks do not give the Department the assurances requested in its telegram no. 605, April 30 as you no doubt realize. Please report the manner in which this Government's objections to this decree and its probable operation were made known to the Argentine Government.

The Admiral's statement concerning the illegal exports to Spain and other countries of considerable quantities of plates and materials would indicate that the supplies for legitimate uses are more than adequate. This matter should be thoroughly investigated by the Embassy with a view to enabling the immediate downward revision of the Argentine allocation of plates and other materials.

HULL

---

[44] Not printed.
[45] Adm. Francisco Stewart, Director of the Argentine State Merchant Marine.

800.857/671 Suppl. : Telegram

The Secretary of State to the Ambassador in Argentina (Armour)

WASHINGTON, June 11, 1942—4 p. m.

848. Your 955, May 21, 9 p. m.[46] Please telegraph whether the decree has been suitably modified or extended for a further period.

HULL

800.857/678 : Telegram

The Ambassador in Argentina (Armour) to the Secretary of State

BUENOS AIRES, June 15, 1942—5 p. m.
[Received 6 : 20 p. m.]

1132. [For] Duggan. Department's 848, June 11, 4 p. m. and 865, June 13, 3 p. m.[47] The Foreign Office has not replied to the Embassy's memorandum of May 8, 1942, which contained the substance of Department's 605 of April 30, 8 p. m. The Ministry of Marine will however issue an order suspending the decree until June 30, 1942, but each request for repairing ships must be filed with the prefect of Maritime Police.

British Embassy advises that Admiral Stewart, Director of the Argentine State Merchant Marine, when consulted a few days ago on the status of the decree, stated that there was nothing to worry about since the decree was not operative.

The British Embassy is of the opinion that there need be no further apprehension about its becoming operative. Embassy understands Department's position in withholding shipments of steel designed for ship repairs but suggests that we be authorized to inform the Argentine Government that shipments are being permitted to come forward on the understanding that the decree number 116,279 will be suppressed or modified in a manner also inimical to our war efforts.

ARMOUR

800.857/678 : Telegram

The Secretary of State to the Ambassador in Argentina (Armour)

WASHINGTON, July 2, 1942—1 p. m.

987. Your 1132, June 15, 5 p. m. In accordance with your recommendation, export licenses have today been issued authorizing exporta-

---

[46] Not printed.
[47] Latter not printed.

tion of 800 steel plates, 2 electric arc welders and other repair materials consigned to Cía. Argentina de Navegación Mihanovich, Ltda. The Steel plates were charged against the Maritime Commission's Repairs and Conversion allocation, in accordance with Administrative Order No. 7, providing for the maintenance of this company's normal operations. You are authorized to inform the Argentine Government in the manner suggested by you. It is important, however, that you follow the ship repair situation closely, in order that the Department will be in a position to recommend future shipments if the need should arise. No further export licenses will be granted for such critical material outside the Board of Economic Warfare's allocation system until the Department hears further from you that the decree has been suppressed or modified in a satisfactory manner.

HULL

800.8830/1754 : Airgram

The Chargé in Argentina (Reed) to the Secretary of State

BUENOS AIRES, August 10, 1942—8 p. m.
[Received August 18—12 : 30 p. m.]

A–68. Local newsprint importers have reported to the Embassy that there is discrimination in the United States against shipments of newsprint to Argentina. One local importer received a letter from the law firm Wilkie, Owen, Otis, Farr & Gallagher, 15 Broad Street, New York, which stated in part :

"The problem of newsprint cargo has now been placed under the control of a central commission and the policy has been decided upon with regard to South American shipments. The Board of Economic Warfare and the War Shipping Administration are allotting so much tonnage for each country, according to Mr. (the name was cut out by the censor). The commission, in the case of unfriendly countries, is using its discretion as to newsprint cargo which shall be allotted."

The Embassy believes that the intimation that Argentina will be discriminated against in the shipments of newsprint is fallacious and that Mr. Wilkie has been misinformed, since the press, which is 95% pro-Ally, is one of the greatest supporters of the Allied cause in Argentina.

The fact that such information is presumably given out to persons outside the Government, is in itself dangerous. The reports invariably reach interested parties here who use the information against the United States. The Embassy would appreciate receiving confirmation that there will be no discrimination in shipments of newsprint to the friendly press in Argentina in order to combat the afore-mentioned rumor.

REED

811.20 (D) Regulations/8407 : Airgram

The Chargé in Argentina (Reed) to the Secretary of State

BUENOS AIRES, August 12, 1942—12 : 15 p. m.
[Received August 20—12 : 45 p. m.]

A–73. Department's telegrams 1170 of August 7, 3 p. m., 1186 of August 8, 8 p. m., 1187 of August 8, 9 p. m.[48] It is the Embassy's understanding of the Pool Agreement[49] that South American participants must contribute all tankers owned or chartered and all petroleum supplies, including stock on hand, local production, and future imports from sources outside of the Pool. The total quantity for which the Pool is able to supply tanker space is then prorated so that each participant will have available in the future the same total percentage quantity of petroleum. The tanker delivered quantity is the prorated percentage less all supplies from local resources.

If the Embassy's understanding of the basic Pool Agreement is correct, which the Department is requested to confirm, should Argentina now join the Pool they would be obliged to give up:

1. All of their Argentine flag tanker tonnage.
2. All tanker tonnage which may in the future accrue to Argentina by purchase or charter.
3. Nearly all benefit from the crude oil which soon will be brought into Argentina from Bolivia.
4. Approximately 40% of present Argentine crude oil production.
5. Nearly all of any increase in production, which might accrue if Argentina were able to purchase production material in the United States.

In return for this very considerable contribution :

1. Argentina would have the knowledge that she had adhered to hemispheric solidarity to the extent that she had handled her petroleum resources in a "fair and equitable" manner, in the eyes of the United States and the other American Republics.
2. The United States would not object to further acquisitions by Argentina of such tanker tonnage as might be impossible for the United States to acquire directly; but in accordance with the Pool principle, all petroleum which might be imported into Argentina in such tankers would be shared by all of the Pool members, by the

---

[48] None printed.
[49] See section entitled "Proposal by the United States for the control of the distribution of petroleum products among the American Republics," *Foreign Relations*, 1941, vol. VI.

additional export from Argentine production of the prorata quantity of petroleum.

3. Argentina might be granted export licenses for sufficient drilling material to maintain her present rate of production, or even to increase it substantially, but in exchange, just as in the case of the acquirement of additional tanker tonnage, the extra production would have to be exported prorata for the benefit of the Pool members.

In view of Argentina's attitude and actions to date, the Embassy has no reason to believe that the Argentine authorities would be willing to join the Pool on the above basis, and therefore believes that it is preferable not to make the direct proposal. In the discussion which the Embassy will hold with the Argentine authorities, the Embassy will make it clear that no more critical materials can be spared nor any export licenses issued, except that if the Argentine Government should decide to collaborate in the petroleum Pool operation, the United States Government would then be prepared to make further sacrifices, which would be justified by the way in which Argentina would lighten the petroleum transportation load now being carried by the United States Government.

Should it be that the Department would welcome the adherence of Argentina to the Tanker Pool on some basis less severe than the Embassy's understanding of the present basis as outlined above, the Department's instructions would be appreciated. For instance, if the Department approves, in the original discussion with the Foreign Office it might be suggested that an acceptable basis for Argentine participation in the Pool would be:

1. That Argentina would assign to the Pool all of her tanker tonnage not required for the coastwise movement of petroleum.
2. Products manufactured from all crude oil production in excess of the monthly average production during the period of July 1, 1941, to June 30, 1942, be exported to the Pool members.

Production material in considerable quantity would then justifiably be released to the Y.P.F.,[50] and to mixed companies to be formed in accordance with the terms of the present petroleum law. It would be agreed that the mixed company charters would be available to both the foreign-owned and the native-owned oil companies now operating in Argentina, so that the best of the governmental reserves would be drilled as soon as possible. (By law, the mixed companies are eligible to drill in the reserved areas.) A participation in this manner by all of the oil operators in Argentina would be sure to result in a greatly increased production within twelve months, and might even make Argentina entirely independent of outside petroleum resources, within a very few years.

---

[50] Yacimientos Petrolíferos Fiscales.

There has been considerable objection on the part of Y.P.F. to the formation of mixed companies, where the other partner is one of the foreign oil companies. It may be pointed out that the existing laws of Argentina provide absolute protection to the national interests, and it is very difficult to see how anything but benefit could accrue to the nation through an all-out effort of this kind. It would be necessary for Argentina to accept the fact that Y.P.F. would be giving up any hope of having a petroleum monopoly, but it is entirely possible that Y.P.F. could retain permanently its present percentage of the market, and form a cartel arrangement with the other oil companies in the country under which they would all participate in supplying the remaining consumption.

A telegraphic reply will be appreciated.

REED

811.20 (D) Regulations/8407 : Telegram

The Secretary of State to the Chargé in Argentina (Reed)

WASHINGTON, August 22, 1942—6 p. m.

1265. Embassy's A–73 of August 12. Your understanding of what full participation in the Pool would mean in Argentina's case is in the main correct. To take the position however that Argentina's own production must be shared with other republics is definitely an extension of the principles upon which the Pool was originally based. All that can fairly be represented without such extension of principle is that no pool tankers will be used to supply any country which is capable of supplying itself from its own production at the same level as the others. From the beginning however, it has been made clear that all pool members must use their oil importing tankers in the common interest on a basis of equality. This would not apply to Argentina's tankers used in her own coastwise crude movement.

The Department believes that the basis suggested by Embassy which contemplates pooling of tankers available for importing and considering all crude production in excess of the last 12 month average as exportable with an understanding as to material to be supplied from here for use by mixed companies in further development of exportable production, might lead to a satisfactory solution. In fact our recent informal discussions here with Catinari [51] of YPF and members of the Argentine Embassy have been along this line. In these discussions Catinari stated that, in his personal opinion, Argentina would not view with favor the exportation of locally produced oil because their proven reserves are insufficient to guarantee continued supply for

---

[51] Juan Norberto Catinari, temporarily in the United States, attached to the Argentine Embassy.

Argentina. He appeared satisfied with the suggestion that this government give assurance that any oil thus exported would be replaced in kind, that is by sale of oil to Argentina, following the war emergency. It is suggested that you include the same provision in your discussions.

It is important that you do not commit this government to supplying any material nor to any other final agreement until so instructed. You should however press your discussions with the utmost vigor along the lines you have indicated and keep Department informed currently by telegram as to developments. If Department is thus informed its discussions and other actions can be shaped and timed to give you the best possible support. Particularly the Department wishes to be kept closely informed as to the reactions of government officials and of YPF to the mixed company idea. It is the Department's opinion that the mixed company plan has fundamental merits which may make it most effective in averting serious difficulties which have been experienced elsewhere.

HULL

800.8830/1754 : Telegram

The Secretary of State to the Chargé in Argentina (Reed)

WASHINGTON, August 24, 1942—10 p. m.

1272. Your airgram A–68, August 10, 8 p. m. There is no discrimination in shipments of newsprint to Argentina. To confirm this, refer to the Department's telegram No. 1234, dated August 17 [*18*], 1942,[53] which stated the Department had made arrangements for the shipment of 1,535 tons of newsprint from the west coast of the United States to Argentina for the newspapers *La Nación* and *La Prensa*. The vessel on which this newsprint was carried was not scheduled to stop at Buenos Aires but was originally scheduled to stop only at Montevideo and Rio. Both Uruguay and Brazil are badly in need of newsprint. The department was successful in having this vessel carry 1535 tons to Buenos Aires.

The Department in conjunction with the Board of Economic Warfare is attempting to effect a system whereby sufficient newsprint will be shipped to each of the consumers in the other American Republics including Argentina in an orderly fashion each month. This was outlined in a circular telegram dated July 11.[53]

It is urgently requested that the information asked for in the circular telegram of July 11 be furnished the Department immediately.

HULL

---

[53] Not printed.

800.8830/1785b : Telegram

The Acting Secretary of State to the Chargé in Argentina (Reed)

WASHINGTON, August 29, 1942—8 p. m.

1298. Due to the critical shipping situation and in view of the fact that the average monthly exports of newsprint to Argentina for the first 6 months of 1942 amounted to 4500 tons, the Department requests urgently the Embassy's comments as to whether 5000 tons per month would not be sufficient in view of the cut in size of newspapers.

WELLES

800.8830/1802a

Memorandum by the Assistant Executive Secretary of the Board of Economic Operations (Corbett)[54]

[WASHINGTON,] September 2, 1942.

The following is the course of discussions between representatives of the Argentine Merchant Marine and the War Shipping Administration. A proposal was made by the Argentine Merchant Marine to the War Shipping Administration for the employment of the former's vessels:

1. Four Argentine ships to be used to Peru and Chile.
2. Four ships, including three ex-German ships, to be used to the west coast of the United States. The Argentines are insistent upon using the three ex-German ships in the west coast, as they state that the Germans will sink them if they use them in the east coast trade.
3. Three refrigerated vessels to be used to Cristobal carrying dairy products and meat.
4. Several ships to be used to Venezuela, Colombia and Mexico on the northbound voyage, carrying cargo from the United States on the southbound voyage.
5. The remainder of the ships to be used directly to New Orleans or Gulf ports.

The War Shipping Administration counter-proposal was as follows:

a. From WSA's point of view, there is no need to establish any United States Pacific coast service from the Argentine. Consequently, it was suggested that the German vessels referred to in point 2 above be used in place of the ships mentioned in point 1, thereby releasing these ships for east coast service.
b. The Reefer ships to be used to Trinidad, Puerto Rico or Cuba with frozen meat.
c. No ships to be sent to Venezuela, Colombia, or Mexico unless our requirements from the River Plate area have been met.

---

[54] Copy transmitted by the Department to the Chargé in Argentina in instruction No. 3137, September 14, 1942.

d. All ships to go to New Orleans.

e. Navy has restricted all neutral shipping in the Gulf to New Orleans. Because of poor bunker facilities, the Argentines desired the WSA to make available approximately 15,000 or 20,000 tons of Norfolk coal in New Orleans. This WSA said it might be possible to do if the Argentines agreed to all other points.

f. The Argentines were informed that we needed approximately 40,000 tons from the River Plate area.

The Argentine reply to these proposals was as follows:

1. In lieu of supplying the Argentines with coal at New Orleans, as mentioned in point (*e*), the War Shipping Administration would, on ships controlled by it, send 7,000 tons of coal a month to Argentina for the Navy and one other consumer whose name I do not have.
2. The Argentine vessels would be loaded southbound in accordance with the Central Bank's program of August 10.
3. The Argentines still desire to use one ship to the west coast of the United States.
4. The Reefer ships would have to be used to Puerto Rico or Cuba, as the Argentines will not send them to Trinidad.

Jack C. Corbett

811.20 (D) Regulations/8407 : Telegram

The Secretary of State to the Chargé in Argentina (Reed)

Washington, September 6, 1942—11 a. m.

1325. Since Department's cable no. 1265 of August 22, officers of the Department have had informal conversations with García Arias [55] and extensive discussions with Catinari, who Department understands has held responsible position in YPF for several years prior to joining Embassy here. Catinari has also spent several days in New York with Petroleum Supply Committee for Latin America acquainting himself with its methods of operation and the statistical oil supply situation in the various American republics concerned. The Petroleum Supply Committee has been very frank and cooperative in giving him an accurate picture of the situation and of aims, accomplishments and problems of the joint supply program. Upon his return from New York Catinari appeared wholly in favor of bringing YPF into this joint program on the basis of using Argentina's importing tankers to assist in supplying other republics and perhaps exporting any oil produced in excess of present rate in return for materials from this country. He seemed strongly disposed to carry on these negotiations at this end and to refer them to Buenos Aires only for final approval.

---

[55] Argentine Chargé.

The Department held a further meeting on September 3 with García Arias and Catinari at which the Minister asked certain questions which would enable him to place the entire question before the Argentine Government. The questions may be summarized as follows:

(1) What political implications would be attached to Argentina's action in becoming a member of the Pool? To this Department answered informally none whatever, beyond the perfectly obvious indication of willingness to assist in maintaining the essential economies of the other American republics.

(2) What is the relation of the national petroleum committees and the Petroleum Supply Committee for Latin America in New York with the various governments? To this the Department replied that matters of broad policy were to be taken up between the governments at a high diplomatic level. Matters of execution would be handled through the Petroleum Supply Committee for Latin America and the national petroleum committees. The national petroleum committees in each case are set up as the government in question desires— usually with a governmental member as chairman.

(3) Would this Government facilitate the acquisition by Argentina of the two Swedish tankers now under negotiation, if Argentina agreed to share their use with other republics? To this the Department answered that if Argentina were to participate fully in the petroleum supply arrangements, this Government would give appropriate assistance to Argentina in the safe passage of the two Swedish tankers.

(4) Assuming that Argentina's share in the so-called pool were to supply Uruguay's requirements, what quantities of oil would be involved and what would be its source? To this the Department answered informally that Mr. Catinari had been furnished information concerning Uruguay's needs.

(5) If Argentina collaborated in the joint supply program in accordance with the principles which have been established for its guidance modified as might be agreed to take Argentina's special circumstances into account, on what basis would this Government supply material for production and refining? To this the Department answered informally that this Government would be likely to make a comparable sacrifice by diverting material from extremely important uses here to Argentina, but that certain subsidiary questions arise in this connection concerning the allocation of this material among and its utilization by the several oil companies operating in Argentina.

Department is inclined to believe that these negotiations should remain in your hands and consequently will as far as possible confine itself to general statements at this end. Since the entire question is of high importance, however, you are requested to press the negotiations as urgently as is permissible. Moreover Department must be kept informed by telegram concerning discussions at your end to avoid confusion in dealings here over which Department does not have complete initiative.

HULL

800.85/770a

The Secretary of State to the Argentine Chargé (García Arias)

WASHINGTON, September 24, 1942.

SIR: Reference is made to conversations and arrangements between the Governments of the United States and of the Argentine Republic which have taken place over the last fifteen months with respect to the placing into operation in inter-American services of enemy vessels. During this period, and principally through the intermediary of the Inter-American Financial and Economic Advisory Committee and in accordance with its plan of August 28, 1941,[56] there have been placed into effective service practically all of the enemy vessels in Argentine ports.

Paralleling the discussions and action relating to the immobilized vessels directly the subject of the Advisory Committee's plan, my Government has taken up with your Government the question of the vessels *Buenos Aires*, *Comodoro Rivadavia* and *Madryn* owned by the Argentina Nueva Compañía General de Navegación, c/o A. M. Delfino y Compañía, Florida 439, Buenos Aires. This company and these vessels have been included both in my Government's Proclaimed List of Certain Blocked Nationals and the British Statutory List and the vessels have consequently been considered by my Government as enemy vessels.

The United States Embassy at Buenos Aires addressed notes to the Argentine Foreign Office relative to this matter on May 27 [*21*] and June 25, 1942.[57] These communications pointed out that it was the view of the United States that in putting these vessels into service all connection with the former ownership should be severed and any proceeds or funds arising therefrom should be effectively blocked for the duration of the war, in accordance with Resolution V of the Third Meeting of Ministers of Foreign Affairs at Rio de Janeiro.[58] Resolutions VII and VIII of the Inter-American Conference on Systems of Economic and Financial Control at Washington in July 1942 [59] reiterated the policy laid down in Resolution V.

On August 12, 1942 the Embassy at Buenos Aires informed the Department that an arrangement had been made to sell the *Buenos Aires* to the S.A.D.E.I.[60] with effective blocking of the proceeds in the Bank

---

[56] For correspondence concerning the resolution and plan of this Committee in 1941, see *Foreign Relations*, 1941, vol. VI.

[57] Neither printed.

[58] For correspondence concerning the meeting held January 15–28, 1942, see pp. 6 ff.; for text of Resolution V, see Department of State *Bulletin*, February 7, 1942, p. 124.

[59] For correspondence concerning the Conference, see pp. 58 ff.; for text of Resolutions VII and VIII, see Pan American Union, Congress and Conference Series No. 39: *Final Act of the Inter-American Conference on Systems of Economic and Financial Control* (Washington, 1942), pp. 19 and 21, respectively.

[60] Sud Americana de Exportación e Importación, S. R. L.

of the Argentine Nation, and recommended that the vessel be deleted from the Proclaimed List. On August 14, 1942 my Government took action ordering such deletion to be published in the next supplement of the List.

With respect to its notes relating to the *Comodoro Rivadavia* and the *Madryn*, which vessels present an entirely parallel case, the Embassy at Buenos Aires received no reply until on September 12, 1942 the press of Buenos Aires reported the purchase of these vessels by the Argentine Navy and State Merchant Marine respectively, the purchase price of 6,400,000 pesos being turned over in free funds to the former owners. The Embassy subsequently received an informal confirmation of these press reports, but to date has received no reply or statement from the Foreign Office.

The Government of the United States is constrained to point out the obvious implications of such payments of free funds to persons, whom it considers as of enemy status and as inimical to the security of the Hemisphere, and to state that it deems such actions to be inconsistent with the Inter-American Resolutions referred to above and with the spirit of the plan of the Inter-American Financial and Economic Advisory Committee, which it recognizes does not apply directly to the two vessels in question. It accordingly requests that the Argentine Government take appropriate steps effectively to control the funds in question.

Accept [etc.]   For the Secretary of State:
SUMNER WELLES

865.85/800 : Telegram

The Acting Secretary of State to the Ambassador in Argentina
(*Armour*)

WASHINGTON, October 17, 1942— 4 p. m.

1563. Your 1769, September 13; 1954, October 9; 1982, October 13.[61] Discussions have been held with the Argentine Ambassador[62] and Admiral Stewart on payments to be made in connection with the ships with the following results:

Admiral Stewart and the Ambassador phoned Fincati[63] and Prebisch[64] Wednesday or Thursday of this week and obtained their informal agreement:

(1) not to make any payments out of this account (Art. 10, Italian-Argentine ship contract) to the Italians until Admiral Stewart's return;

---

[61] None printed.
[62] Felipe A. Espil.
[63] Adm. Mario Fincati, Argentine Minister of Marine.
[64] Raúl Prebisch, general manager, Banco Central de la República Argentina.

(2) that a plan will be devised to control the funds of Delfino [(] plan tentatively suggested by Admiral Stewart is an allowance of about 2,000 pesos per month for living expenses and scrutiny of all other withdrawals from Delfino's accounts) ;

(3) that all payments on Inter-American plan ships (*Esmeralda* and *Lloyd Argentino*) are to be subject to informal approval of you and British Embassy; and

(4) no payments to Vlasov[65] in any form and possibly none to Iterman,[66] depending upon your views.

The Argentines have been trying to move the *Esmeralda* out of Pernambuco, but because the ship is still on the British Statutory List, have been unable to obtain either certificate or agency service from Wilson.[67] On the basis of Argentine notification to Inter-American Committee that ship was taken according to Inter-American plan and Stewart's statements in points (3 & 4) above, British Embassy here is recommending to London delisting of *Esmeralda* and approval of Wilson as agent for ship. This is being done with no prejudice to future action by British and ourselves directly or through Inter-American Committee if above commitments (items 3 & 4) are not honored.

While the above proposals are not all that might be desired, they provide a possible basis for our future handling of these matters, and we have so indicated to the Argentine Embassy. The Argentine Ambassador here is satisfied with the arrangements and you are requested to send your comments.

Shipping agreement, copy of which will be forwarded to you shortly, was initialled by War Shipping Administration and Admiral Stewart yesterday.[68] This agreement has no validity until financial matters relating to ships are satisfactorily settled.

All matters remain in abeyance until arrival next week in Argentina of Admiral Stewart.

WELLES

---

[65] Alexander Vlasov, Rumanian ship owner resident in Buenos Aires; owner of the ship *Esmeralda*.

[66] Isaac Gutman Iterman, Argentine capitalist holding a substantial interest in the Organización Comercial e Industrial Financiera Argentina.

[67] Presumably Capt. Robert A. Wilson, British Naval Attaché at Rio de Janeiro and Caracas.

[68] This agreement on shipping schedules and related matters was arranged by the War Shipping Administration and the Flota Mercante del Estado, an Argentine Government agency; agreement not printed.

835.85/87

Memorandum of Conversation, by the Second Secretary of Embassy in Argentina (Gantenbein) [69]

[BUENOS AIRES,] November 4, 1942.

Participants: Admiral Stewart
Mr. Hughes [70]
Mr. Gantenbein

Messrs. Hughes and Gantenbein called today by appointment upon Admiral Francisco Stewart for the purpose of discussing various of the pending ship matters. After preliminary remarks, Admiral Stewart was handed a memorandum, a copy of which is attached hereto,[71] setting forth the position of the United States with respect to the contemplated payment of 565,000 pesos in free funds to Mr. Isaac Gutman Iterman and to the Organización Comercial e Industrial Financiera Argentina, in which Mr. Iterman has a substantial interest, in connection with the purchase by the Merchant Marine of the three ex-German ships now called the *San Martín, Santa Fé* and *Belgrano*. This memorandum had been prepared after Admiral Stewart, during a courtesy visit at the Embassy several days ago, had stated that he was not familiar with the problem involved in these contemplated payments. After glancing at the memorandum, Admiral Stewart said that it was the impression which he gathered at Washington that the Inter-American Financial and Economic Advisory Committee was disposed to modify the exception provided for with respect to paragraph (*c*) of the Committee's interpretation of article 5 (*d*) of the ship plan. However, he recognized that there was no analogy between the present matter and the *Rio Colorado* case, which Dr. Liaudat of the Central Bank (who is a member of the Merchant Marine board) had previously claimed to be analogous.

Admiral Stewart was told that since Mr. Iterman had a banking business at Santa Fé and presumably loaned the money in question from funds available for investment purposes, it was not seen how he or his financial company could object to accepting in blocked form treasury or other obligations which would be bearing interest and thereby adding to the value of his assets. Admiral Stewart appeared very sympathetic to this consideration and said that it was possible that the Merchant Marine might even make provision for an additional one or two percent interest, which would also be blocked.

---

[69] Transmitted to the Department by the Ambassador in Argentina in his despatch No. 7243, November 6; received November 18.
[70] Thomas L. Hughes, Commercial Attaché.
[71] Not printed.

Reference was then made to the Delfino payment. Admiral Stewart stated that Dr. Torriani, head of the commercial and consular division of the Foreign Office, is having an investigation made concerning the possibilities of freezing the properties which Sr. Delfino purchased with the amount which had been recently paid to him in free funds (which properties now appear to include 1,500,000 pesos paid for acquiring a part interest in the Hotel Richmond in this city). He said that he would see Dr. Torriani this afternoon and attempt to expedite the completion of the investigation.

At this point Admiral Stewart gave an account of events preceding the payments in question. He stated that it was at first desired to buy these vessels for the purpose of maintaining a military force in Patagonia but that difficulties were encountered in finding available funds. Later, however, arrangements for acquiring the ships (primarily for other purposes) were made by the Ministry of Marine, which signed a contract with Sr. Delfino, apparently without adequately appreciating the factors involved in paying Sr. Delfino in free funds. He added that the matter had been complicated by the fact that Sir David Kelly, the British Ambassador, shortly before the actual payment was made, had gone to Admiral Fincati, the Minister of Marine, and had greatly antagonized Admiral Fincati by intimating that Great Britain might curtail its meat purchases from Argentina if the payment were made to Sr. Delfino, which Admiral Fincati felt was an offence against the national dignity. Admiral Fincati, he said, reported the matter immediately to President Castillo, with the result that there was felt to be no alternative to paying the amount in question. (It is understood that Admiral Stewart described the same incident while in Washington.) However, Admiral Stewart also mentioned that President Castillo felt that the Government had to make the payment inasmuch as it was obligated to do so under the terms of the contract to which the Government was a party and which had been made pursuant to a Government decree.

In reply to an inquiry as to the status of the shipping agreement which had been recently negotiated at Washington, Admiral Stewart commented that although the formal signature of the agreement was awaiting the satisfactory solution of the Delfino matter, it had been arranged in Washington that it would be placed in effect following its initialing and that it was, therefore, in effect now.

In regard to the case of the *Esmeralda*, Admiral Stewart said that this vessel was still in Pernambuco. There had been some delay, he said, in moving it to Buenos Aires due to the fact that the Merchant Marine feared that the twelve or thirteen Rumanian seamen on the ship, who were previously employed by Mr. Vlasov, might be instigated by Mr. Vlasov to cause difficulties with reference to insurance, and therefore it was the plan of the Merchant Marine to supply the ship with other seamen. Concerning the claims against the ship to be paid in free funds, Admiral Stewart said that it had been definitely decided that these would not be paid until after the ship arrived in Buenos Aires and until after the United States and British Governments had been consulted with respect to the individual claims. When asked, however, whether it would not be necessary to pay the port dues and perhaps the other taxes of the Brazilian Government, Admiral Stewart did not seem to be familiar with the details of the matter. Regarding the list of claims which had been promised to the Embassy by Dr. Liaudat several weeks ago, Admiral Stewart said that this list would be furnished shortly.

Concerning the purchase of bunkers from the Italian Government in connection with the purchase of the sixteen Italian ships, Admiral Stewart said that these funds would be definitely blocked.

When inquiry was made about the Delfino tugboats, which had previously belonged to the Hamburg American Line, Admiral Stewart stated that it was his understanding that there were twelve of these that had been taken over not from Sr. Delfino's company but through the intermediary of Sr. Delfino as agent of the owners. In any event, he said that the funds had been blocked.

J[AMES] W. G[ANTENBEIN]

800.8830/1968 : Telegram

The Secretary of State to the Ambassador in Argentina (Armour)

WASHINGTON, November 6, 1942—11 p. m.

1674. Embassy's 2188, November 5, 1942, 9 p.m.[73] Department's 1609, October 26, 1942 [73] stated that the Flota is discriminating against certain papers by refusing to carry newsprint and gave as an example the refusal of the Flota to carry 350 tons of newsprint on the *Rio Corrientes* which sailed November 8. Since then, the Flota has refused to carry an additional amount of newsprint for *La Nación*. It was also pointed out to the Embassy that on October 1, there were 7,453 tons of newsprint certified by the Board of Economic Warfare to the War Shipping Administration as eligible for shipment. This newsprint was consigned to papers selected in accordance with Embassy's recommendation 1684, September 2.[73] On October 28, Board of Economic Warfare approved over 8,000 tons of newsprint in accordance with Embassy's 1684. This large amount was approved to make up for possible unshipped or unmanufactured paper from previous months.

---

[73] Not printed.

Of the total amount, *El Mundo* and *Editorial Haynes* had 900 tons approved and *Crítica* had 1,245 tons approved. All newsprint applications in excess of 8,000 tons have been held up as there is no reason to approve newsprint that would exceed available shipping tonnage to any great extent. It is suggested that the Embassy immediately bring to the attention of the appropriate Argentine Government officials the condition existing with respect to the discrimination by the Flota. The Embassy should point out to the complaining papers that newsprint is being equitably made available for export in so far as United States Government agencies are concerned. The Department now awaits the result of the Embassy's investigation as to why the Argentine Government is permitting the Flota to discriminate against certain newspapers.

HULL

800.8830/1995 : Telegram

The Ambassador in Argentina (Armour) to the Secretary of State

BUENOS AIRES, November 9, 1942—10 p. m.
[Received 10:25 p. m.]

2223. Department's 1674, November 6, 11 p. m. *La Prensa* of November 8 quotes Flota Mercante as saying that it will suspend carrying newsprint from the United States, such instructions being attributed to President Castillo. Bares [74] of Flota Mercante today confirmed this but said suspension was temporary only and he anticipated satisfactory solution of matter within a few days. He also denied rumors in local press that October agreement between Flota Mercante and War Shipping prorating had been rejected by Argentine Government.

Argentine Government's plan for handling the newsprint matter may be along the lines of following information supplied by Bedoya of *Crítica* which is based on recent conversation between Castillo and *Crítica* representative.

(1) Proclaimed List will be respected in that newsprint carried by Flota Mercante will not be made available to *Pampero*, *Cabildo*, *Crisol*, *Mattino D'Italia* or *Deutsche La Plata Zeitung*.

(2) Argentine Government probably will buy newsprint and distribute it among newspapers on the basis of recommendations made by the existing Newsprint Advisory Committee, which will be extended to include *Razón*, *Crítica*, *Mundo* and interior papers.

(3) We will not be permitted to allocate newsprint among newspapers.

---

[74] José Bares, of Flota Mercante del Estado.

(4) Swedish newsprint will come in as at present presumably without official control over allocation.

At least part of the reason for the proposed action is the annoyance of the Government, in this case shared by other papers concerning the disproportionately large quantity of newsprint being obtained by *La Prensa*.

Further developments will be reported at earliest opportunity.

ARMOUR

811.20 (D) Regulations/8710 : Telegram

The Secretary of State to the Ambassador in Argentina (*Armour*)

WASHINGTON, November 10, 1942—9 p. m.

1699. Embassy's 1873 of September 28, 1977 of October 13, 2009 of October 15, 2136 of October 31, and 2205 of November 7.[75]

1. Department wishes to make clear that primary objective in present negotiations is to secure effective collaboration of Argentina in the joint effort among republics to insure maximum supply of oil to all republics with limited facilities now available. To this end Department has suggested to other republics particularly those neighboring Argentina that they join in effort to secure such collaboration. Vegh Garzon[76] presumably is acting in interests of his own country and because of familiarity with general situation obtained by recent long visit here Department believes he is in position to make representations in behalf of Uruguay which will be helpful to entire situation. For your information pool committee in New York has commended him highly to Department for cooperative attitude shown. For your further information Department is sending circular telegram[77] to neighboring republics informing them of present negotiations with Argentina both to secure their assistance and to correct certain misunderstandings which are being reported currently to Department.

2. Concerning Embassy's proposed reply to government committee outlined in Embassy's 1873 Department agrees but with understanding as to detail that the following points be considered of importance in the order shown:

(*a*) If Argentina will use or make available for use as described in (*c*) below, the tanker tonnage under its control, except that necessary in its own coastwise trade, this government will do all possible to make available to Argentina sufficient material to enable local pro-

---

[75] None printed.
[76] General Manager, Administración Nacional de Combustibles, Alcohol, y Portland.
[77] Circular telegram of November 11, 1942, not printed ; it indicated the types of fuels to which the principles of the Pool were applicable (800.6363/986a).

duction plus imports from Bolivia to be maintained at the average level of such supplies during the past 12 months.

(*b*) If under the foregoing arrangements the products from local production and refining are not in balance with Argentina's requirements for the various products, tankers will be allocated to bring in the product which is deficient and take away that in excess in such a manner as will maintain Argentina's over-all supply on a tonnage basis in the proportion of the tonnage produced in Argentina plus imports from Bolivia during the past 12 months to the total tonnage consumed by Argentina during the same period.

(*c*) In order to utilize efficiently the tankers made available by this arrangement Argentina will create a committee which in collaboration with national committees which have been created in the other republics for a similar purpose will schedule the Argentina controlled tankers in such a way as will result in their most efficient use in supplying the republics with oil and without upsetting the principle of equality of treatment upon which this supply program has been based.

(*d*) Material made available by this Government for the purpose of maintaining production as described in paragraph (*a*) above will be allocated one half to YPF and one half to American companies now operating in Argentina; and Argentina will facilitate the acquisition, under Argentina's laws, of drilling rights by the American companies which will enable those companies to use the material efficiently in developing new production.

(*e*) If this Government finds it possible to do so it will make available additional material on the basis described under paragraph (*d*) above for the purpose of increasing crude oil production in Argentina to substantially more than the average during the past 12 months with the understanding that during the period of the tanker shortage caused by the war at least two-thirds of the increased production be made available for export to the other republics in accordance with the same principles of most economical use of tankers and equality of treatment as now govern the supply from other sources to those republics.

With regard to Argentina's apparent reluctance to include discussion of mixed companies in present negotiations the Department wishes to make its views clear. This Government has no intention of negotiating particular contracts between any American interests and Argentina. Before releasing any material for Argentina however it will wish adequate assurance from the Government of Argentina that this material will be used to the best possible advantage in increasing oil production and that some arrangement will be reached through which the American companies can participate in those operations on an equal basis with YPF. The Department understands that under existing laws this can be achieved through the formation of mixed companies which are entitled to drilling rights in government reserved lands. This Government wishes assurance that American companies will not be impeded in their efforts to conclude reasonable agreements under those laws.

You understand of course that you are not to commit this Government in any specific way without approval of the Department. Because of the extremely tight material situation here it will be necessary for the Department to have a fairly close estimate of the material involved in the negotiation in order to get assurance of its availability from War Production Board before any commitment is made to the Government of Argentina. It is also important that the quantity of material be held to the absolute minimum.

Reports have reached the Department that some arrangement is under discussion in Argentina according to which two Argentine tankers would be chartered indirectly by certain American oil companies and used to supply Argentina in addition to the indigenous production. It seems hardly necessary to point out that any such arrangement would be completely out of order and that any efforts on the part of an American oil company representative to promote such a plan would be regarded most unfavorably by the Department.

HULL

835.24/822 : Telegram

The Secretary of State to the Ambassador in Argentina (Armour)

WASHINGTON, November 16, 1942—9 p. m.

1739. Your 2142, October 31, 2192, November 6, 2236, November 11, and Department's airgram A–328, November 6.[79] The schedule of exports in Department's memorandum [80] is based upon probable availability of materials. In this respect it differs from the Central Bank schedule. The figure for iron and steel in the Department's memorandum—5000 tons monthly—is maximum. Figure of 4000 tons of tinplate is also maximum. Inasmuch as the plans worked out with the Flota here were to move 40,000 tons of Argentine products to the United States each month, it was necessary for the Department to determine whether it would be possible to provide sufficient United States merchandise to load these boats for the return trip. The schedule contained in the memorandum indicates it is possible, although the distribution may not be according to the Central Bank's economic desires. The 6500 tons of newsprint is important and it is believed that it is within the Flota's capabilities to move this amount if the northbound movement ever attains the 40,000-ton level. Of course, drastic measures by the newspapers to reduce their consumption would in turn reduce the necessity of moving 6500 tons a month. The De-

---

[79] None printed.
[80] Memorandum of September 23, not printed.

partment believes such action on the part of the newspapers would be desirable to the extent that it does not interfere with our political desires.

It will be noted from the schedule that after iron, steel, tinplate, newsprint and coal allocations have been taken care of, this leaves 7500 tons of miscellaneous unallocated commodities, the distribution of which is left up to the Central Bank in accordance with its economic plans. Exceptions could arise where needs of Argentine industries contributing directly to the war effort are involved. Department fully understands the reluctance of the Central Bank and the Flota to provide for more than 1000 tons of newsprint per month. However, you should seek by every means possible to increase the 1000-ton figure of the Central Bank as much as possible, it being understood that the difference between the Central Bank's allotment and your revised minimum requirements can always be carried on Dodero's [81] or American ships going to Uruguay. Naturally, any shipments to Argentina on American vessels are effected at a sacrifice to the war effort, as it reduces our ability to supply friendly countries. It is obvious that, while our licensing procedure has been fully explained to you, our control over the movement of a certain portion of the shipping to move newsprint will insure equitable distribution among the friendly Argentine press.

Taking into consideration Argentina's present stocks of tinplate, it appears that 4000 tons per month is excessive and will be sharply reduced. Consequently, the Central Bank will have that extra tonnage to dispose of among what it considers vital unallocated commodities. Naturally, such a reduction will also increase the ability of the Flota to carry the newsprint.

HULL

835.85/89 : Telegram

The Ambassador in Argentina (Armour) to the Secretary of State

BUENOS AIRES, November 21, 1942—midnight.
[Received November 22—9 : 15 a. m.]

2345. Embassy's despatch No. 7243, November 6.[82] Stewart asked Bohan [83] and Gantenbein [84] and Simon of the British Embassy [85] to call this morning and showed them a contract which had been approved by the Argentine authorities covering the purchase of the three Lloyd Argentina ships. Iterman and his Company have now

[81] A. A. Dodero, official of the Cía. Argentina de Navegación Mihanovich, Ltda.
[82] Not printed.
[83] Merwin L. Bohan, Counselor of Embassy for Economic Affairs.
[84] James W. Gantenbein, Second Secretary of Embassy.
[85] Walter Simon, Financial Adviser and First Secretary of the British Embassy.

agreed to accept payment in blocked form and the contract provides that all payments will be blocked except approximately 540,000 pesos to be repaid to the Merchant Marine for repairs and other expenses recently incurred and 15,000 pesos to be paid to the Argentine Government for taxes.

As in the case of the Danish ships the blocked funds will be released upon the "cessation of hostilities or the concluding of an armistice which will permit the aforementioned vessels to navigate freely". Upon being requested to do so, Stewart agreed to endeavor to have this clause changed to provide as in the Inter-American ship plan and in the case of the Italian ships for blocking until the end of war. This modification would of course be advantageous in the event of reparations after the war. Stewart has promised to furnish the Embassy with a copy of the contract in time for forwarding in the airmail pouch Monday.

He said that he did not know the present status of the Delfino matter and indicated that this was now being handled exclusively in the Foreign Office. The Embassy will discuss the subject there the first part of next week.

Stewart said that the *Esmeralda* was on its way to Argentina and presumably the list of contemplated payments will be submitted to the Embassy within the next few days.

Regarding the payment to the Italian Government for coal and supplies, he reiterated that these funds were being blocked and indicated that the blockade would be in the form provided for in the contract covering the Italian ships.

ARMOUR

103.9164/326 : Telegram

The Ambassador in Argentina (Armour) to the Secretary of State

BUENOS AIRES, November 28, 1942—3 p. m.
[Received 6 p. m.]

2402. Information in Department's 1767, November 19, midnight [86] from War Shipping Administration to Gibson [87] was delivered upon arrival to Flota Mercante, as Gibson is still in Montevideo. Flota Mercante officials discussed matter with Embassy officers on November 26, and stated that while they would do everything possible to abide by agreement with War Shipping Administration, the loading instructions for December placed the Flota in an awkward position.

---

[86] Not printed ; this telegram gave instructions on the commodities to be loaded in certain specified ships (103.9164/288b).
[87] Ray A. Gibson, Agent of the War Shipping Administration.

First, it does not offer "full and down" cargo as mentioned in the agreement. Second, they feel a disproportionately high tonnage has been assigned to zinc concentrates. Since this latter cargo is supplied by one producer only, and since the large tonnage for quebracho is also supplied by a small group, there is relatively little tonnage left to distribute among the country's major exporting groups.

Therefore the Flota Mercante, including the representative of Ministry of Agriculture, has submitted a counterproposal covering 39,250 tons to be transported to New Orleans in December, and the first days of January. This is divided as follows: salted hides 11,500; zinc concentrates 4,200; wool 9,600; quebracho extract 7,000; canned meats 2,600; casein 1,000; linseed 1,000; tallow 1,000; miscellaneous 1,350. (Agriculture insisted on including linseed and tallow.)

The Embassy agrees that the Flota is placed in a difficult position by not carrying cargo which is more evenly distributed among export groups and which would more effectively benefit country's over-all economy. In view of current protests of present Flota administration from certain official and unofficial circles, and probability that any new Flota administration would be less disposed to cooperate with us, it is believed that we should do anything within reason to help them. Therefore information is requested at earliest opportunity as to whether December loading instructions might be revised more along the lines of Flota's counterproposal above.[88]

ARMOUR

MEASURES TAKEN BY THE UNITED STATES TO ELIMINATE AXIS-CONTROLLED AIRLINES IN ARGENTINA [89]

835.796/263a : Telegram

The Acting Secretary of State to the Ambassador in Argentina
(Armour)

WASHINGTON, March 7, 1942—3 p. m.

322. In view of Prebisch's [90] statement that the Argentine Government would block the proceeds of funds resulting from the purchase of French ships in Argentina, as reported in the inclosure to your despatch no. 4199, February 20,[91] the Department suggests that if you perceive no objection, you endeavor to persuade the authorities to

---

[88] In telegram No. 1884, December 3, midnight, the Ambassador was instructed to convey the desire of the War Shipping Administration to cooperate with Flota and to accept, if necessary, certain specified minimum quantities of various commodities for shipping (103.9164/326).

[89] Continued from *Foreign Relations*, 1941, vol. VI.

[90] Raúl Prebisch, General Manager of the Banco Central de la República Argentina.

[91] Despatch No. 4199 not printed, but for memorandum of February 20, by the Second Secretary of Embassy in Argentina, enclosed in the despatch, see p. 455.

block the proceeds should Argentina purchase planes and spare parts from Air France.

WELLES

835.796/243

The Ambassador in Argentina (Armour) to the Secretary of State

No. 4383   BUENOS AIRES, March 11, 1942.
[Received March 16.]

Subject: Further Information on the Corporación Sudamericana de Servicios Aéreos, S. A.

SIR: With reference to the Department's telegram no. 127 of January 29 and the Embassy's telegram no. 188 of January 30,[92] I have the honor to submit further information regarding the question of including the above mentioned airline on the U. S. Proclaimed List.[93]

An official decree dated December 22, 1941, increased this company's subsidy, but at the same time specified a period of 60 days in which to improve its financial situation and to increase its capital so that the majority would be in Argentine hands. Mr. Wm. Barclay Harding of the Defense Supplies Corporation [94] arrived in Buenos Aires shortly after the expiration of the 60-day period, and he discussed this matter with Dr. Bosch, Director General of Civil Aeronautics. Dr. Bosch indicated that the company had not yet completed its reorganization under the terms of the decree. Before returning to Rio de Janeiro, Mr. Harding informed Dr. Bosch that the Embassy would follow up the matter in a short time.

There is attached hereto a copy of memorandum dated March 7,[95] outlining the conversation which Asst. Commercial Attaché Walstrom had with Dr. Castells (Undersecretary of Interior) and with Dr. Bosch. It will be noted that the latter says that a 60-day extension has been recommended. Both of these Argentine officials have expressed the hope, informally, that the inclusion of the Corporación on our Proclaimed List be deferred. While such a reaction might have been expected, it is nevertheless interesting to obtain the personal views of the Argentine officials concerned.

There is also attached hereto a copy of Mr. Walstrom's memorandum dated March 10,[95] reporting an interview with Sr. Antonio

---

[92] Neither printed.
[93] For correspondence on the Proclaimed List, see pp. 280 ff.
[94] The Defense Supplies Corporation operated as a buying agency of the Federal Loan Agency until February 24, 1942, when it was transferred to the Department of Commerce.
[95] Not printed.

Biedma, who recently resigned as the local manager for the Corporación. Sr. Biedma has very strong doubts that the Argentine Government will be able to effect a reorganization of the Corporación in a manner which would actually eliminate the Italian participation, or even reduce it to a minority interest.

There are several arguments both for and against placing the Corporación on the Proclaimed List. One of the arguments against such action is the fact that the U.S. apparently is in no position to arrange for a substitute service, as has been done in other cases where pro-Axis airlines were eliminated. In this connection the following paragraph is quoted from a letter dated February 25 from Ambassador Frost at Asunción, regarding the rumored purchase of airplane engines by the Corporación in Paraguay:

"The question of the Axis affiliations of the Corporación has been a vexatious one, and any light which you may be able to throw upon it will be appreciated. The Corporación's representative here, Manuel Ferreira, S.A., is a very large purely Paraguayan firm which we are disposed to consider friendly and above suspicion. The Corporación's service is greatly needed and greatly appreciated in Asunción. If it disappears because of lack of new engines, or because of inclusion in the Proclaimed List, I believe that it may be well for the general public to have no idea that the result could have been brought about through our interest."

As will be noted in the attached memorandum, the son and the law partner of Acting President Castillo are both connected with the Corporación. Should the company be placed on the Proclaimed List, with the consequent stoppage of gasoline sales by Intava,[98] it is possible that the Acting President would instruct the Argentine company Y.P.F.[99] to supply the Corporación with gasoline henceforth. It will be recalled that several months ago Y.P.F. agreed to supply no more gasoline to airlines on the Proclaimed List, but the inclusion of a nominally Argentine airline on this List might well cause a change in Y.P.F.'s sales policy. Up to this time the Argentine Government has shown little or no formal opposition to the application of Presidential Proclamation 2497 [1] to firms in this country, but there is always the possibility that our black-listing of an Argentine public service might antagonize the Argentine Government in such a manner as to prejudice the smooth operation of the Proclaimed List.

On the other hand, there seems to be no doubt that the Corporación is controlled by Italian interests, and that should it begin to show a

---

[98] International Aviation Associates.
[99] Yacimientos Petrolíferos Fiscales.
[1] Proclamation Authorizing a Proclaimed List of Certain Blocked Nationals and Controlling Certain Exports, July 17, 1941; for text, see Department of State *Bulletin*, July 19, 1941, p. 42, or 55 Stat. (pt. 2) 1657.

profit, these funds would go to Fiat Argentina, which is also on the Proclaimed List. According to a report of October 6, 1941, prepared by the former Director General of Civil Aeronautics (and forwarded with Embassy's confidential despatch no. 3634 of December 3, 1941),[2] the liabilities of the Corporación include 582,000 pesos owing to Ala Littoria and 380,000 pesos to Fiat.

As mentioned previously, the company's present operations constitute little if any threat to hemisphere defense. However, should Brazil decide to sell the Lati[3] planes to the Corporación, or to the Argentine Government, it would permit the establishment of a new service to Rio (competing with Pan American Airways), together with the slight possibility of occasional trips to Italy to obtain replacement parts.

Although, as stated above, there is considerable doubt whether the Corporación can be converted into a real Argentine enterprise, the Government is continuing its demands for further changes. For this reason it may be desirable to withhold action for the immediate future.

The Embassy is also considering the possibility of approaching the Corporación with a proposal whereby its profits would be blocked for the duration of the war, in return for which it would not be placed on the Proclaimed List. However, such a plan should be contingent on a restriction of the company's operations to its present routes.

Respectfully yours,   NORMAN ARMOUR

835.796/265

The Ambassador in Argentina (Armour) to the Secretary of State

No. 4448   BUENOS AIRES, March 17, 1942.
                                  [Received March 24, 1942.]

SIR: With reference to the Department's telegram no. 322 of March 7, 3 p. m., and referring also to the Embassy's despatch no. 4422 of March 13[4] in regard to the possible purchase by Argentina of airplanes and spare parts owned by the Air France, I have the honor to report that this subject was discussed with the Central Bank some days ago and again today. Dr. Edgardo Grumbach, head of the foreign-exchange department of the Central Bank, stated today that his institution had no knowledge whatever of the negotiations in question but had addressed a communication to the Ministry of Finance inquiring

---

[2] Neither printed.
[3] Líneas Aéreas Transcontinentales Italianas.
[4] Latter not printed.

in the matter and suggesting that the proceeds of any such transaction be blocked as in the case of the recent purchase of the Italian ships.

A report is circulating here, although it has not been confirmed, that the son of Acting President Castillo is involved in these transactions, perhaps through the Corporación Sud Americana de Servicios Aéreos S. A., in which he, as well as a former law partner of the Acting President, has an interest (as reported in the Embassy's despatch no. 4383 of March 11, 1942).

Respectfully yours,   For the Ambassador:
                                                                EDWARD L. REED
                                                                Counselor of Embassy

---

835.796/245 : Telegram

The Ambassador in Argentina (Armour) to the Secretary of State

BUENOS AIRES, [March 20, 1942—4 p. m.]
[Received 4 : 32 p. m.]

519. The following telegram has been sent to the Embassy at Rio de Janeiro.

March 20, 4 p. m.   Rumors persist that Corporación Sud Americana de Servicios Aéreos anxious to get Lati planes for extending its airline to Rio de Janeiro and possibly to Europe as mentioned in Embassy's despatch No. 4383 March 11.

Do you think checkmating would release Lati planes to Argentina and do you know whether Corporación or affiliates have recently approached Brazil regarding an Argentine airline to Rio de Janeiro? If so we might forestall such development by putting Corporación on Proclaimed List. Your comments will be appreciated.

Repeated to Department.

ARMOUR

835.796/245 : Telegram

The Acting Secretary of State to the Ambassador in Argentina (Armour)

WASHINGTON, March 26, 1942—10 p. m.

428. Your 519.   For your information, this Government has offered to buy Lati airplanes, all of which have been expropriated by the Brazilian Government. They are now being evaluated. The Department will not recommend inclusion of Corporación on Proclaimed List until you believe this advisable.

WELLES

835.796/249

The Ambassador in Argentina (Armour) to the Secretary of State

No. 4600   BUENOS AIRES, March 27, 1942.
                                              [Received April 6.]

SIR: With reference to the Department's strictly confidential telegram no. 428 of March 26, 10 p. m., I have the honor to report two
recent conversations with the Brazilian Ambassador, Dr. Rodrigues
Alves, regarding Argentine efforts to obtain the Lati planes now in
Brazil, and to outline further considerations with respect to the Corporación Sudamericana de Servicios Aéreos.

On March 23 the Brazilian Ambassador told me of a recent talk he
had had with Dr. Castells, Undersecretary of Interior, who remarked
that Dr. Castillo's elder son, Ramón, had considerable influence with
his father; in fact, the Acting President found it difficult to refuse his
son anything. Dr. Castells then referred to the desire of Ramón
Castillo Jr. to acquire the Lati planes now in Brazil, and said that
the planes were needed by Argentina for use on the airline from
Buenos Aires to Esquel (now being operated by the army air service),
and to maintain communications with isolated army posts along the
Chilean frontier.

After his talk with Dr. Castells, the Brazilian Ambassador was approached by Ramón Castillo Jr. for the purpose of enlisting the Ambassador's cooperation in arranging for the purchase of these Lati
planes. Dr. Rodrigues Alves replied that he thought all of these
planes, with perhaps one exception, were of flimsy wooden construction and hardly suitable for the Argentine army. However, Castillo
Jr. still seemed anxious to acquire them, and said that he was also
interested in getting five or six transport planes from the United
States.

The Brazilian Ambassador said young Castillo had told him that
"a member of the British Embassy" (he could not remember the name
Castillo had given him, and was unable to recognize it afterwards on
consulting the diplomatic list) had told him that if Argentina would
grant nonbelligerent treatment to Great Britain, the British would
then use their influence to get these American planes for Argentina.
Dr. Rodrigues Alves was very insistent that he had clearly understood
young Castillo on this point. However, I have since had the opportunity to discuss this with the British Embassy, which states that the
report is "ridiculous".

On March 24 I had another talk with the Brazilian Ambassador, and
asked him specifically if he thought Argentina intended to use the
Lati planes, if they secured them, for a trans-Atlantic service. He
replied in the negative, saying that young Castillo had assured him the

planes were intended for army use and on the Esquel line. He also said that the local Fiat company had endeavored to obtain the Lati planes by means of an ante-dated purchase agreement, which Brazil refused to recognize.

The Brazilian Ambassador at first seemed favorably disposed to recommending the sale of the Lati planes to Argentina; that they did not amount to much anyway and the Argentine Government had after all permitted the return of the Condor [5] planes to Brazil (this point had also been stressed by young Castillo). Furthermore, some reciprocal gesture by Brazil, negotiated by the son of Dr. Castillo, would be highly appreciated by the Acting President.

With regard to the American planes desired by young Castillo, Dr. Rodrigues Alves admitted that it would be inconsistent under our Government's present policy to furnish such equipment to Argentina, but suggested an ingenious solution whereby we might furnish such planes to Brazil and Brazil in turn could release the Lati planes to Argentina.

I said that I thought our Government would be against any such arrangement permitting the release of the Lati planes to Argentina, adding that I felt sure the Ambassador would agree that if our Government scrupulously adhered, as it was doing, to the plan to furnish all available supplies to Brazil and other republics which had broken relations with or declared war on the Axis powers, it would seem inconsistent for Brazil on its part to furnish planes to Argentina, even though these were old Lati planes which happened to be within their country.

Dr. Rodrigues Alves expressed hearty concurrence with this point of view and said he would present it in this light to Dr. Aranha.

The above information furnished by the Brazilian Ambassador raises several points for speculation. Bearing in mind that young Castillo is affiliated with the Corporación Sudamericana de Servicios Aéreos, some of the parts and motors from these Lati planes unquestionably would have been used to replace worn out equipment on the company's present fleet of three Italian "Macchi" planes. Present operations are from Buenos Aires to Montevideo and to Asunción, but there is a possibility of the line being extended to Rio de Janeiro by the Corporación itself or by a new Argentine company.

In such event, this extension might be a logical link for the rumored airline between Buenos Aires and Europe. According to the local press, one of the matters to be discussed during the forthcoming visit of the Spanish trade mission is the possibility of an airline connecting

---

[5] For correspondence on the removal of Axis influence in the operations of Sindicato Condor, Ltda., see pp. 441–453 *passim* and pp. 766 ff.

Spain and Argentina. Col. Francisco Iglesias, the Spanish aviator who made an extensive flight in 1929, arrived in Buenos Aires on March 24, on his way back to Spain from Lima, where he represented his country at the Fourth Centenary of the Discovery of the Amazon Region. *Pampero* of March 24 comments as follows: "Although his visit does not have an official character, it would not be surprising if he took advantage of the opportunity to consider the possibility of establishing the projected Madrid–Buenos Aires airline."

The interest of Castillo Jr. in acquiring American transport planes is also significant. There is a rumor to the effect that he would like to merge the Corporación with Aerovias Argentinas, the latter company being recently organized to obtain concessions and operate new air routes in Argentina. As reported in the Embassy's confidential despatch no. 3542 of November 21, 1941,[6] this company has a strong board of directors, and while it had been understood that most of them were partisans of ex-President Justo, it is just possible that its directors would be willing to cooperate with the Castillo faction, especially if they could make better progress. In this event, the American planes would presumably be intended for domestic and possibly international routes of the rumored Corporación Aerovias consolidation. It is also reported that the Corporación intends to change its name in the near future.

With specific reference to the Corporación, there is transmitted herewith a translation of a report [6] prepared by Sr. Antonio Biedma, the former manager of this company, mentioned in the Embassy's confidential despatch no. 4383 of March 11. Sr. Biedma is highly regarded in local aviation circles, and he is believed to be a trustworthy source of information. His report offers further evidence that the company is directly controlled by Fiat and Ala Littoria, and that the Acting President's son, as well as his law partner, are closely affiliated with the company.

As mentioned in the Embassy's aforementioned despatch no. 4383, there have been several factors which have restrained the Embassy from recommending the Corporación for the Proclaimed List. To these may be added the possibility of a lawsuit against Intava in the event it is no longer able to supply gasoline, and the disruption of the pooling arrangement between the Corporación and the Uruguayan company Causa [7] on the Buenos Aires–Montevideo daily service.

The refusal of Brazil to release the Lati planes materially reduces the threat of expansion by the Corporación. The only other

---

[6] Not printed.
[7] Compañía Aeronáutica Uruguaya, S.A.

possibilities apparent at this time for establishing new airlines from Argentina to Brazil and Europe are: 1) utilization of the Air France planes for which Argentina has been negotiating, which would first require considerable overhauling of the planes and the probable employment of former Air France pilots, and 2) the establishment of the proposed Spanish-Argentine line, with planes furnished by Spain, which presumably could be discouraged by withholding fuel.

Briefly, the inclusion of the Corporación on the Proclaimed List would probably cause a cessation in operations, provided Intava stopped fuel supplies. However, due to the considerations already mentioned, such action on our part might well cause unpleasant repercussions.

The above factors have been outlined in some detail in order to give the Department full background information, and in the event that future developments require quick action with respect to placing the Corporación on the Proclaimed List.

Respectfully yours,   NORMAN ARMOUR

832.796/844 : Telegram

The Ambassador in Brazil (Caffery) to the Secretary of State

RIO DE JANEIRO, April 1, 1942—5 p. m.
[Received 6 : 20 p. m.]

1114. Reference despatch 4600, March 27, from Embassy Buenos Aires. Aranha[9] remarked to me today that the Argentine Acting President's son is interested in purchasing Lati planes; he said it might be a good thing to let him buy a few. I told him that I definitely did not agree. He then said that he would not permit the sale of any of the planes to the Argentine.

CAFFERY

835.796/249 : Telegram

The Secretary of State to the Ambassador in Argentina (Armour)

WASHINGTON, April 28, 1942—8 p. m.

594. Reference despatch 4600, March 27 and previous regarding Corporación Sudamericana de Servicios Aéreos. We have now postponed Proclaimed List consideration for twice the period originally suggested in January by Dr. Bosch and unless there is a more hopeful prospect of early complete elimination of Axis interest in this company than appears to us here, we believe it will be necessary to propose firm's inclusion on list shortly.

---

[9] Oswaldo Aranha, Brazilian Minister for Foreign Affairs.

Please report precise role occupied by Castillo Jr. in situation and whether you now agree that foregoing action is necessary. For your confidential information, our lack of action on this case has been commented on in high Brazilian official circles.

HULL

835.796/256

The Ambassador in Argentina (Armour) to the Secretary of State

No. 4930   BUENOS AIRES, May 2, 1942.
[Received May 11.]

Subject: Corporación Sudamericana de Servicios Aéreos.

SIR: With reference to the Department's strictly confidential telegram no. 594 of April 28, 8 p. m. regarding the possible inclusion of the above named company on the Proclaimed List, and to the Embassy's telegraphic reply no. 811 of May 2, 3 p. m.,[10] I have the honor to report the following additional information.

Mr. Grant Mason Jr. of the Defense Supplies Corporation arrived in Buenos Aires on the afternoon of April 29 on his way to the United States, and left for Rio de Janeiro on the morning of May 1. In company with Mr. Thomas D. Park [11] and Asst. Commercial Attaché Walstrom, he conferred on April 30 with Dr. Samuel Bosch, director of civil aeronautics, in order to discuss American technical assistance in developing an Argentine civil flying program (referred to in Embassy's confidential despatch no. 4870 of April 27 [12]). At this meeting Dr. Bosch stated his desire to have Mr. Park remain here to help establish an advanced flying school, and also agreed that one or two more American advisers should be obtained, if possible, for a period of one to two months. (See Embassy's confidential despatch no. 4933 of May 2.) [12]

The placing of the Corporación on the Proclaimed List would not be in harmony with our efforts to assist in the general development of Argentine flying. Consequently, the opportunity was taken to inform Dr. Bosch that the airline was still being seriously considered for listing. However, the possible embarrassment or difficulties arising therefrom apparently were not considered serious enough by Dr. Bosch for him to withdraw his request for continued assistance from Mr. Park and other advisers.

Apropos of the 60-day extension granted to the Corporación for improving its situation, Dr. Bosch was questioned as to what progress

---

[10] Latter not printed.
[11] Representative of the Defense Supplies Corporation.
[12] Not printed.

had been made recently.   He asked Messrs. Mason and Walstrom to return to his clinic that evening, when he would show them a report submitted on this subject by the Corporación to the Bureau of Civil Aeronautics.   It was agreed that it might be advisable to invite Dr. Ramón Castillo Jr., son of the Acting President who is affiliated with the company, to this meeting for a frank discussion, but it developed that he was out of the city.

The Corporación report shown to Messrs. Mason and Walstrom by Dr. Bosch outlined the claims of this company as to the manner in which it had complied with the Government's requirements, as set forth in the official decree of December 22, 1941, wherein the airline's concession was revised and the Government made stipulations regarding nationality of personnel and improvement of the company's financial situation.   A translation of this decree was given in the Embassy's report no. 789 of January 22 ("Argentine Aviation Notes").[14]

Article VII, paragraph 2, of this decree reads as follows:

"The president of the board of directors of the company, at least two-thirds of the members or administrators and the manager, should be native or naturalized Argentines with a minimum of ten years citizenship."

The Corporación's report, which apparently was submitted during the first part of April, gave the following revised list of the board of directors:

> Carlos Rueda, president (Argentine);
> Ricardo C. Cranwell, 1st vice-president (Argentine);
> Ramón Castillo Jr., 2nd vice-president (Argentine);
> Roberto Magugliani (Italian);
> Carlos Menendez Behety Jr. (Argentine);
> Wenceslao Escalante (Argentine);
> Francisco Roncoroni (Argentine);
> Enrique Lorenzo Mira (Argentine);
> Pierre Colin Jeannel (French);
> Enrique Mario Vasquez, manager (Argentine).

Dr. Bosch said that the above complied with the Argentine requirements as to nationality, but that he was suspicious that the two foreigners, Magugliani and Jeannel, exerted an abnormal amount of influence in the company's operations, and that he was considering the appointment of a supervisory commission to make sure that the Corporación was administered as a truly Argentine company.   Attention is invited to the enclosure forwarded with the Embassy's confidential despatch no. 4600 of March 27, where it is mentioned that the majority of the directors is either affiliated directly with Fiat or else connected with that company's firm of legal advisers.

---

[14] Not printed.

Article VII, paragraph 3, of the aforementioned decree reads as follows:

"The company shall proceed within the period of 60 days from the date of the present decree: *a*) to clear up its financial situation through the elimination of its balance of losses; *b*) after having amended the statutes to increase the capital under the following conditions: the new investments shall be effected through the issuance of nominative shares, intransferable without authorization of the Executive Power, whose subscribers, in the proportion necessary to constitute an absolute majority of the whole of the firm's capital, should be native or naturalized Argentines with more than 10 years citizenship. Excess shares shall be taken up only by stock companies or private individuals residing in the country."

The Corporación's report said that at the stockholders' meeting of last December 23, it had been resolved to reduce the capital by 70 percent, which would conform with stipulation "a" in paragraph 3, Article VII, of the December 22 decree, since the balance sheet as of September 30, 1941, is understood to have shown a loss of about 585,000 pesos, and the capitalization at that time was approximately 815,000 pesos.

The Corporación's report also said that on March 28 it had been decided to issue two new stock series of 10,000 shares each with a value of 30 pesos per share, in order to raise the company's capitalization to its previous level. (Mr. Mason suggested the possibility that the new capital subscribed might be used to pay off some of the debt to Fiat and Ala Littoria.) The report likewise showed a list of stockholders, and the number of shares held by each. Of a total 27,166 shares of stock, 18,593 or 68.44 percent were held by Argentine citizens, whereas the balance was held by companies and individuals not necessarily Argentine. This also appears to conform with stipulation "b" in paragraph 3, Article VII, quoted above. The list showed that Fiat held a relatively small block of shares, although Dr. Bosch admitted confidentially that it would be possible for Fiat to make fictitious stock transfers to individuals.

Incidentally, in referring to its compliance with other stipulations of the decree, the Corporación mentioned that its insurance had been placed with British Aviation Insurance Company Ltd. and Aviation & General Insurance Company Ltd., 3–4 Lime St., London.

It appears that the Argentine authorities are endeavoring to make the Corporación as Argentine as possible, and that certain progress has been made. It is also evident that Dr. Bosch himself is quite sincere. However, he admitted that it was difficult for him to effect a complete elimination of Italian influence. The Corporación having ostensibly complied with the stipulations in the December 22 decree, and a notable improvement having been effected in the company's financial situation and in the elimination of practically all non-Argentine personnel, it might be difficult for Dr. Bosch to make further demands without antagonizing the friends of the Acting President affiliated with the company.

Nevertheless, it was pointed out to Dr. Bosch that the Corporación apparently was still heavily indebted to Fiat and Ala Littoria, and that the primary interest of at least some of the directors would be in liquidating this obligation to the Italians. Dr. Bosch thought he could demand that this not be done, and that whatever earnings accrued under the revised concession should be used for improving the service and not for paying off questionable commitments incurred previously. Mr. Mason mentioned that when he was a member of the Civil Aeronautics Board, this principle had also been followed in certain cases involving U. S. subsidies to American airlines.

Dr. Bosch was told that while the inclusion of the Corporación on the Proclaimed List might still be considered necessary, some consideration would be given to an arrangement whereby the Corporación would agree to the freezing of its debt to the Italian interests, and the blocking of any profits which might find their way into pro-Axis hands. Dr. Bosch seemed to think that this would be a good solution, and it was the general impression that, should this meet with the approval of Washington, such a proposal would be made to the Corporación by the Embassy.

Dr. Bosch was not fully familiar with certain aspects of the Corporación's reorganization, and as stated above, he further admitted that it might be possible for the company to effect fictitious stock transfers. However, if the company is willing to consider the blocking of its funds, it is believed that this would offer the Embassy an opportunity to demand full details as to its finances.

Previous despatches (Nos. 4383 and 4600 of March 11 and 27) have outlined the reasons for not taking definite action against the Corporación up to the present time. To recapitulate, the principal restraining factors are as follows:

a) Both the son and the law partner of the Acting President are directors of the company, and the placing of the airline on the Proclaimed List might antagonize the Argentine authorities and prejudice the heretofore satisfactory operation of the Proclaimed List in Argentina.

b) It is generally conceded that present operations of the line constitute little or no threat to hemisphere defense. It offers a public service to Argentina, Uruguay and Paraguay, and if it is forced to suspend operations due to inability to get gasoline, apparently we are in no position to offer a substitute service, as we have done in other countries.

Under normal circumstances the Embassy would have recommended the inclusion of this firm on the Proclaimed List. Due, however, to the above mentioned considerations, it is felt that other possible solutions should be explored before taking final action. Consequently, my telegram no. 811 of May 2, 3 p. m.,[16] requested the Department's opinion as to the advisability of a proposal for blocking this company's funds.

Respectfully yours, NORMAN ARMOUR

835.796/266

The Ambassador in Argentina (Armour) to the Secretary of State

No. 5225 BUENOS AIRES, May 28, 1942.
[Received June 5.]

Subject: Personnel of Condor Airline in Argentina.

SIR: With regard to the above subject, I have the honor to refer to the Embassy's telegram no. 964 of May 22 [*21*], 9 p. m.[16] (a copy of which was sent to the Embassy at Rio de Janeiro), and to transmit herewith further information.

The telegram sent on May 16, 7 p. m., from the Embassy at Rio de Janeiro to this Embassy stated that Dr. Bento Ribeiro Dantas of the reorganized Condor company was desirous of discharging all persons in Condor's employ whom we considered undesirable, and that he would shortly consult this Embassy on the matter.

Dr. Dantas called on the Counselor of the Embassy on May 19, and promised to furnish that same afternoon a revised list of the Condor personnel in Argentina. At that time he said he would return on May 22 to obtain whatever opinion we might offer as to any of his employees. His second visit was on May 21, at which time he brought a list of personnel, and said that he would probably be returning to Río de Janeiro on the following morning, unless last minute developments postponed his departure. It was subsequently learned that he did not leave; as mentioned below, he paid a further visit to the Embassy today.

According to the revised payroll furnished by Dr. Dantas on May 21, approximately 38 employees have been discharged within the past few months, practically all of them being Germans. There are about 15 German and Italian employees remaining, and Dr. Dantas says that within a short time most of these will also be discharged, as soon as satisfactory replacements could be trained.

---

[16] Not printed.

It was pointed out to Dr. Dantas that it was obviously his primary concern to see that any dangerous or suspicious employees were weeded out of his new organization, and that he and his company would be the first to suffer if there continued to be a possibility of sabotage or German control. He stated that he realized his responsibility in this connection, and that he was fairly well satisfied with the progress which had been made so far. While up to this time the Embassy has been unable to obtain any detailed information on the remaining personnel employed at the Quilmes airport, we did raise some question as to several officers in the administrative department . . .

[Here follows report on four employees.]

On his visit to the Embassy today, Dr. Dantas supplied further information regarding the general Condor situation. He says the Brazilian Government is anxious for his company to extend services to Buenos Aires (but not to Santiago) as soon as possible and, in fact, the former Argentine Ambassador to Brazil, Dr. Labougle, had expressed the same desire to President Vargas. However, the Argentine Government has not yet given formal approval for the renewal of this service.

Dr. Dantas saw the Minister of the Interior, Dr. Culaciati, yesterday, and during the course of the conversation there was a reference to the four Condor planes which had been grounded at Quilmes airport when the airline suspended service last December. It will be recalled (Embassy's strictly confidential despatch no. 4600 of March 27) that Argentina reluctantly permitted these planes to be returned to Brazil, and three of them were flown back, leaving one here. Dr. Culaciati inferred to Dr. Dantas that the release of these planes was conditioned on the acquisition by Argentina of the Lati planes now grounded in Brazil, but Dr. Dantas denied that there was such an understanding, at least as far as he was concerned.

Dr. Culaciati then referred to the Condor shops at Quilmes. Dr. Dantas informed the Embassy today that the former Lufthansa officials were endeavoring to convince the Argentine army that it should expropriate these shops for Argentina, in which case Dantas thought that the Germans formerly employed by Condor would again be given employment. Dr. Dantas thinks there is a definite possibility that Condor will lose its Quilmes shops, possibly as a *quid pro quo* for permission for Condor to resume its service to Buenos Aires. Apropos of this, he said he made somewhat the following statement to Dr. Culaciati: "When Condor was under German control, and many Germans were employed, Argentina never thought of taking over the Quilmes shops. It seems strange that you should want to do this when we have reorganized our company, and have replaced the former German personnel with Argentines."

Dr. Dantas believes that Ramón Castillo Jr. is still working behind the scenes in connection with Argentine airline pretensions, and that it is not impossible that some form of combination with the Spanish airline Iberia is being contemplated. However, he had no concrete information on this possibility.

Dr. Dantas is remaining in Buenos Aires for a few days longer, in the hope of getting a definite answer from the Argentine authorities regarding resumption of service. With regard to the general problem of replacing undesirable personnel, the Embassy believes that he has proceeded in a fairly expeditious manner considering the circumstances, and that he might have to make a temporary compromise in keeping a few of the questionable employees on the payroll, at least until adequate substitutes can be found.

The Department's opinion would be appreciated as to whether Intava would be licensed to furnish gasoline to Condor in the event it obtains Argentine permission to resume service to Buenos Aires, and whether the complete elimination of all German and Italian employees is a necessary prerequisite to obtaining gasoline from Intava.

Respectfully yours,   For the Ambassador:
                                             EDWARD L. REED
                                             Counselor of Embassy

---

835.796/268

The Ambassador in Argentina (Armour) to the Secretary of State

No. 5396   BUENOS AIRES, June 11, 1942.
                                          [Received June 18.]

Subject: Possible resumption of Lati air service between Argentina and Spain

SIR: With reference to the Department's instruction No. 2466 of June 2,[18] I have the honor to report that recent rumors pertaining to this general subject were mentioned in the Embassy's strictly confidential despatch No. 5322 of June 4.[18]

With regard to the *Berliner Boersenzeitung* report that Argentine pilots would be used between Buenos Aires and Natal, it is questionable whether Brazil would permit Argentine pilots to fly any further north than Río de Janeiro. It is believed that this latter privilege would also be conditioned on Argentine permission for a Brazilian airline, such as Condor, to resume service to Argentina. As mentioned previously, there has been some talk that Brazilian and Argentine airlines would effect a junction at Posadas, in the northeastern part of Argen-

---

[18] Not printed.

tina, in order to establish a new service between Buenos Aires and Río de Janeiro, but there do not appear to have been any definite developments in this connection.

Apart from the periodic rumors as to secret arrivals of long-distance Axis planes in South America, the reported movement of former Lati employees from Brazil to Argentina (see confidential despatches nos. 4299 and 4302 of June 1 and 4, from Office of Military Attaché, Río de Janeiro [20]) lends credence to the possibility that plans for a new South Atlantic air service are being considered.

Constant efforts to obtain more concrete information along this line have been unsuccessful so far, but the Embassy will continue to report information and rumors of a fairly credible nature.

In any event, it is assumed that the U. S. control over gasoline, coupled with the application of general economic measures if necessary, will offer an effective means of blocking any project which appears inimical to our interests.

Respectfully yours,

For the Ambassador:
EDWARD L. REED
Counselor of Embassy

835.796/270 : Telegram

The Ambassador in Argentina (*Armour*) to the Secretary of State

BUENOS AIRES, June 23, 1942—11 p. m.
[Received June 23—8 : 25 p. m.]

1216. Embassy's 519, March 20, 4 p. m.; Department's 428, March 26, 10 p. m.; Embassy's despatch No. 5322, June 4.[21] Officials of Aerovias Argentinas claim Corporación is requesting new airline concession Buenos Aires to Rio de Janeiro via Posadas on basis that Corporación will be able to obtain Lati planes now in Brazil, and that concession may be granted within a few days. Third parties inform Embassy that Aerovias thinks it could obtain this concession if we furnished the planes. However, Aerovias still maintains coy attitude and has not yet formally approached Embassy.

In any event award of concession to Corporación might be blocked if we could unofficially confirm as soon as possible either that the United States had already purchased the Lati planes, or that Brazil definitely will not release them against our objections.

Repeated to Rio de Janeiro.

ARMOUR

---

[20] Neither printed.
[21] Despatch not printed.

835.796/271 : Telegram

The Ambassador in Brazil (Caffery) to the Secretary of State

RIO DE JANEIRO, June 24, 1942—6 p. m.
[Received 6 : 25 p. m.]

2193. Buenos Aires' 1216, June 23, 11 p. m., to Department. Aranha tells me that he will not let the Argentine have the Lati planes.

CAFFERY

835.796/280 : Telegram

The Chargé in Argentina (Reed) to the Secretary of State

BUENOS AIRES, August 7, 1942—6 p. m.
[Received 9 : 23 p. m.]

1532. Intava Company received visit from Colonel Borges, Brazilian Air Attaché, who said his Government instructed him to arrange for monthly purchases of 10,000 sues [*liters?*] 87-octane aviation gasoline for delivery to Condor Airline in Buenos Aires. Intava understands Condor intends to reopen weekly service between Brazil and Argentina as soon as fuel arrangements made. Borges admitted he would have to approach YPF if refused by Intava in which event Embassy believes YPF will agree to supply. Intava replied it would need written Embassy permission before supplying Condor. Borges suggested Ambassador Caffery be consulted if we referred matter to the Department.

With reference to Embassy's despatch No. 5225 May 28, it is believed that a few Germans and Italians are still on local Condor payroll. Embassy will endeavor to secure further information tomorrow. With reference to Department's instructions 2776 July 16 [22] I confess insufficient information as yet to recommend listing of Laspiur.[23]

Please instruct at earliest opportunity if we may authorize Intava to give this gasoline to Borges or Condor, and under what conditions. Repeated to Rio de Janeiro.

REED

835.796/282 : Telegram

The Chargé in Argentina (Reed) to the Secretary of State

BUENOS AIRES, August 11, 1942—1 p. m.
[Received 3 : 26 p. m.]

1553. Embassy's 1532, August 7, 6 p. m. Ribeiro Dantas, president of Condor Airline, now visiting Buenos Aires says Argentine Government willing to pay 4 million pesos for Condor shops and

---

[22] Not printed.
[23] Ernesto Laspiur, general manager in Buenos Aires of Sindicato Condor, Ltda.

installations at Buenos Aires Quilmes airport and that he will accept this offer. Presumably Argentine Army will take over former Condor technical personnel at Quilmes including some Germans recently discharged by Condor. Dantas says Condor had Argentine permit valid until end of the year for service to Buenos Aires, with provision for further study of proposed Argentine-Brazilian mixed company. He thinks latter will not materialize.

Above development will leave Condor with only administrative personnel and small maintenance staff in Argentina. Dantas claims all local personnel now Argentine.

As mentioned Embassy's 1532, participation of Borges is in effect a sale to the Brazilian Government, probably making it difficult for YPF to refuse to sell in the event Intava not authorized to do so. If Intava is granted permission to supply Borges or Condor, suggest that this be on month to month basis.

There remains question of traffic control. Understanding with Condor as to undesirable aliens and merchandise would be advisable. Embassy would also require copy of passenger lists. Should these points be negotiated here for Argentina or in Rio de Janeiro for company as a whole?

An early reply for Intava regarding gasoline would be appreciated. Repeated to Rio de Janeiro.

REED

835.796/280 : Telegram

The Secretary of State to the Chargé in Argentina (Reed)

WASHINGTON, August 14, 1942—7 p. m.

1210. Your 1532, August 7, 6 p. m. and 1553, August 11, 1 p. m. The whole Condor problem has been reviewed with Ambassador Caffery, with whom we have agreed on a formula which he will take up on his return to Brazil.

Intava should furnish no gasoline to Condor under any circumstances, pending further communication from the Department.

HULL

811.20(D) E.D.B./1789 : Airgram

The Chargé in Argentina (Reed) to the Secretary of State

BUENOS AIRES, September 16, 1942—4 p. m.
[Received September 22—4 : 20 p.m.]

A–196. Department's telegram 1141 of July 31, 7 p. m.[24] The Embassy is informed by the Standard Oil Company that their appeal

---

[24] Not printed.

for Ethyl fluid was again refused. It is presumed that the Y.P.F. stock of 27 drums plus the Army reserve of 59 drums is the cause of a prohibition on the shipment of more Ethyl to Argentina. To make sure that the Department is fully informed as to the Embassy's estimate of the effect of cutting off Standard's supplies, the Embassy wishes to note some probable results:

(1) Standard is now using approximately three drums of Ethyl aviation fluid per month, and therefore will be out of stock about the end of November.

(2) This will leave Y.P.F. as the only source of aviation gasoline in Argentina, which will force Corporación, Condor, Aeroposta, and all other local business, into Y.P.F. hands, and take away from the United States any possible means of exerting pressure because of control of the fuel source.

(3) Since Y.P.F. have only 27 drums of Ethyl fluid available for civilian use, and are consuming five drums monthly for current military consumption, it might be that the military authorities would refuse to permit Y.P.F. to deplete their stocks by the additional two drums monthly needed for Pan American. This action would make it unnecessary to draw upon Army reserves until about February, 1943, but it would ground Pan American planes.

(4) There is the possibility that Standard's stock of codimer blending fluid might be requisitioned by Y.P.F. when Standard's Ethyl supplies are exhausted, on the ground that only Y.P.F. had facilities for making aviation fuel. This would make Standard unable to furnish 100 octane fuel for United States purposes if required because of an emergency.

(5) A by-product of this situation would be the elimination of Intava from the market, which would strengthen Y.P.F.'s efforts toward securing a petroleum monopoly.

The 86 drums of Ethyl fluid now held by Y.P.F. would last for 17 months, at the present rate of use. The addition of three drums a month to the consumption, to cover Standard's present production, would exhaust the stocks in 10 months. This difference of 7 months seems to the Embassy scarcely sufficient to compensate for the political and other damage to the United States which might result through cutting off all further supplies of Ethyl fluid to the Standard Oil Company. As you know, their aviation gasoline output is sold through Intava and goes only to consumers approved by the United States.

REED

835.796/293 : Telegram

The Chargé in Argentina (Reed) to the Secretary of State

BUENOS AIRES, September 16, 1942—5 p. m.
[Received September 16—4 : 42 p. m.]

1792. My 1553, August 11, 1 p. m., and Department's 1210, August 14, 7 p. m. Condor plane scheduled to arrive here from Rio de Janeiro this afternoon and return tomorrow. Local newspapers advertising resumption weekly service with FW [25] 4-motored planes.

Condor probably has sufficient gasoline for return trip tomorrow. Also rumored that YPF has been making recent deliveries to Quilmes airport. Intava anticipates further requests for gasoline from Brazilian Air Attaché.

Indication as to Condor's present and future status would be appreciated. Also has Condor been asked to cooperate with this Embassy as to passenger lists and traffic control.

Repeated to Rio de Janeiro.

REED

835.796/301

The Chargé in Argentina (Reed) to the Secretary of State

No. 6729   BUENOS AIRES, September 24, 1942.
[Received October 1.]

SIR: With reference to the Embassy's telegram no. 1792 of September 16, 5 p. m., and the Department's telegram no. 1423 of September 22, 9 p. m.,[26] I have the honor to report certain information relative to the resumption of operations by Servicios Aéreos Condor.

Contrary to information previously obtained and reported in the Embassy's aforementioned telegram no. 1792 of September 16, there was no inaugural southbound service from Rio to Buenos Aires on September 16. However, a Brazilian Junkers Ju–52 plane which accompanied the plane bringing General Justo to Buenos Aires on September 12 was used to make the first northbound trip from here to Rio de Janeiro on September 17. The first Condor southbound plane from Rio, a four-motored Focke-Wulf, arrived here yesterday afternoon with 24 passengers and returned to Rio today with one passenger. The plane arrived at and departed from the "Moron" airport (regularly used by Pan American Airways System) instead of using the former Condor field at Quilmes. About a week ago the Director of Civil Aeronautics, Dr. Bosch, asked the local Pan Ameri-

---

[25] Focke-Wulf.
[26] Latter not printed.

can Airways office if Condor could use the American company's ground facilities, which request was refused.

The Focke-Wulf plane was refueled from drums which bore the markings of Intava and West India, both Standard Oil subsidiaries. However, Intava states that it has not supplied any gasoline to Condor in drums for a long time, and that these drums were either from old emergency stocks which Condor formerly maintained at interior points in Argentina, or else Condor obtained empty drums in the market and filled them from its underground tanks at Quilmes.

Intava estimates that Condor had from 10,000 to 15,000 liters of 87 octane gasoline in its Quilmes tanks when service was suspended last December, but part of this was used up in getting the four Condor planes back to Brazil.

There is also a good probability that the 7,400 liters of gasoline requested from Intava by the Brazilian Air Attaché, and referred to in my telegrams 1623 of August 24, 6 p. m., and 1815 of September 19, 11 a. m.,[27] will be turned over to Condor. These transactions involve the replenishment of gasoline used by three Brazilian planes for their return trips to Brazil, and such quantities would have been ample to carry them all the way to Rio de Janeiro. However, if the present Condor service refuels at Porto Alegre northbound, the 7,400 liters will probably allow six to eight trips from Buenos Aires to Porto Alegre.

Nevertheless, this Embassy believes that it would be difficult to refuse permission to Intava to deliver the 7,400 liters, since the request came not from Condor but from the Brazilian Military Air Attaché, and with payment to be made by the Brazilian Ministry of Aeronautics. In the words of Intava, it "represents a business deal between our interests and a friendly power."

Apart from any Intava gasoline stocks which Condor has been able to accumulate at Quilmes, there are recent reports to the effect that Condor has been obtaining gasoline from the official Argentine petroleum company Y.P.F. The Military Attaché of this Embassy advises that a Y.P.F. truck visited the Quilmes airport on September 10 and stayed for 40 minutes, presumably to fill one or more underground tanks. There have been other reports to the effect that previous deliveries were also made by Y.P.F. The Brazilian Air Attaché intimated to Mr. Petrognani of Intava that Dr. Laspiur, the present Condor general manager in Argentina, had approached Y.P.F. on the matter of gasoline supplies, although the results of such negotiations are not known. Dr. Laspiur is also a lawyer and is understood to have as a partner the legal adviser to Y.P.F., so it is quite possible that he made such an approach.

---

[27] Neither printed.

The Embassy's report no. 1340 of September 9 [28] gave the text of the Argentine decree authorizing Condor to resume service to Argentina. In the confidential section of this report mention was made of certain "conditions and obligations" which are to be complied with by the end of this year. Dr. Ernesto Pueyrredon, managing director of the domestic airline Aeroposta Argentina, recently told a member of the Embassy staff that in addition to the two major conditions referred to in our report (formation of a joint Argentine-Brazilian airline, and sale to the Argentine army of the Condor shops and ground installations at Quilmes) it was his understanding that Condor also is to furnish proof to the Argentine Government that it is now a purely Brazilian company, and that it will relinquish any future plans to extend its line to Chile. (Dr. Pueyrredon also said that each Condor plane returning to Rio over the past several months carried out some extra equipment, which actually belonged to Aeroposta instead of Condor.)

The Department's telegram no. 1423 of September 22 indicates the possibility that Condor will be removed from the Proclaimed List after the arrival in Rio de Janeiro of Messrs. Royce and Duncan,[29] which incidentally brings up the question of the Condor personnel in Argentina. This matter was discussed in detail in the Embassy's strictly confidential despatch no. 5225 of May 28, which also requested the Department's view on the matter. During his latest visit to Buenos Aires in August, the president of Condor, Dr. Ribeiro Dantas, stated that all non-Argentine personnel in his local administrative staff had been discharged and that while there were a few Germans still employed at the Quilmes airport, these would be replaced "as soon as possible"—at any rate they would pass from the employ of Condor as soon as the Argentine army took over the Quilmes shops.

The Embassy's above mentioned despatch no. 5225 of May 28 raised some doubt as to four employees in the administrative section: . . .

[Here follows report that two of the employees had been discharged, one sent on a mission to Chile for Condor, and that information available on the fourth was inadequate to warrant his inclusion on the Proclaimed List.]

Reverting to the matter of gasoline supplies for Condor, it will be recalled that Y.P.F. officials have informed the Embassy on several occasions that the company would not sell to firms on the Proclaimed List. However, for reasons outlined below, we have not discussed the Condor matter with Y.P.F. at this time.

In the first place, Y.P.F. would probably justify its action (assuming that it is really making deliveries) on the grounds that Condor

---

[28] Not printed.
[29] Alexander B. Royce and Francis L. Duncan, representatives of the Federal Loan Agency.

is now a Brazilian company. Also, there is not much use in making an issue of its dealings with Condor at this time if the latter is to be removed from the Proclaimed List in the near future—Y.P.F. would only think that we were trying to save the business for Intava.

Until the Condor matter is definitely clarified, the Embassy also hesitates to threaten Y.P.F. with non-delivery of materials from the U.S. Such a move on our part would end immediately the negotiations now being conducted relative to Argentine petroleum for Uruguay and Paraguay, involving the delivery of production equipment to Y.P.F. Furthermore, if Washington continues to refuse export permits on ethyl fluid for Argentina (see Embassy's airgram A-196 of September 16, 4 p. m.), it is quite possible that Pan American Airways System itself will have to ask Y.P.F. for gasoline. Whether Y.P.F. would be willing to supply is open to some doubt, especially if we force them to stop selling to Condor.

It is also apparent that the Brazilian Government is anxious for the new service to continue operating, and that the Argentine Government will be disposed to cooperate, at least until the end of the year when the present Condor decree expires.

Although the Department, in its telegram 1423 of September 22, indicates that it does not look with favor on the resumption of Condor service to Buenos Aires, or the provision of gasoline in this connection, the fact is that the line is already operating and probably will obtain its future gasoline supplies from Y.P.F. This is an unfavorable reflection on the effectiveness of our Proclaimed List. If Condor is delisted, the Embassy does not see how the company could be prevented from obtaining gasoline. If it is kept on the list, it is believed that the factors outlined in the preceding paragraphs should be considered before we attempt to persuade Y.P.F. not to make any further gasoline sales to this company.

Respectfully yours,

EDWARD L. REED

811.20(D) E.D.B./1789 : Telegram

The Acting Secretary of State to the Ambassador in Argentina *(Armour)*

WASHINGTON, October 7, 1942—5 p. m.

1503. Embassy's A-196, September 16. The Department is informed that six drums are being shipped for the Standard Oil Company of New Jersey.

WELLES

835.796/302 : Telegram

The Ambassador in Argentina (Armour) to the Secretary of State

BUENOS AIRES, October 10, 1942—11 a. m.
[Received 12 : 11 p. m.]

1965. Embassy's report No. 1204,[30] Argentine Aviation Notes, July 17, page 16. As there are reports that the Argentine Government is completing negotiations for the purchase of the 5 airplanes of the Air France (apparently 3 for the Army and 2 for civilian aviation) for approximately 3,000,000 pesos inquiries in the matter were recently made at the Central Bank which in strict confidence has now suggested that the matter be taken up with the Foreign Office. A memorandum was today sent to the Foreign Office inquiring whether in the event of such an operation the purchase price would be blocked.

ARMOUR

835.796/309 : Telegram

The Ambassador in Argentina (Armour) to the Secretary of State

BUENOS AIRES, October 31, 1942—5 p. m.
[Received 5 : 05 p. m.]

2140. Department's 1210, August 14, 7 p. m., and last part of Embassy's confidential despatch 6729, September 24. Intava has been approached by Laspiur local head of Condor Airline regarding possibility of obtaining gasoline. Laspiur says they have enough for only two more trips from Buenos Aires.

It is believed that Condor will go to YPF unless Antiava [*Intava*] is permitted to supply within very near future. Department's comments will [be] appreciated.

Repeated to Rio de Janeiro.

ARMOUR

835.796/309 : Telegram

The Secretary of State to the Ambassador in Argentina (Armour)

WASHINGTON, November 6, 1942—midnight.

1677. Your 2140, October 31, 5 p. m. You are authorized to inform Intava that there will be no objection to supplying Condor, on a spot delivery basis, and until further notice, reasonable quantities of fuel as required for individual flights for the Buenos Aires–Rio service. Condor should not be allowed to accumulate any excess stocks, and a careful record should be kept of deliveries under this authorization.

(Repeated to Rio de Janeiro.)

HULL

[30] Not printed.

835.796/314 : Telegram

The Ambassador in Argentina (Armour) to the Secretary of State

BUENOS AIRES, November 25, 1942—7 a. m.
[Received 10 : 03 a. m.]

2369. Department's 1677, November 6, midnight. Assuming that removal of Condor from Proclaimed List also applies to Argentina Intava desires to know if it should continue to limit supplies on individual flight basis.

ARMOUR

835.796/316a : Telegram

The Secretary of State to the Ambassador in Argentina (Armour)

WASHINGTON, November 30, 1942—8 p. m.

1880. The removal from the Proclaimed List of Condor Brazil does not remove Condor Argentina, which will be handled on its own merits.

Therefore, Intava should continue deliveries of supplies to Condor Argentina on individual flight basis, unless deliveries are made direct to "Cruzeiro do Sul" successor to Condor Brazil, in which case, if you are satisfied, there need be no restrictions on Intava deliveries.

If circumstances warrant, the Department will present the case for delisting Condor Argentina to the Interdepartmental Committee. In the event you recommend this procedure you should submit full information justifying such action.

HULL

DISCUSSIONS CONCERNING THE SEVERING OF COMMERCIAL AND FINANCIAL RELATIONS BY ARGENTINA WITH THE AXIS POWERS

740.00112A European War 1939/7480

Memorandum of Conversation, by the Second Secretary of Embassy in Argentina (Gantenbein) [31]

[BUENOS AIRES,] February 9, 1942.

I called by appointment today upon Dr. Raúl Prebisch, General Manager of the Central Bank, and after preliminary remarks stated that I was calling at the request of the Ambassador in order to have an informal and off-the-record conversation with him regarding

---

[31] Copy transmitted to the Department by the Ambassador in Argentina in his despatch No. 4116, February 10; received February 16.

Resolution V adopted at the Conference of Rio de Janeiro.[32]   I stated that, as he knew, the United States Government attached great importance to this financial and economic resolution and that it was naturally very interested regarding the steps that would be taken by Argentina.

.   .   .   .   .   .

I then referred to Argentina's reservation to the resolution [33] and said that it was not altogether clear to me how the second sentence of the reservation should be interpreted.   More specifically, I asked whether the sentence meant that Argentina would apply future measures only "to firms or enterprises managed or controlled by Axis or foreign belligerent countries not in the American continent."   Dr. Prebisch said that this was not at all the case, that he had drafted the reservation himself and that its purpose was to have the Argentine Government "for political reasons" on record as contemplating the possibility of applying the economic and financial measures not only to the Axis countries but also to other non-American belligerent countries.   When I inquired whether it was therefore to be inferred that Argentina had undertaken to assume all the obligations under Resolution V, the reservation pertaining only to additional applications, Dr. Prebisch replied in the affirmative.

Turning to another matter, I said that it had been gratifying that largely through the good offices of Dr. Prebisch and conversations that the Embassy had had the Banco de la Provincia and the Banco de Avellaneda had adopted measures providing for greater cooperation with the democracies.   I said that this cooperation, however, as well as the cooperation on the part of a substantial number of banks in Buenos Aires, was being neutralized by the fact that certain other institutions, including the Banco de la Nación, were continuing to have relations with black-listed firms and individuals and were, in fact, accepting business which the other banks turned down, besides engaging in other transactions inconsistent with policies pursued by the United States.   I stated that the Ambassador was frankly disturbed about this and that before reporting to the authorities in Washington the part being played by the Banco de la Nación, the Embassy thought that possibly some understanding could be reached with that institution along the lines of the understandings reached

---

[32] For correspondence concerning the Third Meeting of the Foreign Ministers of the American Republics, see pp. 6 ff.   For the Resolutions contained in the Final Act of the Meeting, see Department of State *Bulletin*, February 7, 1942, pp. 117–141 ; Resolution V recommended that the American Republics cut off commercial and financial intercourse with nations signatory to the Tripartite Pact. The Tripartite Pact between Germany, Italy, and Japan was signed at Berlin September 27, 1940, League of Nations Treaty Series, vol. ccIV, p. 386.

[33] For text of reservation to Resolution V, see Department of State *Bulletin*, February 7, 1942, p. 140.

with the Banco de la Provincia and the Banco de Avellaneda. Dr. Prebisch quickly volunteered to have a conversation in the matter with Dr. Jorge A. Santamarina, the president of the Bank.

After referring to previous conversations in regard to negotiations for a new French payments agreement, I asked Dr. Prebisch whether the negotiations were still in the state of suspense. Dr. Prebisch answered in the affirmative and later said that there was no intention to resume the negotiations. I said that that was welcome news inasmuch as there was some fear that Axis activities here might be financed through French francs.

Finally, I referred to the widespread practice here of making payments to and from the Axis countries through Switzerland and said that although we had heard encouraging reports shortly after the adoption of the measure on December 22, which purported to render it more difficult to make payments in this way, more recent reports had been of a less encouraging character. Dr. Prebisch said that Mr. Walter Simon [33a] of the British Embassy had made the same comment and he (Dr. Prebisch) said that he had promised to look into this matter to see what further action might be taken.

740.00112A European War 1939/8046

Memorandum of Conversation, by the Second Secretary of Embassy in Argentina (Gantenbein) [34]

[BUENOS AIRES,] February 20, 1942.

I called by appointment upon Dr. Prebisch again today and began by referring to *El Pampero* and other agencies of Nazi propaganda in Argentina. I stated that the Ambassador had mentioned this subject informally at the Foreign Office once or twice but felt reluctant to make formal representation because of the long-established policy of the United States with respect to freedom of the press. It had occurred to the Embassy, I said, that perhaps an approach to the problem would be through the Central Bank, especially with reference to the Executive Decree No. 110,790 of January 8, 1942, which subjects to the control of the Central Bank "transfers of funds abroad and internal movements of funds which may have a direct or indirect relation to such transfers by firms or enterprises managed or controlled by persons who have the nationality of a country at war or are domiciled in it." In this connection, I referred to the recent report of the Congressional committee investigating subversive activities in

---

[33a] Financial Adviser and First Secretary of the British Embassy in Argentina.
[34] Copy transmitted to the Department by the Ambassador in Argentina in his despatch No. 4199, February 20; received March 3.

Argentina, which made it clear that *El Pampero* and other Nazi papers and news agencies were receiving financial support from the German Embassy and from sources in Germany, and I said that it was well known that a large number of copies of *El Pampero* were being distributed gratis to members of the Argentine armed forces and to government employees as a part of the Nazi propaganda system.

Dr. Prebisch said that he felt entirely in accord with the Embassy in respect to the unsavory nature of *El Pampero* as well as its detrimental influence upon relations between the two countries and stated that he had given considerable thought to what might be done in the matter. Over a year ago, he said, he had informed the Embassy of the source of the newsprint supply of *El Pampero*, and he indicated that our Government had evidently not taken steps to cut off this supply.[35] I commented that this aspect of the matter had been under constant study by the Embassy and by the authorities in Washington, but that the newsprint problem was a very involved and difficult one. Dr. Prebisch then said that the application of any financial action against *El Pampero* would have to be initiated by the Argentine Government, and when asked whether the decree aforecited did not furnish sufficient authorization to go ahead, he said that he was afraid not. Dr. Prebisch stated that his suggestion would be that the Embassy hold the matter in abeyance until after the elections in March and then take it up with the Foreign Office.

. . . I said that the Ambassador had informally inquired at the Foreign Office concerning Argentine action on the various resolutions of the conference [35a] and had been informed that they had been referred to Dr. Ruiz Moreno [36] for an opinion as to whether it was necessary to submit them to Congress for approval. I added that the Ambassador did not, however, feel disposed to make representations concerning Resolution V, largely because he felt that it was assumed that Argentina would take the appropriate action in accordance with its commitments under Resolution V.

In reply to the question whether it was likely that Great Britain would be placed in the same category as the Axis countries in any forthcoming decree in connection with Resolution V, Dr. Prebisch stated that probably all non-American belligerents would be placed in the same general classification, as in the decree of January 8, but that as a practical matter the measure would apply only to the Axis countries.

I then referred to the relations of the Banco de la Nación Argentina with the Axis countries, (which I had also discussed with Dr. Prebisch

---

[35] For correspondence on the newsprint problem, see pp. 400–428, *passim*.

[35a] i.e., the Third Meeting of the Foreign Ministers of the American Republics, held at Rio de Janeiro January 15–28, 1942.

[36] Isidro Ruiz Moreno, Legal Adviser to the Ministry for Foreign Affairs.

on February 9, 1942) and after reminding Dr. Prebisch that he had said that he would welcome such pertinent information on this and other matters as the Embassy might be able to supply, I said that it had come to the attention of the Embassy that about the middle of last December the Banco de la Nación had executed a payments order by the Reichsbank of Berlin for approximately 190,000 pesos. When I said that this may have been for the German Embassy or for propaganda organizations here, Dr. Prebisch said that under a new regulation, the German, Italian and Japanese Embassies were being limited to 200,000 pesos per month for their peso requirements. He said that it would be very difficult for those Embassies to receive more than that amount through banks here. However, when I suggested that perhaps the Embassies could receive pesos through the accounts of others and through peso notes delivered at the Embassy, Dr. Prebisch admitted that that would be a possibility. He promised, nevertheless, to look into the transaction referred to.

Referring to the conversation which the Embassy had had last December, through Dr. Prebisch's good offices, with officials of the Banco de la Provincia, I said that the Embassy had received another report indicating that in the first part of January, the Banco de la Provincia had received from the Banco Alemán here two sums aggregating 52,000 pesos for the account of the Banco Alemán, Barcelona, through the Instituto Español de Moneda Extranjera of Madrid. This, I said, would seem to be a "cloaking" transaction inconsistent with the understanding which the Embassy had reached with the Banco de la Provincia. Dr. Prebisch said that he would look into this matter also.

Turning to the broader question of relations of Argentine banks with black-listed firms, I asked Dr. Prebisch whether there was any policy among the banks here in this regard. I said that the Banco de Avellaneda had given assurances that it would refrain from such transactions and that the American banks, as well as the banks cooperating with the British Embassy, were refraining from operations with firms on the American and British lists. Dr. Prebisch replied that, of course, the Argentine Government had taken no official action in the matter but that transactions with black-listed firms were in general being frowned upon by the Argentine banks. He said that it was realized that the maintenance of relations with black-listed firms would render banks, as well as other commercial organizations, subject to being placed on the black-lists themselves. In this connection, I reminded Dr. Prebisch that the pertinent committee in Washington was becoming more drastic and was frequently calling upon the Embassy for explanations when it received reports that organizations here, including banks, were maintaining relations of this character. Dr. Prebisch said that he would look into this subject to see whether a more effective policy might be worked out here.

Finally, I asked Dr. Prebisch whether in the event that the Argentine Government purchased the French ships here for the newly established Merchant Marine, the proceeds would be blocked, to which Dr. Prebisch replied definitely in the affirmative.

The general impression that I obtained from this conversation was that Dr. Prebisch favors a cooperative policy with the United States in economic and financial matters, and really wants to be helpful, but either feels powerless in the matter or is unwilling to use his influence to force the issue with the Government.

740.00112A European War 1939/8424

Memorandum of Conversation, by the Second Secretary of Embassy in Argentina (Gantenbein) [37]

[BUENOS AIRES,] February 27, 1942.

Dr. Grumbach [38] asked me to call at the Central Bank yesterday, which I did, and after briefly discussing another matter which was relatively unimportant (reported in the Embassy's despatch No. 4272 of today's date [39]), he led the conversation to the recent conference at Rio de Janeiro and the conversations that I had had on February 9 and 20 with Dr. Prebisch (as reported in the Embassy's despatches No. 4116 of February 10, 1942,[40] and No. 4199 of February 20, 1942 [41]), including the operations of the Banco de la Nación. (I gathered that Dr. Prebisch may have asked Dr. Grumbach to discuss these matters with the Embassy.)

As it was evident that Dr. Grumbach was seeking my comments and had nothing in particular to say himself on the subject, I took occasion to state that earlier in the day the Ambassador had informed me that he was becoming increasingly disturbed regarding reports that the Banco de la Nación was not pursuing policies consistent with those of the United States. I said that I had previously discussed these reports with Dr. Prebisch and that the Embassy earnestly felt that unless some remedy could be found for the situation that appears to exist, the authorities in Washington might deem it necessary to give consideration to the placing of the Banco de la Nación on the Proclaimed List, regrettable as this would be.

---

[37] Copy transmitted to the Department by the Ambassador in Argentina in his despatch No. 4279, February 28; received March 10.

[38] Edgardo Grumbach, head of the Foreign Exchange Department of the Central Bank.

[39] Not printed.

[40] See footnote 31, p. 453.

[41] See footnote 34, p. 455.

Dr. Grumbach said that, of course, every step should be taken to avoid this, that he inquired what our policy was with respect to the relations of banks with black-listed firms and individuals. I said that the same principles applied to banks as applied to the other concerns, viz., that if banks maintained relations with firms on the Proclaimed List, they made themselves subject to being placed on the list also. I said that it was useless to obtain commitments from such institutions as the Banco de Avellaneda that they would sever relations with black-listed firms when the latter could receive facilities at other banks, including the largest and most important bank in the country, namely, the Banco de la Nación. Thus far, I told Dr. Grumbach, the authorities in Washington had apparently been somewhat lenient in regard to banks, probably because of the far-reaching implications involved, but exigencies of the war were requiring that a more drastic policy be pursued. I said that there was no intention to interfere in any way in the internal affairs of Argentina or to "penalize" banks or other concerns having relations with black-listed firms, but that our Government felt perfectly justified in saying to its own nationals that they must refrain from maintaining relations with concerns outside of the United States if the latter concerns were giving aid to the enemy. Dr. Grumbach said that he understood our view of this, but that having just returned from a vacation of some weeks, he had not realized that the application of our policy with respect to banks had become tightened to this extent.

Referring to Resolution V of the recent conference at Rio de Janeiro, I said that, speaking off the record, I could say that Argentina's failure to take any action during the month that had elapsed since the end of the conference had caused a distinctly unfavorable impression in the United States and that it was to be feared that unless some action were taken promptly, this impression would become even worse. After referring to the reports here day before yesterday of a critical article by Mr. Turner Catledge of the *Chicago Sun*, I said that I feared that unfavorable comments of that kind would become increasingly conspicuous in the United States if Argentina did not adopt measures pursuant to its commitments at the Rio de Janeiro conference. At this point, I handed Dr. Grumbach a copy of the far-reaching financial and economic decree issued by Ecuador on February 9, 1942, and said that if a country like Ecuador could adopt such measures, it should be far easier for a country with a highly-developed financial structure and machinery, such as Argentina has, to do likewise. (I handed him an additional copy which I said might be of interest to Dr. Prebisch.)

Dr. Grumbach then mentioned the political situation here as a factor, to which I replied that I was afraid that that would not serve to decrease the feeling of impatience in the United States, for it was felt in our country that this war had reached a point where internal politics of countries should be accorded secondary consideration.

Dr. Grumbach made no further comments, but as I left he remarked how busy he was being kept by such matters as priorities, and I gathered the impression that perhaps the Central Bank was beginning to perceive a relationship between priorities, allocations and United States purchases of Argentine products, and the position being maintained by Argentina concerning the Axis countries, and that it might be seeking to ascertain the minimum in the way of financial and economic cooperation that the United States would consider satisfactory.

740.00112A European War, 1939/9617

The Ambassador in Argentina (Armour) to the Secretary of State

No. 4450   BUENOS AIRES, March 17, 1942.
                                                    [Received April 1.]

SIR: With reference to the Embassy's despatch of yesterday [42] reporting authorizations recently granted by the Central Bank for transfers of French francs outside of the Franco-Argentine payments agreement, I have the honor to report that a member of the Embassy staff called this morning upon Dr. Edgardo Grumbach, head of the foreign-exchange department of the Central Bank, and inquired about these transactions.

Dr. Grumbach confirmed that the authorizations had been granted, although he emphasized that the pesos paid for the francs would be deposited in a blocked account. He admitted that the resulting blocked funds could be released for such purposes as expenses of the French Embassy (which, like the embassies of the Axis countries, has been limited to 200,000 pesos per month), but said that the French Embassy could always obtain its peso requirements for expenses by a deposit of francs, so that the release of blocked funds for this purpose would not in reality represent any important facility. When Dr. Grumbach was reminded of the assurances given by Dr. Prebisch to the effect that the negotiations for the renewal of the French payments agreement had been suspended by the Central Bank and that there was no intention of renewing them (Embassy's despatch no. 4116 of February 10, 1942,[43] and previous despatches), and when he was told that the recent authorizations did not seem to be consistent with those assurances, Dr. Grumbach said that, speaking in great confidence and "off the record", the recent action was taken, against

---

[42] Despatch No. 4436 not printed.
[43] Not printed, but see memorandum of February 9, and footnote 31, p. 453.

the wishes of the Central Bank, as a result of instructions from the Ministry of Foreign Affairs.

Dr. Grumbach was told that although our Government had no desire to interfere in any way with Argentine relations with a friendly third country, as had been made clear in the previous conversations, it had hoped that the Argentine authorities would be able to cooperate in this matter with our Government's policy of endeavoring to minimize the foreign exchange made available in the Hemisphere for Axis uses; that while these funds might be blocked they could nevertheless be unblocked for purposes that would represent facilities to the Axis countries; that the very fact that so much interest had been shown to have the authorizations made was in itself evidence that the authorizations represented facilities; and that, indeed, it was feared that the news of the authorizations would be viewed with disappointment in Washington, where the friendly cooperation in regard to the payments agreement had previously been a source of gratification.

.   .   .   .

Mr. Simon thinks that it would be advisable for both of our Embassies to discuss the subject at the Foreign Office and states that the British Ambassador would be disposed to do so if I should take similar action. I am hesitant to do this, in the absence of instructions from the Department, inasmuch as our Government, unlike the British Government, is continuing to maintain diplomatic relations with the Vichy Government. The Embassy has interpreted the Department's telegram no. 1002 of December 2, 9 p. m.,[44] to refer only to very informal conversations with the Central Bank. In the event, however, that the Department should wish me to approach the Foreign Office in the matter, I should welcome instructions in that sense.

Respectfully yours,   NORMAN ARMOUR

740.00112A European War 1939/11741

The American Embassy in Argentina to the Argentine Ministry for Foreign Affairs [45]

[Translation]

AIDE-MÉMOIRE

The Embassy of the United States of America has been informed that blocked funds of the German Reichsbank have been released in the amount of two hundred and fifty thousand pesos at the request

---

[44] Not printed; it instructed the Embassy to use its influence to prevent any agreement that would result in an accumulation of pesos available to the French Government (635.5131/51).

[45] Copy transmitted to the Department by the Ambassador in Argentina in his despatch No. 5031, May 11; received May 23.

of the Siemens Company for the payment of loans contracted with certain Argentine banks by the "Inag" Fábricas Reunidas de Utiles Sanitarios, a subsidiary of the Siemens Company of Germany. It is not known whether one of the local German banks was among the institutions receiving this payment, but irrespective of this consideration the operation served to increase the credit of a German company in Argentina and to furnish the German Government with a potential source of income in this country.

It would seem that the aforementioned transaction is inconsistent with Resolution V of the Rio de Janeiro Conference.

BUENOS AIRES, April 9, 1942.

740.00112A European War 1939/11135

The American Embassy in Argentina to the Argentine Ministry for Foreign Affairs [46]

[Translation]

AIDE-MÉMOIRE

At the time of the collapse of France in June, 1940, there was, it is understood, an accumulation of three or four hundred million French francs in the fund of the Argentine-French payments agreement. Shortly thereafter it was made known that when this fund became exhausted the Argentine authorities would not authorize further transfers of payments to occupied or unoccupied France during the remainder of the war. It has recently come to the attention of the Embassy of the United States of America that authorizations have been granted for two sizable financial remittances to occupied France by the Cervecería Argentina Quilmes and the Banco Hipotecario Franco-Argentino, these funds being transferred entirely outside of the Argentine-French payments agreement.

The Ambassador of the United States has been instructed by his Government to inform his Excellency the Minister of Foreign Affairs and Worship that the United States Government considers the transfers in question to constitute a serious violation of Resolution V of the Rio de Janeiro Conference.

BUENOS AIRES, April 9, 1942.

---

[46] Copy transmitted to the Department by the Ambassador in Argentina in his despatch No. 4874, April 27 ; received May 8.

740.00112A European War, 1939/10635

The Ambassador in Argentina (Armour) to the Secretary of State

No. 4710   BUENOS AIRES, April 11, 1942.
                                          [Received April 25.]

SIR: With reference to the Department's telegram No. 418 of March
25, 11 p. m.,[47] authorizing the Embassy to have conversations regarding war financial cooperation with certain local banks interested in
obtaining credit facilities from the Export-Import Bank of Washington and referring also to the Embassy's telegram No. 645 of
April 10, 3 p.m.,[47] I have the honor to report below conversations
with officers of certain of the banks mentioned in the Department's
telegram No. 377 [*337*] of March 11, 12 noon.[47]

Banco de la Provincia

On April 7 and again on April 9, officers of the Embassy had conversations with Sr. Alberto Tintoré, head of the foreign department
of the Banco de la Provincia, in the course of which reference was
made to the conversation last December at the Central Bank with the
general manager and head of the foreign-exchange department of the
Banco de la Provincia during the visit in Buenos Aires of Mr.
Ravndal [48] and to the letter received from the bank several days thereafter (reported in the Embassy's despatch No. 3825 of January 8,
1942 [47]). In the conversation on April 7, Sr. Tintoré said that he
could say definitely that his institution had no relations with firms
and individuals on the Proclaimed List outside of Argentina, but
that as he was not familiar with the bank's policy as applied to relations with such firms and individuals located within the country, he
would be obliged to consult with other officers of the bank before
giving an answer. On April 9, Sr. Tintoré said that after consulting
with Dr. d'Oliveira, general manager of the bank, he could say that
the policy of his institution was not to grant new credits to parties on
the Proclaimed List and to liquidate by degrees such credits as were
outstanding. He stated that this was consistent with sound banking
practice inasmuch as listed firms, if they should have need for loans,
would probably not be good credit risks. When questioned on the
point, Sr. Tintoré said that even if a firm on the Proclaimed List were
a good risk, and wished credit, it would be the policy of his bank not

---

[47] Not printed.
[48] On November 19, 1941, Christian M. Ravndal was sent by the Department to
the American Missions in South America to discuss export controls, the freezing
of foreign funds, and the Proclaimed List.

to grant it, although he admitted that there might be rare exceptions. In regard to transactions with Europe, he said that the Banco de la Provincia pursued a strict policy of scrutinizing the facts of every case before transferring a payment, and he referred in this connection to what he characterized as the strictly enforced control of the Central Bank through requiring a specific authorization before a payment to Europe could be made. Sr. Tintoré gave evidence of wishing to cooperate fully with the Embassy, including furnishing complete information on any individual cases. (In this regard, see the Embassy's despatch No. 4715 of yesterday's [today's] date [51] regarding a deposit made last January in the Banco de la Provincia by Mr. Frederick J. Gilfillan.) When Sr. Tintoré was told that the Embassy's gratification in receiving his bank's renewed assurances of cooperation would be increased in Washington if they could be confirmed in some form of written communication, he said that he would be glad to inquire of his superiors whether this could be done.

Ernesto Tornquist y Compañia

The Embassy had a conversation on April 7 with Sr. Carlos Alfredo Tornquist, formerly head of the bank and now a member of the Board of Directors, who was accompanied by another director and the head of the foreign-exchange department of the institution. These persons stated emphatically that it was the policy of the bank to desist from all transactions with firms on the Proclaimed List either in Argentina or abroad and said that the bank could be counted upon to cooperate in every way possible with pertinent war measures of the United States. Sr. Tornquist offered to confirm this in a letter to the Embassy. Although a report has been received from a discharged employee of the bank indicating that Sr. Tornquist has subsequently gone to Rio de Janeiro to negotiate an operation involving interests that are ostensibly Belgian but in reality German (a report which the Embassy is now investigating), all other evidence indicates that this institution is pro-democratic and friendly towards the United States.

Banco Polaco Polska Kasa Opieki, S.A.

Dr. Enrique Gruber, President of the above-mentioned bank, informed the Embassy on April 7 that his institution was cooperating completely with our Government and that it had no relations whatsoever with firms or individuals on the Proclaimed List. He said that his bank did a considerable proportion of the Polish business in Argentina and that it could be relied upon to be completely anti-Nazi. When questioned in the matter, Dr. Gruber said that it was true that the bank was not on friendly terms with the Polish Legation but that this was due to its refusal about a year and a half ago to turn the bank

---

[51] Not printed.

over to a representative of the Polish Ministry of Finance who suddenly appeared in Buenos Aires seeking to take over the institution by payment of 900,000 pesos and whose mission the Polish Legation supported. The ownership of the bank, he said, had been placed in escrow during the remainder of the war with the result that the bank could not legally have been sold under these circumstances. Dr. Gruber, who stated that before coming to Buenos Aires to establish the Polish Bank here some ten years ago he had been head of two large banks in Warsaw, claimed that his institution was owned by Polish interests but was not controlled directly or indirectly by the Polish Government.

Banco Francés del Río de la Plata

Sr. Le Prevost, head of the foreign-exchange department of the above bank, called at the Embassy on April 9. He gave assurances that his institution was cooperating in every way with the war financial policy of our Government and that it was granting no credit facilities to firms on the Proclaimed List.

Shaw, Strupp and Company

Mr. Julius Strupp, a partner of the above company (and a naturalized American citizen) called at the Embassy yesterday and gave assurances, as he had done before, that his bank was cooperating fully with our Government. When told that a report had been received that the books of his company for 1941 had not been audited (see Embassy's despatch No. 4217 of February 24, 1942 [52]), Mr. Strupp stated that the British auditors, Deloitte, Plender, Griffiths and Company, were working on the books now and would certify them shortly. He then volunteered the information that Price, Waterhouse had declined to certify the bank's books for the reason that the auditor assigned to the work did not understand banking practices, more especially purchase-and-sale entries relating to the borrowing of bonds for three months at a commission for purposes of tenders by the bank's clients. Although this explanation might well be questioned, it would seem that if Deloitte, Plender, Griffiths and Company are disposed to certify the books, any previous irregularities have now been corrected.

Some time ago Shaw, Strupp and Company gave assurances in writing to the British Embassy concerning cooperation with war measures, and insofar as is known there has been no evidence that those assurances have been violated.

Banco Popular Argentino

Two officers of the Embassy called upon Sr. Quesada, the general manager of this bank, on April 8. Sr. Quesada explained that his

---

[52] Not printed.

bank had no relations with firms and individuals on the Proclaimed List established outside of Argentina, but he indicated that his bank saw no reason why it should desist from such relations within the country.

There is some doubt as to the pro-democratic sympathies of this bank. At least one of its directors is understood to be avowedly pro-Nazi, and Dr. Carlos A. Pueyrredón, the Mayor of Buenos Aires, who is a conservative and whose belief in the principles of continental solidarity may be questioned, is said to have considerable interests in the bank.

All of the banks with whom these conversations were held stated that they continued to have an interest in the financial facilities contemplated, although in general they questioned whether they would be able to avail themselves of such facilities under existing trade conditions.

As the Banco Société Génerale, the Banco de Italia y Río de la Plata, and the Banco Holandés Unido have given secret undertakings to the British Embassy and have, it is reported, been cooperating closely with that mission, no conversations were deemed necessary at this time.

In the Embassy's telegram No. 645 of April 10, 3 p. m., there were recommended as suitable agencies for purposes of the credit plan of the Export-Import Bank of Washington all of the banks mentioned in the Department's telegram No. 337 of March 11, 12 noon, except Argentaría, which can probably best be investigated in the United States in relation to J. Henry Schroeder Banking Corporation, which controls it; The Banco Popular Argentino, which, it is felt, has thus far failed to demonstrate a sufficiently cooperative attitude, as indicated above; and the Banco Español del Río de la Plata. Although the last-named institution is reported to be owned principally within Argentina (at one time it was owned by interests in Spain), it is closely allied with Spanish interests, has subsidiaries in Spain, and is actively engaged in financing Argentine exports to that country, a portion of which, according to recent reports reaching the Embassy, are likely to be proceeding ultimately to Germany or occupied territories. There is reason to believe, therefore, that the institution may be regarded by the Axis countries as a "friendly bank." If further investigations should indicate this to be not the case, the Department will be promptly informed in the premises.

Respectfully yours,   NORMAN ARMOUR

635.116/282 : Telegram

The Ambassador in Argentina (Armour) to the Secretary of State

BUENOS AIRES, April 15, 1942—9 p. m.
[Received 9 : 08 p. m.]

676. Embassy's 1223, October 30.[53] Contending that Argentina's increasingly favorable dollar exchange position would not seem to justify continuation of import embargoes on products of United States origin, in the past 3 months the Embassy has frequently urged in informal conversations with Central Bank officials the removal of these restrictions. The bank yesterday definitely assured the Embassy that on or about May 1 not only will all imports from the United States for which no exchange is now made available be admitted into Argentina, but that the bulk of the exchange rates will be adjusted to extend to United States products no less favorable treatment than that accorded to third countries notwithstanding the exceptions provided for in the related notes to the trade agreement.

ARMOUR

740.00112A European War 1939/11741

The Argentine Ministry for Foreign Affairs to the American Embassy in Argentina [54]

[Translation]

The Ministry of Foreign Affairs and Worship has the honor to address the Embassy of the United States of America acknowledging receipt of its memoranda, dated April 9 last,[55] relative to remittances made to France by the Cervecería Argentina Quilmes and the Banco Hipotecario Franco-Argentino by way of financial services authorized by the Central Bank and in payment of debts contracted with certain Argentine banks by the "Inag", Fábricas Reunidas de Utiles Sanitarios.

In reply, the Ministry of Foreign Affairs and Worship takes pleasure in indicating to the Embassy of the United States of America that on this occasion the Argentine Government wishes to submit the following explanations:

The remittances made to France for purposes of financial services could not be effected by using the francs which the Central Bank has

---

[53] Not printed.
[54] Copy transmitted to the Department by the Ambassador in Argentina in his despatch No. 5031, May 11 ; received May 23.
[55] Ante, pp. 461 and 462.

in the Bank of France in the payments account between Argentina and France for the reason that the amounts available are small and it has been considered advisable to hold these exclusively for taking care of other payments of small amounts. Consequently, for making remittances of financial services to France without employing the aforementioned francs there were three different possibilities:

(a) to give free exchange (Swiss francs, escudos), which in affecting our exchange reserves involved the possibility that those reserves would not be utilized in the final analysis for the purposes for which they were intended;

(b) to give francs, which could have been done by making use of the credit in the Bank of France, in accordance with the terms of the existing agreement. It was not judged advisable to contract debts of this character for providing financial services; and

(c) to authorize the transfer in accordance with the procedure with which we can now make transfers to Germany, Italy and countries with compensation accounts.

This last form of procedure is very simple and does not involve any movement of exchange. It is the one which was chosen for authorizing the services of the Cervecería Argentina Quilmes and the Banco Hipotecario Franco-Argentino. It consists of the following: the Argentine bank which desires to make the transfer seeks a French bank which is willing to sell it francs for this purpose and to receive their equivalent in local currency. *This equivalent in local currency in favor of the French bank is blocked and may not be used in any case for purchasing free exchange.* Only the Central Bank may grant authorization for employing the funds for purely internal expenditures, in accordance with the following purposes;

(a) payments of expenses for cables and postage, imposts, taxes and bank commissions;

(b) current expenses in connection with real estate located in the country which is owned by the holder of the account;

(c) payments to navigation companies and captains of steamships for meeting steamship expenses in Argentine ports;

(d) payments to insurance companies resident in the country provided that they pertain to the fulfilment of reassurance contracts;

(e) payments of taxes and expenses of trade marks or patents registered in the country in the name of owners established in France;

(f) payments of remittances of a personal character (pensions, retirement benefits or family assistance) to residents in Argentina and travel expenses;

(g) payments for subscriptions, notices and publications to or in local newspapers and magazines;

(h) payments of income on securities issued by the French Government provided that the holders of the securities are domiciled in Argentina and acquired them before June 26, 1940; and

(i) purchase of Argentine bonds or securities which are deposited in the country in the name of the owners of the funds.

With respect to the other operation mentioned by the Embassy it deals with the following: the Central Bank authorized that funds blocked in the account of the "Deutsche Ueberseeische", of Berlin be transferred to the firm "Inag" for increasing its capital and amortizing at the same time a debt in the Banco Alemán. This operation is doubly advantageous for Argentina: first, because "Inag" is developing industrial enterprises of great utility for the country: it manufactures X-ray apparatus and dental and surgical instruments; and secondly, because it conforms with the policy being pursued by the Central Bank in endeavoring to have firms of foreign origin which have obligations with the local banks in amounts which are very large in proportion to their capital in the country amortize these debts by degrees.

Therefore, in the operation itself there is nothing which can benefit foreign countries. On the other hand, the adoption of measures of control, however strict these may be, is not aimed at prejudicing legitimate interests, but on the contrary, should guarantee the development of activities useful for the country and place them under protection from acts or interventions capable of adversely affecting the national interests.

There being thus explained the operations mentioned, the Argentine Government rejects the statement of that Embassy which indicates that the aforementioned transfers constitute a serious violation of Resolution V, of the Rio de Janeiro Conference. It should be recalled that in that conference the Argentine Delegation made clear that it was in accord with the need of taking measures of economic and financial control of all internal or external activities of firms or enterprises which might adversely affect, in one way or another, the welfare of the Republics of this continent or the continental solidarity or defense, and therefore it does not consider justified the opinion that there should be included in the obligation contracted at Rio de Janeiro financial operations conducted in the form and for the purposes outlined above.

Consequently, the Argentine Government must necessarily assume that only an incomplete knowledge of the facts has permitted the Government of the United States to furnish that Embassy with necessary instructions for the sending of the memoranda which are herewith replied to.

The Ministry of Foreign Affairs and Worship avails itself of this opportunity to present its compliments to the Embassy of the United States of America.

BUENOS AIRES, May 8, 1942.

740.00112A European War 1939/11741

Draft Memorandum by the American Embassy in Argentina to the Argentine Ministry for Foreign Affairs [56]

[BUENOS AIRES, undated.]

The Government of the United States has carefully considered the memorandum of the Ministry of Foreign Affairs and Worship dated May 8, 1942, which refers to two *aide-mémoires*, of the Embassy of the United States, both dated April 9, 1942, concerning financial remittances from the Cervecería Argentina Quilmes and the Banco Hipotecario Franco-Argentino, to occupied France, and concerning the release of blocked German funds for the benefit of the "Inag" Fábricas Reunidas de Utiles Sanitarios.

With respect to the remittances of the Cervecería Argentina Quilmes and the Banco Hipotecario Franco-Argentino, the aforementioned memorandum appears to assume that it was necessary to make these payments in some form, and after enumerating various possible methods of transfers, it states that the most advantageous form was found to be that which was followed, viz., to arrange for credits in France to be compensated for by an equivalence in Argentine pesos deposited in blocked accounts in this country. The memorandum adds that these blocked pesos may be released only for certain enumerated purposes.

It would appear that, as viewed from any angle, these operations represent facilities to occupied France which could benefit the German authorities, for not only do the payee companies in France receive funds and does the French Bank receive assets in Argentina against which notes may be issued, but also the pesos in Argentina, while initially blocked, may be released for various purposes. The Government of the United States, therefore, continues to consider that these transactions are inconsistent with Resolution V of the Rio de Janeiro Conference, in which all of the American Republics, including Argentina, agreed to recommend the immediate adoption of "any additional measures necessary to cut off for the duration of the present Hemispheric emergency all commercial and financial intercourse, direct or indirect, between the Western Hemisphere and the nations signatory to the Tripartite Pact [57] and the territories dominated by them."

In regard to the operation whereby the "Inag" Fábricas Reunidas de Utiles Sanitarios, a subsidiary of the Siemens Company of Germany, was enabled to repay a loan to the German bank, the Banco Alemán Transatlántico, and to increase its capital in Argentina, the

---

[56] Copy transmitted to the Department by the Ambassador in Argentina in his despatch No. 5031, May 11; received May 23. For the Department's reaction to this draft, see telegram No. 815, June 5, 9 p. m., to the Ambassador in Argentina, p. 481.

[57] League of Nations Treaty Series, vol. CCIV, p. 386.

Government of the United States takes the view that this transaction was inconsistent with Resolution V of the Rio de Janeiro Conference for at least three reasons: (1) it permitted a payment from a blocked fund to a German bank whose interests are admittedly closely identified with those of the aggressor nations and whose liquid resources are by the transaction increased; (2) it permitted the German firm's subsidiary to increase its credit in Argentina by decreasing its banking indebtedness; and (3) by providing for an increase of capital of a German firm, it increased in a corresponding amount the resources in an American country of a company under the control of the German authorities. The Department of State feels that there can be no doubt that all three of these aspects of the operation in question are inconsistent with what the twenty-one American Republics had in mind when they agreed upon Resolution V of the Rio de Janeiro Conference.

As to the considerations in the memorandum with respect to the Argentine national interests involved in the development of industrial enterprises in the country, the Government of the United States has consistently given support to those various inter-American activities serving to facilitate and encourage the development of industry within the republics of the continent. It is believed, however, that Resolution V of the Rio de Janeiro Conference did not contemplate that the interests of national industries would be placed ahead of the interests of continental defense in fulfilling the obligations contracted in that Resolution.

In view of the foregoing considerations, the Government of the United States is confident that the Argentine Government will agree that financial operations of these kinds are not in harmony with the inter-American resolution aforementioned.

840.51 Frozen Credits/6701

Memorandum by the Secretary of State for President Roosevelt [58]

[WASHINGTON, undated.]

PROPOSAL OF THE TREASURY DEPARTMENT TO THE BOARD OF ECONOMIC WARFARE THAT ARGENTINE FUNDS IN THE UNITED STATES BE FROZEN

I. *The nature of the proposal.*

The proposal is that the funds of Argentina in the United States be frozen and that a general license then be issued for purely Argentine transactions. The purpose of the proposed action is twofold:

a. To coerce Argentina into greater collaboration with the war effort of the United Nations.

---

[58] Handed to President Roosevelt May 14, 1942. A notation on the memorandum by the President reads: "C. H. Not in accord with Good Neighbor Policy. F. D. R."

b. To demonstrate to all the other American countries that the United States Government "means business" and will wield its huge economic power to force more effective collaboration. The Treasury memorandum [59] states "it may be that the freezing of Argentine assets should be accompanied by similar action against Chile and that the policy (i.e. freezing) should be based on their continuance of relations with the Axis."

II. *The proposal is one of basic foreign policy.*

Treasury and the Board of Economic Warfare frankly admit that they are not concerned primarily with methods of improving Argentine administration of foreign property but are attempting to force a change in the basic relationships of Argentina and the United States. The technical inadequacy of the proposed freezing order is admitted by all, but it is sponsored by Treasury and the Board of Economic Warfare in the utterly mistaken view that it will coerce Argentina into the line desired by us.

The question raised is clearly one of foreign policy, namely, what is the best way for this Government to bring about better collaboration in the war effort by Argentina. The determination of such a fundamental matter of foreign relations is obviously of proper concern only to the Department of State under the instruction of the President.

III. *Argentine policy regarding hemisphere solidarity.*

The Treasury and the Board of Economic Warfare start from the premise that Argentina is affirmatively working in the interests of the Axis. This is definitely erroneous. The active collaboration of Argentina in some aspects of our war effort is demonstrated by:

1. The offer by the Argentine Government of the use of its ports and territorial waters by the armed vessels of the United States, just as though the United States were not a belligerent.[60]
2. Argentine refusal to permit itself to become the haven of Axis diplomats from the countries which had severed relations with the Axis.
3. Refusal of Argentina to sell aviation gasoline to Axis-controlled airlines.
4. Sale of its strategic materials to the United States.[61]

Nevertheless, Argentina has not collaborated in the way hoped for at the Rio Conference; primarily, it has not severed diplomatic relations with the Axis.

IV. *United States policy toward Argentina and its results.*

In order to persuade Argentina of where its vital interests lie, the United States, since Rio has withheld delivery of military and naval

---

[59] Not found in Department files.
[60] This offer was effected by decrees of December 9 and 13, 1941; see Embassy's despatch No. 3740, December 24, 1941, printed in *Foreign Relations*, 1941, vol. VI, section entitled "Reactions in the other American Republics to the declarations of war between the United States and the Axis Powers."
[61] See pp. 306 ff.

supplies to Argentina unless Argentina agrees to contribute substantially in some acceptable way to the security of the hemisphere, and is furnishing scarce nonmilitary goods only after the needs of the other American republics have been supplied. This policy is bearing fruit. The powerful military and naval elements in Argentina, which really maintain the present Government in power, are beginning to question the desirability of Argentina's present policy. Public opinion, carefully influenced by us, in general is becoming more and more insistent upon a more effective collaboration by Argentina with the democracies.

V. *Effect of freezing Argentine funds in the United States.*

A. If in this situation Argentine funds here were to be frozen, not only would commercial intercourse and the flow of trade, including strategic materials, be hampered but of far greater importance, the Argentine Government would be pushed toward the Axis. Our action would be considered by most Argentineans, even our friends, as a demonstration of the thesis which the Axis is subtly promoting, namely, that the United States, under the guise of hemisphere solidarity, is actually embarked upon a policy of ruthless economic imperialism. Indeed, this action would be received with grisly satisfaction by the Axis, which would view it as a specific result of its efforts to drive a wedge between Argentina and the other American republics.

B. The contemplated measure would likewise produce serious repercussions in the other American republics. The whole basis of our inter-American policy over the past few years has been nonintervention, respect for individual sovereignty, and the reaching of decisions through voluntary agreement. Far from applauding the proposed freezing of Argentine funds as Treasury and the Board of Economic Warfare believe, the other American republics would begin to wonder whether we had repudiated our present policy and returned to the days of the Big Stick. The spectacle of Argentina being beaten over the head with an economic club would in no way advance the confidence in our aims and purposes so painstakingly, but so successfully, built up in the other American republics.

If those countries were to lose confidence in our ability to maintain a broad, tolerant, and collaborative attitude, even in this time of stress, we might well, by dramatic coercion, toss away the results of a decade of careful development in relations and do harm inestimably greater to our war effort than the difficulties flowing from Argentina's lack of full collaboration.

VI. *The problem of Argentine deficiencies of administration of foreign property.*

Those deficiencies which have aroused the Treasury and the Board of Economic Warfare no less than the Department, of course require continual attention and our best efforts to remedy them. Effective control action can immediately be taken by this Government in conjunction with the United Nations regarding some aspects, such as by more thorough navicert control over shipments between Argentina and Spain, or by an amendment to Treasury General Order No. 5 [63] prohibiting the transfer of United States currency from any foreign country to the United States. Other action can be taken through implementation of our blacklist program, and some action can only be taken by the Argentine Government itself. The Department has lost no opportunity to bring to the attention of the Argentine Government the loopholes and weaknesses in its administrative machinery.

C[ORDELL] H[ULL]

740.00112A European War, 1939/11929 : Telegram

The Ambassador in Argentina (Armour) to the Secretary of State

BUENOS AIRES, May 26, 1942—10 p. m.
[Received May 26—8 : 22 p. m.]

982. Embassy's despatch number 4710 of April 11 regarding Export-Import Bank credits. Central Bank states that the Banco de la Provincia de Buenos Aires is not included in list of allocations just received from the Import-Export Bank and expresses the opinion that it would have unfortunate effects if this bank which is the second largest here and semi-governmental should be left out. The Embassy concurs and in view of apparent cooperative attitude of the Banco de la Provincia as reported in aforementioned despatch and number 4924 of May 1 [64] recommends that the Central Bank be advised of inclusion by telegram.

ARMOUR

840.51 Frozen Credits/6809

The Ambassador in Argentina (Armour) to the Secretary of State

No. 5278   BUENOS AIRES, June 1, 1942.
[Received June 18.]

SIR: With reference to the Department's circular telegram of April 7, 9 p. m.,[64] requesting monthly reviews of developments in Argentina

---

[63] This refers to General Ruling No. 5, amended May 19, 1942, and September 3, 1943. See 5 *Federal Register* 2159 ; 7 *Federal Register* 3770 ; 8 *Federal Register* 12286.

[64] Not printed.

concerning the freezing of Axis assets and other control measures, and referring also to the Embassy's despatch No. 4926 of May 1, 1942,[65] I have the honor to report the following:

General

Another month has elapsed since the Río de Janeiro Conference without the Argentine Government evidencing any appreciable disposition to adopt measures in accordance with Resolution V of that conference. Virtually the only development of this nature during May was a circular (No. 283) of the Central Bank, dated May 7, 1942, providing restrictions on remittances abroad by drafts, travellers' checks, etc., presumably in order to provide the Bank with a better check on the destination of funds sent abroad (the Embassy's despatch No. 5085 of May 14, 1942 [65]), but it remains to be seen whether this measure will be used effectively against the Axis countries.

Some encouragement may be found in the fact that Dr. Irigoyen, the Under Secretary of Finance, took occasion to mention to me briefly at the opening of Congress on May 28 that the outlook for greater foreign-funds control here was now more promising. Similarly, Dr. Irigoyen in a conversation with an officer of the Embassy on May 19 intimated that there might be developments here with respect to Resolution V of the Rio de Janeiro Conference in about two weeks thence (the time of the opening of Congress had not yet been announced), and it seems not unlikely that he had in mind legislation to be introduced in Congress shortly after its opening, especially as he had indicated in a conversation with Messrs. Meltzer and Towson [66] during their visit here some weeks ago that the Government felt that it did not have authority to go further in the control of financial transactions with or for the benefit of the Axis countries without Congressional legislation. While Dr. Irigoyen's recent remarks have offered some encouragement, there is, of course, the possibility that the position that the Government must await authorization from Congress before taking additional steps or enforcing more strictly existing measures has been adopted as a convenient means of avoiding responsibility and with a belief that the Conservative-controlled Senate might obstruct the enactment of such legislation.

The attitude of the Argentine Government in the whole matter of Axis-funds control was evidenced in its memorandum of May 8, 1942, sent to the Embassy in reply to representations concerning transfers of funds to occupied France and the release of blocked funds here for

---

[65] Not printed.
[66] Bernard D. Meltzer, Assistant to Assistant Secretary of State Acheson, and Norman E. Towson, Assistant Director of Foreign Funds Control, Department of the Treasury, on special mission to certain of the American Republics.

the benefit of a German bank and an Argentine subsidiary of the Siemens Company (the Embassy's despatch No. 5031 of May 11, 1942 [69]). The Argentine memorandum appeared to justify the operation of releasing blocked German funds on the grounds of benefits that Argentina would derive, and while stating that "therefore, in the operation itself there is nothing which can benefit foreign countries," the memorandum did not even attempt to give reasons why Axis interests would not profit by the transaction to the detriment of continental defense.

[Here follows a lengthy discussion of Argentine market for looted United States currency.]

Argentine Market for Looted United States Securities

With respect to looted United States securities, the Embassy has been endeavoring through a competent investigator to find a "black market" for these here, but it appears that any such market is not large, and there is no available evidence that considerable amounts of such securities are being offered for sale in Buenos Aires. In fact, the only securities selling at large discounts that it has been possible to locate have been two relatively small blocks of Imperial Oil (quoted on the New York Curb Exchange) and International Petroleum (quoted on the New York Stock Exchange). In this connection, it is reported here that a large proportion of the United States securities purchased in Europe in recent years have been held for safekeeping in the United States. Argentine securities imported into this country from Europe must, as has been previously reported, be declared and placed under the control of the Central Bank.

Respectfully yours,   NORMAN ARMOUR

811.51/4202 : Telegram

The Secretary of State to the Ambassador in Argentina (Armour)

WASHINGTON, June 4, 1942—9 p. m.

804. Your 983, May 26, 11 p. m.[69] While the difficulties of tracing the history of bank notes and preventing smuggling into Argentina are recognized, these difficulties are no greater in the case of Argentina than in the case of other countries. It would seem necessary that a few unfortunates may have to suffer by reason of these difficulties in order that the essential purpose of the Treasury restrictions may be realized; namely to prevent the Axis powers from liquidating

---

[69] Not printed.

looted currency through the facilities of other countries, particularly the American Republics. The same considerations are present with respect to the effect of Central Bank control upon the exchange market. Furthermore, it is believed that the establishment and proper administration of appropriate controls by the Central Bank would considerably minimize the possibility of injury to legitimate interests.

With respect to travelers bringing dollar notes into Argentina, the Department approves of the position taken by the Embassy's officer in his conversation with Grumbach. Such currency brought into Argentina by European travelers is currency against which the Treasury measure is aimed and there would seem to be no reason why persons leaving Europe could not travel with other forms of money such as dollar drafts, et cetera, which it is not believed would interfere too greatly with the "customary" practice. United States Customs authorities are allowing for the time being a $250 exemption for each person entering the United States, plus a like amount for each accompanying dependent. Such an exemption is necessary in this country since dollar currency is the legal exchange medium and a refusal to permit reasonable amounts to be brought in free of restriction might cause hardship. There would seem to be no reason for a similar exemption in the case of dollar currency brought into Argentina, since other recognized mediums of exchange are readily available.

With respect to the holdings of banks and exchange shops under the control of the Central Bank, it is not believed that any general exemption can be granted but the *bona fides* of the holdings and the fact that they were acquired prior to the close of business on May 19, together with the adequacy of the controls adopted by Argentina, will be taken into consideration by the Treasury in any application for their release. The same considerations are applicable to dollar notes bought in good faith for non-banking and non-speculative purposes before the news of the Treasury restriction became generally known in Argentina.

That part of the Department's circular telegram May 27, 10 p. m.[70] concerning the regulations adopted by the Brazilian authorities with respect to the use of American bank notes in Brazil sent in code should not be disclosed as being the procedures which are being followed in Brazil since the Department was informed in strict confidence and has not been advised of any public announcement by the Brazilian authorities on this aspect of the matter.

HULL

---

[70] Not printed.

840.51 Frozen Credits/6701

The Secretary of State to the Ambassador in Argentina (Armour)[71]

No. 2480   WASHINGTON, June 4, 1942.

SIR: Reference is made to the telegram, no. 680, May 14 [*15*], 1942, 6:00 p. m., "From the Secretary to the Ambassador".[72] There are now enclosed:[73]

(1) A memorandum of the Treasury Department dated May 12, 1942, proposing the freezing of Argentine funds because of the pro-Axis financial and commercial transactions which are occurring in Argentina either because of the failure of the Argentine Government to impose adequate controls, or to apply effectively the controls which have been put into operation;

(2) A memorandum of the Department of Justice dated May 12, 1942, entitled "Axis Funds and Financial Activities in Argentina".

As you know, it is of paramount importance to eliminate pro-Axis financial and commercial transactions which are being executed in Argentina. To accomplish this, not only is it necessary for the staff of the Embassy effectively to implement the various control measures which have been adopted by our Government, but it is also necessary to induce, if possible, the Argentine Government to adopt complementary controls in accordance with the provisions of Resolution V adopted at the Rio Conference. This Department, and the other interested government agencies, view with grave concern the pro-Axis transactions which are being carried on in Argentina and the uncooperative attitude of the Argentine Government. It is, therefore, suggested that you personally follow questions raised by action designed to strengthen United States control measures or to induce the Argentine Government to carry out the commitments embodied in Resolution V.

I

In communications between the Embassy and the Department, and in discussions between various missions from Washington and the Embassy, measures which would strengthen United States controls have, of course, been suggested from time to time. In accordance with those suggestions, and with steps already taken by the Embassy, further vigorous action along the following lines, among others, is an indispensable prerequisite to increasing the effectiveness of our controls:

(1) In so far as possible, a careful check should be made regarding the liquidation of looted currency and securities, with a view to im-

---

[71] The file copy of this instruction bears the following notation: "Returned to FF (Mr. Hiss) to be given to Mr. Meltzer to deliver to the Ambassador in person." Donald Hiss was Chief of the Foreign Funds Control Division.
[72] Not printed.
[73] Enclosures not attached to file copy.

plementing General Ruling No. 5, as amended.[74] (Reference is made to the circular telegram of May 18, 1942.[75]) Information regarding the specific firms or persons or other channels direct or indirect through which such currency and securities are flowing, and information regarding serial numbers, or any other identifying marks on such currency or securities would, of course, particularly facilitate the administration of that Ruling.

(2) A careful check should be made of holding companies, dubious exchange houses, and other firms which are suspected of being engaged in cloaking activities. Evidence of cloaking by firms in Argentina should, of course, result in their immediate recommendation for inclusion on the Proclaimed List. Such evidence regarding firms in the United States or firms in Argentina suspected of having accounts in the United States should, of course, be submitted as a possible basis for *ad hoc* freezing by the United States Treasury Department. That Department is making an investigation regarding the material under item 2 of its memorandum and has been requested to submit information or suggestions which would aid investigation by members of the Embassy staff.

(3) Investigation should be made of the amount of remittances to Axis territory directly, or indirectly through neutral countries. It is suggested that information might be secured through the Central Bank or otherwise, regarding remittances to each neutral country for the last four years. These figures might be analyzed in the light of the trade balances between Argentina and the countries involved, and an estimate might be made of the amount of remittances not referable to "legitimate trade transactions" which have been made to Axis territory directly, or indirectly through neutral European countries. In this connection, it is, of course, significant that officials of the Central Bank and the Argentine Government have repeatedly stated that remittances to neutrals are limited to those connected with "legitimate trade transactions". An explanation of the transactions which are deemed "legitimate trade transactions" by the Argentine authorities should also be submitted.

(4) A careful check should be made of the progress of negotiations between the Argentine Government and the Spanish trade mission. Any significant development should be reported to the Department by telegram.

(5) A careful check should be made on the possible flow of goods between Europe and Argentina, with a view to recommending the strengthening of the navicert system.

(6) A careful check should be made of all transactions which appear to involve, directly or indirectly, an Axis interest. Important transactions should be reported in summary by telegram, but details on all of the transactions described above should be sent by air mail.

Reports to the Department on the foregoing items, including suggestions for remedial action, should be kept current. In addition, an immediate report on the accuracy of the facts set forth in the attached memoranda is requested.

---

[74] See footnote 63, p. 474.
[75] *Post*, p. 789.

II

The Argentine Ambassador to the United States has already been informed of the Treasury proposal, its rejection and the view of the United States Government that Argentina's cooperation under Resolution V has been unsatisfactory in character. In addition, you should make strong representations to the Argentine Government regarding its failure to implement Resolution V by severing commercial and financial intercourse direct or indirect between Argentina and the nations signatory to the Tripartite Pact and its failure to take measures to eliminate financial and commercial activities which are prejudicial to the welfare and security of the American republics. It is requested that, in the first instance, this matter should be taken up with the President of Argentina to insure his receiving a proper report of the attitude of this Government.

The Department is also preparing an instruction suggesting representations to be made to the Argentine Government concerning pro-Axis activities in Argentina, in fields other than commercial and financial. It is suggested that you do not seek an interview with the President until you have received that instruction and are prepared to make representations concerning both the matters covered herein and in that instruction.

Your representations regarding Resolution V should, unless you perceive some objection, include reference to the following:

(1) As a result of Argentina's failure to implement Resolution V and the consequent inadequacy of Argentine controls, the nations signatory to the Tripartite Pact, the territories dominated by such nations, and the nationals and partisans of both, are executing financial and commercial transactions in Argentina, or through the use of Argentine facilities, which prejudice the welfare and security of the American republics.

For illustrative purposes, unless you perceive some objection, you may refer to the following transactions (and similar transactions of which the Embassy is aware) which have been executed in Argentina with the apparent approval or knowledge of the Argentine Government, notwithstanding that those transactions run directly counter to Resolution V, since they prejudice the welfare and security of the American republics by increasing the strength of the signatories to the Tripartite Pact:

(a) With the authorization of the Argentine monetary authorities, remittances have been made to Axis nationals to service Argentina's external debt owed to the residents of Axis countries. (Despatch no. 4925 dated May 1, 1942.[76])

(b) Substantial private remittances have been made to, or for the benefit of, firms or persons in Axis territory.

(c) Substantial transfers have been made to occupied France, contrary to assurances by the Central Bank that no payments

---

[76] Not printed.

would be made outside of the Argentine-French payment agreement. Although the pesos which may be made available to French banks as a result of such transfers are blocked, it is the understanding of the United States Government that such funds may, under existing Argentine controls, be freely unblocked and used for purposes which prejudice the welfare and security of the United States and the other American republics.

(2) As a further result of Argentina's inadequate controls, shipments of material from the United States to Argentina, and the extension of public or private credit by the United States to Argentina may directly or indirectly increase the economic and financial power of Axis agents and other Axis partisans in Argentina who are executing commercial and financial transactions which are inimical to the security and welfare of the American republics. In determining allocations of increasingly scarce material and shipping space and in its total commercial and economic relations with Argentina, the United States Government will be compelled to give appropriate weight to this fact—that shipments from the United States and other transactions between the United States and Argentina may, in the absence of appropriate controls by Argentina, directly or indirectly increase the economic and financial power of the enemies of the United States and of the other American republics.

(3) The United States Government would be constrained to view the future continued failure of Argentina to carry out the commitments embodied in Resolution V adopted at Rio de Janeiro as a definitive indication of Argentina's intention neither to fulfill the obligations, nor to gain the benefits, of the several inter-American instruments with respect to commercial and economic matters, to which she is a party.

It is requested that a copy of any note or *aide-mémoire* which is transmitted to the Argentine Government be submitted to the Department and that the Department be kept fully informed of developments.

Very truly yours,   For the Secretary of State:
                                     DEAN ACHESON

740.00112A European War, 1939/11741 : Telegram

The Secretary of State to the Ambassador in Argentina (Armour)

WASHINGTON, June 5, 1942—9 p. m.

815. Your despatch no. 5031.[77] Draft reply approved, but the following suggestions are submitted:

1. At the end of the first sentence of the third paragraph, add "Although the use of blocked funds may be limited to purposes not inherently undesirable in themselves, the release of such funds to Axis partisans has the effect of increasing the free funds available to them and such increased funds may be used directly for purposes which prejudice the welfare and security of the American republics."

---

[77] See footnote 56, p. 470.

2. Page 2, Item (c) of the Argentine note indicates that transfers are still being made directly to Axis territory. The Department has been under the impression that such transfers had been stopped through the denial of the required licenses. If such is not the case, you should object to them even more vigorously than to transfers to France. Please clarify this point by telegram.

HULL

840.51 Frozen Credits/6701

The Assistant Secretary of State (Acheson) to the Ambassador in Argentina (Armour)

WASHINGTON, June 6, 1942.

DEAR NORMAN: I am asking Messrs. Cochran [78] and Meltzer to carry this personal letter to you so as to explain certain aspects of the situation here in Washington with respect to Argentina.

As you know, the Treasury Department in a meeting of the Board of Economic Warfare recommended that the freezing controls of this country be applied generally to Argentina. As you also know, this proposal was definitely rejected and there is no intention to have that decision modified. In this connection Mr. Welles feels that it will be desirable to make clear to you one point covered in the instructions [79] which Messrs. Cochran and Meltzer are presenting to you personally. In paragraph (2) on page 2 [80] it is stated that firms in the United States or in Argentina who are found to be engaged in cloaking activities should be reported to the Department with a view toward having the United States Treasury apply *ad hoc* freezing controls to their activities. This does not mean that there would be any general freezing of Argentina but merely refers to the practice which is now being followed regarding the activities of all persons wherever resident who are found to be acting for or on behalf of enemy countries. Persons who are frozen by this manner may engage in transactions in so far as they are subject to the jurisdiction of the United States only pursuant to license.

When Treasury's proposal was made it was fortunate that Mr. Meltzer was available to the Department in as much as his information and knowledge, resulting to a great extent from his recent trip to Buenos Aires and his work with the Embassy, made it possible to present without delay a reasoned analysis of the Treasury proposal.

Having failed in its efforts to freeze Argentine funds, the Treasury Department then complained about the inadequacy of the informa-

---

[78] H. Merle Cochran, of the Department, on special mission to Argentina June 8–July 23, 1942.
[79] Instruction No. 2480, June 4, p. 478.
[80] Paragraph (2) under section numbered I.

tion on Argentine financial and commercial matters and strongly urged that at least three Treasury officers be sent to Argentina to study this subject and report directly to Treasury. In dealing with this suggestion it was fortunate that Mr. Meltzer had recently visited the Embassy and could report favorably on the work which it was carrying out.

The Treasury proposal was met by a counter-proposal of the Department to assign Messrs. Cochran and Meltzer temporarily to Buenos Aires for the purpose of assisting the Embassy in preparing the report requested in the Department's instructions and to work on other matters as explained in my telegram of June 6, 1942.[81]

I am sure that Messrs. Cochran and Meltzer will do everything in their power to be of maximum assistance to you and the Embassy.

Sincerely yours, DEAN ACHESON

<hr />

740.00112A European War, 1939/11929 : Telegram

The Secretary of State to the Ambassador in Argentina (Armour)

WASHINGTON, June 8, 1942—11 p. m.

827. Reference your 982, May 26 regarding Banco de la Provincia. The Department feels that the desire of the bank to be included in the Export-Import Bank's approved list should be used to obtain from the bank a written statement approved by the board of directors that : (1) The bank will grant no new credits or overdrafts to Proclaimed List persons, (2) the bank will proceed immediately and definitely to eliminate existing credits and overdrafts of this nature (in this connection the bank should give its oral agreement to furnish to the Embassy full information concerning the existence of all such credits and overdrafts), (3) the bank will inform the Embassy before making any remittance to any Axis occupied or controlled country or to any European neutral country if any person in any Axis occupied or controlled country has an interest, giving the Embassy the full details of the contemplated transaction, (4) the bank will cooperate with the Embassy in cases of intended transfers to foreign countries where there might be any doubt as to possible benefit to enemies of the allied nations.

The Department appreciates the cooperative attitude displayed by Tintoré[82] and d'Olivera[83] but feels that in practice government pressure through Sánchez Sordono [*Sorondo*][84] would nullify their good intentions.

<hr />

[81] Telegram No. 819, not printed.
[82] Alberto Tintoré, head of the Foreign Department of the Banco de la Provincia.
[83] General Manager of the Banco de la Provincia.
[84] President of the Banco de la Provincia.

Please forward your opinion concerning the desirability of obtaining an agreement along these lines as a condition of the inclusion of the Banco de la Provincia in the Export-Import Bank's approved list. It should be understood that in the event the Banco de la Provincia does not strictly comply with the above assurances the facilities of the Export-Import Bank will be withdrawn.

Your opinion is also requested as to the advisability of obtaining similar assurances from all banks to be included in the Export-Import Bank's approved list. It is thought that formal rather than informal assurances might strengthen the Embassy's position with regard to banks which in the past may have been engaged in questionable activities.

HULL

840.51 Frozen Credits/6784 : Telegram

The Ambassador in Argentina (Armour) to the Secretary of State

BUENOS AIRES, June 15, 1942—midnight.
[Received June 16—2 : 48 a. m.]

1146. Embassy's 1134, June 15, 7 p. m.[85] The Ministry of Finance has issued a press release together with three decrees reported in the evening papers implementing Resolution V.

The press release, bearing the caption "measures of economic and financial control resulting from the fifth recommendation of the consulative meeting at Rio de Janeiro," notes that the "fifth recommendation refers to the cutting off during the present continental emergency of all commercial and financial intercourse between the Western Hemisphere and the nations signatory to the Tripartite Pact and the territories dominated by them as well as suspending commercial and financial activities prejudicial to the welfare of the American Republics." Later it states that "Doctor Acevedo [86] declared that the decrees signed today have been issued in accordance with the fifth recommendation at Rio within the spirit of the Argentine reservation which of course does not affect the scope and efficacy of the control but which strengthens it." After outlining the contents of the decrees, the press release reports that according to Doctor Acevedo his Ministry is preparing a draft law which will be soon submitted to Congress to enable the adoption of still further measures and in a final paragraph states that the Minister concluded "by saying that in that way the executive power has evidenced its firm purpose of fulfilling within its powers the obligations contracted at Rio concerning everything

---

[85] Not printed.
[86] Carlos Alberto Acevedo, Argentine Minister of Finance.

that pertains to the welfare of the nation or of the other American Republics and to continental solidarity and defense".

The decrees which are dated today in general give the Ministry of Finance and the Central Bank far-reaching discretionary powers of control although freezing of funds is not specifically provided for. Decree number 122712 signed by the Acting President and seven Ministers authorizes the naming of supervisors or interventors in any enterprise "which belongs to non-American belligerent foreigners or whose activities are in any way connected with non-American foreign belligerent countries or citizens["]; provides for the recommendation by a commission of penalties and other measures when there are found to be cases deemed inimical to the national or continental interests; and increases the control over the external and internal movement of funds granted the Central Bank in the decree of January 8.

Decree number 122713 signed by the Acting President and the Minister of Finance authorizes the Central Bank to require sworn statements of any persons or firms engaging in any way in transactions abroad as to details of their operations and provides for penalties for false declarations.

Decree number 122714 with the same signatures extends to operations with all non-American countries the control provided by decree number 66230 of June 26, 1940; provides that from 30 days from the date of the decree all parties in the country maintaining in their power assets or open accounts in the names of parties in non-American countries must furnish the Central Bank with a sworn declaration containing pertinent information; gives the Central Bank broad powers to require the transfer of such assets to authorized banks or on institutions and provides for penalties.

The texts with translations of the above will be transmitted in Wednesday's airmail pouch.[87]

Tonight Grumbach invited an officer of the Embassy to call at his home and explained these various measures. He indicated that the Central Bank had drawn them up and that while it had hoped that it might be able to obtain 80% of them from the Government it secured all that it asked for. While the measures do not differentiate between the non-American belligerent countries, he volunteered the comment that this was owing to political consideration but that it was the intention to apply them only against the Axis countries. When asked for an indication as to the policy in other respects that would be applied in utilizing these powers he said that he thought that Prebisch might be disposed to furnish the Embassy with confidential information on the point tomorrow. However, he emphasized the difficulties that had confronted the Central Bank in the administration

---

[87] Despatch No. 5481, June 17, not printed.

of foreign funds control in the past because of what was felt to be insufficient powers and expressed the belief that now it had broad powers with which it could go ahead.

I believe that it would be highly desirable if the fullest publicity possible could be given to these measures and if there could be thus encouraged the efforts that are being made here to offer greater collaboration.

ARMOUR

840.51 Frozen Credits/6837 : Telegram

The Ambassador in Argentina (Armour) to the Secretary of State

BUENOS AIRES, June 20, 1942—5 p. m.
[Received 10 : 38 p. m.]

1196. Embassy's 1146, June 15, midnight. Cochran, Gantenbein, and Meltzer had long and frank conference yesterday with Prebisch and with the Central Bank's representatives to Conference, Gagneux and Grumbach, regarding adequacy of decrees. Bank officials appeared anxious to learn of criticism of decrees which might be made in Washington and of methods for improving them. Following is a summary analysis of decrees and of conversations :

1. Decrees do not increase authority to block assets of Axis nationals and partisans in Argentina. However, bank officials stated that an earlier decree number 110,790 (see despatch 3865, June [*January*] 13 [88]) blocking of funds of Axis nationals as such and of any other person or firm, irrespective of nationality, in Argentina, which carries on pro-Axis activities. The basis for such blocking which was admitted to be tenuous as a matter of interpretation, is as follows : Since such firms or persons may make external transfers, their internal operations are "related" to external transfers and hence subject to blocking control under decree 110,790. Bank officials asserted that this power has already been exercised, and will submit full particulars. Previously the bank in discussions with the Embassy had questioned whether the decree conferred this power.

2. Bank officials also state that accounts, cash, and securities in the name of residents of Germany and Italy, as well as Japan, are blockable under earlier measures and are submitting memorandum regarding these measures and their practical operation. Since the Embassy, Department, and Treasury previously had not been aware of the authority allegedly conferred by such measures, the memorandum will be carefully studied and a report on the existence and applications of the authority will be submitted.

---

[88] Not printed.

3. In discussing decree number 122,712 and the interventor system, the following deficiencies were brought to bank officials' attention:

(*a*) Interventors are authorized only to watch and report. Interventors require but do not have authority to prevent or suspend any transaction which appears undesirable. In the absence of such authority, undesirable transactions may be executed while the interventor's reports are traveling through the time consuming administrative process established by decree 122,712.

Bank officials replied that a bill endowing interventors with such powers was about to be introduced into Congress, and that a firm would probably refrain from completing the transactions questioned by an interventor because of the fear that such action would result in the immediate blocking of all of its assets by the bank (see item 1 above).

(*b*) Present decree, even if supplemented by that bill, places upon interventors burden of discovering undesirable transactions. This will be extremely difficult in view of deceptive devices which Axis firms have contrived. It was suggested that all operations of firms in which interventors are placed be blocked and that only licensed transactions be permitted. In this way the burden of justifying doubtful transactions would be imposed upon the firm under intervention (bank officials in reply to an inquiry stated that article 1 was applicable to a firm or person, ostensibly Argentine, who was suspected of engaging in undesirable activities).

4. In discussing decree 122,714, following points were made:

[(*a*)] Article 2 was not broad enough because it was limited to intangibles, to formal rather than beneficial ownership, and to persons resident in Axis territory rather than to Axis nationals or partisans in Argentina. Bank officials adverted to administrative and political difficulties involved in census of property held by or for all Axis nationals in Argentina. It was then suggested that census could initially be confined to property of persons or firms carrying on or suspected of, undesirable activities. This suggestion was favorably received.

(*b*) In reply to an inquiry, bank officials stated that authorized banks, under article 3, included German banks. They sought to explain away this anomaly on the ground that all banks were controlled by Central Bank and that would justify political position of Axis banks insured [*insuring*] their compliance with Central Bank regulations.

(*c*) Bank officials stated that all property covered by article 2 "blocked" and agreed to submit full particulars regarding practical effect of such blocking.

In their earlier informal conversations with Ministry of Finance and Central Bank officials Cochran and Meltzer had been assured of the sincere desire of these officials to implement Resolution V. The new decrees were cited as concrete evidence. Further proof of this determination was promised. Yesterday the bank officials welcomed the criticisms discussed above.

These officials indicated a reluctance to seek legislation which would confer more specific authority to control internal transactions lest this intensify existing political criticism that the Central Bank has excessive power over the country's economy. However, the bank officials promised immediately to attempt to tighten the decrees. They could not say yesterday whether this would be through revision of the bills about to be introduced or through regulations issued under the existing decrees or under any new enabling legislation. They appeared anxious to strengthen their administration of foreign property in order both to stop undesirable transactions and to enable their delegation in Washington to meet questions and criticisms offered by other countries.

The bank officials were informed that the Embassy prior to the issuance of the decrees had received instructions which would be the basis of representations to appropriate officials of the Government. It was suggested to the bank officials that such representations particularly while the administration of the decrees was in a formative state, might assist the bank in achieving its program by making the Argentine Government agreeable to a vigorous implementation of Resolution V.

A full analysis of decrees and report on a wide range of other subjects covered in conversations will follow by next courier.

Please send copy to Secretary of Treasury.

ARMOUR

840.51 Frozen Credits/6784 : Telegram

The Secretary of State to the Ambassador in Argentina (Armour)

WASHINGTON, June 23, 1942—6 p. m.

932. Your 1146, June 15, midnight. Please express to the appropriate Argentine officials this Government's appreciation of the steps taken by Argentina to implement Resolution V as evidenced by the three recently issued decrees. However, you should indicate discreetly that this Government hopes that the administration of these decrees will result in the implementation of the aims of Resolution V to the fullest extent and that any subsequent decrees or legislation which may be found necessary will be speedily enacted.

Due to the fact that the decrees by their terms apply to allied nations outside the Western Hemisphere as well as to the Axis powers, the Department does not feel that it should encourage any publicity until the Argentine Government is prepared publicly to clarify its position on this point.

HULL

840.51 Frozen Credits/7398

Memorandum of Conversation, by the Second Secretary of Embassy in Argentina (Gantenbein) [89]

Mr. Hughes [90] and Mr. Gantenbein called on Dr. Prebisch by appointment today in regard to various matters concerning foreign-funds control and related matters. It was pointed out to Dr. Prebisch that several months ago the Embassy had informed the Central Bank that it had been instructed to discuss with the banks interested in obtaining certain credits from the Export-Import Bank their relations with the firms on the Proclaimed List and that after inquiring whether the Central Bank would be disposed to obtain the desired information, the Embassy was informed that it was preferred that it discuss the matter directly with the interested banks. It was noted that several weeks ago he, Dr. Prebisch, had expressed disapproval of a sentence in the standardized form which the Embassy was asking the banks to sign in the matter * on the theory that this was tantamount to assuming powers of control that had been given to the Central Bank by various measures (including the decrees of June 15 and 17, 1942); that the Embassy had not subsequently discussed such a commitment with those banks which had not already subscribed to it; that on August 1, Dr. Louro [91] had informed the Embassy of his (Dr. Prebisch's) disapproval of the Embassy's action in requesting of the Banco de la Provincia, by instruction, information concerning its outstanding credit accounts with firms on the Proclaimed List now and a year ago; and that the Embassy was in a quandary as to how to obtain this information. Dr. Prebisch said that the Central Bank was placed in a delicate position in the matter and that while he and his Bank had every wish to be cooperative, this "interference" by the Embassy was creating an unfavorable impression.

Dr. Prebisch was told that, as had been said on previous occasions, the Embassy had not the slightest intention or desire to interfere in the banking affairs of Argentina; that it did not see any semblance whatsoever of interference in asking for this information from a bank that had applied for a credit in the United States, especially in view of the fact that the Central Bank had expressly asked the Embassy to discuss the matter directly with the banks; but that if the Central

---

[89] Copy transmitted to the Department by the Ambassador in his despatch No. 6000, August 5; received August 17.

[90] Thomas L. Hughes, Commercial Attaché.

*Namely, the commitment that the banks would consult with the Embassy before making remittances to Axis-occupied or controlled countries or to any European neutral country if any person in any Axis-occupied or controlled country had an interest, giving the Embassy the full details of the contemplated transaction. [Footnote in the original.]

[91] Alfredo Louro, official of the Banco Central.

Bank took the position that it did not now wish the Embassy to seek the information, it would be appreciated if the Central Bank would furnish the data itself.

Dr. Prebisch said that he would endeavor to obtain the information, and when asked whether he would also obtain figures relating to the Banco de la Nación, the Banco Español del Rio de la Plata, and the Banco Popular Argentina, irrespective of the Export-Import Bank credits, he replied that he would try to obtain these also, although he added that in all cases he could furnish only the global figures and not the amounts according to the names of the firms receiving the credits.

At this point, Dr. Prebisch asked whether the United States Government took the position that no credits should be granted to firms on the Proclaimed List, even if the national economy would be thereby prejudiced. He was told in reply that it would seem that the best solution for all parties in such cases would be the appointment of interventors who would see to it that the firms in question did not apply resources to Axis uses, and that under such circumstances there would not seem to be the same objection to the granting of credit facilities by Argentine banks. Dr. Prebisch indicated that he was in sympathy with this position and that it was his intention to proceed along the lines of the reorganization in the Martini & Rossi and Pirelli cases. In this connection, he said that the interventors in the initial thirteen firms, as well as the special inspectors in the two German banks (the Embassy's Despatch no. 5790 of July 21, 1942 [93]) had already commenced their work.

When asked whether there were any recent developments regarding the two draft laws covering the expropriation and management of certain enterprises which were to have been submitted to Congress some weeks ago (the Embassy's Despatch no. 5598 of July 1, 1942,[93] page 3), Dr. Prebisch replied in the negative, (insofar as he knew).

Dr. Prebisch's attention was then invited to the dollar-currency control in Argentina, more specifically to the fact that while the Central Bank had given assurances that the dollar-currency market would be closed, with the exception of purchases and sales of up to $100 for travelers traveling to and from the United States, various exchange houses were continuing to quote dollar notes and that in fact a student departing for the United States was known to have purchased $700 in currency from such an establishment yesterday. Dr. Prebisch promised to look into this matter at once and indicated that such transactions would be stopped immediately.

J. W. G[ANTENBEIN]

[BUENOS AIRES,] August 5, 1942.

---

[93] Not printed.

740.00112A European War, 1939/15861

The Chargé in Argentina (Reed) to the Secretary of State

No. 6001 BUENOS AIRES, August 6, 1942.
[Received August 17.]

SIR: Referring to the Department's telegrams no. 877 of June 15, 6 p. m. and no. 1094 of July 22, 8 p. m., and the Embassy's telegram no. 1469 of July 29, 11 p. m.,[94] in regard to credits to be extended to certain Argentine banks by the Export-Import Bank of Washington covering uninsurable risks and concerning also the desire of the Department that these institutions furnish assurances of cooperation with war-time financial measures of the United States, I have the honor to report that following the receipt of the Department's telegram under reference the Embassy requested the institutions included in the Embassy's telegram no. 645 of April 10, 3 p. m.,[95] excluding the local branches of the two American Banks, to execute a form embodying the four points contained in the Department's telegram no. 827 of June 8, 11 p. m. A copy and English translation of the form are enclosed herewith.[95]

All of these institutions have now either signed the form or furnished assurances of cooperation in some other form. Shaw, Strupp and Company, Ernesto Tornquist and Company, the Banco Holandés Unido, the Banco Polaco P.K.O., the Société Générale, and the Argentaría S. A. de Finanzas have returned the form after signing it or have supplied a statement embodying in more or less the same terms the substance of the form.

The Banco Francés del Río de la Plata has informed the Embassy that it is not at this time interested in the credit facilities in question, but it has nevertheless voluntarily furnished a statement, a translation of which is enclosed herewith.[95]

The Banco de Italia y Río de la Plata has been reluctant to execute the undertaking desired as it has considered this to be inconsistent with the control exercised by the Central Bank, including the bank's recent Circular No. 293 of July 4, which prohibits banks from furnishing certain information to institutions other than the Central Bank. However, the Banco de Italia y Río de la Plata has been especially cooperative with the British Embassy for some months as this Embassy has reported in its despatches nos. 4050 of February 3, 1942, and 4211 of February 24, 1942.[96] Señor Doretti, the General Manager of the institution, called at this Embassy several weeks ago and explained that his bank was willing to cooperate in every way

---

[94] None printed.
[95] Not printed.
[96] Neither printed.

with this mission, and he has subsequently furnished a letter dated July 10, 1942, signed by himself and the President of the bank, a copy and translation of which are enclosed.[98] Inasmuch as it is understood that the Banco de Italia y Río de la Plata is in practice complying with all of the points mentioned in the form, it is recommended that the statement of this bank be accepted for purposes of the Export-Import Bank credits.

Concerning the Banco de la Provincia, the Embassy has discussed this matter a number of times with Señor Alberto Tintoré, head of the Foreign Department of the bank (reference is made also to the conversations on April 7 and April 9 reported in the Embassy's despatch no. 4710 of April 11 last). The Banco de la Provincia has consistently taken the position that while it has not been granting any new credits to firms and individuals on the Proclaimed List, it cannot, as a semi-official bank (one-half of its stock is owned by the Province of Buenos Aires, and it is the fiscal agent of the Province) give the desired assurances concerning the immediate elimination of existing credits and overdrafts. Sr. Tintoré has also volunteered the information in a spirit of frankness that there were instances, although they were few, in which his bank was obliged to advance credit to the Province which the latter might, in turn, make available to firms on the Proclaimed List for such purposes as public works, but that this was a matter over which the Bank had no control.

As to the furnishing of figures of outstanding credit accounts with firms on the Proclaimed List, the Bank was apparently prepared to supply the total figures both now and a year ago, but on August 1, the Central Bank informed the Embassy that it would consider this inconsistent with the Central Bank's own control over Argentine banks. The matter was discussed yesterday with Dr. Prebisch, the General Manager of the Central Bank, who indicated that he would have the figures for Proclaimed List accounts of the Banco de la Provincia furnished the Embassy through the Central Bank (as well as figures for certain other banks irrespective of the Export-Import Bank credits (as was reported in the Embassy's despatch no. 6000 of August 5, 1942 [99]). As soon as the Embassy receives these figures, which it is understood will be supplied within the next few days, it will transmit them to the Department by telegraph.

With respect to the approval of the undertaking of the Banco de la Provincia by its board of directors, it appears that it will not be possible to obtain this under existing conditions. As the Department is aware, the President of the Bank, Dr. Sánchez Sorondo, is sympathetic towards the totalitarian countries and is not friendly towards the United States, and if Dr. D'Olivera, the General Manager, should

---

[98] Not printed.
[99] Not printed, but see footnote 89, p. 489.

permit the matter to be aired at a meeting of the board, there is little doubt that it could cause serious complications, including impairment of Dr. D'Olivera's cooperation with our Government. Dr. D'Olivera takes the position that he has full authority to sign the declarations and that therefore nothing would be gained by presenting the subject to the board. It has also been emphasized, and Dr. Prebisch confirmed this yesterday, that the President of the Banco de la Provincia has very little power in the administration of the Bank, and in support of this statement there have been cited the Bank's statutes, which do in fact, appear to give the President only limited powers. It is reported that Dr. Sánchez Sorondo spends but very little time at the Bank, and then only to attend meetings.

In regard to the desired commitment that the Bank consult with the Embassy before making any remittance to Axis countries or to neutral countries if for the benefit of Axis interests, Dr. Prebisch had previously requested that the Embassy not ask for such an undertaking in the future as the Central Bank considered that this would conflict with its own control, especially by virtue of the powers conferred by the decrees of June 15 and June 17.

Although the signed undertaking (copy and translation enclosed herewith)[1] of the Banco de la Provincia, even if the promised figures show a material decrease in all credit accounts with Proclaimed List firms and individuals, falls short of the commitments requested in the Department's telegram no. 827 of June 8, 11 p. m., it is believed that it is as satisfactory as can be obtained under present conditions. Moreover, it is feared that if this bank should not now be placed upon the approved list of the Export-Import Bank, there would be a serious danger not only that the Banco de la Provincia would feel less inclined to pursue a cooperative policy but also that the Central Bank, which has manifested special interest in having the former included, would feel offended in the matter. Further although less important factors in the case are the facts that the Banco de la Provincia is the second largest bank in the country, that it is considered an exceptionally well managed institution, and that it has just received much favorable publicity here on the occasion of the renewal of its contract with the Province until 1986. It is, therefore, recommended that if the figures to be submitted are not, in the circumstances, definitely unsatisfactory, the Banco de la Provincia be at least tentatively included in the list of the Export-Import Bank, but with the understanding that the Embassy be furnished through the Central Bank with figures of Proclaimed List credit accounts every six months.

Respectfully yours, EDWARD L. REED

---

[1] Not printed.

811.515/1530 : Telegram

The Chargé in Argentina (Reed) to the Secretary of State

BUENOS AIRES, August 18, 1942—7 p. m.
[Received August 18—7 p. m.]

1591. Embassy's 1518, August 5, 8 p. m., and despatch No. 6125, August 14.[2] The Central Bank has informed the Embassy that it has decided to (1) issue a resolution probably tomorrow or the day after to be published in the *Official Bulletin* stating that dollar notes may not be negotiated by any one in Argentina without authorization of the Central Bank; (2) specifically inform the bank's exchange houses and agencies probably by a circular that they may not negotiate dollar notes without previous authorization of the Central Bank except in amounts up to $100 for travelers to and from the United States; (3) request the competent authorities to make an investigation with a view to prosecuting infractions of the foregoing; and (4) give general publicity in the premises through a press announcement.

REED

740.00112A European War, 1939/15861 : Airgram

The Secretary of State to the Chargé in Argentina (Reed)

WASHINGTON, August 28, 1942—6 : 05 p. m.

A-103. Your despatch 6001, August 6. The Department is not disposed to accept the modified undertaking of the Banco de la Provincia as set forth in your despatch under reference. This decision has been reached with the full realization that if the Banco de la Provincia is not included in the approved list, the Central Bank will not permit the other banks to participate in the credits of the Export-Import Bank.

It is believed in a situation of this kind, where the facilities of an instrumentality of this Government are being made available, that this Government is fully justified in insisting upon an undertaking on the part of the recipients of the benefits of these facilities which will afford some degree of assurance that the recipients will cooperate in the economic warfare policies designed to strengthen the security of the Western Hemisphere.

The modified undertaking of the Banco de la Provincia falls far short of the four points outlined in the Department's 827, June 8, 11 p. m., which the Department considers to be the minimum requirements of a satisfactory undertaking. It does not even contain an assurance that no new credits or overdrafts will be granted to Proclaimed List nationals; it merely states that the Banco de la Provincia will

---

[2] Neither printed.

not invest the proceeds of the credits received from the Export-Import Bank in operations benefiting such nationals. It is true that in a backhanded manner, the Banco de la Provincia has stated that it has decided "not to conduct credit operations with new 'enlisted' clients" but this at most means that the bank will not take new undesirable accounts and in no way limits the bank in granting new credits, et cetera, to the numerous Proclaimed List accounts already on the bank's books. The second point in the Department's suggested undertaking is not answered at all. The Banco de la Provincia does not agree in any way to eliminate existing credits and overdrafts of Proclaimed List nationals; it merely refers to the fact that such credits and overdrafts are being reduced due to the curtailing of the business of Proclaimed List nationals, which fact is in no way attributable to any policy of the bank. The third and fourth points of the Department's suggested undertaking are evaded by reference to the purported controls of the Central Bank, which, as you well know, have as yet shown no signs of being enforced effectively.

The undertaking of the Banco de Italia y Río de la Plata is likewise considered unsatisfactory. It is so vague in its terms as to be practically meaningless. If that bank is as cooperative as you state and is in effect complying with all the points of the Department's suggested undertaking, it is difficult to understand why it does not wish to confirm this in writing.

It is believed that a further approach to Prebisch might result in the giving of satisfactory undertakings by both the Banco de la Provincia and the Banco de Italia y Río de la Plata. You should indicate to Prebisch that the points embodied in the Department's suggested undertaking represent the putting into operation of the basic provisions of the resolutions of the recent Inter-American Conference on Systems of Economic and Financial Controls [3] and that the Central Bank, having subscribed to these resolutions, should certainly not want to place any obstacles in the way of activating them. You should also indicate to Prebisch that undertakings by the individual banks will afford the Central Bank ancillary and independent method of enforcing the Central Bank's own controls. With respect to the psychological argument that the giving of undertakings by the individual banks is inconsistent with the controls exercised by the Central Bank, you should inform Prebisch that the known pressure exerted by the Foreign Office leaves the Department with no alternative but to recognize that the Central Bank's controls of necessity have to be relaxed frequently irrespective of what the independent desires of the Central Bank may be. It is believed that this

---

[3] For correspondence concerning this Conference, see pp. 58 ff. For text of resolutions, see Pan American Union, Congress and Conference Series No. 39: *Final Act of the Inter-American Conference on Systems of Economic and Financial Control* (Washington, 1942).

argument, if cautiously presented, will in no way offend the Central Bank and may well strengthen the hand of the Central Bank in its attempts to resist the pressure of the Foreign Office. In the event, however, that the above outlined approach to Prebisch should prove fruitless, it may be that the Central Bank, as the agency in which the control over banking operations is centralized, will be willing to give the appropriate undertaking on behalf of all the interested banks.

Should the appropriate undertaking be forthcoming from the Banco de la Provincia, the Department is willing to forego the approval by the bank's board of directors provided the undertaking is signed by D'Olivera and you are satisfied that he has full power to sign.

The Department has noted that the Banco del Río de la Plata is not interested in the credits at this time. As a consequence, its name will not be included in the approved list with the understanding that it may be included at a future date, if it so desires, upon the giving of an appropriate undertaking.

For your information, the Export-Import Bank has informed the Department that for non-political reasons the Banco Polaco P.K.O. is not being included on the approved list.

Please proceed on this matter in the manner above outlined and keep the Department fully informed. The Export-Import Bank is being informed that pending further developments the Banco de la Provincia, the Banco de Italia y Río de la Plata and the Banco del Río de la Plata [4] should not be included in the approved list.

HULL

811.515/1549 : Telegram

The Chargé in Argentina (Reed) to the Secretary of State

BUENOS AIRES, August 29, 1942—1 p. m.
[Received 4:14 p. m.]

1658. Embassy's 1625 August 24, 8 p. m.[5] The Central Bank has issued a resolution announced in its circular No. 303 dated August 28, 1942, stating that in order to conduct operations of any nature in United States dollar notes the interested parties must obtain previous authorization of the Central Bank except for amounts up to $100 previously provided for in cases of travelers to and from the United States. The full text is being sent by air mail.

REED

---

[4] In airgram A–168, September 4, the Chargé in Argentina stated that the Embassy knew of no such institution as the "Banco del Río de la Plata". (740.00112A European War, 1939/17071)
[5] Not printed.

835.51/1514 : Telegram

The Secretary of State to the Chargé in Argentina (Reed)

WASHINGTON, September 16, 1942—11 p. m.

1385. Despatch no. 6137, August 14, 1942.[6] Central Bank's authorization of the remittance of Reichsmarks to Berlin is of deep concern to the Department. It is assumed that you have informed or will inform the Central Bank that this transaction is clearly inconsistent with Resolution No. I adopted by the recent Inter-American Conference in Washington[7] and that it is viewed with disfavor by the Department. You may also in your discretion state that authorization of transactions of this character must inevitably raise doubts concerning the general application of Argentine controls in accordance with the Resolutions adopted by the Inter-American Conference.

The British are sending similar instructions to Simon.[8]

HULL

840.51 Frozen Credits/7907

The Chargé in Argentina (Reed) to the Secretary of State

No. 6720

BUENOS AIRES, September 23, 1942.
[Received October 6.]

SIR: Referring to the Embassy's despatches nos. 5790 of July 21, 1942, and 5979 of August 5[9] (page 2), in regard to the placing of "interventors" in thirteen Axis-controlled firms here by authority of Decree no. 122,712 of June 15, 1942, I have the honor to report that occasion was taken in a conversation at the Central Bank this morning to ask Dr. Alfredo Louro of that institution what the results of these investigations had thus far been. Dr. Louro, who appeared to speak with much frankness, stated that the first phase of the investigations, consisting of efforts to ascertain to what extent contributions were being made by these German organizations for political purposes, was now virtually completed and that the interventors had reported almost no irregularities. Dr. Louro mentioned as perhaps the principal disclosure the fact that the Merck Company had made a payment to the Nazi newspaper El Pampero but said that this was connected

---

[6] Not printed.

[7] Inter-American Conference on Systems of Economic and Financial Control, June 30 to July 10, 1942; Resolution I aimed at severing completely all financial and commercial ties between the Western Hemisphere and the Axis.

[8] Walter Simon, Financial Adviser and First Secretary of the British Embassy in Argentina.

[9] Neither printed.

with advertizing which had been contracted for previous to Decree No. 110,790 of January 8, 1942 (see the Embassy's despatch no. 3865 of January 13, 1942 [11]). According to Dr. Louro, there have been contributions to various German organizations, such as athletic clubs, but he said that these were considered to have bona fide commercial or good-will value and were not of a political character. He stated that one of the thirteen firms had asked for permission to make a lump contribution to the German "Winterhilfe" fund (the Embassy's despatch no. 6722 of August [*September*] 23, 1942 [11] but that the bank had denied this request, taking the view that the contributions should be made directly by individuals within the firm.

Dr. Louro said that the next phase of the investigation would have as its purpose the ascertaining of the extent to which political activities are being financed through misleading commercial guises, such as over-payments for merchandise and services, portions of which might be used for financing German activities. He remarked that this would naturally be a more difficult task than the investigation concerning contributions.

As to the personnel being used in the investigations, Dr. Louro stated that the interventors were well-qualified income-tax inspectors, that at least one such inspector was assigned to each concern, and that it was intended to have these same persons continue with the next phase of the investigations.

The Embassy will continue to keep in close contact with the Central Bank in regard to the investigations and will not fail to make available to the appropriate officers of that institution such data in the Embassy's files concerning the experiences of the United States in analogous cases as might seem helpful.

According to Dr. Louro, a list of additional German firms to be intervened is now being prepared by the Central Bank.

Respectfully yours,   EDWARD L. REED

740.00112A European War, 1939/17071 : Airgram

The Secretary of State to the Chargé in Argentina (Reed)

WASHINGTON, September 24, 1942—6 : 30 p. m.

A–193. Your airgram A–168, September 4, 6 : 10 p. m.[12] In view of the information contained in your airgram under reference, it would appear that insistence upon the desired undertakings would

---

[11] Not printed.
[12] Not printed; it replied to the Department's airgram A–103, August 28, p. 494. In this reply the Chargé stated: "The Embassy feels that to push further at this time for more comprehensive commitments or improvements in form in the written undertakings would entail very definite risks of adverse repercussions that would be far out of proportion to the possible increased benefits." (740.00112A European War, 1939/17071).

have adverse political repercussions. Consequently, the Department is disposed to let the matter drop.

The Department upon re-examining the present attitude of the Argentine Government and the present administration of Argentine financial controls suggests that you approach the Central Bank and inform them that as satisfactory undertakings cannot be obtained from the Banco de la Provincia, the Banco de Italia y Río de la Plata, and the Banco Francés del Río de la Plata, and as the Central Bank does not wish the facilities of the Export-Import Bank to be made available to any Argentine banks unless these banks are included, this Government after carefully considering the problem will withdraw the offer of the Export-Import Bank credit arrangements made to any banks in Argentina and regard the present negotiations with all banks in Argentina as closed.

HULL

840.51 Frozen Credits/7907 : Telegram

The Acting Secretary of State to the Ambassador in Argentina (Armour)

WASHINGTON, October 13, 1942—4 : 45 p. m.

247. Your despatch no. 6720, September 23, 1942. All contributions by business enterprises to pro-Axis organizations can, of course, theoretically be attributed to commercial motives and the desire for business goodwill. However, it is believed that in a large majority of the cases an examination of the activities of the organizations involved and of the commercial advantage which could reasonably be expected to flow from contributions would indicate that the primary motive behind contributions is political, rather than economic. In this connection it would be helpful if the Central Bank would furnish the Embassy with a list of the contributions involved and if the Embassy would examine those contributions with a view to determining their commercial justification, if any. For example, contributions by a producer of raw materials, as distinguished from a retailer, would be difficult to attribute to commercial motives.

With respect to Dr. Louro's statement that the Bank would deny firms authorization to make contributions to the German "Winterhilfe" fund, but that the bank took the view that such contributions should be made directly by individuals within the firm, it should be observed that Resolution VII passed by the Inter-American Conference on Systems of Economic and Financial Control reaches transactions by natural persons, as well as those by business enterprises, if those transactions prejudice the political and economic independence or security of the hemisphere. It would seem, therefore, that under that Resolution, if contributions by firms or enterprises are banned on political grounds, individuals should also be prohibited from making those contributions. It is, of course, immaterial, from the standpoint of hemispheric security, whether a contribution to an undesirable organization is made by a business firm as a firm, or by individuals within that firm. It is suggested that you call this fact to the attention of the appropriate officers of the Central Bank.

Please keep the Department informed.

WELLES

811.515/1661 : Airgram

The Ambassador in Argentina (Armour) to the Secretary of State

BUENOS AIRES, October 28, 1942—6 : 50 p. m.
[Received November 4—5 p. m.]

A–319. Department's telegram No. 1489, October 3, 7 p. m.[14] The Embassy agrees that it would be desirable to include on the Proclaimed List any exchange houses continuing to trade in dollar currency in violation of the established Argentine control and it will submit recommendations in this sense when such cases are learned of in the future. However, the raid by the Central Bank on October 8 has apparently served to stop for the present unlawful dollar currency trade in the exchange shops, as reported in the Embassy's telegram No. 2003 of October 14, 11 p. m., and despatch No. 7092 of October 26.[15]

ARMOUR

840.51 Frozen Credits/8384

The Counselor of Embassy for Economic Affairs in Argentina (Bohan) to the Secretary of State

No. 7223
BUENOS AIRES, November 4, 1942.
[Received November 19.]

SIR: Referring to the Department's circular telegram of April 7, 9 p. m.[14] requesting monthly reviews of developments in regard to the freezing of Axis assets and other control measures, and with reference also to the Embassy's despatch no. 6819 of October 1 last,[14] I have the honor to submit the following report for the month of October:

The principal developments have been in the field of dollar-currency control. On October 8, inspectors of the Central Bank raided fifteen

[14] Not printed.
[15] Neither printed.

exchange shops that were more or less openly violating the Argentine prohibitions on trade in United States currency and the Central Bank has subsequently kept the situation so well under control that the black market has become small and very restricted (Embassy's telegram no. 2003, October 14, 11 p. m. and despatch no. 7092 of October 26, 1942 [16]). This action was taken after the Embassy had discussed the matter on a number of occasions at the Central Bank, furnishing the Bank with a copy of a report of an extensive investigation made into the operations of the exchange shops, and after the subject had been taken up with the Foreign Office by a note dated October 5, 1942, pursuant to the Department's telegram no. 1489 of October 3, 7 p. m.[17]

Following the reduction from $250 to $50 as the amount which travellers may take with them into the United States, the Central Bank informally advised the banks and exchange shops that they should decrease from $100 to $50 the amount of dollar currency which travellers proceeding from here to the United States may purchase in the local market, and it is understood that definite instructions in the matter will be issued shortly.

By a circular (No. 310) dated October 16, 1942, the Central Bank has required the banks that send dollar currency to the United States in accordance with the established procedure to report these shipments to the Central Bank. It will be recalled that the Bank had informed the Embassy on October 10 that it could not furnish, for checking purposes, the figures for currency shipments as it did not have these figures (Embassy's despatch no. 6972 of October 14, 1942 [17]). Presumably the Central Bank had not required these reports originally because of its wish to avoid giving any appearance to the public of being involved in the individual shipments, realizing that in many of these cases the currency would not be released.

No important freezing measures have been adopted during the month.

With respect to the "interventors" and special inspectors in various German firms and the two German banks here, it was reported on October 31 by an employee of a German concern that, as a result of the address at Boston of the Under Secretary of State on October 8 [18] and conversations which the Embassy had at the Central Bank (Embassy's airgram No. A–301 of October 22 and despatch no. 7118 of October 27, 1942 [16]) the Central Bank had given very strict instructions to the interventors and inspectors. The same informant added that the Central Bank had made a thorough investigation of the

---

[16] Neither printed.

[17] Not printed.

[18] For text, see Department of State *Bulletin*, October 10, 1942, p. 808; for the reaction of the Argentine Government, see memorandum of October 10 from the Argentine Embassy, p. 210.

Banco Alemán Transatlántico, going through correspondence as well as financial statements, and that as a consequence the law firm of Blousson and Mosciaro, which represents the Banco Alemán Transatlántico and a large number of other German concerns, had decided to advise its clients to remove from their places of business all incriminating papers. The same informant stated that Sr. Pahlke, manager of the German firm Tubos Mannesmann, a Proclaimed List national, was collecting such documents for the purpose of taking them to his home. (As soon as the Embassy receives a report that the papers have been thus removed it will inform the Central Bank and suggest that the Bank may wish to search Sr. Pahlke's home.)

The Embassy has been supplied by Mr. Lansing Wilcox, Resident Vice President of the First National Bank of Boston, with the following interesting figures showing the adverse effects of the war upon the deposits of the two local German banks and the Italian-controlled Banco Francés e Italiano (all three of which are on the Proclaimed List) during a period when most local banks experienced unusual prosperity:

	July 1939 Pesos	September 1942 Pesos
Banco Alemán Transatlántico	76, 000, 000	46, 000, 000
Banco Germánico de la América del Sud	47, 000, 000	31, 000, 000
Banco Francés e Italiano para la América del Sud	43, 000, 000	27, 000, 000
	166, 000, 000	104, 000, 000
All Banks	4, 020, 000, 000	5, 340, 000, 000

In the latter part of October, the Central Bank after representations by this Embassy and the British Embassy, declined to authorize the transfer locally of a large amount of securities, reported to be worth a million pesos, held here by a resident of Monte Carlo, as well as the transfer by the same party of a smaller amount to the Italian Consul at Lausanne (Embassy's despatch no. 7124 of October 28, 1942 [21]).

With respect to the blocking of funds paid for the purchase of ex-Axis ships, reference is made to the purchase by the Argentine Merchant Marine of the *Esmeralda* (Embassy's despatch no. 7019 of October 17, 1942 [21]).

Respectfully yours,   MERWIN L. BOHAN

---

[21] Not printed.

840.51 Frozen Credits/8412

The American Embassy in Argentina to the Argentine Ministry for Foreign Affairs [22]

MEMORANDUM

The Embassy of the United States of America has been informed by its Government that following the recent severing by the French Government at Vichy of diplomatic relations with the United States,[23] the Government of the United States has deemed it necessary to discontinue allowing the French Government and its agencies to have access to dollar funds held in their names in the United States. Also, all of France within continental Europe has been declared by the United States Government to be enemy territory for purposes of restrictions against communicating and trading with the enemy. Previously only occupied France had been regarded as enemy territory. This action has been taken by the Secretary of the Treasury by means of an amendment of the definition of "enemy territory" in General Ruling No. 11 of the Treasury Department,[24] which had been promulgated pursuant to the Trading with the Enemy Act and pertinent regulations relating to the freezing of funds.

Inasmuch as the Government at Vichy is known to be controlled by the governments of the aggressor countries, more especially by the German Government, it is hoped that the Government of Argentina will see fit to adopt similar economic and financial measures with respect to France and assets of the French Government within Argentina, with a view particularly to preventing the large withdrawals of funds which may be attempted immediately. Similarly, it is hoped that appropriate controls may be applied to the properties of any French nationals within Argentine territory who are known to be giving support to the aggressor nations either directly or through other countries, including those dominated by the aggressor nations. Such collaboration on the part of Argentina would necessarily add much to the effectiveness of the steps taken by the United States Government.

BUENOS AIRES, November 10, 1942.

---

[22] Copy transmitted to the Department by the Chargé in Argentina in his despatch No. 7292, November 12; received November 21.
[23] See telegram No. 1651, November 8, 8 p. m., from the Chargé in France, vol. II, p. 201.
[24] 7 *Federal Register* 2168.

811.515/1705 : Telegram

The Ambassador in Argentina (Armour) to the Secretary of State

BUENOS AIRES, November 18, 1942—4 p. m.
[Received 5 : 45 p. m.]

2310. Department's 1716, November 12, 7 p. m.[25] The Embassy is informally notifying the Central Bank that while it assumes that the exchange houses will continue to abstain from trading in dollar currency in accordance with the Central Bank's regulations, our Government has requested of the Embassy for Proclaimed List purposes the names of any firms that may do otherwise in the future. Also the Embassy is discreetly letting the possibility of listing be known among the principal exchange houses. It is believed that this procedure will accomplish the desired purposes and will avoid any feeling on the part of the Central Bank that the Embassy is interfering in its own control measures concerning dollar currency which at least for the moment are proving effective.

ARMOUR

811.515/1746

The Argentine Under Secretary for Foreign Affairs (Gache) to the American Ambassador in Argentina (Armour)[26]

[Translation]

BUENOS AIRES, November 19, 1942.

MR. AMBASSADOR: I have the pleasure to address Your Excellency in order to refer to the note of your Embassy No. 791, dated October 5 last, in which it was indicated that there had come to the attention of your Government the fact that various exchange houses and agencies of this country were not complying with the regulations issued on the subject of dollar notes.

I beg leave to inform Your Excellency that the Ministry of Finance, to which the aforementioned note had been referred for action, has advised the Foreign Office that steps have been taken to verify these acts and that, without prejudice to the measures adopted against the houses which have violated the existing regulations, there are being studied the possibilities of regulating the functioning of the agencies engaging in the purchase and sale of foreign notes and coins and of making provision for the fulfillment of certain requirements which will assure correctness and responsibility in such operations. There are at the same time being prepared certain measures intended

---

[25] Not printed.
[26] Copy transmitted to the Department by the Chargé in Argentina in his despatch No. 7546, December 1 ; received December 9.

to make as strict as possible the control over the entry and departure into and from the country of every kind of notes and securities.

I avail myself [etc.] ROBERTO GACHE

835.51/1525 : Telegram

The Secretary of State to the Ambassador in Argentina (Armour)

WASHINGTON, November 20, 1942—6 p. m.

1772. Your 2099, October 27, 11 p. m.; Department's despatch no. 3388, October 28, 1942.[27] Unless you perceive some objection, please address a communication to the Foreign Office protesting against the authorization of remittances to the head office of the Banco Hipotecario in France and point out the following:

Shortly after the collapse of France in June 1940, there was an accumulation of three or four hundred million francs in the account of the Central Bank under the Argentine-French Payments Agreement. Subsequently this Government was informed that when this fund became exhausted, Argentina would not authorize further transfers of payments to occupied or unoccupied France for the duration of the war. On April 9, 1942 it was learned that authorization had been granted for two substantial financial remittances to occupied France and that these remittances were entirely outside the Argentine-French Payment Agreement. The Foreign Office was informed that this Government considered these remittances a violation of Rio Resolution V. The Foreign Office, under date of May 8, 1942, submitted a memorandum to the effect that the remittances in question did not constitute a violation of Resolution V. This Government, after giving careful consideration to this memorandum, presented the reasons which, in its judgment, made it necessary for it to continue to consider the transactions involved inconsistent with Resolution V.

This Government has recently learned that the Argentine authorities have authorized further remittances of substantial amounts by the Banco Hipotecario Franco-Argentina to its head office in France and that these remittances are to be effected outside the French-Argentine Payments Agreement. For the reasons which this Government has previously presented remittances made by the Banco Hipotecario in the past have afforded facilities in France which might benefit the aggressor nations. Accordingly, even before the recent developments in France, it was the carefully considered view of this Government, that the authorizations in question were inconsistent not only with Resolution V adopted in Rio but also with resolutions adopted by

---

[27] Neither printed.

the Washington Conference. As a result of recent developments in France, it is now even clearer to this Government that such remittances in the future would benefit the aggressor nations. Indeed such remittances can no longer, in their practical effect, be distinguished from remittances direct to Germany. Accordingly, their authorization would be viewed with the greatest concern by this Government. It is hoped that the renewed expression of this Government's views, together with new developments in France, will result in denial of authorizations for such transactions in the future.

HULL

840.51 Frozen Credits/8454 : Telegram

The Ambassador in Argentina (Armour) to the Secretary of State

BUENOS AIRES, November 24, 1942—midnight.
[Received November 25—1 : 50 a. m.]

2367. Department's 1708, November 11, midnight [*11 p. m.*].[28] The Embassy after a full consideration of all factors definitely recommends that the Banco de la Provincia and the Banco de la Nación not be subject to *ad hoc* freezing at this time.

While the intercept and other material dealing with the operations of the banks may justify freezing, the action, directed against the two largest banks in this country, one a governmental institution and the other a semi-governmental one, would unquestionably alienate the Central Bank, gravely imperil the negotiations now under way looking towards the over-all control of subversive activities in Argentina and the cutting off of all code communications with Europe, and possibly precipitate serious reprisals against American interests in Argentina.

The Embassy has the same objective in mind as the Treasury Department, namely, cutting off all financial transactions with enemy territory and enemy nationals, as well as all transactions either direct or indirect, of benefit to the Axis. It admits that in attempting to attain this objective it can probably count but little in the line of active cooperation of the Government but it feels that any hope of accomplishment would be destroyed by the proposed action of the [Treasury?].

The Economic Counselor this afternoon discussed without gloves the entire subject of financial controls with Prebisch who definitely stated that he had sufficient powers to limit remittances in accordance with the provisions of Resolution I of Washington Conference. He is willing to examine with us possibility of tightening these con-

---

[28] Not printed; this instruction transmitted a proposal of the Treasury Department to apply freezing action or revoke licenses of certain firms (840.51 Frozen Credits/8222).

trols to the point where they will be satisfactory to Treasury Department. He further offered to carry out an inspection of all foreign dollar holdings, including securities, of Argentine banks and to block any found to be the property of the Axis; he is also willing unofficially to recognize the Proclaimed List outside of Argentina in connection with approval or disapproval of remittances and to give every facility to carry out a study of Argentine controls in relation to Rio and Washington Resolutions. As concerns credits and loans to Proclaimed List nationals within Argentina by Argentine banks Prebisch stated that so far he had no power to discriminate although he has already used his influence to the end that loans not be provided for expansion and he is willing to discuss the extension of the interventor system and other measures of control.

The Embassy does not wish to prophesy success for its proposed program of action. It feels, however, that a joint study of the control system here, to which Messrs. Mann and Skelton [29] would be assigned, holds more possibilities for constructive attainment than the freezing of the two banks.

I therefore recommend most strongly that the proposed action should not be taken.

ARMOUR

840.51 Frozen Credits/8477 : Telegram

The Ambassador in Argentina (Armour) to the Secretary of State

BUENOS AIRES, November 25, 1942—10 p. m.
[Received November 25—10 p. m.]

2382. My 2368, November 24, midnight.[30] This afternoon the Central Bank outlined its position with reference to action reported in Department's 1775, November 20, 9 p. m.[30] Central Bank stated that it felt only two avenues were open to the Treasury Department, (1) either to consider Argentina as a neutral country and apply the controls in that manner, or (2) to consider Argentina as a member of the hemisphere block and have confidence in the controls exercised by the Central Bank. The bank recognized that Argentina actually fell in neither of these categories. In his [*its?*] judgment it could not totally cut off financial relations with the Axis until political relations had been broken by the Government, but felt that it had made an honest attempt to cooperate in the implementation of the Washington Resolutions and that it had not fallen far short of compliance with those Resolutions. It admitted that it had been unable to go as far as

[29] James Harold Mann and Byron George Skelton, Special Assistants in the Department of State assigned to the Embassy in Argentina.
[30] Not printed.

the Treasury might desire, but felt that the cooperation given the United States by the Central Bank was far from neutral and even hazardous considering Government's position.

It stated that the action taken by the Treasury Department against the Banco de la Provincia and the Banco de la Nación was a very grave step since, if the action had been taken as a result of remittances by those banks, the Treasury Department should have penalized the Central Bank which was the responsible party rather than the institutions themselves. Furthermore should any remittances have been made by the banks without the approval of the Central Bank the matter then became one for action by the Central Bank rather than by the Treasury Department. The Central Bank stated that it must request information of the Treasury Department as to the concrete reasons for having taken the action since, unless it could tell the local banks exactly why the action had been taken, its moral authority would be completely undermined.

The offer made yesterday by Prebisch to study the entire situation with officers of the Embassy was re-emphasized and the bank stated that it would give every facility for a thorough joint survey. It is willing clearly to define the extent to which it can go so that the Treasury Department will know exactly what is possible, but it feels that the Treasury Department will have to work either with or against the bank.

The Embassy feels that at the present moment neither the Treasury nor the Department is in possession of sufficient facts to determine definitely whether the cooperation of the Central Bank is of greater value than the sum total of remittances which take place and it feels that it would be extremely unwise for any drastic action to be taken by the Treasury Department until the facts are established. The Embassy is not requesting an indefinite stay of action on the part of the Treasury, but it does request a reasonable time in which to go to the bottom of the entire question of financial controls.

The bank is ready to start discussions and it requests an immediate reply with regard to the specific charges against the Banco de la Provincia and the Banco de la Nación. The Embassy wishes to warn the Department that the conversations which have taken place were completely without protocol and hence the information given herein regarding the attitude of the Central Bank should not be discussed in any way with the Argentine Embassy in Washington and must otherwise be kept confidential.

A reply to the Central Bank's request and an authorization to enter into discussions with the bank would be appreciated by Saturday at the latest.

ARMOUR

840.51 Frozen Credits/8477 : Telegram

The Secretary of State to the Ambassador in Argentina (*Armour*)

WASHINGTON, November 28, 1942—7 p. m.

1846. From Acheson. Your 2367,[32] 2368 [33] and 2382.[34] The Department concurs with the recommendations in your 2367. The information which was the basis for denying new credits to the Banco de la Provincia and the Banco de la Nación is being revised and will probably be made available to the Central Bank. Please do not make any commitments in this connection. It may be desirable to indicate that the two banks and the Central Bank must already be aware of the reasons underlying the Treasury action.

You are authorized to undertake with the Central Bank such discussions of the Argentine controls as you deem appropriate. It is requested, however, that you not give the impression that the extension of United States controls will be suspended until the discussions are completed. In connection with these discussions, you might point out to the Central Bank that it would be helpful if the Department, as a first step, could be promptly furnished with the following information regarding the two banks:

a) The volume of remittances effected by each bank to Europe during the last year, broken down by countries, with an indication of the volume of remittances in which a Proclaimed List interest was involved.

b) The volume of remittances effected to or for Proclaimed List nationals within this hemisphere during each month since the promulgation of the Proclaimed List.

c) The average volume of credits which each bank has had outstanding to Proclaimed List interests within this hemisphere each month since the promulgation of the Proclaimed List, broken down by countries.

d) The amount of credits which have been extended to, or renewed for, Proclaimed List interests each month since the promulgation of the Proclaimed List.

Please promptly inform the Department regarding the Central Bank's reaction to the request for this information and indicate the time when it will be available.

A more detailed reply follows. [Acheson.]

HULL

---

[32] Dated November 24, midnight, p. 506.
[33] Not printed.
[34] *Supra.*

840.51 Frozen Credits/8477 : Telegram

The Secretary of State to the Ambassador in Argentina (Armour)

WASHINGTON, December 11, 1942—10 p. m.

1933.   Your 2382, November 25; Department's 1846, November 28. Treasury action denying new credits to the Banco de la Provincia and the Banco de la Nación is based on information which reveals that these institutions have engaged in the following activities of benefit to the Axis:

(a) *Banco de la Provincia.*

1. Has received deposits for and executed payments to official and non-official agents of Germany, Italy and Japan.

2. Has performed numerous services for German, Italian and Japanese banks in Argentina, such as receiving accounts and making remittances on behalf of such banks and extending facilities to their clients in cooperation with the Axis banks.

3. Has made numerous remittances to Axis and Axis-occupied territory.

4. Has made collections for, extended credit to, and rendered numerous other services for Proclaimed List nationals.

5. Has refused to sign an undertaking to grant no new credits to Proclaimed List persons and to eliminate existing drafts and overdrafts of such persons. The proposed undertaking was submitted to all the banks in Argentina in connection with a plan for extension of credit by the Export-Import Bank.

6. Has for over a year regularly published a full-page advertisement in extreme pro-Axis propaganda publication.

7. The Embassy has reported that the President of the institution has clearly demonstrated his Nazi sympathies and has been associated in business transactions with known pro-Axis individuals.

(b) *Banco de la Nación.*

1. Has transferred funds to Axis territory, notably remittances to Italy on behalf of the Italian Foreign Exchange Institute and remittances of reichsmarks to the Deutsche Verrechungskasse.

2. Has executed payments to Italian and German officials in Argentina.

3. Has transferred funds to neutral countries, particularly Switzerland and Portugal, for the account of enemy banks.

4. Has transferred funds for Proclaimed List banks and other Proclaimed List nationals.

5. Has extended credit facilities to Proclaimed List firms.

6. Has for over a year regularly published full-page advertisement in extreme pro-Axis propaganda journal.

The foregoing evidence shows clearly that the banks have engaged in widespread activities directly and indirectly beneficial to the Axis nations. It should be pointed out that under these circumstances the United States obviously cannot indirectly increase the economic resources and power of its enemies by furnishing its facilities for the support of such objectionable activities.

You may in your discretion present all or part of the above information to the Central Bank. You may perhaps feel that point no. 5 under the Banco de la Provincia should not be raised since the undertaking in question was submitted by the United States solely in connection with the proposed Export-Import Bank transaction and without any intimation that a refusal to sign would be considered as a reason for applying sanctions against the bank. It is suggested also that before submitting the above information a further check should be made with the Embassy's files and with the British Embassy for the purpose of securing any additional information which you may wish to present along with the data contained herein.

HULL

840.51 Frozen Credits/8477 : Airgram

The Secretary of State to the Ambassador in Argentina (Armour)

WASHINGTON, December 14, 1942—2 : 20 p. m.

A–468. Your 2367, November 24; your 2382, November 25; and Department's 1846, November 28, 7 p. m. The following is sent for your information and for such use as you may deem appropriate:

(*a*) The Department must reject the view of the Central Bank that the latter's approval of transactions which benefit the enemy insulates the commercial banks consummating those transactions against the application of United States controls. The logic of the Central Bank's position would immunize all pro-Axis Argentine entities against United States controls since their pro-Axis activities often involve the tacit acquiescence or the affirmative approval of the Argentine Government.

(*b*) The Department welcomes Prebisch's proffer of cooperation so far as it goes, and approves the joint study. However, the following considerations create some doubt as to the good faith of the proposal and some suspicion that it may be a delaying action and no more.

1. The Central Bank for a long time has claimed adequate authority to cut off pro-Axis remittances. However, as a matter of administration, that authority has not always been exercised, and some remittances benefiting the Axis have been going forward from Argentina. Whether those remittances result from pressure by the Foreign Office or the Ministry of Finance upon the Central Bank, or from the Bank's own attitude does not change the fact that these remittances are aiding the enemy.

2. Although a joint study of the Argentine controls may be useful, it seems clear that as a result of the Embassy's continuing efforts, discussions between the Central Bank and special missions from the Department, and the Washington Conference, Prebisch is already well aware of our objectives and of the deficiencies in existing Argentine control measures. It would appear that it is not informa-

tion the Central Bank needs but the willingness, or the authority from the Foreign Office, to eliminate pro-Axis transactions. It is recognized, of course, that there are some marginal cases which the Central Bank may handle along lines designed to protect allied interest, notwithstanding that the Foreign Office might pursue a different approach. However, basically, the policy of the Central Bank will, of course, be governed by Argentina's overall foreign policy. It would therefore seem necessary to secure the support of the Foreign Office before a substantial strengthening of the Argentine controls will be effected.

3. With reference to the Central Bank's statement that its influence has been exerted to prevent expansion of the commercial activities of Proclaimed List nationals, the Department would welcome the Embassy's comments as to whether the bank's claim is well founded. In this connection it will be helpful to know whether Proclaimed List nationals who are not vulnerable to our controls and who are in a position to expand their commercial operations have experienced any difficulty in securing the necessary credit. With respect to Proclaimed List nationals adversely affected by our controls, there would, of course, be little occasion for expansion, and if such cases arose, it would appear that prudent private banking would dictate against the expansion of credit to such Proclaimed List nationals.

4. Thus far, the Argentine interventor system does not appear to have been more than a ceremony—except for its possible deterrent effect. In connection with any discussions of that system, it would seem desirable to emphasize the need for making it an effective anti-Axis weapon in these cases where it is used, as well as for extending its use.

(c) The Bank's promise to inspect all foreign dollar holdings of Argentine banks and to block any found to be the property of the Axis is not entirely clear. If by the "Axis" is meant the Axis Governments, the promise is very narrow and even a good faith effort at performance will probably not be very fruitful. However, if the "Axis" includes the property of all pro-Axis individuals, e.g., all persons on the Proclaimed List, a vigorous inspection by the Bank may prove very useful.

HULL

835.51/1530 : Telegram

The Ambassador in Argentina (Armour) to the Secretary of State

BUENOS AIRES, December 17, 1942—5 p. m.
[Received 6 : 55 p. m.]

2575. Department's instruction 2895, August 3, 1942; 2789, July 17, 1942; [35] and Embassy's 2382, November 25, 10 p. m., 1942. In conversations yesterday with officials of the Central Bank regarding Argentine financial controls, officials of the Embassy pointed out that

---

[35] Neither printed.

the remittance of 1,909,000 pesos to Germany, Italy, France (occupied and unoccupied) and occupied countries during August, September, October and November this year for family aid was contrary to Resolution I of the Washington Conference. Central Bank officials insisted that this was not true and that they had made their position clear on this point to the Treasury during the Conference and that their position in general on financial controls was clearly outlined in a memorandum handed to Foley on July 2, 1942.[36] They vigorously maintained that the entire memorandum constituted the interpretation of the reservation finally drafted by Argentina to the resolutions passed at the Conference, and that such memorandum was so terminated [construed?] by representatives of Department and Treasury. Gagneux [37] stated that he had fully explained Argentina position to Collado,[38] White, Pehle, and Bernstein.[39] Central Bank admits that this memorandum was not generally known to other delegates at the Conference as a reservation but insists that a gentleman's agreement was made between themselves, Department and Treasury. Embassy does not so understand the document as written nor as commented upon in the instruction transmitting it as being a reservation. Bank considers such memorandum a reservation, has acted upon that basis in the past and intends to act upon that basis in the future.

Please discuss with Treasury and telegraph comments relative to Central Bank position indicated above as soon as possible because conversations with bank cannot progress until point clarified. If Argentine understanding is not in accord with that of Department and Treasury, please phrase telegram so that paraphrase may be given to Central Bank.

ARMOUR

835.51/1530 : Telegram

The Secretary of State to the Ambassador in Argentina (*Armour*)

WASHINGTON, December 26, 1942—7 p. m.

2021. Your 2575, December 17, 5 p. m. Memorandum submitted to Department and Treasury during conference was merely a statement of Argentine controls as they then existed and was discussed with the Department and Treasury on that basis. It was a statement of the

---

[36] Not printed; Edward H. Foley was General Counsel of the Department of the Treasury. A copy of the memorandum was submitted also to the Department of State.

[37] Edmundo Gagneux, Assistant General Manager of the Central Bank.

[38] Emilio G. Collado, Executive Secretary of the Board of Economic Operations of the Department of State.

[39] Harry D. White and John W. Pehle, Assistants to the Secretary of the Treasury; Bernard Bernstein, Assistant General Counsel, Department of the Treasury.

Argentine position but was not at any time considered by the Treasury or the Department as an interpretation of the reservation finally drafted by Argentina and was not discussed as such with the Argentine delegates. Gagneux's statement that a gentleman's agreement was made between the Argentine delegates, the Department and the Treasury is contrary to our understanding and any such agreement would obviously be counter to the procedure of international conferences if not known by all of the delegates. Please inform Gagneux that Department and Treasury have never considered the memorandum referred to as an interpretation of the reservation finally drafted by Argentina and that a continuance of the remittances referred to will be regarded by the Department and the Treasury as inconsistent with the resolutions adopted at the conference.

HULL

AGREEMENT BETWEEN THE UNITED STATES AND ARGENTINA PROVIDING FOR THE WAIVER OF PASSPORT VISA FEES, SIGNED APRIL 15, 1942

[For text of the agreement, signed at Buenos Aires, see Department of State Executive Agreement Series No. 266, or 56 Stat. (pt. 2) 1578.]

BOLIVIA

ASSISTANCE BY THE UNITED STATES TO BOLIVIA IN DEFENSE MEASURES

710. Consultation 3/489 : Telegram

The Chargé in Bolivia (Dawson) to the Secretary of State

La Paz, January 26, 1942—8 p. m.
[Received 11 : 55 p. m.]

40. Following telegram has been sent to the Embassy, Rio de Janeiro.

"January 26, 8 p. m. For the Under Secretary.[1] Your January 24, 5 p. m. Acting Minister for Foreign Affairs[2] this afternoon showed me telegram sent yesterday to Bolivian Minister for Foreign Affairs[3] in Rio de Janeiro authorizing him to announce that Bolivian Government confirmed its intention to break off relations with Axis Powers. Telegram went on to tell Anze he should secure following commitments from you as preliminary to issuance of decree enacting rupture used [*sic*].

1. Guarantee that United States would protect Bolivia from aggression by Axis Powers against the 'other nations'.
2. Increase in capital of Bolivian Development Corporation[4] to 'at least $40,000,000'.
3. Increase in prices for Bolivian minerals sold to Metals Reserve and substitution of f.o.b. Chilean ports for c.i.f. United States ports in tin contract.[5]

Acting Minister for Foreign Affairs stated to me that actual breach would take place within 2 or 3 days if these conditions were met. It seems obvious that Anze exceeded instructions in his speech at Plenary session announcing rupture . . .

. . . .

I have an interview with the President[6] at 11 a. m. tomorrow at which I shall endeavor to present matters in such a light as to secure

---

[1] Sumner Welles was representing the United States at the Third Meeting of the Foreign Ministers of the American Republics at Rio de Janeiro, January 15–28, 1942 ; for correspondence on this Meeting, see pp. 6 ff.
[2] Justo Rodas Eguino.
[3] Eduardo Anze Matienzo.
[4] For correspondence concerning this Corporation, see section entitled "Program for economic cooperation between the United States and Bolivia", pp. 592 ff.
[5] See *Foreign Relations*, 1940, vol. v, pp. 524 ff.
[6] Gen. Enrique Peñaranda y del Castillo.

immediate issuance of decree breaking relations. Will submit full report thereafter.

Repeated to Department as my 40, January 26, 8 p. m."

DAWSON

---

710. Consultation 3/503 : Telegram

The Chargé in Bolivia (Dawson) to the Secretary of State

LA PAZ, January 27, 1942—3 p. m.
[Received January 28—3 : 50 a. m.]

41. My January 26, 8 p. m.[8]   President assured me today that indication in telegram from Acting Minister for Foreign Affairs to Anze that its three points were prerequisite to breaking off relations with Axis Powers was result of hasty drafting; that points were merely outline of economic and defense aid which it was hoped the United States would be able to give Bolivia in due course.

The President stated categorically that decree breaking off relations would be issued in 2 or 3 days at the latest and that delay was due solely to necessity for first taking steps to protect mines and other strategic points and to deal with dangerous Axis nationals. In support of this he mentioned minor sabotage which has been attempted in last few days.

The President also showed great perturbation over vulnerability of Bolivian mines to attack by carrier-based Japanese aircraft having received note from Japanese Chargé d'Affaires making threats if relations are broken.

He asked me to ascertain whether it would be possible to secure temporary stationing in Bolivia of at least a flight of United States Army pursuit planes pending the arrival of planes and anti-aircraft artillery which Bolivia has requested under Lend-Lease.[9] He stressed that this should not be taken as offering of air bases and that actual use of planes for patrol and other purposes would be by agreement between their commander and Bolivian military authorities. He added that he was not now making a request for such planes but would make it if they were available and details would be arranged.

If planes could be made available from Canal Zone or elsewhere I believe it would have very beneficial effect. Their presence would bolster morale of weak Bolivian Government and people and might have salutary influence on Chile and Argentina. Undoubtedly some

---

[8] *Supra.*

[9] For correspondence on Lend-Lease negotiations between Bolivia and the United States, see *Foreign Relations*, 1941, vol. VI, section under Bolivia entitled "Negotiation of a Lend-Lease Agreement with Bolivia, signed December 6, 1941."

means of considering planes and personnel as part of military aviation mission [10] could be worked out if thought desirable.

My impression from conversations yesterday and today is that Bolivians hoped to get definite commitments from us on three points before breaking off relations but that they have abandoned this in fear that economic cooperation will be endangered if they delay breach, having gotten this idea from telegrams from Anze and Zulme.

They are, however, honestly panicky about sabotage and possibility of attack. That they have been warned of possibility of sabotage continually since December 7 by Legation and have taken no action until faced by necessity for breaking off relations is beside the point. What is essential now is to calm them and help them organize to deal with possible danger.

In addition to arrangements if possible for sending of United States Army Air Corps detachment recommend strongly that an experienced field officer of Air Corps be sent immediately to head aviation mission (present chief is in Panama on sick leave and will probably not return) . . .

. . . .

Summary of important points above sent to Under Secretary at Rio de Janeiro as my January 27, 3 p. m.

DAWSON

---

710. Consultation 3/587

The Chargé in Bolivia (Dawson) to the Secretary of State

No. 1639   LA PAZ, January 29, 1942.
                                        [Received February 5.]

SIR: With reference to the third paragraph of my telegram No. 41 of January 27, 3 p. m., in which it was stated that the Bolivian Government had received a note from the Japanese Chargé d'Affaires ad interim threatening Bolivia if diplomatic relations should be broken off, I have the honor to report that this note was read to me by the Acting Minister of Foreign Affairs in the presence of the President on January 27.

The note, couched in execrable Spanish, partook of the nature of an ultimatum. It started out by referring to the "glorious Japanese victories" and the forthcoming consolidation of the "Greater East Asia Sphere of Co-Prosperity", said that Japan expected to renew its commercial relations with the countries of Latin America "even before the termination of the War", remarked that the United States had promised to buy Latin American surplus raw products and to

---

[10] For correspondence, see *Foreign Relations*, 1941, vol. VI, section under Bolivia entitled "Agreement between the United States and Bolivia for a military aviation mission . . ."

furnish its countries with needed finished materials but would be unable to do so because of its critical economic position, added that Japan had no designs upon Latin America, commented upon the fact that "certain discussions are going on at Rio de Janeiro", stated that "the countries of South America do not appear to take a breach of relations seriously" but that Japan does as a step toward which would lead inevitably to War "with grave prejudice to those foolhardy enough to take the step" and warned Bolivia that, if it should break off relations, the consequences would be its own responsibility.

The Peruvian Minister to Bolivia [12] has informed me that he has been advised that his Government had received an "impertinent" note from the Japanese Minister in Lima warning it of the consequences of a breach of relations. It would thus appear that the note delivered in La Paz was a circular sent from the Japanese Foreign Office to its missions in South America or the local Chargé d'Affaires' interpretation of general instructions.

The Acting Minister of Foreign Affairs told me today that neither the Italian Minister nor the German Chargé d'Affaires ad interim had made any representations to the Bolivian authorities in regard to a possible breach of relations, either by note or orally, as reported in my despatch No. 1640 of January 29, 1942,[13] mild representations in this sense have, however, been made by the Papal Nuncio.

Respectfully yours,   ALLAN DAWSON

740.0011 European War 1939/19143

The Bolivian Chargé (Dorado) to the Secretary of State

[Translation]

WASHINGTON, January 29, 1942.

EXCELLENCY: I have the honor to inform Your Excellency that I have received instructions from my Government to communicate to Your Excellency that there was signed yesterday the Decree by which diplomatic relations between my country and Germany, Italy, and Japan were severed.

The attitude of my Government is based on the Declaration issued by the Second Consultative Meeting of the Ministers of Foreign Affairs held at Habana,[14] in which it was agreed to give a continental character to any act of aggression against an American country, and on the Recommendation concerning severance of relations with Axis

---

[12] José Enrique Bustamante y Corzo.
[13] Not printed.
[14] Resolution XV of the Final Act of this meeting held July 21–30, 1940; Department of State *Bulletin*, August 24, 1940, pp. 127, 136.

countries approved by the Third Consultative Meeting at Rio de Janeiro.[15]

Your Excellency will realize that my country, by this action, reaffirms its spirit of cooperation and continental solidarity, giving effect to the commitments contracted during inter-American conferences.

I take advantage [etc.] CARLOS DORADO

740.0011 European War, 1939/19143

The Secretary of State to the Bolivian Chargé (*Dorado*)

WASHINGTON, January 30, 1942.

SIR: I have received your communication of January 29, 1942 informing me, under instructions from your Government, that the Bolivian Government has severed diplomatic relations with Germany, Italy, and Japan.

This welcome information has been given to the President of the United States and he has sent the following telegram directly to His Excellency the President of the Republic of Bolivia:

"The Chargé d'Affaires of Bolivia in Washington has officially informed this Government that Your Excellency's Government has severed diplomatic relations with Germany, Italy, and Japan.

"This action by the Government of Bolivia reaffirms again in a very practical manner the attitude of the people and Government of Bolivia toward the aggressor nations which threaten the safety of the institutions and principles of this Hemisphere.

"The firm stand taken by Your Excellency and Your Excellency's Government in support of practical and effective inter-American solidarity, and the very real contribution made by Your Excellency's Minister of Foreign Affairs at the Consultative Meeting in Rio de Janeiro, have greatly strengthened the spirit of collaboration which now exists between the Republics of this Hemisphere.

"Permit me, Excellency, in sending you my own best wishes, to express my confidence in the continued effectiveness of cooperation between our two Governments in the defense of the Hemisphere."

The firm position taken by the Bolivian Government in severing relations with Axis powers is profoundly gratifying to me personally, and I wish to express my confidence in the effective results that will inevitably flow from this increasingly strong collaboration between the Republics of the Hemisphere.

Accept [etc.] For the Secretary of State:
A. A. BERLE, JR.

---

[15] Resolution I of the Final Act of this meeting held January 15–28, 1942; Department of State *Bulletin*, February 7, 1942, pp. 117, 118.

710. Consultation 3/590

The Chargé in Bolivia (Dawson) to the Secretary of State

No. 1661   LA PAZ, February 2, 1942.
                                            [Received February 7.]

SIR: I have the honor to refer to my telegrams Nos. 40 of January 26, 8 p. m., and 41 of January 27, 3 p. m., both in regard to negotiations at Rio de Janeiro between the Bolivian Minister of Foreign Affairs and the Undersecretary in regard to certain economic questions affecting Bolivia and the United States.

As I reported to the Undersecretary at Rio de Janeiro in a telegram dated January 28, 1 p. m., which was not repeated to the Department, I have seen most of the exchange of telegrams between the Bolivian Minister of Foreign Affairs, in Rio de Janeiro, and his Government covering the various problems discussed at Rio de Janeiro, i. e., the question of Bolivia's breaking diplomatic relations with the Axis powers, that of the establishment of a Bolivian Development Corporation and that of the settlement of the Standard Oil problem in Bolivia.[16] Some of these telegrams were shown to me by the President and others by the Acting Minister of Foreign Affairs.

Prior to Dr. Anze Matienzo's departure for Rio de Janeiro, I had had extensive conversations with him about all of these matters. He had assured me of his complete support for a general breach of relations with the Axis powers by all of the American Republics. As stated in my telegrams Nos. 6 of January 5, 2 p. m.,[17] and 13 of January 7, 7 p. m.,[18] to the Undersecretary, Dr. Anze Matienzo had made it clear that he hoped to get Mr. Welles to sign some sort of a commitment for implementing the plan of economic cooperation between the two countries and to make an attempt to settle the Standard Oil question while at the Rio de Janeiro Consultative Meeting.

It was in order to present the Legation's and Economic Mission's considered opinion as to the best method of dealing with the first point and having a concrete proposal ready for consideration by Mr. Welles instead of relying on Dr. Anze Matienzo's rather vague ideas that Mr. Bohan [19] prepared the general outline of a Bolivian Development Corporation embodied in my telegram No. 5 of January 5, 11 a. m.[20] This seems to have formed the basis of the agreements on

---

[16] For correspondence on the negotiations between Bolivia and the Standard Oil Co., see pp. 586 ff.

[17] Not printed.

[18] *Post*, p. 586.

[19] Merwin L. Bohan, Chief of the U. S. Economic Mission to Bolivia.

[20] Not printed; for correspondence on the economic cooperation program, see pp. 592 ff.

this point signed by Mr. Welles and Dr. Anze Matienzo at Rio de Janeiro.[21]

So far as the Standard Oil question was concerned, Dr. Anze Matienzo told me that he had secured President Peñaranda's permission to take the matter up at Rio de Janeiro somewhat against the President's own judgment but that he was willing to stake his political future on reaching a settlement and pushing it through on his return from Rio de Janeiro. In our conversations, we discussed possible formulas and amounts which might be paid which coincide closely with the agreement finally reached between Dr. Anze Matienzo and Mr. Herman A. Metzger, representative of the Standard Oil Company of New Jersey, as quoted in the Department's telegram No. 39 of January 28, 9 p. m.[22]

It seemed advisable to have Mr. Bohan go to Rio de Janeiro to assist in the conversations since he was the originator of the plan for a Bolivian Development Corporation and since the carrying out of any commitments which might be made at Rio de Janeiro would fall to the Economic Mission and the Development Corporation. Furthermore, I had discussed with him at length the ideas of Dr. Anze Matienzo concerning a Standard Oil settlement and it seemed that he could assist in that matter also. I accordingly telegraphed to the Undersecretary at Rio de Janeiro under date of January 9, 3 p. m.,[23] suggesting that Mr. Bohan be detailed to Rio de Janeiro to assist in the conversations with Dr. Anze Matienzo. The Undersecretary replied in a telegram of January 13, 1 p. m.,[23] asking that Mr. Bohan go to Rio de Janeiro immediately and this was confirmed by the Department in its telegram No. 17 of January 14, 2 p. m.[23] Mr. Bohan left on the latter date.

I had also arranged with Dr. Anze Matienzo before his departure to have Mr. Guillermo Mariaca go to Rio de Janeiro if Mr. Bohan were detailed there. Mr. Mariaca is the Bolivian official who has been most sensible in his approach to the Standard Oil problem and has for years endeavored in every way possible to support a settlement when no other Bolivian authority would touch the matter. It seemed evident that ensuring his advice for Dr. Anze Matienzo would be helpful toward the objective of a fair settlement.

On January 26 after the Consultative Meeting was under way, the Acting Minister of Foreign Affairs, Mr. Justo Rodas Eguino, showed me telegrams from Dr. Anze Matienzo in which the latter described in general terms the agreements he was reaching with the Undersecretary

---

[21] See pp. 592–595.
[22] *Post*, p. 587.
[23] Not printed.

in regard to the Bolivian Development Corporation, covering an authorized capital of $25,000,000 and a loan from the Export-Import Bank of $10,000,000, as well as the proposed Standard Oil settlement. Dr. Anze Matienzo urged strongly that the Bolivian Cabinet take action to break diplomatic relations with the Axis powers and that he be authorized to announce at the Consultative Meeting that this had been done.

When he handed me these telegrams, Mr. Rodas Eguino also showed me his reply, stating that it had been drawn up at a Cabinet meeting and approved by the President and Cabinet. This reply did not touch on the Standard Oil questions. It told Dr. Anze Matienzo that he could announce at the Consultative Meeting that the Bolivian Government confirmed its intention to break relations with the Axis powers (not that it had done so) and asked him to secure commitments from the Undersecretary that:

1. the United States would guarantee Bolivia against any aggression by the Axis powers or *other nations;*
2. the capital of the Bolivian Development Corporation should be $40,000,000 instead of $25,000,000;
3. prices for the Bolivian minerals sold to the Metals Reserve Company would be raised, and
4. these prices would be figured f.o.b. Chilean ports (they already are in the tungsten contract but not in the tin contract) instead of c.i.f. New York.

It was stated clearly in the telegram to Dr. Anze Matienzo that these were to be considered as a "preliminary" to breaking relations. While the telegram did not say when the Bolivian Government would break relations with the Axis powers, Mr. Rodas Eguino told me that this would take place within two or three days *if* the above conditions were met.

I accordingly telegraphed a summary of the telegram and conversation to the Undersecretary and repeated this to the Department as my telegram No. 40.[25] I suggested that no commitments be made to Dr. Anze Matienzo until the breach in relations had actually taken place . . .

The Undersecretary's reply of January 27, 4 p. m.,[26] which does not appear to have been repeated to the Department, stated that Dr. Anze Matienzo had made no suggestions to him touching in the slightest degree on the points outlined above. He added that it was the understanding in Rio de Janeiro, confirmed by press reports, that relations between Bolivia and the Axis powers had been broken on January 26.

From this telegram and subsequent conversations with Mr. Rodas Eguino and President Peñaranda, it seems obvious that Dr. Anze

[25] Dated January 26, 8 p.m., p. 515.
[26] Repeated to the Department as telegram No. 63, January 27, 6 p.m.; not printed.

Matienzo did not comply with his Government's instructions because
(a) of his realization that its desires could not be met and (b) his willingness to fight through ratification of the agreements he was reaching
with Mr. Welles on his return to La Paz with the assistance of Mr.
Luis F. Guachalla, Bolivian Minister to the United States, a member
of his delegation who has considerable prestige in Bolivia through
his successful representation of Bolivian interests in the United States.
It likewise appears probable that Dr. Anze Matienzo deliberately
declared that his Government had broken relations with the Axis
powers in an attempt to force its hand, realizing that the Government
was wavering and being convinced himself of the advisability of such
action as promptly as possible. These actions of Dr. Anze Matienzo
were, of course, in the real interest of improved relations between the
two countries and required very considerable courage. I reported the
above conclusions to the Undersecretary in a telegram dated January
28, 1 p. m., but did not repeat it to the Department.

In the meantime, concerning the question of the supposed breach
in relations, Dr. Anze Matienzo's statement at Rio de Janeiro had
caused his Government considerable anxiety. Relations had *not* been
broken and the Bolivian Government was not certain when it would
take the action and yet it did not wish to disavow its Minister of
Foreign Affairs completely. It consequently . . . issued an official
communiqué, published in the morning press of January 27, 1942,
reading as follows, in translation:

"In accordance with the decision taken at the last Cabinet meeting,
the Foreign Office has instructed the Bolivian delegation at Rio de
Janeiro to state at the Consultative Meeting of American Foreign
Ministers that the Government ratifies its adherence to the formula,
already approved, recommending the breaking of relations with the
Axis powers. Consequently, the decree putting this attitude into effect
will be promulgated in due course."

On January 27, 1942, I saw President Peñaranda in the company of
Mr. Rodas Eguino and presented certain arguments to him in favor of
an immediate breach of relations. These appeared to have some effect
on him and he promised me that the appropriate decree would be
forthcoming within two or three days, assuring me that the telegram
to Dr. Anze Matienzo setting forth the commitments he should get
from the Undersecretary were not, as stated in the telegram, a prerequisite to a breach of relations but merely an outline of what the
Bolivian Government hoped the United States would do for Bolivia
eventually. The President explained that the delay in issuing the
decree was caused solely by the necessity for taking precautionary
measures to prevent sabotage, etc., by Axis elements. The foregoing

was reported to the Department in my telegram No. 41 [27] and likewise in summary to the Undersecretary.

The President interrupted a Cabinet meeting to hold this half-hour conversation with me. The decree breaking off relations with the Axis powers was issued thirty hours later. Cabinet officers inform me that my conversation with the President and the fact that Dr. Anze Matienzo had stated that Bolivia had broken off relations were the two deciding factors, the President not having been certain whether Bolivia should not delay indefinitely and follow Argentina and Chile's lead until the conversation.

Either Dr. Anze Matienzo has not yet fully informed his Government of the agreements he reached at Rio de Janeiro with Mr. Welles and Mr. Metzger, or it has not understood them. Unfortunately, instead of awaiting his arrival, not scheduled until mid-February because of a trip to Buenos Aires, or that of Mr. Guachalla, who is due in La Paz tomorrow, the Bolivian Government spokesmen have made wild statements as to what was agreed upon at Rio de Janeiro, including statements that Bolivia would get a credit of $40,000,000 in connection with the Development Corporation instead of the $10,000,000 which was agreed upon (this is apparently based upon the fact that Dr. Anze Matienzo was asked to have the authorized capital made $40,000,000 in lieu of $25,000,000; Mr. Rodas Eguino has persisted in disregarding the difference between authorized capital and the conditional Export-Import Bank Loan of $10,000,000 to the Corporation despite my continued efforts to make him understand the difference).
. . . There is enclosed a translation of an interview [28] granted by the Acting Minister of Foreign Affairs to *El Diario* and published in the January 28 edition of that newspaper which will repay careful reading . . .

A further example of the Bolivian Government's loose giving of publicity to its aspirations instead of the realities may be found in an official communiqué with regard to the Standard Oil settlement issued by the Office of the President and published in the morning press of February 1, 1942. This reads, in translation:

"The Government has received a suggestion in the sense of paying the Standard Oil Company $1,000,000 in exchange for all of the plans and studies carried out by the Company (in Bolivia). It would furthermore be declared that neither Bolivia nor the Standard Oil Company has any claims pending, the right of Bolivia to its petroleum being thus accepted.

---

[27] Dated January 27, 3 p.m., p. 516.
[28] Not printed.

"Simultaneously, the Export-Import Bank would lend us a first instalment of $5,500,000 for the development of our petroleum industry, which sum would be increased as necessary. This credit would be independent of others already agreed upon for help to mining, agriculture and communications.

"This subject will be definitely decided after consideration of the report which will be made by the Foreign Minister, Dr. Eduardo Anze Matienzo."

Mr. Rodas Eguino has shown me much of the telegraphic correspondence exchanged between him and Dr. Anze Matienzo in regard to the Standard Oil question. Dr. Anze Matienzo informed him of the proposed terms whereby $1,500,000 plus interest from March 1937 would be paid by the Bolivian Government to the Standard Oil Company and the Export-Import Bank would open a credit of $5,000-000 for Bolivian petroleum development. To this, the Bolivian Government replied suggesting that the payment to the Standard Oil Company be reduced to $1,000,000 and the credit from the Export-Import Bank increased to $5,500,000. Dr. Anze Matienzo answered that this was impracticable. Nevertheless, the Bolivian Government has now announced to its public that the terms being considered are the ones it would like, not those signed by its representative at Rio de Janeiro. Incidentally, Mr. Rodas Eguino informs me that it was not the Government's intention to say anything about the Standard Oil settlement until Dr. Anze Matienzo's return but that it was felt necessary to do so since the fact that a settlement was under consideration had leaked from Cabinet meetings into the press and the Government thought it was essential to "give the public the true facts."

Fortunately, the press had accepted the idea of a Standard Oil settlement without too much opposition and public opinion also seems to be inclined in the same sense, although the picture will undoubtedly change somewhat when it is found that the terms are not as favorable as the Bolivian Government has irresponsibly announced. However, now that the fundamental step of breaking relations with the Axis powers has been taken, Bolivia can no longer hold off and present the possibility of such a breach as a *quid pro quo* for further concessions. Once Dr. Anze Matienzo and Mr. Guachalla arrive and the matter is taken up in the Cabinet definitely, I believe that they, with such assistance as Mr. Bohan, Mr. Mariaca, and I can offer them, will be able to overcome obstacles and get the agreements approved. However, the situation will not be an easy one. . . .

Respectfully yours,   ALLAN DAWSON

824.24/450

The Bolivian Chargé (Dorado) to the Secretary of State

WASHINGTON, February 24, 1942.

EXCELLENCY: In compliance with instructions which I have received from my Government, I have the honor to request of Your Excellency's Government a favorable decision on the following matter:

In conformity with the Agreement of December 6, 1941,[29] inspired by the Declaration of Lima [30] and the need for attending to the defense of the Americas, the United States proposed to transfer to the Republic of Bolivia arms and munitions of war up to an approximate total value of $11,000,000, it having been decided that the quota for the first year should cover $3,000,000 in military material for the army of Bolivia.

The Ministry of National Defense and the General Staff of the Bolivian army, in accordance with the suggestions of the Chief of the American Army Air Mission, Colonel Edward H. Porter, and taking into account the situation through which the country is passing at present with relation to problems of continental defense and its own security, have considered the urgency of introducing changes in the application for armament, for which reason my Government requests that of Your Excellency to employ its valued recommendation before the proper authorities in order that the Bolivian request, which is given concrete form in the following points, may be decided on favorably:

1. That the credit of $3,000,000 established as the first quota be allotted in full for the acquisition of aviation training material.

2. That the application submitted to the War Department in Washington by the Bolivian Purchasing Commission be accepted in full, in view of the fact that no substitutions can be made for the material included in the said application, because of the special flying conditions in Bolivia, due to the altitude.

This petition is repeated, in view of the fact that the War Department at Washington has placed in its specifications the supplying of certain types of airplanes that could not be used in my country without serious danger to the life of the Bolivian and American pilots who expect to receive the training planes to open an active period of training.

---

[29] The Lend-Lease Agreement between the United States and Bolivia; see *Foreign Relations,* 1941, vol. VI, section under Bolivia entitled "Negotiation of a Lend-Lease Agreement with Bolivia, signed December 6, 1941."

[30] Declaration of the Principles of the Solidarity of America, approved December 24, 1938, *Report of the Delegation of the United States of America to the Eighth International Conference of American States, Lima, Peru, December 9–27, 1938* (Washington, Government Printing Office, 1941), p. 189.

The reasons forming the basis for the previous request were set forth to the Hon. Sumner Welles, Under Secretary of State, and the Hon. Laurence Duggan, Adviser on Political Relations of the exalted Department of which you are in charge, by General David Toro, ex-President of Bolivia and head of the Bolivian Military Purchasing Commission, and also by Colonel Oscar Moscoso, Military and Air Attaché of this Legation, during the interviews which the high officials mentioned were good enough to grant us a few days ago. Further, Colonel Moscoso is sending to Mr. Duggan today a Confidential Memorandum in which data on Bolivian aviation are given.[31]

My Government hopes that Your Excellency's Government will receive this suggestion favorably, in view of the fact that Bolivia is the principal source of supply of tin and tungsten, "strategic minerals" which the United States of America, Great Britain and the other United Nations need for the production of arms.

The principal mining centers in Bolivia may be subjected to surprise attacks by air, which can easily be made by an enemy from airplane carriers which approach the coast. Three hours of flight would be enough to place the airplanes over Catavi, Oruro, Potosí and other important mining centers which produce not only tin and tungsten but zinc, lead, antimony, copper, etc. If the enemy should reach his objective, the supplying of Bolivian minerals to the United States of America would be entirely interrupted. Bolivia has no means of anti-aircraft defense, and it is urgent to attend to this common danger by hastening the organization of a good military aviation school.

Because of her strategic location within the geography of the continent, Bolivia can, in accordance with any joint plan for defense, be converted, with the aid of the United States of America, into a great future air base, the position of which in the center of the Continent, in the heights of the Altiplano and with easy access to the coasts, would represent a factor advantageous to American aviation.

Bolivia, furthermore, an inland country with few means of communication and consequently with her economic, political and social life unarticulated, today faces grave problems in connection with national unity, due to the lack of contacts between the various regions of her territory. To augment military and civil aviation is consequently a program on which action is urgently needed for any Government which attempts to carry out a constructive plan for the benefit of the whole.

In accordance with all the preceding, I respectfully request Your Excellency to recommend to the War Department that my Govern-

[31] Not printed.

ment's application be decided in harmony with the urgent needs of Bolivia, whose attitude of loyal friendship and frank support toward the United States of America is well known to Your Excellency.

I avail myself [etc.]   CARLOS DORADO

824.248/208

Memorandum of Conversation, by the Adviser on Political Relations (Duggan)

[WASHINGTON,] April 17, 1942.

The Ambassador [32] inquired whether there was anything I could tell him with regard to the desire of his Government to obtain antiaircraft equipment and certain detachments of planes to protect vital installations in Bolivia.

I told the Ambassador that a translation had been made of his note [33] and the matter was under consideration by the appropriate authorities of the Government. I added that our preliminary exploration made it appear as though this equipment, were it to be available, would probably have to be furnished out of Bolivia's Lend-Lease allocation. I impressed upon the Ambassador that there was no assurance yet, however, that the equipment could be spared owing to the extremely heavy demand for antiaircraft guns and for planes of the type desired by his Government.

The Ambassador then stated that, under the arrangements contemplated by his Government, it might not be necessary at this time to turn the equipment over to Bolivia. With respect to the planes, his Government was prepared to accept the assignment of these squadrons as part of the United States Aviation Mission. The planes together with pilots, mechanics, and any other necessary personnel, under this arrangement would be stationed in Bolivia theoretically as a part of the United States Aviation Mission but actually there to protect Bolivian vital installations from air attack and to perform other missions important to this Government. The Ambassador then explained that although it was impossible so to state in the note, what his Government had in mind in effect was the establishment of aviation bases in Bolivia. On account of the central location of Bolivia in South America, his Government thought that this Government might be very glad to station squadrons in Bolivia that would be in a position to immediately proceed to any neighboring country for whatever purpose, at a moment's notice, thereby saving what might be very valuable time.

The Ambassador stated that his Government was prepared to agree to similar arrangements in connection with the antiaircraft guns,

[32] The Bolivian Ambassador, Luis Fernando Guachalla.
[33] Not printed.

namely, that United States detachments accompany these guns and set them up and man them.

With respect both to the planes and guns, a later determination could be arrived at by the two Governments as to whether they would be turned over to Bolivia.

In concluding, the Ambassador referred to the interest in this general question shown by the President when he received Señor Guachalla as Ambassador. Señor Guachalla said that the President himself asked the Ambassador what Bolivia was doing to protect its tin mines. The President emphasized that it was vital to the successful prosecution of the war that nothing happen to these mines.

I thanked the Ambassador for his courtesy in amplifying orally the intent and purpose of his note. I told him that his views would immediately be brought to the attention of the Acting Secretary of this Department and appropriate high officials in the other Departments.

824.24/437 : Telegram

The Chargé in Bolivia (Dawson) to the Secretary of State

LA PAZ, April 24, 1942—5 p. m.
[Received 7: 21 p. m.]

270. My 43, January 28, 6 p. m.[34] Minister of Foreign Affairs this afternoon showed me telegram he is sending Guachalla based on pessimistic reports from Toro to the Minister of Defense[35] that lend-lease equipment for Bolivia will be held down in amount and delayed in delivery. The Minister pictures anarchy in Bolivia if full lend-lease requests are not met.

While the telegram is special pleading and grossly exaggerated I do believe it would be advisable to deliver 8 or 10 airplanes to Bolivia well before August 6 when Congress next meets for domestic political effect as well as some dual purpose machine guns for mounting on trucks ordered by Bolivian Army which have received export clearance. Expediting shipment of trucks would also be helpful.

Toro and Guachalla also complain about failure to appoint military instruction mission to replace expelled Italian mission. If at all possible rapid assignment of at least part of mission would be advisable as staff schools are disrupted and we should quickly counteract Italian influence on officers.

Toro also complained about treatment Bolivian Army pilots are receiving in the United States. I outlined situation and suggested that attempts be made through Bolivian Embassy in Washington to make them learn English so that they would be eligible for Army training.

---

[34] Not printed.
[35] Gen. Miguel Candia.

I explained to Foreign Minister as I have before to the Minister of Defense that lend-lease shipments must necessarily be subordinated to our own war necessities and that I was sure everything possible was being done to fill Bolivian needs but that they should understand delay.

DAWSON

824.24/443

The Chargé in Bolivia (Dawson) to the Secretary of State

No. 2046   LA PAZ, April 30, 1942.
                                                            [Received May 8.]

SIR: I have the honor to refer to my telegram No. 270 of April 24, 5 p. m., with regard to an interview with the Bolivian Minister of Foreign Affairs, Dr. Eduardo Anze Matienzo, in which he made certain complaints concerning the Bolivian Government's dissatisfaction, based on reports of General David Toro, Chief of the Bolivian Military Mission to the United States, with the progress of arrangements for Lend-Lease aid to Bolivia and other matters involving military cooperation. These complaints were outlined in a telegram to the Bolivian Embassy in Washington with instructions for them to be taken up with the Department.

The Foreign Minister appeared particularly perturbed over a statement from General Toro that the amount of aviation equipment to be turned over to Bolivia under Lend-Lease has been cut from a value of $3,000,000 to one of $1,000,000 and that only some 36 planes will be covered by this latter sum. He stated that what Bolivia needed was airplanes and anti-aircraft artillery and that this news was most disappointing. He also referred to a commitment which he said had been made to him by the Under-Secretary at the Rio de Janeiro Consultative Meeting to the effect that all that Bolivia needed for protection of its mines would be made available to it and that this would be done at the expense of the United States, not under Lend-Lease. The Minister said that this alleged commitment covered the anti-aircraft artillery his Government wanted but that General Toro had advised him that the United States Army authorities with whom he was dealing had insisted it would have to come out of Lend-Lease, that delivery would be much delayed and that they were not prepared to agree to turning over as much of such material as was essential.

While the Legation is not informed of the nature of the conversations on the subject between Mr. Welles and Dr. Anze Matienzo at Rio de Janeiro, it seems possible that the latter misunderstood the tenor of the Under Secretary's remarks. It would be of assistance in overcoming the somewhat unreasonable attitude of the Bolivian authorities if the Legation could be advised what commitment, if any, was made. It would also be appreciated if the Legation could be informed as to the nature of the cut from $3,000,000 to $1,000,000 mentioned by the Foreign Minister. As the Lend-Lease agreement of December 6, 1941, called for deliveries of not more than $3,000,000 in the first year, to cover all matériel, it occurs to the Legation that what may have happened is that the Army has informed General Toro that not more than $1,000,000 worth can be supplied.

This morning, the Assistant Military Attaché of the Legation called on the Minister of Defense, General Miguel Candia, and was met with complaints similar in nature to those by the Foreign Minister to me. On the subject of planes, the General insisted that it was necessary that all of the 36 planes now promised should be delivered in Bolivia by some time in July so that he could have them all in the air for a monster parade and review he is planning for August 6, 1942, the Bolivian national holiday. He also insisted on the need for additional aviation equipment up to a value of $3,000,000 at a later date. How the 36 planes would be gotten to Bolivia in view of the shipping shortage or how they would be flown on August 6th when Bolivia does not have 36 properly trained military pilots was not touched on by the General.

The General also discussed the Bolivian Army's alleged need for anti-aircraft artillery although he did not mention the supposed commitment made at Rio de Janeiro for this to be paid for entirely by the United States. This idea of anti-aircraft defense is an *idée fixe* with the Bolivian military authorities who pretend to envision attacks from Japanese carriers on Bolivia's mines. Actually, of course, the worst vulnerability of these is to sabotage, to guard against which the Bolivian Government has taken few measures. . . .

In the conversation between General Candia and the Assistant Military Attaché this morning, the latter made reference to a telegram he had just received from the War Department to the effect that the members of the Military Instruction Mission had been chosen and would be ready for departure for Bolivia as soon as the contract for their services was signed. To this the General replied that the present military school year was far advanced and that he consequently did not want the Military Instruction Mission until the beginning of the next school year, in February 1943. The Department will note that this stand is completely at variance with the complaints of General Toro and the Foreign Minister and their insistence that the Mission be sent at once. This lack of coordination in the Bolivian Government is not unusual.

It has just been learned reliably by the Legation from a confidant of the Minister of Defense that an offer has been received by the Bolivian Government from Argentine sources for the purchase of the old

Junkers equipment now in the hands of the Bolivian Army. This equipment consists of two JU–86's, one equipped as a transport and the other as a bomber but convertible easily into a cargo carrier, plus the remnants of two or three Junkers which have been in accidents but something from which could be salvaged. The Argentine offer is said to have stated that the planes would be used in Bolivia. If this provision were serious, the only answer which occurs to the Legation is that the Argentine interests have plans for starting some sort of an air line in lowland eastern Bolivia (the JU–86's are not adapted to altitude flight such as would be necessary for use on the plateau) possibly in part to carry the rubber they are trying to contract in competition with the Rubber Reserve Company. In any event, the opening of a new air line in eastern Bolivia would be in direct competition with Lloyd Aéreo Boliviano in which the United States has a direct interest since the line has been rehabilitated with funds furnished by the Defense Supplies Corporation and is managed by Pan American-Grace Airways.[36]

It occurs to the Legation that, in view of the Argentine offer, it might be advisable, before turning over to Bolivia any Lend-Lease matériel, to consider asking for a commitment that neither this nor any other Bolivian military equipment would be disposed of to another country or to foreign private interests (this latter suggestion might, however, be overcome should the Bolivians desire by having any Argentine purchasers organize in Bolivia as a Bolivian corporation). It will be remembered that there is a provision in the L. A. B. contract whereby its Junkers cannot be disposed of without consent of the Defense Supplies Corporation.

The Department will recall from its instruction No. 510 of March 16, 1942,[37] to the Legation that the Bolivian Government has already sold at least $1,328,000 worth of rifles and rifle ammunition to the Free Belgian Forces and the British Government. This was obviously in anticipation of receiving Lend-Lease equipment which could replace it. It will be recalled further that, under the Lend-Lease Agreement, Bolivia is to receive $11,000,000 worth of matériel and repay not more than $2,000,000 over a period of six years. This readiness to take advantage of our proposed loan leads to the belief that the Argentine offer for airplanes might very easily be accepted if precautions to prevent it are not taken. In any event, the Legation feels that it would not be unreasonable to ask Bolivia to pay the $1,328,000 to the United States on Lend-Lease as the latter equipment is delivered instead of following payment schedules set forth in the Lend-Lease Agreement.

---

[36] For correspondence on the elimination of German influence in Bolivian commercial airlines, see *Foreign Relations*, 1941, vol. vi, section under Bolivia entitled "Elimination of German influence in Bolivian commercial airlines."
[37] Not printed.

Such procedure is, however, probably not practicable because of the terms of the Agreement.

The Department will also recall from the Legation's telegram No. 287 of October 10, 1941,[38] that the Bolivian Government signed a contract with one Henry Koopman, a German agent who, it has been learned, was acting for Japanese principals, for sale of the so-called scrap iron, held by the Bolivian Army including many usable trucks. In view of the Bolivian insistence on the need for trucks from Lend-Lease funds (see paragraph 2A of my telegram No. 43 of January 28, 6 p. m.[38] and subsequent correspondence), this also does not have a particularly pleasant odor. As the Department was informed (see my despatch No. 1181 of October 10, 1941),[38] the Koopman deal was put through despite the Legation's pointing out in advance to General Candia that Koopman and his associates were suspected of being German agents. . . .

Respectfully yours,　　　　　　　　　　　　　ALLAN DAWSON

824.24/437 : Telegram

The Secretary of State to the Chargé in Bolivia (Dawson)

WASHINGTON, May 16, 1942—9 p. m.

281. Your 270, April 24, 5 p. m. The text of the contract for the Military Instruction Mission is now receiving the consideration of the War Department, which has selected five officers for this Mission. You will be informed by cable as soon as the contract is signed and the officers are ready to depart.[39]

The Munitions Assignments Board has approved the allotment to Bolivia of 15 primary, 17 basic, and 10 advanced training planes, deliveries of which are scheduled to begin in July and end in October. The Bolivian Embassy has submitted its Government's request for 22 additional planes. This request will be given every consideration by the Board, consistent with the production and demand situation obtaining during the next 6 or 9 months. It is suggested that the Bolivian Government submit its request again during the period of delivery of the 37 planes.

The Bolivian Government's order of trucks is receiving the attention of the Department, which will send you further information on this subject.

---

[38] Not printed.
[39] The contract was signed on August 11, 1942; the Embassy was notified by Department's telegram No. 533, August 11 (824.20/228a).

With reference to army pilots, the Department assumes you refer to pilots who will bring to Bolivia the planes to be acquired in the United States. The War Department reports that it will give these pilots the necessary training.

HULL

824.248/227

The Ambassador in Bolivia (Boal) to the Secretary of State

No. 517   LA PAZ, August 21, 1942.
[Received August 28.]

SIR: I have the honor to report an interview this morning concerning Lend-Lease equipment for Bolivia between General Miguel Candia, Bolivian Minister of National Defense, and Lieutenant Colonel Donald N. Wackwitz, Chief of the United States Army Aviation Mission to Bolivia, which was also attended by Colonels Coello and Jordan, the two ranking officers in the Bolivian Air Corps.

General Candia had asked Colonel Wackwitz to call in regard to the airplanes to be sent shortly from the United States to Bolivia under the Bolivian-United States Lend-Lease agreement and to plans to be made for ferrying them from the United States and using them in Bolivia. General Candia had received word from General David Toro, Chief of the Bolivian Military Mission to the United States, that the original quota of 59 planes for Bolivia in 1942 had been cut to 38 and that delivery of the remaining planes would have to be postponed until 1943. This seemed to disturb the General greatly and Colonel Wackwitz reports that he pounded the table and said that he would not accept the reduction. Colonel Wackwitz attempted to explain that the need for planes for actual war purposes and training in the United States necessitated the curtailment but this seemed to have little effect. Colonel Wackwitz informs me that the interview terminated with General Candia saying that he would send a telegram to General Toro instructing him to protest to the War Department and say that Bolivia could not agree to the reduction in Lend-Lease deliveries this year!

.   .   .   .

Colonel Wackwitz has for months been trying to impress upon the Bolivian Army authorities the need for providing hangar and other facilities for the planes which are to come to Bolivia under Lend-Lease without any visible success. That the bulk of the 38 planes the Bolivian Army is to receive in 1942 will be without shelter and thus subject to rapid deterioration and that the Bolivian Army does not now have sufficient trained pilots to utilize satisfactorily even that number of planes does not prevent General Candia from insisting on more.

Despite the absurdity of General Candia's stand, it does seem worthwhile for the Department and the War Department to explain patiently to Ambassador Guachalla and General Toro the situation making the decrease in Lend-Lease deliveries necessary.

Respectfully yours, For the Ambassador:
ALLAN DAWSON
First Secretary of Embassy

824.248/243 : Telegram

The Ambassador in Bolivia (Boal) to the Secretary of State

LA PAZ, December 7, 1942—11 a. m.
[Received 2 : 56 p. m.]

1152. Reference Embassy's telegram 1095, November 24, 9 a. m.[42] Thirteen of the fifteen training airplanes arrived at La Paz December 6, one having been delayed in Lima because of damage caused by motor failure on the take-off. The airplane flown by Colonel Coello which was damaged at San José, Costa Rica, is still being repaired there by Taca.[43] Coello was brought back to La Paz as a passenger. None of the pilots was hurt during the trip. The pilots were met at the airport by a large and festive crowd, including President Peñaranda and the Minister of National Defense. I believe arrival of these airplanes will have an excellent effect as a concrete example of lend-lease deliveries and hemisphere defense cooperation.

BOAL

824.24/655

The Secretary of State to the Bolivian Ambassador (Guachalla)

WASHINGTON, December 11, 1942.

EXCELLENCY: Reference is made to Your Excellency's note of December 3, 1942 [42] enclosing a check on the Riggs National Bank of Washington, D. C., drawn to the order of the Treasurer of the United States in payment for defense articles delivered in accordance with the second article of the Lend Lease Agreement signed between the Governments of the United States of America and Bolivia on December 6, 1941.

I am informed that the Office of Lend Lease Administration is in the process of drawing up schedules of deliveries of defense articles made to the various governments and that it is the intention at some future date to submit such schedules to the various governments for

---

[42] Not printed.
[43] Transportes Aéreos Centro-Americanos.

their approval and for payment of the sums due for articles actually delivered. Until such schedules are prepared and checked, it will be impossible for my Government to determine how much is owed by your Government under the terms of the Lend Lease Agreement. My Government interprets Article II of the Lend Lease Agreement as only requiring payment by your Government for defense articles which have actually been delivered and I am informed that deliveries to your Government have as yet been of small magnitude compared with the amount of your Government's check.

Until the schedules referred to above are presented to your Government the Government of the United States does not consider that any amounts are due by your Government under the terms of the Lend Lease Agreement. May I suggest therefore that any payments by your Government await presentation of schedules of articles delivered by my Government, and may I return to you with my Government's deep appreciation the check enclosed with your note under reference.

Accept [etc.] CORDELL HULL

AGREEMENT PROVIDING FOR A MILITARY MISSION FROM THE UNITED STATES TO BOLIVIA, SIGNED AUGUST 11, 1942

[For text of the agreement, signed at Washington, see Department of State Executive Agreement Series No. 267, or 56 Stat. (pt. 2) 1583.]

NEGOTIATION FOR THE PURCHASE BY THE UNITED STATES OF STRATEGIC MATERIALS FROM BOLIVIA [45]

811.20 Defense (M) Bolivia/46

The Chargé in Bolivia (Dawson) to the Secretary of State

No. 1531 LA PAZ, January 6, 1942.
[Received January 12.]

SIR: I have the honor to report that one of the first and most widespread of Bolivian reactions after the formal entrance of the United States into the War was that, with the possibility of its being cut off from Malayan tin and Chinese tungsten, there was a wonderful opportunity for Bolivia to get higher prices for its tin and tungsten

---

[45] Continued from *Foreign Relations*, 1941, vol. VI. For correspondence regarding the purchase of Bolivian rubber, see *post*, pp. 560 ff.

despite the stipulation as to prices in the respective contracts with the Metals Reserve Company.[46]

There has been for the past four weeks a marked campaign in the local press to this end. The campaign has been indulged in not only by the ultra-nationalistic newspapers and those under some degree of German influence, such as *La Calle*, *La Noche* and *El Diario*, but also by *Ultima Hora*, normally entirely friendly to the United States and the Allied cause. . . .

La Razón, the sole newspaper maintaining the thesis that the present agreements should be honored to the letter, has pointed out that a contract is a contract and that, if the War were over, the United States would keep its word and continue to buy Bolivian tin and tungsten at what would then be prices far higher than the prevailing world ones. It has been met by its journalistic rivals with hoots of derision and the claim that of course the United States would not be foolish enough to do any such thing as well as the always clinching argument that *La Razón* has sold out to foreign "imperialism".

The newspaper campaign and analogous talk by the man in the street was to be expected but it is rather disappointing that Cabinet officers have taken a similar stand in conversations with me. Both the Minister of Foreign Affairs, Dr. Eduardo Anze Matienzo, and the Minister of Economy, Mr. Alberto Crespo . . . have on several occasions expressed to me the hope that the Metals Reserve Company would be willing to consider an "adjustment" of the tin and tungsten contracts to provide for higher sales prices. They have based their arguments on slightly different grounds than the newspaper campaign, alleging that costs have risen greatly since the two contracts were entered into whereas the tungsten contract calls for a fixed price and the tin contract practically does so.

I have replied to them that it seems to me there may be some merit in their argument as regards tin but that the contract covering that provides for the possibility of adjusting prices in clause (*a*) under the heading "Price". I have suggested that the Bolivian Government, with the assistance of the principal mining companies, might compile figures as to costs for submission to the Metals Reserve Company as the basis for a request that the buying price of tin of the Metals Reserve Company be raised. So far as I have been able to ascertain, nothing has yet been done in this regard.

The Department and the Metals Reserve Company are, of course, aware that one of the major reasons for increased costs of mining in Bolivia is the extremely burdensome tax structure in the form of huge

---

[46] An instrumentality of the Reconstruction Finance Corporation under the Federal Loan Agency ; for correspondence concerning these contracts, see *Foreign Relations*, 1940, vol. v, pp. 524 ff., and *ibid.*, 1941, vol. vi, section under Bolivia entitled "Negotiations for the purchase by the United States of strategic metals from Bolivia."

export and so-called additional taxes as well as taxes on profits and the provision whereby mining companies turn over a large share of their foreign exchange to the Government. These taxes are on a sliding scale so that as prices received by the companies for their minerals rise, a greater and greater share is taken by the Government. If it is shown that Bolivian mining costs have risen materially since the tin contract was signed, which there is reason to believe is the case (wages have been increased considerably, supplies and equipment from the United States are generally more expensive and prices for imported foodstuffs, necessary for the functioning of the mines, have risen), it is to be hoped that it will be possible to secure some form of a standstill or freezing agreement from the Bolivian Government covering the tax structure so as to ensure that the bulk of any increase in prices will go to the companies to make up for their higher costs rather than into the coffers of the Bolivian Government.

As regards the tungsten contract, I have taken a different stand with the Bolivian authorities who have mentioned it informally to me. From information from the tungsten producers themselves, it is obvious that the price now being received is adequate for an excellent profit in almost all cases. There is a general scurry among the larger mine owners to take up options on small tungsten properties and to find new opportunities for investment in the field. This would hardly be the case if the price of $21 per unit contained in the present three-year contract were not a fully adequate one.

Consequently, in my conversations with the Ministers of Foreign Affairs and Economy and the Manager of the Banco Minero, Mr. Santiago Schulze, I have pointed out (1) that the tungsten contract is a fixed price one with no provisions for adjustment of the price, (2) that the price is obviously a good one, (3) that the Bolivians have already received a marked rise in the price in the change from a price of $17 to one of $21 after agreement had been reached on the first, (4) that the tungsten contract is only six months old so that there has been no marked increase in costs since it was signed and (5) that the Peruvian and Argentine producers have recently signed contracts [47] at a $21 price showing that it is still adequate.

Interestingly enough, the press campaign for revision of the contracts with the Metals Reserve Company has centered largely on the tungsten rather than the tin contract. In none of it has there been the slightest indication of a conception that, if the United States and

---

[47] For correspondence on the purchase of Peruvian exportable metals by the Metals Reserve Company and the acquisition of strategic goods from Argentina by the United States, see *Foreign Relations*, 1941, vol. VII, section under Peru entitled "Agreement between the Metals Reserve Company and Peru . . ." and *ibid.*, vol. VI, section under Argentina entitled "Negotiations for an agreement on the purchase of exportable surpluses of strategic materials from Argentina."

Great Britain need Bolivian tin and tungsten, they are the only buyers to whom Bolivia can sell nor of the fact that Bolivian desire for a change in prices is futile unless the Metals Reserve Company is agreeable. Furthermore, there has been no consideration of the fact that were prices to be raised it would be natural for the term to be made indeterminate instead of fixed, as at present. . . . they want every advantage, both higher prices and that of security in the event of an early termination of the War. I have, however, pointed out to the Bolivian authorities with whom I have talked that they could hardly expect to have both advantages. This plus the arguments outlined in the preceding paragraph seem to have been moderately effective and I have heard nothing from them as to a desire for amendment of the tungsten contract for some days.

The press campaign as to revision of the tungsten contract has been based on the falsest premises imaginable. Assertions have been made, for example, that the United States is buying tungsten from Peru, Mexico and Argentina for $30 per unit and more. These allegations having gone without answer, I addressed a note to the Foreign Office on December 11, 1941, pointing out that the Metals Reserve Company actually had contracts with Peruvian and Argentine producers at $21 per unit and that we were buying from Mexican producers at the same price. The substance of this was furnished to the press two days later by the Foreign Office. Thereafter, the attacks on the contract mostly took another form, concentrating on the idea that no contract should have been made at all and that Bolivia would have been far better off to sell its tungsten on the open market and take advantage of rising prices, ignoring the fact that there are no rising prices, the market being controlled by the United States and Great Britain.

It is of interest in this general connection, that the tungsten producers themselves have had several meetings to discuss the situation and that it was the general consensus of opinion among them that they did not desire an increase in price but would like an extension of the term of the contract at the present, or an even lower, price so as to give them security for further capital investments. If the parties to a contract are satisfied with it there would seem to be no valid reason for objection on the part of uninvolved bystanders but logic is, of course, not a factor in this situation.

The only defenses of the tungsten contract which had been published were editorials and articles in *La Razón* written by staff members ignorant in mineral matters and two articles by Senator Edmundo Vasquez, who was Minister of Economy when the tungsten contract was signed; his statements were largely apologia for himself. I consequently thought it advisable to get some of the facts before the public and encouraged the publication of the enclosed article,[48] written by

---

[48] Not reprinted.

"An Old Miner", in *La Razón* on January 4, 1942. While the article has its flaws, it was naturally written in a vein and style to make it comprehensible to the average Bolivian reading it. It at least presents certain facts which have not previously been aired in public. A more technical or scholarly exposé would have been ineffective.

Respectfully yours,   ALLAN DAWSON

811.20 Defense (M) Bolivia/47m : Telegram

The Secretary of State to the Chargé in Bolivia (*Dawson*)

WASHINGTON, January 21, 1942—6 p. m.

26. Your no. 21, January 14, 5 p. m.[49] Department finds little merit in Hochschild's[50] assertions and believes that prices offered in Department's cable December 30, noon,[51] are more than fair. Nevertheless, it is desired to control purchase of Bolivian antimony in this country and it is feared that a unilateral fixing of ceiling prices would defeat this end. If we are not in a position to supply the British with antimony, we can raise no objection to their purchasing in Bolivia, and this might affect prices very adversely.

It has been decided today that Office of Production Management will enforce Order M–63 so that all antimony entering this country will be purchased by the Metals Reserve Company. If British purchasing can be held off, no further definitive action will be taken until conversation with Hochschild who, it is understood, arrives here 28th. Meanwhile however, Office of Price Administration will call a trade meeting to discuss price ceiling.

The following ideas have been advanced: (1) To drop negotiations, establish ceiling prices and inform British they are free to purchase in Bolivia; (2) to inform Hochschild that ceiling to be adopted will in all probability be considerably less than offer made in the December 30 cable, but that offer still stands open for immediate acceptance; and (3) to pay the prices asked by Hochschild as described in your cable of December 18, 4 p. m.[52] (it is very doubtful whether Federal Loan Agency would approve this third alternative plan).

Department is anxious to come to reasonable bilateral agreement and would appreciate any suggestions and advice you can offer in the premises.

HULL

---

[49] Not printed.
[50] Mauricio Hochschild, head of a firm of widespread connections, which dealt in tungsten, lead, zinc, and other commodities.
[51] Sent as telegram No. 1, January 2, 1942; not printed.
[52] Telegram No. 392, not printed.

811.20 Defense (M) Bolivia/52 : Telegram

The Chargé in Bolivia (Dawson) to the Secretary of State

LA PAZ, January 22, 1942—3 p. m.
[Received 6 : 33 p. m.]

31. Department's 26, January 21, 6 p. m. Either first or second plan seems satisfactory if modified by agreement with British for them to keep out of Bolivian market competitively; second appears to Legation to be preferable. It is obviously as much to their interest as to ours for prices to be held down to a reasonable level. If Metals Reserve were the only authorized purchaser for the United Nations all Bolivian antimony should flow to the United States except perhaps for very small amounts to Argentina and we could keep our commitments to the British by turning over to them amount agreement [agreed] upon. A less satisfactory solution would be for British to establish ceiling prices equivalent to ours.

Department's desire for reasonable bilateral agreement is shared by Legation but unfortunately not be [by] Hochschild or Banco Minero. Crux of matter is that antimony comes almost entirely from small producers and that Hochschild and Banco Minero want to make utmost possible profit as middlemen.

Inslee,[53] Bohan[54] and Worcester[55] are absent but from earlier conversations I feel that they would concur in the above. Pixley[56] and Oberbillig[57] do.

DAWSON

811.20 Defense (M) Bolivia/83 : Telegram

The Chargé in Bolivia (Dawson) to the Secretary of State

LA PAZ, February 28, 1942—noon.
[Received 7 : 27 p. m.]

121. My 31, January 22, 3 p. m. Hochschild representatives and Banco Minero inform me that they are willing to accept antimony price offers of $1.84 to $2.21 per short unit f.o.b. Chilean ports which they say Metals Reserve has made but that Bolivian Government in Cabinet session 2 days ago instructed Banco Minero not to accept in the hope that refusal would result in Metals Reserve's eventually agreeing to higher prices originally requested by Hochschild and Banco Minero. Conversation with Minister of Economy confirms this in general terms.

---

[53] Joseph A. Inslee, member of the United States Economic Mission to Bolivia.
[54] Merwin L. Bohan, Chief of the United States Economic Mission.
[55] John Worcester, attached to the Economic Mission.
[56] Rex A. Pixley, Assistant Chief of the Economic Mission.
[57] Presumably Ernest E. Oberbillig, official of the Board of Economic Warfare.

From what can be gathered here . . . antimony shippers are satisfied with terms suggested.

I trust that Metals Reserve will be adamant in negotiations and inform Bolivian Legation in Washington that antimony ceiling will be adopted if negotiations are not promptly concluded. Furthermore, extending copper prices agreed upon with Chile to Bolivian production should not be considered in my opinion unless satisfactory antimony contract is first signed.

It would be helpful if the Legation could be kept advised in general, of course, of antimony negotiations instead of having to depend upon partial and perhaps inaccurate reports from Bolivian sources. It may be that Bridgman [58] has written fully to Inslee but latter is out of town.

DAWSON

811.20 Defense (M) Bolivia/83 : Telegram

The Acting Secretary of State to the Chargé in Bolivia (Dawson)

WASHINGTON, March 3, 1942—5 p. m.

118. Your no. 121, February 28, noon. Department in entire agreement with you. Hochschild, who was empowered to negotiate by the Banco Minero, accompanied by Foy, Vice President of the Chemical Bank, who was authorized by the Banco to sign negotiations made firm offer to Metals Reserve which was formally accepted by latter. Both Hochschild and Foy now confirm that the deal was definitely closed.

Bolivian Chargé d'Affaires [59] here has been orally informed that if the generous terms are not confirmed at once, the negotiations will be off, no contract will be made and Office of Price Administration and other agencies will act unilaterally.

Please bring the above situation immediately to the attention of the Bolivian Government and cable their reaction.

WELLES

811.20 Defense (M) Bolivia/112

The Bolivian Ambassador (Guachalla) to the Acting Secretary of State

WASHINGTON, March 18, 1942.

EXCELLENCY: I am pleased to inform Your Excellency of the signing of a contract for eleven months, to December 31, 1942, between

---

[58] G. Temple Bridgman, Executive Vice President of the Metals Reserve Company.
[59] Raúl Diez de Medina.

Metals Reserve Company and the Banco Minero and Mauricio Hochschild, S.A.M.I., dated March 18, 1942, covering all Bolivian antimony and antimony lead concentrates and ores except as specified.[60] I have the honor to inform Your Excellency that my Government fully approves this contract and guarantees the fulfillment of the provisions.

I have added my signature to the contract to which the Banco Minero is a party in accordance with special instructions received from that important institution in my country which in turn represents according to Law, Bolivian enterprises in their relations abroad.

My Government will effect the necessary control over exports by prohibiting the export of antimony and antimony-lead concentrates and ores, in accordance with the authority granted to the Minister of Finance [61] by the decree of the President of Bolivia promulgated July 31, 1941, except to the United States, the United Kingdom or to purchasers in the other American Republics having parallel systems of export control.

Please accept [etc.] LUIS GUACHALLA

811.20 Defense (M) Bolivia/153b : Telegram

The Secretary of State to the Chargé in Bolivia (Dawson)

WASHINGTON, April 28, 1942—9 p. m.

242. At a meeting today the Metals Reserve Company hinted at its willingness to revise the tin contract to a price of 60¢ gross, f.o.b. Chilean ports. By gross is meant a Straits basis, that is, 60¢ less 1½¢. Nothing definite could be said because it was not felt desirable to be definite until the British had had an opportunity of presenting their views on this price; and the British Embassy here is awaiting further instructions from London. To our surprise, the Bolivian Ambassador stated that his instructions were to stand on a 60¢ net price. The meeting broke up on the understanding that the interested departments and agencies would consult among themselves and reconvene the meeting in the near future. It will be noted that the price which Metals Reserve may be willing to pay, that is 60¢ gross, f.o.b. Chilean ports, represents (a) an absolute increase in the price of 10¢ per pound plus (b) the shipping and insurance costs from Chilean ports to Texas City and (c) plus the complete assumption of liability to provide shipping by Metals Reserve Company instead of the present arrangement which puts the responsibility for providing shipping on the shippers.

In the light of the information which you have furnished us, the 60¢ gross price, f.o.b. Chilean ports, appears to be generous. Your

---

[60] In a note of March 25, 1942, the Ambassador gave notice of the signing of a similar contract covering copper (811.Defense (M) Bolivia/128).

[61] Joaquín Espada.

opinion as to the course which the Department should follow will be appreciated.

It appears that a system of control over export prices from the United States will be soon complete and in view of this fact, it was suggested to the Bolivian Ambassador and the producers that the contract should run to December 31, 1943. Your opinion on this point is also requested.

Reference the Department's telegram of yesterday on the subject of the rubber negotiations,[62] the Bolivian Ambassador here has telegraphed to La Paz suggesting that he be given authority to discuss the rubber agreement in Washington. This appears to the Department to be desirable and if you can assist in any way in obtaining a favorable reply to the Ambassador's suggestion, it would be helpful.

HULL

811.20 Defense (M) Bolivia/155 : Telegram

The Chargé in Bolivia (Dawson) to the Secretary of State

LA PAZ, May 3, 1942—11 a. m.
[Received May 4—3 : 42 a. m.]

286. Department's 242, April 28, 9 p. m. Price and terms which Metals Reserve hinted might be offered seem to satisfy us and we feel from conversations with major producers that they would be satisfied with them. Bolivian Government as usual is trying for its own purposes to get maximum concessions exceeding miners' hopes. We strongly urge Department and Metals Reserve not to raise proposed offer as we think it is eminently fair.

None of the Department's telegrams contain any reference to our repeated suggestions that commitments be obtained from the Bolivian Government as to its taxation and exchange policies. Our support of the above price is not based on any idea of generosity but on our reasoned estimate of what is necessary to restore profit margin for producers and thus maintain and stimulate production. If Bolivian Government cuts profits by increasing tax rates or adds to costs by strengthening boliviano part of these effects will be lost as was the case at the time of the tungsten contract. . . . We trust that the Department and Metals Reserve have these possibilities fully in mind and will take proper safeguards.

If effective export price ceilings are to be in effect we see no objection to fixed price until December 31, 1943, although a yearly price adjusted to a cost margin seems more satisfactory to us.

It is inferred from next to last paragraph of Department's 238, April 27, 8 p. m.,[63] that tungsten price adjustment is still under con-

---

[62] Telegram No. 238, April 27, 8 p.m., p. 564.
[63] *Post*, p. 564.

sideration. We can see utterly no justification for an increase at present for this mineral. Taxes are far higher than on tin having been increased at the time of tungsten contract. We feel strongly that taxes should be reduced rather than price increased.

DAWSON

811.20 Defense (M) Bolivia/313

Memorandum by the Acting Chief of the Division of Defense Materials (Finletter) [64]

[WASHINGTON,] May 26, 1942.

Your instructions are requested on the following question. Under a contract dated November 4, 1940 Metals Reserve Company agreed to purchase from certain Bolivian producers 18,000 tons of tin annually for a period running five years from July 1, 1940. The price for the first year ending July, 1941 was 48½ cents per pound c.i.f. United States ports. Thereafter the price was to be determined by a formula which has become inoperative by reason of the Japanese conquest of the Eastern Straits tin producing area. Metals Reserve Company has continued to pay the 48½ cents price since the formula became inoperative.

The Bolivians have asked for an increase in the price by reason of the fact that the price formula has been rendered inoperative. They point to increased costs both in the machinery needed for the mining operations and in the general standard of living. Dawson of the Legation at La Paz and the American economic mission in Bolivia advised in February that in their opinion a price of 57 cents per pound c.i.f. United States ports would compensate for the increase in costs since the signing of the contract. This price was offered, but the Bolivians insisted on a price of 60 cents *f.o.b. Chilean ports.* The Bolivians thus were asking for (*a*) an absolute increase in the price from 48½ cents per pound to 60 cents per pound; (*b*) the assumption by Metals Reserve Company of transportation and insurance costs from the Chilean ports to the United States ports, or an estimated additional 2.35 cents per pound; (*c*) the assumption by Metals Reserve Company of the risk of increases in shipping and insurance costs; and (*d*) the assumption by Metals Reserve Company of the risk that ships may not be available to carry the tin from West coast South American ports to United States ports.

---

[64] Addressed to the Adviser on International Economic Affairs (Feis), who indicated agreement as to immediate negotiating procedure; to the Executive Secretary of the Board of Economic Operations (Collado), who agreed with Mr. Feis; and to the following who indicated no opinion: Chief of the Division of the American Republics (Bonsal), the Adviser on Political Relations (Duggan), the Assistant Secretary of State (Acheson), and the Under Secretary of State (Welles).

These demands of the Bolivians have met with serious resistance both from the Metals Reserve Company and the Board of Economic Warfare. The English, whom we consulted by reason of the fact that their contract with the Patiño Company provided that they were obligated to pay the same price as that paid by Metals Reserve Company, were also opposed to the increase. Allan Dawson at La Paz, in consultation with the Bohan mission, opposed the payment of this 60 cents f.o.b. Chilean ports price. There seemed, however, to be important reasons for making this concession. The Bolivian Ambassador made a strong case in terms of the political situation in Bolivia. Furthermore, the need of this country and Great Britain for tin is such that it seemed desirable to err on the side of an overpayment. Accordingly, due to the insistence of the Department, the Metals Reserve Company, the Board of Economic Warfare, and the English agreed to the payment of the 60 cents f.o.b. Chilean ports price. They even agreed to make this price retroactive to January 1, 1941 [1942?]. The Department and Metals Reserve also agreed, at the insistence of the Bolivian Ambassador, to abandon the plan (which had previously been determined upon, with the approval of Mr. Duggan) for making the tin price conditional upon the reaching of a favorable agreement with Bolivia as to rubber. The only demand which was made was that the contract run until December 31, 1943, that is for a period of about nineteen months.

This was communicated to the Bolivian Ambassador who reported that the producers felt that the contract should run for only seven months, that is to December 31, 1942. His reason for this was that he felt that increasing costs in Bolivia rendered it unwise to extend the contract further than that date. We pointed out to him that recently the Office of Price Administration has fixed ceiling prices on exports for substantially all machinery and equipment and that this should prevent any substantial increase in the cost of mining operations to the producing miners in Bolivia. The Ambassador, however, after consultation with the producers, stated that he could not accept the offer and insisted that nothing less than a contract at 60 cents f.o.b. Chilean ports, price retroactive to January 1, 1942, and running only to December 31, 1942 would be accepted.

I reported this to Messrs. Clayton (RFC)[65] and Rosenthal (BEW).[66] They agreed to consider it and have now reported that they desire to refuse this demand of the Bolivian Government. I told them that I would refer the matter to you for your decision.

---

[65] W. L. Clayton, Assistant Secretary of Commerce; the Reconstruction Finance Corporation was transferred to the Department of Commerce February 24, 1942.

[66] M. S. Rosenthal, Assistant Executive Director, Board of Economic Warfare.

My own opinion is that the demand should be refused, in the absence of political factors in Bolivia with which I am not familiar.

THOMAS K. FINLETTER

811.20 Defense (M) Bolivia/196 : Telegram

The Secretary of State to the Ambassador in Bolivia (Boal)

WASHINGTON, June 15, 1942—5 p. m.

359. Your 417, June 11, 1 p. m.[67] The present status of the tin price negotiations is that a complete proposal has been made to the Bolivian producers which this Government considers to be eminently fair and from which it has no expectation of receding.

While it is believed that it would be most systematic and effective to continue all of the negotiations in Washington, it is believed that you might be of definite assistance in this matter by indicating clearly to the Bolivian authorities the view in the preceding sentence.

HULL

811.20 Defense (M) Bolivia/219

The Bolivian Ambassador (Guachalla) to the Secretary of State

WASHINGTON, June 29, 1942.

EXCELLENCY : I refer to the conversations between our two Governments regarding the amendatory contract [68] entered into today by Metals Reserve Company, an agency of the Government of the United States, providing, among other things, for an increase in the basic price paid by that Company for tin purchased from Bolivian tin producers, under the five-year contract signed on November 4, 1940. The increase in price is designed to compensate the producers for increased costs in production and to stimulate the production of tin in Bolivia.

In view of the purpose of the increase in price, I wish to confirm that during the remaining life of the contract of November 4, 1940, as so amended, the Bolivian Administration, in keeping with the established policy of fostering the development of the mining industry of Bolivia, will use its best efforts to the end that the tax and other related policies of the Government of Bolivia will not be so applied as to eliminate or weaken the stimulus to the production of tin which the increased price under the revised contract is designed to insure, and consequently that the Bolivian Administration will use its best efforts to the end that the Government of Bolivia will not by such

---

[67] Not printed.
[68] English text not printed ; for Spanish text, see *Boletín Oficial del Ministerio de Relaciones Exteriores*, No. 10, May–December, 1942, p. 99.

policies cause a modification under the increased price of the percentages of the sales proceeds which go to the Government and the tin mining industry respectively under the existing price.

The amendatory contract also provides for the purchase by Metals Reserve Company of the entire Bolivian production of tin ore and concentrates (less the quantity thereof sold for export to buyers in the United Kingdom) up to a total of 30.000 tons per year, as more fully set forth in the amendatory contract. I have the honor to confirm that the Government of Bolivia will adopt all measures necessary during the remaining term of the contract to limit the export of tin from Bolivia to the United States or to the United Kingdom except for the export of not exceeding twenty-five tons of fine tin monthly to Chile and except as otherwise be agreed upon between the Government of Bolivia and the Government of the United States.

I am happy to assure you that the Government of Bolivia will use its best efforts to cause the maximum possible production of tin to be attained in Bolivia during the term of the contract and to that end, in accordance with existing legislation, it will encourage the improvement of wages and living conditions of the workers in the mines.

In view of the mutual economic advantages of the contract of November 4, 1940, as amended, I have the honor to inform Your Excellency that my Government fully approves this contract and guarantees the fulfillment of its terms on the part of the various Bolivian signers thereof.

Duly authorized I have added my signature to that of the producers of Bolivian tin in representation of the Banco Minero de Bolivia, Government agency that represents, according to law, numerous small enterprises in their relations abroad.

Likewise, I beg to inform Your Excellency, that the following individuals have been invested with due authority to negotiate the terms of and to execute the contract entered into on today's date: for Compagnie Aramayo de Mines en Bolivie, Mr. Carroll A. Wilson, its representative; for Compañía Minera de Oruro Group, Mr. Mauricio Hochschild, its agent; for Compañía Minera Unificada del Cerro de Potosí, Mr. Mauricio Hochschild, its President; for Asociación Nacional de Mineros Medianos, Mr. Jorge E. Zalles, its representative.

I avail myself [etc.]   LUIS GUACHALLA

811.20 Defense (M) Bolivia/291d : Telegram

The Secretary of State to the Ambassador in Bolivia (Boal)

WASHINGTON, July 17, 1942—11 p. m.

459. In view of the great difficulties encountered by you in your negotiations, it is the view of the Department that you have achieved

a major accomplishment in securing the signature of the rubber agreement and your efforts in this respect have been very much appreciated.

In view of the favorable outcome, the Department is prepared to obtain serious and sympathetic consideration here of the revision of the tungsten agreement suggested by the Minister of Economy. In substance the suggested revision involves a change in price to $24 f.o.b. Chilean ports and an extension of the agreement for 3 years beyond its present termination. Your views on the merits of the suggested revision are requested.

HULL

811.20 Defense (M) Bolivia/207

The Secretary of State to the Ambassador in Bolivia (Boal)

No. 159   WASHINGTON, July 24, 1942.

SIR: Reference is made to the Department's telegram no. 397 of June 26, 1942, and to the Embassy's despatch no. 41 of June 6,[69] regarding a proposed agreement with Bolivia for the purchase of cinchona bark. There are enclosed two signed copies of this proposed agreement.[70] If agreeable to the Bolivian Government, please have the appropriate authority sign both copies, retaining one and returning the other to the Department.

The Department hopes that the Bolivian Government will agree to the proposed agreement in its present form. A preliminary draft which was presented to Señor Alberto Crespo, Bolivian Minister of National Economy, on July 8 had been drawn up in the light of the Embassy's despatch under reference as well as supplementary data made available by Mr. William Pennock[71] in conversations with officials of the Department. At Señor Crespo's suggestion, Department officials discussed the draft agreement in the light of changes suggested by Señor Crespo, Señor Dr. Don Luis Fernando Guachalla, Bolivian Ambassador, and Señor Don René Ballivian, Commercial Attaché of the Bolivian Embassy here. Señor Ballivian has read the present draft and has stated he believes that it embodies all of the important suggested changes, and that it is possible his Government may sign it in its present form.

The principle underlying the proposed agreement is that for a three-year period the United States will buy all cinchona bark and quinine products produced in Bolivia, with certain exceptions, in re-

---

[69] Neither printed.
[70] Not printed.
[71] Drug production technician of the Office of the Coordinator of Inter-American Affairs.

turn for Bolivian restriction on their export to countries other than the United States. The Defense Supplies Corporation,[72] or its agent, would be the sole purchaser of bark and products in Bolivia. It would purchase not only for its own account, but its agent would purchase also for the account of the Bolivian plant, as well as for the account of those authorized to export to Argentina and Chile. It is thought that the provisions of paragraph 1 (a), regarding the requirements of the Bolivian plant, and of paragraph 7 (b), have met the objections of the Bolivians to the provisions of earlier drafts relating to the bark supply of the Bolivian plant and the legitimate antimalarial needs of neighboring countries.

Through the option granted Defense Supplies for the purchase of bark containing less than two percent quinine sulphate, the United States will be in a position to assist in the exploration of this undeveloped part of Bolivia's cinchona resources. This can be done through improving the extraction process of the Bolivian plant enabling it to process this low-content bark efficiently. The technical expert which Defense Supplies promises to make available to the Bolivian plant will work on this problem.

It is hoped that Bolivia will agree to the prices included in paragraphs 2 (a), (b), and (c) and to the methods of payment provided in paragraphs 2 and 3. In arriving at these prices, an attempt has been made to set a figure for the aggregate product, in its raw and finished forms, which will be of the utmost benefit to Bolivia and the United States in the present emergency and at the same time does not overlook the possibility that Bolivia at some undetermined future date may again have to compete with the former Dutch monopoly. Furthermore, the acknowledged needs of large parts of Bolivia's population as well as of our own for quinine and quinine salts have been kept uppermost in mind in arriving at these suggested prices.

With these considerations in mind, the Embassy may, if necessary, urge upon the Bolivian Government the advantage of judging these prices in terms of the aggregate yield rather than focusing attention on one price considered separately from the others. The bark price of $12.50 per kilogram of sulphate content is less than the present market and, considered by itself and without relation to the sulphate price in paragraph 2 (b) and the alkaloid prices in 2 (c), would seem to be disadvantageous to Bolivia. When considered in connection with the prices for sulphate and the other alkaloids, however, and particularly when it is recalled that efforts will be made to expand the production and distribution of the alkaloids, the bark price offered seems reasonable. In this connection, the Embassy is advised that

---

[72] An instrumentality of the Reconstruction Finance Corporation operating under the Secretary of Commerce.

the Defense Supplies Corporation is purchasing 500 kilograms of the 15-percent by-product mass resulting from the processing of the bark at the Bolivian plant, the purpose being to make an analysis of this product here.

As regards the price of $23.50 per kilogram offered for quinine sulphate, it is equivalent to the United States price less an item of 13½ cents added as a surcharge by the Dutch Kina Bureau. By an odd coincidence, it equals what are understood to be the costs of shipping, insurance, etc., between Arica, etc., and the United States. As regards the prices offered for the alkaloid by-products of the extraction process, they are in the same proportion to the price obtained by the Bolivian plant as the respective weights of the by-products are to the total mass.

It is not believed that the other paragraphs of the proposed agreement need elaboration. The reasons for offering the services of a technician to study and make recommendations for the improvement of the processing at the Bolivian plant are obvious. Likewise, it is clear why the services of a plant pathologist are needed and why it is believed to be to the advantage of Bolivia to accept this offer. The provisions of paragraph 6 for experimental plantings and for their enlargement, in case they are successful, are for securing the future supply of cinchona bark not only for the Bolivian plant but also for the Western Hemisphere generally.

The Bolivian representatives expressed a desire for a longer term for the proposed agreement than the thirty-six months provided in paragraph 11. Their attention was drawn to the option which Defense Supplies would have in the event that the war had not come to a conclusion at the end of three years. In proposing a purchase agreement for even three years, the United States is taking some risk, and by the same token Bolivia is relieved of market considerations during this same period. While it is not possible to state in advance that Defense Supplies would exercise its option at the end of three years, the continuance of the emergency war situation, which calls for the agreement in the first place, would suggest the likelihood that it would do so.

Simultaneously with the despatch of this instruction, the Bolivian Embassy here is transmitting a Spanish translation to its Government in La Paz. The Embassy is urged to exert its best efforts without delay to obtain the agreement of the Bolivian Government. Please do not fail to keep the Department informed of the progress of the negotiations.

Very truly yours, For the Secretary of State:
DEAN ACHESON

811.20 Defense (M) Bolivia/303 : Airgram

The Ambassador in Bolivia (Boal) to the Secretary of State

LA PAZ, August 1, 1942.
[Received August 7—11 : 36 a. m.]

A–11. Department's instruction no. 159 of July 24, 1942. Proposed quinine agreement being presented to Bolivian Government but Embassy is of opinion that prices offered are inadequate to stem reduction in production and are certainly insufficient to increase production. It has been noted that Department recognizes that bark price offer is less than the present market (in this connection Bolivian speculators' price, presumably for delivery in Argentina, has risen to equivalent of $16) but that it is felt prices for sulphate and other alkaloids, as well as proposed efforts to expand production and distribution of alkaloids, are sufficient compensation. This general thesis might be supportable if alkaloids other than sulphate were produced by local factory and if purchases of bark and of alkaloids were to be made from same persons or organization; however, only alkaloid factory produces is sulphate and bark dealings will be carried on through middlemen with Indian gatherers while sulphate purchases will be made from factory. Sulphate prices could not possibly offer inducement to gatherers and it is to be feared that low bark price will result in collection of only most available and highest yield bark with consequent drop rather than temporary increase in production probable.

Also, present prices quoted and being received by factory are $29 per kilo of quinine sulphate containing 98% quinine and $5 per kilo of alkaloid mass containing about 16% quinine sulphate (in place of $3 price of early July as reported in Embassy's telegram no. 524 of July 9, 4 p. m.[74]). These prices are for delivery at factory and do not include packaging. Our offer of $23.50 per kilo for quinine sulphate is less and even though factory's production costs would be lower on basis of suggested bark price "judging prices in terms of aggregate yield" might still lead Bolivian Government and factory to oppose contract unless we offer higher prices. (Department will recall that large bark producers are politically more potent than persons interested in factory.) In any event, some bargaining will probably be necessary before agreement on terms can be reached.

The annual allowance of 120 tons of bark for the factory with the possibility of it being increased to 300 tons seems to the Embassy rather generous. It is true that the contract draft provides for purchase of alkaloids and that if operations of factory are sufficiently efficient it might be preferable to purchase alkaloids in place of bark, but as pointed out in Embassy despatch 41 [74] there is at least some

---

[74] Not printed.

doubt as to the possibilities of efficient operation of the factory with its present equipment and personnel. The fact that no alkaloids other than sulphate are being at present separated would seem to support thesis of inadequate equipment and improper operation; factory states that these products can be produced "only with elaborate laboratories". Priester [75] reports confidentially that director of Dutch quinine trust while here in August 1939 to consider Government's offer to sell factory, stated it was "completely worthless". While it has undoubtedly been improved since then it is to be doubted that it now represents peak in quinine production efficiency.

One possibility which may not have received consideration would be for Defense Supplies Corporation to purchase from factory total alkaloid mass (not sulphate) and to complete the alkaloid separation in United States. Local factory's inefficiency is most apparent in its separation of sulphate and by handling this part of process in United States we might be able to avoid large part of waste now being experienced and still leave a place for the factory in the general scheme. Technical aid would be of assistance to factory in even the mass extraction process although as stated above this is most efficient part of factory's operations. It might be possible even to so improve factory that all the bark might be processed here with resultant alkaloid mass being shipped to United States.

BOAL

811.20 Defense (M) Bolivia/303 : Telegram

The Secretary of State to the Ambassador in Bolivia (Boal)

WASHINGTON, August 12, 1942—7 p. m.

536. Reference your airgram A–11, August 1, we expected that some bargaining would be necessary on the proposed quinine agreement. In your discretion, you are authorized to increase prices to $14 per kilogram for quinine calculated as sulphate, USP X, in bark which contains 3% or more of such quinine. You may then offer for bark containing less than 3% but containing a total of 3% or more of total crystallizable alkaloids out of cinchona on the basis of the amount of such total alkaloids contained in the bark as follows: 12 cents per pound for bark containing from 3% to 4% of such alkaloids, 13 cents for bark containing 4% to 5%, 14 cents from 5% to 6%, and 15 cents for bark containing 6% or more of such total alkaloids.

If these prices are not sufficient to obtain a contract, please ask Bolivians to submit firm offer on entire price structure to be relayed to us with your recommendations.

---

[75] J. E. Priester, representative of the Dutch quinine trust.

We believe prices for sulphate and alkaloid mass now offered are reasonable because we plan to take entire output of factory. Our reasoning is that alkaloid mass is of little value to the factory and they should accept lower quinine price to dispose of alkaloid mass at this good figure. Processing costs on mass are heavy but we expect to reduce it to other alkaloids here.

We agree annual allowance to factory is large and can only be made provided we get entire output and privilege of increasing operating efficiency. We hope ultimately to have factory produce quinine sulphate and totaquina under recent U.S. pharmacopoeia.

As regards the suggestion in your airgram A–15 of July 31,[76] the Defense Supplies Corporation is giving it favorable consideration. Details of its decision will be transmitted by telegraph without delay.

HULL

811.20 Defense (M) Bolivia/334 : Telegram

The Secretary of State to the Ambassador in Bolivia (Boal)

WASHINGTON, August 20, 1942—4 p. m.

563. Refer your 693, August 18.[77] It is suggested that you advise Zapata [78] that there is every intention of undertaking an intensive development program immediately after an agreement is signed. It is impossible to estimate precisely the cost of this program but you may give assurances that it will be pushed vigorously and that we shall invest what is necessary to obtain significantly increased quantities of cinchona. If you feel that a specific commitment will facilitate an early agreement, you may commit $300,000 as the minimum amount that will be spent for this purpose. In addition, private firms have expressed considerable interest in the matter.

HULL

811.20 Defense (M) Bolivia/219

Memorandum by the Assistant Chief of the Division of Defense Materials (Cissel)

Reference is made to the note from the Bolivian Ambassador to the Secretary of State dated June 29, 1942, in connection with the amendatory contract entered into on that day by Metals Reserve Company providing, among other things, for an increase in the basic price paid

---

[76] Not printed; the suggestion was that the Defense Supplies Corporation buy out the Dutch quinine interests in Bolivia (811.20 Defense (M) Bolivia/297).

[77] Not printed; it reported that the Bolivian Foreign Office wished for a commitment from the United States to provide funds for developing the quinine industry (811.20 Defense (M) Bolivia/334).

[78] Raúl Espejo Zapata, head of the Political Economic Section of the Bolivian Foreign Office.

by that Company for tin purchased from Bolivian tin producers. This will confirm that it is understood between the Governments of Bolivia and of the United States that, under the terms of the amendatory contract, exports of tin from Bolivia will be limited to the United States or to the United Kingdom except for the export of not exceeding twenty-five tons of fine tin monthly to Chile and except as may otherwise be agreed upon between the Governments of Bolivia and of the United States.

WASHINGTON, August 27, 1942.

824.6354/337

The Ambassador in Bolivia (Boal) to the Secretary of State

No. 682   LA PAZ, October 1, 1942.
                                                 [Received October 12.]

SIR: I have the honor to refer to the Embassy's despatch No. 647 of September 22, 1942,[79] and to transmit herewith a copy in full translation of the Bolivian Foreign Office's note dated September 25 in reply to my note of September 21,[80] which protested a violation of the tin contract.

It will be observed that the Foreign Office's note confirms the information that the Minister of National Economy had rescinded the export permit for the 25 tons of tin ore which was destined for shipment to Argentina, of which fact the Department was advised by the Embassy's telegram No. 860, September 25, 5 p. m.[79]

The Foreign Office note also contains the welcome assurance that the necessary steps are being taken to avoid any exportations of minerals in the future which would not conform to existing contracts.

Respectfully yours,   PIERRE DE L. BOAL

811.20 Defense (M) Bolivia/415 : Telegram

The Acting Secretary of State to the Ambassador in Bolivia (Boal)

WASHINGTON, October 6, 1942—4 p. m.

710. There is a growing feeling within the Department that the cinchona negotiations with Bolivia are being deliberately prolonged or at the best are being made the subject of a temporizing policy on Bolivia's part. The receipt of the Embassy's telegram 831 of September 17, 11 a. m.[79] gave rise to the hope that negotiations would be speeded up and that the Bolivian Government would shortly give

---

[79] Not printed.
[80] Neither printed.

its reactions to our proposals. The absence of any indication of Bolivian desires, other than those mentioned in the Embassy's telegram under reference, tends to confirm our impression that the negotiations continue to languish.

The extreme urgency of increasing our quinine supplies has been mentioned from time to time and only the imperative need to develop available sources of cinchona bark in the most efficient manner prompts the Department to refer to it again. The high quinine content of Bolivian bark, the existing extraction facilities in Bolivia, the potentialities of increased extraction efficiency, and the possibilities of expanding bark production through plantations all make the early conclusion of a cinchona agreement with Bolivia an objective of the highest priority. Equally important is the need for steps to assure the use of American cinchona resources for anti-malarial needs only. We believe that the proposals made to Bolivia will attain these objectives while assuring Bolivia over the next 3 years favorable conditions for developing its cinchona and quinine industries.

The Department urges you to consider these cinchona negotiations of the highest importance. If it is not possible to receive from Minister Crespo without delay a more definite expression of the form he would like to see the contract take, please advise the Department immediately. Would it be advisable to withdraw our proposal and request a statement from Minister Crespo of the points which he should like to see covered in an agreement? If it is inadvisable to withdraw the proposal, but the urgency of the matter should be brought to the attention of the Bolivian Government, would it be advisable to call in Ambassador Guachalla and drive home the importance of the matter with him? Even after discounting the effect of the existing political situation, it is still believed that it is reasonable to expect a prompt reply from Minister Crespo and a willingness to negotiate, which would clear up outstanding points without delay.

Your comments are solicited and it is hoped that the Department may receive without delay by telegraph your recommendation for pushing the negotiations through to a successful and speedy conclusion.

WELLES

S11.20 Defense (M) Bolivia/476: Airgram

The Ambassador in Bolivia (Boal) to the Secretary of State

LA PAZ, October 9, 1942—3 p. m.
[Received October 14—2:05 p. m.]

A–108. Reference Department's telegram No. 710, October 6, 1942, 4 p.m. As indicated in the Embassy's telegram 898, October 6, 1942, 4

p. m.,[84] the reluctance of the Bolivian Minister of Economy to hasten the negotiation of a quinine contract has been due to the very unstable political situation and the unusual pressure on him and his office, since he is continuing to act temporarily as Minister of Finance during the latter's illness. In view of the urgency of this matter, however, as indicated in the Department's telegram under reference, I again emphasized today to the Minister of National Economy the importance which my Government attributes to the conclusion of a contract which will facilitate the exportation of Bolivian quinine to the United States. The Minister of Economy said that he would do everything possible to give the Embassy on Wednesday, October 14, the counter-proposals with respect to the provisions of the proposed contract, which the Embassy has been hoping to obtain from him for some time. It is understood that the principal quinine producers and the quinine factory in La Paz have agreed among themselves to counter-proposals which they have given to the Minister of Economy for his use in presenting counter-proposals to the Embassy.

The Minister of Economy commented this morning that he had had an opportunity to discuss the proposed quinine agreement with national Deputies from the quinine producing districts, and that he had the definite impression that there would probably not be much difficulty in obtaining the approval of the Congress to the agreement. The Minister of Economy commented further that if for any reason the agreement could not be acted on by this Congress prior to termination of the present session (which will probably close before the end of the year), the agreement could be put immediately into effect by decree and could be presented to the next Congress for approval.

With respect to the prompt purchase of available cinchona bark prior to the conclusion of the agreement, it would be possible for Priester to obtain a considerable quantity if he were authorized to pay the prices indicated in the Embassy's Airgram No. A–98, October 2, 1942, 4:45 p. m.[84] Priester has already been able to obtain approximately 14 tons of cinchona bark through the application of his unusual experiences in such purchasing.

If the Department has under preparation any new or revised provisions for the proposed quinine agreement which would provide for the processing of all Bolivian cinchona bark in La Paz, it would be appreciated if they could be sent promptly to the Embassy for consideration in the imminent discussions with the Minister of Economy.

BOAL

---

[84] Not printed.

811.20 Defense (M) Bolivia/476 : Telegram

The Secretary of State to the Ambassador in Bolivia (Boal)

WASHINGTON, October 23, 1942—6 p. m.

765. Refer Department's 738, October 16, 4 p. m.[87] Amendments have been prepared to the proposals submitted to the Bolivian Government for the purchase of cinchona bark and anti-malarial products. The text of the amended proposal will be forwarded to the Embassy as soon as possible. In the meantime, you are authorized to inform the Bolivian Government that the amended proposal will be along the following lines:

1. Defense Supplies Corporation will be committed to the principle that all possible cinchona bark shall be processed in Bolivian plants and that one of the express purposes of the agreement will be the further development and expansion of the cinchona bark processing industry in Bolivia;

2. Prices for anti-malarial products will be revised upwards;

3. A minimum sum of $300,000 will be spent in putting the agreement into effect;

4. Defense Supplies Corporation will agree to sell atabrine to Bolivia at $4.50 per thousand tablets, f.o.b. New York.

None of the previous offers made in the original proposal will be withdrawn in the amended proposal.

With reference to (1) above, information is desired on the present capacity of Bolivian plants and plans for expansion.

HULL

811.20 Defense (M) Bolivia/496 : Telegram

The Ambassador in Bolivia (Boal) to the Secretary of State

LA PAZ, October 24, 1942—11 a. m.
[Received 1 : 45 p. m.]

966. Department's 738, October 16, 4 p. m.[87] Minister of Economy disclosed during conversations yesterday afternoon he is now dubious that any cinchona bark agreement can be put through Congress this session. He expressed opinion it might be much more effective for our Government to negotiate individual purchase contracts with producers rather than attempt to secure congressional approval of an agreement with the Bolivian Government. I now believe it advisable that a purchasing agency be set up immediately to negotiate individual contracts with local producers before price goes higher and other complications arise. Explanatory airgram follows.

BOAL

---

[87] Not printed.

811.20 Defense (M) Bolivia/509 : Telegram

The Secretary of State to the Ambassador in Bolivia (Boal)

WASHINGTON, November 14, 1942—6 p. m.

832. Reference Department's 765, October 23, 6 p. m. and Embassy's 983, October 28, 11 p. m.[88] We are airmailing copies of a revised cinchona proposal and of proposed contracts with cinchona producers and with the Government quinine factory.

We agree in principle to the suggestions made in your telegram under reference, except point 1 as to prices.[89]

The revised proposed agreement between Defense Supplies and Bolivia is not greatly different, except in form, from the original proposal. Where changes in substance do occur, it is felt that they are in Bolivia's favor. This is notably so in the case of prices of antimalarial products, the offer for quinine sulphate USP XII having been revised upward from $23.50 to $28.34 per kilogram, f. o. b. ocean steamer Arica.

For various reasons, none of the Government agencies concerned deem it wise to accede to the price demands being made by Bolivian producers for high-content bark. Our offers for other bark are now being analyzed. While we want to increase available quinine supplies as much as possible, this does not obscure the unfortunate repercussions upon our over-all economic relations with Bolivia which would probably result from giving in on bark prices. Moreover, to do so would necessitate generalizing these concessions to other countries with whom agreements have been or are being made. In this connection and for your confidential information, Bolivia's relative importance as a source of cinchona bark has definitely receded as a result of information recently obtained on other sources.

You are aware of our preference for an agreement with the Bolivian Government rather than a number of contracts with producers and with the factory. For this reason and for those sketched above, you are authorized and instructed, upon receipt of the documents, (1) to withdraw the original proposed cinchona agreement and (2) to replace it either by the revised proposal or by the program suggested in your telegram under reference, whichever appears to offer the best chance of acceptance.

HULL

---

[88] Latter not printed.
[89] Point 1 proposed an $18 price for the bark that exceeded 3 percent sulphate content.

NEGOTIATION AND APPLICATION OF AN AGREEMENT CONCERNING THE BOLIVIAN EXPORT OF RUBBER

811.20 Defense (M) Bolivia/109a : Telegram

The Acting Secretary of State to the Chargé in Bolivia (Dawson)

Washington, March 18, 1942—1 p. m.

161. Rubber Reserve Company [91] is prepared to enter into commitment with Bolivian Government to purchase entire production of rubber in Bolivia except for an appropriate amount (to be agreed upon) necessary for domestic consumption, at 30⅝ cents United States currency per pound f. o. b. ocean carrying vessel at Belém, Brazil, for Beni hard fine cut classified rubber with appropriate differentials for other grades. Purchases would be paid for on basis of cash against shipping documents endorsed "on board" ocean carrying vessel at Belém and such other places, as may be deemed advisable by Rubber Reserve and Bolivia and subject to final price adjustment based on quality inspection and net certified weights determined at port of entry in United States. The term of the agreement shall be to December 31, 1946, unless sooner terminated by mutual consent, price paid being subject to change after expiration of first 2 years if conditions change. The Government of Bolivia would agree to restrict export licenses to Rubber Reserve Company or its nominees and to restrict expansion of rubber manufacturing facilities and to curtail rubber manufacturing as soon as possible. The exportation of manufactured rubber, if any, would be restricted to the United States. Bolivia would agree to use its best efforts to cause maximum amount of rubber to be produced and made available for sale to Reserve. Local labor would be financed locally for necessities for collecting rubber. Some governmental agency, if desirable, would be designated as the single buying agency, otherwise sales would be made through usual trade channels now in existence. Price on sales to Rubber Reserve would also be fixed as local sales price.

Foregoing proposal corresponds generally to agreements entered into with Brazilian Government on March 3.[92]

For your information we understand certain American republics are negotiating to acquire rubber production in some Latin American countries. Please consult immediately Bolivian authorities and request their immediate consideration of proposal. If Bolivian authorities agreeable in principle to sale of rubber to United States, Rubber Reserve willing to enter into an agreement immediately to acquire it;

---

[91] An instrumentality of the Reconstruction Finance Corporation under the Department of Commerce.
[92] See bracketed note, and telegram No. 640, March 13, 7 p. m., to the Ambassador in Brazil, p. 692.

and upon consummation of purchase arrangement are prepared to discuss with Bolivian authorities any useful joint arrangements to increase rubber production.

WELLES

811.20 Defense (M) Bolivia/110 : Telegram

The Chargé in Bolivia (Dawson) to the Secretary of State

LA PAZ, March 20, 1942—6 p. m.
[Received 11 : 32 p. m.]

193. Department's 161, March 18, 1 p. m. Presented rubber proposal to Ministers of Foreign Affairs and Economy.[93] Their immediate reaction was that price was too low explaining they had received higher offer from Argentina without specifying price. They also object to exclusive provisions stating that in any event they would want to sell Santa Cruz rubber to Argentina because of difficulty of communications from Santa Cruz to the Amazon. (There have been no exports from Santa Cruz for last 10 years.) Furthermore they indicated they would desire commitments for help propriety [*sic*] establishing plantation rubber as well as in financing of labor and expansion of needs ($1,500,000 has been talked of in Government circles).

I did not include provisions for exception for domestic ties [*tires?*] or commitments as to restricting manufacture in my [apparent omission] as there is no manufacture in Bolivia and these would merely give additional points on which Bolivians could raise objection. If contract is made commitment to sell us all Bolivian production would seem to serve our purpose.

Press campaign similar to tungsten campaign [94] has already started alleging that rubber is now quoted in Buenos Aires at $2.70 per kilo as compared to $1.30 in New York and that Bolivia should not make long term exclusive contract with the United States at low price. There has been no leak as to our negotiations but press has jumped to conclusion that Bolivian Government is contemplating rubber contract as a result of issuance of supreme decree March 16 prohibiting sale of rubber abroad without approval of Ministry of Economy.

Present production of rubber in Bolivia is about 1,000 tons per annum and I do not see how it can be increased much beyond 3000 tons in any appreciable future because of lack of labor in rubber regions.

DAWSON

---

[93] Eduardo Anze Matienzo and Alberto Crespo Gutiérrez, respectively.
[94] See despatch No. 1531, January 6, from the Chargé in Bolivia, p. 536.

811.20 Defense (M) Bolivia/110 : Telegram

The Acting Secretary of State to the Chargé in Bolivia (Dawson)

WASHINGTON, March 28, 1942—9 p. m.

177. Your 193 of March 20. The following is for your information in carrying on negotiations with the Bolivian officials.

As you undoubtedly perceive, it is urgently necessary that entire Bolivian production of rubber be assured to us. An agreement has been entered into with Brazil at a specified price and negotiations are under way with the other producing countries at equivalent prices. Any substantial increase to Bolivia might require changes in these other prices.

The Rubber Reserve proposal involves a 5-year commitment, thus assuring to Bolivia a steady demand which should be an important offset to any temporarily higher offer.

Negotiations with the other producing countries are proceeding much more satisfactorily, and the Bolivian position is causing unfavorable reaction here.

You may use in your discussions such of the foregoing as in your judgment would aid in negotiating.

Rubber Reserve Company will agree to pay premiums of 2½ cents per pound for all rubber in excess of 2,500 tons and up to 4,500 tons purchased by Rubber Reserve annually and of 5 cents per pound for purchases over 4,500, such premiums to be paid to the Bolivian Government and used for expansion of production of wild rubber.

In addition Rubber Reserve would establish a fund of $1,125,000 to be available for increasing wild rubber production, premiums paid as above provided being credited against the funds. It is not now feasible to permit the fund to be used for expansion of plantation rubber, because of the complex nature of this problem and of its bearing on the post-war situation. Also this is a long-range development which seems to be more a subject for consideration by the Bolivian Development Corporation.[95]

We understand that the Santa Cruz rubber you refer to represents only a small part of the total production. While communication from Santa Cruz to the Amazon may be difficult, can it be arranged at extra expense? Any such expense would be a justifiable increase in price over the Brazilian price. A possible method of effecting the reimbursement of this additional expense might be to have the Bolivian Government pay the additional costs and obtain reimbursement from Rubber Reserve.

---

[95] For correspondence concerning American aid to Bolivia involving this Corporation, see pp. 592 ff.

We agree with your decision on the matters referred to in the second paragraph of your 193.

WELLES

811.20 Defense (M) Bolivia/137 : Telegram

The Chargé in Bolivia (Dawson) to the Secretary of State

LA PAZ, April 18, 1942—6 p. m.
[Received April 19—5 : 03 p. m.]

257. Department's 205, April 11, noon,[96] et ante. Rubber trade accord with Argentine. Offers are now 50 cents per pound or more apparently delivered in Buenos Aires although this is not clear. There are at least six representatives of Argentine business in La Paz trying to buy rubber or producing properties. Some shipments of rubber from the Beni to Buenos Aires via Manaos are already under way. Arrival of two Argentine Government experts mentioned in telegram No. 688, April 17, 1 p. m. from the Embassy at Buenos Aires [96] will undoubtedly make situation still more difficult.

. . . .

It is my understanding that Beni Up River Fine has always drawn a substantial premium in the world markets over Number One Plantation.

I would suggest a proposition along the following lines as perhaps sufficiently attractive to interest Bolivia:

Commitment of Bolivia to sell and the United States to buy all Bolivian rubber (this would hardly be accepted unless we take care of Argentina as suggested below).

Term of 5 years.

Price of 35 cents per pound for Beni Hard Cut Fine Classified at Bolivian border less actual weight deductions. Other grades to be purchased at differential identical with past trade usage.

Advance of $500,000 with promise of as much more as may be necessary for fomenting rubber conditions, organizing supplying of rubber gatherers, et cetera, to be administered through Bolivian Development Corporation or experienced special field representative of Rubber Reserve Company.

Bonus of 5 cents per pound on all rubber exports to be applied to repayment of advance. Funds from this bonus to go to the Bolivian Government after full repayment of advance.

Additional bonus of 5 cents per pound on all rubber exports if these exports exceed 1500 tons per annum, this bonus to go to producers. Publicity could be given the additional bonus so as to help rubber gatherers to get added wages.

While I realize these are stiff terms from our point of view even they will be insufficient if Argentines, as seems likely, want rubber

---

[96] Not printed.

enough to raise ante. Is there no possibility of making a deal with Argentina whereby it would withdraw from [the Bolivian market?] and we would guarantee it say 50% of its normal imports these to be supplied by us from Brazil, Bolivia or wherever most convenient?

If something of this sort is impossible and we cannot meet Argentine price it might be better to withdraw our offer, let Argentina have Bolivian rubber and concentrate on Brazil. As Argentina would not offer as much if we were out of the market this would at least prevent price spiral in competition in Bolivia. If price is boosted materially here Brazil will undoubtedly demand upward revision of our price agreement with it.

As stated in my 216, March 30, 5 p. m.,[98] premium proposals contained in Department's 177, March 28, 9 p. m., have not been presented pending further word from the Department. Difficulties I see in the telegram are that (1) proposed fund would apparently be advanced to Bolivian Government which could not be trusted to use it properly, (2) there would thus be no direct incentive to producers to increase production and (3) the Argentine-Bolivian production can be increased to 2500 tons in which case there would be no opportunity for repayment of fund.

A prompt decision is vital as situation is daily becoming more difficult and complex.

DAWSON

811.20 Defense (M) Bolivia/137 : Telegram

The Secretary of State to the Chargé in Bolivia (Dawson)

WASHINGTON, April 27, 1942—8 p. m.

238. Your 257 April 18. Your suggested proposal has been carefully considered. Only difficulties are with respect to price and bonus payments. It does not seem feasible at this time to pay more than established in our agreements with Brazil and Peru. The method of taking care of additional costs of production, inaccessibility of rubber supplies, supplying rubber gatherers, etc. has been to make payments therefor from the fund proposed to be established by Rubber Reserve Company. We apparently did not make clear the nature of the fund. It is not a loan repayable by the Bolivian Government, and represents merely a commitment by Rubber Reserve Company to expend up to this amount for increasing rubber production. There will be no obligation on Bolivia with respect to its repayment; however, premiums paid are deducted from the balance of the fund not theretofore expended. The figure of $1,125,000 was an estimate made here of the amount which might reasonably

---

[98] Not printed.

be expended to increase production. But, for your information only, if additional sums can profitably be spent for this purpose, resulting in increased production there will probably be no difficulty in making provisions for them.

It is agreed that the fund might best be spent under the direction of Rubber Reserve Company, or some other American governmental agency operating in Bolivia, if this is acceptable to Bolivia.

In the agreement with Brazil a base price was fixed for the highest grade, the agreement providing that other grades were to be at appropriate differentials. A preliminary schedule fixed for this purpose has now been revised after discussion with the Brazilian authorities, and on the basis of the revised schedule, the price payable to Bolivia for Beni Upriver Fine would be 32¼ cents per pound f.o.b. vessel at Belém, Brazil and 39 cents per pound f.o.b. vessel at Belém for Beni Hard Fine on washed and dried basis as stated in Department's 205 of April 11.[99] Rubber Reserve advises that Beni Upriver Fine has not drawn a premium in world markets over first grade plantation rubber. It is agreed that other grades would be purchased at differentials based on past trade usage.

In view of the general difficulties we have requested Mr. Douglas Allen and Raymond Bogardus, representatives now in Brazil of Rubber Reserve Company, to go to La Paz as soon as possible to aid you in negotiations. They may be accompanied by Messrs. Manifold and Roberts.[1] These men all have full background on the rubber situation and should give you substantial assistance. They intend to leave Belém within the next few days.

In conversation Friday with Guachalla,[2] we indicated to him the great urgency for our acquisition of the Bolivian rubber production and the unfortunate political reactions here if this production should go to Argentina. We said that a decision by Bolivia to sell to Argentina was certain to have importance in the development of economic relations between the two countries. The talk then touched on the fact that discussions were going on for revision of our tin and tungsten purchasing agreements with Bolivia. We threw out the suggestion indirectly but sufficiently clearly that if the Bolivian Government worked out the rubber production in accordance with American requests, it would facilitate our endeavor to meet Bolivian requests as regards tungsten and tin.[3] At the end of a general review of various factual features of the three supply questions, the Ambassador stated he would be glad to do anything he could to aid in concluding satis-

---

[99] Not printed.

[1] Courtland B. Manifold, representative, and James C. Roberts, assistant to the President, Rubber Reserve Co.

[2] Luis Fernando Guachalla, Bolivian Ambassador in the United States.

[3] For the opinion of the Chargé in Bolivia (Dawson) on this suggestion, see his telegram No. 286, May 3, 11 a. m., p. 544.

factory agreements on all three matters and said he would immediately cable his Government.

Pending the arrival of Allen, we suggest that you do everything possible to delay any agreement with Argentina. In view of the time element, we think it is impossible to initiate with Argentina at this time any negotiations as to its acquisition of rubber from the producing countries.

HULL

811.20 Defense (M) Bolivia/152 : Telegram

The Chargé in Bolivia (Dawson) to the Secretary of State

LA PAZ, April 30, 1942—11 a. m.
[Received 4 : 28 p. m.]

280. Department's 238, April 27, 8 p. m. Argentines have already bought at least 175 tons of rubber. Shipments are now being made by air to Cochabamba taking advantage of low LAB [5] freight rate and thence by rail to Buenos Aires. Price of recent market reported reliably to have been 56 cents per pound c.i.f. Buenos Aires which works out about 48 cents f.o.b. Beni.

DAWSON

811.20 Defense (M) Bolivia/165 : Telegram

The Secretary of State to the Chargé in Bolivia (Dawson)

WASHINGTON, May 16, 1942—2 p. m.

275. Your 308 of May 9.[6] As advised in our 257 of May 9,[6] the 5 year guarantee of prices is satisfactory. It is also agreed in principle that the excess transportation costs referred to may be absorbed in some way by Rubber Reserve Company.

The fund referred to by you has been already agreed to in no. 177 of March 28 and no. 238 of April 27. It is contemplated that such fund would be expended under the direction of some United States governmental agency, and this was stated in our 238 of April 27.

The price premiums for volume were intended to be equitably related to present and potential volume of production on the same basis as in Brazil. Is there any feeling that the figure of 2500 tons and 4500 tons contained in 177 of March 28 are not equitable for this purpose?

While it is believed that the negotiations will be expedited through conversations with Guachalla here to give him background explanations which he in turn can pass on to his Government, it appears

---

[5] Lloyd Aéreo Boliviano.
[6] Not printed.

doubtful that he would be in a position to accede on the major points. In view of Ambassador Boal's imminent arrival at La Paz and his first hand knowledge of the rubber situation here, it is suggested that this should assist in reaching a conclusion of the rubber agreement promptly and it is one of the first matters to be taken up by him.

Repeat to Lima as 421 for Allen.

HULL

811.20 Defense (M) Bolivia/189 : Telegram

The Ambassador in Bolivia (Boal) to the Secretary of State

LA PAZ, June 2, 1942—6 p. m.
[Received 11 : 10 p. m.]

379. Department's May 26, 1 p. m.[7] Bolivian Government is awaiting receipt by La Paz representative of Beni Rubber Producers of instructions from his principals before proceeding with negotiations. Embassy has seen advance copy of these instructions which suggest :

(1) Five-year minimum term for contract.

(2) Prices equivalent to those in Brazilian and Peruvian contracts.

(3) Provision for larger producers to ship uncut balls to New York as they have in the past with guarantee of 3% shrinkage.

(4) Bonuses of 2½ cents per pound on exports over 1,000 tons per annum and 5 cents over 2,000 tons, these to be prorated among exporters.

(5) Absorption by Rubber Reserve of excess freight from Villa Murtinho to Pará over cost from Xapuri via Acre to Pará.

(6) Payment by Rubber Reserve of storage costs at Pará after 30 days' delay in shipment.

(7) Commitment as to priorities for and assistance in securing supplies and equipment needed for rubber production.

(8) Promise of 750 tons of shipping space per annum for Brazil nuts and 10 for raw hides and skins; this provision stated to be indispensable.

(9) Agreement to ship to Bolivia sufficient manufactured rubber articles for its needs (Embassy understands that Government wishes guarantee that 30% of raw rubber exports will be returned in form of tires, et cetera).

(10) Joint governmental plan of economic assistance for rubber development including improving river and land communications.

These points seem to be covered in proposals Rubber Reserve or to be adaptable thereto except for points 4 and 8. The 15% increase mentioned in second paragraph of Department's 300 should satisfy producers in lieu of point 4 which indicates misunderstanding as to nature of bonuses. Point 8 probably not feasible because of shortage

---

[7] Telegram No. 300, not printed; it authorized certain increases in price and premiums to be offered to Bolivia in order to effect an agreement (811.20 Defense (M) Bolivia/179).

shipping space but Roberts has suggested that Rubber Reserve might possibly purchase some nuts and hold them unshipped.

We fear that the Bolivian Government will insist on percentage arrangement for tires as indicated under point 9 instead of the vague assurances contained in Department's circular of May 18, midnight.[8] Would appreciate instructions on this point.

With reference to the last paragraph of Department 300, Roberts, while in Riberalta conferring with rubber producers, stated that provided that rubber agreement was signed, Rubber Reserve would absorb differential in freight from Bolivia to Pará as compared with Acre to Pará but could not cover any future increases in freight rates. His statement was based on conversation with Allen in Lima and his understanding that latter had received instructions authorizing this by telephone from Washington. In view of this situation, believe that commitment should be made.

BOAL

811.20 Defense (M) Bolivia/189 : Telegram

The Secretary of State to the Ambassador in Bolivia (Boal)

WASHINGTON, June 8, 1942—9 p. m.

334. Your 379 of June 2.

1. Contract should expire December 31, 1946, to be consistent with other rubber contracts. This is not, however, an important issue.

2. Agreed, except that entire 15 percent increase referred to in the Department's telegram 300 of May 26 [9] should go to producers. The price of 39 cents plus approximately 15 percent has now been fixed at 45 cents per pound.

3. Because of the lack of familiarity here with the various types and grades of Bolivian rubber, it is very desirable that in the agreement as initially signed the price be given only for Beni Hard Fine, washed and dried, and for Castilloa scrap with a provision that prices for other types and grades be fixed at appropriate differentials from the specified price based on past trade practice. It is planned to have representatives of Rubber Reserve go to Bolivia as soon as possible after the execution of the agreement, and these representatives would be in a position to agree on prices for these other types and grades, including the price for uncut balls. Since all prices are on the basis of f. o. b. Brazilian ports, it will be unnecessary to have any guarantee with respect to shrinkage in transit from Brazilian

---

[8] Printed in vol. VI, section under Colombia entitled "Negotiation of an agreement between the Rubber Reserve Company and Colombia . . ."

[9] See footnote 7, p. 567.

ports to this country, but this will be a factor in determining the price which will be agreed upon. Past trade practice in this connection will, of course, be given effect to.

4. Your suggestion that 15 percent increase takes care of this is agreed with. However, if essential to obtaining execution of contract you are authorized to agree that the premiums are to be based on the lower figures of 1,000 and 2,000 tons. However, such premiums are not to be prorated among exporters but paid to Government of Bolivia to be used by it in increasing quantity and improving quality of rubber production.

5. Satisfactory, so long as agreement does not cover future increases in freight rates from Villa Murtinho to Pará.

6. Satisfactory.

7. A general undertaking will be given that this Government will use its best efforts so far as consistent with conduct of war, to arrange to furnish necessary supplies and equipment. It is out of the question to give a flat commitment in this respect, for reasons apparent to you. Any "assistance" of a financial nature would be limited to expenditures from the fund of $1,125,000, which can be supplemented to the extent required in reasonable projects for increasing rubber production.

8. It is unlikely that shipping could be made available for Brazil nuts. In any event they are thought here to be directly competitive with rubber and they are of no value as strategic materials. The same question has arisen in Brazil. It is in substance a problem caused by the factors referred to in the Department's circular telegram of May 27, 6 p. m.,[10] and it will have to be handled on the basis there referred to. The hides are not of the quality used here, but the amount seems unimportant one way or the other and they should not be permitted to be an important issue. Under ordinary circumstances very little attention would be paid to this proposal, and there is no disposition here to give it favorable consideration. However, your comments are requested.

9. It is regretted that nothing more definite can be agreed to than the assurances contained in the Department's circular telegram of May 18.[11] In addition to the factors outlined in that telegram, it will be readily apparent to you that shipping difficulties alone would make impossible an unconditional agreement in this respect. The only feasible alternative seems to be that being followed in Ecuador[12] where Ecuador's obligation to sell crude rubber is conditioned on there being

---

[10] Not printed.

[11] See footnote 8, p. 568.

[12] For correspondence on the negotiations with Ecuador concerning rubber, see vol. VI, section under Ecuador entitled "Negotiation and application of an agreement concerning the production and export of Ecuadoran rubber."

available to Ecuador rubber products, including tires and tubes, in amounts sufficient to satisfy its indispensable requirements.

10. Acceptable so long as Rubber Reserve retains control over and direction of expenditure of $1,125,000 fund.

HULL

811.20 Defense (M) Bolivia/197 : Telegram

The Secretary of State to the Ambassador in Bolivia (Boal)

WASHINGTON, June 17, 1942—11 p. m.

367. Your 415 of June 11.[13] It is urged that every effort be made to sign agreement prior to departure of Ministers of Finance and Economy.[14]

You are authorized to offer the following prices: Crude Beni Fine, cut and classified, 36¾ cents, which is believed to be at the proper differential from the 45 cent price you refer to; Castilloa Scrap, or Bolivian Caucho, 27½ cents; Smoked Sheet, 48¼ cents.

Question of handling Brazil nuts is being considered further here, but it is suggested you continue to try to keep it out of negotiations. In general it may be said that problem appears primarily to relate to present stocks on hand which are tying up capital and it is expected that necessary relief in this situation could be afforded.

HULL

811.20 Defense (M) Bolivia/203 : Telegram

The Ambassador in Bolivia (Boal) to the Secretary of State

LA PAZ, June 18, 1942—3 p. m.
[Received 10 : 23 p. m.]

449. My telegram No. 415, June 11, 11 a. m.[13] and my telephone call to Finletter[15] this morning. The Foreign Minister prior to leaving La Paz today informed me that he had just received a communication from the Bolivian Embassy at Buenos Aires transmitting a written proposal by the Argentine Government for an agreement to buy all of Bolivia's rubber production. The proposal he said is for a term of 5 years. Price according to Minister of Economy is specified by the Argentine Government at 39 cents for crude classified at present, f.o.b. Villa Murtinho as compared with our price of 36¾ cents f.o.b. Belém. Cost of transportation from Villa Murtinho to Belém is about 7 cents.

---

[13] Not printed; this telegram indicated delays in concluding a rubber agreement.
[14] Joaquín Espada and Alberto Crespo Gutiérrez, respectively. They were coming to the United States to discuss plans for financial and economic cooperation; see pp. 592 ff.
[15] Thomas K. Finletter, Acting Chief, Division of Defense Materials.

He said that in paragraph No. 4 of the Argentine proposal the Argentine Government stated that it would be part of the agreement that it would use its best efforts to maintain the present flow of sugar, wheat, rice, meat, manufactured products, and hunting weapons to Bolivia and to prevent any obstruction from arising in their delivery.

The Foreign Minister stated that the latter paragraph was considered as a veiled threat that a stoppage of these necessities might occur if the Argentine offer were disregarded. He said, however, that he would instruct the Bolivian Embassy in Buenos Aires to advise the Argentine Foreign Office that an agreement on rubber had already been reached in principle with the United States.

Repeated to Buenos Aires.

BOAL

811.20 Defense (M) Bolivia/214 : Telegram

The Ambassador in Bolivia (Boal) to the Secretary of State

LA PAZ, June 25, 1942—3 p. m.
[Received June 26—1:45 a. m.]

476. Reference paragraph "d" of my 470, June 24, 7 p. m.[16] Minister of Economy objects to article 8 of the proposed agreement as subject for domestic action not for contractual relations with Reserve.[17] He states that he agrees with objectives of article and that Bolivian Government intends to take steps along the lines suggested but that insertion of article would place difficulties in the way of approval of agreement as a whole especially if producers are required to sign.

It is my feeling that economic condition of gatherers can best be improved and equitable real wages established through proper control of $2,125,000 fund on ground by Reserve. Greatest problem at present is that gatherers are always in debt to companies which advance them food and supplies. This situation can be more effectively remedied by Reserve through use its fund than by Bolivian Government promises and without possible bad results of insisting on latter. The Department will appreciate that the fact that this article is in neither Peruvian nor Brazilian agreement might open the Government here to criticism from the opposition if included for Bolivia alone. Increased opposition strength in the next Congress suggests advisability of not offering grounds for political debate.

The President has put forward any suggestions to offer to La Paz to June 28 or June 29 in order to deal with rubber problem and to

---

[16] Not printed.
[17] Article 8 was a provision concerning fair wages and supplies for rubber gatherers.

give instructions to Ministers of Economy and Finance before departure for Washington June 30. If question raised in my 470 and the present telegraph can be resolved before the week end it should probably be possible have agreement ready for signature by latter date unless new unforeseen difficulties arise.

Tentative draft agreement as discussed with Minister of Economy this morning is being forwarded by tomorrow's courier.

BOAL

811.20 Defense (M) Bolivia/228 : Telegram

The Ambassador in Bolivia (Boal) to the Secretary of State

LA PAZ, July 2, 1942—10 p. m.
[Received July 3—1 : 27 a. m.]

497. For Finletter. Today I saw the Foreign Minister who returned to La Paz yesterday. He explained that he has discussed the rubber contract with the President and considers they are now ready to conclude but feel some provision must be made to cover their situation vis-à-vis Argentina which, through the Bolivian Ambassador in Buenos Aires,[19] has made it clear again that if Bolivia cuts them off without any contractor [contract] despite their offer of a 5 years' contract, economic reprisals may be expected. The Foreign Minister suggested that payment of 150 tons annually for "neighboring countries" be made in our contract with the provision that the situation be re-examined with view to adjustment by mutual consent at the end of the first year.

The Foreign Minister had at first suggested that 15% of Bolivian production be set aside for export to neighboring countries but I pointed out that this would unfairly [apparent omission] our cooperation to increase production.

The Foreign Minister appreciates that subtracting 150 tons annually would probably mean proportionate reduction in development funds to be supplied by us but says that in view of Argentine stranglehold on Bolivia's food supply and oil transportation system he considers contract must include the 150 tons as a gesture. He adds that even if this gesture is not satisfactory to Argentina it will place him in a position to stand his ground against further intimations of unrestrained pressure.

As an Argentine representative may arrive in the next few days it would be most helpful to have the Department's reply as early as

---

[19] Adolfo Costa du Rels.

possible tomorrow with a view to trying to reach a conclusion before his arrival which might complicate matters.[20]

BOAL

811.20 Defense (M) Bolivia/241 : Telegram

The Ambassador in Bolivia (Boal) to the Secretary of State

LA PAZ, July 9, 1942—midnight.
[Received July 9—2 : 16 p. m.]

521. My 512, July 7, noon.[21] The Foreign Minister informs me that the Argentine Ambassador [22] called at the Foreign Office this morning and stated that the Argentine Government has made a proposition to the American Government through the American Embassy in Buenos Aires regarding Bolivian rubber production and asked that the conclusion of any agreement with the United States here be delayed pending a reply by our Government to the Argentine proposal. The Foreign Minister said that he saw no option but to agree to await our reply.

Under the circumstances I would appreciate your telegraphing me the substance of our reply to Argentina as soon as possible to show to the Foreign Minister in order to remove this as a reason for delay in signature.

BOAL

811.20 Defense (M) Bolivia/244 : Telegram

The Secretary of State to the Ambassador in Bolivia (Boal)

WASHINGTON, July 11, 1942—6 p. m.

444. Understand from telephone conversation with Ambassador that you have received telegram from Buenos Aires informing you that the Argentine Government has discussed with the American Ambassador in Buenos Aires the possibility of Argentina making an agreement, on terms approved by the United States Government, for the acquisition by Argentina of the Bolivian rubber production. The Department desires to proceed with the proposed rubber agreement between Bolivia and Rubber Reserve Company and accordingly does not desire to consider any arrangement whereby this production would be made available to Argentina.

---

[20] Notation on file copy indicates that a reply was made by telephone on July 3 but does not give the nature of the reply. Article 3 of the agreement signed on July 15, however, contains a provision for an annual quota of 150 tons for export to neighboring countries ; for text, see p. 576.
[21] Not printed.
[22] Avelino Aráoz.

Your 530 of July 10.[23] First suggestion as to change in wording of paragraph 4 of Note is approved. It is assumed clause at end of paragraph 4 beginning "and the Government of Bolivia would limit the consumption" remains unchanged.

HULL

811.20 Defense (M) Bolivia/269

The American Ambassador in Bolivia (Boal) to the Bolivian Minister for Foreign Affairs (Anze Matienzo)[24]

No. 43   LA PAZ, July 15, 1942.

EXCELLENCY: As Your Excellency is aware, my Government is desirous of fomenting the production of raw rubber in the Western Hemisphere and of acquiring the maximum possible amount of this product in furtherance of the common defense effort. I have the honor consequently, under instructions from my Government, to present the following proposal:

(1) In order to stimulate the development of the crude rubber resources of Bolivia, the Rubber Reserve Company, an agency of my Government established as a corporation under the laws of the United States, would set up a fund of $2,125,000 to be available for the purpose of increasing the wild rubber production in Bolivia, including the improvement of river and land communications in the rubber-producing regions. Control over and direction of expenditure of this fund would be exercised in agreement with the Government of Bolivia by the Rubber Reserve Company which would furnish special technicians for the purpose of utilizing the fund in the most efficient manner practicable to the end of fomenting and facilitating production of wild rubber in Bolivia.

(2) The Government of the United States and the Government of Bolivia would collaborate fully for the purpose of increasing the output of Bolivian crude rubber. The Government of the United States would arrange to furnish technicians to aid in the development of the production of smoked sheet rubber and also would use its best efforts to make possible the acquisition by producers in Bolivia of the necessary equipment for such production as soon as practicable.

(3) The Government of Bolivia would agree to allow only the Rubber Reserve Company or persons or organizations named by it to export rubber from Bolivia, except as otherwise provided in the agreement between them mentioned below, and to encourage the highest possible production of rubber and the export to the United States of the largest amount possible.

---

[23] Not printed; this telegram refers to changes in wording sought by Bolivia with respect to rubber manufactured goods (811.20 Defense (M) Bolivia/244).

[24] Copy transmitted to the Department by the Ambassador in his despatch No. 310, July 17; received July 22.

(4) The Government of the United States would meet the needs of Bolivia in manufactured rubber articles within the limits of equitable cooperation permitted by the present situation and the Government of Bolivia would limit the consumption of crude rubber and the use of rubber products to the extent necessary to permit the maximum contribution to the defense of the Hemisphere.

(5) The Rubber Reserve Company would enter into an agreement for the purchase of all rubber produced in Bolivia until December 31, 1946, excluding exceptions made in the agreement. The prices stipulated in the agreement would be based on present costs of production and would be reconsidered on the basis of equity if there were any general revision of rubber prices in similar agreements of the Rubber Reserve Company with other countries.

(6) In furtherance of Resolution XXX adopted at the Rio de Janeiro Consultative Meeting of Foreign Ministers,[25] the Government of the United States would extend to development work in the valleys of the Amazonian tributaries of Bolivia and adjacent regions the good offices of the Health and Sanitation Division established by the Office of the Coordinator of Inter-American Affairs to carry out a program of improving health and sanitation conditions in cooperation with governmental agencies of the other American Republics.

The foregoing proposals would appear to further substantially the effectiveness of Resolution II of the Rio de Janeiro Consultative Meeting wherein each of the signatory powers undertook to collaborate with the other American Republics to the fullest degree possible in the mobilization of its economic resources with the special objective of increasing the production of those strategic materials essential for the defense of the Hemisphere against armed aggression and for the maintenance of the economics of the American Republics.

I am authorized by my Government to reiterate to Your Excellency its earnest desire to assist Bolivia in obtaining such manufactured products, foodstuffs and raw products as are essential for the maintenance of the national economy of Bolivia and its readiness to take such steps toward this end as may be consistent with its war effort if a serious impairment of Bolivia's present sources of such supplies should occur.

On behalf of the Government of the United States and in accordance with the conversations which I have had with officials of the Government of Bolivia, I have the honor to request that the Government of Bolivia give consideration to the above proposals.

I avail myself [etc.]   [File copy not signed]

---

[25] For correspondence concerning this meeting, held January 15–28, 1942, see pp. 6 ff.; for text of the Final Act of the Conference, see Department of State *Bulletin*, February 7, 1942, p. 117.

811.20 Defense (M) Bolivia/269

The Bolivian Minister for Foreign Affairs (Anze Matienzo) to the American Ambassador in Bolivia (Boal)[26]

[Translation]

La Paz, July 15, 1942.

Mister Ambassador: I acknowledge receipt of Your Excellency's kind note, dated today, in which are formulated a plan for the development of the production of rubber in Bolivia and a project for economic collaboration between the United States of America and my country, in furtherance of the Second Resolution of the Third Consultative Meeting of Ministers of Foreign Affairs of the American Republics at Rio de Janeiro.

2. I take pleasure in informing Your Excellency that the competent organisms of my Government have studied this proposition and are ready to cooperate in said development work in accordance with the specific propositions which Your Excellency's note mentions.

3. I am convinced that this program will constitute a fundamental step toward the carrying out of mutually advantageous economic relations between our two countries as is contemplated in the Resolution adopted at the Rio de Janeiro Conference.

I avail myself [etc.]   Ed. Anze Matienzo

811.20 Defense (M) Bolivia/269

Agreement Between the Rubber Reserve Company and the Government of the Republic of Bolivia[26]

This Agreement, made and entered into this fifteenth day of July, 1942, by and between the Rubber Reserve Company (hereinafter called "Reserve") an Agency of the United States Government and a corporation existing under the laws of the United States of America and having an office for the transaction of business in Washington, D. C., party of the first part, and the Republic of Bolivia (hereinafter sometimes called "Bolivia"), party of the second part;

Witnesseth:

1. Reserve agrees to establish or cause to be established an agency (hereinafter called the "Agency") which shall be authorized to assist in developing the rubber resources of Bolivia and to acquire and sell all types of rubber and rubber products produced within the territory of the Republic of Bolivia. Reserve and Bolivia agree that the

---

[26] Copy transmitted to the Department by the Ambassador in his despatch No. 310, July 17; received July 22.

Agency shall have all powers necessary and appropriate to the performance of these functions.

2. Bolivia recognizes the large rubber requirements of the United States for the war emergency and agrees that the Agency shall have the exclusive right to export rubber from the Republic of Bolivia, with the exceptions provided for in Article 3 of this agreement. Bolivia agrees to use its best efforts to bring about the maximum production of rubber and to cause it to be sold to the Agency, and to take effective measures for the purpose of conserving rubber and directing it into essential war time uses, including measures to prevent the hoarding of rubber and rubber products.

3. Reserve agrees that the Agency will buy and Bolivia agrees that it will cause to be sold to the Agency all of the rubber, with the exception of a quota for export to neighboring countries, produced within the territory of the Republic of Bolivia which is not required by the Republic of Bolivia for domestic use and consumption. The quota for export to neighboring countries shall be 150 tons per calendar year.

Until the exact capacity and costs of production in the provinces of Larecaja and Caupolicán of the department of La Paz can be established, the production of these provinces exported through the city of La Paz, will not be included in the present agreement, Bolivia undertaking for its part to have this production included in the agreement as soon as commercial and industrial conditions permit. It is further mutually agreed that the exports under this provision shall not exceed 60 tons a year and that in the event that production should exceed this amount, the contracting parties may proceed to an adjustment of the aforementioned conditions by mutual consent.

It is further mutually agreed that the rubber production from the triangle formed by the rivers Tarvo and Paraguá in the Department of Santa Cruz exported through Puerto Suárez will not be included in the present agreement for the first year of its life, at the end of which time the question of the production from this triangle will be rediscussed with a view to reaching a mutual accord. It is further provided that the total exports of rubber from the provinces of Larecaja and Caupolicán and from the aforementioned triangle plus the above mentioned quota for neighboring countries, constituting all exceptions from this contract, shall not be in excess of 250 tons per annum, Reserve to be entitled to and to receive all rubber produced in all areas of Bolivia with the exception of said maximum of 250 tons.

Regulations for the administration of the quota for export to neighboring countries shall be established by common accord between Reserve and Bolivia and the figure of 150 tons shall likewise be subject to adjustment by mutual consent of Reserve and Bolivia at the end of the first year of the life of this agreement.

The amount required for domestic use and consumption in Bolivia shall be determined by mutual agreement between Reserve and Bolivia. Should it become possible, during the period of this agreement, for Bolivia to establish a domestic tire factory, the quota for domestic use and consumption will be subject to adjustment by mutual consent.

4. Reserve and Bolivia agree that the base price to be paid by the Agency for purchases of rubber hereunder shall be forty-five (45) cents, U.S.A. currency per pound, f.o.b. Belém, Brazil, or f.o.b. Chilean or Peruvian Pacific Ocean ports as designated by Reserve for Beni hard fine on a washed and dried basis, and thirty-seven and one-eighth (37⅛) cents, U.S.A. currency per pound, f.o.b. Belém, Brazil, or f.o.b. Chilean or Peruvian Pacific Ocean ports as designated by Reserve, for usual good quality crude Beni, fine, cut and classified, with appropriate differentials for other types and grades (which shall include forty-eight and one-quarter (48¼) cents for smoked sheet rubber); and twenty-seven and one-half (27½) cents, U.S.A. currency per pound, f.o.b. Belém, Brazil, or f.o.b. Chilean or Peruvian Pacific Ocean ports as designated by Reserve, for usual good quality Castilloa scrap (as understood in trade circles in New York City) with appropriate differentials for other types and grades (said base price together with said differentials being hereinafter referred to as the "Fixed Price"). Reserve agrees to advance to producers substantially eighty per cent of the Fixed Price (after deducting export taxes, freight and other charges to the ocean port of shipment) upon delivery (a) at air or river ports designated by Reserve, (b) at rail head for transportation to Pacific Ocean ports or (c) at border rail head of the Madeira–Mamoré Railroad for transportation to Belém, title however, not to pass to Reserve until delivery f.o.b. ocean port. Reserve further agrees to absorb all freight costs from (a) air or river ports designated by Reserve, (b) rail head for transportation to Pacific Ocean ports or (c) border rail head of the Madeira–Mamoré Railroad for transportation to Belém which are in excess of two and one-quarter (2¼) cents per pound, understood to be approximately the present freight cost from Acre to Belém. If the Agency purchases rubber at internal points other than those specified above, the price to be paid by it shall be the Fixed Price less appropriate differentials to cover transportation to such specified points, transportation from them to ocean ports on a basis of two and one-quarter (2¼) cents per pound and customary handling charges.

In addition to the aforesaid prices Reserve agrees to make premium payments on account of purchases and sales of rubber in the Republic of Bolivia as follows:

Two and one-half (2½) cents per pound for all of the rubber so purchased and sold in excess of fifteen hundred (1500) long tons and not in excess of twenty-five hundred (2500) long tons during any one calendar year of this agreement;

And five (5) cents per pound for all of the rubber so purchased and sold in excess of twenty-five hundred (2500) long tons during any one calendar year of this agreement.

The amounts of any premiums so paid may be deducted from the unexpended balance of the development fund provided for in clause seven of this agreement. Bolivia agrees that all premiums not so deducted shall be used by the Government of the Republic of Bolivia or an appropriate agency thereof for the purpose of financing the immediate expansion of production and improvement of quality of wild rubber in the territory of the Republic of Bolivia.

5. It is understood that purchases by the Agency f.o.b. Belém or Chilean or Peruvian ocean ports shall be on the basis of cash against shipping documents endorsed "on board" ocean carrying vessel at the designated port destined for continental ports of the United States of America, provided however that in the event the shipping space to be provided by the Agency in any such case is not available within thirty days after notice to the Agency of the readiness of the rubber for shipment, the rubber shall be stored in a place at the port to be designated by the Agency and the Agency will arrange for payment for the rubber against warehouse warrants or receipts of other documents of title (in lieu of ocean bills of lading) acceptable to the bank negotiating the payment draft and in any such cases such payment shall be at the f.o.b. price less any export duties and taxes and charges for loading on board ship in effect at the date such payment is made; storage charges in this event will be paid by the Agency.

6. It is understood that Bolivia will cause to be established the Fixed Price for all sales of rubber for domestic use or consumption in the Republic of Bolivia.

7. Reserve agrees to establish a development fund of two million, one hundred and twenty-five (2,125,000) dollars to be expended by Reserve in its discretion in accord with Bolivia on developing and increasing the production and improving the quality of rubber in Bolivia, the methods of producing it and the stimulation of conditions favorable to maximum rubber output. The Agency will appoint an adviser designated by Bolivia and satisfactory to the Agency whose duty it shall be to advise the Agency upon methods of securing maximum rubber production in Bolivia.

It is mutually agreed that the amount of the development fund will be reduced by seventy-five thousand (75,000) dollars per annum during the maintenance of the quota of 150 tons for export to neighboring countries provided for in Article 3 of this agreement with the annual reduction being increased or decreased five hundred (500) dollars for each ton by which the export quota is augmented or cut.

8. Reserve agrees to use its best efforts so far as consistent with the conduct of the war to facilitate the furnishing of necessary supplies and equipment for the maintenance and expansion of the Bolivian rubber industry.

9. It is mutually agreed that existing contracts for the purchase of Bolivian rubber which have not been filled may be taken over by Reserve with payment to be made on the terms contained in such contracts.

10. Reserve agrees to purchase during the calendar year 1942 up to five hundred (500) long tons of Brazil nuts produced in Bolivia, and now owned in Bolivia or Brazil by Bolivian producers at a price to be mutually agreed upon by Reserve and Bolivia but in no case less than the price to be paid by Reserve for Brazil nuts under similar agreements with other countries, this purchase being in the nature of relief to such producers during the year 1942 to facilitate readjustment of their production and the labor now engaged therein with a view to utilizing them in developing vegetable oil or other products, preferably strategic, until such time as the world market for Brazil nuts shall again be normal.

11. The term of this agreement shall be for a period beginning with the date hereof and ending December 31, 1946, unless sooner terminated by the mutual consent of the parties hereto.

ED. ANZE MATIENZO
JOHN WORCESTER

811.20 Defense (M) Bolivia/291f : Telegram

The Secretary of State to the Ambassador in Bolivia (*Boal*)

WASHINGTON, July 17, 1942—5 p. m.

455. From Rubber Reserve. Reference rubber agreement.[28] Pending establishment of purchasing organization in Bolivia, we are planning to buy at agreement prices from large producers through their customary New York selling agents. Also during this interim it is desirable that you purchase pursuant to the provisions of article 4 of the agreement all miscellaneous lots of rubber which are available. For this purpose we are immediately establishing a fund of $100,000 with the Bank of Bolivia available to the Ambassador or his nominee. In this connection cable Rubber Reserve weekly the total tons purchased with this fund together with the amount of rubber stocks in each location so purchased and not exported. Pending establishment official prices for grades other than those specified in the agreement it is suggested that the following fob ocean ports

---

[28] *Supra.*

prices be used: Crude Beni hard fine uncut, 36⅛; Crude Bolivian hard fine cut and classified, 36½; Crude Bolivian Hard Fine uncut, 35½; Crude Beni and Bolivian Medium, 33½; Crude Beni and Bolivian Coarse, 26½; Crude Bolivian Weak Fine cut and classified, 34⅞. Article 9 of the Rubber agreement provides that Rubber Reserve may take over at the contract price any pre-existing contracts for the purchase of Bolivian rubber. You are requested to investigate the possibility of taking over any such contracts and are authorized to take them over if possible. We call to your attention that contracts providing for the exportation of rubber to countries other than the United States cannot be fulfilled if the exportation would be in excess of the 250 ton quota stipulated in paragraph 3 for the calendar year 1942. James C. Roberts, Assistant to the President, Rubber Reserve Company, expected to arrive La Paz about July 21 and will be followed within 2 weeks by additional Rubber Reserve personnel. Mr. Roberts will remain in Bolivia a sufficient length of time to organize Rubber Reserve activities. Upon Roberts' arrival suggest he be designated Ambassador's nominee for $100,000 fund. Worth, rubber technician, instructed join Frantz [29] promptly as possible. He is now available to leave Porto Velho for Riberalta as soon as he can secure transportation. Suggest use Frantz and Worth for buying if necessary. Have cabled Embassy Lima requesting them to offer Priester [30] position as Assistant to the Representative of the Rubber Reserve Company in Bolivia at an annual rate of compensation of $6,000 per year plus living allowance of $7 per day while away from La Paz on official business. Have requested Priester to return La Paz as promptly as possible. [Rubber Reserve.]

HULL

811.20 Defense (M) Bolivia/284 : Telegram

The Ambassador in Bolivia (Boal) to the Secretary of State

LA PAZ, August 1, 1942—7 p. m.
[Received 11:48 p. m.]

591. For Rubber Reserve from Roberts. During the last week we have learned by inquiry that, prior to the signing of the Rubber Agreement, the Bolivian Government had issued export permits for shipments to Argentina and Chile totaling 1050 tons. Most of the holders are not rubber producers but speculators who are using the permits as options. As a result of this situation, the three men we have in the Beni and Pando now trying to contract for rubber have

---

[29] Bruce Worth and Harvey R. Frantz were field technicians for the Rubber Reserve Company.
[30] J. E. Priester represented the Dutch quinine trust in Bolivia.

not been able to obtain any as the holders of the permits are paying more.

This situation has been explained to the Minister of Foreign Affairs Matienzo, Under Secretary of Economy Suaz Nabar, and Acting Minister of Economy Sanjines on the basis, first, that article 3 of the agreement defines that not more than 250 tons per calendar year could not [sic] be exported to countries other than the United States and, therefore, that not more than $11\frac{1}{24}$ths of this amount could go out after the signing of the contract. If the permits were allowed to run, they in effect make the contract ineffective as far as this calendar year is concerned as the amount yet to be purchased and shipped against them will probably absorb the remainder of this year's supply. We have implied that we cannot ask Washington to execute present orders for supplies for Bolivia which are sorely needed in Brazil unless we are assured that the letter of the agreement will be followed.

Secondly, that article 9 requires that Rubber Reserve be given an opportunity to buy existing contracts. We have talked with two holders of permits who advise they would be glad to sell to us instead of Argentina provided the Bolivian Government would give them legal basis for canceling their Argentine obligations.

Sanjines agreed this morning to issue a decree to the effect that no exports will be permitted unless bona fide and notarized purchase contract and sales contract dated prior to the signing of the agreement is presented to the Economy. As regards point 2, Sanjines agreed to explore a method whereby his Government can allow these permit holders to break their Argentina obligations.

It might be helpful if advantage were taken of the stay in Washington of Minister of Economy Crespo and Minister of Finance Espada to impress upon them the necessity of strict adherence to terms of Rubber Agreement in connection with general program of economic cooperation. Recommendations by them to their Government would aid us materially in our efforts. This situation explains why we have not been anxious give you approval to execute pending supply orders of Bolivian producers.

Repeated to Allen. [Roberts.]

BOAL

811.20 Defense (M) Bolivia/307 : Telegram

The Secretary of State to the Ambassador in Bolivia (Boal)

WASHINGTON, August 10, 1942—8 p. m.

532. Your 618, August 8.[31] At a meeting today with Ambassador Guachalla and Minister Crespo, it was indicated that it was the view

---

[31] Not printed.

of this Government that the terms of the Rubber Agreement were clear with respect to exports after the date of its signature and that all that remained to be done was to implement the agreement. It was pointed out that the agreement contemplated that exports could be made thereafter only to United States, with the exception of not exceeding 250 tons annually. It was also pointed out that the agreement specifically provided that Rubber Reserve is entitled to take over existing contracts and, subject to approval of Roberts, Rubber Reserve desires to take over such contracts. The Ambassador and the Minister were told that the situation was regarded as very serious and the matter was presented to them in such a way as to leave no doubt as to the possible effect on other pending negotiations of failure to reach a satisfactory result.

Minister Crespo advised that he would immediately cable his Government asking that the contract be implemented in accordance with its terms. It is suggested that you take similar action. In this connection, it would be agreeable to this Government to have 250 tons calculated on the basis of a fiscal year, beginning with the date of the agreement, instead of on a calendar year basis.

HULL

811.20 Defense (M) Bolivia/316 : Telegram

The Ambassador in Bolivia (Boal) to the Secretary of State

LA PAZ, August 12, 1942—6 p. m.
[Received August 13—12 : 28 a. m.]

631. For Duggan [32] and Finletter. Reference Department's telegram No. 532, August 11 [*10*], 8 p. m. The Foreign Minister assured me this morning that his Government would carry out the Rubber Agreement scrupulously; that no more than a proportionate part of the 250 tons for this year specified in the agreement would be exported for the period July 15 to December 31; that all existing contracts would be called in for revision in order that Rubber Reserve could take over such as they have delivered; that hoarding of rubber by cloaked German interests would not be permitted and a decree implementing the Rubber Agreement had been signed. This decree, I gather, is the one which was drafted by the Government in consultation with Roberts and is not wholly satisfactory. The Ministry for Foreign Affairs confidentially ascribed the present difficulties to the extensive issuance of export licenses in Crespo's name just prior to the signing of the agreement.

He read me a telegram that he had just sent to Crespo which is in the sense of the above conversation as regards the Bolivian Government's intention with respect to carrying out the Rubber Agreement.

---

[32] Laurence Duggan, Adviser on Political Relations.

I am telegraphing separately *en clair* under telegram No. 632 [33] the Spanish text of the legalized copy of the decree which has been transmitted to me by the Foreign Minister this afternoon.

I believe that Rubber Reserve can proceed under this decree, however, to examination and acquisition of existing contracts with the Ministry of Economy. As I anticipate that there will be further difficulties arising out of the interests of contract holders and the large number of export permits granted, I respectfully recommend that some form of contingency clause be included in agreements favoring Bolivia in Washington so that continuance from month to month of prices and benefits will depend upon faithful execution of rubber agreement here. It is also recommended that Crespo be impressed with the desirability, when he arrives here, of securing the issuance of a decree in substitution of the one under reference conforming to the outline satisfactorily concluded with the Foreign Minister on August 8.

I gather that the Foreign Minister himself had no objection to that form and that the difficulty lay rather in the Ministry of Economy. I shall telegraph tomorrow whether or not the decree given in my telegram 632 has been published here.

BOAL

811.20 Defense (M) Bolivia/346 : Telegram

The Secretary of State to the Ambassador in Bolivia (Boal)

WASHINGTON, August 27, 1942—noon.

591. Your 723, August 24, 1 a. m., and 720, August 22, noon.[34] The Department has expressed its concern to the Bolivian Ambassador with respect to the possibility that the rubber agreement may be subjected to modification or delay in its application by reference to the Bolivian Congress. The Bolivian Ambassador was informed that, while this Government did not wish to presume to make suggestions concerning purely domestic Bolivian procedure for endorsement of the agreement, there was no indication at the time of the negotiation of the agreement that anything further than the signature of the representatives of the two Governments was needed to make it effective. It was emphasized to the Ambassador that this Government attributes especial importance to the prompt application of the rubber agreement not only as a means of obtaining a vital strategic material but as an integral part of the program of cooperation with Bolivia typifying the reciprocal action necessary for success of the program.

HULL

---

[33] Not printed.
[34] Neither printed.

811.20 Defense (M) Bolivia/517

The Ambassador in Bolivia (Boal) to the Secretary of State

No. 784 LA PAZ, October 27, 1942.
[Received November 3.]

SIR: I have the honor to enclose a copy of a contract [35] which was signed on October 19, 1942, between the authorized representatives in La Paz of the Rubber Reserve Company and the Banco Agrícola of Bolivia providing principally that the funds to be provided to rubber producers in Bolivia to finance increased production will be loaned through the Banco Agrícola, but that the Rubber Reserve Company shall be the sole purchaser of rubber production in Bolivia.

The Banco Agrícola, according to the provisions of the contract, is to receive all of the interest paid on the loans by the rubber producers, in return for which the Banco Agrícola is required only to assume a maximum risk of 25 percent of the loans and to perform the detailed services of the collections and checking on the manner in which specific amounts of funds are expended.

The Rubber Reserve Company considers this contract to be advantageous principally because it includes the agreement of the Banco Agrícola that the Rubber Reserve Company shall be the sole purchaser of Bolivian rubber production. Also, it is definitely advantageous to the Rubber Reserve Company to be relieved of the accounting details of handling the large loans that are being made to producers. It is expected that these loans to be handled by the Banco Agrícola may total between 50,000,000 Bolivianos and 100,000,000 Bolivianos (approximately between $1,000,000 and $2,000,000).

It will be noted that the contract provides that the Rubber Reserve Company shall sell to the Banco Agrícola the 250 metric tons per annum that is to be available for shipment from Bolivia to countries other than the United States. It is expected that the Banco Agrícola will realize a comparatively large profit on this amount of rubber.

Respectfully yours, PIERRE DE L. BOAL

811.20 Defense (M) Bolivia/535 : Telegram

The Ambassador in Bolivia (Boal) to the Secretary of State

LA PAZ, November 16, 1942—10 p. m.
[Received 10 : 47 p. m.]

1061. The Senate today passed a resolution formulated by the Finance Company and the Constitutional Committee to the effect that as the Rubber Agreement is in accordance with the wishes of rubber producers it need not have congressional sanction and also emitting

---

[35] Not printed.

the opinion that the operations of the Banco Agrícola are administrative and do not need legal approval. "Our private agreement with the Banco Agrícola is on file with Rubber Reserve".

The resolution which the Senate passed and sent forward to the President seemed to imply that the Government should call in the rubber producers and have them sign the approval of the agreement and the Government is preparing to do this as soon as possible. Rubber Reserve representative here is arranging to bring producers to La Paz for this purpose by plane.

BOAL

GOOD OFFICES OF THE DEPARTMENT OF STATE IN NEGOTIATIONS BETWEEN BOLIVIA AND THE STANDARD OIL COMPANY [36]

824.50/49 : Telegram

The Chargé in Bolivia (Dawson) to the Secretary of State

LA PAZ, January 7, 1942—7 p. m.
[Received 10 : 07 p. m.]

13. For the Under Secretary.[37] My 6, January 5, 2 p. m.[38] In conversation today Minister of Foreign Affairs [39] made it clear that he is most anxious to bring something concrete back from his meeting with you in Rio de Janeiro [40] to counteract criticism that American economic cooperation is a myth.

He stated that what he has in mind on Standard Oil problem is an agreement with you on a lump sum settlement (he indicated $1,000,000 as his idea of a proper amount) and at the same time an agreement for a credit of about $2,500,000 from the Export-Import Bank for oil fields development and roads to petroleum region.

He said that he thought only method of settling Standard Oil question was for it to be done rapidly and presented as a *fait accompli* to the Bolivian public since any opportunity for debate would bring failure as in prior attempts. There is much to be said for this point.

On the off chance that a formula for settlement of the oil problem can be found, matter of credit for oil fields development etc., might be included in the development of the idea described my No. 5, January 5, 11 a. m.[41] by the addition of aid to the petroleum industry as one

---

[36] Continued from *Foreign Relations*, 1941, vol. VI.
[37] Sumner Welles.
[38] Not printed.
[39] Eduardo Anze Matienzo.
[40] Third Meeting of the Foreign Ministers of the American Republics, January 15–28, 1942 ; for correspondence, see pp. 6 ff.
[41] Not printed ; for correspondence on the economic cooperation program, see pp. 592 ff.

of its authorized activities. Incidentally our best information is that at least $5,000,000 would be needed for proper development of oil fields as a self-liquidating project and that sum suggested by Anze would be wasteful since it would not accomplish objective.

DAWSON

824.6363 St. 2/560a : Telegram

The Secretary of State to the Chargé in Bolivia (Dawson)

WASHINGTON, January 28, 1942—9 p. m.

39. Your 13, January 7, 7 p. m. The Bolivian Minister of Foreign Affairs informed Mr. Welles at Rio de Janeiro that he had been authorized by the President of Bolivia [42] to enter into an immediate arrangement for the settlement of the Standard Oil dispute. He presented the draft of a suggested Agreement between the Bolivian Government and the Standard Oil Company in which provision was made for payment of a specific amount to the Company for all of the rights, interests and properties in Bolivia of the Company and its Bolivian subsidiary. The Minister of Foreign Affairs suggested that the total amount of the payment might be $1,000,000.

After discussion of the matter between the New York office of the Standard Oil Company, Mr. Metzger [43] in Rio de Janeiro, Mr. Welles, the Department, the Bolivian Minister of Foreign Affairs and presumably the Bolivian Government, certain modifications in the form of the Agreement were made. The Standard Oil Company has now informed the Department that arrangements were completed for the signature on January 27 of the following Agreement [44] signed by the Bolivian Minister of Foreign Affairs on behalf of the Bolivian Government and by Mr. Metzger on behalf of the Standard Oil Company of Bolivia and the Standard Oil Company of New Jersey:

"The Government of Bolivia will pay to the Standard Oil Company (New Jersey) the sum of $1,500,000, United States Currency, at the State Department in Washington, for the sale of all of its rights, interests and properties in Bolivia and those of its subsidiary, Standard Oil Company of Bolivia, as they existed immediately prior to March 13, 1937 and likewise for the sale of its existing maps and geological studies which are the result of its explorations in Bolivia. This payment will be made with interest at the rate of 3 percent per annum, from March 13, 1937, within 90 days from the date of the Supreme Resolution of the Republic of Bolivia putting this Agreement into effect.

---

[42] Gen. Enrique Peñaranda y del Castillo.
[43] H. A. Metzger, Standard Oil Company representative in Rio de Janeiro.
[44] For the Spanish text of the agreement and the resolution of approval by the Council of Ministers of Bolivia, see *Boletín Oficial del Ministerio de Relaciones Exteriores*, No. 9, January–April 1942, p. 129.

"The Government of Bolivia, the Standard Oil Company (New Jersey), and the Standard Oil Company of Bolivia declare that upon the payment of the amounts referred to immediately above, no issue will remain pending between them and that there will be no occasion for any claims or counter-claims of whatsoever character, since the fulfillment of the present agreement, which has been freely entered into, shall be regarded as having terminated satisfactorily and amicably all the differences between the Bolivian Government and the companies.

"Signed in duplicate in Spanish and English at Rio de Janeiro, Brazil, on January 27, 1942."

The Standard Oil Company informed the Department that it was its understanding that the Bolivian Government intended to put the Agreement into effect by a decree and without consulting the legislative branch of the Bolivian Government. Please use your influence in every appropriate and tactful way to press for the immediate issuance of the supreme decree that will terminate the Standard Oil problem in Bolivia.

While it is assumed that the Agreement was signed in Rio de Janeiro on January 27, the Department has not received final confirmation of this fact.

HULL

824.6363 St. 2/564 : Telegram

The Bolivian Minister for Foreign Affairs (Anze Matienzo) to the Secretary of State

LA PAZ [undated].
[Received February 12—12:18 a. m.]

I have the honor to communicate to Your Excellency that my Government today approved the agreement between the Government of Bolivia and the Standard Oil Company of New Jersey signed at Rio de Janeiro January 27 of the current year.[45] In this connection I cherish the assurance that the relations between our respective countries will be as hitherto and even more cordial in the future for our mutual benefit.

I present to Your Excellency [etc.]   E. ANZE MATIENZO

824.6363 St. 2/576 : Telegram

The Chargé in Bolivia (Dawson) to the Secretary of State

LA PAZ, March 2, 1942—noon.
[Received 5:22 p. m.]

124. My 114, February 25, 4 p. m.[46] Opposition to Standard Oil settlement has started on the ground that approval by the Cabinet

---

[45] The agreement was put into effect by a decree of February 24, 1942.
[46] Not printed.

alone is unconstitutional and that it must be submitted to Congress, which will not meet until August, to be put into effect. The Government seems to be wavering in its intention to carry the settlement through and make payment within 90 days of supreme resolution. I am, of course, making every effort to convince it to comply with its commitment.

.   .   .   .

Despatch follows.

DAWSON

824.6363 St. 2/579 : Telegram

The Chargé in Bolivia (Dawson) to the Secretary of State

LA PAZ, March 7, 1942—noon.
[Received 5 : 44 p. m.]

141. For the Acting Secretary. My 127, March 3, 5 p. m.[47] Foreign Minister inquires whether it would be possible to use blocked sterling funds of Bolivia in Great Britain arising from sales of Patiño[48] tin for payment to Standard Oil.

He says that payment will be made in any case but that he desires if possible to forestall criticism by pointing out use of blocked funds constituted benefit to Bolivia. I have told Minister that I do not consider his suggestion practicable but he has requested me to take it up personally with you. Please instruct me what reply you wish made. I see utterly no merit in suggestion for the following reasons:

1. Doubt as to whether British and Standard Oil would agree, and inevitable delay in making payment which would result from necessary quadripartite negotiations;

2. Fact that so far as I can ascertain Bolivia does not have on hand sufficient blocked sterling to cover Standard Oil payment, having disposed of most of last year's accumulation to neighboring countries under clearing agreements and would thus in effect be trading on futures;

3. Further fact that it has large surplus of dollars available.

If question were to be raised it should have been done at Rio de Janeiro. My feeling is that if, as expected Export-Import Bank petroleum credits are forthcoming before Congress meets in August, opposition which Bolivian Government professes to fear will by then have become unimportant and that letter suggested in my 127 is adequate support for Government in the meantime.

Idea of utilizing blocked sterling funds for Standard Oil payment originated in fertile mind of Finance Minister.[49] What he is really

---

[47] Not printed.
[48] Patiño Mines and Enterprises, Inc.
[49] Joaquín Espada.

interested in is insuring freeing of all funds of this sort, future as well as present. Legation and Economic Mission [51] have given consideration to means whereby this might possibly [be] done to mutual advantage and will discuss it in a despatch but feel that it has no place in the Standard Oil settlement.

DAWSON

824.6363 St. 2/579 : Telegram

The Acting Secretary of State to the Chargé in Bolivia (*Dawson*)

WASHINGTON, March 11, 1942—6 p. m.

143. Your 141, March 7, noon and 144, March 9, noon.[52] Please inform the Minister of Foreign Affairs that I agree with you that his suggestion is not practicable. You may, if appropriate, mention that the United States has considered sympathetically the blocked sterling problems of Bolivia, and that in the past the Department interceded in a small way with the British in connection with the utilization of blocked sterling in acquiring grain from Argentina.

WELLES

824.6363 St. 2/589 : Telegram

The Chargé in Bolivia (*Dawson*) *to the Secretary of State*

LA PAZ, April 1, 1942—6 p. m.
[Received April 2—12:40 a. m.]

219. My 194, March 21, 2 p. m.[53] After numerous conversations by Bohan [54] and me with President, Cabinet officers and others involved, Cabinet yesterday decided unanimously to make Standard Oil payment as soon as possible and Banco Central directors approved loan to Government of $1,750,000 with which to make payment. The payment thus will be made by the Government itself as provided in Rio de Janeiro agreement and not by YPFB [55] as recently contemplated. Am assured by personal letter that payment will be made in Washington next week, probably April 7, regardless of whether $2,000,000 so-called stabilization credit bill of Export-Import

---

[51] For correspondence on the work of this Mission, see pp. 592 ff.
[52] Latter not printed; this telegram indicated that the Foreign Minister now realized that it was impractical to use blocked sterling (824.6363 St. 2/581).
[53] Not printed.
[54] Merwin L. Bohan, Chief of the U. S. Economic Mission.
[55] Yacimientos Petrolíferos Fiscales Bolivianos.

Bank to Banco Central is forthcoming although they hope for it and Guachalla [56] has been optimistic as to chances of securing it.

While situation has changed thus since my 213, March 28, 2 p. m.,[57] Bohan and I still recommend strongly that credit be offered. Our reasons are:

(1) It will take ground from latest accounts oppositionists' allegation that payment to Standard Oil endangers reserves of Banco Central and help our friends to stand firm.

(2) The credit will probably not be used as Banco Central is not likely to want to pay 4% interest when it does not really need the money and can get short term credits from New York commercial banks cheaper.

(3) With the form of guarantee we have suggested there would be no risk.

(4) And most important. It will be months before any of the credits from the Import Bank to Bolivian Development Corporation can be opened. With congressional elections only a month off the story already current that the Bolivian Government is paying Standard Oil but that the promised aid from the United States Government is a fable will be spread and probably result in losses to Government in elections unless evidence to the contrary is produced. An announcement of a $2,000,000 credit would counteract this effectively, as we have said before this is really a political not an economic matter. Weak and bad as the Government is it does cooperate within limits and it is to our interest to help it unobtrusively instead of playing into the hands of the opposition which is much less friendly.

DAWSON

824.6363 St. 2/601a : Telegram

The Secretary of State to the Chargé in Bolivia (Dawson)

WASHINGTON, April 22, 1942—9 p. m.

227. Payment of $1,729,375 was delivered to the Standard Oil Company (New Jersey) on April 22. Maps and geological studies now in possession of Department are being delivered to Ambassador Guachalla. The Embassy at Buenos Aires is being instructed by telegraph to deliver maps and geological studies in its possession to the Bolivian Ambassador there or such person as he may designate.

HULL

---

[56] Luis Fernando Guachalla, Bolivian Ambassador in the United States.
[57] *Post*, p. 597.

PROGRAM FOR ECONOMIC COOPERATION BETWEEN THE UNITED STATES AND BOLIVIA[58]

824.50/44

The Secretary of State to the Chief of the United States Economic Mission to Bolivia (Bohan)

WASHINGTON, January 21, 1942.

The Secretary of State refers to telegram no. 5, January 5, 1942, 11 a. m.,[59] from the Chief of the United States Economic Mission to Bolivia, suggesting that there be established in Bolivia a managing and technical organization to supervise the carrying out of the program of economic and financial cooperation with Bolivia which will be formulated by the Economic Mission and suggesting the general outline of such an organization.

The Department will give careful consideration to the suggestion that there be established a managing and technical organization, but it is believed that the advisability and nature of such an entity will depend upon the nature and variety of projects eventually recommended by the Economic Mission and approved by the two Governments. It is suggested that the final report of the Economic Mission might include a detailed recommendation on this subject. The Department agrees that it would not be advisable to discuss this subject with Bolivian officials at this time.[60]

Pending the organization of a control entity, the Department would of course assist in every possible way in carrying out any specific recommendations the Economic Mission may make for the assignment of technical experts to assist in rapid increases in production of strategic minerals.

La Paz Embassy Files, 851A

The Under Secretary of State (Welles)[61] to the Bolivian Minister for Foreign Affairs (Anze Matienzo)

RIO DE JANEIRO, January 27, 1942.

MY DEAR MR. ANZE MATIENZO: I have the pleasure of enclosing a Memorandum Agreement and a Memorandum, both dated January

---

[58] Continued from *Foreign Relations*, 1941, vol. VI.
[59] Not printed.
[60] The discussion on the proposed corporation and other projects for the economic development of Bolivia was resumed by the representatives of both countries at the Third Meeting of the Foreign Ministers of the American Republics at Rio de Janeiro January 15–28, 1942; for correspondence on this Meeting, see pp. 6 ff.
[61] Under Secretary Sumner Welles was representing the United States at the Third Meeting of the Foreign Ministers of the American Republics at Rio de Janeiro.

27, 1942, relating to the formation of a corporation to carry out a program of economic cooperation between the United States and Bolivia and the extension of credits to that corporation by the Export-Import Bank of Washington.

I feel sure that the steps which we have taken in Rio de Janeiro, important as these are, represent but the prelude to a long-term and mutually beneficial program of economic cooperation between our countries.

Believe me

Yours very sincerely, SUMNER WELLES

[Enclosure 1]

MEMORANDUM

The attached Memorandum Agreement on credits to be furnished for agricultural, mining and other industries and for transportation, is made with the understanding that the present commitment of the Export-Import Bank of Washington is limited to a maximum initial amount of ten million dollars, United States currency.

It is also understood that, in connection with the statutes and by-laws of the corporation, mentioned in paragraph four, one-half of the membership of the Board of Directors will be appointed by the Government of Bolivia from a list submitted by the Export-Import Bank of Washington. It is further understood that the president of the corporation is to be a Bolivian and the general manager, appointed by the Board in agreement with the Export-Import Bank, a citizen of the United States of America.

RIO DE JANEIRO, January 27, 1942.

[Enclosure 2]

MEMORANDUM AGREEMENT

1. The Government of the United States agrees to furnish the Government of Bolivia with a credit for the purpose of aiding the Government of Bolivia in the development of its agricultural, mining, and other industries and in the construction of adequate means of transportation within Bolivia.

2. The Government of Bolivia agrees to create immediately a corporation which will be charged with the preparation of plans and the administration and management of the funds mentioned in paragraph one above as well as any funds furnished to the corporation by the Bolivian Government. The corporation will be authorized to operate with a capital of $25,000,000 U. S. currency.

3. The corporation will draw on the Export-Import Bank of Washington for the funds to finance the plans mentioned in paragraph two above, once those plans are approved by the Governments of Bolivia and the United States, in the amounts necessary and under the conditions to be set forth in the respective loan contracts.

4. The statutes and by-laws of the corporation shall be drawn by a special committee to be set up in La Paz. Upon approval, by both Governments, of the statutes and by-laws, the Government of Bolivia will immediately authorize the formation of the corporation.

5. The Governments of Bolivia and the United States will, immediately upon the creation of the corporation, take steps to resolve the question of communications between Cochabamba and Santa Cruz and to aid the mining industry.

RIO DE JANEIRO, January 27, 1942.

La Paz Embassy Files, 851A

The Bolivian Minister for Foreign Affairs (Anze Matienzo) to the Under Secretary of State (Welles)

[Translation][62]

RIO DE JANEIRO, January 27, 1942.

DEAR MR. WELLES: I take pleasure in enclosing the Spanish text of the Agreement [63] which we reached during our conversations on the procedure for rendering the financial and technical assistance which the Government of the United States undertakes to furnish to the Government of Bolivia for the purpose of developing Bolivian mining and other industries, agriculture, and systems of transportation.

Although the Agreement, dated today, does not mention the problem of monetary stabilization in Bolivia, I understand that this problem will be considered in due course, in conformity with the pertinent paragraph of the Memorandum of the Department of State dated August 1, 1941,[64] fully accepted by my Government.

I also understand that, as soon as the execution of any communications or agricultural project and the form of assistance for mining are agreed upon, the Government of the United States will make such arrangements as may be advisable to supply promptly sufficient amount of the necessary materials which are to be acquired in the United States.

The Agreement confirms the desire of the Parties to solve the problem of communications between Cochabamba and Santa Cruz as

---

[62] Supplied by the editors.
[63] For English text, see *supra*.
[64] See telegram No. 127, August 1, 1941, 3 p. m., to the Minister in Bolivia, printed in *Foreign Relations*, 1941, vol. VI, section under Bolivia entitled "Proposed program for economic cooperation between the United States and Bolivia."

soon as the Bolivian corporation mentioned in paragraphs 2 *et seq.* thereof is established. You are very well aware of the necessity of solving this problem and the statements which you were good enough to make to me with respect to the matter assure me that the necessary work will be begun in a short time.

It is understood, in my opinion, that the fact that the amount of 25 million dollars is allocated for the capital of the corporation that is the subject of the Agreement does not limit to that amount the development program and I do not doubt that the results of the initial operations of the corporation will be so satisfactory that new credit contracts may be concluded with the Export-Import Bank of Washington, since the idea of a plan for long-term cooperation referred to in the aforesaid Memorandum of August 1, 1941 may be correctly interpreted only in this manner.

It has given me very great satisfaction to enter into this first Agreement with you and thus create new opportunities in the field of relations between Bolivia and the United States. Consequently, I have the honor to express my appreciation for the noble spirit of understanding and friendship manifested by you at all times and to make known to you how confident I am that, in the future, agreements of greater promise will be concluded between our two countries for their mutual advantage and benefit.

I avail myself [etc.]   [File copy not signed]

La Paz Embassy Files, 851A

The Under Secretary of State (Welles) to the Bolivian Minister for Foreign Affairs (Anze Matienzo)

RIO DE JANEIRO, January 27, 1942.

MY DEAR MR. ANZE MATIENZO: Confirming our verbal understanding, I am pleased to inform you that the Export-Import Bank of Washington has agreed to extend a credit of up to $5,500,000 U.S. currency for the development of the petroleum resources of Bolivia. This is in addition to the initial credit of $10,000,000 for agricultural, mining, and other industries and for transportation, mentioned in the Memorandum of January 27, 1942.

The Export-Import Bank informs me that it will make the necessary loan contracts with the corporation referred to in paragraphs two and three of the Memorandum Agreement of January 27, 1942, once the plans for the development of the petroleum industry have been approved by the Government of Bolivia and accepted by the Export-Import Bank.

Believe me

Yours very sincerely,   SUMNER WELLES

La Paz Embassy Files, 851A

The Bolivian Minister for Foreign Affairs (Anze Matienzo) to the Under Secretary of State (Welles)

[Translation][65]

RIO DE JANEIRO, January 27, 1942.

MY DEAR MR. WELLES: I take pleasure in acknowledging receipt of your courteous letter of this date, whereby you were good enough to inform me that, according to our verbal understanding, the Export-Import Bank of Washington has agreed to extend a credit of $5,500,000, United States currency, for the development of the petroleum resources of Bolivia, in addition to the initial cost of $10,000,000 mentioned in your Memorandum of January 27, 1942.

You add that the Export-Import Bank will make the necessary loan contract with the Corporation referred to in paragraphs 2 and 3 of the Agreement of Janury 27, 1942 as soon as the plans for the development of the petroleum industry are approved by the Government of Bolivia and accepted by the Export-Import Bank.

My Government attaches special importance to the Bolivian petroleum industry and is certain that the initial assistance now agreed on will serve as a basis for its effective development and as a source of income that will permit a broad policy of credits directed toward the economic reconstruction of Bolivia. With this plan in mind, my Government has temporarily engaged the services of an American expert, who is now in La Paz studying the reorganization of that industry in its various aspects. However, in order to carry out this program completely, my Government now requests the technical cooperation of the Government of the United States, which it is fully confident will be extended.

In expressing to you how much I appreciate your valued influence and decided support, I have [etc.]   [File copy not signed]

824.50/75a : Telegram

The Acting Secretary of State to the Chargé in Bolivia (Dawson)

WASHINGTON, February 23, 1942—10 p. m.

103. The Export-Import Bank has prepared drafts of the charter and by-laws of the Bolivian Development Corporation which will be sent to you within a few days for the possible assistance of the com-

---

[65] Supplied by the editors.

mittee in La Paz that has been charged with the preparation of these documents.[66]

WELLES

824.51/1170 : Telegram

The Chargé in Bolivia (Dawson) to the Secretary of State

LA PAZ, March 26, 1942—11 a. m.
[Received 12:50 p. m.]

203. My 194, March 21, 2 p. m.[67] Understand that Bolivian Government has telegraphed Bolivian Minister in Washington [68] to request a so-called stabilization loan of $2,000,000. Suggest no action pending receipt of a telegram from the Legation discussing entire situation which will be sent this afternoon.

DAWSON

824.51/1171 : Telegram

The Chargé in Bolivia (Dawson) to the Secretary of State

LA PAZ, March 28, 1942—2 p. m.
[Received 6:52 p. m.]

213. My 194, March 21, 2 p. m.,[67] and 203, March 26, 11 a. m. With regard to the request of the Bolivian Ambassador that a $200,000,000 [*$2,000,000*] stabilization credit be granted the Banco Central for a period of 2 years, the Legation and the Economic Mission feel strongly that this credit should be granted immediately but upon the following terms: Definite hypothecation of Banco Central gold held by New York Federal Reserve Bank instead of general security of Banco's reserves which we understand has been offered; 1 year with renewal clause. Government expects to pay 4% interest.

The reserve position of the Banco Central expressed in enough [*sic*] currency was as follows on March 25: Total, $15,400,000; gold $8,200,-000 of which $3,000,000 held in New York; blocked and free pounds $3,100,000; $2,700,000; other currencies $1,400,000.

---

[66] These drafts were forwarded by the Department on March 2 to the Legation and were returned by the Chargé with his despatch No. 1936, April 6 (not printed) ; the United States Economic Mission in Bolivia reviewed the documents, making some changes. The purpose of the Corporation, according to the charter, was the development of the natural resources of Bolivia, including the improvement of agriculture, mining, forestry, commerce, industry, transportation, and public works. Broad powers to effect this purpose were accorded to a Board of Directors composed of six members, of whom three were to be Bolivian citizens. (824.50/85)

[67] Not printed.

[68] Luis Fernando Guachalla.

There is no real economic justification for this credit. The Legation and the Economic Mission recommend that it be granted however for the following reasons:

(1) It would assure Standard Oil settlement since the credit should not be opened until after the payment is made;

(2) There would be no risk involved with the security suggested by us;

(3) The way would be cleared for the proper financing of the Development Corporation to which the Minister of Finance [70] has promised in writing $3,000,000 per annum for the duration of the war;

(4) It should bring to an end the growing and now serious campaign to the effect that American aid is a myth;

(5) The position of the two Cabinet officers who have loyally supported Standard Oil and economic cooperation agreements [71] reached at Rio de Janeiro would be strengthened;

(6) Refusal of credit would result in Cabinet crisis with one of two equally unfortunate results:

(a) Resignations of the Ministers of Foreign Affairs and Economy [72] who are definitely committed to the Standard Oil payment irrespective of the result of the stabilization loan application or

(b) Resignation of Minister of Finance so that his party, whose leader started the attack on constitutionality of Standard Oil settlement procedure, could make political capital in coming electoral campaign out of alleged threat to currency and further disseminate allegations of American non-cooperation.

It is respectfully urged that immediate consideration be given to this problem and that we be advised of decision by March 31 if possible because of coming Bolivian holidays and desirability of having this troublesome question settled before political attacks make it more difficult.

DAWSON

824.51/1171 : Telegram

The Acting Secretary of State to the Chargé in Bolivia (Dawson)

WASHINGTON, April 6, 1942—5 p. m.

195. Your 213, March 28, 2 p. m., and 219, April 1, 6 p. m.[73] The Acting Secretary is today transmitting the following communication to the Bolivian Ambassador:

---

[70] Joaquín Espada.

[71] For agreement with the Standard Oil Company of New Jersey, see telegram No. 39, January 28, 9 p. m., to the Chargé in Bolivia, p. 587; for the economic agreement, see note of January 27 to the Bolivian Minister for Foreign Affairs, p. 592.

[72] Eduardo Anze Matienzo and Alberto Crespo Gutiérrez, respectively.

[73] For latter, see p. 590.

"Reference is made to the request of your Government for the cooperation of the Government of the United States in establishing an arrangement for the stabilization of the boliviano–dollar rate of exchange.

I am pleased to inform you that the Secretary of the Treasury has indicated that the Treasury Department is agreeable in principle to the conclusion of a stabilization arrangement with the Government of Bolivia and the Banco Central de Bolivia involving up to $2,000,000. The Secretary of the Treasury has further indicated that he is prepared to enter into at once conversations regarding the details of such an arrangement."

WELLES

824.51/1174 : Telegram

The Chargé in Bolivia (Dawson) to the Secretary of State

LA PAZ, April 11, 1942—11 a. m.
[Received 5:45 p. m.]

233. The Cabinet yesterday approved drafts of charter and bylaws of Development Corporation as attached to my despatch No. 1936, April 6.[74] The draft contract between Corporation and the Government will be somewhat modified and revised copies will be airmailed next week.

DAWSON

824.51/1175 : Telegram

The Chargé in Bolivia (Dawson) to the Secretary of State

LA PAZ, April 13, 1942—6 p. m.
[Received 8:58 p. m.]

242. Department's 195, April 6, 5 p. m. Despite the daily promises which have been made to us for 12 days that Standard Oil payment would be made promptly no steps have actually been taken to this end so far as we can ascertain. . . . We are, of course, continuing our efforts and payment may possibly be effected at any time.

We respectfully suggest that (1) "stabilization" arrangement under no circumstances be concluded until Standard Oil payment is actually made, and (2) that it be made on no other basis than hypothecation of $3,000,000 gold held by Banco Central in New York as suggested in my 213, March 28, 2 p. m.

It is noted from the communication from the Acting Secretary to the Bolivian Ambassador quoted in the Department's 195, that a stabilization arrangement with the Banco Central and the Bolivian Government is contemplated. In cases of provisions of Chase Bank loan contract of May 31, 1942 [*1922*], with Bolivian Government to the effect

---

[74] See footnote 66, p. 597.

that Bolivia shall contract no further external loans unless certain stipulations are complied with we think a loan to the Government might be attacked legally and feel that a loan to the Banco Central direct is preferable although guarantee by Government would appear unobjectionable.

DAWSON

824.51/1177: Telegram

The Chargé in Bolivia (Dawson) to the Secretary of State

LA PAZ, April 16, 1942—2 p. m.
[Received 11:50 p. m.]

248. My 242, April 13, 6 p. m. and previous. Minister of Finance informed me yesterday that Bolivian Ambassador in Washington had advised that interest on proposed stabilization loan would be 1½% instead of 4% and said that Banco Central would consequently use it. He has been giving impression in conversations and press interviews that loan will be for revolution of boliviano instead of stabilization. Any strengthening of boliviano would partially nullify effects of increased tin price (see my telegram 245, April 14, 4 p. m.[75]). Strongly urge that Treasury, Metals Reserve[76] and Department confer as these problems are intimately related.

Minister of Finance also said that he expected part of loan to be used for setting up government-controlled company to carry needed mining supplies. While I feel that such a company is essential, other funds will be available and stabilization funds should certainly not be utilized for the purpose.

My idea in recommending loan was purely as a gesture since under terms suggested by me credit would only have been used if absolutely economically necessary to maintain exchange position of Banco Central. I hope that no definite commitment has been made on an interest rate of 1½% since this would be an open invitation to Bolivian Government to raid Banco Central using equivalent of these funds for purposes not related to currency stabilization and thus in effect increasing the total foreign obligations due the United States under the program of economic cooperation. If the Treasury is not committed I again urge that the interest rate be made high enough and the collateral sufficiently ironbound so that the loan will only be used in case of necessity and for stabilization (the safe way to accomplish this is to make terms severe). Otherwise it would add another burden to the future foreign exchange position of Bolivia and increase the difficulties which will be present in any case in the repayment of the

[75] Not printed.
[76] The Metals Reserve Co. was an instrumentality of the Reconstruction Finance Corporation under the Department of Commerce.

credits to which the Export-Import Bank is already committed. These credits will be controlled through the Bolivian Development Corporation whereas the stabilization loan if diverted will be under no control whatsoever.

As I have pointed out before the operation was intended solely to assure settlement of the Standard Oil question through guaranteeing exchange position of Banco Central. . . .

DAWSON

824.51/1175 : Telegram

The Acting Secretary of State to the Chargé in Bolivia (Dawson)

WASHINGTON, April 16, 1942—11 p. m.

216. Your 242, April 13, 6 p. m.

1. The negotiation of a stabilization arrangement with the Treasury will take several weeks, a draft of contract not yet having been handed to the Bolivian Ambassador for transmission to La Paz.

2. Stabilization arrangements entered into by the Treasury must directly involve the Government. They are in no sense loans, which our Treasury is not directly empowered to make. They are rather monetary arrangements in which the Treasury on request purchases Bolivian currency which is held for its account by the Bolivian Treasury or Central Bank, which in turn is credited with the dollar equivalent at the Federal Reserve Bank of New York. The arrangement calls for the repurchase of the bolivianos by Bolivia for dollars under certain terms and conditions at the request of our Treasury. Provision would be made for periodic meetings to consider the boliviano–dollar exchange relationship and other relevant monetary matters. They provide a basis for complete collaboration by the monetary authorities of the two countries.

3. Since the Treasury holds bolivianos, it is not felt desirable to request additional security in the form of gold. A loan against gold is hardly more than a mere facility since the Federal Reserve Bank or any commercial bank under appropriate conditions and with a nominal rate of interest would be prepared to make such an advance. The type of operation contemplated by the Treasury provides a real secondary reserve for seasonal or special balance of payments fluctuations, and would strengthen the boliviano both for psychological and directly economic reasons.

Please continue your efforts to accomplish the transfer of the Standard Oil payment, and inform the Department of any developments.[77]

WELLES

---

[77] With regard to payment to the Standard Oil Company of New Jersey, see telegram No. 227, April 22, 9 p. m., to the Chargé in Bolivia, p. 591.

824.51/1193 : Telegram

The Ambassador in Bolivia (Boal) to the Secretary of State

LA PAZ, June 15, 1942—4 p. m.
[Received 10 : 33 p. m.]

435. My 424, June 13, noon.[79] Note from Foreign Office dated today[79] states that Bolivian Government, that is Cabinet, has approved charter and bylaws. No direct mention is made of approval of proposed contract between Bolivian Development Corporation and Bolivian Government although it is stated that Cabinet action enables Bolivian Government to form Corporation and to sign contract between it and Corporation.

Note adds that approval of charter and bylaws and granting of legal recognition of Corporation are acts within administrative competence of Bolivian Government but that contracts both between Bolivian Government and Corporation and with Export-Import Bank as well as law authorizing them will be submitted to next Congress meeting August 6 for its approval.

Copy of note being sent by air mail.

BOAL

824.50/148

The Under Secretary of State (Welles) to the Ambassador in Bolivia (Boal)

WASHINGTON, August 12, 1942.

DEAR PIERRE: Now that the conversations with the Bolivian Ministers of Finance and National Economy are drawing to a close, I am sending you for delivery to Dr. Anze Matienzo an acknowledgment of his letter of July 15, 1942.[79] I expect that by the time this letter reaches you, you will have received information from the Department by telegraph concerning the final results of the discussions, so that the enclosed reply to the Minister of Foreign Affairs[79] will by then be appropriate.

In order to assist the two Ministers as much as possible in the presentation in La Paz of the results of their discussions, we are endeavoring to include in the exchange of notes at the end of the discussions reference to all of the recent cooperative arrangements which have been worked out both in La Paz and in Washington. I believe these arrangements have been sufficient to permit an impressive presentation to the Bolivian public.

---

[79] Not printed.

Consistent with your suggestion, the Bolivian Ministers are being informed that the Government of the United States will at the appropriate time give every consideration to the practicability, under conditions then existing, of extending credits (up to $15,000,000) for the second stage of the long-term program recommended by the Economic Mission. The Ministers are being informed, however, that before such action is taken, completion of the first stage of the program should be assured. The Economic Mission has estimated that the second stage of the long-term program should comprise approximately $20,000,000 in expenditures.

It has not been considered practical to increase at this time the specific commitments of Export-Import Bank credits which were promised at Rio de Janeiro,[80] since the scarcity of materials necessary for carrying out the developments is so serious that there is little prospect of being able to obtain such materials in the predictable future for projects beyond those included in the first stage of the program. The developments in the first stage of the program appear, in any event, to be sufficiently ample to make a very definite contribution to development of the Bolivian national economy. I believe, moreover, that the statements made to the two Ministers in the note which the Secretary of State will address to the Minister of Finance at the end of his visit in Washington will provide the Ministers with adequate material for favorable publicity.

With very best wishes [etc.]   SUMNER WELLES

824.50/144

The Secretary of State to the Bolivian Minister of Finance (Espada) and the Bolivian Minister of National Economy (Crespo Gutiérrez)

WASHINGTON, August 14, 1942.

EXCELLENCIES: It has been deeply gratifying to discuss with Your Excellencies the many aspects of economic and financial cooperation between Bolivia and the United States. I believe that the arrangements resulting from these discussions should be of great economic benefit to our two countries, and that these measures of cooperation should at the same time contribute to the strengthening of inter-American solidarity.

The Government of the United States has given careful consideration to the recommendations of the United States Economic Mission

---

[80] Reference is to the conversations between representatives of the United States and Bolivia which took place at the time of the Third Meeting of the Foreign Ministers of the American Republics at Rio de Janeiro, January 15–28, 1942.

which has recently completed its studies in Bolivia, and this Government now believes that the recommendations of the Economic Mission comprise a practicable plan for systematic specific developments in Bolivia which will result in general improvement in the Bolivian national economy.

The Economic Mission has outlined a long-term program totaling approximately $88,000,000 for improved communications, increased production of agricultural, livestock and other basic industries, for irrigation projects to contribute to these agricultural developments, for the further stimulation of the mining industry, and for the further development of the Bolivian petroleum industry. The Economic Mission has assisted Your Excellencies in the arrangements for establishing a Bolivian Development Corporation which would act as a central agency for the carrying out of these developments and for the provision of expert assistance in studying additional projects.

In view of the decision of the Government of the United States that the recommendations of the Economic Mission constitute a practicable working plan, this Government is prepared to extend promptly through the agency of the Export-Import Bank of Washington the credits which were the subject of conversations at Rio de Janeiro between the representatives of the Governments of Bolivia and the United States. As contemplated in these conversations, these credits will be extended under a loan agreement to be signed between the Bolivian Government, the Bolivian Development Corporation and the Export-Import Bank of Washington, as soon as the Bolivian Development Corporation is legally constituted.

The first stage of the $88,000,000 long-term program recommended by the Economic Mission includes developments which it is estimated will involve the utilization of $26,125,000, of which $12,000,000 is allotted to roads; $6,625,000 to agriculture; $5,500,000 to petroleum; $1,000,000 to mining; and $1,000,000 to health and sanitation. Of the funds required for these developments, the credits to be extended by the Export-Import Bank will comprise $15,500,000. It is understood that the Bolivian Government would provide funds in the amount of $9,000,000 to the Bolivian Development Corporation for the program of economic development, by three annual appropriations of $3,000,000 per annum, in addition to which the Bolivian Government would provide a special fund of $1,500,000 for highway developments. Additional funds for the $26,125,000 first stage of the program would be provided by the amount of $2,125,000 established by the Rubber Reserve Corporation of the Government of the United States (in accordance with the terms of the agreement signed with the Bolivian Government on July 15, 1942[81]), with a view to the

---

[81] *Ante*, p. 576.

further development of rubber production in Bolivia; and by the grant of $1,000,000 made by the Government of the United States through the Office of the Coordinator of Inter-American Affairs for the development of health and sanitation projects in Bolivia.

Of the total financial resources of $29,125,000 involved in the first stage in the program, the Government of the United States would accordingly provide $18,625,000 and the Government of Bolivia would provide $10,500,000. The apparent margin of $3,000,000 is considered the minimum amount necessary for working capital and to assure funds for the systematic amortization of the obligations of the Corporation.

The recommendations of the Economic Mission with respect to the number, nature and size of the projects to be included in the first stage of the program were based in considerable part upon considered estimates of the availability of necessary materials and supplies. The machinery, materials and supplies that it would be necessary to import into Bolivia to complete the projects in the first stage of the program are becoming increasingly scarce, and it will of course be recognized that progress in carrying out the projects will be contingent upon the availability of specific materials and equipment when applications are received for priorities and export licenses that may be required. The Government of the United States will of course make every effort to facilitate the exportation to Bolivia of such equipment and materials.

The Government of the United States will be glad to enter into conversations with the Government of Bolivia with respect to additional cooperative financing of highway work in the event it is found that the $12,000,000 allotted for highway developments in the first stage of the program is not sufficient to complete the projects which are approved. Likewise, the Government of the United States will be glad to enter into similar conversations with respect to cooperative financing of the Villamontes irrigation project when plans are prepared for that project. These conversations will of course be dependent upon (1) the economic justification of the projects which have not as yet been thoroughly studied, (2) the availability of the materials which it may be necessary to import from the United States, and (3) the availability of sufficient labor in Bolivia to carry out the projects without affecting mining production or the completion of projects that have been previously approved.

In accordance with the recommendations of the Economic Mission, the Government of the United States will at the appropriate time give favorable consideration to the practicability, under conditions then existing, of extending through the appropriate credit institution up to $15,000,000 in credits for the financing of the second stage of the long-term program, which stage the Economic Mission has estimated should comprise approximately $20,000,000 in expenditures. It is believed, however, that before such action is taken, completion of the first stage of the program should be assured.

I believe that the additional measures of cooperation between Bolivia and the United States which have been arranged concurrently with the visit of Your Excellencies are a further outstanding indication of the close relationship that has been developed between the economies of our two countries. These measures include the offer of the Treasury Department of the United States to enter into a monetary stabilization arrangement involving up to $2,000,000 for the stabilization of the dollar–boliviano exchange relationship, and the agreement of the Export-Import Bank of Washington to establish special short-term credits of up to $2,000,000 for the Banco Central of Bolivia.

The arrangements which have been made for the purchase from Bolivia by the Rubber Reserve Corporation of the United States of all rubber produced in Bolivia (with the exception of not exceeding 250 tons annually) should, I believe, prove to be of great practical benefit to our two countries.

Likewise, the revision of the agreement which provides for the purchase by the Metals Reserve Company of the United States of a specific part of Bolivian tin production [82] should, I believe, contribute markedly to the attainment of the mutual objectives of our two governments. I am confident that the $1,300,000 so far extended in credits by the Metals Reserve Company and the Export-Import Bank of Washington for the development of further mineral production in Bolivia will be found of practical utility in effecting increased production and recovery of those minerals.

The arrangements that are now being made for revision of the agreement by which the Metals Reserve Company of the United States purchases Bolivian tungsten should likewise redound to the benefit of Bolivia while providing the United States with continued assurance of increasing supplies of this vital strategic material.

I am firmly convinced that the independence of all of the American republics depends upon the victory of the United Nations, and the actions of the Bolivian Government in facilitating in every way the supplying of strategic minerals and eliminating Axis activities within the frontiers of Bolivia are practical and effective indications that the Bolivian Government shares this view. I have been gratified by the arrangements which have been made with Your Excellencies for extension of control over commercial and financial operations of persons and entities whose activities are inimical to the security of the

---

[82] For correspondence on negotiations for the purchase by the United States of Bolivian strategic materials, see pp. 536 ff.

hemisphere. The cooperation of Bolivia in measures of mutual security such as these has been deeply encouraging to the Government of the United States in the prosecution of the war.

Accept [etc.] CORDELL HULL

824.50/145

The Bolivian Minister of Finance (Espada) and the Bolivian Minister of National Economy (Crespo Gutiérrez) to the Secretary of State

[Translation]

WASHINGTON, August 14, 1942.

MR. SECRETARY: We have been honored to receive Your Excellency's note of today's date, summarizing the results of our discussions during the past few weeks concerning measures of economic and financial cooperation between Bolivia and the United States. We agree with Your Excellency that these conversations have resulted in arrangements which should be of great economic benefit to our countries and which at the same time contribute definitely toward the strengthening of inter-American cooperation.

The recommendations of the United States Economic Mission have been considered by us in their various aspects, and we agree that these recommendations comprise a practicable working plan for economic developments in Bolivia. We likewise agree that the establishment of a Bolivian Development Corporation should provide an efficient means by which these developments can be carried out. It is the intention of the Bolivian Government to give every possible assistance in facilitating the establishment and the operations of the Corporation.

In view of the large amounts of materials and financing that would be involved in the execution of the entire long-term program recommended by the Economic Mission, which totals approximately $88,-000,000, the recommendation of the Economic Mission that the program be carried out by degrees, or in stages, appears logical, utilizing in the first stage of the program $26,125,000, of which $12,000,000 will be allotted to highways; $6,625,000 to agriculture; $5,500,000 to petroleum; $1,000,000 to mining; and $1,000,000 to health and sanitation.

As outlined in Your Excellency's note, the Bolivian Government is prepared to allot funds in the amount of $9,000,000 for the capital of the Bolivian Development Corporation, such funds to be provided during three consecutive years at the rate of $3,000,000 per annum. In addition, the Bolivian Government is prepared to provide $1,500,-000 for the use of the Bolivian Development Corporation in carrying out highway developments.

The Government of Bolivia agrees that the credit of $15,500,000 which the Government of the United States has agreed to extend through the Export-Import Bank of Washington for the developments in the first stage of the long-term economic program should constitute an exceptionally useful form of cooperation between the United States and Bolivia. Likewise, the additional funds provided by agencies of the Government of the United States—$2,125,000 for assistance in increasing production of rubber, and the grant of $1,000,-000 for health and sanitation projects—will be of great assistance in these specific fields of activity. The offer of the Treasury Department of the United States to enter into a monetary stabilization arrangement involving up to $2,000,000 for the stabilization of the dollar-boliviano exchange relationship is in itself fully appreciated by our Government, but because of the difference in views concerning certain provisions of the proposed arrangement, this matter must be postponed for further detailed consideration. The agreement of the Export-Import Bank of Washington to establish special short-term credits of up to $2,000,000 for the Banco Central of Bolivia, should also be a very beneficial measure of financial cooperation between the United States and Bolivia.

The favorable disposition of Your Excellency's Government to enter into conversations with the Government of Bolivia with respect to additional financing of highway work in the event it is found that the $12,000,000 allotted for highways in the first stage of the program is not sufficient to complete the projects which are approved, is likewise a foresighted measure of cooperation. In this respect, we have the honor to inform Your Excellency that the Government of Bolivia has decided to allot a special fund of $1,500,000 for highway works in order that the important construction of the Sucre–Camiri highway may be carried out. Likewise, the favorable disposition of the Government of the United States to enter into conversations with the Government of Bolivia concerning cooperative financing of the Villamontes irrigation project, when the plans for that project are prepared, reveals in our judgment a high spirit of collaboration on the part of Your Excellency's Government which we are pleased to recognize. These conversations, both with respect to highway works and with respect to irrigation works, will depend, as has been agreed, on the three requirements mentioned by Your Excellency in the note to which we are pleased to reply.

Our Government is certain that the financial cooperation of the United States, which Your Excellency mentioned with respect to the carrying out of the second stage of the long-term program, will encounter no obstacle in becoming opportunely practicable, since the Government of Bolivia is expecting the best results from the plan which is to be initiated and it has the fullest confidence that it will be able to depend always upon the assistance of the United States.

The Government of Bolivia is of course aware of the very great need in the United States for materials for the manufacture of war matériel. Since the Economic Mission, however, based its decisions concerning the projects to be included in the first stage of the program upon the estimated availability of equipment and materials in the United States, the Government of Bolivia is confident that the Government of the United States will make every effort to facilitate the exportation to Bolivia of the necessary equipment and materials.

The Government of Bolivia is on its part doing everything possible to facilitate and increase the provision to the United States of the strategic materials which are produced in Bolivia. We agree with Your Excellency that the recent arrangements for the exportation of practically the entire Bolivian rubber production to the United States, the recent revision of the agreement concerning the sale of a large proportion of Bolivian tin production to the United States, and the present discussions concerning revision of the arrangements for shipment of Bolivian tungsten to the United States should all constitute very practical measures for implementing this policy of the Bolivian Government.

The Government of the United States may be sure that it is the intention of the Government of Bolivia to continue and to extend the measures of control over commercial and financial operations of persons and entities whose activities are inimical to the security of the hemisphere.

We are pleased to inform Your Excellency that we have discussed with the President of the Foreign Bondholders Protective Council [83] the possible inauguration of discussions with a view to servicing the Bolivian dollar debt. As a result of this preliminary exchange of views, we believe that it may soon be possible to find a mutually acceptable basis for subsequent formal discussions.

We avail ourselves [etc.]
JOAQUÍN ESPADA
ALBERTO CRESPO GUTIÉRREZ

824.50/156

The Bolivian Ambassador (Guachalla) to the Secretary of State

WASHINGTON, August 14, 1942.

EXCELLENCY: I have the honor to refer to the arrangements which are being made between Their Excellencies, Dr. Joaquín Espada, Minister of Finance of Bolivia, and Señor Alberto Crespo Gutiérrez,

---

[83] Francis White.

Minister of National Economy of Bolivia, and the Export-Import Bank of Washington for the establishment of the Corporación Boliviana de Fomento, and for the extension to the Corporación of a credit of $15.500.000 authorized by the said Export-Import Bank.

I am pleased to inform you that the draft of the proposed charter and by-laws of the Corporación Boliviana de Fomento has now been approved by the Bolivian Government in the form in which it was recently submitted to the Export-Import Bank of Washington. It is expected that this draft of the charter and by-laws will be adopted upon the establishment of the Corporación soon after the Ministers of Finance and National Economy return to La Paz.

The proposed agreement between the Republic of Bolivia and the Corporación Boliviana de Fomento [84] has likewise been approved by the Bolivian Government. Moreover, the text of the proposed loan agreement between the Republic of Bolivia, the Corporación Boliviana de Fomento and the Export-Import Bank of Washington [84] has been approved by the Minister of Finance and the Minister of National Economy. Both agreements will be submitted without change to the National Congress of Bolivia with a view to their prompt approval or ratification.

Accept [etc.]   LUIS GUACHALLA

824.50/166 : Telegram

The Secretary of State to the Ambassador in Bolivia (Boal)

WASHINGTON, September 29, 1942—7 p. m.

693. Your 867 and 869 September 28.[85] Neither the Department nor the Export-Import Bank would wish to proceed with the Bolivian Development Corporation in the absence of Congressional approval. Furthermore, the Export-Import Bank would not be in a position to make funds available under the proposed contract without such approval. It seems clear from your telegram no. 865 of September 28,[84] from Article 18 of the draft contract between the Bolivian Government and the Corporation enclosed in the Department's instruction no. 247 of August 27, 1942,[84] and from the Bolivian Ambassador's note of August 14, 1942 a copy of which was enclosed in instruction 223 of August 19, 1942 [86] that Congressional ratification is essential to the functioning of the Corporation.

---

[84] Not printed.
[85] Neither printed; these telegrams indicated that the Bolivian Congress had not acted and that the Ambassador was in doubt as to whether the agreements were in force (824.50/166, 811.20 Defense (M) Bolivia/443).
[86] Instruction not printed.

The Department and Rubber Reserve consider that the Rubber Agreement is already in effect and that it is not subject to Congressional approval. Should the Agreement be submitted to Congress and disapproved, the entire problem would have to be reexamined.

The Department perceives no direct relationship between the Rubber Agreement and the Development Corporation Agreements. However, the failure of Bolivia to carry out its commitments under the Rubber Agreement would necessarily have an unfavorable effect upon the entire program of economic cooperation.

It is desired that you keep the Department currently informed on all matters affecting the Corporation.

HULL

824.50/174 : Telegram

The Ambassador in Bolivia (Boal) to the Secretary of State

La Paz, October 8, 1942—11 a. m.
[Received 1 : 38 p. m.]

907. Referring to my 901, October 6, 6 [7] p. m., and my 904, October 7, 1 p. m.[87] The Finance Committee of the Chamber of Deputies yesterday reported favorably the resolution on the Development Corporation in the form given in insert 3 of my 901. The Committee's report specifically mentions that the approval in the revised form relieves the Chamber from the necessity of considering the text of the tripartite agreement,[88] authorizes the Executive to sign the tripartite agreement and gives specific approval to the contract between the Bolivian Government and the Corporation.

Embassy hopes Department and ExImbank will find this form acceptable as the alternative would be long discussions and delay in functioning of Corporation. Understand Guachalla has been instructed to discuss matter with Department.

BOAL

824.50/175 : Telegram

The Ambassador in Bolivia (Boal) to the Secretary of State

La Paz, October 9, 1942—4 p. m.
[Received 6 : 42 p. m.]

911. Substance of Department's 718 and 719 of October 8 [89] given to Minister of National Economy this morning. He expressed the

---

[87] Neither printed.
[88] Agreement between the Republic of Bolivia, Corporación Boliviana de Fomento, and the Export-Import Bank, not printed.
[89] Neither printed; in these telegrams the Department transmitted suggestions of changes that the Export-Import Bank wished the Bolivian Congress to consider (824.50/173, 174).

opinion that no difficulties would be encountered in incorporating the Export-Import Bank's suggestions in Chamber's resolution of approval. By coincidence while I was with him, he was called to come to the Chamber immediately as the Development Corporation was then under discussion in secret session.

I now feel more hopeful regarding speedy action on the matter.

BOAL

824.50/194 : Telegram

The Secretary of State to the Ambassador in Bolivia (Boal)

WASHINGTON, November 25, 1942—10 p. m.

871. Your 1094, November 24, 1942.[92] The Department and the Export-Import Bank have reached the conclusion that the proposed law as well as any legislation proposed by the Bolivian Government should conform to the provisions of the contracts already agreed to by the two governments if it is to result in the implementation of those contracts.

The text of the law clearly does not conform to the understanding reached with the Bolivian Mission for the following reasons:

1. Complete autonomy in the Corporation with freedom to select projects for submission to Export-Import Bank for approval and to carry such projects into effect when approved is basic to the credit commitment. Therefore, Article 9 of the proposed law which provides for the appointment of a Federal Comptroller to handle the resources destined to the execution of the works and to the administration of the Bolivian Development Corporation is directly contrary to the basic understanding of the credit.

2. Likewise Article 6, in detailing specific projects, limits the powers of the Corporation to select projects contrary to the theory of the credit. Funds will not be available under the credit for any project unless such project is approved by Export-Import Bank, and no project will be approved unless submitted by the Corporation in detail in accordance with the terms of the agreement.

3. Export-Import Bank cannot approve any extension of credits under a law which indicates a commitment—even in principle—for a possible credit of $15,000,000 in addition to the present $15,500,000, or which states such credits may be in the nature of revolving funds. In discussions with the Bolivian Mission it was definitely understood these points went beyond the Bank's commitment and would not be mentioned. There is, however, nothing to prevent the Congress from authorizing the Executive to contract a general credit in excess of the $15,500,000, provided such authorization does not indicate any commitment on the part of the Bank for such additional amount.

---

[92] Not printed; it transmitted text of law approved by Bolivian Chamber of Deputies authorizing the Executive to borrow funds for the Bolivian Development Corporation (824.50/194).

4. Department's Cable 719 of October 8 [93] remains unchanged and any legislation should conform to the suggestions contained therein and the comments made above, if the Export-Import Bank is to be expected to give favorable consideration to the proposed credits.

The foregoing observations are for your background information and guidance in replying to any further inquiries that may be made by Bolivian officials. While the Department of course regrets that the proposed law in its present form will not facilitate the rapid conclusion of the agreements previously reached between the two Governments, you should carefully avoid any action which might be construed as an attempt on the part of this Government to influence the Bolivian Congress or intervene in any way in a matter of internal legislation.

HULL

824.50/212

The Bolivian Ambassador (Guachalla) to the Secretary of State

WASHINGTON, December 22, 1942.

EXCELLENCY: On August 14 I confirmed to Your Excellency that the proposed loan agreement, as prepared by the Export-Import Bank of Washington, between the Bolivian Government, the Export-Import Bank and the Bolivian Development Corporation had been approved in form and content by Their Excellencies, Dr. Joaquín Espada, Minister of Finance of Bolivia, and Sr. Crespo Gutiérrez, Minister of National Economy of Bolivia, and that the contract between the Bolivian Government and the Bolivian Development Corporation had been approved by the Bolivian Government in the form in which it was submitted to the Export-Import Bank and that the two proposed agreements would be submitted without change to the National Congress of Bolivia for the necessary authorizing legislation.

I have the honor to advise Your Excellency that both Houses of the Bolivian Congress have passed and the President on December 3 promulgated a law to authorize the signing of the tri-partite loan agreement between the Bolivian Government, the Export-Import Bank of Washington and the Bolivian Development Corporation, and a law to authorize the signing of the contract between the Bolivian Government and the Bolivian Development Corporation.

---

[93] Not printed; it stated that the Export-Import Bank did not wish to draft or to assume responsibility for Bolivian enabling legislation for the Bolivian Development Corporation, but the Bank did offer observations on the Bolivian drafts, objecting to linking present loan to any additional loan authorizations, proposed rotating credits, and draft limitation on life of the loan. Provisions for the enabling legislation were suggested. (824.50/173)

The Government of the United States and the Export-Import Bank have requested a clarification of the legislative acts with reference to their effect upon the understanding reached between the Export-Import Bank and the Bolivian Government as to the operations of the Bolivian Development Corporation contemplated by the two agreements.

I take this opportunity to assure Your Excellency on behalf of my Government that the legislative acts referred to above and as now promulgated authorize the signing of the two above mentioned contracts in their present form without change in any of their provisions.

I also take this opportunity to assure Your Excellency on behalf of my Government that the legislative acts will not necessitate any change in the operations or the method of operation of the Bolivian Development Corporation as contemplated by the two said agreements. In this respect my Government has authorized me to give formal assurances to your Government that, so long as any portion of the credit established by the Export-Import Bank remains available to the Corporation or has not been repaid, the functions of the "contralor fiscal" as provided in Article 9 of the law authorizing the loan agreement with the Export-Import Bank of Washington will be exercised exclusively by the three members of the Board of Directors of the Bolivian Development Corporation nominated by my Government, who in the performance of their duties shall be responsible to the Government of Bolivia. In acting in their capacity of "contralor fiscal" as contemplated by said legislative act, the three Bolivian directors will have the responsibility and obligation of examining all of the accounts of the Corporation and will prepare and submit reports of the handling of the funds, the execution of the works and the financial condition and administration of the Corporation to the Comptroller General of the Republic for his approval. The functions of such directors in their capacity as "contralor fiscal" will therefore be such as will be consistent with their responsibility to my Government and with the duties and powers as directors as prescribed by the charter and bylaws.

Further, I have been authorized by my Government to give formal assurances to your Government that the provisions of the legislative acts do not stipulate nor will my Government impose any limitations upon the functions, powers or duties of any of the officers or directors of the Bolivian Development Corporation as set forth in its charter and bylaws.[94]

Accept [etc.]   LUIS GUACHALLA

---

[94] These assurances were accepted as satisfactory by the Secretary of State in a note dated December 24, 1942 (824.50/212).

EFFORTS TO SECURE COOPERATION OF THE BOLIVIAN GOVERNMENT IN THE CONTROL OF FINANCIAL TRANSACTIONS INVOLVING THE AXIS

740.00112A European War, 1939/5953

The Chargé in Bolivia (Dawson) to the Secretary of State

No. 1521   LA PAZ, January 5, 1942.
                                        [Received January 9.]

SIR: I have the honor to refer to the Legation's despatches Nos. 1422 and 1445 of December 12 and 15, 1941,[95] in connection with the Supreme Decrees of December 10, 11 and 12, by the terms of which the funds of those German, Italian and Japanese firms included in the Proclaimed and Statutory Lists for Bolivia were supposed to have been frozen by the Bolivian Government and to report that lax administration of the decrees has nullified almost completely their expected effects.

In the first place, the interventors who were supposed to have been appointed to control the operations of these firms have not been named; although it was not expected, even by Bolivian Government officials, that really effective control would be exercised by these interventors, their appointment would have been at least an indication of an attempt at proper administration of the decrees by Governmental authorities. In the second place, far from effectively freezing the funds of such listed firms, local banks have now been authorized by the Ministry of Finance to discount notes for them and to lend them money; an example of this is a note in the amount of Bs. 476,075 discounted by the Banco Central on December 29 for Kyllmann Bauer y Cía.[96] According to the authorization of the Ministry of Finance banks may now extend loans to listed German, Italian and Japanese firms as long as such loans are made "under control"; the fact that there is no machinery for such "control" seems not to have been considered by the Ministry.

The reason offered by the Ministry of Finance and the local banks for their failure to enforce the freezing order is that many of the firms whose funds are supposedly blocked are so important to the economy of the country that their operations must be permitted to continue. While in some few cases this may be true and a reorganization of certain firms may be desirable in order to eliminate their undesirable elements and to permit their continued operation, it is not believed that the Bolivian Government's failure to at least attempt an enforcement of its freezing order can be excused on these grounds.

---

[95] Neither printed.
[96] A Proclaimed List firm.

The Legation is of the opinion that . . . this situation can be corrected and a more effective control exercised over local firms included in the Proclaimed List. (Reorganization would, of course, be one of the possible measures of control.) However, it is my opinion that it would be desirable to delay conversations on the subject with responsible officers of the Bolivian Government until after the Consultative Meeting of the Foreign Ministers of the American Republics scheduled for January 15 in Rio de Janeiro.[97] If, as is to be hoped, a concerted stand is made by the South American countries, including Bolivia, against the Axis powers, it is believed that effective action by the Bolivian Government against Axis firms within the country can much more easily be encouraged.

It is trusted that the Department will approve my delaying action in this matter until after the Rio de Janeiro meeting.

Respectfully yours,   ALLAN DAWSON

740.00112A European War, 1939/6395

The Secretary of State to the Chargé in Bolivia (Dawson)

No. 541   WASHINGTON, March 30, 1942.

The Secretary of State refers to the Legation's despatch no. 1575 of January 15, 1942 [98] and to earlier despatches relating to the ineffectiveness of the Bolivian Government's administration of the freezing regulations. It is noted that the Legation concludes that purchases of properties from persons on the Proclaimed List would not furnish an adequate solution to the problem of restricting the influence of the present owners without a more effective blocking of the proceeds and that, consequently, it is the Legation's opinion that the best method of handling the changes in ownership would be for the Bolivian Government to vest title in itself of Axis-owned or controlled properties situated in Bolivia for the duration of the war.

In this connection the attention of the Legation is called to Resolution V [99] of the Third Meeting of the Ministers of Foreign Affairs of the American Republics at Rio de Janeiro in which it is recommended that all transactions of whatsoever nature which are inimical to the security of the Western Hemisphere be prevented. The Resolution goes on to indicate possible measures to be taken in cases seriously affecting the national interest. Within the United States, as the Legation has been informed from time to time, action has been taken to freeze entirely the assets of undesirable individuals and to prevent entirely undesirable transactions, requiring individual licenses for all

[97] For correspondence concerning the Third Meeting of the Foreign Ministers of the American Republics, see pp. 6 ff.
[98] Not printed.
[99] Department of State *Bulletin*, February 7, 1942, p. 124.

transactions of undesirable persons or firms. In certain cases firms have been granted licenses to do business subject to specific limitations and provided that full reports are filed with the Treasury Department. In other cases of large entities carrying out operations deemed essential or important to the economy or war effort of the United States, reorganizations have been required, and in some cases individuals placed in the firms by the Treasury Department. In one case, as a last resort, the Government of the United States took over the ownership and control of General Aniline and Film Corporation, under an arrangement whereby the question of compensation was postponed until such time as the Secretary of the Treasury deems appropriate, as explained in the Department's circular telegram of February 17, 1942.[1] This action was taken as a last resort because it was thought that this was the only way in which the enterprise could be effectively controlled and because it was thought inadvisable in the national interest to require the company to cease all operations and liquidate its business.

740.00112A European War 1939/10867

The Chargé in Bolivia (Dawson) to the Secretary of State

No. 2007   LA PAZ, April 23, 1942.
                                                           [Received April 30.]

SIR: I have the honor to refer to my confidential despatches Nos. 1873, 1874, and 1909 of March 20, March 21 and March 28, 1942, respectively,[2] reporting foreign exchange transactions carried out by Kyllmann, Bauer y Cía. with the cooperation of the Banco Central de Bolivia, and to respectfully suggest that, as a means of convincing the Banco Central of its past mistakes, banks in the United States be approached, perhaps informally, with reference to the possibility of their not making any more collections than necessary through the Banco Central.

The Department will recall the numerous despatches which have been written reporting sales of dollar exchange by the Banco Central to various Proclaimed List Nationals; although this has been stopped in large part . . . sales of Argentine peso and Peruvian sol exchange have increased tremendously. (Such Argentine and Peruvian exchange is of course available to Bolivia only by reason of the fact that this country is receiving a large supply of free dollars from the United States in return for its tin and tungsten; Bolivia's balance of trade with both Peru and Argentina is extremely unfavorable.) It is true, of course, that the banks have been given carte blanche to do as they

---

[1] Not printed.
[2] None printed.

please in this matter (see my No. 1575 of January 15, 1942,[3] enclosing a copy of a letter written by the Minister of Finance [4] to all the banks in which he suggested that they decide for themselves whether or not to observe the Government's freezing decree) but it is the Banco Central more than any of the others which has taken advantage of the anomalous situation to enrich its coffers.

. . . .

In this connection it has occurred to the Legation that perhaps one effective means which might be employed would be for American banks no longer to make their collections, at least for La Paz, Cochabamba and Oruro, through the Banco Central. In all of these cities the Banco Mercantil has a branch and could satisfactorily handle the business; as suggested in previous despatches, the manager of this bank is completely friendly and cooperates in every way possible with the Legation. In all the other interior cities except Sucre only the Banco Central operates and in Sucre the other bank is the Banco Nacional, the manager of which is Nazi in sympathy (see my despatch No. 1957 of April 10, 1942 [3]).

However, probably ninety percent of the foreign collection business is done in La Paz, Cochabamba and Oruro, and unquestionably the Banco Central would suffer considerably if that particular source of its income were temporarily cut off. In addition to the commission which it enjoys on such collections most importers purchase their foreign exchange from the bank which is making the collection and this is of course another source of profit which would be affected if the Banco Central were to experience a sudden decrease in its foreign business.

There seems to be no question that the manager of the Banco Central and the Minister of Finance would quickly realize the significance of what was happening. Their first reaction probably would be at the end of the month, when no doubt they would deduce from a study of the bank's report that importations from the United States had suffered a sharp reduction. However, after observing that during the same period of time the collection business of the Banco Mercantil, and the Banco Nacional in La Paz, had experienced a corresponding increase it hardly seems possible that they would not be struck by the coincidence. A conversation with the Legation would undoubtedly result with, it is to be trusted, a satisfactory solution for both parties.

It appears to the Legation that the main advantage in taking action of this kind is the unobtrusiveness with which the desired end might

---

[3] Not printed.
[4] Joaquín Espada; enclosure missing from Department files.

be achieved. As far as anyone in Bolivia except the Legation is concerned American banks, by some coincidence, all would have made a purely commercial decision at more or less the same time to deal with some bank in Bolivia other than the Banco Central. There would have to be no publishing of names or other obvious action, and there would be no necessity to tell anyone what was happening; however, the Banco Central would understand.

For the Department's information Mr. Edward G. Miller, of Assistant Secretary Acheson's office, while in La Paz a short time ago suggested that perhaps the above action might be effective if the Legation considered it advisable; since Mr. Miller's departure nothing has occurred to make it seem less desirable that the Banco Central be brought to task for its unfriendly operations.

Respectfully yours, ALLAN DAWSON

740.00112A European War 1939/10867

The Department of State to the Bolivian Embassy

AIDE-MÉMOIRE

Repeated reports have been received by this Government from sources which are thoroughly reliable which clearly indicate that the Banco Central de Bolivia, wholly owned by the Bolivian Government, continues to grant exchange to firms in Bolivia whose activities are inimical to the security of the Western Hemisphere. The exchange granted to these firms in turn is remitted to German banks in Argentina and Peru. The continuance of these practices by the Banco Central, which appears to be contrary to Resolution V adopted at the Third Meeting of the Ministers of Foreign Affairs of the American Republics, will raise difficulties in connection with the operation of the stabilization agreement about to be signed between the two governments. This matter has been repeatedly discussed by the representatives of the United States Embassy in La Paz with the manager of the Banco Central [5] but such transactions are still permitted to be undertaken.

The Department of State would appreciate assurances on the part of the Government of Bolivia that the Banco Central de Bolivia will desist from any further operations of the type mentioned above.

WASHINGTON, May 20, 1942.

---

[5] Humberto Cuenca.

811.51/4249 : Telegram

The Ambassador in Bolivia (Boal) to the Secretary of State

La Paz, June 13, 1942—1 p. m.
[Received 8 : 55 p. m.]

425. Department's circular telegrams of May 18 [7] and May 27 [8] regarding currency. Bolivian Foreign Office and Minister of Finance notified promptly in accordance with Department's instructions but no action as yet taken; even local banks have not been officially informed by Bolivian authorities and warned concerning the acceptance of dollar currency although Embassy has advised them informally.

Embassy has learned from manager of the Banco Central that he is concerned with reference to disposal of some $15,000 in dollar currency which bank has. In this connection Department will recall numerous despatches of the Legation and Embassy concerning dealings of Banco Central with Axis and Proclaimed List nationals. Respectfully suggest that any attempts of Banco Central or its manager to dispose of these funds be subjected to closest scrutiny and that origin of currency be most carefully investigated.

BOAL

811.515/1411 : Telegram

The Ambassador in Bolivia (Boal) to the Secretary of State

La Paz, July 6, 1942—5 p. m.
[Received 10 : 06 p. m.]

507. Department's circular telegram June 23, 11 p. m., and Embassy's telegram No. 469, June 24, 6 p. m.[9] Decree issued by Bolivian Government June 29, made public July 4, provides control over United States currency in accordance with Department's suggestions; presume Banco Central will soon begin under the terms of decree accepting currency for transmittal to the United States. In the meantime, there is no market, official or free, for dollar currency and consequently no exchange rate. No large blocks known to be seeking markets.

Text of decree follows by air mail.

BOAL

---

[7] *Post*, p. 789.
[8] Not printed ; this circular telegram announced measures taken by Brazil at the request of the United States to control use of American bank notes (811.51/4188).
[9] Neither printed.

811.515/1411 : Telegram

The Secretary of State to the Ambassador in Bolivia (Boal)

WASHINGTON, July 10, 1942—8 p. m.

440. Your 507, July 6, 5 p. m. The currency problem was discussed with Cuenca July 8. He insisted that he did not receive notice of the United States controls over currency until June 14 after he had cabled Buenos Aires for information and had himself approached the Embassy. Apparently this was due to the delays inherent in notifying the Foreign Office and the Minister of Finance about this Government's controls.[10]

In light of Cuenca's vehement insistence that he did not receive prompt notice, his further statement that he suspended the purchase of dollar currency immediately after he did receive notice and the small amount involved, the Department feels that Treasury cannot refuse to take the $15,000 which the Central Bank now holds. The Department recognizes the need for bringing pressure on the Central Bank but feels that under the present circumstances such pressure will have to be exerted in other ways. Accordingly, Cuenca is being informed today that Treasury will accept the $15,000.

The agreement to accept the $15,000 is predicated upon the assumption that Bolivia has now instituted complete controls over dollar currency along the lines previously suggested by the Department and will effectively enforce such controls. Cuenca is apparently unaware of the fact that such controls have already been instituted. Treasury is handing him a memorandum outlining the types of controls which this Government desires to see instituted in order that he may take appropriate steps to put such controls into effect to the extent that this has not already been done.

Please cable whether the Department's assumption is correct and confirm whether the Central Bank is now refusing to purchase dollars and is accepting such currency on a collection basis only.

HULL

811.515/1449

The Ambassador in Bolivia (Boal) to the Secretary of State

No. 284
LA PAZ, July 13, 1942.
[Received July 18.]

SIR: I have the honor to refer to the Department's telegram No. 440 of July 10, 1942, 8 p. m., as well as to the Embassy's telegram in

---

[10] The Ambassador in reply to this assertion observed in his telegram No. 534, July 13, noon, that the Embassy note on the subject had been delivered to the Minister of Finance on May 29 and that the delay was due to the failure of the Minister to advise the banks (811.515/1434).

reply, No. 534 of July 13, 12 noon,[12] and to the Embassy's despatch No. 247 of July 8, 1942,[13] all referring to the control measures instituted by the Bolivian Government for the purpose of transmitting United States currency to the Treasury Department.

As stated in the Embassy's telegram and despatch under reference, the controls instituted by the Bolivian Government are believed to be satisfactory and to be working effectively. However, it has occurred to the Embassy that it may be of interest to the Department to know that the Banco Central has the apparent intention of using the foreign dollar exchange turned over to it under the control measures in its own name. As will be recalled, the control measures provide that all dollar currency turned over to the bank by individuals will be deposited to the bank's own account in New York, and once the funds are released by the Treasury Department, the Banco Central will carry out the respective liquidation with the individual who makes the deposit here. It has been learned through reliable sources that the Banco Central has announced to depositors that it will not return the dollars either as traveler's checks or in drafts to the original owners, but will purchase the dollars at the official rate of exchange, which is 46 bolivianos to the dollar. Since the street rate has risen to as high as 52 bolivianos to the dollar, the benefits to the bank in securing dollar exchange at the lower figure are obvious.

Respectfully yours,　　　　　　　　　　　　　　　Pierre de L. Boal

840.51 Frozen Credits/7047 : Telegram

The Ambassador in Bolivia (Boal) to the Secretary of State

La Paz, July 13, 1942—2 p. m.
[Received July 14—12 : 05 a. m.]

535. Department's instruction 81, June 25 and Embassy's despatch No. 254, July 9.[14] Embassy has learned through unimpeachable source on Banco Central's own Board of Directors that contrary to information in despatch under reference Finance Minister Espada now in the United States instructed Banco Central prior to his departure through a communication addressed to bank's directors on July 1 that sales of foreign exchange may be continued to listed nationals for the purpose of importations, specifically naming Axis-owned firms Bernardo Elsner, Juan Elsner, and Kyllmann Bauer as approved recipients of such facilities. Espada's instructions prohibit only transfers of funds to other banks which are Axis controlled.

---

[12] See footnote 10, p. 621.
[13] Not printed.
[14] Neither printed.

It is respectfully recommended that entire question of sales of foreign exchange to listed nationals as brought out in the Department's *aide-mémoire* of May 20 be called to both the attention of Espada and the Banco Central's manager, Cuenca, for the purpose of their agreeing to some effective action before their return to Bolivia. Report following.

BOAL

840.51 Frozen Credits/7047

The Secretary of State to the Ambassador in Bolivia (Boal)

No. 162   WASHINGTON, July 28, 1942.

The Secretary of State refers to the Embassy's despatches no. 69 of June 15, 1942, no. 149 of June 25, 1942, and no. 223 of July 22 [*2*], 1942,[15] and to the Embassy's telegram no. 535 of July 13, 1942, and to previous correspondence in connection with the ineffectiveness of the Bolivian controls of inimical firms in that country.

The Secretary of State also refers to the visit to Washington of Mr. Humberto Cuenca, General Manager of the Central Bank of Bolivia, for the purpose of attending the Inter-American Conference on Systems of Economic and Financial Control which was held in Washington from June 30 to July 10, 1942.[16] A circular instruction outlining the results of this conference will shortly be transmitted to the missions.

At the first working session of the conference, each delegate was asked to explain the steps already taken by his Government to implement Resolution V adopted at the Third Meeting of the Ministers of Foreign Affairs at Rio de Janeiro. Mr. Cuenca stated in substance that although Bolivia had promptly adopted a freezing decree, it had been found impracticable to apply its provisions rigorously to certain large German commercial firms which are essential to his country's economy, owing to their predominance in the distribution of prime necessities in certain outlying areas. He stated that he hoped that the conference would look sympathetically upon Bolivia's special predicament in the field of economic and financial controls of politically undesirable firms.

Thereafter certain members of the United States delegation discussed the situation privately with Mr. Cuenca. It was explained that this Government viewed with concern the continued operation, with the consent of the Bolivian Government, of dangerous organizations, such as the Elsner firms and Kyllmann, Bauer. It was stated that while Bolivia's problems may be difficult because of the past

---

[15] None printed.
[16] For correspondence concerning this Conference, see pp. 58 ff.

importance of these firms, nonetheless this appeared to be a situation which could be promptly remedied by action on the part of the Bolivian Government to foster other clean organizations to take over the functions of the German firms and ultimately to eliminate them. Mr. Cuenca stated that he had given the matter serious consideration and that although he himself is completely anti-Nazi and would like to wipe out the German firms, there is neither sufficient technical skill nor financial resources available in Bolivia to enable the Bolivian Government to take this action on its own initiative without assistance from the United States. It was explained to him that this Government would be pleased to consider, with representatives of the Bolivian Government, the question of financial assistance and the elimination of German firms, and there was again strongly emphasized the necessity of the Bolivian Government's taking strong action to this end. At one point in these conversations Mr. Cuenca stated that he felt it incumbent upon him to make a general reservation to any resolutions adopted at the conference calling for strong controls over the Axis financial and commercial transactions within the American republics, but he did not press this question further and made no reservation to any of the resolutions adopted.

Upon receipt of the Embassy's telegram no. 535 of July 13, it was decided that instead of discussing the problem further with Mr. Cuenca, it would be desirable to arrange for a meeting between the Ministers of Finance and National Economy and Mr. Cuenca, together with certain responsible officers of the Department. This meeting was held on July 16, and a copy of the memorandum of conversation is transmitted herewith [17] for the Embassy's information. It will be noted that neither the Minister of Finance nor Mr. Cuenca was able to attend this meeting, but that it concluded in the determination to pursue the discussions further in the effort to arrive at a concrete formula for the elimination of German firms.

The Embassy will be informed of further developments in connection with this matter.

840.51 Frozen Credits/7047

The Secretary of State to the Ambassador in Bolivia (*Boal*)

No. 248   WASHINGTON, August 27, 1942.

The Secretary of State refers to the Department's instruction no. 162 of July 28, 1942 concerning the ineffectiveness of Bolivian control of certain firms in Bolivia whose activities are inimical to the defense of the American republics.

---

[17] Not printed.

This matter was recently discussed further at a meeting in which the Bolivian Ministers of Finance and National Economy,[18] the Bolivian Ambassador at Washington,[19] and officers of the Department participated. It was agreed at the meeting that the Bolivian Ministers of Finance and National Economy would meet with the managers of certain large Bolivian commercial organizations soon after the return to La Paz of the Ministers, to determine the financial requirements for a program in which these Bolivian commercial organizations would open branches in areas of Bolivia now served in large part by commercial organizations which are included on the Proclaimed List of Certain Blocked Nationals.

The Bolivian Ministers of Finance and National Economy stated that, as soon as information might be available as a result of such a meeting with the managers of Bolivian commercial organizations, they would inform the American Embassy at La Paz so that the Embassy could inform the Department of State concerning the amounts of credits which the Export-Import Bank of Washington might be requested to provide for the expansion of the Bolivian commercial organizations.

The Bolivian Minister of Finance also stated that he would arrange for the introduction of appropriate legislation at the present session of the Bolivian Congress which would provide the Bolivian Government with authority to expropriate Axis property in Bolivia. The Bolivian Ministers of Finance and National Economy likewise stated that, as soon as the Bolivian commercial organizations should be in a position to provide the necessary commercial services in the areas now served by organizations on the Proclaimed List, drastic action would be taken to curtail the activities of such organizations on the Proclaimed List. It was mentioned that one such measure would be the refusal to such organizations of exchange necessary for payments for imported merchandise.

811.51/5105

The Ambassador in Bolivia (Boal) to the Secretary of State

No. 545 La Paz, August 31, 1942.
[Received September 10.]

Sir: I have the honor to refer to the Embassy's despatch No. 247 of July 8, 1942,[20] forwarding a copy of a Supreme Decree dated June 29, establishing a control of dollar currency in Bolivia, and especially to Article 3 of that decree which made compulsory the deposit

[18] Joaquín Espada and Alberto Crespo Gutiérrez, respectively.
[19] Luis Fernando Guachalla.
[20] Not printed.

with the Banco Central of all dollar currency in Bolivia by July 15. It will be recalled (see Embassy's despatch No. 435 of August 10, 1942 [22]) that a subsequent decree was issued following up this matter and prohibiting all transactions in United States dollar currency.

The Embassy is now in receipt of a note from the Foreign Office stating that several individuals and firms were unable to make the necessary arrangements for the deposit of their currency before July 15 and are asking special permission to do so now. The Foreign Office, remembering the Department's statement (see circular telegram of June 19, 11 a. m. [p. m.] [22]) that "the Treasury is expected to refuse applications for the release of currency which is not promptly forwarded to the United States", has asked that the Treasury agree to accept applications for the release of at least some $5,000 in additional currency which has not as yet been accepted by the Banco Central for forwarding to the United States. According to the Foreign Minister, the Ministry of Finance will carefully supervise this additional operation, will accept currency only from firms and individuals not suspected of being anti-American and not included in the black lists of the allied countries, and will see that the source of the currency is established beyond question.

It is respectfully recommended, in view of the small amount of dollar currency which will no doubt be involved as well as the evidently sincere expressions of the Ministry of Finance to do everything possible to avoid accepting currency from persons or firms whose activities might be considered inimical to allied interests, that the request of the Foreign Office, if at all possible, be given favorable consideration. The Embassy of course understands that the Treasury is still accepting applications for the release of currency but sympathizes with the desire of the Bolivian Government to secure a definite statement to the effect that applications covering the currency which it now desires to forward will not be summarily refused.

Respectfully yours,   PIERRE DE L. BOAL

840.51 Frozen Credits/7802

The Department of State to the Bolivian Embassy

AIDE-MÉMOIRE

Thoroughly reliable sources have reported to this Government that the Banco Central de Bolivia, wholly owned by the Bolivian Government, is continuing to grant exchange facilities to firms in Bolivia whose activities are inimical to the security of the Western Hemisphere. This situation continues despite the assurances contained in

---

[22] Not printed.

the note of His Excellency the Ambassador of Bolivia, dated June 11, 1942,[23] in which was quoted a letter dated June 3, 1942, from His Excellency Eduardo Anze Matienzo, Minister of Foreign Relations of Bolivia. In that letter, the Minister of Foreign Relations stated that the Government of Bolivia would do everything necessary to prevent the irregularities set forth in the *aide-mémoire* of the Under Secretary of State of the United States, dated May 20, 1942, which dealt specifically with the granting of exchange facilities by the Banco Central de Bolivia in the manner aforementioned.

The Government of the United States is confident that the Government of Bolivia wishes to give practical effect to Resolution V adopted at the Third Meeting of the Ministers of Foreign Affairs of the American Republics and that the Government of Bolivia will wish to make certain that its instructions to the Banco Central are so comprehensive as to prevent the granting of exchange to any firms, whether located within or without Bolivia and regardless of nationality, whose activities are believed to be inimical to the security of the American Republics.

In view of the foregoing and of the events since the date of the aforementioned *aide-mémoire*, including the adoption of resolutions at the recent Inter-American Conference on Systems of Economic and Financial Control which implemented Resolution V adopted at the Third Meeting of the Ministers of Foreign Affairs, this Government would greatly appreciate receiving renewed assurances from the Government of Bolivia that the Banco Central de Bolivia will not engage in any further operations of the type mentioned in the preceding paragraph.

WASHINGTON, September 22, 1942.

840.51 Frozen Credits/7815

The Bolivian Embassy to the Department of State

The Bolivian Embassy refers to an *Aide-Mémoire* of the State Department dated September 22, 1942, regarding the exchange facilities which the Banco Central de Bolivia continues to grant to firms inimical to the security of the Western Hemisphere, despite the assurances contained in a letter of the Bolivian Ambassador addressed to the Honourable Sumner Welles, Under Secretary of State of the United States of America,[24] in which was quoted another letter, received by the Ambassador from His Excellency Eduardo Anze Matienzo, Minister of Foreign Affairs of Bolivia, stating that the Government of

---

[23] Not printed.
[24] Dated June 11, 1942, not printed.

Bolivia would do everything necessary to prevent the irregularities mentioned in an *Aide-Mémoire* of the Under Secretary of State of the United States of America, dated May 20, 1942, regarding said exchange facilities.

2. In reply, the Bolivian Embassy wishes to confirm the confidence expressed in the *Aide-Mémoire* of the Department of State dated September 22, 1942, to the effect that it is the firm intention of the Government of Bolivia to comply with the provisions contained in Resolution V adopted at the Third Meeting of the Ministers of Foreign Affairs of the American Republics and with those contained in the resolutions of the recent Inter-American Conference on Systems of Economic and Financial Control which implemented said Resolution V of the Rio de Janeiro Meeting.

3. However, at the present time [the Embassy] is unable to explain the reasons why exchange facilities are still being granted to firms inimical to the security of the Western Hemisphere and has, therefore, consulted the matter with the Bolivian Government. Until more accurate information on the matter is made available, it anticipates to explain why said facilities are being granted by recalling that, during an interview of their Excellencies the Ministers of Finance and of National Economy of Bolivia with the Honourable Dean Acheson, Assistant to the Secretary of State of the United States, it was pointed-out that great difficulties were entailed in the immediate substitution of some important firms inimical to the security of the Western Hemisphere by others of Bolivian or friendly nationality, a fact that was accepted as evident by the Honourable Dean Acheson.

4. As soon as a reply is received from the Bolivian Government this Embassy will be glad to again approach the State Department on the subject.

WASHINGTON, September 22, 1942.

811.51/5105 : Airgram

The Secretary of State to the Ambassador in Bolivia (Boal)

WASHINGTON, September 23, 1942—7 : 15 p. m.

A–78. Your despatch 545, August 31. It is suggested that you inform the Foreign Office that the several individuals and firms who were unable to deposit their currency prior to July 15 now be allowed to make such deposits for forwarding to the United States on a collection basis. Treasury has stated that it will not view the failure of these persons and firms to make their deposits before July 15 as per se sufficient grounds for denying the applications for release. Treasury, however, does not wish to authorize local liquidation of the currency in view of the fact that such action might establish an unwise precedent.

With respect to the suggestion that the Minister of Finance will do everything possible to avoid accepting currency from undesirable persons or firms, it should be noted that the acceptance of such currency for forwarding to the United States on a collection basis may be advisable since the currency will be effectively withdrawn from circulation and can be blocked in this country for reasons other than failure to deposit before July 15.

It is assumed that the foregoing will satisfy the desires of the Bolivian Foreign Office. If this should not be the case, please inform the Department.

HULL

840.51 Frozen Credits/8110

The Department of State to the Bolivian Embassy

AIDE-MÉMOIRE

The Government of the United States is again constrained to advise the Government of Bolivia that thoroughly reliable sources report that the foreign exchange facilities of the Banco Central de Bolivia continue to remain available to firms in Bolivia whose activities are considered inimical to the security of the Western Hemisphere, and that the exchange obtained by such firms is currently being utilized by them to effect the importation of substantial quantities of marketable commodities from Argentina, Chile, and Peru. This Government regrets that these transactions persist despite the provisions of Resolution V of the Third Meeting of the Ministers of Foreign Affairs of the American Republics and the resolutions of the Inter-American Conference on Systems of Economic and Financial Control. The continuation of such a course of action on the part of the Banco Central can only be injurious to hemispheric security.

His Excellency, the Ambassador of Bolivia to the United States, and His Excellency, Eduardo Anze Matienzo, Minister of Foreign Relations of Bolivia, have heretofore assured this Government that the Government of Bolivia would take all steps necessary to prevent the Banco Central from engaging in such transactions. It is hoped that henceforth the Bank will not grant foreign exchange to any firm whose activities are inimical to the security of the American Republics. Although some of the objectionable firms to which the Banco Central sells foreign exchange may be essential to the economy of Bolivia, it is submitted that the aspects of hemispheric security are of such magnitude that this Government continues to hope that a program will be formulated under which such firms may be eliminated in favor of enterprises which will bulwark, rather than threaten, that security.

WASHINGTON, November 19, 1942.

840.51 Frozen Credits/8762

The Ambassador in Bolivia (Boal) to the Secretary of State

No. 933   LA PAZ, December 4, 1942.
[Received December 15.]

SIR: I have the honor to refer to the Department's circular telegram of April 7, 1942, 9 p. m.,[25] which requested monthly reports concerning local developments with regard to the enforcement of measures for the control of Axis nationals, and to the Embassy's despatch No. 813 of November 5, 1942,[25] which reviewed the situation up to the end of October.

As will be recalled, during September and October the continued political crisis prevented Government leaders from giving much attention to the possibilities of creating more effective controls, in spite of the interest evidenced on several occasions by Minister of Finance Dr. Joaquín Espada and Minister of Economy Alberto Crespo Gutiérrez in accomplishing something worthwhile along these lines. Furthermore, Dr. Espada's illness during those two months, when he spent part of the time in Buenos Aires, prevented him from instituting any new policies in his Ministry. Dr. Espada returned to work shortly after the middle of November. During the final week of November the Cabinet resigned and Congress adjourned. With the recent naming of a new Cabinet, which includes both Dr. Espada and Crespo in their old posts, the political crisis has been eased, and it is now expected that the Ministers may be more willing to take up the problem of adopting new measures for the control of Axis commercial interests through foreign exchange control and the encouragement or actual setting up of nation wide competitive organizations.

Meanwhile, the Embassy has continued to rely on its own initiative in order to carry on economic warfare against Axis interests in Bolivia.

[Here follows a detailed description of offending business firms.]

A tentative proposal being drafted at this Embassy for the organization of an official Bolivian Corporation to assist in the elimination

---

[25] Not printed.

of large Proclaimed List firms and aid acceptable firms in the expansion of their operations is still in a formative stage.

Respectfully yours,

For the Ambassador:
ROBERT F. WOODWARD
Second Secretary of Embassy

AGREEMENT BETWEEN THE UNITED STATES AND BOLIVIA PROVIDING FOR A HEALTH AND SANITATION PROGRAM, SIGNED JULY 15 AND 16, 1942

[For text of the agreement, signed at La Paz, see Department of State Executive Agreement Series No. 300, or 56 Stat. (pt. 2) 1864.]

BRAZIL

COOPERATION BETWEEN THE UNITED STATES AND BRAZIL ON CERTAIN MEASURES FOR HEMISPHERE DEFENSE [1]

832.248/317 : Telegram

The Secretary of State to the Ambassador in Brazil (Caffery)

WASHINGTON, January 17, 1942—9 p. m.

147. Your no. 2018, December 12.[2] The War Department makes the following proposal (The Under Secretary,[3] it is understood, was advised of the project before the War Department was able to confirm it) :

1. This Government will assign to the United States Military Mission 2 B–18 and 10 P–36 airplanes for operation in the northeast area by United States Army personnel under the supervision and direction of the military mission for training of Brazilian military personnel.

2. The crews delivering the planes will return to their stations leaving however seven qualified enlisted men for indispensable service and maintenance.

3. The planes will be delivered upon formal acceptance of the offer on the part of the Brazilian Government (which it is hoped can be expedited) at the time and place indicated by the Brazilian Government. Seven to ten days should be allowed for issuance of orders and commencement of the movement after receipt by the War Department of the Brazilian acceptance.

[Here follows information concerning the flight plan, and the personnel, equipment, and armament of the planes.]

HULL

---

[1] Continued from *Foreign Relations,* 1941, vol. vi, sections under Brazil entitled "Cooperation between the United States and Brazil on certain measures for Hemisphere defense" and "Negotiation of a Lend-Lease Agreement between the United States and Brazil, signed October 1, 1941." For additional information on this subject, see Stetson Conn and Byron Fairchild, *The Framework of Hemisphere Defense,* in the series *United States Army in World War II: The Western Hemisphere* (Washington, Government Printing Office, 1960), pp. 303 ff.

[2] Not printed ; this communication was addressed by Gen. Lehman W. Miller, the Military Attaché in Brazil, to the War Department through the Department of State. It concerned the plans to protect Natal and Pernambuco. (832.248/317)

[3] Under Secretary of State Sumner Welles was in Rio de Janeiro at this time as representative to the Third Meeting of the Foreign Ministers of the American Republics; for correspondence concerning this Meeting, see pp. 6 ff.

740.0011 European War 1939/18611 : Telegram

The Under Secretary of State (Welles), Temporarily at Rio de Janeiro, to the Secretary of State

RIO DE JANEIRO, January 18, 1942—6 p. m.
[Received January 19—6 : 17 a. m.]

21. For the President. The highlights of the situation are approximately as follows: Two days before my arrival in Rio de Janeiro President Vargas called together his Cabinet and his highest military and naval authorities and told them that he had reached the decision that, both from the standpoint of the highest interests of Brazil as well as from the standpoint of the commitments which Brazil had previously made, Brazil must stand or fall with the United States. He stated that any member of the Government who was in disagreement with this policy was at liberty to resign his position. He received a unanimous vote of approval though the Chief of the General Staff [4] and the Minister of War [5] both of whom had during the earlier months of the war been unquestionably under the belief that Germany would triumph stated that Brazil's ability to defend herself was very limited and one of the chief reasons for this was the fact that notwithstanding the repeated efforts which the Brazilian Army had made to obtain armaments and munitions from the United States and notwithstanding the repeated assurances which had been given by the United States Government that such help would be forthcoming, up to the present time nothing but token shipments from the United States had been made. They stressed particularly the point that even the few small tanks which had been sent [were] without armament and were consequently practically useless. Both the Minister for War and General Góes Monteiro, however, stated that in their considered opinion the policy announced by President Vargas was the only correct policy for Brazil to follow. (I know from outside sources that both Generals have made statements to exactly the same effect to representatives of the Axis Powers and to representatives of the Argentine and Chilean Governments.)

In the course of his statement of policy to his Cabinet, President Vargas emphasized significantly that his Government did not have to depend upon the Armed Forces of the Republic for the control of subversive activities, even including any attempt at a local uprising by German or Italian sympathizers. He told his Cabinet that the Brazilian people were 100% in agreement with the policy upon which he had decided and that the people themselves would be able to take care of any attempts at Axis-inspired uprisings.

---

[4] Gen. Pedro Góes Monteiro.
[5] Gen. Eurico Gaspar Dutra.

Since that moment the attitude of the Brazilian Government could not have been finer nor more firm from our point of view. The Brazilian press has cooperated completely in everything we have wanted and the atmosphere consequently created both by the press and by open public sympathy with the United States has needless to say been enormously helpful at this time.

President Vargas has stated to the Argentine Foreign Minister[6] that the Brazilian Government supports the United States completely and that the Brazilian Government considers it indispensable that a joint declaration by all the American Republics for an immediate severance of relations with the Axis Powers be adopted at the Conference. He has sent a personal message to that effect by courier to the Acting President of Argentina[7] and he is presently using all of Brazil's very great influence in Chile in order to bring the Chilean Government in line. It is not too much to say that had it not been for the strong and helpful position taken by President Vargas and by Aranha[8] four of the other South American Republics would probably have drifted in the direction of Argentina.

Last night President Vargas sent for me and after I had expressed my deep appreciation of all that he had been doing to cooperate with us he said that as I knew the decisions of his Government had been taken and that the decisions were final. He continued that as Aranha had told me earlier in the evening the latter had received during the day letters addressed to him on [from] the German, Italian, and Japanese Ambassadors. These letters, whose texts I had seen stated, bluntly, in the case of the German Ambassador and in a more veiled fashion in the case of the Japanese and Italian Ambassadors that if Brazil undertook to break diplomatic relations she could anticipate a state of war with the Axis Powers. (The letters were regarded as personal by the Brazilian Government and they are therefore anxious that no publicity should be given to their contents as yet.)

President Vargas then went on to say that the decision reached by the Brazilian Government implied inevitably that she would soon be actually at war. He said that the responsibility which he had assumed on behalf of the Brazilian people was very great. He said that it was peculiarly great because of the fact that notwithstanding all his efforts during the past 18 months to obtain at least a minimum of war supplies from the United States I myself knew what the result of his effort had been. He said that he felt that in view of the present circumstances he could depend upon you better than anyone else to understand his crucial difficulties. He went on to

[6] Enrique Ruiz-Guiñazú.

[7] Ramón Castillo.

[8] Oswaldo Aranha, Brazilian Minister for Foreign Affairs.

say that obviously Brazil could not be treated as a small Central American power which would be satisfied with the stationing of American troops upon its territory, but that Brazil rather has a right to be regarded by the United States as a friend and ally and as entitled to be furnished under the Lend-Lease Act [9] with planes, tanks, and coast artillery sufficient to enable the Brazilian Army to defend at least in part those regions of northeastern Brazil whose defense is as vitally necessary for the United States as for Brazil herself.

In view of the nature of the conversation I regarded it as inexpedient to take up with the President the issue of the stationing of United States forces in northeastern Brazil in line with the understanding which I reached with General Marshall before I left Washington. Personally I have no doubt that this issue can be met successfully and that the Brazilian Government will agree thereto provided the Brazilian Army is given at least a minimum of matériel requested by President Vargas.

The conversation I had with the President was at a large gathering and I could only speak with him for a few moments. He has asked me to come to see him alone tomorrow, Monday, evening at 6 o'clock. I should like to be specifically authorized by you to state in the course of that conversation that I have communicated directly with you and that you have authorized me to say to him as Chief Executive of one great American nation to the Chief Executive of another great American nation and also as a personal friend that if the President will give me a list of the minimum requirements needed urgently by the Brazilian Army for the proper protection of northeastern Brazil you will give orders that the items contained in that list will be made available to the Brazilian Government at the first possible moment subject only to the exigencies of the present defense requirements of the United States of America and to any subsequent modifications that may later be agreed upon by the United States and Brazilian General Staffs.

As I know you will appreciate the issue involved is one of the highest national importance. . . . Like all armies, the Brazilian High Command is not inclined to be enthusiastic about getting into war if they have none of the basic elements for defense. If they are not promptly given the necessary assurances and if they are not able to see with their own eyes before long some concrete evidences of help coming, exactly that kind of a situation which the Nazis could use to their best advantage will be created.

---

[9] Act of March 11, 1941; 55 Stat. 31. For correspondence on the negotiation of the Lend-Lease Agreement between the United States and Brazil, signed October 1, 1941, see *Foreign Relations*, 1941, vol. VI; for text of further agreement, signed March 3, 1942, see *post*, p. 815.

The problem is one of such critical importance that I have felt it necessary to bring it to your attention immediately. I shall deeply appreciate it if you can let me have a favorable reply before my interview with President Vargas tomorrow evening.

. . .   .

WELLES

832.24/634

President Roosevelt to the Under Secretary of State (Welles), Temporarily at Rio de Janeiro [10]

[WASHINGTON, January 19, 1942.]

WELLES: Your 21: [11] Tell President Vargas I wholly understand and appreciate the needs and can assure him flow of material will start at once. He will understand when I say there are shortages in a few items which I do not trust to putting on the wire but which are soon to come into production. I want to get away as soon as possible from token shipments and increase them to a minimum of Brazilian requirements very quickly.

Tell him I am made very happy by his splendid policy and give him my very warm regards.

I will send list of immediate shipments in separate code message.

ROOSEVELT

832.24/619 : Telegram

The Secretary of State to the American Delegation at the Third Meeting of the Foreign Ministers of the American Republics

WASHINGTON, January 19, 1942—10 p. m.

34. Personal for Mr. Welles. Reference your 21, January 18, 6 p. m., and Duggan's telephone conversation of today with Caffery.[12]

The following information regarding Lease-Lend material for the Brazilian Army has been provided by General Marshall: [13]

Starting now five primary training planes will go forward each month. Deliveries have been made of 50 percent of the primary

---

[10] This communication written in the President's own hand appears to have been transmitted to the Adviser on Political Relations (Duggan), who made the following notation: "Unable to reach Mr. Welles or anyone on his immediate staff, I telephoned the President's message to Mr. Caffery [Ambassador in Brazil]. Mr. Caffery stated that he was going to join the President [of Brazil] and Mr. Welles in a few minutes and would therefore have an opportunity to give the message to Mr. Welles."

[11] Dated January 18, 6 p. m., p. 633.

[12] Concerning the telephone conversation, see footnote 10, above.

[13] Gen. George C. Marshall, Chief of Staff, U.S. Army.

trainers and those which will be sent now are the remainder. Unless we are able to increase production, 50 basic trainers will not be available until beginning in August. At present production rates, combat planes will not be available for release until fall.

The War Department will notify regarding harbor defense equipment in the near future. Another survey is being made to see if any can be transferred to Brazil from present installations.

Ten light tanks, 30 motorcycles, 31 scout cars, 74 ¼-ton trucks or jeeps and 20 ambulances are now being released for Brazil. Arms and ammunition for weapons on all combat vehicles is likewise being released. A total of 65 light tanks will be shipped at the rate of 10 per month. In February 200 ¼-ton jeeps will be shipped and in March 250. These are weapon carriers as well as scout carriers. Twenty ½-ton weapon carrier trucks will be shipped in February and 100 each month thereafter until a total of 410 has been reached. A total of 380 1½-ton cargo trucks are to be shipped beginning with 90 in February and 90 each month thereafter. A total of 557 ½-ton cargo trucks will be released beginning with a shipment of 182 in February and 100 each succeeding month. Forty-nine 2½-ton prime mover trucks will be shipped at the rate of five a month beginning in February.

For your information the United States troops now engaged and troops now embarking are making very heavy demands daily for ammunition. It is suggested, however, that you limit comment on this situation to the most general terms.

HULL

832.24/651 : Telegram

The Ambassador in Brazil (Caffery) to the Secretary of State

RIO DE JANEIRO, January 31, 1942—2 p. m.
[Received 6 : 05 p. m.]

303. For the Under Secretary. I had a satisfactory talk with General Eduardo Gomes.[14] He emphasized his interest in obtaining the spare parts (item 1 of Air Ministry memorandum[15]).

Souza Costa,[16] when he told me goodby this morning, emphasized that the principal object of his visit to Washington is "procurement of necessary armament".

CAFFERY

---

[14] Commander of the 2d Air Zone and Director General of Airways, Brazilian Ministry of Aeronautics.
[15] Not printed.
[16] Arthur de Souza Costa, Brazilian Minister of Finance.

832.248/340 : Telegram

The Ambassador in Brazil (*Caffery*) *to the Secretary of State*

[Extracts]

Rio de Janeiro, February 3, 1942—8 p. m.
[Received February 4—5 : 27 a. m.]

334. For the Under Secretary. Referring to the 10 P–36 and the 2 B–18 airplanes about which there has been a great deal of correspondence, the Chief of Cabinet of the Air Ministry [17] now writes as follows to the Chief of our Air Mission [18] here :

"In order to issue instructions to the Air Force staff and to the command of the 2d Air Zone as to the grouping of P–36 and B–18 airplanes in the northeast of Brazil the Ministry of Aeronautics desires that in accordance with the cooperation agreement signed between the United States and Brazil [19] the following points be fixed.

1. The arrival of 10 airplanes P–36 and 2 airplanes B–18 is expected, these planes to be sent by the American Government to Brazil in accordance to the request made by the Minister for Air, that airplanes be furnished to guard the northeast.

In accordance with the agreements made and due to the present impossibility of the furnishing of modern airplanes to be acquired by the Brazilian Government it has been decided that the airplanes in question would continue to be property of the American Government, being utilized by the personnel of the F. A. B.[20] for training and eventual use.

2. In order to define the situation of the above-mentioned planes that are going to constitute an aeroplane grouping, the Ministry of Aeronautics desires that the following points be crossed in the following manner :

1. Period of adaptation of the planes by the F. A. B. personnel. (*a*) Nature of adaptation according to program in detail presented by the Chief of the U. S. M. M. and approved by the Minister; (*b*) duration—not to exceed 6 weeks; (*c*) grouping conferred [*sic*] with during the adaptation and its subordination; one superior officer of the F. A. B. directly subordinated to the command of the 2d Air Zone. The American officers will administer the instructions in accordance to the approved program.

2. After the adaptation period : (*a*) Situation of the planes : The Brazilian Government will take the entire responsibility as to the material indemnifying the American Government for any damage occurred. [(*b*)] Grouping command : After the adaptation period the command will continue to be exercised by a superior officer of the F. A. B. directly subordinate to Air Minister. (*c*) The officers of the U. S. M. M. will return to Rio against [*sic*] this period and any suggestions that the U. S. M. M. may have to

---

[17] Presumably Col. Dulcidio Cardoso.
[18] Col. Thomas D. White.
[19] For a general statement of the terms of this agreement, see *Foreign Relations*, 1941, vol. vi, section under Brazil entitled "Cooperation between the United States and Brazil on certain measures for Hemisphere defense", footnote 2.
[20] Brazilian Air Force.

make as to the instruction or use of the referred to grouping will be sent through the aeronautics staff.["]

[Here follows an explanation of mutual dissatisfactions of American and Brazilian officers over the air defense of Brazil.]

Referring to the last paragraph of the note quoted above from Colonel Cardoso, I recommend that the Minister of Air's [20a] condition be accepted.

CAFFERY

832.24/668b : Telegram

The Secretary of State to the Ambassador in Brazil (Caffery)

WASHINGTON, February 5, 1942—2 p. m.

276. From the Under Secretary. Please deliver personally to President Vargas the following message from me. (Please see that Aranha has a copy of it at the same time that you hand it to President Vargas.)

"Immediately upon my return to Washington I received the authorization of President Roosevelt to inform the necessary authorities of the Government of the United States of the President's desire that Your Excellency's requests be promptly complied with and that those authorities be informed of the President's wish that your requirements be met immediately.

In studying the military needs of Brazil, it now seems perfectly clear that instead of 100 million dollars, at least 150 million dollars will be required. I am happy to assure Your Excellency now that an additional 50 million dollars can be made available to Brazil and this Government will adjust its agreement with the Brazilian Government accordingly. During the visit of Minister Souza Costa to Washington, this new agreement can be concluded. Pending, however, the formalities of such an agreement, this Government will procure the additional material with the understanding, of course, that nothing will be sent to Brazil that does not receive the prior approval of your Government.

In addition to the list which I had the honor of giving Your Excellency during my recent visit to Rio de Janeiro there will be sent to Brazil before the first of March the following items:

Telescope sights	117
7 inch projectiles	282
Tetryl	2, 500 pounds
Scout cars	31
Tanks completely equipped with guns and machine guns	20
30 caliber ammunition	360, 000 rounds
Tracer Ammunition	90, 000 rounds
45 caliber ball ammunition	30, 000 rounds
37 mm A.P. shell	3, 000

[20a] Joaquin Pedro Salgado Filho.

Ambulances	20
2½ ton trucks	360
¼ ton command reconnaissance cars	274
½ ton weapons carrier trucks	40
Tank trucks	10
1½ ton trucks	180
4 ton trucks	26
Motorcycles	30
Lodestar Lockheed	1
Fairchild primary trainers	30

An additional 15 primary trainers will be sent at the earliest possible moment.

We will start shipment of basic trainers in February and complete total of 50 at earliest possible moment.

In addition to Beechcraft transports already delivered we can deliver two additional transports a month. I believe this schedule can be substantially increased and am bending every effort to get this done.

While we are moving our fighters, dive bombers and bombardment planes into the battle areas, nevertheless our production is on the increase and these combat craft will be sent at the earliest possible date.

Amphibian and patrol planes, bombs and spare parts should reach you at an early date. Bi-motor Beechcraft also are under way.

Your naval requests are being handled here promptly and Navy today has advised me that a substantial amount of naval equipment can be shipped immediately. I will let you know as soon as possible about the details of this.

I have conferred this morning with your Ambassador [21] and with General Amaro Bittencourt.[22] The latter informs me that in addition to the material above listed, the Brazilian Government urgently requires first, 5,000 6-inch projectiles; second, armament and munitions for the 10 tanks and 10 scout cars already in Brazil; third, a priority for the completion by the Baldwin Locomotive Company of twelve 7-inch cannon.

I have submitted these three requests immediately to Mr. Hopkins [23] who has full authority to deal with these questions, and through whose assistance by direction of the President the above statement is sent to you, and Mr. Hopkins has assured me that these matters will be satisfactorily attended to before the conclusion of today. General Amaro during the course of today will receive direct word on these points.

I am glad to inform Your Excellency that due to the President's directions I have found the most excellent cooperation with regard to the requirements of your Government from both the War and the Navy Departments.

In conclusion, may I state that if at any moment the urgent requirements of the Brazilian Government as set forth in the memoranda Your Excellency gave me are not being satisfactorily met, I

---

[21] Carlos Martins.
[22] Brazilian Military Attaché in the United States.
[23] Harry L. Hopkins, Special Assistant to President Roosevelt.

shall appreciate it if you will have word sent to me directly and I can assure you that it is the desire and the policy of this Government to see to it that every question be immediately and satisfactorily solved in the interest of the Brazilian Government.

Please accept the assurances of my highest consideration and of my lasting personal friendship."

General Amaro tells me that with the inclusion of the three points mentioned in the latter part of my message to the President, the desires of the Brazilian war department will be fully met. There will be no trouble in so far as the Navy Department is concerned. The outstanding gap, of course, is the question of the combat planes, but I feel sure that some progress can be made along this line in the immediate future.

In your conversation with the President, please make it doubly clear that if for any reason he is not wholly satisfied with this response, all he has to do is to let me know through you and I feel positive that everything necessary can be done at this end to meet the situation.

Please telegraph me the result of your conversation. [Welles.]

HULL

832.24/673 : Telegram

The Ambassador in Brazil (Caffery) to the Secretary of State

RIO DE JANEIRO, February 7, 1942—noon.
[Received 6:55 p. m.]

371. For the Under Secretary. Aranha told me Thursday afternoon he was going the same evening to the Rezopolis.[24] He asked me to give your message [25] (when it came) to Fraga [26] to take to him at the Rezopolis and he would take it to President Vargas the next day at Petropolis.

I telephoned Aranha yesterday morning that I was proceeding to Petropolis and suggested that he meet me there: he did. When I showed him your telegram he said "That's just the old run around. You can't show that to President Vargas. Welles told him that you would give us equal treatment with England, Russia, China—you are doing nothing of the kind; you are dumping a lot of trucks on us; giving us nothing we need for the defense of the northeast: anti-aircraft guns, artillery, combat planes. Tell Welles he had better just file this away and forget it. Our military people are going to raise hell with many I told you so's. President Vargas will never believe the State Department again".

---

[24] Reference presumably is to the resort town, Teresopolis (Therezopolis).
[25] See *supra*.
[26] Presumably Edgar Fraga de Castro, an official in the Brazilian Ministry for Foreign Affairs.

I made several appropriate observations and stuck to my guns that I would see Vargas.

I saw Vargas who asked me to convey to you his appreciation and gratitude. He said, "My offhand opinion is very good indeed (of course I will consult my technicians). Welles is carrying out his promises to me. This is not all we need but the fact that he is getting it to us before the first of next month demonstrates his good faith (which I have never doubted). Thank him for me and thank also President Roosevelt for his cooperation. Tell Welles that we shall be expecting this material as fast as he can send it.

I have full confidence that he appreciates our other urgent needs, especially how badly we need artillery and anti-aircraft guns at Fernando de Noronha, Natal, etc.; and that without combat planes we will be helpless in the northeast". (See General Miller's memorandum to me dated January 19, 1942 of which you have a copy entitled "Immediate needs of Brazilian Army and Air Force for defense northeast Brazil".[27] [)]

As I left he repeated, "Tell Welles of my high appreciation and of my full confidence in him".

Aranha was waiting for me and when I told him of the results of my conversation he said "I hope that he keeps to that opinion".

CAFFERY

832.24/674 : Telegram

The Secretary of State to the Ambassador in Brazil (Caffery)

WASHINGTON, February 9, 1942—5 p. m.

307. From the Under Secretary. Your 371, February 7, noon. I showed your telegram to the President yesterday. He was much amused by it.

Please tell Aranha from me that for once his uncanny intuition has been in error. This is no "run around" and there is not going to be any "run around".

There has been created here in the Government a new board known as the Munitions Allocations Board of which Harry Hopkins is the head and of which General Burns[28] is the executive chief. This Board is subordinate only to the President and is superior to every other branch of the Government dealing with matters in this field.

I have just conferred with General Burns by instruction of the President and I have arranged with General Burns to have his first meeting this afternoon with Souza Costa. The needs of the Brazilian War Ministry, Aviation Ministry and Ministry of Marine will be

---

[27] Not found in Department files.
[28] Maj. Gen. J. H. Burns.

taken up in order and before the end of this week, a satisfactory agreement as to future deliveries will be reached in each case. I have emphasized to General Burns the requirements mentioned in your telegrams 377, February 7, 6 p.m., and 379, February 7, 8 p.m.[29] He understands the picture fully.

For the reasons above set forth, the next 3 or 4 days will be of particular importance in finally clearing up the assignment of armament and munitions for the Brazilian Government. In accordance with the request contained in my telegram to you 276, February 5, 2 p. m., please telegraph me any further specific requests or amendments which President Vargas may have to make with regard to my message to him.

I am very much encouraged by the determination on the part of the competent authorities here to give Brazil ample satisfaction naturally within the limits of what is possible and reasonable under present circumstances. [Welles.]

HULL

810.20 Defense/2059 : Telegram

The Ambassador in Brazil (Caffery) to the Secretary of State

RIO DE JANEIRO, February 11, 1942—10 p. m.
[Received February 12—12 : 12 a. m.]

414. The Brazilian Navy Department agrees to the operation of naval vessels from Rio de Janeiro and Santos as desired in the second paragraph of Department's 312, February 9, 11 p. m.[30]

It would not be expedient for me to take up the matter of operation of planes with the Air Ministry before I have replies to my Nos. 377, February 7, 6 p. m., and 379, February 7, 8 p. m.[29]

CAFFERY

810.20 Defense/2059 : Telegram

The Secretary of State to the Ambassador in Brazil (Caffery)

WASHINGTON, February 13, 1942—9 p. m.

351. Your 414, February 11, 1942, 10 p. m. Navy inquires whether the consent of the Brazilian Navy Department applies also to the British Naval vessels. It is important that they should be included in this permission as they constitute an integral part of the naval patrol.

HULL

---

[30] Neither printed.
[29] Not printed.

832.248/340 : Telegram

The Secretary of State to the Ambassador in Brazil (Caffery)

WASHINGTON, February 16, 1942—6 p.m.

371. From the Under Secretary. General Marshall and the War Department in general are most desirous of taking immediate action in accordance with the outline in your no. 334, February 3, 8 p. m., with respect to the 10 pursuits and 2 bombers; and they are exceedingly grateful to the Air Ministry for its cooperation in this regard and its sympathetic recognition of the problems of personnel and equipment faced by our Army. The Air Ministry's willingness to shorten the period of adaptation, thus permitting the rapid release of our much needed personnel, coincides exactly with the program of the War Department, which sincerely appreciates this mark of collaboration.

In brief, the War Department accepts the Air Ministry's proposal in its broad outline. The minor differences from that proposal in the following outline are merely dictated by the need for fitting it in with our legislation and particularly our war plans, which the War Department feels confident the Air Minister will readily understand.

1. On signal of the Brazilian Government 2 B–18's and 10 P–36's together with crews, maintenance personnel, equipment and ammunition will be sent to the Natal area for delivery to the United States Air Mission and for training of Brazilian personnel and operation under the supervision of the Air Mission.

2. Personnel accompanying the ships will, under the Air Mission's supervision, conduct the instruction of the Brazilian personnel in the operation and maintenance of the airplanes and will return to the United States when the Brazilian authorities consider that the Brazilian personnel has acquired the necessary training. It is repeated that the War Department greatly appreciates the Air Ministry's cooperation in fixing this period of adaptation at a maximum of 6 weeks. Anything which can be done further to shorten the period will be helpful.

3. When the Air Ministry is satisfied that the FAB personnel has acquired the desired training, the title to the airplanes and accessory equipment will, in accordance with the procedure fixed by legislation, be transferred to the Brazilian Government, at a reasonable valuation, under the terms of the new expanded Brazilian-United States lend lease agreement now being negotiated.

To perfect plans for the flight the War Department asks for the following specific information: (a) the exact place in the northeast area to which the airplanes shall be flown, and (b) the designation of the Brazilian personnel or agency in that area who will receive the group and will work out the details of the cooperative arrangements there. Upon receipt of the instructions of the Brazilian Government and approval of the foregoing the War Department will promptly dispatch the ships to Brazil. [Welles.]

HULL

832.248/341 : Telegram

The Secretary of State to the Ambassador in Brazil (Caffery)

WASHINGTON, February 18, 1942—9 p. m.

388. You will, the Department feels sure, be interested in having the following information which reveals the understanding on the part of the military and lend lease authorities of Brazil's defense needs:

1. Ten AT–6 "advanced training airplanes" will be flown to Brazil within a few days by United States Army crews of one pilot and one co-pilot per plane (some Brazilian air personnel at present in the United States may accompany the American crews). The United States personnel will remain for a short period of instruction, the length of which should be determined by the Air Ministry. These planes, while officially designated as trainers, are in effect combat aircraft useful for oversea missions. Each carries three .30 caliber machine guns and four 100-pound bombs. The ammunition, it is understood, will be transported by sea. The Brazilian Minister of Finance and General Bittencourt and Colonel Ararigboia[32] are delighted with the offer.

2. The 50 Vultee basic trainers requisitioned by the Brazilian Aeronautical Mission and scheduled for delivery over a period of several months will now be made available to Brazil from February production.

3. With reference to your despatch 6401 of January 31, 1942,[33] the question of the 10 twin-engined Beechcraft for the Brazilian Army Airmail Service is now on the agenda of the Munitions Allocations Board to determine whether improved delivery schedules are possible. In this case however it should be pointed out that this plane is barely coming into production, and the type of engines required by this ship is extremely hard to obtain. Optimism with regard to the improvement of the delivery schedules is not yet therefore justified.

HULL

---

[32] Col. Armando de Souza e Mello Ararigboia, Brazilian Air Attaché in Washington.
[33] Not printed.

832.24/703 : Telegram

The Ambassador in Brazil (Caffery) to the Secretary of State

RIO DE JANEIRO, February 18, 1942—midnight.
[Received February 19—3 : 55 a. m.]

479. For the Under Secretary. Aranha showed me this morning the confidential report to President Vargas of the Minister of War on the material promised in Department's 276, February 5, 2 p. m. While showing more appreciation than Aranha showed (my telegram No. 371, February 7, 12 noon) still he made some of the same criticisms Aranha made; and remarked that "even the 25,000,000 had not yet been deposited", et cetera.

I should appreciate any further information available in regard to the three requests made by General Amaro Bittencourt as additional "urgent requirements" of the Brazilian Government; also as to the present status of the material promised before the first of March; also as to the present status of spare parts mentioned in my 377, February 7, 6 p. m.[34]

CAFFERY

810.20 Defense/2092c : Telegram

The Secretary of State to the Ambassador in Brazil (Caffery)

WASHINGTON, February 18, 1942—midnight.

392. The Commanding General, Caribbean Defense Command,[35] has advised the War Department as follows:

"My responsibilities in the Caribbean theatre make essential a much broader intelligence coverage than now exists, not only of the Caribbean theatre, but also south to include Peru and Brazil to the fifth parallel of South Latitude. This additional territory is the location of Axis activity and potential Axis air and ground observations which may become very dangerous to the Caribbean theatre."

The War Department has now informed this Department that it would like to station at Manáos, Brazil, 2 Grumman amphibians (O-A9) and 8 officers and 4 enlisted men to carry out air surveillance flights. The planes would carry armament.

Without sounding out the Brazilian Government, please give the Department your views as to the best approach to the Government in order to attain the objective of the War Department.

HULL

---

[34] Not printed.
[35] Maj. Gen. Frank M. Andrews.

832.24/703 : Telegram

The Acting Secretary of State to the Ambassador in Brazil (Caffery)

WASHINGTON, February 21, 1942—8 p. m.

427. Your 479, February 18, midnight. In my judgment, satisfactory arrangements regarding urgently needed military and naval matériel have been arrived at, including all of the matériel contained in my message to President Vargas.[36] The President has personally interested himself in the matter, being fully aware of the importance to the war effort of the wholehearted cooperation of President Vargas and the Government of Brazil.

Dr. Souza Costa, who, of course, has been advised at every step by General Amaro, has informed me that he regards as satisfactory the arrangements concerning naval matériel. He has also expressed satisfaction with the arrangements regarding aviation matériel now that the 50 Vultee BT–15's have been made available. He naturally hoped to be able to secure some combat aircraft but appreciates the critical demand for combat planes by troops of the United Nations now actually fighting. A few combat planes will be made available.

With regard to ground matériel, instructions have been issued to have all of this matériel scheduled for delivery during January and February assembled at New Orleans for shipment on a Brazilian vessel March 7. Moreover, in addition to the 20 light tanks which will be ready for shipping on this vessel there will be assembled for delivery during March at New Orleans or whatever other port Brazil selects an additional 30 light tanks. Thereafter, the regular scheduled delivery of 10 per month will be maintained until 65 tanks are turned over. I regard this arrangement concerning tanks as the utmost that could be obtained. The extent to which we have gone to make these light tanks available is clear from the fact that they have been taken away from our own troops, which, on account of heavy deliveries to forces fighting the Axis in Libya, in Russia, and in the Far East, are already insufficiently supplied.

As a further indication of our desire to share available matériel with the Brazilians, four antiaircraft guns, complete with fire control and a reasonable amount of ammunition, are being immediately made available. These guns have a range, I am told, of 30,000 to 35,000 feet. Dr. Souza Costa has requested such guns for the protection of Natal, Belém and Fernando de Noronha. These guns have been protecting a plant making a vital piece of equipment.

With regard to the three urgently needed items mentioned in my telegram no. 276, February 5, 2 p. m., the Brazilians have accepted 1,000 armor-piercing and 4,000 high-explosive 6-inch shells.

---

[36] Presumably message transmitted in Department's telegram No. 276, February 5, 2 p. m., p. 639.

Armament and munitions for the 10 tanks and 10 scout cars already in Brazil will be available for shipment on March 7. Finally, the highest priority has been given for the modification of the 7-inch gun carriages.

With regard to the spare parts mentioned in your 377, February 7, 6 p. m.,[37] a request has today been presented to Mr. Hopkins that he make them immediately available, and this will be done.

Dr. Souza Costa has also raised the question of a specific delivery schedule for the other important items, such as light and medium tanks and antiaircraft and antitank guns, for which requisitions have been filed. Including aircraft, these items are among the most difficult to furnish, since they are precisely the implements most needed by forces now engaged in fighting. With the augmentation of production it should be possible to make some deliveries on these items during the coming months, and the War Department has stated that it anticipates all the items in which Dr. Souza Costa has expressed particular interest can be made available to Brazil prior to the end of the present calendar year. It is, however, utterly impossible, in view of the war situation, as well as shipping difficulties to make firm commitments now regarding monthly deliveries. I will explain this to Dr. Souza Costa when he returns from New York on Tuesday.

I suggest that you go over the foregoing with President Vargas, not only to convey to him the factual information but to give him an idea of the extent to which the President went to make available this equipment, particularly the tanks and the four antiaircraft guns. Please assure the President that every proper effort will be made to assure the delivery of the other equipment for which requisitions have been filed during the balance of the year but that it is not possible at this precise moment to develop a fixed delivery schedule for the tight items such as light and medium tanks and antiaircraft and antitank guns, and that this will have to be agreed upon after the departure of Dr. Souza Costa.

WELLES

811.248/357 : Telegram

The Acting Secretary of State to the Ambassador in Brazil (Caffery)

WASHINGTON, February 21, 1942—9 p. m.

428. From my personal telegram no. 427, of February 21, 8 p. m. I think you will agree that the requests of the Brazilian Government with regard to urgently-needed military and naval matériel have been met. As soon as President Vargas is apprized of the results of the conversations of Dr. Souza Costa I would appreciate your tak-

---

[37] Not printed.

ing up with him at once the matters which follow hereafter. The President attaches the greatest importance to the conclusion immediately of these arrangements with the Brazilian Government since they will make possible the rapid ferrying of large numbers of planes to north Africa and the Far East where they are critically and urgently needed. The rapid passage of these planes and their immediate arrival at fighting fronts will have an important bearing on the course of the military operations now taking place.

The desires of the War Department are as follows:

(1) The War Department states that it is impossible for proper servicing to be given to the planes crossing the Atlantic from Brazil to Africa under the existing arrangement whereby the service personnel of Pan American Airways services the aircraft. In the first place, Pan American personnel is not sufficient to take care of the large number of planes now flying in groups and which frequently require overnight servicing. In the second place, Pan American personnel is not familiar with the servicing of military planes. The War Department is desirous therefore of sending service personnel as follows: 300 to Belém, 300 to Natal, and 150 to Recife. This personnel would cover the following functions: administrative, communications, maintenance, supply, messing, weather, and other technical details. The men would be in uniform but completely unarmed. They would have no security function of any kind.

(2) The War Department would like permission to construct quarters; barracks; administrative, technical and other similar accommodations at each of the above-listed localities to accommodate the Air Corps Ferrying Command squadrons concerned, plus an average of 100 transient United States Government personnel. This construction at the present time can be accomplished expeditiously by contract through Pan American Airways, Inc. Such construction should be located immediately adjacent to the land airdromes at Belém, Natal, and Recife.

(3) Under existing arrangements the prior approval of the Brazilian Government must be obtained for all flights of United States military aircraft except the 3-times-a-week ferry service. Although the Brazilian Government has been most cooperative and attentive in granting permissions, it would enormously facilitate matters if a blanket permission could be granted. Weather conditions frequently make it impossible for planes to fly at the stipulated times. Moreover, the more people who know of these flights the greater the opportunity of the Axis learning of their number, type, et cetera.

The War Department, therefore, would like to secure the privilege of the free and unrestricted use of a corridor along the north coast of Brazil and as far south as Recife for the movement of military aircraft. This corridor has been defined as follows: a strip along the coast of the northeastern portion of Brazil from the border of French Guiana at Cabo d'Orange to Belém, thence continuing southeastward along the coast to Natal and thence southwestward along the coast to Recife, the strip to be approximately 100 miles in depth from the ocean in order to provide for easier navigation and to avoid flight interferences due to weather. If granted, the War Department would move its planes along this corridor without requesting the usual notification through diplomatic channels but information regarding plane movements would be furnished directly to Brazilian commanders at Belém and Natal by Air Corps Ferrying Command officials at those places. It is contemplated that aircraft would move at the rate of approximately 50 per day eastbound and a lesser number westbound.

(4) Permission is desired to construct underground bulk storage with pipeline connections to dispersed lesser storage for approximately 1 million gallons of gasoline at Belém and Natal, and approximately 500,000 gallons of gasoline at Amapa, Fortaleza and Recife to support the movement of combat echelons and United States' military air transportation as distinguished from local operations.

(5) Permission is requested to lengthen the runway to approximately 6,000 feet on Fernando de Noronha Island; to station a detachment of approximately 50 officers and men from the Recife Air Corps Ferrying Command squadron thereat for the final inspection of certain types of aircraft to be flown across the South Atlantic; and to stock this airdrome with approximately 500,000 gallons of gasoline supplies, spare parts, communications and weather facilities, including the necessary housing thereat.

The War Department, of course, is confident that the Brazilian Government will provide local Brazilian security forces to safeguard the United States movements along this corridor as well as the stockages of fuel and facilities incident thereto along the corridor and on Fernando de Noronha Island.

The War Department suggests that it should be helpful in securing favorable action on the points mentioned above by making the two following offers:

The Air Corps Ferrying Command will arrange to provide invaluable flight training for selected members of the Brazilian air force, acting in the capacity of copilot on 10 United States' military transport type airplanes operating from Miami to Natal and return.

The Air Corps Ferrying Command will provide invaluable training to selected technicians of the Brazilian air force at Belém and Natal by instructing such technicians in the maintenance of the latest types of combat aircraft being flown over the route.

Following the receipt of a favorable reply to these various propositions General Olds, Commanding General of the Air Corps Ferrying Command, will be glad to proceed at once to Brazil to confer in detail with Minister Salgado and General Gomes in order to insure that the entire plan of operation is put into effect to the full satisfaction of the Government of Brazil.

Needless to say, I recognize the extent of cooperation which President Vargas and his Government is being called upon to lend, but am confident that he will unhesitatingly accord the privileges requested on account of his understanding that we must cooperate, one with another, to the fullest extent possible in order to attain the defeat of the totalitarian nations. It has not been easy to convince our

Army that tanks should be taken from our own troops which are still very insufficiently supplied to send to Brazil. Nor has it been easy to persuade the Army that the four antiaircraft guns should be removed from a vital defense plant leaving that plant without any antiaircraft protection to be sent to Brazil. The President, however, has decided that this matériel be given to Brazil because of considerations broader than the purely military which demand today the closest working relationship between the two Governments. I feel certain that President Vargas will consider the requests embodied in this telegram in that same spirit. They are far-reaching and they require a greater measure of cooperation from Brazil than ever before requested in this field but this cooperation is vital to the winning of the war in which Brazil and the United States are equally interested.

WELLES

811.248/358 : Telegram

The Ambassador in Brazil (Caffery) to the Secretary of State

RIO DE JANEIRO, February 23, 1942—4 p. m.
[Received 6 : 55 p. m.]

558. For the Under Secretary. I shall take up your 428, February 21, 9 p. m., with President Vargas at an early date.

Aranha showed me on Saturday a report he had drawn up for President Vargas regarding the three Marine detachments at Recife, Belém and Natal, defending their presence there on the ground that they were "service personnel" and only "service personnel," insisting that they were not guards or active Marines in any sense of the word. He said that after he submitted this report to President Vargas, President Vargas finally approved the presence of the three detachments.

Also only last week the Air Ministry was endeavoring to set up obstacles in the way of our continuing our ferry service, et cetera, over northeast Brazil; however, I believe that situation has now been righted.

I am not saying these things as a pessimist, but only to bring out that this is not going to be easy.

CAFFERY

811.248/358 : Telegram

The Acting Secretary of State to the Ambassador in Brazil (Caffery)

WASHINGTON, February 24, 1942—10 p. m.

451. Your 558, February 23, 4 p. m. I fully understand the immense difficulties which are involved. However, in your conversa-

tion with President Vargas certain points should be made entirely plain.

1. This Government has just given concrete evidence to Brazil of the fact that even at great sacrifice to itself it is doing everything possible to supply Brazil with her naval and military requirements.

2. The defeat of the Axis powers is clearly as much in the interest of Brazil as it is in the interest of the United States.

3. The ability of the United States effectively to assist in turning the Japanese tide in the Far East depends to a desperately large extent on our ability to rush the bombing planes rapidly to the Far East. For that reason our Ferry Service must be expanded rapidly in northeastern Brazil in order to take care of the largely increased amount of planes we are now sending. In order to carry this out effectively we have got to have trained and experienced technicians to do the job. That is the sole reason why this request is being made. If members of the Brazilian Air Force were properly trained and experienced to do this work we would be asking them to do it for us.

4. In accordance with the terms of the suggestion made, the expansion of our Ferry Service will give Brazilian pilots an extraordinarily valuable opportunity for practical training in the handling of combat planes.

5. I feel confident that if General Olds can go personally to Brazil once you have prepared the foundation for such discussion, he can reach a satisfactory understanding through personal contacts with Salgado and Eduardo Gomes.

6. The time element, as President Vargas will realize, is of the utmost importance. Every day now counts.

WELLES

832.24/719 : Telegram

The Acting Secretary of State to the Ambassador in Brazil (*Caffery*)

WASHINGTON, February 26, 1942—2 p. m.

465. Your 588, February 25, 5 p. m.[39] The Minister of Finance and General Amaro state to me that they are completely satisfied with the arrangements entered into with this Government covering military and naval matériel. The Brazilian Ambassador informs me that in the telephone conversation which he had yesterday evening with Aranha, the latter informed him that the impression of the Brazilian Government was "very good".

WELLES

---

[39] Not printed.

832.24/723 : Telegram

The Ambassador in Brazil (Caffery) to the Secretary of State

RIO DE JANEIRO, February 26, 1942—6 p. m.
[Received 9 : 38 p. m.]

609. For the Under Secretary. Your telegram 276, February 5, 2 p. m. Are all items listed in third paragraph of your message to President Vargas distinct from the items named in paragraph four of the text of Department's 34 to American delegation, January 19, 10 p. m.? In other words, what specifically has been set aside for or delivered to Brazilian Army, aside from aircraft?

Also reference Department's telegram 388, February 18, 9 p. m., please confirm that planes mentioned under number 1 are AT-6['s].

CAFFERY

832.24/723 : Telegram

The Acting Secretary of State to the Ambassador in Brazil (Caffery)

WASHINGTON, February 28, 1942—8 p. m.

506. Your 609, February 26, 6 p. m. Yesterday afternoon I handed to Souza Costa the memorandum quoted hereafter recapitulating the understandings and arrangements arrived at through his conversations with regard to the furnishing of armament to Brazil.[40] I am happy to inform you that Souza Costa has since advised me that not only he but also General Amaro consider that the arrangements as set forth in the memorandum with regard to both immediate deliveries and deliveries during the remainder of 1942 are 100 percent satisfactory. Souza Costa cabled a statement in this sense to President Vargas last night. This helpful report should create a favorable atmosphere for taking up the various requests desired by the Ferry Command.

WELLES

811.248/395a : Telegram

The Acting Secretary of State to the Ambassador in Brazil (Caffery)

WASHINGTON, March 2, 1942—4 p. m.

515. With regard to the additional facilities desired by the Ferry Command in northeastern Brazil, I have today received a further communication from the War Department which reads as follows:

---

[40] Memorandum not printed; the understandings consisted of a promise to provide Brazil with some 60 primary and advanced training planes, 10 pursuit planes, and 2 bombers. Armament and ammunition for 10 light tanks and scout cars were offered as well as a small quantity of armor piercing shells and high explosive rounds. Some 50 light tanks and a few anti-aircraft guns were to be ready in the immediate future with many more available in the fourth quarter of the year.

"Referring to the additional facilities required in northeast Brazil for the ferrying of aircraft through this area, I am advised that the American Section of The Joint Board for northeast Brazil [41] has presented to General Ary Pires, President of the Board, a specific proposal for the provision of housing and storage facilities and the improvement of access roads at Amapá, Belém, São Luíz, Fortaleza, Natal, Recife, Maceió, and Bahia at an estimated cost of $2,700,000. I understand that General Pires concurs in this program and that it has received the informal consideration of the War Ministry. I also am advised that the Joint Board has discussed the assignment of an officer of the Corps of Engineers to northeast Brazil to supervise this program in collaboration with an engineer officer of the Brazilian Army assigned for this purpose.

2. In view thereof, it is requested that the consent of the Brazilian Government be obtained to the airport construction program in the amount of $2,700,000 as recommended to the Joint Board by the American Section and to the assignment of an officer of the Corps of Engineers to northeast Brazil to supervise and coordinate the construction activities now being undertaken through Pan American Airways.

3. The War Department is prepared to make the construction equipment being utilized in this program available to the Brazilian Government for use in the construction of defense works in Northeast Brazil as the extended construction program is completed."

Please take up this suggestion as a part of the whole arrangement proposed for northeastern Brazil.

You will realize, I know, how urgent the matter is and how vital the War Department considers the expansion of its facilities for ferrying. I can only reiterate that every day counts.

I have seen the text of a telegram sent by President Vargas to Souza Costa which the latter showed me regarding the arrangements for the immediate furnishing of naval and military material and for the commitments undertaken by this Government under the Lend Lease agreement for the furnishing of military supplies for the balance of the current year. The message made it emphatically clear that the President was wholly satisfied. Souza Costa informed me that this message was sent after President Vargas had consulted with General Dutra.[42] In view of this, it would seem to me necessary to try and use the present opportunity for the completion of these Ferry Command arrangements which after all are more in the immediate interest of Brazil than they are in the interest even of the United States. Please do your utmost to get me some immediate and favorable reply.

WELLES

---

[41] This Joint Board originated with the recommendation of the Chief of Staff of the Brazilian Army in which the American Chief of Staff concurred on October 29, 1941.

[42] Minister of War.

810.20 Defense/2228a : Telegram

The Acting Secretary of State to the Ambassador in Brazil (Caffery)

WASHINGTON, March 12, 1942—9 p. m.

624. I am sending you by air mail portions of three memoranda relating to Brazil handed me by the War Department in connection with certain projects for the construction of additional airports by Pan American Airways.[43] If you concur, General Olds will take this matter up with the Brazilian authorities at the same time he discusses with them the details of the questions regarding which President Vargas has already given general approval.

Since it is now well known throughout the Americas that the airport development program of Pan American Airways under the original program was financed by this Government, and in view of the changed situation, I think that such negotiations as may be required with the Brazilian Government should be conducted by this Government rather than by Pan American Airways as was done in the first program. Specific details on the work proposed to be done on each site have been requested of the War Department and will be forwarded as soon as received.

As you will note from one of the memoranda, the War Department is ready to consider that the funds necessary for the construction work to be done at Montes Claros, Carolina, Caravellas and Barreiras be either lent or given to the Brazilian Government in order that that Government might perform this work rather than Pan American Airways. The idea of the War Department is that possibly the Brazilian Government would be pleased and, therefore, more cooperative generally and specifically in connection with the improvement of the other airports in Brazil which are of greater strategic importance to this Government. The War Department would, of course, be glad to lend the Brazilian Government such engineers and advice as might be requested. Would you please telegraph me whether, in your opinion, the Brazilian Government would be pleased at this prospect, particularly if the funds are donated for the purpose, so that the War Department can prepare an adequate statement for your use in taking the matter up with the Brazilian authorities.

WELLES

---

[43] War Department memoranda not printed; portions of these memoranda were transmitted to the Ambassador in Brazil by Mr. Welles in a letter of March 13, 1942 (not printed).

832.248/373 : Telegram

The Ambassador in Brazil (Caffery) to the Secretary of State

RIO DE JANEIRO, March 25, 1942—2 p. m.
[Received 5 : 25 p. m.]

1025. For the Acting Secretary. President Vargas informed me today that his military experts believe that an attack on the northeast of Brazil can be expected by August this year, not with the intention of invading Brazil, but for the purpose of destroying airports, installations, et cetera, used by the ferry command. He added that his Air Force are insisting on the absolute necessity of immediately obtaining the following combat equipment which was requisitioned from us under Lend-Lease on October 4 last: 40 pursuit planes P–47, P–39, or P–40E; 28 medium bombers B–25; 285 bombers A–24, and 14 patrol flying boats PBY, 6 of which should be amphibian.

He personally requested me to bring this matter to your attention and added that General Olds could confirm the critical need for this material. You may recall that Olds, in his telegram to General Arnold [47] (my 948 of March 12 [19] 9 p. m.[48]), stated that ["] smallest immediate requirements for protecting Brazilian-American activities in Recife, Belém, Natal and Fernando de Noronha about 30 P–39 or P–40, 15 B–25, 15 A–24 airplanes." General Olds recommended that at least part of this equipment be made available while General Gomes is in the United States.[49] Olds suggested that the United Nations now receiving this equipment should be induced to pro-rate it to Brazil for obvious reasons (my despatch 6808, March 21 [48]).

CAFFERY

832.248/376 : Telegram

The Acting Secretary of State to the Ambassador in Brazil (Caffery)

WASHINGTON, March 30, 1942—7 p. m.

820. Your No. 1025, March 25, 2 p. m. I submitted this question immediately to General Arnold. I have this morning received a reply from him which reads as follows:

"Replying to your letter of March 26th, during the stay of General Gomes in the United States discussions were held covering the Natal and Northeast Brazil situation. General Gomes agreed with me that while there is danger of an invasion of that area, the chances are that the worst that will probably happen will be a nuisance raid.

---

[47] Lt. Gen. Henry H. Arnold, Chief of the U.S. Army Air Forces, and Deputy Chief of Staff for Air.
[48] Not printed.
[49] Brig. Eduardo Gomes was on an official visit to the United States at this time to confer on the development of ferry routes between the United States and Brazil.

Everyone agrees that 30 Pursuit and 15 Medium and Light Bombardment airplanes would be very desirable as a complement for the Natal area. Unfortunately there are more insistent demands for these airplanes elsewhere in combat zones where they are employed by troops in contact with and operating against the enemy. As a compromise, I informed General Gomes that we would send to the Natal area six P-40's and six B-25's at once. He was very appreciative and when the difficulties covering the operation of so few planes over so many points were explained to him he was apparently quite satisfied.

In order that the maximum benefit may be obtained from these six P-40's and six B-25's, it was decided that American crews would man and maintain the planes pending the time when Brazilian crews could take them over, at which time the American combat and maintenance crews would be returned to the United States.

In the meantime, the question of air defense for the Natal area is still an open one and the solution of this question is subject to change, depending upon the trend of the war."

I suggest that until General Gomes has had an opportunity of talking over with President Vargas and other officials of the Brazilian Government the results of his trip to Washington, you might well refrain from making any direct reply to the message from President Vargas. After you have, yourself, talked with General Gomes, however, and if he is apparently satisfied with the situation as indicated in General Arnold's above-quoted communication, you may then consider it expedient to give a message along the lines of this letter to President Vargas.

WELLES

811.3332/128 : Telegram

The Acting Secretary of State to the Ambassador in Brazil (Caffery)

WASHINGTON, April 10, 1942—8 p. m.

931. In view of the reported presence of enemy submarines off the Brazilian coast, the Navy Department urgently requests blanket permission to operate United States Navy patrol planes from the land fields at Fortaleza and São Luiz without prior notification. Notification by the local United States naval commanding officer at Natal to the local authorities would of course be made at the time of beginning the operations. The area of particular interest is roughly that stretch of the coast between São Luiz and Fortaleza.

This request does not involve the use of additional planes but only the amphibian planes operating from Natal at present.

You may use your discretion in approaching Brazilian authorities. Urgent reply requested.

WELLES

810.20 Defense/2418 : Telegram

The Acting Secretary of State to the Ambassador in Brazil (Caffery)

WASHINGTON, April 16, 1942—midnight.

989. Your 1202, April 9, 4 p. m.[52]   While the War Department is willing to pay for the construction by the Brazilian Government of the airfields at Caravellas, Montes Claros, Carolina, and Barreiras, it would, of course, prefer to be relieved of this obligation since these airports have no present military value.   If, however, an offer to construct these airfields with United States Government funds will assist you materially in obtaining the necessary permission for the other airport development projects and other matters desired by the War Department, you are authorized to inform the Brazilian Government that the required funds will be made available.

It should however be thoroughly understood by the Brazilians that (1) United States aircraft will have free access to these fields, and (2) that materials and machinery for their construction cannot be furnished for probably a year or more (all machinery and material available is currently needed for work on airfields of greater strategic importance).

The Department believes that the construction of the airports mentioned should be tied into the future development of Brazilian commercial aviation and of the regions served, rather than represented as having any immediate military value.

WELLES

810.20 Defense/2527 : Telegram

The Acting Secretary of State to the Ambassador in Brazil (Caffery)

WASHINGTON, April 19, 1942—4 p. m.

1022. In connection with the permission previously granted by the Brazilian authorities for the operation of United States Navy patrol planes from Maceió, Aratu (Bahia), Recife and Natal and, in order to provide accommodations for flight and ground crews as well as to assure adequate storage and maintenance facilities, the Navy Department urgently desires that permission be obtained from the Brazilian Government for the construction of the following additional aviation facilities:

(a) At Maceió a seaplane base; at Aratu (Bahia) a seaplane base; at Recife a landplane base; at Natal a landplane base.

In the case of each of the foregoing the following will be required: Barracks, messing and sanitary facilities for 50 officers and

---

[52] Not printed.

300 men; a radio building; a nose hangar; additional underground storage adequate for 50,000 gallons of gasoline; two ammunition magazines and additional land sufficient to provide for all of the facilities aforementioned.

(b) It is also desired to construct a seaplane base at Natal, the requirements for which will be identical with those enumerated above, except that barracks, messing and sanitary facilities for only 25 officers and 200 men are needed. Thus, at Natal, both landplane and a seaplane bases are contemplated.

The Navy Department does not desire, for the present, that permission be obtained for the erection of any facilities at Rio de Janeiro or Santos.

It is contemplated that the new facilities would be constructed under a contract with the Pan American Airways, Incorporated. These would, of course, be additional to the work now being performed by that company under the original contract of November 2, 1940, consisting primarily of the construction of surfaced runways for each landplane base, a ramp for each seaplane base and surfaced parking areas and gasoline storage at all of the bases and the recent supplemental contract.

While the additional area of land required at the four bases will vary somewhat according to the terrain and other local factors, it is estimated that approximately 30 acres, exclusive of the area required for magazines, will be needed in each instance. Owing to the necessity for placing magazines at a distance of between 1,000 and 2,000 feet from other structures, a study will have to be made at each base in order to determine, on the basis of security, accessibility and land requirements, the most suitable location. It is proposed that, in accordance with previous practice, the land will be purchased by and title taken in the name of the Pan American Airways, Incorporated.

In view of the urgency of this matter, you are requested in your discretion at once to endeavor to obtain the desired permission of the Brazilian authorities and to reply by telegraph.

WELLES

832.20/390a : Telegram

The Secretary of State to the Ambassador in Brazil (Caffery)

WASHINGTON, May 11, 1942—8 p. m.

1195. From the Under Secretary. I have this morning received the following memorandum from General Marshall:

"The situation in the Recife–Natal–Fortaleza region as to the development of an effective Air force for the protection of our line of communications is growing more and more serious. We have placed in that region, for the Brazilians, the following planes:

> 10 P–36s (pursuit)
> 6 P–40s (modern pursuit)
> 2 B–18s (2-engine old medium bombers)
> 6 B–25s (2-engine highly modern bombers)

Lieutenant Colonel Thomas B. Hall, Air Corps, is our senior Air officer there charged with training Brazilians in the operation of these planes. To give you a first-hand picture of the existing conditions I am quoting from a personal letter of Colonel Hall to one of his friends in the War Department, which has accidentally come to my attention.

'The troubles are the following: no 100-octane gasoline, and we have not flown for a week. Another is lack of pilots—there are only three who have taken instruction on the B–18s, and about five actually flying the old P–36s.

Colonel Macedo has requested more pilots and no action has been taken. No thought has yet been given to such a thing as training bombardiers or navigators, or even co-pilots.

The B–25s (medium bomber) have been here almost a week and Macedo has been the only officer even to look at them. Even Macedo has not wanted to fly.

The worst thing is over the matter of where the units will be stationed; that is as much in the air as when you left and it prevents us from taking any steps towards the establishment of the gunnery range or the bombing range, or to make any revetments, etc. Our people who came down here full of vim and vigor and ready to set the world on fire are about to give up after sitting around in this place doing nothing. It is a shame and it makes one sick to see that fine equipment lying idle, but there has never been stronger proof of our stand.

The lack of organization, equipment and pilots makes the airplanes useless. As far as I can determine, nothing is being done about it either. The lack of enthusiasm of the Brazilians to fly the planes is the thing which surprises me most.'

It seems evident from the foregoing that we can expect practically no patrol protection in support of our Navy over the Brazilian waters off the coast of Northeastern Brazil. With the present submarine menace this is a very serious matter involving both heavy losses of tonnage and the repercussions of Latin America due to our failure to protect shipping. There is also the deadly hazard of sudden Fifth Column events in that area, to cut off our air communications with the Near and Far East and to menace the Panama Canal.

With reference to the last comment, we consider it of great military importance to have an immediate aerial reconnaissance of the Amazon above Manaos in the Rio Branco–Rio Negros area. Our proposal was that we would fly the planes with Brazilian co-pilots and a partial Brazilian crew to make this reconnaissance. The Air Minister agreed. General Gomes canceled this agreement and stated that Brazil would make the reconnaissance for us in 4 days. Actually this reconnaissance would require 28 days of flying 10 hours daily, using 8 airplanes having a 1600-mile range, and operating from Manaos. The '4-days' reply really stated an absurdity. The region referred to is a vast natural landing ground from which an attack on vital installations of the Panama Canal could be launched.

These matters are growing so deadly serious that, as Chief of Staff, I feel that something must be done immediately or we must frankly accept the possibility of a disastrous development in the Panama-Brazilian theater.

The War Department has made real sacrifices in many directions to satisfy Brazilian requirements in military equipment in support of the position taken by the State Department that a definite betterment of the situation in Northeast Brazil would result. We have relieved officers at the request of our Ambassador—officers of superior qualifications. I have changed the assignments of officers in the War Department concerned with the Brazilian situation because they had become so convinced that our failure to secure the necessary precautionary measures would result in a disaster in that region that their feelings were too intense to facilitate negotiations.

. . . I, therefore, request that you instruct our Ambassador in Rio to present again to the Brazilian Air Ministry the urgent necessity for utilizing to the maximum advantage the American planes and instructors now in Brazil. Specifically, he should secure agreements for the use of both American and Brazilian pilots and crews for the immediate detailed and effective reconnaissance of the Amazon area. Also, arrangements should be made to undertake without further delay the training of Brazilian pilots and crews in the use of the 24 American planes, using American personnel as instructors. It is especially important that during the training period, the matériel and personnel (American pilots and bombardiers) involved, should be utilized in extending patrol activities off the Brazilian coast. I suggest that General Eduardo Gomes should be included, if possible, in any conferences held on the matter."

Please telegraph me your reactions. In view of the very serious concern shown by General Marshall in this regard, I think it imperative that you take as effective action as in your judgment may be possible. This issue seems to me one that, under normal conditions, you would wish to lay personally before President Vargas, but, of course, I do not know if the present state of his health is sufficiently good to make this possible. [Welles.]

HULL

832.20/398 : Telegram

The Ambassador in Brazil (Caffery) to the Secretary of State

RIO DE JANEIRO, May 16, 1942—4 p. m.
[Received 6 : 32 p. m.]

1669. For the Under Secretary. Referring again to Department's 1195, May 11, 8 p. m., the Cabinet are in agreement that the Air Ministry must seriously endeavor to rectify the situation at Fortaleza described by Colonel Hall.

Salgado has invited my attention to letters he received from Colonel Hall which present a very different picture. (I of course understand that Hall did not feel in position to put the facts before the Air Minister.)

Aranha told me this morning that Salgado is ordering 60 additional pilots to proceed to Fortaleza.

CAFFERY

[A political-military agreement between the United States and Brazil entered into by an exchange of notes dated May 23 and May 27, 1942, at Rio de Janeiro, not printed, provided among other provisions, for the establishment of two Brazilian-American Technical-Military Mixed Commissions, one in Brazil and the other in the United States. For information on the negotiation of the agreement and the establishment of the two Commissions, see Stetson Conn and Byron Fairchild, *The Framework of Hemisphere Defense*, in the series *United States Army in World War II: The Western Hemisphere* (Washington, Government Printing Office, 1960), pp. 317–319.]

832.24/881a : Telegram

The Secretary of State to the Ambassador in Brazil (Caffery)

WASHINGTON, May 27, 1942—9 p. m.

1364. From the Under Secretary. Against the opposition of our own Navy, and only due to personal instructions given by the President, arrangements were finally made by the Navy Department to escort to Trinidad the five Brazilian vessels loaded with lend-lease material. It was clearly understood by the Brazilian Embassy here that the commanders of these vessels would scrupulously obey the orders given by the convoying authorities.

I have just received the following letter from the Vice Chief of Naval operations: [59]

"As you will recall arrangements were made to escort five Brazilian vessels loaded with lend-lease material as far as Trinidad. I am enclosing herewith a memorandum [60] which I believe you should have as apparently two of the Brazilian vessels the *Midosi* and *Tiradentes* are proceeding without escort through the Caribbean, and in the unfortunate event that either is torpedoed, this information may prove of value. In the meantime there appears there is nothing you can do as the matter has been taken up with the Brazilian Naval Attaché."

I have communicated this information to the Brazilian Ambassador, who is informing President Vargas by direct cable. The Ambassador is suggesting that the Brazilian Navy, through the Brazilian Naval Attaché in Washington, assume jurisdiction over the commanders of these vessels in the place of the agents of Lloyd Brasileiro.

[59] Vice Adm. Frederick J. Horne.
[60] Not found in Department files.

I know you appreciate the sacrifice which the convoying of these vessels involves to us at the present time. If these vessels are sunk, the loss will be very great from the standpoint of the Brazilian Army. Moreover, each one of the vessels had guns which we had supplied and American armed guards on board which we had lent. The unwillingness of the captains of these Brazilian ships to obey the orders issued to them by the American naval authorities seems to me nothing short of criminal in the light of circumstances. I hope you will take this matter up vigorously and support the Ambassador's recommendation that the Brazilian Navy should assume the responsibility and that none of these vessels should proceed except under orders given directly to them by the Brazilian Navy in cooperation with our own naval authorities. [Welles.]

HULL

832.20/403 : Telegram

The Ambassador in Brazil (Caffery) to the Secretary of State

RIO DE JANEIRO, May 28, 1942—9 p. m.
[Received 10 : 15 p. m.]

1807. My 1649, May 15, 5 p. m.[61] The Minister for Air is back from the northeast; he reports that the deficiencies in the situation are being rapidly corrected; he reports also that the B–25's are on submarine patrol duty sometimes more than 8 hours per day; frequently with mixed crews.

He requests that Major Bennett, Captain Westbrook and Lieutenants Billon, Toulinson, Beloso and Heraes be retained another month for instruction purposes and that American mechanics and radio technicians be retained for instruction and maintenance purposes.

He requests additional B–25's to assure continuance of the program of cooperation (in view of the wear and tear on present equipment).

He insists that we supply antiaircraft machine guns for the defense of patrol and ferry command bases.

Details on all this by airmail.

CAFFERY

832.20/403 : Telegram

The Secretary of State to the Ambassador in Brazil (Caffery)

WASHINGTON, June 12, 1942—7 p. m.

1513. From the Under Secretary. Your 1807, May 28, 9 p. m. I have received today from the Deputy Chief of Staff[62] a reply to

---

[61] Not printed.
[62] Lt. Gen. Henry H. Arnold.

the suggestions contained in your telegram under reference, which I submitted to him.

The pertinent portion of this reply reads as follows:

"With reference to the request for the extension of the duty of the United States Army Air Force pilots and enlisted personnel, their original instructions were to remain until proper transition of Brazilian pilots had been completed, and I will, in consequence, authorize them to remain another month as requested, although the situation with respect to trained Air Corps personnel is extremely critical at this time in our own armed forces.

With respect to additional B–25's, the present procurement status of these aircraft precludes further deliveries of this type. I could not recommend additional transfers to Brazil at present, nor do I believe that the Munitions Assignment Board would authorize such transfers. However, I am informed that the Munitions Assignment Board has allotted to the Brazilian Government 18 A–29 Lockheed Light Bombers and 28 A–31 Dive Bombers, for delivery from August through December of this year, inclusive. These aircraft are suited for the missions now being performed by the B–25's, and may be employed to supplement and augment present operations.

With respect to antiaircraft machine guns, the adequate defense of the airfields in Northeast Brazil has been studied by the War Department and will be discussed in the conference of the Joint Brazil-United States Defense Commission which will meet in Washington in the near future."

[Welles]
HULL

810.20 Defense/2954

The Ambassador in Brazil (Caffery) to the Secretary of State

No. 7792   RIO DE JANEIRO, June 29, 1942.
                            [Received July 9.]

SIR: With reference to my telegram No. 1617, May 13, 5 p. m. and the Department's reply No. 1267, May 18, midnight,[63] and also to War Department construction of air installations at certain places in Brazil, I have the honor to transmit herewith a translation of a pertinent, self-explanatory note from the Foreign Minister dated June 25.[64] (The decree-law mentioned, No. 3462, was transmitted in the Embassy's Voluntary Report prepared by the Assistant Commercial Attaché under date of August 1, 1941.[64])

It will be noted that the Brazilian authorities lay down the condition that the construction of the Navy facilities at Recife, Natal, Maceió and Bahia be effected by Panair do Brasil, S. A. and they insist

---

[63] Neither printed.
[64] Not printed.

that title to all land acquired in connection with Army or Navy installations be vested in the Brazilian Government.

It will also be observed that the authorities favor our Government's donating to Brazil all buildings and other tangible results of our program the use of which is of course guaranteed to us during the present war.

Respectfully yours, JEFFERSON CAFFERY

740.0011 European War 1939/23852

The Brazilian Ambassador (*Martins*) *to the Secretary of State*

[Translation]

No. 375/940.(00) WASHINGTON, August 22, 1942.

MR. SECRETARY OF STATE: Under instructions of my Government, and in accordance with the procedure adopted and the undertakings assumed in the Pan American Conferences of Buenos Aires and Lima, as well as in the meetings of Foreign Ministers, I have the honor to inform Your Excellency that, on the night of the fifteenth to sixteenth of the present month, there were torpedoed, twenty miles off the coast of Sergipe, five Brazilian passenger vessels which were plying from one Brazilian port to another carrying, among others, pilgrims on their way to the São Paulo Eucharistic Congress.

2. One of the vessels, the *Baependy*, was carrying a troop contingent of one hundred twenty men who were not on the way to any war zone, having simply been transferred from one military region of the country to another.

3. Prior to this criminal act, with the loss of many lives, there had already been torpedoed by Axis submarines thirteen Brazilian vessels in international traffic.

4. At that time our attitude was one of simple protest against the violation, in these unnecessary and brutal acts, of the rules of law and of the principles of humanity which govern warfare on the high seas.

5. On this occasion, where the number of victims was of several hundreds, including women and children, the aggression was directed against our coastwise shipping and was carried into Brazilian waters against essentially peaceful navigation which, by its very nature, is devoid of any objective susceptible of favoring any belligerent nation, even American, or of injuring the interests of any third parties. They were passenger vessels and none was either operating in a war or blockade zone, or could be suspected of carrying cargoes for any of the adversaries of the Axis powers, since their ports of destination were exclusively Brazilian.

6. Their sinking off the Brazilian coasts is undisputably an act of direct aggression against Brazil and results in the extension of the war to South America.

7. By virtue of this fact, the Brazilian Government, through the Spanish Embassy and the Swiss Legation, has notified the governments of Germany and Italy that, in spite of its consistently pacific attitude, it is not possible to elude the fact that those countries have practiced against Brazil acts of war, creating a condition of belligerency which we are forced to recognize in the defense of our dignity, of our sovereignty, of our safety and of that of America, and to resist those acts to the extent of our strength.

I avail myself [etc.]   CARLOS MARTINS PEREIRA E SOUSA

740.0011 European War 1939/23741c : Telegram

The Secretary of State to the Chargé in Brazil (Simmons)

WASHINGTON, August 22, 1942.

2405. The following telegrams have today been sent:

"His Excellency Getulio Vargas, President of the United States of Brazil, Rio de Janeiro.

I have been informed that the United States of Brazil has today recognized that a state of war exists between Brazil on the one hand and Germany and Italy on the other hand.

On behalf of the Government and people of the United States I express to Your Excellency the profound emotion with which this courageous action has been received in this country. This solemn decision more firmly aligns the people of Brazil with the free peoples of the world in a relentless struggle against the lawless and predatory Axis powers. It adds power and strength, moral and material, to the armies of liberty. As brothers in arms, our soldiers and sailors will write a new page in the history of friendship, confidence, and cooperation which has marked since the earliest days of independence relations between your country and mine.

The action taken today by your Government has hastened the coming of the inevitable victory of freedom over oppression, of Christian religion over the forces of evil and darkness.

I send you my warmest personal regards and expressions of the fullest confidence in the success of our common cause.

Franklin D. Roosevelt"

"His Excellency Oswaldo Aranha, Minister for Foreign Affairs, Rio de Janeiro.

I have received a note from the Brazilian Ambassador in Washington [66] informing me that the Government of Brazil recognizes that a state of war exists between Brazil on the one hand and Germany and Italy on the other hand.

---

[66] Dated August 22, supra.

The people of the United States welcome the people of Brazil as brothers in arms and salute their high resolve and defiant courage in taking a position unequivocally at the side of the embattled freedom-loving nations of the world. Today a heavy blow has been dealt the Axis Powers, moral no less than military, when a great, peaceful and law-abiding nation is driven by unprovoked acts of ruthless barbarity to take up arms in self-defense. It comes as no surprise to my countrymen that the proud Brazilian Nation has chosen the risks and hardships of battle when confronted with wanton attacks on its sovereign dignity and rights.

The action of the Axis powers in attacking your great country and people is a further demonstration of the fact that those Powers will strike at any peace-loving nation as and when to do so will serve their purpose of world conquest, regardless of considerations of humanity and international law. It also brings into bold relief the basic principle upon which the solidarity of the American republics rests, namely, that an attack against any one of them is an attack against all of them. Each of the twenty-one American Republics are today equally in danger.

Together our two countries will face the future with serene confidence and high hearts.

I take pleasure in sending Your Excellency renewed assurances of my high personal esteem.

Cordell Hull"

HULL

740.0011 European War 1939/23806 : Telegram

The Chargé in Brazil (Simmons) to the Secretary of State

RIO DE JANEIRO, August 26, 1942—5 p. m.
[Received 8 : 05 p. m.]

3250. Department's 2414, August 24, 3 p. m.[67] Aranha says Brazilian Government entirely disposed to adhere to the agreement,[68] as well as to act in accordance with our wishes "now or in the future" to the best of its ability, in furthering the war effort. He will study text of declaration and Mexican communication before communicating with us further in the matter.

SIMMONS

---

[67] Not printed.

[68] This agreement was the Declaration by United Nations of January 1, 1942, according to which the signatories pledged themselves to use their full resources against the Axis, cooperate with other signatory governments, and not make a separate peace. Brazil became eligible to adhere when she declared war against the Axis. For text of Declaration, see vol. I, p. 25; for correspondence concerning the Declaration, see *ibid.*, pp. 1 ff.

832.248/417 : Telegram

The Ambassador in Brazil (*Caffery*) to the Secretary of State

RIO DE JANEIRO, August 27, 1942—10 p. m.
[Received August 28—1 : 30 a. m.]

3289. My 3274, August 27, 6 p. m.[70] Admiral Ingram [71] has strongly recommended that either Army-manned or Navy-manned squadron Hudson land-based medium bombers be sent Recife with all despatch with orders to report to his command "under [doctrine?] of paramount interest"; this squadron to be taken over by Brazilian personnel as soon as they qualify "thus releasing ours".

In view of the existing situation at Recife and the cooperation being furnished by Brazilian patrol planes and in view of statements made by Harry Hopkins in connection with the furnishing of lend-lease material and the desirability of Brazil's declaring war, I recommend that these planes be sent to Recife as recommended by Admiral Ingram.

CAFFERY

832.248/422 : Telegram

The Secretary of State to the Ambassador in Brazil (*Caffery*)

WASHINGTON, September 6, 1942—2 p. m.

2623. Your 3434, September 4, 5 p. m.[70] War Department states that the question of expediting delivery of combat airplanes to Brazil has been discussed by Joint Brazilian–United States Defense Commission, which recommended an advance of delivery dates. In pursuance of this recommendation, the War Department has advanced the delivery dates of 18 A–29 medium bombers to be used by Brazilian air force for anti-submarine patrol, so that delivery will be completed by the end of October instead of the end of December. The Defense Commission is also studying the acceleration of delivery dates on other types of planes for Brazil. In deciding this matter, it will be necessary to consider the ability of Brazilian air force to absorb these planes and establish necessary ground crews and facilities for their efficient maintenance and operation.

The question of delivering the 18 A–29 planes by United States Army training crews is also receiving earnest and sympathetic consideration. It is expected that a decision will be reached early this week. For your own information, War Department states that there is a shortage of training crews owing to the need of this personnel for combat operations in other parts of the world. It is hoped, how-

---

[70] Not printed.
[71] Vice Adm. Jonas H. Ingram, Commander of the South Atlantic Force.

ever, that it will be possible to send one of these crews for each three planes delivered in Brazil.

With reference to the defense needs of the bases, the Defense Commission will recommend to War Department the assignment of small caliber anti-aircraft guns. The critical need for large caliber anti-aircraft artillery in other theaters prevents allocation of any such material at this time. HULL

810.20 Defense/3261

The Under Secretary of State (Welles) to the Ambassador in Brazil (Caffery)

WASHINGTON, September 22, 1942.

DEAR JEFF: On receipt of your letter of August 31,[72] I requested the War Department to send me for transmission to you, any available documents on the activities of the Joint Brazil–United States Defense Commission which would give you up-to-date information on this subject and assist you in your conversations with Brazilian officials.

I have received from the War Department copies of seven recommendations made by this Commission, and I am enclosing them herewith.[73] The War Department tells me that with reference to recommendation number one, it has taken necessary action to provide for the delivery before the first of November of all the eighteen A–29 light bombing planes which are needed for active duty on the Northeast coast of Brazil. Recommendations two to five inclusive must be approved by the Brazilian authorities before action can be taken by the War or Navy Department. Action on recommendations six and seven is now pending in the War Department.

You will be glad to hear that the Brazil–United States Defense Commission is functioning smoothly and harmoniously. The Brazilian members are taking great interest in the Commission's work and are, I am told, most cooperative in suggesting subjects for recommendation and in drafting the texts.

I shall endeavor to keep you informed of important developments. Believe me [etc.] SUMNER WELLES

---

[72] Not printed.
[73] Not printed; the recommendations included (1) expediting delivery of 18 A–29 planes, (2) defining the area and persons within the jurisdiction of military police, (3) locating Brazilian purchasing agencies in Washington, (4) submitting Brazilian defense purchases to the Joint Commission, (5) placing shipping problems in the hands of the War Shipping Board, Lloyd-Brasileiro, the Joint Defense Commission, etc., (6) specifying the numbers of guns and teaching personnel, and (7) indicating the number of personnel for teaching the use of the 18 A–29 and 28 A–31 planes to be delivered to Brazil. On October 30th the Joint Commission made three further recommendations: (8) establishing a disassembly and crating plant for planes at Recife, (9) establishing three station hospitals at Brazilian ports, and (10) organizing a joint military commission to be located at Rio de Janeiro. (832.248/431, 832.20/475)

740.0011 European War 1939/24470 : Telegram

The Ambassador in Brazil (Caffery) to the Secretary of State

RIO DE JANEIRO, September 24, 1942—6 p. m.
[Received 9 : 34 p. m.]

3800. Department's 2807, September 23, 9 p. m.[74] Aranha is under the impression that there have been set up at Washington councils and boards consequent upon the declaration. He asked me what they are.

He repeated that Brazil has no interest in the United Nations; but a great deal of interest in cooperating with us. "If you want us to sign" he said, "we will sign. Should this be done with some formality; and where. Spell out to me exactly what you want us to do."

(This is a typical Aranha sort of move.)

CAFFERY

740.0011 European War 1939/24470 : Telegram

The Secretary of State to the Ambassador in Brazil (Caffery)

WASHINGTON, September 26, 1942—7 p. m.

2854. Your 3800 of September 24. No councils or boards have been set up at Washington consequent upon the United Nations Declaration.

Embassy's telegrams of August 26 [75] and September 10 [76] indicate that Brazil decided to adhere to United Nations Declaration and that Aranha was studying Declaration and Mexican communication of adherence. In reply to his query as to what he should do, you may refer again to the Mexican communication for form of adherence. After Brazilian willingness to adhere has been received here arrangements could be made for appropriate public ceremony at Washington and if desired, simultaneously Rio, together with our reply thereto [sic].

I believe that Aranha will realize the obvious advantages of having formally associated together in the United Nations Declaration all powers engaged in the struggle for victory over Hitlerism.

HULL

---

[74] Not printed; in this telegram the Ambassador was asked as to Brazil's adherence to the United Nations Declaration. For Aranha's initial viewpoint, see telegram No. 3250, August 26, 5 p. m., from the Chargé in Brazil, p. 667.
[75] Telegram No. 3250, p. 667.
[76] Not printed.

810.796/900

The Acting Secretary of State to the Brazilian Ambassador (Martins)

WASHINGTON, October 19, 1942.

EXCELLENCY: I have the honor to refer to Your Excellency's note no. 263/588.5 of May 2, 1942 [77] and to conversations that have taken place between members of Your Excellency's staff and officers of the Department of State and of the War Department concerning the request of the Brazilian Minister for Air that arrangements be made for the training in the United States of Brazilian military pilots. We understand that the purpose of this training is to enable the Brazilian graduates to serve as instructors in the Brazilian Air Force.

I am happy to confirm the informal agreement reached between your Minister Counselor,[78] your Air Attaché,[79] and officials of the State and War Departments outlined below:

(1) The War Department will furnish the instruction and all equipment, except that of a personal nature, required for this training. All expenses, such as transportation, subsistence allowances, et cetera, will be for the account of the Brazilian Government.

(2) In each entering class, from ten to fifteen Brazilian students will be accommodated, it being understood that the number in the first class will not exceed ten.

(3) Eligibility for this instruction is contingent on

(a) satisfactory completion of the equivalent of the primary phase of military flight training, as given in the United States. The student should be fully prepared to enter the basic training course on arrival in this country;

(b) meeting the United States Army Air Force physical standards;

(c) satisfactory scholastic preparation, particularly in the sciences, and a working knowledge of English.

(4) Each pilot, before his departure from Brazil, will be tested for flight ability by the Brazilian Air Force, in consultation with the United States Military Mission.

(5) It is desirable, but not essential, that these students should arrive in the United States at least two weeks prior to the day on which their flight training is to commence.

(6) The War Department will provide training as above to one hundred thirty students. This agreement will therefore include the class to begin on June 28, 1943 and may be renewed thereafter as mutually agreeable.

(7) The United States War Department and the Brazilian Air Ministry reserve the right to cancel this agreement, or to propose amendment thereof, on thirty days notice, in writing, by the War Department to your Air Attaché, or by your Air Attaché to the War

[77] Not printed.
[78] Fernando Lobo.
[79] Col. Armando de Souza e Mello Ararigboia.

Department, respectively. In the case of cancellation by the War Department, for reasons not now foreseen, the cancellation shall not affect students already in the United States, or who have departed from Brazil for the United States.

(8) Basic training is to be followed by Advanced training. The Advanced training will be distributed between single-engine and twin-engine training as currently provided for United States students.

(9) Beginning dates of classes for which these Brazilian students are eligible are as follows:

November 12, 1942	March 22, 1943
December 15, 1942	April 24, 1943
January 16, 1943	May 26, 1943
February 18, 1943	June 28, 1943

I should be gratified to receive Your Excellency's confirmation of the Brazilian Air Ministry's agreement with the foregoing.[80]

Accept [etc.]   SUMNER WELLES

832.248/434 : Telegram

The Ambassador in Brazil (Caffery) to the Secretary of State

RIO DE JANEIRO, October 27, 1942—6 p. m.
[Received 11 : 30 p. m.]

4413. For the Under Secretary. I received today the following self-explanatory memorandum from Colonel Hall, head of our air mission here:

"(1) On the occasion of your passage through Recife on your return from the United States, Brigadiero Eduardo Gomes made the urgent request that the delivery of the Lockheed bi-motor bomber aircraft (A–29) be accelerated because of the important task of anti-submarine patrol.

Admiral Ingram and General Walsh [81] sent strong messages urging the rapid delivery of the airplanes. On my visit to Rio at that time the Air Minister reiterated the great necessity for the airplanes. About 3 weeks ago notice was received that six of the airplanes were ready to leave the States very soon. As yet, not one has been delivered.

(2) This failure not only to heed the request for accelerated delivery, but to comply with the original terms of the delivery schedule, has had deeply-felt results in the Brazilian Air Force as you probably know. It has particularly caused Brigadiero Gomes great distress and anxiety.

He is charged with a huge responsibility in furnishing air patrol for shipping and by no means has the equipment to properly accomplish the job. He as well as ourselves realizes that the combat

---

[80] No reply found in Department files.
[81] Gen. Robert L. Walsh was in charge of United States aviation activities in northeastern Brazil.

fronts are of first importance but it is believed that the airplanes scheduled for delivery could be spared.

(3) Undoubtedly you are completely aware of the situation and the Air Minister has probably discussed it thoroughly. This is written only to add my request that all possible steps be taken to bring about, at the least, fulfillment of the schedule."

CAFFERY

832.248/434 : Telegram

The Secretary of State to the Ambassador in Brazil (Caffery)

WASHINGTON, October 31, 1942—1 p. m.

3320. From the Under Secretary. Your 4413, October 27, 6 p. m. According to information obtained from the War Department, the Munitions Assignments Board has approved the assignment of 18 of these planes for delivery in October and 10 in November. They were in process of manufacture for the British and before delivery can be made to Brazil, they must receive certain additional necessary accessories. This work is now being completed, and every effort is being made to expedite the delivery of these airplanes to Brazil. [Welles.]

HULL

832.20/475

The Under Secretary of State (Welles) to the Ambassador in Brazil (Caffery)

WASHINGTON, November 7, 1942.

DEAR JEFF: On September 18 [22] I sent you in response to your request copies of Recommendations 1 to 7, of the Joint Brazil–United States Defense Commission.[82] I said that Recommendations 2 to 5 required the approval of the Brazilian authorities before action could be taken by our War or Navy Department and that action on Recommendations 6 and 7 was pending in the War Department. We have now heard from the War Department that the senior member of the Brazilian delegation has reported that the Brazilian Government has approved these recommendations. In addition, Recommendations 6 and 7 have received the War Department's approval and action is being taken to put them into effect.

Recommendations 8 to 10 have been made by the Defense Commission. They have been approved by the War Department and are being forwarded to Rio de Janeiro in order to obtain the approval of the Brazilian Government. I am enclosing a copy of each.[82] Recommendation No. 10 relates to the establishment of the Brazilian-Amer-

---

[82] Not printed, but see footnote 73, p. 669.

ican technical military mixed Commissions and is therefore of considerable interest and importance.

Believe me [etc.]   SUMNER WELLES

832.20/479

The Ambassador in Brazil (Caffery) to the Secretary of State

No. 9548   RIO DE JANEIRO, December 23, 1942.

SIR: Referring to previous reports of the setting up in Rio de Janeiro of the Joint Brazil–United States Military Mixed Commission, I have the honor to report that Aranha asked me this morning if our representatives are here in Rio, adding that the Brazilian Government is now ready to set up the Commission. He said that he will notify me in a few days and we can have some sort of informal ceremony in his office to get things going.[83]

Respectfully yours,   JEFFERSON CAFFERY

AGREEMENT PROVIDING FOR A NAVAL MISSION FROM THE UNITED STATES TO BRAZIL, SIGNED MAY 7, 1942

[For text of the Agreement, signed at Rio de Janeiro, see Department of State Executive Agreement Series No. 247, or 56 Stat. (pt. 2) 1462.]

ARRANGEMENTS TO PROCURE FOR THE UNITED STATES STRATEGIC MATERIALS FROM BRAZIL[84]

811.20 Defense (M) Brazil/221

The Ambassador in Brazil (Caffery) to the Secretary of State

No. 6384   RIO DE JANEIRO, January 30, 1942.
                                            [Received February 3.]

SIR: I have the honor to report that the Embassy has recently reviewed the operations of the first six months of the United States–Brazil Strategic Materials Agreement[85] with the view to formulating suggestions which might be of value in the adoption of a procurement program in Brazil to meet war needs in the United States.

Probably the most important accomplishment of the agreement, prior to the entrance of the United States into the war, was the

---

[83] In despatch No. 9606, December 30, the Ambassador reported that this ceremony took place in Aranha's office on that day (832.20/481).

[84] Continued from *Foreign Relations*, 1941, vol. VI.

[85] See telegrams Nos. 460, May 13, 3 p. m., and 466, May 14. 8 p. m., from the Ambassador in Brazil, *ibid.*, section under Brazil entitled "Arrangements to procure for the United States strategic materials from Brazil."

shutting-off of Axis sources of supply for strategic materials. The actual procurement policies followed by the purchasing agencies have been, with the exception of two or three commodities, very limited in scope. No purpose would be served by reviewing the cases of lost opportunities either in the actual procurement of needed materials or in the development of future sources of supply. It should be mentioned, however, that whatever validity there may have been for an over-cautious buying policy on the part of the purchasing agencies, it is apparent that a basic change in procurement policies and methods of administration is essential to the war effort.

The changed situation would appear to dictate an expansion in the list of commodities which should be made subject to bilateral agreement between the United States and Brazil and a reconsideration of the quantitative undertakings for certain of the commodities now included in the Agreement.

The Embassy assumes that the objectives of the authorities in the United States are to maximize the production and exportation to the United States and allied nations of Brazilian strategic materials, and to adapt this program in such a manner as to maintain amicable relations with Brazil and to minimize points of friction. The attainment of the first objective is in a large measure dependent upon the second.

Taking into consideration the importance of the time element, it would appear that the most effective type of program requires a revision of procurement policies on the part of the government purchasing agencies, a more effective organization within the Brazilian Government and an administrative organization in Brazil of American governmental representatives which would make possible a maximum of correlation and integration of effort. Procurement policies, to be most effective, should get away from the concepts of world market prices which are in many cases greatly influenced by conditions in countries having efficient and well-established production. Each commodity should be studied separately and consideration given to the adoption of any device which would expand output, subject, of course, to the qualification that a larger supply of a given Brazilian commodity is of value to the war program. Such devices might include increased prices, bounties for all production above a normal level, long-term contracts to make projects more attractive to Brazilian capital, advances for equipment and other working capital requirements, and possibly outright investment.

A number of Brazilian Government agencies are concerned in one way or another with the production and distribution of Brazilian materials and the Embassy has in the past experienced many delays in attempting to obtain action expeditiously on matters which are intimately connected with the Strategic Materials Agreement. The Embassy is hopeful that in accordance with Resolution II of the Third Meeting of the Ministers of Foreign Affairs of the American Republics,[86] the Brazilian Government will adopt practical measures which will permit more rapid action. The Embassy has already informally approached the Brazilian Government with a proposal to form a joint defense materials committee to meet periodically and to be composed of the Chief of the Economic Section of the Ministry of Foreign Affairs, the Director of Exchange of the Bank of Brazil and the Commercial Attaché of the Embassy.

The growing recognition of the need to correlate and integrate the work of representatives from different government agencies in Washington who are currently in Brazil or who will arrive in the future, resulted in a meeting held at the Embassy on January 26, 1942, and attended by Wayne C. Taylor, Under-Secretary of Commerce, Emilio G. Collado and Howard J. Trueblood of the Department of State, Carl Spaeth of the Board of Economic Warfare, Warren Lee Pierson, President of the Export-Import Bank and Mr. Donnelly and Mr. White of the Embassy.[87] It was pointed out at this meeting that with the rights which the United States had acquired to monopolistic purchases of Brazilian strategic materials, there had been created a corresponding obligation on the part of the Government of the United States to so administer its procurement program as to minimize points of friction and to eliminate factors which tended to create dislocations in Brazil's national economy. It was mentioned that decisions made in Washington from day to day and communicated to New York to be transmitted to a purchasing agency in Brazil to buy or to cease buying, frequently resulted in unnecessary disturbances in Brazil. It was further pointed out that there were many factors involved in a procurement program for a given commodity; that these included not only those of direct purchases, but also of rail transportation, storage, water transportation, correlation with British purchases, and a multitude of intergovernmental problems. It was mentioned that frequent and unanticipated changes in buying policy made in Washington and communicated directly to the purchasing agency in Brazil had had unfavorable political repercussions which could have been avoided had the matter been first referred to the Embassy.

---

[86] For correspondence concerning this meeting at Rio de Janeiro, January 15–28, 1942, see pp. 6 ff.; for text of the Final Act of the Meeting, see Department of State *Bulletin*, February 7, 1942, pp. 117–141.

[87] Walter J. Donnelly, Commercial Attaché, and Ivan B. White, Third Secretary of Embassy and Vice Consul.

At the same time, it was recognized that a number of government agencies in Washington were sending representatives to Brazil to make mining, agricultural or transport studies, and that their activities should be made subject to supervision and directed into channels where they could give the most direct assistance to the expansion of output of needed materials.

It was likewise agreed that there should be organized within the Embassy a defense materials unit to correlate and integrate all of these activities and to provide a more adequate statistical and research service.

Finally, great importance was placed on the formation of a company subsidiary to the Federal Loan Agency (as are the commodity companies such as the Metals Reserve Company), organized on a geographical basis in Brazil, to handle all procurement activities for the Federal Loan Agency. Such a company should be given, within the framework of broad policies formulated in Washington, necessary authority to make decisions locally and to act promptly and effectively in taking advantage of every opportunity to increase the flow of needed materials to the United States. It is believed that such an organization, with adequate powers, would be able to assume the initiative in developing worthwhile projects and that many of the delays currently being experienced through the necessity of referring details to the United States could be avoided.

There is enclosed a chart [88] of the proposed organizational set-up for the defense materials program in Brazil, as agreed upon at the meeting under reference. In regard to the question of communications, it was thought that all matters of general policy, as well as matters which involve any change in buying policy should be channelized through the Embassy. There is, of course, no objection to direct correspondence on detailed matters, which in no way relate to a change in policy or to intergovernmental matters, between the Federal Loan Agency and its subsidiaries and the procurement organization in Brazil.

I would appreciate the comments of the Department and other interested agencies in regard to the organizational plan under reference.

Respectfully yours,

.For the Ambassador:
JOHN F. SIMMONS
Counselor of Embassy

---

[88] Not printed.

811.20 Defense (M) Brazil/219c : Telegram

The Secretary of State to the Ambassador in Brazil (Caffery)

WASHINGTON, January 31, 1942—1 p. m.

242. As you know, one of the matters which Mr. Warren Pierson plans to negotiate while at Rio de Janeiro is a proposed financing by the Reconstruction Finance Corporation of the opening of the Itabira mine and the improvement of the rail facilities running from that mine to the Port of Victoria. The Itabira mine is located on one of the largest low phosphorous iron ore deposits in the world, but due to the lack of capital and lack of proper rail facilities, it has never been put into commercial production.

Mr. Pierson is also planning to negotiate with the Brazilian authorities and private companies a loan to enable the Central Railway to carry larger quantities of manganese and iron ore to the port of Rio de Janeiro and also to finance the improvement of the loading facilities at the port of Rio de Janeiro. This proposal with the Itabira plan constitute one unitary project.

Since Mr. Pierson's departure, the Department has been studying these projects further and it has become apparent that the successful completion of these negotiations is of the utmost importance to the British-American war effort. It is hoped that if Mr. Pierson's negotiations are successful, there will be made available in increasing quantities up to a total of 50,000 tons or more monthly of low phosphorous ore. At the moment the combined British-American supply of such low phosphorous ore is approximately 35,000 tons a month below current needs of United States and Great Britain. This low phosphorous ore goes into the making of high grade steels necessary for the construction of guns, tanks, armor piercing shells, and various other war weapons. The successful conclusion of the project with respect to the Central Railway would increase substantially the available manganese and iron ore from the mines feeding the Central Railway. This iron ore is used for a different purpose than the Itabira ore but it and the manganese are considered to be of an importance equal with that of the Itabira project.

The Department accordingly believes that it is necessary to strengthen the negotiations which Mr. Pierson is expected to carry on by establishing these negotiations at a high level where commercial considerations, methods of negotiation and questions of cost will be of minor importance. It is therefore suggested for your consideration that unless the Under Secretary of State [89] or you have done so

---

[89] Under Secretary Sumner Welles attended the Third Meeting of the Foreign Ministers of the American Republics at Rio de Janeiro and returned to the United States on January 29.

already, you speak to Foreign Minister Aranha about these two projects and inform him that in the view of this Government rapid and comprehensive development of the mines and communications under efficient management can only be secured by the direct intervention of the Brazilian Government. It is further suggested that you regard these two projects as of the highest importance and that you take an active and leading position in the negotiations with respect to them. In the meantime the Department will discuss the matter with Souza-Costa [90] on his arrival in Washington.

HULL

811.20 Defense (M) Brazil/220 : Telegram

The Ambassador in Brazil (Caffery) to the Secretary of State

RIO DE JANEIRO, February 2, 1942—11 p. m.
[Received February 3—12:30 a. m.]

327. For the Under Secretary. Department's 242, January 31. I have discussed these projects with Aranha [91] who expressed real interest. He and Souza-Costa told Pierson on Sunday that the Brazilian Government would cooperate.

We have all agreed that Costa will discuss details familiarizing Pierson (who is accompanying him to the United States) and other officials of our Government in Washington this week.

The plan of action as agreed upon in principle provides (1) Brazilian Government to acquire Victoria E. A. Railway; (2) our Government to arrange for priorities and finance purchase of railway equipment; (3) dollar loan to be amortized by shipment of ore [apparent omission] freight rebates; (4) Brazilian Government to finance milreis expenditures; (5) American engineers to cooperate in reconstruction and administration of railway; (6) Itabira mines to be operated by a company composed of Brazilians, Americans, British.

We need Costa's cooperation to settle the railway problem and his assistance will depend upon the success of his mission to the United States especially in connection with the procurement of armaments and Lend-Lease assistance.[92]

Pierson also reached an understanding with the British Embassy here which he will explain upon arrival.

CAFFERY

---

[90] Arthur de Souza Costa, Brazilian Minister of Finance.
[91] Oswaldo Aranha, Brazilian Minister for Foreign Affairs.
[92] Under the Lend-Lease Act of March 11, 1941; 55 Stat. 31. For correspondence on the negotiation of the Lend-Lease Agreement between the United States and Brazil, signed October 1, 1941, see Foreign Relations, 1941, vol. VI; for text of further agreement, signed March 3, 1942, see post, p. 815.

811.00 Defense (M) Brazil/263 : Telegram

The Ambassador in Brazil (Caffery) to the Secretary of State

RIO DE JANEIRO, February 20, 1942—1 p. m.
[Received 1 : 23 p. m.]

495. For the Under Secretary. Aranha agrees with me that the Brazilian Government should appoint a small but well-selected committee of officials of the Ministries of Foreign Affairs and Finance and the Bank of Brazil to administer the strategic materials agreement. However, he is reluctant to name the committee and to give it broad powers without the approval of Souza Costa.

I am told that the Ministry of Finance is responsible for the unnecessarily long delays in passing on our requests to add commodities to the agreement. As the situation is becoming worse I strongly recommend that you ask Souza Costa to telegraph Aranha requesting him to name the committee. It would also be helpful if Souza Costa would instruct his Ministry to despatch pending cases at once.

CAFFERY

811.20 Defense (M) Brazil/276b : Telegram

The Acting Secretary of State to the Ambassador in Brazil (Caffery)

WASHINGTON, February 25, 1942—2 p. m.

454. In keeping with Resolution II of the Rio de Janeiro Meeting of Foreign Ministers, conversations have been held with Souza Costa and his colleagues, in which the Brazilian Ambassador participated, looking to the establishment in Brazil of an organization under Brazilian Governmental sponsorship and control to increase the production of strategic materials and other natural resources. The new organization would examine all feasible projects for such development and would see that those recommended be effected either by existing enterprises in Brazil or, where suitable entities do not already exist, by new organizations which would be established for that purpose.

The overall organization would be a non-profit one. It would utilize to a very considerable degree United States expert assistance. In addition to funds for local expenditures to be supplied by Brazil, a substantial line of dollar credit would have to be allocated by the Federal Loan Agency to be drawn against as needed for dollar expenditures in connection with specific projects. The Federal Loan Agency would, of course, have the right to approve or disapprove specific undertakings. For your strictly confidential information, the amount now under discussion is $100,000,000, and, while it is anticipated that this sum will be forthcoming, it is not as yet definitely committed.

Agreement in principle has been reached here with the Brazilians on the aforedescribed plan. Souza Costa is telephoning Aranha and said that, if his Government approves, we will proceed rapidly with an exchange of notes to formalize the matter.

Quite aside from the urgent need for the materials to be produced and the stabilizing effect on hemisphere economy, it is believed that the public announcement of a program of the kind described, particularly one involving such a high line of credit, should have a salutary effect on the Brazilian public, as well as in the public minds of the other American republics.

Discussions are also proceeding between Souza Costa, the Department and the Export-Import Bank, of a plan and agreement for development of Itabira Mines and connected railway.

WELLES

811.20 Defense (M) Brazil/263 : Telegram

The Acting Secretary of State to the Ambassador in Brazil (Caffery)

WASHINGTON, February 26, 1942—midnight.

477. Your 495, February 20. Subject matter of the first paragraph of your telegram has been discussed with the Minister of Finance. It was his opinion, which the Department shares, that the appointment of such a committee might appropriately be deferred until the conclusion of negotiations now going on in Washington which may result in an agreement for the establishment of a development corporation by the Government of Brazil. This development corporation might make the selected committee to which you refer unnecessary.

Detailed discussions have been held with Dr. Dantas [94] and with other members of the Mission on the various commodities subject to the strategic materials agreement, and, as suggested in the second paragraph of your 495 and in your 565 of February 24,[95] the Brazilian Mission has been requested to telegraph to Rio suggesting that pending cases on proposed additions of commodities to the overall agreement be expedited.

Your 513, February 21.[96] It is understood that the cotton linters agreement has been approved and that the Minister of Finance is telegraphing today to this effect.

[94] Garibaldi Dantas, Brazilian cotton expert.
[95] Latter not printed.
[96] Not printed.

Your 530, February 21.[97]   The Minister of Finance has informed
the Department that he will propose, probably today, an increase
in the price of rubber over that set out in Department's 313 of February 9,[98] as well as certain other modifications in the proposal of the
Rubber Reserve Company.

WELLES

[For texts of an exchange of notes between the Acting Secretary
of State (Welles) and the Brazilian Minister for Finance (Souza
Costa) concerning the mobilization of the productive resources of
Brazil and the extension of credit by the United States, dated March
3, 1942, see Department of State Executive Agreement Series No.
370, or 57 Stat. (pt. 2) 1314.]

811.20 Defense (M) Brazil/365 : Telegram

The Acting Secretary of State to the Ambassador in Brazil (Caffery)

WASHINGTON, March 28, 1942—6 p. m.

813. Your 1030 March 25, 5 p. m.[97]   On March 11 there was transmitted to Souza-Costa a memorandum outlining proposals from
Defense Supplies Corporation with respect to Brazilian burlap, castor
beans, ipecac and rotenone, and also outlining the status of negotiations
with respect to certain other Brazilian materials.   Through an over-
sight this memorandum was not transmitted to you.   The full text
follows.

"The Department of State has been informed by the Defense Supplies Corporation that it is prepared to make proposals for the purchase of certain Brazilian products, as follows:

Burlap: Defense Supplies Corporation would agree that it or
its nominees would purchase, and the Brazilian Government
would sell or cause to be sold to Defense Supplies Corporation or
its nominees, the exportable surplus of Brazilian burlap meeting
standard United States Government specifications for comparable constructions of Indian burlap, in any amount up to 50
million yards shipped during 1942 and in any amount up to 100
million yards shipped during 1943.   The price would be 12.9
cents per yard for 40-inch 10-ounce burlap delivered in 1942 and
12 cents per yard for 40-inch 10-ounce burlap delivered in 1943,
both prices to be f.a.s. Santos, prices for other constructions to
bear the same relation to the prices fixed for 40-inch 10-ounce
construction as in the price schedule covering burlap issued by

---

[97] Not printed.
[98] *Post*, p. 691.

the United States Office of Price Administration, a copy of which is attached. Payment would be made in the amount of 80% of the purchase price against delivery of on-board bills of lading and in the amount of 20% against delivery of inspection certificate covering inspection after arrival at United States port. The Government of Brazil would agree to provide ocean shipping space, at United States Maritime Commission rates, for at least 50% of the amount shipped in any year.

Castor Beans. Defense Supplies Corporation would agree that it or its nominees would purchase, and the Brazilian Government would agree to sell or cause to be sold to Defense Supplies Corporation or its nominees, the exportable surplus of Brazilian castor beans in any amount up to 200,000 metric tons shipped during the next 12 months, at a price of $75 per metric tons f.o.b. steamer at Brazilian ports payable against delivery of on-board bills of lading. In lieu of castor beans, there may be delivered the equivalent in the form of castor oil (of such quality and at such price as shall be agreed upon between the Government of Brazil and Defense Supplies Corporation). The Government of Brazil would agree to provide ocean shipping space, at United States Maritime Commission rates, for at least 50% of the amount shipped during the contract period.

Ipecac. In case purchases by interests in the United States, the British Empire, and other American Republics which have systems of export control similar to that of Brazil, do not absorb all of the exportable surplus of Brazilian ipecac during the next 18 months, Defense Supplies Corporation would agree to acquire the ipecac not so absorbed during such period in any amount up to 90 metric tons at a price of $2 per pound in the case of Matto Grosso quality, and of $1.40 per pound in the case of Minas quality, in each case f.o.b. any Brazilian port, payable against delivery of on-board bills of lading.

Rotenone. In case purchases by interests in the United States, the British Empire, and other American Republics which have systems of export control similar to that of Brazil, do not absorb all of the exportable surplus of Brazilian powdered timbo, having a crude rotenone content of not less than 5%, during the next 18 months, Defense Supplies Corporation would agree to acquire the timbo not so absorbed during such period in an amount up to 4 million pounds at a price of $16\frac{1}{2}$ cents per pound f.o.b. any north Brazilian port, payable against delivery of on-board bills of lading.

The Brazilian Government would undertake, with respect to each of the foregoing products and during the period of the agreement of Defense Supplies Corporation to purchase such product as aforesaid, to restrict, through the issuance of export licenses and other adequate control regulations, the exportation of such product except to Defense Supplies Corporation or its nominees or (in the case of any exportable surplus of such product not purchased by Defense Supplies Corporation or its nominees pursuant to this agreement) to interests in the United States, the British Empire, and other American Republics which have systems of export control similar to that of Brazil.

Defense Supplies Corporation has advised the Department that it desires to acquire silk from Brazil, but that it does not at present have sufficient information on which to base an offer. It is suggested that the Brazilian Government arrange to furnish to the American Embassy at Rio de Janeiro full information with respect to Brazilian silk, including information as to present and potential production and as to quality.

The Department understands that the Agricultural Attaché of the Brazilian Embassy in Washington[2] will communicate in the near future with the Division of Defense Materials of the Department to discuss Brazilian hides and wool.

The American Embassy at Rio de Janeiro, with Mr. F. M. McAshan, representing the Federal Loan Agency, will be carrying on negotiations with the Brazilian Government concerning the acquisition of babassu nuts by interests in the United States."

With regard to hides, wool and babassu nuts, no specific proposals are under consideration at the present time. In consultation with McAshan, however, you are requested to discuss the situation with respect to each of these commodities with the appropriate Brazilian authorities and transmit to the Department any specific proposals which might be advanced by the Brazilians. In the case of babassu nuts, some concern has been expressed here over the possibility that a development program for this product would divert labor from the production of rubber, which is more urgently needed. This aspect should be explored with the Brazilians. In addition, you are requested to inform the Department of any recent developments in connection with the General Mills babassu program.

WELLES

811.20 Defense (M) Brazil/471 : Telegram

The Ambassador in Brazil (Caffery) to the Secretary of State

RIO DE JANEIRO, April 16, 1942—8 p. m.
[Received April 17—1 : 16 a. m.]

1298. For Clayton[3] and Finletter.[4] I have been told that President Vargas told Souza Costa yesterday that he approved of the negotiations to date relating to the rubber program[5] and Itabira and Victoria Minas projects. He also authorized Souza Costa to:

(1) Take possession in the name of the Federal Government of the Victoria Minas Railway, and the Itabira Mines.

---

[2] Paulo Fróes da Cruz.
[3] W. L. Clayton, Special Assistant to the Secretary of Commerce.
[4] Thomas K. Finletter, Acting Chief, Division of Defense Materials, Department of State.
[5] For correspondence concerning the rubber procurement and rubber conservation program, see pp. 691 ff.

(2) Organize immediately two corporations, one for the railway and another for the mines, similar to the corporate setup of the national steel plant.

(3) Reach an immediate agreement with the present operators of the railway and mines so as not to further prejudice their interests.

[The remainder of this telegram, here omitted, is concerned with the rubber program.]

CAFFERY

811.20 Defense (M) Brazil/752 : Telegram

The Ambassador in Brazil (Caffery) to the Secretary of State

RIO DE JANEIRO, June 22, 1942—5 p. m.
[Received 6:56 p. m.]

2157. Department's 1429, June 4, 5 p. m.[6] Are we authorized to exchange notes with the Foreign Office along the following lines: (1) create a United States Purchasing Commission in Brazil to acquire strategic materials and other products; (2) arrange for storage in Brazil and subsequent exportation to the United States; and (3) request exemption from all insurance requirements, taxation and fiscal regulatory requirements.

The Minister of Finance approves the plan and is confident the Foreign Office will raise no objections. Please rush telegraphic reply.

CAFFERY

811.20 Defense (M) Brazil/752 : Telegram

The Secretary of State to the Ambassador in Brazil (Caffery)

WASHINGTON, June 23, 1942—10 p. m.

1639. Your 2157, June 22, 5 p. m. You are authorized to exchange notes with the Foreign Office along the lines suggested.

It is planned that rubber will not be handled through this purchasing commission. A special arrangement is planned by the Board of Economic Warfare and the Rubber Reserve Company[7] whereby Allen[8] will be designated by both these Agencies as head of the rubber program in Brazil. It is assumed that nothing in the proposed notes will interfere with these arrangements.

HULL

---

[6] Not printed.
[7] The Rubber Reserve Company was a purchasing agency of the Department of Commerce.
[8] Douglas H. Allen, Special Assistant to the President of the Rubber Reserve Company.

841.244/1a : Circular telegram

The Secretary of State to the Diplomatic Representatives in Argentina, Brazil, Uruguay, and Paraguay

WASHINGTON, June 27, 1942—10 p. m.

In view of the combined needs of the United Nations for meat products and with a view to reaching the most effective procurement and allocation of canned meat, it has been agreed between the British and American Governments that all purchases of canned meat in Argentina, Brazil, Paraguay, and Uruguay for the United Nations will be made by the Ministry of Food of the United Kingdom. All quantities of canned meat purchased by the Ministry of Food under the arrangement is to be allocated to the United Kingdom, to the United States, and otherwise in such manner as may be agreed from time to time between the United States Department of Agriculture and the Ministry of Food. Such purchases as are allocated to the United States will be paid for directly to the local suppliers in dollars at the official equivalent of the sterling price fixed by the relevant Ministry of Food contract.

In your discretion, please inform the appropriate authorities of the foregoing arrangement, stressing that it has been reached only because of the pressing need for the most efficient organization of the procurement of an important food item. If you believe that it is preferable that the arrangement should come to the attention of the Government only indirectly as a result of cessation of direct purchases from the United States, you need not communicate the foregoing but in such event please inform the Department.

HULL

811.20 Defense (M) Brazil/828

Press Release Issued by the Ambassador in Brazil (Caffery) to the Brazilian Press, July 3, 1942 [9]

ESTABLISHMENT OF A UNITED STATES PURCHASING COMMISSION IN BRAZIL

Ambassador Jefferson Caffery announced today that in order to carry out the various agreements between the Governments of Brazil and the United States, and in anticipation of new agreements between the two Governments, the United States Government, after consulta-

---

[9] Copy transmitted to the Department by the Ambassador in his despatch No. 7866, July 7, 1942; received July 13.

tion with the Brazilian Government, and with their approval, has decided to establish a United States Purchasing Commission in Brazil, with headquarters in Rio de Janeiro. The Commission will acquire and export the strategic materials and other products covered by the agreements.

The United States Purchasing Commission will represent the Metals Reserve Company, the Defense Supplies Corporation, the Commodity Credit Corporation, the Rubber Reserve Company, and other procurement agencies of the United States Government. The Commission will be under the jurisdiction of the American Embassy.

The purchase of minerals and metals, which has been efficiently handled during the past year for the Metals Reserve Company by the Rio de Janeiro office of Leonard J. Buck Inc., will be under the control of the new Commission. The entire staff and organization of the Leonard J. Buck office will be taken over as a part of the United States Purchasing Commission and will, in the future, handle the purchase of minerals and metals through the Commission.

The United States Purchasing Commission will have its offices in the Edificio Metropole, Avenida Presidente Wilson 165, 7th. floor. The Commission will function early in July.

811.20 Defense (M) Brazil/926 : Telegram

The Ambassador in Brazil (Caffery) to the Secretary of State

RIO DE JANEIRO, July 31, 1942—9 p. m.
[Received 9 : 22 p. m.]

2819. The cocoa and coffee agreements have not been signed owing to last minute developments in shipping deal. However Brazilian Government accepts the six agreements covering babassu, castor, burlap, ipecac, cotton linters and rotenone and will announce today they have been signed.[10]

CAFFERY

---

[10] Copies of the notes covering these agreements were transmitted to the Department by the Chargé in his despatch No. 8098, August 4, 1942 (not printed). They included detailed provisions on the following : Chronological period or periods in which they were to apply; participation of the Defense Supplies Corporation, the Commodity Credit Corporation and the Banco do Brasil; preclusive purchases by the United States and export embargoes by Brazil so as to exclude the Axis; price formulae; responsibility for the payment of taxes and storage charges; provision for deterioration of the commodity, method and timing of payments, inland transportation, and financial backing for developing producing facilities. (811.20 Defense (M) Brazil/994)

For information in Portuguese concerning these agreements, see Ministério das Relações Exteriores, *Relatório de 1942* (Rio de Janeiro, 1944), pp. 33–41.

832.5018/7 : Telegram

The Ambassador in Brazil (Caffery) to the Secretary of State

RIO DE JANEIRO, August 31, 1942—7 p. m.
[Received September 1—3 a. m.]

3333. For Collado.[11] Department's 2424, August 24, midnight.[12] Messrs. McClintock[13] and LeCron[14] with Mr. Keeler, Agricultural Attaché, have worked out with the Minister of Agriculture, Dr. Apolonio Salles, a proposed agreement for the stimulation of production of foodstuffs in Brazil, especially in the Amazon area, and north and northeastern Brazil, including Bahia, where war and transport difficulties have created deficiencies in foodstuffs.

A draft agreement was approved by President Vargas and Cabinet at meeting Saturday, August 29, and is to be prepared for final signature at Foreign Office September 3. Signatories would be myself, Oswaldo Aranha, Apolonio Salles, and Nelson Rockefeller.[15]

The agreement provides for the establishment of a Brazilian-American food production commission to consist of two members, one a Brazilian representing the Minister of Agriculture and the other the American chief food production specialist to be nominated by the Coordinator's Office, to carry out a program to be drawn up by the Ministry of Agriculture with the collaboration of the American specialists.

The Brazilian Government will make available during 1942 a special appropriation of 5,000 contos, equivalent to $250,000; in 1943, it will make available an equal sum. In addition, it will direct toward the purposes of this program the expenditure of approximately 11,500 contos in 1942 and 11,500 contos in 1943, from the regular budgets of the Ministry of Agriculture. Total Brazilian Government funds to be expended for the purposes of the program over 2-year period will thus total approximately $1,400,000.

The Coordinator's Office will provide food production specialists as needed, and will contribute $1,000,000 in 1942, of which $500,000 is to be deposited shortly after the signing of the agreement, and $500,000 to be made available on deposit of the initial contribution of 500,000 contos by the Brazilian Government. The second contribution of $1,000,000 by the Coordinator will be made during the first half of September 1943.

---

[11] Emilio G. Collado, Executive Secretary of the Board of Economic Operations, Department of State.
[12] Not printed.
[13] John C. McClintock, Assistant Coordinator of Inter-American Affairs.
[14] James D. LeCron, Director of the Food Supply Division of the Office of the Coordinator of Inter-American Affairs.
[15] Coordinator of Inter-American Affairs.

The Brazilian Ministry of Agriculture will make available for the carrying out of the program all equipment, buildings and land of the Division of Vegetable Production Development of the Ministry, as well as the technical collaboration of all other necessary agencies of the Ministry of Agriculture. These include such agencies as the Instituto Agronomico do Norte in Belém and assures cooperation with Camargo [16] as well as other agricultural institutions whether federal or state.

Please request Lockwood, Coordinator's Office,[17] to instruct Garst [18] to proceed to Rio de Janeiro to arrive not later than September 12. Arrangements are being made for Garst, LeCron and Keeler to accompany the Minister of Agriculture to northeastern states, and Amazon Basin, leaving Rio de Janeiro around September 16.

As we desire to sign the agreement in Rio de Janeiro on September 3, immediate confirmation authorizing me to sign is requested.[19]

CAFFERY

811.20 Defense (M) Brazil/1574 : Telegram

The Ambassador in Brazil (Caffery) to the Secretary of State

RIO DE JANEIRO, October 6, 1942.
[Received October 6—8 p. m.]

4023. My 4014 [*4015*], October 6.[20] I released the following statement to the American press today.

"American Ambassador Jefferson Caffery and Brazilian Foreign Minister Oswaldo Aranha signed three agreements today providing for the purchase by the United States of Brazilian coffee, cocoa, Brazil nuts and another agreement with respect to the manufacture of rubber goods.[21]

Ambassador Caffery said that the coffee and cocoa transactions would be handled through established commercial channels and in accordance with existing commercial practice. The coffee agreement provides that the United States through the Commodity Credit Corporation will purchase or underwrite the entire unshipped portion of the United States quota for Brazilian coffee which expired September 30, 1941, and in addition guarantees Brazil the purchase by the United States of 9,300,000 bags of the 1943 Brazilian quota year.

---

[16] Felisberto Camargo, Director of the Instituto Agronomico do Norte.
[17] John E. Lockwood, General Counsel of the Office of the Coordinator of Inter-American Affairs.
[18] Jonathan Garst, field representative of the Coordinator's Office.
[19] Authorization was given in Department's telegram No. 2519, September 1, 1942.
[20] Not printed.
[21] Copies of these agreements were transmitted to the Department by the Ambassador in his despatch No. 8678, October 7, not printed. For information in Portuguese concerning these agreements, see Ministério das Relações Exteriores, *Relatório de 1942*, pp. 33–41.

The cocoa agreement provides that the United States will purchase about 1,300,000 of Baia cocoa between October 1942 and March 1943. These purchases will be made by the Commodity Credit Corporation.

Under the Brazil nut accord the Rubber Reserve Company of the United States will buy as much as 10,500 tons of existing stocks produced in the 1942 season.

Agreement on manufactured rubber goods will aid the other American Republics to meet their essential needs for products of this commodity, and provides other readjustments of crude rubber prices for the 5-year period of the agreement.[22]

Commenting on the agreements Ambassador Caffery said: 'The agreements speak volumes for the farsighted administrations of Presidents Franklin D. Roosevelt and Getulio Vargas, and afford one more realistic example of the vast range of practical cooperation between Brazil and the United States. They go far toward removing as far as humanly possible the uncertainties of war, and their depressing effects on these industries'."

Translation Souza Costa's speech follows.[23]

CAFFERY

832.51/2113a : Telegram

The Secretary of State to the Ambassador in Brazil (Caffery)

WASHINGTON, November 27, 1942—midnight.

3719. For West [24] from Pierson.

1st: Failure to organize Companhia Vale do Rio Doce [25] is creating serious legal difficulties and moreover is holding up important interdepartmental arrangements. We urge therefore that formal organization be completed at earliest possible moment, even if necessary to delay until later date the full dress ceremony which Brazilian officials seem to desire.

2d: (a) The inability to obtain and ship materials and equipment as promptly as originally contemplated is certain to postpone date upon which full deliveries of ore can begin. This naturally reduces period during which Eximbank will be able to obtain reimbursement.

(b) In effort to expedite program Eximbank is approving use of dollar credit for items not foreseen when agreement was made.

(c) Proposed ore purchase contracts contain *force majeure* clauses which, if exercised, will further limit period during which Bank may expect reimbursement.

---

[22] See pp. 691 ff.
[23] In telegram No. 4028, October 6, 1942, from the Ambassador in Brazil, not printed.
[24] Robert K. West, Engineering Consultant of the Export-Import Bank.
[25] This company was a Brazilian Government corporation which by acquiring the Itabira Mines and the Victoria Minas Railway was to be the Government instrumentality for increasing ore production; the United States was represented on its board of directors by Robert K. West and B. H. Blanchard.

For foregoing reasons we feel that it is only equitable for Brazil to extend reimbursement period from 20 years to 30 years. This will involve merely substituting 30 for 20 annual notes and, of course, 30 instead of 20 interest notes. Will you please broach this subject to Pinheiro [26] pointing out reasons for suggestion?

3d: Because of changes in local situation I feel that you should return to Washington for brief period for consultation. I hope this may be after formal organization of Company, but if this is to be further delayed, perhaps you can come to Washington prior to date of organization. [Pierson.]

HULL

NEGOTIATIONS CONCERNING THE PRODUCTION, PURCHASE, AND DISTRIBUTION OF BRAZILIAN RUBBER AND RUBBER PRODUCTS

832.6176/171 : Telegram

The Secretary of State to the Ambassador in Brazil (Caffery)

WASHINGTON, February 9, 1942—midnight.

313. Your 283, January 29, 11 p. m.[27] The following from Rubber Reserve: [28]

"Rubber Reserve will agree to buy all available rubber until June 30, 1944 at a base price of 39 cents f.o.b. Belém for acre fine, on a washed and dried basis, with appropriate differentials for unwashed types and lower grades.

"The above agreement is subject to the following conditions: (1) Assurance from the Brazilian Government that it will put forth utmost effort to encourage production and flow of rubber from all Brazilian markets to Rubber Reserve Company; (2) Export licenses to be restricted to Rubber Reserve or its nominees; (3) All rubber produced to be sold to Rubber Reserve on above price basis, except amount required for domestic consumption; (4) The base price of 39 cents f.o.b. Belém with similar differentials is to be established by Brazilian Government for domestic consumption.

"Rubber Reserve Company will establish representation in such Brazilian markets as may be necessary to expedite purchase and flow of rubber to United States.

"In view of existing conditions affecting rubber supplies please confer appropriate government officials and advise early as possible."

With reference to (2) above, the Priorities Division of the War Production Board on January 23 last issued an order [29] restricting the sale of rubber by dealers to Rubber Reserve Company and conversely

---

[26] Israel Pinheiro, superintendent of the Itabira project.
[27] Not printed.
[28] The Rubber Reserve Company was a purchasing agency of the Federal Loan Agency until February 24, 1942, on which date it was transferred to the Department of Commerce.
[29] 7 *Federal Register* 511.

restricting purchases of rubber in the United States to Rubber Reserve Company. Accordingly, so far as the United States is concerned, the necessary machinery has already been established.

HULL

[An agreement between the Government of the United States and the Brazilian Government for increasing the production of rubber in Brazil was effected by exchange of notes between the Under Secretary of State (Welles) and the Brazilian Minister of Finance (Souza Costa), signed at Washington, March 3, 1942. For texts of notes, see Department of State Executive Agreement Series No. 371, or 57 Stat. (pt. 2) 1318.]

811.20 Defense (M) Brazil/327 : Telegram

The Acting Secretary of State to the Ambassador in Brazil (Caffery)

WASHINGTON, March 13, 1942—7 p. m.

640. Following from Rubber Reserve:

"The following Agreement was signed by Rubber Reserve Company and the Republic of Brazil on March 3d:

'This Agreement, made and entered into as of this 3d day of March, 1942, by and between Rubber Reserve Company, an Agency of the United States Government, (hereinafter called "Reserve"), a corporation existing under the laws of the United States of America and having an office for the transaction of business in Washington, D. C., party of the first part, and the Republic of Brazil (hereinafter sometimes called "Brazil"), party of the second part;

WITNESSETH:

1. Brazil agrees to establish, or cause to be established, a single selling agency (which will be the Bank of Brazil or some other Brazilian Government Department or Agency, such selling agency being hereinafter referred to as the "Selling Agency"), located at Belém, Para, and at such other places as may be deemed desirable by Reserve and Brazil, with appropriate authority to acquire and sell crude rubber produced within the territory of the Republic of Brazil (such crude rubber being hereinafter referred to as the "Rubber").

2. Reserve agrees to make such arrangements as may be necessary for the purchase of the Rubber, it being understood that all such purchases shall be on the basis of cash against shipping documents, f. o. b. Belém, Para, or such other places as may be deemed desirable by Reserve and Brazil. All of the rubber so purchased shall be subject to a final price adjustment based on quality inspection and net certified weights determined at the port of entry in the U. S. A.

3. During the term of this agreement, Reserve agrees to buy and Brazil (acting through the Selling Agency) agrees to sell all of the Rubber which is not required by the Republic of Brazil for domestic consumption or use.

4. Reserve and Brazil agree that the base price for all purchases and sales of the Rubber under paragraph 3 hereof shall be thirty-nine (39¢), U. S. A. currency, per pound, f. o. b. Belém, Para, for Upriver Acre Fine, on a washed and dried basis, with appropriate differentials for unwashed types and lower grades (said base price, together with said differentials being hereinafter referred to as the "Fixed Price"); provided, however, that after the expiration of the first 2 years of the term of this agreement the Fixed Price shall be subject to such adjustment from time to time as Reserve and Brazil may mutually agree is appropriate by reason of any changed circumstances affecting the world price of crude rubber.

In addition to the base price above referred to, the Rubber Reserve Company will pay premiums as follows: 2½¢ per pound for all rubber in excess of 5,000 tons and up to 10,000 tons purchased hereunder by the Rubber Reserve Company during any one year of this agreement; a premium of 5¢ per pound for all rubber purchased hereunder in excess of 10,000 tons during any one year of this agreement. All premiums so paid,

(a) shall be credited against the $5,000,000 fund of the Rubber Reserve Company referred to in paragraph 1 of the note of His Excellency, the Brazilian Minister of Finance, addressed to the Acting Secretary of State of the United States of America, dated March 3, 1942, and,

(b) shall be turned over by the Brazilian Government to the Instituto Agronomico do Norte, or other department or agency of the Brazilian Government having similar functions, to be utilized for the immediate expansion of the production and improvement of quality of raw wild rubber in the Amazon Valley and adjacent regions.

5. It is understood that Brazil intends to establish, or cause to be established, the Fixed Price for all purchases and sales of the Rubber for domestic consumption or use.

6. Brazil agrees that it shall use its best efforts to cause the maximum amount of the Rubber to be produced and to be made available for sale to Reserve.

7. Brazil, recognizing the large requirements of rubber in the United States for the war emergency, agrees to restrict to the United States of America, the exportation of the rubber in raw and manufactured form from the Republic of Brazil, provided that arrangements shall be made for the purchase by the United States of manufactured rubber at prices to be mutually agreed upon. Reserve agrees that all rubber purchased by it hereunder shall be disposed of only in accordance with the regulations of the War Production Board or some other Agency of the United States Government having similar authority.

8. Reserve agrees that it shall use its best efforts to expedite the purchase and exportation of the Rubber which Reserve is obligated to buy under paragraph 3 hereof.

9. The term of this agreement shall be for a period beginning with the date hereof and ending on December 31, 1946, unless sooner terminated by the mutual consent of the parties hereto.' End of Agreement.

Rubber Reserve Company is also prepared to pay the following prices, F. O. B. Belém, for the different grades of rubber, and is establishing a letter of credit through the Reconstruction Finance Corporation so that the Bank of Brazil may draw against such letter of credit as rubber is shipped from Brazil on ocean going vessels destined for Continental U. S. A. ports:

Acre Washed	39¢
Upriver Washed	38⅝
Islands Washed	38⅝
Acre Cut Classified (Crude)	30⅝
Upriver Cut Classified (Crude)	30¼
Islands Cut Classified (Crude)	28⅛
Sernamby Rama Washed	28⅛
Sernamby Rama Crude	20
Sernamby Cameta Washed	29⅝
Sernamby Cameta Crude	15½
Caucho Washed	33½
Caucho Crude	24

and Rubber Reserve Company will pay the following prices, U.S.A. Currency, per pound, F. O. B. São Salvador (Bahia) and such other Brazilian ocean ports, as Reserve and Brazil may mutually agree upon for the following grades of rubber:

Ceara Scrap (Crude)	17¢
Mangabeira (Crude)	17

Please advise Brazilian Government and Bank of Brazil accordingly. Also advise Rubber Reserve Company if Brazil proposes to provide for shipping arrangements or if Reserve is expected to do so. Suggest Brazilian Government be encouraged to expedite selling arrangements so that exports can be started to United States."

WELLES

811.20 Defense (M) Brazil/328 : Telegram

The Ambassador in Brazil (Caffery) to the Secretary of State

RIO DE JANEIRO, March 14, 1942—4 p. m.
[Received 6 : 15 p. m.]

871. For Rubber Reserve. Department's number 640, March 13, 7 p. m. Will Firestone Tire and Rubber Company and Goodyear Tire and Rubber Company here continue to act as buying agents for Rubber Reserve under agreement?

Please rush reply.

CAFFERY

811.20 Defense (M) Brazil/328 : Telegram

The Acting Secretary of State to the Ambassador in Brazil (Caffery)

WASHINGTON, March 17, 1942—3 p. m.

671. Your 871 of March 14. Firestone and Goodyear will not continue to act, as Rubber Reserve will deal directly with Bank of Brazil.

WELLES

811.20 Defense (M) Brazil/335 : Telegram

The Ambassador in Brazil (Caffery) to the Secretary of State

RIO DE JANEIRO, March 17, 1942—9 p. m.
[Received 11:20 p. m.]

916. For Rubber Reserve. Department's 640, March 13, 7 p. m. I have informed the Brazilian Government and the Bank of Brazil. Dr. Truda of the Bank of Brazil [30] is of the opinion that the Government will expect Rubber Reserve to provide for shipping arrangements.

Dr. Truda says that the Government must promulgate a decree law establishing a single selling agency. He will discuss this and other matters with Souza Costa [31] who is returning today.

Dr. Truda intends to establish buying offices at Belém and Manáos to purchase at the fixed price less a small discount for expenses of the selling agency, reselling only to established consumers within Brazil and to Rubber Reserve. He will maintain a uniform selling price for domestic and export trade. He estimates domestic consumption at a maximum of 10,000 tons annually.

Dr. Truda is in complete agreement with the provisions of paragraph 3. He says that Brazil has recently exported 165 tons to Venezuela, 20 tons to Chile, and that the Government will authorize shipment of 150 tons to Argentina which were purchased several months ago but he will not approve other requests.

He will adopt measures to prevent hoarding rubber by non-consumers.

CAFFERY

811.20 Defense (M) Brazil/355

The Ambassador in Brazil (Caffery) to the Secretary of State

No. 6764

RIO DE JANEIRO, March 18, 1942.
[Received March 23.]

SIR: I have the honor to refer to the Department's telegram No. 623, of March 12, 8 p. m.,[32] transmitting a note from the Reconstruction

---

[30] Leonardo Truda, Director of the Export-Import Section of the Bank of Brazil.
[31] Arthur de Souza Costa, Brazilian Minister of Finance, had been in Washington arranging for the purchase of defense materials.
[32] Not printed.

Finance Corporation for the Bank of Brazil relative to the $10,000,000 credit for the purchase of Brazilian rubber. The note was delivered to the Bank of Brazil on March 13, 1942.

I enclose copies of the letter of acknowledgment of the Bank of Brazil, and copies of the notice of registration of the credit.[33] The only difference between the note of the Reconstruction Finance Corporation and the credit registered by the Bank of Brazil is that the bank provides for three negotiable copies of the bill of lading, whereas the Reconstruction Finance Corporation calls for only two copies. Mr. McAshan[34] perceives no objection to the procedure, provided the Bank of Brazil will forward the third negotiable bill of lading to the Federal Reserve Bank, when one of the first two negotiable bills of lading has been received in the United States.

Please request the Rubber Reserve Company to confirm acceptance of the letter and enclosures of the Bank of Brazil.

The Bank of Brazil has suggested that original draft and documents referred to in the Department's telegram mentioned above be forwarded by air, second draft and documents by boat mail and third negotiable bill of lading to remain with the bank to be forwarded to the Federal Reserve Bank when one of the above originals has been received in the States. This suggestion is made to provide for the contingency of both remittances going astray.

Respectfully yours,
　　　　　　　　　　　　　　　　　　For the Ambassador:
　　　　　　　　　　　　　　　　　　JOHN F. SIMMONS
　　　　　　　　　　　　　　　　　　Counselor of Embassy

811.20 Defense (M) Brazil/335 : Telegram

The Acting Secretary of State to the Ambassador in Brazil (Caffery)

WASHINGTON, March 24, 1942—6 p. m.

749. Your 916 of March 17. Proposal of Dr. Truda to permit export of 150 tons of rubber to Argentina would appear to violate terms of notes and rubber purchase agreements, as substance of these is that after date of signature Brazil will permit exportation of rubber only to this country. You are requested to point this out to Dr. Truda and obtain his cooperation in preventing this shipment.

　　　　　　　　　　　　　　　　　　　　　　　　　　　WELLES

---

[33] Neither printed.
[34] S. Maurice McAshan, representative of the Defense Supplies Corporation, a purchasing agency of the Department of Commerce.

811.20 Defense (M) Brazil/361 : Telegram

The Acting Secretary of State to the Ambassador in Brazil (Caffery)

WASHINGTON, March 27, 1942—10 p. m.

799. "Your 1008, March 24, 2 p. m.[35] Suggestion that Rubber Reserve station inspectors at Belém and Manáos to approve final quality and weights before shipment of rubber not practicable at present time.

Rubber Reserve agrees to amend letters of credit to permit single selling agency to draw for value rubber, less F. O. B. charges, in case export shipment not made within 30 days after rubber available for shipment, provided rubber stored in public warehouse acceptable to bank of Brazil and warehouse receipt delivered to American Consul at time of payment.

Rubber Reserve authorizes you to negotiate amendment to differentials contained Department's 640 March 13 within limits reported in Embassy's telegram 689, March 4,[36] but not over 19½ cents for crude Mangabeira and crude Manicoba or Ceara. Rubber Reserve recommends that differentials for both crude and washed Cameta also crude and washed Caucho be negotiated at or near the prices quoted for these grades in Department's 640, March 13.

Reply will be made at later date to suggestions connection Article 7 agreement."

WELLES

811.20 Defense (M) Brazil/361 : Telegram

The Acting Secretary of State to the Ambassador in Brazil (Caffery)

WASHINGTON, March 30, 1942—10 p. m.

822. Your 1008 of March 24.[35] Circular telegram of March 28 [37] which was repeated to you concerning the rubber situation generally will indicate the belief here that the manufacture of rubber articles in Brazil should be drastically limited. The fact that the other South American republics cannot obtain tires from the United States does not mean that they should be able to get them from Brazil. The reason they cannot get the tires is that on an overall basis, considering the essential needs of the United States, the United Kingdom and the American republics, there is not sufficient rubber to make them. The factors outlined in the circular telegram demonstrate the necessity for making fully effective the provision of the agreements with Brazil

---

[35] Not printed.
[36] Latter not printed.
[37] Printed in vol. VI, section under Colombia entitled "Negotiation of an agreement between the Rubber Reserve Company and Colombia . . ."

that the maximum amount of rubber will be made available to the United States after providing appropriate amounts for internal consumption.

We understand that the rate of rubber manufacture in Brazil has increased tremendously in the last few months. In view of Brazil's undertaking referred to above, limitations on this would seem appropriate, as well as the institution of other measures of the kind referred to in the circular telegram.

Mr. Douglas Allen, the Rubber Reserve representative now on his way to Rio, as advised by the Department's telegram 800 of March 27,[39] will be prepared to discuss these matters.

WELLES

811.20 Defense (M) Brazil/515 a : Telegram

The Secretary of State to the Ambassador in Brazil (Caffery)

WASHINGTON, April 25, 1942—midnight.

1076. For Donnelly:[40] Confirming telephone conversation of today:

1. It appears to the Department to be necessary to reach an agreement as soon as possible as to the manufactured products to be purchased by the Rubber Reserve Company.

2. As to manufactured products, the Department suggested to you, and it is believed that you agree, that there should be two restrictions as to these products which should be included within the agreement to be made with the Brazilian Government.

3. The first restriction should be as to the types of the products to be manufactured. The test which is suggested is that the same standards should apply in Brazil as apply in the United States. As we said, this principle has been readily accepted by Peru in recent negotiations which have just been concluded,[41] and we have suggested the same standard to certain other American republics who have indicated a willingness to go along with this principle of equality of use. This accordingly would mean that in the proposed Brazilian agreements some effort should be made to limit the types of goods to be manufactured so as to eliminate luxury products to the same extent that the manufacture of these goods is limited in the United States.

---

[39] Not printed.
[40] Walter J. Donnelly, Commercial Attaché.
[41] For correspondence regarding these negotiations, see vol VI, section under Peru entitled "Cooperation between the United States and Peru in the mobilization of the economic resources of Peru; agreement for purchase by the Rubber Reserve Company of surplus Peruvian rubber."

4. The second limitation would be to limit the quantity of such permissible goods as might be manufactured. It is obvious that there must be a quantitative limitation as well as a qualitative limitation. It is accordingly suggested that having arrived at the categories to be manufactured, actual quantity limitations be set up.

5. The next point which we wished to make in the telephone conversation is that it appears to the Department to be urgently desirable to reach an agreement as to internal consumption of raw rubber in Brazil at the earliest possible time. The Peruvian agreement provides for an actual number of tons which is to represent the total consumption of raw rubber in Peru. This figure, as has been stated, is based on the principle of equality of uses in the United States and Peru. The principle has, it is believed, been recognized by the United States–Brazilian agreement as to rubber, but it now remains to translate this general commitment into an actual tonnage. For the same reasons which motivate us to request an early agreement as to manufactured rubber, we urge that an early settlement be made of the actual amounts of raw rubber to be reserved for internal consumption in Brazil. We also think it advisable for you to discuss with appropriate Brazilian officials the adoption of a rationing scheme which would make tires available only for essential uses.

6. As explained to you by telephone, the reason for the Department's sense of urgency in the above matters is the fact that there have been reports of various attempts to make forward contracts as to both raw and manufactured rubber with the Brazilian producers and manufacturers. The Department desires to prevent the creation of such agreements which might constitute *faits accomplis* which would interfere with the application of the principles above referred to.

7. We realize the necessity, which you referred to during the telephone conversation, of trying to agree upon figures for the requirements of the other American republics from Brazil so that any restrictions which might be reached in your negotiations could be agreed upon by Brazil after consultation and in agreement with the other American republics. The Department has attempted to get these figures as to both amount and types of raw and manufactured rubber, but as yet has not had much success. The Department will, however, attempt to obtain these figures for you and obtain agreements where possible.

HULL

811.20 Defense (M) Brazil/525: Telegram

The Ambassador in Brazil (Caffery) to the Secretary of State

RIO DE JANEIRO, May 1, 1942—6 p. m.

[Received 10:52 p. m.]

1486. For Finletter,[42] Newhall,[43] Clayton,[44] Klossner,[45] from Allen. Department's 1076, April 24 [*25*], midnight, and my 1442, April 28, 9 p. m.[46] Following agreement reached at meeting with Brazilian rubber manufacturers and members Brazilian Commission subject approval Finance Minister.

1. Annual over-all quota 10,000 tons dry weight rubber and reclaim.

2. Minimum of 25% of quota to be devoted to manufacture essential products for export to apply against essential Western Hemisphere requirements as determined by Washington thereby in effect establishing maximum internal quota of 7,500 tons.

3. Rubber Reserve to purchase exportable surplus tires and tubes at equivalent of net Rio de Janeiro dealer prices as approved by Brazilian Government.

4. Export of tires and tubes to countries other than United States prohibited effective immediately regardless of licenses outstanding. Necessary instructions already issued by Finance Minister.

5. Manufacturers miscellaneous rubber goods willing discontinue manufacture non-essentials and restrict exports to the United States provided prices agreed upon and orders placed for tires and other essential rubber products.   Advisable United States give earliest possible assurance these countries with respect supply essential requirements.

Roberts [47] remaining Rio de Janeiro until end next week to conclude negotiations miscellaneous products will then join us Lima. Urgently need information requested our telegram 1225, April 10, midnight [48] about miscellaneous rubber products for meeting with manufacturers May 7. Telegraph basic information if cannot be airmailed.

Official price schedules have been published in Brazil thereby facilitating resumption shipment.

Believe proportion exportable surplus may run higher than 25% because of acute shortage gasoline and drastic gasoline rationing which already has materially reduced non-essential driving and demand for tires.

---

[42] Thomas K. Finletter, Acting Chief, Division of Defense Materials.
[43] Arthur B. Newhall, Chief, Rubber and Rubber Products Branch, War Production Board.
[44] W. L. Clayton, Assistant Secretary of Commerce.
[45] Howard J. Klossner, official of the Rubber Reserve Company.
[46] Latter not printed.
[47] James C. Roberts, assistant to the President of the Rubber Reserve Co.
[48] Not printed.

Strong diplomatic pressure being brought to bear upon Brazil by other Latin American countries to supply essential export products.

6. All manufacturers willing use approximately same proportion reclaim as now used in United States when available.

7. Brazil desires develop maximum possible domestic supply reclaim and requests United States facilitate shipment pan reclaim equipment.

Telegraph if pan reclaim can be satisfactorily used in same proportion as digested reclaim in United States of America.

8. Brazilian Commission is recommending 2-year suspension of duties and other obstacles to importation and use of reclaim from the United States. Brazil willing use reclaim from the United States to extent their domestic supply inadequate to comply with paragraph 6.

9. Brazil to undertake campaign to bring about economy in use of rubber products.

10. United States to facilitate shipment materials needed by rubber manufacturing industry with respect to which Brazil is dependent upon United States.

11. United States to give assurance to Brazil with respect to supply rubber goods essential for Brazilian military and industrial purposes or equipment for manufacture thereof. [Allen.]

CAFFERY

811.20 Defense (M) Brazil/516 : Telegram

The Secretary of State to the Ambassador in Brazil (Caffery)

WASHINGTON, May 6, 1942—10 p. m.

1164. Your 1442 of April 28 [49] and 1486 of May 1. For Donnelly and Allen. All here concur in feeling that you have obtained excellent results in your negotiations with respect to internal consumption and manufactured products.

The agreement outlined in your 1486 of May 1 is in general satisfactory.

Under points 2 and 3 it is understood that Rubber Reserve purchases the exportable surplus of tires and tubes and then uses them in supplying essential Latin American requirements.

The wording of point 5 is not clear as it refers to the advisability that the United States give earliest possible assurance to "these countries" with respect to the supply of essential requirements. It is assumed that you refer to other Latin American essential requirements for miscellaneous rubber goods. In the agreement with Peru, this Government agreed to collaborate with Peru with the view of assur-

---

[49] Not printed.

ing to Peru an equitable distribution of supplies of rubber products available to United States and Peru on the basis of relative needs and of the present emergency. It is probable that similar assurances will be given to the other countries which have broken with the Axis.

Following is estimated use of miscellaneous rubber products in long tons of crude rubber content during 1940: Argentina 145; Bolivia 30; Chile 195; Colombia 126; Ecuador 21; Panama 36; Paraguay 3; Peru 58; Uruguay 29; Venezuela 147.

Following is estimate of 1942 requirements for essential needs of miscellaneous rubber products in long tons of crude rubber content: Argentina 50; Bolivia 38; Chile 158; Colombia 76; Ecuador 6; Panama 12; Paraguay 6; Peru 59; Uruguay 27; Venezuela 82. No breakdown of products is available at present time.

The estimate of Argentina's requirements is recognized as low, but it is felt that with strict limitation in Argentina there is sufficient rubber in stock to care for requirements for rest of year, except for a small allocation to cover special types of products.

These figures represent only present intention here and it should not be implied that this country is to be bound to supply such amounts to these other countries.

The answer to the question under point 7 depends on the product for which the reclaim is to be used. Goodyear and Firestone have been asked to furnish additional information on this question and it will be transmitted on receipt.

With respect to points 9 and 10, the United States will agree to do everything possible to facilitate these shipments so far as consistent with the relative emergency needs of the two countries.

HULL

811.20 Defense (M) Brazil/780 : Telegram

The Ambassador in Brazil (Caffery) to the Secretary of State

RIO DE JANEIRO, May 13, 1942—3 p. m.
[Received 6 : 30 p. m.]

1615. For Finletter, Clayton, Newhall, Klossner. Mr. Bouças[50] informs us that he understood the 5-million-dollar fund referred to in clause 4 of the rubber agreement of March 3[51] and in numbered paragraph 1 of Souza Costa's note to Mr. Welles dated March 3[52] was to be in addition to the quantity premium payable on rubber in excess of 5,000 and 10,000 tons annually. Mr. Bouças stated that

[50] Valentim Bouças, in charge of all matters pertaining to rubber in the Brazilian office of Coordinator of Economic Mobilization.
[51] See telegram No. 640, March 13, 7 p. m., to the Ambassador in Brazil, p. 692.
[52] Department of State Executive Agreement Series No. 371, or 57 Stat. (pt. 2) 1318.

his understanding reached in Washington was that the premiums would be paid over to the Instituto Agronomico do Norte or the new rubber Institute and not used as a credit against the 5-million-dollar fund.

We had understood that the premiums as due would be credited against any part of the 5-million-dollar fund which had been used in Brazil for the purpose of increasing rubber production until that part of the 5-million-dollar fund so used had been covered after which any such premium would then be paid outright to the appropriate Brazilian governmental agency.

In order to avoid serious misunderstanding at this end it is urgently requested that you telegraph your interpretation as soon as possible.

CAFFERY

811.20 Defense (M) Brazil/606 : Telegram

The Ambassador in Brazil (Caffery) to the Secretary of State

RIO DE JANEIRO, May 19, 1942—4 p. m.
[Received May 20—1:03 a. m.]

1696. Department's 1245, May 16, 2 p. m.[53] The Minister of Finance on April 28 (see my 1442, April 28, 9 p. m.[53]) instructed the Director of the Export-Import Department of Bank of Brazil to prohibit the exportation of crude rubber in any form and tires and tubes except to the United States. The Minister of Finance confirmed the instruction in writing last week and he again instructed the Bank of Brazil to cancel all applications for the exportation of these products.

With regard to the letter from the American Embassy in Buenos Aires the shipments referred to were made under licenses obtained prior to the agreement of March 3 between Brazil and the United States.

The other cases referred to in the Department's telegram are covered by the prohibition cited in the first paragraph.

CAFFERY

811.20 Defense (M) Brazil/538 : Telegram

The Secretary of State to the Ambassador in Brazil (Caffery)

WASHINGTON, May 21, 1942—5 p. m.

1301. In further reply to your 1576, May 9.[54] Rubber Reserve is prepared to purchase all miscellaneous rubber items already manu-

---

[53] Not printed.
[54] Not printed; in this telegram the Ambassador sought clarification of certain points in the rubber agreement of March 3 (811.20 Defense (M) Brazil/538).

factured and in process and all future items made available during the life of the Agreement of March 3 at net dealer prices now prevailing in Brazil, subject to change by mutual agreement.

In so far as practicable Agreement should provide for purchase of essential items, the production of which is permitted under the terms of W.P.B. permissive order M–15–b, as amended,[55] copies of which are being sent. Wherever possible, these items should be produced in accordance with W.P.B. specifications as set forth in order M–15–b, as amended.

The agreement with Rubber Reserve should provide that Rubber Reserve Company is entitled to change the items on the list and specifications therefor with due protection to the interests of the manufacturer. Rubber Reserve will make the necessary arrangements to finance the acquisition of these items and their storage in Brazil. It is understood that this offer applies only to those manufactured goods produced within the quota fixed by agreement for Brazil's domestic industrial consumption of crude and reclaimed rubber.

The agreement is not limited to the acquisition of essential products. This is for two reasons. In the first place we do not have here detailed information as to Brazilian production facilities for miscellaneous products, and hence cannot determine to what extent it would be feasible to manufacture items regarded here as essential. Second, we do not have detailed information as to the requirements of the other Latin American Republics for miscellaneous products. For these reasons Rubber Reserve Company is planning to send to Brazil in the very near future a representative familiar with conservation policies here who will aid in changing over to the manufacture of essential items, and we can proceed with the obtaining of the necessary information for the other Latin American Republics. In the meantime, however, Rubber Reserve Company desires to acquire all manufactured products not required for domestic consumption in Brazil.

Repeat to Lima for Allen as no. 43.

HULL

811.20 Defense (M) Brazil/721a : Telegram

The Secretary of State to the Ambassador in Brazil (Caffery)

WASHINGTON, June 13, 1942—6 p. m.

1532. Your 1804 of May 28.[56] The general purpose of the development fund of 5 million dollars is to make available in Brazil funds for taking all action necessary to increase the production of raw rubber

---

[55] 6 *Federal Register* 6406.
[56] Not printed.

as fast as possible. Implied in this general purpose, however, is the limitation that the fund is not to be used unless, and only to the extent, it is needed for this purpose.

The fund is primarily available for subsidies without obligation of repayment. Included in such subsidies, per the terms of paragraph 4 of the agreement of March 3, 1942, are premiums for raw rubber purchased by the Rubber Reserve Company. These premiums are to be credited against the fund and turned over to the Brazilian Government to be expended by that Government for raw rubber development projects.

Where a request is made for a subsidy from the fund the governing consideration should be the importance of the project for which the subsidy is requested to expeditious production of raw rubber. Subject to this consideration, however, the following may also be taken into account: (1) Whether the project is commercially feasible on a profit basis without subsidy or with only partial subsidy; (2) If it is, whether there is assurance that it will be undertaken at the earliest possible moment regardless of a subsidy.

The fund is also available for loans. As in the case of subsidies, the governing consideration in passing upon a request for a loan is the importance of the project for which the loan is sought to expeditious production of raw rubber. Subject to this consideration, however, the following may also be taken into account: (1) Whether the project is such as is financed by loans according to the usual practice of the industry; (2) Whether the project is a sound risk according to ordinary standards of banking practice; (3) If it is a sound risk whether there is assurance that it will be financed by private sources of capital at the earliest possible moment. The amount of loans granted should be deducted from the fund in the same manner as subsidies in order to determine the balance on hand at any particular given time; but moneys received in repayment of the principal of such loans immediately should be returned to the fund and become available for re-expenditure.

It is suggested that in so far as possible requests for loans to finance projects which are commercially sound be granted from special funds to be set up by the Rubber Reserve Company. This would prevent undue depletion of the 5 million dollar fund which may be used to finance any project necessary to expedite raw rubber production regardless of how bad a commercial risk the project may be.

In accordance with what has been said previously with respect to granting subsidies from the fund, and for more specific guidance with respect to the same, the following are suggested as illustrative of projects meritorious of subsidy: This list is merely illustrative and is by no means to be considered as exhaustive.

(1) The improvement of transportation and communication facilities, such as acquisition of vessels, building of roads into remote rubber producing areas (e. g., those in Matto Grosso), construction of airfields, and provision of short-wave radio transmitters to agents at key points within the Amazon Basin.

(2) The preparation of facilities for tappers moving into production areas is likewise a primary expenditure to be met from the fund. This would include the building of houses and barracks, construction of supply and medicine depots (including launch dispensaries), movement of foods and medicines into the selected areas, and organization of subsistence agriculture (including provision of seeds and implements) in so far as necessary to assure food supplies and minimize import requirements from outside the Amazon system.

(3) Distribution by public authority of food, tools, medicines and supplies for the tappers controlled so far as necessary to assure that they reach the tappers.

(4) As the program expands, large-scale immigration into the Amazon may become essential. It is contemplated that this will involve large-scale preparations in advance of settlement and possibly subsidization of transport into the area and of operations there during a preliminary period.

In as much as the fund is set up to provide for direct developmental costs, salaries and general administrative overhead of Rubber Reserve officers in Brazil shall not under any circumstances be met from the fund.

With respect to arrangements heretofore proposed, on the basis of the foregoing the following treatment would be accorded. The supplies referred to in your 1484 of May 1 [58] appear to be commercially profitable and only a financing problem is involved. The 500,000 dollar fund made available for that purpose will accordingly be restored to the fund to the extent repaid. On the other hand, the credit of $50,000 opened to build barracks and pay transportation does not appear to be a commercial undertaking and hence would be paid for out of the fund and reduce the amount thereafter to be available. The $500,000 made available for special loans pursuant to Department's 1269 of May 18 [58] would be on the same basis as the $500,000 made available for financing the purchase of supplies. The expenditures of $50,000 each for projects approved by McAshan in Department's 1365 of May 27 [58] would also presumably not be commercial propositions and hence paid for outright and finally from the fund.

Please advise whether you and McAshan concur in the foregoing.

HULL

---

[58] Not printed.

811.20 Defense (M) Brazil/820 : Telegram

The Ambassador in Brazil (Caffery) to the Secretary of State

RIO DE JANEIRO, July 10, 1942—8 p. m.
[Received 9 : 27 p. m.]

2480. For Finletter and Allen, Rubber Reserve. Presidential decree law of July 9 created Banco de Credito da Borracha with capital of 50,000 contos of which Brazilian Government will subscribe 55%, Rubber Reserve 40% and Brazilian public 5%. The three directors will consist of two Brazilians and one American. Brazilian Government has approved appointment E. E. Longas, American director, but has not yet named its directors, one of which will be president of bank.

Proportionate stock ownership was changed without our knowledge from the original agreement of 50–50 participation. Bouças explains that new setup is necessary under corporation law requirements of Brazil. Brazilian authorities have assured us that no loans, commitments or undertakings will be concluded without written approval of American director. This is the first time under existing banking legislation that Brazil has permitted foreign stockholders and director and as such represents important concession to United States and is so interpreted here.

If we had been consulted in advance we would have approved the change in proportionate stock ownerships. We regard the decrees and statutes of the bank as satisfactory and feel that the measures will greatly facilitate financing of entire rubber program.

Text by air mail.

CAFFERY

811.20 Defense (M) Brazil/935 : Telegram

The Chargé in Brazil (Simmons) to the Secretary of State

RIO DE JANEIRO, August 1, 1942—8 p. m.
[Received August 2—3 : 27 a. m.]

2832. For Clayton, Finletter, Hays,[59] Bicknell[60] from Allen, McAshan, Micou.[61] Confirming telephone conversation of today with Cooke,[62] Brazil has requested that tires and tubes for shipment from Brazil to American countries other than the United States be not purchased by Rubber Reserve but be sold and shipped by Brazil to

---

[59] Paul R. Hays, Chief, Rubber Division, Board of Economic Warfare.
[60] J. W. Bicknell, Vice President, Rubber Reserve Company.
[61] Creswell M. Micou, in charge of the interests of the Board of Economic Warfare in Rio de Janeiro.
[62] R. C. Cooke, official of the Rubber Reserve Company.

such countries under an agreement between Brazil and Rubber Reserve whereby Brazil would agree that shipments of tires and tubes from Brazil to each such country would not exceed the quota established by the United States for the essential needs of each such country.

The reason for this request by Brazil is that Brazil desires to retain its normal trade relations with the countries concerned and does not wish to appear to have such trade under the direct control of the United States. In this connection the Brazilian Foreign Office has sent a strong note to the Embassy expressing this point of view and taking the position that the rubber agreement between Brazil and the United States only contemplated that Brazil would sell the United States its exportable surplus of crude and manufactured rubber to fill the needs of the United States but not for redistribution by the United States to other American countries. Brazilian Government feels so strongly on this matter that they withheld export permits covering shipment of tires to Peru now in process of loading but we were able to have them agree to issue the licenses upon the understanding that this whole question would be explored with a view to considering an adjustment of the present arrangements for the purchase of tires and tubes in Brazil by Rubber Reserve for distribution to other American countries.

The agreement with Brazil limiting consumption of crude rubber within Brazil and the relating agreement to purchase tires and tubes is set forth in Allen's letter to Bouças originally dated April 27, 1942, later slightly changed and redated May 2.[63] This letter must be read in conjunction with memorandum presented to Brazilian Commission April 28, 1942, setting forth the principles agreed upon. Both of these documents are attached to Allen's report number 3, item number 8.[64] The agreements referred to have been recognized by Brazil in practice but have not been officially confirmed. Brazil has not yet taken the position that the agreement is not in effect It must be remembered, however, that the agreement for limitation of consumption of crude rubber within Brazil was a wholly voluntary act of cooperation by Brazil and was agreed to by Brazil despite the specific provisions of the rubber agreement between Brazil and the United States which contemplated the expansion of rubber manufacture in Brazil. In view of this situation it is important that the United States avoid any appearance of dictation or arbitrary control and as long as Brazil specifically agrees to keep its sales and shipments of tires and tubes to other American countries within the quotas established by the United States the main purpose of the

---

[63] Not found in Department files; for terms of the agreement, see telegram No. 1486, May 1, 6 p. m., from the Ambassador in Brazil, p. 700.

[64] Not found in Department files.

United States is accomplished. Furthermore, the request of Brazil is in our opinion, in accord with the understanding set forth in the memorandum of principles agreed upon by Rubber Reserve and Brazil which was the foundation for the agreement set forth in Allen's letter to Bouças.

If the request of the Brazilian authorities is granted it should be made clear that it is without prejudice to our rights under paragraph 7 of the main Rubber Agreement of March 3.[65]

In any case we will attempt to negotiate early next week an agreement permitting Brazilian manufacturers and exporters to buy and ship from Rubber Reserve present stocks in Brazil in order to liquidate our stocks first before new production is exported. We will also endeavor to arrange for the continuance of the system whereby we purchase all tires and resell to foreign or Brazilian buyers for exportation since Mr. Cooke has informed us that Brazil's production is approximately equivalent to total requirements of other Western Hemisphere Republics. To facilitate these discussions please cable third quarter allocations each Western Hemisphere Republic so far arranged and prospects arranging allocations any others.

If we are unable to make these arrangements suggested by Cooke then we recommend granting Brazil's request outlined in early part of this cable and subject to the conditions set forth, otherwise we fear the breakdown of the entire consumption agreement. [Allen, McAshan, Micou.]

SIMMONS

811.20 Defense (M) Brazil/959 : Telegram

The Secretary of State to the Ambassador in Brazil (Caffery)

WASHINGTON, August 12, 1942—10 p. m.

2251. Your despatch 8073, July 31,[66] and telegrams 2832, August 1 and 2855, August 3.[67] There are certain distinct and important advantages which the present arrangements on Brazilian manufactured products afford to Brazil. In the first place, Brazil is assured a market for these products for the term of the contract at a price fixed by Brazil. Under the arrangements now in effect Rubber Reserve has purchased almost 3 million dollars worth of Brazilian tires. Rubber Reserve pays cash immediately. The manufacturer does not have to wait for shipping to be available before getting his money. Rubber Reserve buys the tires and puts them in warehouses and pays the warehouse charges, an arrangement which permits normal operations by the manufacturers unaffected by the shipping situation.

---

[65] See telegram No. 640, March 13, 7 p. m., to the Ambassador in Brazil, p. 692.
[66] Not printed.
[67] Telegram No. 2855 not printed.

The manufacturers in turn are able to keep their workers steadily employed. They are assured a guaranteed market for 5 years, at a time when Brazil's consumption of tires has been tremendously reduced and when demand in the other countries cannot be considered assured. It seems to us unlikely that Brazil could obtain similar undertakings from other sources.

It should also be kept in mind that this Government is supplying to the manufacturers various materials required in tire manufacture, such as bead wire, which Brazil cannot obtain elsewhere. This Government is also giving sympathetic consideration to the application by the Goodyear Company of Brazil to export machinery for manufacturing rubber belting.

Acting in reliance on the arrangements worked out by Allen, and complied with in practice by the Brazilian authorities, Rubber Reserve has made commitments to furnish tires in specific amounts to Colombia, Peru and others. This Government also gave undertakings to all the other American Republics to supply their indispensable requirements for tires. See the Department's circular telegram of May 18.[68] These undertakings were entered into at the urgent request of the Brazilian Government, and it was assumed the exportable surplus of Brazilian tires would be available to fill them. Even if the understanding set forth in Allen's letter of May 2 [69] was not formally acknowledged, there can be no ambiguity about the meaning of paragraph 7 of the March 3 agreement, which Bouças advised had been cleared by telephone with President Vargas. Moreover, the second paragraph of Allen's memorandum handed to Souza Costa, Bouças and Truda on April 28 [70] leaves no doubt as to the intentions and understanding of this Government in making the arrangements proposed to Brazil.

Aside from the advantages of the present system to Brazil and without regard to its contractual status, the following considerations appear to us to make the abandonment of the present system inadvisable.

1. This Government has no desire to limit or interfere with Brazil's trade relations with the other American Republics, or to obtain control of any of those relations as such.

2. There is a limited and small amount of rubber products available for the indispensable needs of the American Republics. It is urgently necessary that the distribution of available supplies should be made equitably and based upon the essential wartime requirements of the countries.

---

[68] Printed in vol. VI, section under Colombia entitled "Negotiation of an agreement between the Rubber Reserve Company and Colombia for the purchase of Colombia's exportable surplus of rubber."

[69] See footnote 63, p. 708.

[70] Not found in Department files.

3. The Brazilian Government will appreciate that an equitable distribution can be attained only through the exercise of adequate controls. A particular purchaser should not get a disproportionate number of tires. Information as to sizes and types must be considered in each case to determine whether the order is justified. Sales should not be made to undesirable purchasers. Shipments should be arranged so as to coordinate available shipping space with consumption needs. Supplies should be integrated so as to make a pool available to meet orders for various sizes and types. Otherwise there will be inefficiency in filling orders. Rubber Reserve is prepared to create that pool and to maintain balanced inventories.

4. It has taken this Government 2 years to establish adequate controls for exports from this country. Operation under the control machinery is understood and accepted by the various importing countries.

5. The establishment of quotas for exports from Brazil without further implementation is not sufficient. It is extremely doubtful whether Brazil would strictly uphold the quota system under the stress of diplomatic or internal political pressure. In any event certain requirements for tires and other rubber products must be furnished from this country (including, in the case of Brazil, tires for airplanes and other equipment for the Brazilian armed forces) because they cannot be manufactured in Brazil. Information as to shipments from Brazil and the United States must be coordinated so as to be available in passing on any particular shipment from either country.

6. The contract now being negotiated with Mexico [71] contemplates that Mexico will sell to the United States its exportable surplus of manufactured products. Venezuela might conceivably become an exporter of tires. It is therefore quite clear that some single entity must administer the distribution of tires available for export from this country, Brazil, Mexico and any other exporting country.

7. A control system might be established in the Embassy, but this would result in duplication of personnel and in almost endless checking back and forth between the Embassy and the agencies here.

8. As a theoretical matter the administrative entity might best be an inter-American commission. It appears to us hopeless to expect that such a commission could function efficiently at any time in the near future. This Government is prepared to consider the establishment of such an agency if it is considered necessary. Until it is established, however, the disposition of tires from Brazil should remain subject to supervision by this Government, which is the only entity now in a position to provide that supervision.

9. The substance of the present arrangement is this: The Government of the country to which the tires are to be shipped issues a certificate of necessity to an importer in that country. The importer in turn forwards the certificate together with his order to an exporter either in Brazil or in this country. The exporter forwards an export application to the Office of Exports Control of the Board of Economic Warfare and if the order is approved Rubber Reserve sells the tires to the exporter who carries out the transaction with the importer.

---

[71] For correspondence concerning these negotiations, see vol. VI, section under Mexico entitled "Agreement between the Rubber Reserve Company and Mexico . . ."

The exporter thus has all the contacts with the importer in the normal commercial manner, the transaction merely being subject to approval of the export here not with respect to its business aspects but for the purpose of maintaining an equitable distribution of a scarce material.

You will note that orders can be placed either with Brazilian exporters or exporters in this country. The latter were included because importers of tires in the consuming countries were accustomed to deal with exporters in this country and Brazil has not heretofore been an exporter of tires. This latter fact of course means that it is not accurate for Brazil to talk about maintaining normal trade relations. Brazil actually wants to build up new relations; this Government naturally has no opposition to this objective. If agreement to continued purchase and distribution of Brazilian tires by Rubber Reserve could be achieved through exclusion of exporters in this country, that would not be an insurmountable obstacle providing orders already placed and accepted by Rubber Reserve from exporters in this country are executed.

If it would be more satisfactory to the Brazilian Government to have the application filed with the Rubber Reserve office in Rio de Janeiro, that would be entirely acceptable here. Of course in that event the application would be forwarded to the Board of Economic Warfare here for consideration.

Rubber Reserve would also be entirely agreeable to making available to the appropriate Brazilian agencies information as to orders received, shipments made, etc.

10. In order to avoid implications of the kind referred to in paragraph 9 of the note from the Foreign Office of July 25, 1942,[72] Brazil might notify the other Republics that the Governments of Brazil and of the United States have agreed that there would be available, in Brazil or in the United States, a specified quota for the next quarter and that such quotas might be obtained by following the procedure referred to above. In this way Brazil would get credit for supplying the needs and at the same time the orders would be subjected to the controls regarded here as necessary. Quotas for the next quarter have been sent with Rubber Reserve's letter of August 1 to McAshan.

11. The substance of the foregoing is that it is desirable to continue the present arrangements, possibly excluding exporters in this country from the procedure and possibly providing for the filing of applications with the Rubber Reserve office in Rio. It is felt here that a change to a quota system administered by Brazil will result in a complete breakdown in the conservation program now well under way in the other American Republics.

Please inform McAshan and Micou of foregoing. It is concurred in by Ambassador Caffery, Donnelly, Rubber Reserve and Board of Economic Warfare.

(Please repeat to Allen.)

HULL

---

[72] Not printed.

811.20 Defense (M) Brazil/1045 : Telegram

The Chargé in Brazil (Simmons) to the Secretary of State

RIO DE JANEIRO, August 15, 1942—7 p. m.
[Received 10:05 p. m.]

3069. For Cooke, Rubber Reserve, from McAshan. Refer today's telephone conversation. As result of numerous conferences Brazilian authorities, Souza Costa's Commission proposes to confirm in writing their full agreement to the terms and methods set out in our letter to them of August 10 (copy airmailed you August 10 [73]), provided that we agree to an exchange of notes between Brazilian Foreign Office and American Embassy, Rio, setting out following conditions:

(1) Rubber Reserve will indicate monthly to the Commission for the Control of the Washington Agreements [74] the quantities of tires available that may be exported to the American Republics.

(2) By mutual agreement, the Commission for the Control of the Washington Agreements and Rubber Reserve will determine the countries to which these exportations shall be made, with the establishment also of the respective quantities.

(3) The exportations shall be made directly from exporter to importer, that is, through the normal channels of trade.

(4) The Government of Brazil shall have the exclusive responsibility of making the communications to those interested governments with respect of the quotas granted to each of them.

(5) For other manufactured rubber products which are or come to be manufactured in Brazil the Governments of Brazil and the United States agree to establish a plan to supply the other countries of this hemisphere under the same conditions established for tires and tubes.

They further read us their proposed announcement approximate translation being as follows:

"In accordance with the rubber agreement between Brazil and the United States dated March 3 which gives the United States the right to purchase the entire exportable surplus of Brazilian crude and manufactured rubber, the Government of Brazil in cooperating with the United States has arranged to assume a part of the responsibility of supplying the essential requirements of other American countries for those rubber manufactured articles which can best be made in Brazil and best shipped from Brazil. Quantities of such articles are to be made now in advance on a quarterly basis to the countries of destination. The commitment for . . . . . quarter . . . . . year for shipment from Brazil to country will be . . . . . passenger tires and tubes and . . . . . truck tires and tubes."

[73] Not found in Department files.
[74] Organization established by the Brazilian Government to supervise the production and dispatch of strategic commodities to the United States.

Regarding condition number 2 above the Brazilian Commission has agreed verbally to a full clearance with Washington in advance in order to follow Washington's global allotment for each country less the quantity which can best be supplied from the United States instead of from Brazil. Although the Brazilian authorities have so far declined to put this specifically in the exchange of notes it may be possible to obtain such a commitment from them in a separate letter to our Embassy.

Regarding number 3 above the Brazilian Commission has agreed on the Certificates of Necessity procedure in Department's telegram 2251, August 12, provided certificates can be cleared through Rubber Reserve, Rio de Janeiro.

Micou has requested that above conditions particularly number 2 be cleared with Colonel Lord [75] and Peurifoy [76] for possible effect on Board of Economic Warfare program for allocating essential requirements to other American countries.

We would appreciate your clearing the above counterproposal with interested Agencies and Departments in Washington and telegraphing or telephoning your instructions. [McAshan.]

SIMMONS

811.20 Defense (M) Brazil/1084 : Telegram

The Chargé in Brazil (Simmons) to the Secretary of State

RIO DE JANEIRO, August 20, 1942—9 p. m.
[Received August 21—12 : 42 a. m.]

3166. For Cooke, Rubber Reserve, from McAshan. Discussed at length with Bouças late yesterday procedure for tire and tube exports. While he agrees to export price control and commits himself personally to accept allocations sent us in advance of each quarter by Washington, he cannot put in writing the fact that Brazil will follow quotas fixed by the United States only. Furthermore, Commission entirely unwilling to agree that Certificates of Necessity be sent from Rio de Janeiro to Washington for processing but insist this be done here between Rubber Reserve representatives and Commission, with which we are inclined to agree.

They want a formal meeting with us to conclude this whole procedure by Monday at latest. Are we authorized conclude arrangement based on above, further that exchange of notes per our telegram 3069, August 15, 7 p. m., will take place promptly between Brazilian Foreign Office and American Embassy, Rio? [McAshan.]

SIMMONS

---

[75] Col. Royal B. Lord, Assistant Director of the Board of Economic Warfare.
[76] John E. Peurifoy of the American Hemisphere Exports Office, Department of State.

811.20 Defense (M)/1084 : Telegram

The Secretary of State to the Ambassador in Brazil (Caffery)

Washington, August 21, 1942—11 p. m.

2396. For McAshan. Your letter 341, August 10,[77] and telegrams 3069, August 15, 3166, August 20. Following are conclusions after further discussions by Department, Board of Economic Warfare, Rubber Reserve and Donnelly, for which please try to secure Brazilian acceptance.

1st. If Brazilian tires are to be distributed equitably and on basis of indispensable needs, agreement on all transactions should be obtained from Washington. It is suggested that applications and orders be presented by the Commission for the control of the Washington Agreements to Rubber Reserve, Rio de Janeiro. The latter can then informally advise Rubber Reserve, Washington, by telegraph or otherwise, of facts necessary for passing judgment. The agreement between the two Governments need not, of course, refer to anything except approval by Rubber Reserve, Rio de Janeiro. It is believed here that, through special arrangements with Board of Economic Warfare, each transaction could be processed here within 48 hours after receipt. The reason for this procedure is that there is believed to be only insufficient information in Rio de Janeiro for adequate consideration of the applications to be expected. It does not have the names of people on the Proclaimed List in the other countries; this list changes from day to day. It is not in a position to pass on the importance of particular projects for which tires may be needed; Washington has detailed information as to the purpose and status of these projects.

2d. Washington should have the right to approve and if need be to direct allocations. It has made commitments to the other American Republics. A general commitment was made in the Department's circular telegram of May 18,[78] and in all agreements with the rubber producing countries this Government has agreed to use its best efforts to supply specified tonnages of rubber products. In addition this Government has agreed with certain of the countries to furnish specific numbers of tires. In the agreement with Colombia, for instance, this Government undertook to supply 20,000 tires immediately and 30,000 tires within a year. Emergency allocations were made to Peru, Chile and the Dominican Republic in specific amounts. In making these allocations this Government relied on the availability of Brazilian tires. What happens if the disposition of Brazilian tires is not in accord with our commitments?

---

[77] Not found in Department files.
[78] Printed in vol. VI, section under Colombia entitled "Negotiation of an agreement between the Rubber Reserve Company and Colombia . . ."

Further we do not know whether Brazil could withstand the anticipated diplomatic and domestic pressure, and believe that it may find it advantageous to be relieved from it.

We regret that it therefore seems impossible to concur in the proposed procedure. It is suggested that, if possible, you delay any final action until Donnelly's return; he is fully informed as to our position and concurs in it.

HULL

811.20 Defense (M) Brazil/1182 : Telegram

The Ambassador in Brazil (Caffery) to the Secretary of State

RIO DE JANEIRO, August 31, 1942—midnight.
[Received September 1—6 : 18 a. m.]

3343. For Levy,[79] Cooke, Bicknell, from Hays, Micou, McAshan. Bouças Commission agreed this evening to recommend to the Minister[s] of Foreign Affairs and Finance [80] an exchange of notes between the Brazilian Foreign Office and the American Embassy Rio as follows:

"1. Considering the Agreement of March 3, signed in Washington between Brazil and the United States, by which the American Government agreed to acquire from Brazil all of the exportable surplus of crude and manufactured rubber, and considering further that, within the spirit evidenced at the Third Conference of Foreign Ministers of the American Republics, there exists a necessity for real cooperation between all of the countries of the Americas, the Governments of Brazil and the United States resolve to establish, by mutual agreement, a system for determining the allocations for supplying tires and tubes to the nations of the Western Hemisphere;

2. For the purpose of taking care of the wartime requirements and having in mind the defense of the Americas, within an over-all plan of supply, the American Government, using the statistical services which it has at its disposal to determine the requirements of the American Republics, relative to tires and tubes, will propose to Brazil the allocations which Brazil should supply to the other American Republics;

3. On these conditions, periodically and by mutual agreement with the United States, Brazil will make known, directly, to the other interested countries the allocations fixed for each quarter;

4. Exportation will be made directly from exporter to importer, namely, in the normal channels of trade;

5. For the other rubber manufactured articles which are or may be produced in Brazil, the Governments of Brazil and the United States mutually agree to establish a place [*plan?*] for supplying the nations of this hemisphere following the same methods established for tires and tubes."

---

[79] Robert Levi, of the Board of Economic Warfare.
[80] Oswaldo Aranha and Arthur de Souza Costa, respectively.

We are not positive that the Minister of Foreign Relations will accept the last sentence of paragraph 2 quoted above, but the Control Commission is so recommending. May we confirm to them officially that you accept the above wording for an exchange of notes establishing the conditions governing the mechanics of the exportation of manufactured rubber products from Brazil under the main Rubber Agreement of March 3?

If so, please be prepared to cable us the allocations for the third and fourth quarters of 1942 covering tires and tubes to be supplied from Brazil to each other Western Hemisphere country, for prompt submission to the Brazilian authorities as soon as they confirm their acceptance.[81]

Bouças Commission has also agreed to write a separate letter confirming that Certificates of Necessity will be submitted to Rubber Reserve Rio for approval before any export permits will be granted, and Rubberrof [Rubber Reserve] Rio will have time to clear all such certificates with Washington by cable. Further, the Bouças Commission will confirm to us in that separate letter that exporters resale prices to other American countries will not be more than 10% above the price at which Rubber Reserve releases tires and tubes stocks to those exporters, both based f.o.b. steamer Brazilian ports. [Hays, Micou, McAshan.]

CAFFERY

811.20 Defense (M) Brazil/1355a : Telegram

The Secretary of State to the Ambassador in Brazil (Caffery)

WASHINGTON, September 15, 1942—10 p. m.

2721. It is considered urgent here that immediate agreement be reached with the Brazilian Government for the establishment of mutually satisfactory prices for the purchase of rubber products by the United States (presumably Rubber Reserve Company) as contemplated by paragraph 7 of the Rubber Agreement of March 3rd. Prices have been established for the purchase of tires but we think we should now endeavor to establish prices for other manufactured rubber products.

There has been correspondence between Korkegi [82] and Rubber Reserve regarding the problem of curtailing production of nonessential rubber products such as rubber thread, rubber toys and the like. The present object of the Rubber Reserve and BEW [83] is not only to obtain

---

[81] In telegram No. 2563, September 3, 1942, 10 p. m. (not printed), the Department transmitted the reply from the Rubber Reserve Company (811.20 Defense (M) Brazil/1182).

[82] Hani Jacob Korkegi, representative of the Rubber Reserve Company in Brazil.

[83] Board of Economic Warfare.

the cooperation of the Brazilian Government in the curtailment of the manufacture of nonessential rubber products but also to assist in the conversion of existing facilities to the production of essential rubber products. To this end Rubber Reserve stands ready to purchase existing surplus stocks of manufactured rubber products held by manufacturers and upon specific recommendations of the United States Purchasing Commission in Brazil, and assuming that such curtailment can be accomplished, Rubber Reserve will help in the conversion depending upon the merit in each case.

Some system of control should be established by the Brazilian Government to restrict so far as possible the manufacture of miscellaneous rubber goods except tires and the possible prohibition of the manufacture of nonessentials such as cut thread, toys and the like. It would seem appropriate that the Brazilian Government exercise the suggested control of the allocation of crude rubber to the manufacturers and that the appropriate agency of this Government assist in such control by the licensing of shipments of chemicals and supplies to such manufacturers from this country.

That this matter is of great urgency is shown by Korkegi's reports that the manufacture of non-essential rubber products in Brazil is definitely on the increase, as illustrated by an account of the increase of the production of rubber thread in the case of one manufacturer from 800 kilograms to 1400 kilograms per day, and that the present exportable surplus of rubber thread alone is estimated at 35 tons per month.

HULL

811.20 Defense (M) Brazil/1521

The Assistant Chief of the Division of Defense Materials (Cissel) to the Chief of the Division of the American Republics (Bonsal)

[WASHINGTON,] October 2, 1942.

MR. BONSAL: Telegram 3937, October 1 from Rio [84] requested that we telephone Donnelly and Russell [85] with respect to the tire and tube agreement. This was done this morning. Donnelly advised that they had had an extended conference with the Foreign Minister yesterday and had obtained complete agreement on the tire and tube contract in the form submitted by Allen with the changes requested in the Department's telegram of September 24.[86] Several additional changes were suggested by Aranha. Most important was as follows:

---

[84] Not printed.
[85] James A. Russell, official of the Rubber Reserve Company.
[86] Telegram No. 2827, not printed; in it the Department recommended a number of changes in the phraseology of the agreement (811.20 Defense (M) Brazil/1392).

The agreement now provides that 25% of tires manufactured in Brazil will be sold to the United States. Brazil wishes the right to increase or decrease this figure, so long as the manufacture does not exceed 10,000 tons. Donnelly stated that the Foreign Minister had made a very strong statement to the effect that strict conservation of tires would be instituted in Brazil and that in his opinion it is unwise to attempt to get a better arrangement on this point. In view of this and in view of the fact that the lack of petroleum has automatically reduced the use of tires in Brazil, it was decided to accept the proposal.

The other changes were accepted, and Donnelly was instructed, with the concurrence of Rubber Reserve Company, Board of Economic Warfare and myself on behalf of the Department, to proceed with the execution of the agreement,[87] which is expected this afternoon or tomorrow morning.

While the subject was not mentioned specifically, I gathered from the telephone conversation that any difficulty with respect to Bouças' proposed resignation had been eliminated.

832.796/1032 : Telegram

The Ambassador in Brazil (Caffery) to the Secretary of State

RIO DE JANEIRO, October 3, 1942—5 p. m.
[Received 11 p. m.]

3970. Department's 2894, September 30, 11 p. m.[88] As reported in my telegram 3841 of September 26, 5 p. m.,[88] permission was officially granted for route Miami–Manáos. No contract between Defense Supplies Corporation and Brazilian Government for this service is necessary, and Defense Supplies Corporation may proceed to make contract with carrier.

---

[87] Copies of the exchange of notes of October 3, 1942, between the American Ambassador in Brazil and the Brazilian Minister for Foreign Affairs which constituted the agreement were transmitted to the Department by the Ambassador in his despatch No. 8678, October 7, 1942, not printed. According to its terms the United States was to determine the allocation of tires and tubes for the other American Republics, and Brazil was to determine the portion she could supply and communicate the allocations to the other American Republics. The normal channels of trade were to be employed. In addition this agreement embodied a ratified form of agreement reached on April 30. According to the latter the essential requirements of Brazil, the United States, and the American Republics were to be provided by a reserve of 10,000 tons of crude rubber of which Brazil was entitled to 75% and from which Brazil was also entitled to acquire the quotas of the other American Republics for export to them. The Rubber Reserve Company was to purchase all tubes and tires not essential for internal consumption in Brazil. Brazil agreed to discontinue the manufacture of non-essential products. The United States was not to export to Brazil's neighbors. Efforts were to be made by Brazil to make extensive use of reclaimed rubber and by the United States to supply essential materials for the rubber manufacturers. (811.20 Defense (M) Brazil/1634)
[88] Not printed.

We are awaiting expected favorable action from Air Minister [89] on routes Pará–Iquitos and Manáos–Guajará Mirim. This will authorize Defense Supplies Corporation to contract with any Brazilian airline it desires for these routes. As in the case of the Manáos–Miami route no contract between the Defense Supplies Corporation and Brazilian Government is necessary.

As soon as the general agreement covering air transportation for the rubber program is approved (this will probably be delayed 1 week because of Air Minister's absence in Buenos Aires), the Ministry for Air will name officials in Rio de Janeiro and Manáos to work out details with appropriate officials of Defense Supplies Corporation and Rubber Reserve in these cities, on the basis of the general agreement. By details, are meant specific approval for the construction of airports at mutually selected sites, et cetera.

The entire matter of the agreement covering air transportation activities for the rubber program has been carried out directly by the Ministry for Air, as a step implementing the rubber agreement signed in Washington March 3. Ministry for Air and Finance Ministry believe that an exchange of notes between you and the Foreign Office is unnecessary, and Embassy believes insistence on such a procedure might complicate and delay matters.

A copy and translation of the draft agreement which has been favorably reported by the Director of Civil Aviation [90] (it is also agreeable to Bouças and the Minister of Finance), and is awaiting final sanction by the Minister for Air, is being forwarded by air mail today.[91]

CAFFERY

811.20 Defense (M) Brazil/1764a : Telegram

The Secretary of State to the Ambassador in Brazil (Caffery)

WASHINGTON, October 27, 1942—10 p. m.

3259. Your 4325 of October 22, 3 p. m.[92] The Department and the other interested agencies in Washington will be glad to examine jointly with the Brazilian and Uruguayan Governments the tire requirements of Uruguay as estimated by the Uruguayan authorities.

With regard to other countries such as Colombia, Venezuela, Peru, Ecuador and Bolivia the allocations were reached by agreement between the governments of those countries in each case with the United States.

---

[89] Joaquim Pedro Salgado Filho.
[90] Adroaldo Junqueira Ayres.
[91] In despatch No. 8652, October 3, 1942, not printed.
[92] Not printed.

The resentment in the other American republics arises from the delay in shipping the agreed allocations; this delay is caused solely by the protracted negotiations and delays in Rio. Argentina has offered gleefully to enter agreements to supply tires to Ecuador, etc. in case we fail to fulfill our obligations.

The Department understands that the Uruguayan case may be a special one, for political or other reasons of importance to Brazil; but before "reconsideration of the entire tire allocation plan" we would like to have specific information from you whether the Brazilian resentment is against the several bilateral tire allocation agreements, mentioned above; or whether you are recommending at the insistence of the Brazilian Government to scrap and negotiate again the agreement in the exchange of notes of October 3, 1942 (enclosures 4 and 8 of your despatch 8678 of October 7, 1942),[93] especially paragraphs 1 and 5.

The joint objective of the Brazilian and the United States Governments in the general agreement of March 3, 1942 and the manufactured rubber goods agreement of October 3, 1942 was to make the maximum of crucially needed rubber available to the joint war effort without sacrifice to the essential needs of the other American republics (which are to be supplied from the most accessible source).

You will, we are sure, understand why the Department is loath to have "the entire tire allocation plan" reconsidered. If, nevertheless, you still think the Brazilians have valid objections please furnish the Department the full story.

Hull

811.20 Defense (M) Brazil/1872 : Telegram

The Ambassador in Brazil (Caffery) to the Secretary of State

Rio de Janeiro, November 12, 1942—7 p. m.
[Received 9 : 55 p. m.]

4721. For Duggan.[94] My telegram No. 4608, November 7, 4 p. m.[95] The Venezuelan Ambassador called yesterday to say he had received a telegram from the President of Venezuela instructing him to arrange for the immediate shipment of tires and tubes to Venezuela. The Ambassador was surprised to learn from the Foreign Office that there was no allocation for his country for the fourth quarter and inquired if this was correct. I told him that one of my experts would call on him to explain the situation.

---

[93] See footnote 87, p. 719.
[94] Laurence Duggan, Adviser on Political Relations.
[95] Not printed.

The tire and tube situation here is unsatisfactory. It is evident that unless we can assure the Foreign Office that each American country has agreed to the allocation and that it is not unilateral action on our part, the Foreign Office will be under constant pressure from representatives of American Republics here and will not be in a position to justify the allocations. This may lead to the repudiation of the agreement to the extent that the Brazilian Government will authorize the exportation of tires and tubes to other countries independent of the allocations.

In Department's telegram 3021, October 10, 2 p. m.[96] it was implied that allocations of tires and tubes to a number of countries had either been reached by agreement or in the case of certain countries with whom the United States has rubber agreements, the allocation represented the amount stimulated [*stipulated*] in such agreement to cover internal consumption. If such is the case it is amply apparent from statements made by the Ambassadors of these countries in Brazil that neither they nor their Governments understand the situation.

Aside from its effects on Brazil, it would seem desirable that the United States endeavor to arrive at allocations by consultation and agreement with each country.

Aranha has instructed the Commission for Control of Washington Agreements to "insist with the American authorities here" that Uruguay and Venezuela receive allocations for the fourth quarter for 4,000 and 5,000 tires and tubes respectively.

I have observed an increasing resentment on the part of my American colleagues here to what they call "arbitrary" action of our Government in dictating the allocations and products they may receive from Brazil.

CAFFERY

811.20 Defense (M) Brazil/1908 : Telegram

The Ambassador in Brazil (Caffery) to the Secretary of State

RIO DE JANEIRO, November 16, 1942—6 p. m.
[Received 11 : 18 p. m.]

4784. My telegram No. 2237, June 26, 4 p. m.[96] Souza Costa told me yesterday that Aranha is determined to ship the 600 tons of crude rubber to Chile which he promised the Chilean Government during the Pan-American Conference here in January and which he alleges was approved by our Government; also that the Chilean Embassy here has already acquired 90 tons for prompt shipment to Chile. Costa said he had strongly opposed the proposed sale of the rubber

---

[96] Not printed.

to Chile on the ground that it violated the rubber agreement with the United States, but that Aranha has taken the position that it is an agreement between two governments and that he as Minister of Foreign Affairs committed the Brazilian Government and that therefore Costa as Minister of Finance has nothing to do with it.

Aranha told Souza Costa that he would resign rather than to break his agreement with Chilean Government. We are reliably informed that the Chileans have had no success in buying additional crude rubber in Brazil and that Aranha is so aroused he might even compel firms to meet the requirements of Chile. Allen and I have reviewed the situation and feel that we should obtain factual information regarding the crude rubber requirements of Chile and recent purchases of crude rubber by Chile from Bolivia and other countries. If we can clearly establish that Chile's requirements of crude rubber taking into consideration the consumption of manufacturing equipment now available there does not exceed 100 tons annually which is Allen's recollection, we could use this point most effectively in our discussion with Aranha and follow up with the obvious observation that the excess of 500 tons might find its way into Argentina or be exchanged for Argentine tires and tubes or other essential products. It would assist if we could assure Aranha that Chile has been given a specific assurance that their essential requirements of tires and tubes will be supplied from the United States or Brazil. These points could be used to supplement our basic contention that in the absence of any specific exception in the basic rubber agreement of March 3, 1942, that any outstanding commitments on that date on the part of Brazil were nullified.

I have no recollection of the United States Government at any time giving its express or implied approval to the reported transaction between Brazil and Chile, but I would like to have the Department's specific assurance in this regard.

CAFFERY

811.20 Defense (M) Brazil/1908 : Telegram

The Secretary of State to the Ambassador in Brazil (Caffery)

WASHINGTON, November 24, 1942—9 p. m.

3672. Embassy's 4784, November 16. Chile's stocks crude rubber recently estimated 400 to 500 tons. Pre-war normal consumption was approximately 400 tons per year including many nonessential items production of which is no longer permitted in this country and is discouraged in Brazil. It is estimated here that Chile's requirements crude rubber for essentials do not exceed 200 tons per year including 35 tons for retreading. Chile is not to receive machinery from this country for manufacture of tires. Department is telegraphing Santiago to check Washington's requirement estimates and details of Chile's recent imports. This information will be telegraphed to you. In any case, it would be deplorable were Chile to receive additional 600 tons from Brazil, an excess which no doubt would be re-exported to Argentina as evidenced by a pending transaction in which Corporación de Fomento, Chile, is to supply crude rubber to Pirelli,[98] Argentina and receive a return of 50 percent by weight in bicycle tires. Assurance to supply Chile's essential requirements conveyed to Chile in Department's circular telegram of May 18,[99] and reiterated in Department's telegram to our Embassy which announced third quarter emergency allocation available from Brazil, stating that orders placed under this allocation would supersede orders previously placed in Brazil. An attempt will be made to reach an understanding with Chilean authorities regarding Chile's rubber requirements and use this understanding as basis for future allocations.

You have Department's assurance that this government at no time approved sale of rubber by Brazil to Chile except to fulfill Chile's essential wartime requirements under the usual allocation procedure.

HULL

811.20 Defense (M) Brazil/2045½

Memorandum by Mr. Arthur A. Compton, Division of the American Republics, to the Adviser on Political Relations (Duggan)

[WASHINGTON,] December 1, 1942.

MR. DUGGAN: At your request I have gone over the attached material [1] relating to the arrangements we have under our various rubber agreements to supply the needs of the other American republics for raw rubber or rubber manufactured goods. Although incomplete, the attached material reveals a story somewhat as follows:

1. Immediately after the basic rubber agreement of March 3 with Brazil, the United States was compelled to purchase all of the existing stocks and future output of manufactured rubber from Brazil in order to prevent a big boom in Brazilian rubber maufacture and indiscriminate export to the other American republics. In the specific negotiations for this purchase and contract, it was agreed that exportable surpluses of tires, tubes, and miscellaneous rubber goods should be used (at least in part) for supplying the essential requirements for these items to the other American republics as agreed in the contracts made with other rubber producing countries in the hemi-

---

[98] An industrial firm composed of a considerable network of companies in several countries.

[99] Printed in vol. VI, section under Colombia entitled "Negotiation of an agreement between the Rubber Reserve Company and Colombia . . ."

[1] Not attached to file copy of memorandum.

sphere. In consideration of this provision, Brazil agreed to reduce its rubber manufacture and its internal consumption of manufactured rubber goods in order to leave more raw rubber for export to the United States.

2. It was then agreed that the method of supplying the essential needs of the other American republics for raw and manufactured rubber from both the United States and Brazil would be as follows:

(*a*) The United States would determine, on the basis of the statistics available to it, the quarterly allocations of manufactured rubber goods to supply the essential needs of the other American republics.

(*b*) Brazil would announce these allocations, and

(*c*) the other American republics could then proceed to purchase (within the allocation announced) from either the United States or Brazil, their essential manufactured rubber goods through the regular commercial channels.

(*d*) Control over these purchases is to be maintained through clearance with the Rubber Reserve Company in Washington of all purchases from either Brazil or the United States (the actual granting of the certificate permitting export being in the hands of the government of the country from which the rubber is to be exported.)

3. The foregoing procedures have given rise to the difficulties outlined in the Ambassador's telegrams 4325 of October 22, 3 p. m.[2] and 4721 of November 12, 7 p. m., directed to you personally. It is my feeling that although both internal Brazilian politics and politics played by the other American republics have a large part in these difficulties, the major problems would be solved if we could accomplish two things:

(*a*) It is necessary to make available to the Brazilian Government the information used in arriving at the allocations established by us for the other American republics in order that the Brazilian Government may be in a position to defend these allocations (which *they* announce) against the inroads of political pressure from the other American republics.

(*b*) It is further of the greatest importance in reducing the political pressure from the other Americas (which thrives and grows on misunderstandings and delays) to provide for the complete and definite understanding (as far in advance as possible) by each of the other Americas of the quarterly allocations applying to them, and to provide to the greatest extent possible for the rapid and efficient delivery of the rubber purchased by each of the other Americas under these allocations.

4. Although I am not in a position to recommend the specific technical details of how these ends should be accomplished, I would recommend by way of suggestion that every consideration be given to the following possibilities:

---

[2] Not printed.

(*a*) The establishment in Washington of a joint Brazilian-United States rubber commission, which among other things would serve the following purposes:

i. It would serve as a source of information to the Brazilian Government on the statistics and considerations involved in arriving at the final rubber allocations so that the Brazilian Government would be in a position to defend these allocations which they are now obliged to announce, and

ii. It would serve also as a body which could arbitrate any difficulties or differences of opinion as to these allocations which may be raised in Brazil by any of the other American republics. (In this connection any statistics available to Brazil which do not coincide with ours would be useful in bringing to light any possible misinformation on which our own statistics may be based.)

(*b*) The careful consideration is strongly urged of the possibility of consulting the governments of the other American republics as to what they believe their essential rubber requirements are. These estimates and their justifications could then be examined in the light of the information available to the United States (supplemented by any information available to Brazil) and altered or cut down accordingly. This procedure would, to my way of thinking, put us in a much firmer position as regards our justification for "dictating" to the other Americas what their needs are. They would then at least feel that they had had a chance to present their story. This, to me, seems most important.

(*c*) The working out of a clear procedure for the joint announcement by the United States and Brazil (perhaps by the suggested joint commission) of the quarterly allocations applying to each of the other Americas in such a way that no misunderstanding will be possible as to the actual amounts of these allocations and as much explanation thereof as may be possible in order to satisfy any complaints which may be received with respect to these allocations.

(*d*) The provision in so far as possible of a clearly understood and efficiently operating delivery service both from the United States and from Brazil for the rubber goods purchased under these rubber allocations.

NOTE: The foregoing comments are intended to apply to the ultimate ironing out of the long-range difficulties which seem to be involved in the present rubber arrangements. As regards the specific problems of Uruguay, Venezuela, Chile, etc. raised in Ambassador Caffery's wires to you, I believe they will have to be ironed out as well as may be possible by whatever specific action can be taken immediately.

In this connection it is interesting to note that we are not even sure that all of the announcements of the fourth quarter allocations have yet been made even though we are now entering into the last month of the fourth quarter. It is further pointed out that deliveries have not yet been made on all of the third quarter allocations. Such delays have lent fuel to the present flare-up and serve to emphasize the necessity of immediate and farsighted action to apply to the announcement and prompt delivery of the allocations for the forthcoming year. Actually these announcements should already have been made and each day that goes by creates increased potential difficulties for next year.

811.20 Defense (M) Brazil/2243a : Telegram

The Secretary of State to the Ambassador in Brazil (Caffery)

WASHINGTON, December 26, 1942—4 p. m.

4060. For Russell, Donnelly, from Allen. This will confirm telephone conversation advising you that the text of the agreement between Rubber Reserve and Semta [3] had been approved by Board of Economic Warfare, Rubber Reserve and State Department with the few slight changes given you over the telephone and authorizing you to sign the agreement. We also confirm authority to provide up to $150,000 for construction of reception and other facilities for whatever organization of the Brazilian Government undertakes the responsibility of caring for and placing the labor transported into the Amazon by Semta. You are also authorized to purchase up to 25,000 tons of staple foodstuffs to create a food reserve in the Amazon. You are also authorized to lease such additional storage facilities at Belém, Manáos or other points on the Amazon for storage of the foodstuffs, rubber supplies and equipment. Suggest endeavor to transport to the Amazon not less than 15,000 tons of foodstuffs within the next 30 days and the entire quantity by February 15. We have discussed with João Alberto [4] the equipment needed for the movement of 50,000 workmen by Semta and their transportation on the Tocantins River and we have arranged here for a large number of shallow draft boats suitable for transporting labor which can be used on the Tocantins and also on the São Francisco and Parnahyba Rivers. I am planning to arrive in Belém around January 1st or 2d and João Alberto is planning to arrive around January 8 and expects to spend a few days at Belém. Suggest desirability of Bouças and Doria being available at Belém at that time. [Allen.]

HULL

---

[3] The agreement between the Rubber Reserve Company and Semta (the Brazilian organization for the mobilization of workers of the Amazon) provided that the latter assemble at Belém, Pará, 50,000 rubber workers at the expense of the Rubber Reserve Company; text of the agreement is quoted in Embassy's telegram No. 5334, December 15, 1942, not printed.

[4] João Alberto Lins de Barros, Brazilian Coordinator of Economic Mobilization.

811.20 Defense (M) Brazil/2130 : Telegram

The Secretary of State to the Ambassador in Brazil (Caffery)

WASHINGTON, December 26, 1942—7 p. m.

4063. Embassy's 5334, December 15.[5] Department approves the form of agreement with the changes agreed upon by Allen and Donnelly in telephone conversation on December 17.

Before operations are undertaken under the agreement, it is believed advisable that Embassy secure clear understanding of the following matters:

(1) As to the methods that will be used for recruiting the labor in question.

(2) As to the fact that the labor obtained shall be placed in employment through an agency of the Brazilian Government and that the Brazilian Government will hold itself responsible for the working conditions of the laborers and the terms of the labor contracts that may be entered into. These of course should be discussed with the Rubber Reserve Company.

(3) That the Brazilian Government will take all necessary measures to see that suitable reception and arrangements are worked out for handling the laborers upon their arrival in Belém and their eventual placement in the producing areas with such financial and technical advice from the Rubber Reserve as may be requested.

The Department's approval of the arrangement is based on the belief that the rubber shortage is so serious and has such military importance as to justify emergency arrangements of this kind. Nevertheless it is felt that the local representatives of the Rubber Reserve Company must follow its execution extremely closely and that the Embassy should at all times keep itself fully informed and satisfy itself that this whole program is being carried out in such a way as to avoid the grave consequences which might otherwise ensue.

HULL

811.20 Defense (M) Brazil/2236 : Telegram

The Ambassador in Brazil (Caffery) to the Secretary of State

RIO DE JANEIRO, December 28, 1942—6 p. m.
[Received 8 : 45 p. m.]

5509. Department's 4063 December 6 [*26*], 7 p. m.

(1) The laborers will be recruited by Semta. Brazilian Government officials are now organizing the program.

(2) The Brazilian Government will be responsible for the working conditions of the laborers, the terms of labor contracts, et cetera, and the laborers will be placed in employment through an agency of the

---

[5] Not printed.

Brazilian Government. All of these points have been cleared with the Rubber Reserve Company.

(3) Reception facilities, housing, supplies of foodstuffs, medicines, et cetera, at Pará will be handled by agencies of the Brazilian Government and the Rubber Reserve's responsibility will be restricted to financial and technical advice as may be requested. The Embassy and the Rubber Reserve Company here will follow the execution of the plan extremely closely. A representative of the Rubber Reserve will make periodic trips to the labor recruiting areas, Belém and the Amazon River and will keep the Embassy currently informed of the progress of the work.

CAFFERY

811.20 Defense (M) Brazil/1908 : Telegram

The Secretary of State to the Ambassador in Brazil (Caffery)

WASHINGTON, January 12, 1943—6 p. m.

122. Department's 3672, November 24. Department has been advised by Embassy at Santiago that 50,247 kilograms washed crude rubber arrived Valparaiso December 13, consigned to Corporación de Fomento, shipped from Santos, Brazil, November 17, by Arthur Dianna y Compañia Limitada.

The Department's information on Chile's crude rubber supply and demand was contained in Department's 3672, November 24.

The shipment referred to is in violation of the rubber agreement. As indicated in Department's 3672 it consists of rubber not needed by Chile and at least part of which will probably reach Argentina in finished form.

Under the circumstances you are requested to take the matter up with the Minister of Foreign Affairs expressing the view that the shipment violated the rubber agreement and protesting such violation, especially when Chile has no justifiable need for the rubber and when Brazil and this Government have undertaken to supply and are supplying Chile's needs for tires and other rubber products.

HULL

AGREEMENT BETWEEN THE UNITED STATES AND BRAZIL PROVIDING FOR THE DEVELOPMENT OF FOODSTUFFS PRODUCTION, SIGNED SEPTEMBER 3, 1942

[For text of the agreement, signed at Rio de Janeiro, see Department of State Executive Agreement Series No. 302, or 56 Stat. (pt. 2) 1875.]

EFFORTS OF THE UNITED STATES TO SECURE FAIR PARTICIPATION WITH BRAZIL IN THE CANADIAN COTTON MARKET

(See under Canada, Volume I, pages 565–586.)

DISCUSSIONS BETWEEN THE UNITED STATES AND BRAZIL CONCERNING SHIPPING PROBLEMS

800.8830/1380 : Telegram

The Ambassador in Brazil (Caffery) to the Secretary of State

RIO DE JANEIRO, February 7, 1942—2 p. m.
[Received 2 : 57 p. m.]

375. My telegram No. 4, January 1, 8 p.m.[6] Dr. Herbert Moses, President of the Brazilian Press Association, strongly urges quick action in obtaining shipments of newsprint for Brazilian newspapers. He says that situation of *A Noite*, Government-sponsored paper, is acute, and the *Jornal do Commercio* will have to close unless it receives newsprint within 25 days. Further that he had been informed that newsprint loaded on Lloyd Brasileiro ships in New York had been removed on orders of our Maritime Commission. Our investigations reveal that supplies of newsprint here are very low.

CAFFERY

800.8830/1380 : Telegram

The Secretary of State to the Ambassador in Brazil (Caffery)

WASHINGTON, February 10, 1942—7 p. m.

316. Your 375, February 7, 2 p. m. The Maritime Commission has issued no such orders as those mentioned in your telegram under reference.

The Maritime Commission informs the Department that 100 tons of newsprint for the *Jornal do Commercio* is on a Lloyd Brasileiro boat which departed in January. Lloyd Brasileiro now carrying approximately 600 tons of newsprint on each of its ships sailing from the United States. The Maritime Commission gives assurances that it will attempt to transport the requirements of *A Noite, Jornal do Commercio* and other Brazilian papers if you will send immediately a report giving the present status of all outstanding Brazilian orders for newsprint.

Maritime Commission informed that paper supplies for Brazil are utilizing shipping space allocated to fill 1941 orders.

HULL

---

[6] Not printed.

832.8595/1 : Telegram

The Ambassador in Brazil (Caffery) to the Secretary of State

RIO DE JANEIRO, March 11, 1942—5 p. m.
[Received 6 : 35 p. m.]

797. Aranha [7] tells me that the Government has ordered all Brazilian boats to take refuge in nearest ports. He says that they will arm those in Brazilian ports. He asks if we can do anything about helping to arm those in United States ports.

CAFFERY

832.8595/1 : Telegram

The Acting Secretary of State to the Ambassador in Brazil (Caffery)

WASHINGTON, March 14, 1942—midnight.

656. Your 797, March 11, 5 PM and 830 March 12, 8 PM.[8] The Maritime Commission will be pleased to arm the six Brazil merchant ships now in United States ports and the two ships due shortly. As soon as these have been armed it will be glad to continue to arm Brazilian ships at the rate of four per month if the Brazilian Government desires us to do so and is willing to send them to the United States ports indicated by our naval authorities. Payment for this can be made in cash or taken out of Brazil's lend-lease appropriation.[9]

The Ambassador and his Naval Attaché [10] have been informed in the premises and are requesting instructions. It would be desirable for them to be authorized to handle the matter with the Maritime Commission and other authorities rather than for the authority to be given to the Lloyd Brasileiro.

Although the Maritime Commission has shown the greatest reluctance to consider providing gun crews for these ships I am prepared to take the matter up on the basis of providing gun crews for these ships on the southbound trips to Brazil. Thereafter, of course, it will be the responsibility of the Brazilian Government to provide gun crews. I have informed Martins in this sense.

WELLES

---

[7] Oswaldo Aranha, Brazilian Minister for Foreign Affairs.
[8] Latter not printed.
[9] For correspondence on the negotiation of the Lend-Lease Agreement between the United States and Brazil, signed October 1, 1941, see *Foreign Relations*, 1941, vol. VI; for text of further agreement, signed March 3, 1942, see *post*, p. 815.
[10] Carlos Martins and Comdr. Edmundo Jordão Amorim do Valle, respectively.

832.8595/4 : Telegram

The Ambassador in Brazil (Caffery) to the Secretary of State

RIO DE JANEIRO, March 16, 1942—7 p. m.
[Received 8:45 p. m.]

888. For the Acting Secretary. My 855, March 13, 10 p. m.[11] Aranha keeps after me as to what we are doing to insure maritime communications.

CAFFERY

832.8595/4 : Telegram

The Acting Secretary of State to the Ambassador in Brazil (Caffery)

WASHINGTON, March 27, 1942—midnight.

807. Your 888, March 16, 7 p. m. Navy Department states that it has cabled the Naval Attaché of your Embassy [12] to offer to the Brazilian authorities all practicable assistance in routing Brazilian merchant vessels en route to the United States.

At present the British Naval Control Service is routing all Brazilian merchant ships whose masters so request. However, the United States Navy is assigning officers to all principal ports in the other American republics with instructions to be prepared to assume full control of routing in this area about July 1. In the meantime United States Naval Attachés and Observers in such ports as they are stationed will be glad to render any available assistance of this kind.

WELLES

800.6363/618a : Telegram

The Acting Secretary of State to the Ambassador in Brazil (Caffery)

WASHINGTON, April 18, 1942—9 p. m.

1016. For military reasons tanker sailings from Gulf and Caribbean points to the East Coast of the United States and the East Coast of South America are being cancelled. The duration of this measure cannot be stated at the present time but may extend over a period of from a month to 6 weeks. Studies are now under way to determine the adequacy of stocks of petroleum products in the country to which you are accredited and when these studies are completed the best means of meeting emergency requirements during the period mentioned will be communicated to you.

Pending the receipt of this fuller information and instructions, you should use the foregoing information only if absolutely necessary in your confidential discussions with Government officials.

WELLES

---

[11] Not printed.
[12] Rear Adm. Augustin T. Beauregard.

832.852/23 : Telegram

The Ambassador in Brazil (Caffery) to the Secretary of State

RIO DE JANEIRO, June 3, 1942—8 p. m.
[Received 8 : 55 p. m.]

1886. The Foreign Office has received a telegram from the Brazilian Embassy in Washington stating that the United States Government is interested in renting the Lloyd Brasileiro ships capable of operating between Brazil and the United States. Also that the Brazilian ships would use Brazilian crews and Brazilian flag. The Embassy further stated that our Government would insure the ships and reimburse Brazilian Government for any losses.

The Foreign Office is telegraphing today accepting proposal in principle.

CAFFERY

800.8830/1601 : Telegram

The Ambassador in Brazil (Caffery) to the Secretary of State

RIO DE JANEIRO, June 6, 1942—2 p. m.
[Received 2 : 45 p. m.]

1916. My despatch 7478 [*7477*], May 29.[13] President Vargas has sent me word through his secretary of his particular desire to ameliorate newsprint situation. He has requested that our Maritime Commission give this matter special and urgent attention.

CAFFERY

800.8830 Brazil/38a : Telegram

The Secretary of State to the Ambassador in Brazil (Caffery)

WASHINGTON, June 8, 1942—9 p. m.

1464. The following is our tentative southbound shipping program to Brazil:

Coal

The War Shipping Administration will attempt to provide space for 50,000 tons of coal a month to Brazil. It will be incumbent upon Brazilian shipping to move an additional 25,000 tons a month. The Department estimates that this amount of coal from the United States will be adequate for Brazilian requirements if ore movement over Central do Brasil is reduced and if other economies are made in the use of coal. Your comments on this estimate would be appreciated. We shall also make efforts to have the British divert some coal shipments to Brazil. Deadweight tonnage available for coal from the United States for the present month is approximately 76,000.

---

[13] Not printed.

Other Dry Cargo

Shipping available for other dry cargo to Brazil is approximately 39,800 deadweight tons. Assuming that 75 percent of this figure represents cargo carrying capacity, the Department has suggested to the Maritime Commission that the resulting 30,000 tons be apportioned in the following manner: iron and steel, 25.8 percent; tinplate, 10.0; newsprint, 13.3; wood pulp, 10.0; machinery, 4.1; copper and brass, 1.6; naval stores, 4.1; sulphur, 2.0; caustic soda and soda ash, 4.1; fertilizers, 3.7; other essentials, 21.3.

Your comments on the above would be appreciated and should be in the Department not later than June 10. Should you differ substantially with the Department's estimates, corrective measures can be applied by the W.S.A. during the remainder of the month. At the same time, please indicate applicability of tonnage allocation and percentage distribution to July shipments.

Our understanding is that five Brazilian ships will leave for United States ports in June. Thirteen United States or United States-controlled vessels are allocated to this trade.

HULL

832.852/23 : Telegram

The Secretary of State to the Ambassador in Brazil (Caffery)

WASHINGTON, June 11, 1942—10 p. m.

1500. Your 1886, June 3, 8 p. m. The Brazilian Government has informed Martins that it desires to have negotiations for these vessels carried on through you. All concerned here agree. To assist you in conducting these negotiations, the War Shipping Administration and the Department are sending representatives to Rio. You will be advised later of the exact date of their departure.

Referring to Department's circular telegram 1366 of May 27, 6 p. m.,[14] the above-named representatives will be prepared to discuss with you the present status of the plans mentioned therein.

HULL

832.852/23 : Telegram

The Secretary of State to the Ambassador in Brazil (Caffery)

WASHINGTON, June 18, 1942—midnight.

1588. Department's 1500, June 11, 10 p. m. Mr. Myron L. Black and Mr. Jack C. Corbett representing the War Shipping Administration and the Department, respectively, will depart from Miami by plane on June 20 for Rio. Mr. E. G. Rose, War Shipping Ad-

---

[14] Not printed.

ministration's marine surveyor, will arrive sometime later from Venezuela.

Please arrange for single room accommodations at Copacabana-Palace for Black and Corbett.

HULL

800.8830/1639

The Ambassador in Brazil (Caffery) to the Secretary of State

No. 7751

RIO DE JANEIRO, June 24, 1942.
[Received June 30.]

SIR: I have the honor to report, as of possible interest to the Department, that the Canadian Trade Commissioner, Mr. Glass, told me on June 23 that he had received a confidential telegram from his government in Ottawa stating that six Lloyd Brasileiro ships are now in southern United States ports and are refusing to accept newsprint that is available for loading there because the freight rates on newsprint are lower than on other cargo. Mr. Glass also said that these ships are supposed to lift 600 tons of newsprint on each voyage.

He is now trying to check this information with local sources.

Respectfully yours,

For the Ambassador:
JOHN F. SIMMONS
Counselor of Embassy

800.6363/716 : Telegram

The Secretary of State to the Ambassador in Brazil (Caffery)

WASHINGTON, June 26, 1942—5 p. m.

1680. Your 1909, June 5.[15] Department has today requested Petroleum Supply Committee for Latin America to regard all petroleum products necessary in connection with production and transportation of raw rubber in Brazil, including transportation of food or other supplies for maintenance of communities or areas essential to maximum rubber production, as war essential in the sense in which this term is used in paragraph 4 (*b*) of Department's circular cable of May 2, 1942.[15] Department suggested that Supply Committee request the Pool Committee [16] in Brazil to make estimate of the types and quantities of petroleum products required in the services just mentioned as a basis for furnishing these supplies in addition to the

[15] Not printed.
[16] See section entitled "Proposal by the United States for the control of the distribution of petroleum products among the American Republics," *Foreign Relations*, 1941, vol. VI.

normal pool supplies which are now subject to rationing. You should give the Pool Committee all assistance possible in this connection.

You should inform the Brazilian Government of this action and state that supplies of petroleum products now on hand may be utilized in the services described to the full extent necessary in security maximum raw rubber for the United Nations and that quantities of oil thus used will be replaced without penalty to regular pool supplies.

For your information there is a committee here on which are represented various agencies of this government including this Department which deals with the classification of requirements for petroleum products from the standpoint of importance to the war effort.

While the Department appreciates the difficulties which confront you in adequately explaining to the Brazilian Government the problems of oil supply it is requested that you do not commit this government to guaranteeing full oil supplies for any class of consumption except when specifically authorized to do so. The reason for this is that rapidly changing war conditions require corresponding reappraisals of the relative essentiality of oil consuming services and the presently critical tanker situation makes it imperative that oil transportation be kept in close adjustment with the demands of highest priority.

Hull

800.6363/786 : Telegram

The Secretary of State to the Ambassador in Brazil (Caffery)

Washington, June 29, 1942—midnight.

1721. When you communicate to the Government of Brazil Department's circular telegram of this date [17] you should state in addition that this Government has in mind the importance to the war effort of certain oil consuming activities in Brazil in addition to those already included in the war essential category for which full oil supplies are furnished. One example of such consideration on the part of this Government is seen in Department's telegram 1680, June 26, in which assurance is given of intention to supply the full requirements of petroleum products necessary for maximum production and transportation of raw rubber. This Government is awaiting the arrival of General Barbosa [18] for discussion of other oil consuming activities which should similarly be classified as war essential.

Despite these efforts on the part of this Government to alleviate the burden which world wide tanker shortage has brought upon Brazil it

---

[17] Not printed; in this telegram the Department warned that tanker shortage was not temporary and that domestic consumption of oil and gasoline must be reduced (800.6363/775a).

[18] Gen. Horta Barbosa, President of the Brazilian National Petroleum Council.

must be noted that the record of gasoline consumption within Brazil during the first 4 months of this year in comparison with consumption during the same period in 1941 does not indicate that any effective measures were taken by the Brazilian Government during the early part of this year to conserve this important product. On the contrary the figures available to this Government show that the use of gasoline during that 4 month period was 4.3 per cent greater in 1942 than in 1941 instead of approximately 20 per cent less as had been recommended by this Government.

The Department has observed with satisfaction that conservation measures recently introduced have reversed this trend and the month of May shows a substantial reduction in gasoline use although the first 5 months total is still approximately the same as the corresponding total in 1941.

The Department is confident that the commendable program of conservation indicated by the reduced consumption in May will be continued and intensified in order that the civilian supplies during the remainder of 1942, at less than one half the 1941 rate, will not critically disturb the national economy. In stating that no improvement in the oil transportation situation is foreseen earlier than the end of this year the Department does not magnify the seriousness of the tanker shortage.   HULL

832.6363/428 : Telegram

The Ambassador in Brazil (Caffery) to the Secretary of State

RIO DE JANEIRO, June 30, 1942—3 p. m.
[Received 4 : 12 p. m.]

2294. Aranha told me this morning that the President called him in yesterday on the gasoline situation: The President said Horta Barbosa had informed him that it would be necessary to lay up all private cars in Brazil at once; there is no diesel oil; fuel oil is practically exhausted, et cetera, et cetera.

CAFFERY

832.852/35 : Telegram

The Ambassador in Brazil (Caffery) to the Secretary of State

RIO DE JANEIRO, July 21, 1942—5 p. m.
[Received 9 : 28 p. m.]

2638. Department's 1957, July 19, 1942.[19] Negotiations are progressing satisfactorily. We have postponed discussion of details of commodities pending definite agreement on ships. Conversations

---

[19] Not printed.

envisage charter of at least 13 ships and operation of not less than 28 additional ships between Brazil and the United States. Aranha and Souza Costa [20] at first held out for right of Brazilian Government to load M–63 products on 28 ships regardless of our shipping priority list, but when I refused to yield they agreed to give preference to strategic materials.

Aranha stated again that President Vargas is disposed to make available to President Roosevelt several Brazilian passenger ships as troop transports. He has asked me to write him a letter indicating President Roosevelt's interest in the matter. Does the Department approve? [21]

Aranha and Souza Costa are anxious to conclude the negotiations promptly and to give nation-wide publicity to the commodity program and only brief and general reference to the ships. They see in the commodity program a means of strengthening their political positions which are insecure as a result of the recent political developments here. I told Aranha that I would inform Department regarding the publicity program. What are the Department views?

CAFFERY

800.8830 Brazil/64a : Telegram

The Secretary of State to the Ambassador in Brazil (Caffery)

WASHINGTON, July 22, 1942—midnight.

1999. Up to July 22, bookings have been arranged on ships sailing in July for 2,875 tons of newsprint destined to Brazil.

HULL

800.85/725b : Telegram

The Secretary of State to the Ambassador in Brazil (Caffery)

WASHINGTON, July 31, 1942—1 p. m.

2096. As the Embassy is no doubt aware, the vessel *Esmeralda* [22] is presently immobilized in the port of Pernambuco. This was the former Roumanian vessel *Oltul*, the name of which is contained in the list of immobilized vessels which was a part of the plan agreed to by the Inter-American Economic and Financial Advisory Committee on August 28, 1941. [23] In addition to the *Esmeralda*, the *Tropicus*, pres-

---

[20] Arthur de Souza Costa, Brazilian Minister of Finance.
[21] The Department indicated approval of the proposed letter in its telegram No. 2006 of July 23, 1942 (832.852/35).
[22] See telegram No. 1563, October 17, to the Ambassador in Argentina, p. 417.
[23] For correspondence concerning the resolution and plan of this committee, see *Foreign Relations*, 1941, vol. VI, section entitled "Resolution and plan of the Inter-American Financial and Economic Committee . . ."

ently in the United States, and the *Omega*, now in Lisbon, are owned by the same person. The United States is requisitioning the *Tropicus* and is asking Panamá to requisition the *Omega*. You are instructed to bring the question of the vessel *Esmeralda* to the attention of the Minister of Foreign Affairs, to inform him of the action which this Government has taken with reference to the other vessels mentioned, and suggest that it would be advisable in the interests of all concerned for the Government of Brazil to take over the *Esmeralda* as an immobilized vessel under the plan referred to above.

The three vessels referred to above belong to one Vlasov, formerly a Roumanian citizen and now an Argentine. For somewhat over a year now, this Government and the British Government have been negotiating with Vlasov and the Argentine Government with a view to placing these ships in service. It appears that the British began negotiations with the agents of Vlasov in the spring of 1941 for the use of the three ships. An informal agreement was arrived at and Vlasov was permitted to transfer his vessels from Roumanian to Panamanian registry. Thereafter Vlasov acquired Argentine citizenship and registered the *Tropicus* and *Esmeralda* in Argentina. On February 2, 1942 an arrangement was worked out whereby the British would charter the *Omega* and Moore-McCormack's Argentine subsidiary would charter the other two vessels. This arrangement was satisfactory to the British, to this Government, to the Argentine Embassy here, and apparently to the owner of the vessels. The Argentine Government, however, refused to allow the agreement to be carried out.

As you know, Vlasov is on the Proclaimed List and the Statutory List. Information this Department has received from Lisbon indicates strongly that Vlasov's representative there is working for the Axis.

It should be pointed out also that the Department has been informed that the British will consider the three ships mentioned as having reverted to their former status as enemy ships unless the agreement referred to is carried out. This Government will take no steps to alter this position. Corbett has full information.

HULL

800.8830 Brazil/78a : Telegram

The Acting Secretary of State to the Ambassador in Brazil (Caffery)

WASHINGTON, August 29, 1942—10 p. m.

2496. The Department will do its utmost to obtain space for shipment to Brazil of 3900 tons of newsprint in August and September. However, due to the critical shipping situation and to the fact that the average monthly shipments of newsprint for the first 6 months of

1942 to Brazil amounted to 1946 tons, the Department requests the Embassy's comments on urging the curtailment of the number of editions and size of newspapers by approximately 30 per cent, limiting future monthly shipments to 2500 tons. It has been reported that Brazilian newspapers have made no cut in the number of editions or size as yet.

WELLES

800.85/752 : Telegram

The Secretary of State to the Ambassador in Brazil (Caffery)

WASHINGTON, September 14, 1942—7 p. m.

2710. Your 3570, September 12, 5 p. m.[24] The Department fails completely to understand the difficulties with the wording of the charter and exchange of notes relating to the shipping arrangements. It was the Department's impression that the Brazilians were all ready to sign more than a month ago except for the one question relating to replacing vessels after the war. The charter which you are now discussing is exactly the old charter with a very generous modification with respect to replacing vessels after the war.

HULL

800.85/753 : Telegram

The Secretary of State to the Ambassador in Brazil (Caffery)

WASHINGTON, September 16, 1942—8 p. m.

2732. Your 3601, September 14, 9 p. m.[25] The suggested changes with respect to articles 3, 4, and 5 are satisfactory to the War Shipping Administration.

The new article 9, replacing article 8, is not satisfactory because of its reference to new vessels. The War Shipping Administration is unable to agree to give Brazil even a qualified right to new vessels as replacements for old vessels which may be lost. They are unable to understand why the Brazilian Government should not be satisfied with replacement by vessels of similar tonnage, size, and characteristics, as they will then be restored to their original position.

It is noted that the new article 9 would obligate the United States to replace vessels listed in article 3 whether loss is caused by marine or war risk, whereas our original suggestion was limited to war risks. There is no objection to expanding the commitment of the United States provided that it is definitely understood that we are concerned

---

[24] Not printed; it reported that the Brazilians were displeased by some of the wording and with some articles of the proposed ship charter (800.85/752).
[25] Not printed.

with total losses from marine risks and not with ordinary damage from marine risks.

With reference to the suggested changes in article 1 of the bareboat charter, the War Shipping Administration suggests that the term "way ports" be changed to read "nearby ports" and omitting the term "between the two countries". This language would permit calls to Uruguayan ports without making direct reference to such ports in the charter itself.

HULL

800.8830 Coal/191a : Airgram

The Secretary of State to the Ambassador in Brazil (Caffery)

WASHINGTON, September 17, 1942—12 : 30 p. m.

A–241. The Department has been discussing with the War Shipping Administration the whole question of coal shipments to Brazil, which constitutes the most difficult shipping problem with reference to the American republics. The following tabulation shows the status of coal shipments in August and those projected for September :

(All figures in thousands of long tons)

	Total	Lloyd Brasileiro	WSA and Other Vessels
August	*45	16	*29
September			
August carryover	11	10	1
September proper	63	3	60
Total	119	29	90

It will be recalled that the proposed schedule envisaged 20,000 tons a month in Lloyd Brasileiro vessels and 50,000 tons in United States-controlled and other vessels. The War Shipping Administration, as you will note, is planning to make up in September most of its August deficiency (11,000 tons of which actually sailed out on September 1 and was included in the 62,000 ton figure cabled to you).

It is imperative that Lloyd Brasileiro carry its own part of the load if the total shipping schedule of 70,000 tons of coal and 28,000 tons of other cargo is to be met. Prospective sailings of Lloyd Brasileiro boats in September and October are very few. This places the major part of the burden on the United States shipping tonnage.

In this connection you might point out to the Brazilian authorities that the Lloyd Brasileiro is always reluctant to carry low value cargo, such as coal, newsprint, rails for the steel mill at Itabira, fire brick

---

*After deducting cargo diverted to Trinidad, Department's 2624, September 7. [Footnote in the original; telegram No. 2624 not printed.]

(which it refused utterly to carry), and other similar materials going largely to official Brazilian projects.

HULL

800.85/761 : Telegram

The Ambassador in Brazil (Caffery) to the Secretary of State

RIO DE JANEIRO, September 22, 1942—4 p. m.
[Received 10 : 05 p. m.]

3754. My telegram No. 3737, September 21, 8 [9] p. m.[26]

(1) Aranha is taking the proposed shipping agreement to President Vargas this afternoon.

(2) He showed me a list which he is preparing of "benefits" Brazil has received from the United States which he will show to the President and Cabinet.

(3) Aranha told me that he has notified the Argentine Government that Argentine merchant ships touching Brazilian ports must have no crew members of German or Italian nationality, nor even naturalized Germans and Italians on board.

(4) Aranha told me that he has notified the French Embassy here that they can forward no more telegrams in cipher [27] as the French authorities at Dakar have withdrawn the cipher privileges of the Brazilian Consuls at Dakar.

(5) Aranha showed me a number of recent telegrams from Chile; he observed that his Ambassador there [28] believes that the situation has improved but he believes that the Chileans "are fooling us".

CAFFERY

800.8830 Coal/191a : Airgram

The Secretary of State to the Ambassador in Brazil (Caffery)

WASHINGTON, September 25, 1942—7 : 20 p. m.

A–288. Reference is made to Department's airgram A–241 of September 17 in which reference was made to the fact that the Lloyd Brasileiro was really not cooperating fully in the transportation of goods between the United States and Brazil. The War Shipping Administration has recently detailed for the Department some of its difficulties. These are:

"1. There is an urgent need for better cooperation between the War Shipping Administration and Lloyd Brasileiro, with particular refer-

---

[26] Not printed.
[27] For correspondence on the efforts to curb Axis activities through the control of communications, see pp. 108 ff. and pp. 186 ff.
[28] Samuel de Souza Leão Gracie, Brazilian Ambassador in Chile.

ence to the character of cargo lifted by the Brazilian and the American controlled vessels in this trade. There is a tendency on the part of the agents to await the assignment of American controlled vessels before disclosing information with respect to their own prospective sailings. The agents claim that they are unable to get the information from Brazil.

2. There is a rather well-founded suspicion on our part that the Brazilians are interested in higher paying freight and that some of their apparent operating difficulties may spring from a desire to avoid handling undesirable cargo such as newsprint and coal.

3. There is a definite need for the reaching of some understanding with the Brazilians with respect to the number of vessels earmarked for trade between Brazil and the United States and some undertaking to continue to operate a minimum number of vessels in this trade."

Of course, item 3 would be cleared up in part if the proposed ship deal with the Brazilians is made. Even in this case, however, there is no firm undertaking to put any more ships into the United States trade to replace any which may be sunk. There continues a belief in Washington that there are additional Brazilian vessels in non-essential trades or not regularly operating which could be added to the Brazilian-United States service.

The Department would appreciate your comments and requests that in your discussions with the Brazilians on shipping matters that occasion be taken to bring home these points.

HULL

800.85/772 : Telegram

The Ambassador in Brazil (Caffery) to the Secretary of State

RIO DE JANEIRO, October 1, 1942—11 a. m.
[Received noon.]

3923. Ship deal officially consummated today with the exchange of notes between Aranha and myself.[29] Brazilians say that there will be no publicity here.

I will telegraph later regarding commodity transactions.

Please send surveyors requested in my 3787, September 23, 6 p. m.[30]

CAFFERY

---

[29] Copies of the notes and the charter were transmitted to the Department by the Ambassador in his despatch No. 8629, October 1, 1942, not printed. The agreement of September 30 provided for the chartering by the United States Government of 13 vessels owned by the Brazilian Government and the placing under the protection of American convoys 23 other ships flying the Brazilian flag. Provisions were included concerning the increase in the number of ships in the Brazilian-American trade, the loss of ships and compensation therefor, recruiting of personnel, etc. (800.85/775)

[30] Not printed.

800.8830 Brazil/78a : Telegram

The Acting Secretary of State to the Ambassador in Brazil (Caffery)

WASHINGTON, October 6, 1942—6 p. m.

2960. Please cable urgently a reply to Department's telegram no. 2496 of August 29, 1942, in which there were requested the Embassy's comments on limiting future monthly shipments of newsprint to 2,500 tons. If the Embassy agrees to the monthly shipment of 2,500 tons, please airgram monthly a distribution by consignees of the 2,500 tons of newsprint. This monthly airgram should reach the Department by the first of the month preceding the month in which the newsprint is to be shipped.

WELLES

800.8830 Brazil/87 : Telegram

The Ambassador in Brazil (Caffery) to the Secretary of State

RIO DE JANEIRO, October 10, 1942—5 p. m.
[Received 7 : 27 p. m.]

4108. Department's 2960, August [*October*] 6, 6 p. m. Last June (Department's 1464, June 8, 1 [*9*] p. m.) the Embassy informed the Brazilian Press Association that every effort was being made to arrange for newsprint shipments at the rate of 3,500 tons a month, "the minimum Brazilian requirement". The large cut now contemplated would have an unfavorable reaction here. The Bank of Brazil has requested as a rock bottom figure an allocation of 3,000 tons of newsprint for October (my 3666, September 17 [31]). Stocks are practically nonexistent. Shipments to Brazil from the first of the year to August 30 totaled only 13,468 tons an average of but 1,683 tons per month. Shipments for the last 3 months of that period were critically low, viz: 171 tons in June, 341 in July and 951 in August.

Shipments of 3,500 tons per month for at least a few months would be desirable so that reasonable minimum stocks could be built up; and it is recommended that thereafter the figure should not be less than 3,000 tons per month.

All papers have already considerably cut their stocks and reduced their circulation.

CAFFERY

---

[31] Not printed.

800.8830 Brazil/87 : Telegram

The Acting Secretary of State to the Ambassador in Brazil (Caffery)

WASHINGTON, October 14, 1942—7 p. m.

3083. Your 4108, October 10, 5 p. m. Please cable urgently monthly distribution by consignees of 3,500 tons of newsprint for November and December and 3,000 tons thereafter. The Department will support shipments of these amounts in accordance with Embassy's recommendation.

Since August 20, 10,539 tons have been approved by the Board of Economic Warfare and 5,057 tons were actually shipped in September in accordance with information supplied to the Department by the War Shipping Administration.

Circulation figures and extent of stock reductions would be appreciated.

WELLES

832.852/59 : Telegram

The Ambassador in Brazil (Caffery) to the Secretary of State

RIO DE JANEIRO, October 21, 1942—7 p. m.
[Received 11 : 02 p. m.]

4316. For Douglas and Radner, War Shipping Administration,[32] from Graham.[33] Tanker *Itamaraty*, Minister of Foreign Affairs and Brazil Maritime Commission now propose:

1. The Brazilian Government shall charter the tanker *Itamaraty* to the United States Government "as is, where is" at a nominal rate for the duration of the hostilities on the same basis as 13 ships.
2. The cost or [of] repairs of the vessel including classification shall be borne by the United States Government.
3. The vessel shall be fully insured against war and marine risks by the United States Government.
4. In case the vessel is lost the United States Government shall pay $1,200,000 out of the insurance to the Brazilian Government.
5. If not lost the vessel shall be delivered in class to the Brazilian Government free of liens and encumbrances 30 days after the end of the hostilities.

With the Ambassador's approval we had a long conference yesterday with officials of the Ministry of Foreign Affairs. The subject of passenger vessels and joint working out of mutual problems were discussed. Brazilians fear that if more ships, particularly passenger, are turned over to us they may find themselves in grave difficulties in coastwise movement, particularly of troops, laborers and

---

[32] Lewis W. Douglas, Deputy Administrator, and William Radner, General Counsel.
[33] Chalmers G. Graham, field representative, War Shipping Administration.

supplies to northern Brazil. We assured them that if they give us the passenger ships some basis could be worked out for meeting whatever current needs of the two countries might arise thereafter. We suggested the prompt establishment of a joint Brazilian-American shipping adjustment group to handle such matters. The idea was well received. We feel that the establishment now of such a group is a necessary requirement to cover the operations of the 23 ships under article III of the agreement of September 30 [34] and also to take care of the use of our vessels in local coastwise trade when needed by Brazilians and when they would otherwise move in ballast as in the case of the *Galveston*, as well as to take care of operations of any passenger and other vessels we might hereafter acquire. At present no machinery is set up for operations under article III and we believe we will not get passenger vessels except under agreement to afford their use by Brazil when the need is shown.

The Ministry urged haste in disposition of *Itamaraty*. We believe whatever we do with respect to this vessel can be effectively used as a lever to acquire possibly passenger and other vessels; therefore, please bear this fact in mind in replying to this telegram. Please telegraph data relative to condition, the cost of repairs and value of *Itamaraty*.

With reference to the use of our vessels in Brazilian coastwise trade, we believe every effort should be made by us to afford such use when desired by Brazil, which will waive coastwise laws because the needs in this trade, particularly in north Brazil, are interfering with our obtaining more Brazilian tonnage.

We will meet with Aranha Friday afternoon, therefore please telegraph reply to reach us not later than Friday morning. [Graham.]

CAFFERY

832.852/44 : Telegram

The Ambassador in Brazil (Caffery) to the Secretary of State

RIO DE JANEIRO, November 4, 1942—7 p. m.
[Received 11 : 35 p. m.]

4556. For the Under Secretary. My 4282, October 20, 3 p. m.[35] Dr. Andrade Queiroz, secretary to President Vargas called Donnelly [36] and Graham of War Shipping Administration to the Palace yesterday to discuss the passenger ship proposal. He said that the President had decided to transfer to us without any restrictions or conditions, and not to be returned to Brazil, four Lloyd passenger ships (the

---

[34] Not printed, but see footnote 29, p. 743.
[35] Not printed.
[36] Walter J. Donnelly, Counselor of Embassy for Economic Affairs.

Pedro I, Santos, Bage, Raul Soares) provided we agree to supply rails and accessories not rolling stock for the proposed railway line to connect the Central do Brazil Railway at Montes Claros in the State of Minas Geraes, with the Leste Railway at Contendas (Bom Jesus dos Meiras) in the State of Bahia, a distance of approximately 500 kilometers. He said that President Vargas and the General Staff of the Brazilian Army regard the project as of vital importance as auxiliary land service for the transport of troops, supplies, et cetera, and as a substitute for a water route and that its completion would make possible an all-rail service between central Brazil to a point north of Natal. He said that President Vargas was unwilling to release more passenger ships at this time owing to the need for the ships for the transportation of troops and supplies along the Brazilian coast. He said that President Vargas does not wish to consider the plan as commercial but as the mutual effort of the two Governments to improve and facilitate inland and ocean transportation for the defense of the Americas. We attempted several times to ascertain the terms under which they would expect us to furnish the rails but the reply was always the same, namely, Vargas does not wish to consider it as a commercial proposition. It was evident, however, that they expect us to supply the rails at our expense in exchange for the complete and unrestricted transfer of the passenger ships to us.

He expressed the hope that our Government would make a prompt decision.

Dr. Queiroz has instructed the Director of the Railway Department of the Brazilian Government to furnish us with detailed information regarding the railway project. Preliminary information obtained from Mr. West, the railway expert attached to the Embassy, indicates that the uncompleted stretch is 600 and not 500 kilometers, that it would involve the furnishing of approximately 50,000 tons of rails and accessories, also that it would take 2 to 3 years to complete the job following the arrival of the equipment in Brazil. Dr. Queiroz did not specify any time element for delivery of the rails and did not make this a condition for immediate release of the ships. The need for importation of the rails is not immediate and will depend upon the construction of the roadbed.

It was agreed that the surveyors of the War Shipping Administration at present in Rio would survey two of the passenger ships now here. This is being commenced today. One of the other passenger ships is scheduled to arrive here shortly from Europe and the fourth is en route to Buenos Aires and will return in about 25 days.

Dr. Queiroz said he would appreciate my conveying President Vargas' message to President Roosevelt and requesting an early reply. Detailed information regarding the railway project will be telegraphed after our meeting with the Director of the Railway Department.

CAFFERY

832.852/63 : Telegram

The Ambassador in Brazil (Caffery) to the Secretary of State

RIO DE JANEIRO, November 17, 1942—4 p. m.
[Received November 18—3 : 14 a. m.]

4807.   Rose requests that following telegram be delivered to Radner, Brierley,[37] War Shipping Administration:

At a meeting today between representatives of Lloyd Brasileiro, the Embassy and the War Shipping Administration held for the purpose of speeding up the turnover of the chartered vessels, it was concluded that the most expeditious manner would be for us to take delivery of the vessels in the United States.

The Lloyd Brasileiro raised the point of the cost of repairs in the United States to comply with article 5 of the Charter Party. Of the 13 vessels chartered: 1 has been delivered; 1 is about to be delivered; 2 are in very poor conditions, namely, the *Minas Loide* and the *Ceara Loide*. The condition of the last two vessels is such that considerable repairs would be necessary here prior to the vessels' departure in class; it was tentatively agreed that these two vessels should remain here, the requirements of article 5 of the Charter Party to be completed here prior to delivery to us of these two vessels. Repair costs incidental to article 5 for the three vessels which are en route to the United States would be covered under the lump sum mentioned hereafter.

The remaining six vessels would be placed in safe condition here, including dry docking, cleaning and painting the bottom and drawing the tail shaft, all for the account of Lloyd Brasileiro inasmuch as these vessels would be in the employ and under the direction of Lloyd Brasileiro until delivered to us in United States.

It was suggested that the Brazilian Government would agree to lump-sum payment of $150,000 for repairs to the nine vessels. From conditions seen on the vessels available here, it is felt that this is a fair estimate of costs in Brazil. The excess cost, which would be offset by the much faster turnover. Lloyd Brasileiro would agree to dry dock, clean bottom, draw tail shaft and place all vessels here and not yet delivered in seaworthy condition for the voyage to the United States as expeditiously as possible.

---

[37] Daniel S. Brierley, Ship Surveyor.

The *Ceara Loide* and the *Minas Loide*, two vessels which are not out of class and require major repairs of boilers, decks, et cetera, and which from observations will not be delivered to us for approximately 3 to 4 months, are to remain here until this work is completed by Lloyd Brasileiro for their account. The time and cost to prepare these vessels for a safe voyage would be practically the same as required for a turnover to us, and these repairs in the United States would be excessive.

The following is a breakdown of the 13 vessels: 1 has been delivered and 1 will be delivered shortly; 2 are being repaired in Rio; and there are 9 which it is felt can be delivered to us in a reasonable time, of which 3 are now en route to the United States.

The *Golaz Loide* has been delivered to us, and the *Recife Loide* is expected to be delivered within the next 10 days.

The *Gavea Loide* and *Bahia Loide* should be ready to proceed within the next 10 days to the United States for delivery there.

The *Vitoria Loide* is sailing coastwise and should not require much time upon her return here for the voyage to the United States.

The *Pelotas Loide* and *Norte Loide* have temporary certificates in British corporation.

The *Su Loide* will require putting through class; she is now out of class.

In each case the three last-named vessels can be given a temporary certificate to proceed to United States and there undergo and complete class requirements.

The *Rio Loide*, *Apa Loide* and *Pirai Loide* are now en route to the United States.

The *Ceara Loide* and *Minas Loide* are to remain here until completion of their repairs.

After carefully analyzing all possibilities, it is suggested, for your consideration, that, if we are to have any despatch, that we agree to accept a maximum lump-sum payment of $350,000 for all expenditures for the nine vessels mentioned and additional expenditures incurred, with the exception of those for the *Minas Loide* and *Ceara Loide*, to be for our account.

Please telegraph your views of the proposal, particularly as Lloyd Brasileiro have definitely informed us that due to lack of mechanics, material and equipment, the delivery of the vessels to us here in accordance with article 5 will be considerably delayed. [Rose.]

CAFFERY

832.852/63 : Telegram

The Secretary of State to the Ambassador in Brazil (Caffery)

WASHINGTON, November 20, 1942—10 p. m.

3622. From Cushing,[38] for Rose, SD 461. Referring to Embassy's 4807.[39] It is understood that *Recife Loide* will be delivered in 10 days, and that *Golaz Loide* has been delivered already. *Apa Loide*, *Pirai Loide*, *Rio Loide*, en route to the United States at present, within 10 days sailing to the United States are *Baia Loide* and *Gavea Loide*. The *Norte Loide*, *Pelotas-Loide* with temporary certificates, and *Su Loide* which is temporarily out of class, to proceed under temporary certificates to New York later. Now out of class are the *Ceara Loide* and *Minas Loide*. *Vitoria Loide*, now operating coastwise to shortly proceed to the U. S. It is understood that proposal is for the *Ceara Loide* and *Minas Loide* to remain in Rio to complete repairs and class requirements. Delivery to be made at Rio of *Recife Loide* and *Golaz Loide*. Nine vessels remaining to be repaired and delivered with U. S. agreed price $350,000 Brazilian account. Repairing, classing, and delivery at Rio of the *Minas Loide*, *Ceara Loide* for our account. We do not understand why we should accept these costs which may run into considerable amount as from your statement these vessels require major repairing. It would appear from analysis of proposal that it would be more fair and reasonable as well as more advantageous in our efforts to speed delivery at [*if*] Brazil's proposal of $150,000 for estimated repairs be expected [*accepted*]. This we understand you to feel represents fairly Brazil repair costs on the nine vessels mentioned with delivery in U. S. and in accordance with contract Brazil to complete the *Minas Loide* and the *Ceara Loide* will [*still*] at Rio for their account. [Cushing.]

HULL

832.852/46 : Telegram

The Ambassador in Brazil (Caffery) to the Secretary of State

RIO DE JANEIRO, November 23, 1942—11 a. m.
[Received 1 p. m.]

4904. Department's 3591, November 18, 8 p. m.[40] President Vargas is unwilling to let us have the six ITA[41] vessels for the following reasons:

---

[38] J. E. Cushing, Assistant Deputy Administrator in Charge of Ship Operations, War Shipping Administration.
[39] *Supra.*
[40] Not printed.
[41] Classification of Brazilian passenger vessel.

(1) They are still the property of the Lage interests [42] which have not been taken over by the Brazilian Government but which are administered by an interventor named by the Government. The Brazilian Government is asking an appraisal of the Lage properties including the vessels and the Lage interests have valued the vessels at $300 per dead weight ton which is absurdly high.

(2) The vessels are suitable for coastwise service and not ocean service and are indispensable to the maintenance of coastwise trade. The Maritime Commission inform us that two of the ITA ships are tied up for repairs.

At a meeting Saturday with the Brazilian Maritime Commission, at which Dr. Andrade Queiroz represented President Vargas, they offered to let us have four ships but I told them I could not even submit a proposal to Washington for less than five ships and after some discussion they agreed to turn over to us the following vessels: *Pedro II*, oil burner; *Almirante Alexandrino*, oil burner; *Bage*, coal; *Pedro I*, coal; *Siqueiro Campos*, coal. Four of the vessels are now in Rio de Janeiro and the *Almirante Alexandrino* is in Manáos.

Rose will return to Rio de Janeiro November 22 from Uruguay and will be available next week to survey the vessels, provided the proposal appeals to the Department and the War Shipping Administration. The Maritime Commission states that the *Bage* and *Pedro I* can be converted into oil burners in the United States within a few weeks.

President Vargas and other officials of the Government are concerned over the increasing need for coastwise shipping for the transportation of troops, foodstuffs and other supplies to the northeast (they are transporting them now), and they assert that in ceding the five vessels to us they will have reached the limit to which they can go without prejudicing coastwise trade. The Maritime Commission referred to the possibility of withdrawing 1 of the 23 ships included in the recent agreement for coastwise service, but I told them that it would be inadvisable to make any alterations in the agreement, and they finally accepted our point of view.

Although they have never said so in so many words, it is obvious that they will ask us to make available to them up to 40,000 tons of rails in exchange for the 5 ships.

Dr. Andrade Queiroz has put off his vacation until November 25. If possible, I would like to receive a reply from the Department before his departure because if there is any chance of reaching an agreement in principle, I might be able to arrange for the early release of the ships.

CAFFERY

---

[42] Lage Shipbuilding Yards.

832.852/46 : Telegram

The Secretary of State to the Ambassador in Brazil (Caffery)

WASHINGTON, November 28, 1942—9 p. m.

3740. Your 4904, November 23. The vessels mentioned have been studied by the War Shipping Administration and the War Department, and because of their age and lack of speed, agencies mentioned do not believe that they would be suitable for the purposes which they have in mind. As you undoubtedly realize, the vessels are to be used as troop transports in inter-island routes. Therefore, the question of their suitability for ocean service is of no great significance.

Please impress upon the Brazilians that these vessels are urgently required in the prosecution of the war.

As stated in Department's 3591,[44] in view of the Army's interest, officials of the War Production Board and the War Shipping Administration are prepared to discuss arrangements for the production and transportation of up to 40,000 tons of rails. However, authorities here do not believe it possible to enter into a discussion involving the production and transportation of this amount of material unless the Brazilians are prepared to turn over all six vessels. As previously stated, this Government would much prefer to acquire these vessels either through purchase or charter, in which case it would be interested in any part of the six vessels which the Brazilian Government feels might be released without prejudicing coastwise trade.

It is also the opinion of those here who are acquainted with Brazilian shipping that the withdrawal of these vessels from Brazilian trade would not seriously damage coastwise service if other Brazilian vessels were efficiently used and allocated without regard to commercial aspects to the most important Brazilian coastwise trades. The presentation of this view is left to your discretion.

Please emphasize in your discussion of this matter with the Brazilians that these vessels would represent a real contribution to our war effort at a time when such a contribution is needed.

HULL

832.852/64 : Telegram

The Secretary of State to the Ambassador in Brazil (Caffery)

WASHINGTON, December 2, 1942—8 p. m.

3784. SD 538 for Rose and Donnelly from Admiral Land.[45] Reference our SD 495, Department's 3703.[44] You are authorized to

---

[44] Not printed.
[45] Vice Adm. Emory S. Land, Administrator, War Shipping Administration.

supplement previous exchange of notes dated September 30, 1942 [46] and charter parties signed on October 20, 1942 so as to provide as follows:

"In consideration of the payment by the owner to the charterer of the sum of $350,000 United States currency the charterer agrees to accept and the owner agrees to deliver to the charterer at ports mutually agreed upon in the United States of America, the following vessels: *SS Norte Loide, SS Su Loide, SS Vitoria Loide, SS Apa Loide, SS Gavea Loide, SS Pelotas Loide, SS Pirai Loide, SS Rio Loide, SS Baia Loide.*

The charterer agrees to make all necessary repairs to said vessels to make the same seaworthy and up to classification as chronicled for in article Nos. 2, 5, 6 of the aforesaid charter parties. It is further agreed that all other terms and conditions of the said charter parties shall remain in full force and effect."

We do not understand your reference to proviso WSA assume cost of War Risk and total loss insurance. If the reference is intended to mean that Brazilian Government will require same war risk and total loss insurance protection for the period of north bound voyage prior to delivery as they are entitled to receive after delivery we are agreeable to this concession if same absolutely necessary to close transaction although we would prefer not to make the concession if possible. Please proceed accordingly and advise. [Admiral Land.]

HULL

832.852/47 : Telegram

The Ambassador in Brazil (Caffery) to the Secretary of State

RIO DE JANEIRO, December 5, 1942—11 a. m.
[Received 2 : 41 p. m.]

5152. Department's 3740, November 28, 9 p. m. Aranha and Celestino [47] believe that President Vargas will eventually let us have the ITA ships. The President instructed Celestino last night to discuss the plan with the Brazilian Maritime Commission and to request them to consider the ships from the standpoint of BRT instead of as a business proposition. The President inquired of Celestino as to the rail project and emphasized the importance of Brazil receiving up to 40,000 tons within 1 year.

President Vargas instructed Celestino to delay his trip to the United States in order to be present in Rio de Janeiro during the conversations relating to the passenger ships. Celestino has canceled his reservations for December 7 but hopes to depart for Washington before December 15.

CAFFERY

---

[46] See footnote 29, p. 743.
[47] Mario Celestino, a director of Lloyd Brasileiro.

800.8830 Brazil/112 : Airgram

The Secretary of State to the Ambassador in Brazil (Caffery)

WASHINGTON, December 23, 1942—6:10 p. m.

A–674. Embassy's 5384, December 17, 1942, 11 p. m.; and 5407, December 18, 1942, 11 p. m.; and Department's 3935, December 15, 1942.[49]

Three shipments of newsprint have left during the last month, 1385 tons on the *Sea Serpent*, the steamer mentioned in Department's 3935, 247 tons on the *Anita*, which left on or about December 3, 1942, and 198 tons on the *Moormacrey*, which left at the same time. However, nine ships are scheduled to sail between now and January 3, 1943 carrying a total of 3639 tons divided as follows: consigned to customers of Murray Simonsen, 1385; Anglo Brasileira, 755; T. Janer, 1065; and miscellaneous, 434. This constitutes a revision from the schedule outlined in Department's 3935 and includes newsprint from St. Maurice Valley consigned to Anglo Brasileira, of which some is presumably for *O Globo*. Due to the critical shipping situation and the curtailment of space, the Department instructed the Embassy in telegram 2496, August 29, 1942 and 3083, October 14, 1942 to submit a recommendation as to the distribution of 3500 tons for November and December, 1942 and 3,000 tons thereafter to various consignees, and the Embassy submitted recommendations in various telegrams, the last of which, no. 4840, November 18, 1942, 8 p. m.,[50] requesting distribution among three consignees the total figure of which was altered in Embassy's 4915, November 23, 1942.[50] The Board of Economic Warfare has continued to cooperate with the Department in approving applications for freight space for newsprint in accordance with Embassy's recommendations and to certify the applications to the War Shipping Administration as eligible for shipment. However, after the War Shipping Administration publishes the list of approved applications for freight space as eligible for shipment, it is then incumbent upon the shippers or the importers' agents themselves to make the necessary contracts with the steamship operators for the actual freight space on board vessels. (See Comprehensive Export Control Schedule No. 10, page 118, paragraph 13.) With respect to newsprint, the Embassy will note that newsprint was placed under general license on October 9, 1942 and to ship newsprint all that was required was an approved application for freight space.

Apparently, it is the Embassy's impression that the Department actually allocates shipping space, and this misapprehension has resulted in the exchange of numerous telegrams and a great deal of

---

[49] None printed.
[50] Not printed.

confusion on the subject of newsprint shipments. As stated above, the Department has nothing to do whatsoever with the actual loading of ships. The Department merely attempts to expedite the approval, by the appropriate agencies charged with shipping, of the necessary applications for freight space. When these applications for freight space are approved, it is then up to the shippers or the agents of the importers to make the actual arrangements with the steamship operators for the lifting of the cargo.

Sufficient newsprint has now been approved with an "A" shipping priority, as an indirect result of the Department's intervention, to take care of the requirements of all consumers in accordance with the most recent recommendation of the Embassy.

The Department realizes the serious situation as a result of irregular shipments and has called this to the attention of the War Shipping Administration.

HULL

832.852/48 : Telegram

The Ambassador in Brazil (Caffery) to the Secretary of State

RIO DE JANEIRO, December 29, 1942—3 p. m.
[Received 6 : 19 p. m.]

5530. Department's 4043, December 23, midnight.[51] President Vargas now says that he is willing to let us have the ITA ships. However, a number of his high officials, including Souza Costa, are opposing this: They say that Brazil cannot spare those ships at this time. Aranha says that is true but he is in favor of letting us have them anyway, as a distinctly war measure.

Aranha is to discuss the whole matter this afternoon with the President and especially what the President will ask from us if he definitely decides to let us have the ITA's.

CAFFERY

832.852/49 : Telegram

The Ambassador in Brazil (Caffery) to the Secretary of State

RIO DE JANEIRO, December 31, 1942—6 p. m.
[Received January 1, 1943—2 : 33 a. m.]

5568. Embassy's telegram 5530, December 29. I have received the following personal letter from Aranha:

"In accordance with our last conversation I take pleasure in the hope of confirming to Your Excellency the statement that President Vargas—complying with the request made to him by President Roosevelt

---

[51] Not printed.

and Your Excellency—has authorized me to communicate to Your Excellency that powers were granted to me to study and make delivery of the Brazilian 'ITA' boats which he decided to turn over to the American Government for urgent purposes.

Your Excellency, who has such a good knowledge of our necessities, can well appreciate the difficulties which will result to our shipping and trade with the north of Brazil from the loss of these six ships.

Another important point which is also known to Your Excellency is the question of the safety of northeastern Brazil. Brazil does not have complete means of communication by land for that region. The program designed and initiated by the Government to complete such a communication system with the city of Natal, Rio Grande do Norte, has suffered constant interruptions due to the lack of railway materials.

Not so much from the standpoint of compensation but to remedy such a great handicap—made even worse as Your Excellency will be the first to recognize by ceding the best ships of our already deficient Merchant Marine—I ask Your Excellency to submit to President Roosevelt for consideration a statement of the most urgent Brazilian necessities connected with the transportation problem: Construction of the following railway stretches:

[Here follows the remainder of Mr. Aranha's letter which is a detailed description of the railway routes and the needed construction materials and equipment; also, one paragraph of the Ambassador's comment on certain details.]

Aranha has been very vague about the terms of the transaction.

He keeps on saying, "the ships are yours", but he declines to give us details, presumably because he prefers to await receipt of our offer. However, he has requested me to find out the c.i.f. Brazilian port cost of the rails and has also expressed the hope that our Government would turn them over to his Government on the basis of Lend-Lease.

I recommend that the Department discuss the rail project with R. K. West who may be reached through Ex-Im Bank.

[Here follows another passage dealing with materials and equipment.]

Of the six ITA ships, five are available and acceptable. The *Itaquice* will require a minimum of 6 to 8 months to repair here due principally to renewal of stripped engine parts such as liners, heads, et cetera. If you are not interested in *Itaquice*, we may be able to substitute the passenger vessel *Pedro II* belonging to Lloyd Brasileiro, built in Glasgow in 1910, now classed in Bureau Verit as 6129 gross tons, reported to make about 16 knots at 90 tons of fuel oil. Log shows usual maximum speed 14 knots 72 tons fuel, 832 tons bunkers. Survey here shows vessel in general good condition. Passenger capacity 325.

In my opinion the Brazilian authorities would be willing to reach an agreement based upon the exchange of the ships for the rails and accessories, and our assurances that we would facilitate the granting of priorities for the equipment specified in item 2 of Aranha's letter.

CAFFERY

DISCUSSIONS BETWEEN THE UNITED STATES AND BRAZIL CONCERNING THE APPLICATION OF THE PROCLAIMED LIST

740.00112A European War, 1939/7599

The Ambassador in Brazil (Caffery) to the Secretary of State

No. 6518
RIO DE JANEIRO, February 14, 1942.
[Received February 19, 1942.]

SIR: I have the honor to refer to the Department's circular telegram of January 28, 1942, 11: 00 p. m.,[53] and to the Department's Instructions No. 2104 of January 29, 1942, and No. 2136 of February 5, 1942,[54] both in connection with cases under consideration for inclusion in the Proclaimed List for Certain Blocked Nationals.

Consultations that have been carried on with Brazilian Government officials have resulted in the active functioning of the Committee referred to in Embassy's telegram No. 335 of February 3, 10: 00 p. m.[55] It will be recalled that this Committee consists of the Chief of the Economic and Commercial Division of the Ministry of Foreign Affairs,[56] the Director of Exchange of the Bank of Brazil[57] and the Commercial Attaché of the Embassy.[58]

The Committee's first meeting took place in the Embassy several days ago, and although no definite policy was outlined, several important agreements in connection with the Proclaimed List were reached.

(1) The Embassy agreed that pending review by the Committee, mentioned above, it would request the Department to suspend action on all cases that have been recommended for inclusion in the Proclaimed List, but which have not as yet been included in that list. The Committee will review these cases, and either remedial or preventive steps agreed upon by the Committee will be taken locally, or the cases will be again recommended to the Department for inclusion in the Proclaimed List. This procedure should prevent an unnecessary increase in the size of the Proclaimed List, and at the same time gives promise of a more direct approach to control of cloaking and other objectionable activities.

---

[53] *Ante*, p. 285.
[54] Neither printed.
[55] Not printed; the Committee mentioned was responsible for Proclaimed List matters in Brazil.
[56] Mário Moreira da Silva.
[57] Francisco Alves dos Santos Filho.
[58] Walter J. Donnelly.

(2) The Embassy will continue to submit recommendations to the Department for the inclusion of firms and individuals in the Proclaimed List, but hereafter, each case will be reviewed by the Committee before a recommendation for inclusion is submitted by the Embassy. It is evident that if the Brazilian authorities, represented on the Committee, do not object to our recommending to the Department that such cases should be included in the Proclaimed List, it is a strong indication that these cases should be included, and I urgently request that all cases so submitted be agreed to by the Interdepartmental Committee.[59]

(3) Certain cases now included in the Proclaimed List are being referred to the Embassy by the Ministry of Foreign Affairs. Remedial steps that will enable the Embassy to recommend that these cases be delisted are being facilitated by the full cooperation of the Bank of Brazil and of the Foreign Office. These offices are enforcing control and corrective measures, which the Embassy, acting individually, could hardly hope to effect.

(4) The Bank of Brazil is studying the question of controls to be set up over Japanese agricultural producers so that Brazil's social and economic structure shall not be interfered with, and at the same time, we shall be enabled to attain the objectives of the Proclaimed List.

(5) In general, the Committee is opposed to inclusion of individuals in the Proclaimed List, and will, unless such action will not achieve our objectives, recommend that such individuals be included in the Confidential List.[60]

I am hopeful that the active cooperation of the Brazilian authorities, extended to us through the Committee, will enable us to remove from the Proclaimed List, under conditions fully satisfactory to us, many troublesome cases now included in it. I must urge, however, that the Interdepartmental Committee, take immediate action on such cases that will be submitted by the Embassy with the recommendation that they be delisted.

I also anticipate that through the work of the Committee, the Proclaimed List will become much more effective, and that we will be in a better position to achieve the results we have been striving for.

In accordance with the plan outlined above, a direct reply will not be submitted to the Department's Instructions Nos. 2104 and 2136.[61] Airmail Despatches No. 6509 and No. 6517 [61] are being submitted today. These despatches contain recommendations for inclusion in the Proclaimed List and in the Confidential List. It is recommended that the Department take immediate action on these cases so that those recommended for inclusion in the Proclaimed List shall appear

[59] The administration of the Proclaimed List was the joint responsibility of the Secretary of State, the Secretary of the Treasury, the Attorney General, the Secretary of Commerce, the Board of Economic Warfare, and the Coordinator of Inter-American Affairs.

[60] For an explanation of the difference between the Confidential List and the Proclaimed List, see letter of March 30 from Assistant Secretary of State Acheson to the Ambassador in Brazil, p. 760.

[61] Neither printed.

in Supplement No. 1 to Revision No. 1, which will shortly be published.

The Director of Exchange of the Bank of Brazil suggested that [at] this first Committee meeting that a representative of the British Embassy be invited to attend subsequent meetings of the Committee. He approached the British Embassy in the matter, and that office has shown its willingness to cooperate and to work with the Committee, and has informed London accordingly. It is anticipated that hereafter, both Embassies will reach agreement on cases before they are presented to the Committee for consideration, and that henceforth, recommendation for inclusion in the respective lists will be submitted at the same time by each office.

The Department's circular telegram of February 12, 5:00 p. m.,[62] in connection with cooperation with the British Embassy on Proclaimed List matters will be answered in more detail shortly.

Respectfully yours,

For the Ambassador:
JOHN F. SIMMONS
Counselor of Embassy

740.00112A European War, 1939/7599 : Telegram

The Acting Secretary of State to the Ambassador in Brazil (*Caffery*)

WASHINGTON, March 4, 1942—11 p. m.

547. Reference your despatch 6518, February 14, 1942.

1. It is necessary to maintain control over Proclaimed List actions in Inter-Departmental Committee here. We fully agree on necessity and desirability of consultation and full exchange of information with Brazilian authorities on cases and while as practical matter we must and will give great weight to their views the collaboration should be on basis of consultation rather than necessity for securing agreement before inclusion of cases on Proclaimed List or confidential list. Full reports should be furnished on cases proposed for addition and deletion and also on cases postponed, giving reasons and precise statement of corrective or control measures actually applied by Brazilian authorities on specific cases.

2. We are concerned about tendency to consider confidential list as permanent alternative control for many cases outside categories stated Department's air mail circular instruction of November 25, 1942 [*1941*].[62] Confidential list control not adequate or desirable as substitute for Proclaimed List. Personal air mail letter from Acheson to Ambassador [63] will explain fully factors involved here.

---

[62] Not printed.
[63] *Infra.*

3. Dr. Souza Costa [65] received telegram from President Vargas March 2 as follows "Newspapers are publishing a new list of Brazilian firms included in the American Black List. This matter, of great concern to our industries and commerce, must be examined carefully. We do not know the sources of information used by American authorities in compiling the Black List. Unknowingly they may be acting on biased information arising from rivalry and intrigue. Under the existing regime of full cooperation with the United States of North America, it is desirable that we understand each other in everything, including this matter, of utmost importance to our development and expansion." Does this mean that President was not informed by Brazilian authorities about consultative procedure? In your discretion please bring operation of consultations to President's attention and reassure him concerning recent additions to list. Dr. Souza Costa is absent from Washington now but we are endeavoring to arrange for thorough discussion of situation with him March 10. Please report fully your interpretation and evaluation of this development and current situation regarding maintenance of strong Proclaimed List policy which in last analysis is necessary if we are to be able to justify and be reasonably successful here in our unending efforts to meet the essential requirements of Brazil and the other American republics.

WELLES

740.00112A European War, 1939/7599

The Assistant Secretary of State (Acheson) to the Ambassador in Brazil (Caffery)

WASHINGTON, March 30, 1942.

MY DEAR MR. AMBASSADOR: We have given a great amount of thought to the developments and suggested procedures concerning cooperation with the Brazilian authorities on Proclaimed List matters set forth in despatch no. 6518 of February 14, 1942.

This entire question is of such importance that I want to bring to your attention personally some of the considerations which we must reckon with here. I have kept in close touch with the Proclaimed List work and I am familiar with the difficult situation with which you and Mr. Donnelly have had to contend in carrying out a strong Proclaimed List policy in Brazil. In determining Proclaimed List policy here we have started with the assumption that neither we nor Brazil can afford to permit the Proclaimed List to be made a major issue between us. We have adjusted our procedures and policies on several important instances to meet this consideration. My present fear is

---

[65] Arthur de Souza Costa, Brazilian Minister of Finance.

not that we will not be able to make fair allowance in the future for the exigencies of certain important cases but rather that the Department's, and in turn the Embassy's, ability to keep the situation in effective balance will be impaired here unless the handling of these matters in Brazil is kept generally in harmony with the underlying realities here.

These realities are summed up in the fact that under the President's proclamation of July 17, 1941 [66] the maintenance of the Proclaimed List is vested in five other departments and agencies in addition to this Department. This is because the Proclaimed List is an instrument for administering controls which are vested in other departments and agencies—export control in the Board of Economic Warfare, priority and allocation control in the War Production Board, freezing control in the Treasury, etc. The task has been to find a common list which would free these controls as much as possible from the restraints of separate political intelligence services and permit the greatest freedom of commercial and financial transactions with persons not on a single published list. At the time the list was established trade had come almost to a standstill because no business man here could find out whether a prospective customer would pass the profusion of secret and separate lists.

In order to produce uniformity and simplicity of administration here, the work of administering the Proclaimed List has been carried out through the Department's Division of World Trade Intelligence and an interdepartmental committee. The committee passes on all cases proposed for addition and deletion and as a practical matter the unanimous agreement of all members must be achieved on each case, not merely because the head of each of the interested agencies and departments must sign the orders promulgating the supplements to the Proclaimed List, but to maintain the authority of the list and prevent the establishment of a host of supplementary lists beyond the Department's control. In order to maintain reasonably uniform listing standards and to prevent ill-considered actions, the committee members have been under instructions from their respective agencies to act only on recommendations which are supported with adequate substantiating information or reasons. While this has required education, both of the committee and some reporting officers in the field, the fact is that the committee has found no difficulty in taking speedy and unanimous action on cases which were adequately reported. This has been true of both additions and deletions. Experience to date has shown clearly that an extremely careful policy on deletions is necessary if the list is to be administered with fairness and effectiveness.

---

[66] Department of State *Bulletin*, July 19, 1941, p. 42.

All this is by way of saying that the Department is not by any means a "free agent" on these matters and that we must carry these other independent departments and agencies with us. In fact, the actual economic warfare licensing control powers are vested, as I have said, not in the Department but in the other agencies. The Department has sought and so far maintained—but not without a struggle—the primary administrative responsibility for the preparation of the list. I am confident that the best of the argument is with us in this matter, but there can be no question that our retaining this control depends upon the continued harmonious functioning of the interdepartmental mechanism and on the Department's ability and willingness to pursue a strong Proclaimed List policy. Furthermore, the interdepartmental authority affords the Department and the missions an essential element of protection against the political pressures which might well result in either emasculating the list or in seriously impairing the Department's effectiveness in other diplomatic affairs if it bore the onus of resisting such pressures on its sole responsibility.

I have gone into this background at some length to bring out why it is imperative that the consultative procedures which have been arranged with the Brazilian authorities should be truly consultative and must leave with the Proclaimed List Committee here the authority to take such action as seems necessary under all the circumstances, including, of course, the views of the Brazilians and the concrete corrective and control measures which they are prepared to apply to specific cases.

I am fearful that if recommendations for the Proclaimed List are restricted to only those cases on which the Brazilian authorities have no objection, we shall find that they are composed mainly of little fellows or people without political influence. There has already been considerable criticism on this score, and if the other agencies became convinced that the Department's leadership was producing this result, they would secede and go their own way with lists of their own, producing a situation far worse than anything the Brazilians have feared. Needless to say we all recognize the necessity for taking important political considerations into account in exceptional cases, but if this is to be done such cases must be the exceptions rather than the rule. As a matter of practical internal politics we can see how it will be very difficult for the Brazilian officials to agree to many cases being placed on the Proclaimed List. However, if they are prepared to check our information against theirs through the joint consultations and then let the decision and the onus of listing rest with us, their position would seem to be less vulnerable, particularly when they can subsequently intercede on a firm's behalf to have the case considered for deletion on the basis of corrective measures taken by the firm or the government.

Despatch no. 6518 states that the local committee is generally opposed to inclusion of individuals on the Proclaimed List and suggests use of confidential list for most such cases. This raises the whole question of how far we can and should go in operating our controls on the basis of a confidential list. We are in full agreement that individuals who are connected with Proclaimed List firms but who would not be listed otherwise should generally be placed on the confidential list merely as potential cloaks. However, if an individual or a firm is engaged in inimical activities so that its transactions should be subject to effective control, the confidential list is not an adequate control measure. I will only mention the most important reasons why this is so:

1). The list cannot be kept confidential with respect to the people actually affected by the list. As soon as licenses are denied to the firm, the persons concerned complain to this government or to their government and all the controversies of public listing ensue.

2). To be an effective control measure the list would have to be put in the hands of

- (*a*) at least six departments.
- (*b*) all collectors of customs.
- (*c*) all Federal Reserve Banks.
- (*d*) all large banks doing foreign business.
- (*e*) all diplomatic missions and consulates in the countries affected.
- (*f*) large United States business firms in the countries affected.
- (*g*) British and Canadian governmental agencies and missions.

3). It provides for no control over exports to the United States by undesirable firms unless consuls use it to deny invoices, in which event the existence of firms on the list is known at once.

4). A confidential list creates so much confusion among American business houses here and abroad that these houses frequently refuse to take foreign commitments when there is, as at present, a surplus of domestic orders. This aspect is particularly serious today when we are almost forced to ask firms to maintain essential business with the American republics.

5). A confidential list cannot be worked along with general licenses, all of which must be revoked if the control is to be in any measure as complete as the Proclaimed List. Today the Board of Economic Warfare still permits many items to move under general licenses to the American republics and the Treasury Department, generally speaking, permits all transactions incidental to inter-American trade to move under general license if the person or firm is not on the Proclaimed List. The Department, and I am sure the other American republics, would be most reluctant to see these general licenses withdrawn, but that is precisely what will be done if we begin a general practice of placing numerous important cases on the confidential list rather than on the Proclaimed List. The Treasury Department at present does not operate on a confidential list but they will insist on doing so if the Proclaimed List is to be seriously compromised. I am reasonably certain that if we get a profusion of covert controls there will be no inter-American trade.

A confidential list as contemplated in the circular air mail instruction of November 25, 1942 [1941] [67] is admittedly of limited utility, but our belief is that it is probably worthwhile if used as a check on potential cloaks and as supplementary to rather than as an alternative control for the Proclaimed List.

The whole situation as we see it comes down pretty much to this: a strong Proclaimed List is a *sine qua non* of getting essential goods to Brazil as our production and licensing authorities cannot justify the domestic sacrifices involved unless there is reasonable assurance that the goods are only going to persons and firms known to be affirmatively friendly to hemispheric defense and our war aims; it is important for the Department and the diplomatic missions to maintain a strong guiding hand on Proclaimed List policies, but this can only be done by preserving the interdepartmental cooperation through the Proclaimed List committee, and any attempt to delegate this authority to the field or to put the Committee in the position whereby it is supposed to act upon mere recommendations from the missions rather than upon full information will surely result in each of the licensing authorities going their independent ways and probably in a demand for independent field people to handle the reporting on these matters.

I went over all of this with Dr. Souza Costa who appeared to be satisfied and stated several times that all President Vargas asked was an opportunity for the Brazilian officials to be heard before action was taken here. But our interview was hurried and neither Duggan [68] nor Dickey [69] nor I felt that we brought home to him the alternative to the Proclaimed List which would result from administrative separatism here. In particular I don't believe we were successful in explaining to him the vital connection between the maintenance of a strong Proclaimed List and our common efforts to get essential goods to Brazil. The American people and most of the people in the other American republics simply would not understand nor long tolerate a policy on our part which resulted in our severely limited exports being made available indiscriminately to our friends and pro-Axis elements. Such a policy would be unfair to our friends in Brazil and in the long run decidedly unrealistic politics for all of us. It seems to us that this is the crux of the matter which in some way we must

---

[67] Not printed.
[68] Laurence Duggan, Adviser on Political Relations.
[69] John S. Dickey, Acting Chief, Division of World Trade Intelligence.

get home to the Brazilian officials if we are to secure their sympathetic tolerance, if not their acceptance of a strong Proclaimed List.

With warm regards,

Most sincerely yours,   DEAN ACHESON

740.00112A European War, 1939/9549 : Telegram

The Ambassador in Brazil (Caffery) to the Secretary of State

RIO DE JANEIRO, April 1, 1942—10 p. m.
[Received 11: 55 p.m.]

1123. I recommended to Aranha [70] today that the two Governments reach an agreement with respect to the operation of the Proclaimed List. He repeated his objections to the policy but pointed out that in view of changing conditions in Brazil and the increasing military and economic cooperation between the two Governments that he now has no objection to our continuing the Proclaimed List but that we should keep in mind that the policy should be directed only against our common enemy.

He referred to other problems in the commerce between the two countries and said that he would appoint a commission composed of myself, Souza Costa, himself and any other persons we might designate together with our advisers to review cases and to make final decisions on all phases of our trade including the Proclaimed List. He said we would meet April 6 to discuss plans.

In view of Aranha's decision I may shortly recommend action on the accumulation of Proclaimed List cases which have been postponed because of the attitude of the Brazilian Government which I have not been in a position to strongly oppose lately owing to the necessity for the full cooperation of the Brazilian Government in obtaining military concession so vital to our war effort.

CAFFERY

740.00112A European War, 1939/10321 : Telegram

The Ambassador in Brazil (Caffery) to the Secretary of State

RIO DE JANEIRO, April 17, 1942—5 p. m.
[Received 11: 25 p. m.]

1306. My telegram No. 1041 [*1123*], April 1, 10 p. m. Aranha arranged for a meeting on April 16 at the office of the President of the Bank of Brazil [71] to discuss Proclaimed List problems. Those present included Aranha, Finance Minister Souza Costa, the President of

---

[70] Oswaldo Aranha, Brazilian Minister for Foreign Affairs.
[71] João Marques dos Reis.

the Bank of Brazil, the Director of Exchange, the Chief of the Economic and Commercial Section of the Foreign Office, myself and my Commercial Attaché.

Following a long discussion of the Proclaimed List policy as applied to Brazil, the Brazilians decided to (1) waive all objections to continuance of the Proclaimed List policy and administration and to collaborate with us in this work, and (2) name a Consultative Committee consisting of the Director of Exchange, the Chief of the Economic and Commercial Section of the Foreign Office and my Commercial Attaché. The President of the Bank of Brazil at the request of Aranha will keep in close touch with the Committee on behalf of the Brazilian Government. The Committee will (*a*) examine the present list with a view to determining the types of control that should be adopted over Axis commercial interests in Brazil; (*b*) make recommendations to nationalize such interests, including banks; (*c*) confer on choice of personnel to control these Axis interests; and (*d*) suggest cases for listing and delisting.

Aranha and Souza Costa favor the taking over of important Axis interests in the near future and they may recommend a policy similar to the Alien Property Custodian plan in the United States. They stressed the importance of absolute secrecy in handling these cases.

This collaboration is an important development in our relations with Brazil with respect to the Proclaimed List and more effective foreign funds control in Brazil.[72]

The first meeting of the Committee will take place today.

CAFFERY

INTEREST OF THE UNITED STATES IN THE ELIMINATION OF AXIS INFLUENCE FROM BRAZILIAN AIRLINES [73]

832.796/720a : Telegram

The Secretary of State to the Ambassador in Brazil (Caffery)

WASHINGTON, January 8, 1942—3 p. m.

60. Press reports state Condor [74] has been expropriated. Is there any basis for these reports? If so please furnish available details.

HULL

---

[72] For correspondence on the cooperative effort of the United States and Brazil to control international financial transactions involving Axis interests, see pp. 789 ff.

[73] Continued from *Foreign Relations*, 1941, vol. VI.

[74] Sindicato Condor, Ltda., Brazilian airline in which German interests had had powerful influence.

740.0011 European War 1939/18525 : Telegram

The Ambassador in Brazil (Caffery) to the Secretary of State

RIO DE JANEIRO, January 14, 1942—5 p. m.
[Received 5 : 50 p. m.]

139. Aranha [75] says that the Italian Ambassador [76] told him yesterday that if Brazil broke off diplomatic relations with the Axis Powers, Japan would declare war against Brazil and implied that difficulties might ensue with the Japanese colonies here. Aranha in reply in effect said : "So what?"

The Italian Ambassador insisted again that the Lati [77] planes be allowed to return to Italy, alleging that an agreement exists among the warring powers that commercial planes may not be shot down. Aranha says he made him an evasive answer to this.

CAFFERY

740.0011 European War 1939/18525 : Telegram

The Secretary of State to the Ambassador in Brazil (Caffery)

WASHINGTON, January 21, 1942—5 p. m.

169. Your 139, January 14, 5 p. m. With respect to the second paragraph of your telegram, as you are aware, the Department's position continues to be based upon the military (not commercial) nature of Lati and its service.

HULL

832.796/767 : Telegram

The Ambassador in Brazil (Caffery) to the Secretary of State

RIO DE JANEIRO, February 3, 1942—7 p. m.
[Received 8 : 40 p. m.]

333. For the Under Secretary.[78] The Minister for Air [79] and General Eduardo Gomes [80] have continued to insist that Condor has been reorganized and is now a Brazilian company. General Gomes used a specially chartered Condor plane yesterday to fly to the northeast.

The Porto Velho–Rio Branco service in the Acre territory is about to start again and they expect to put other routes into service at an early date also to get their radio stations operating again.

---

[75] Oswaldo Aranha, Brazilian Minister for Foreign Affairs.
[76] Ugo Sola, Italian Ambassador in Brazil.
[77] Lineas Aéreas Transcontinentales Italianas.
[78] Sumner Welles.
[79] Joaquim Pedro Salgado Filho.
[80] Commander of the 2d Air Zone and Director General of Airways, Brazilian Ministry of Aeronautics, representing Brazilian interests in the construction of air bases in northeast Brazil by United States interests.

As you know the feeling here against Panair [81] is very high and the Brazilian authorities resent what they believe is an attempt to secure a monopoly in Brazil for Panair. The principal Brazilian officials especially Aranha are determined that Condor shall operate as a Brazilian company; and they assert that it is now Brazilian. They will be asking soon for gasoline as soon as they have used up what they have left.

The local Panair people asked me today if I would object to their buying a Condor plane; I have not yet answered them.

CAFFERY

832.796/773 : Telegram

The Ambassador in Brazil (Caffery) to the Secretary of State

RIO DE JANEIRO, February 4, 1942—8 p. m.
[Received 10 : 18 p. m.]

348. Department's 236, January 29 [82] and my 342, February 4.[83] Salgado says he will requisition the planes at once and will appoint a commission to evaluate. He will turn the planes over to us as soon as we agree on price and will give us legal title thereto.

He says there are seven planes scattered at Rio de Janeiro, Pernambuco and Natal. He will furnish us with specifications, et cetera, as soon as the commission gets underway.

Salgado has just returned from São Paulo and gave me this information over the telephone. He insisted on getting a commitment that we would buy if he requisitioned (at a reasonable price of course).

CAFFERY

832.796/767 : Telegram

The Secretary of State to the Ambassador in Brazil (Caffery)

WASHINGTON, February 4, 1942—11 p. m.

275. Your 333, February 3, 7 p. m. The Department is of course extremely anxious to cooperate with the Brazilian Government in every way possible to ensure the successful reorganization and operation of Condor as a Brazilian company. A definitive proposal is currently being worked out and will be shortly submitted to you for your comment.

---

[81] Panair do Brasil, subsidiary of Pan American Airways.

[82] Not printed; this telegram conveyed the interest of the United States military authorities in obtaining a number of planes of the Italian Transcontinental Air Lines, whose operations had been curtailed (832.796/759).

[83] Not printed; it reported that the Fiat-Argentina firm was also interested in obtaining the equipment of the Italian company, but the Bank of Brazil rejected the offer (832.796/769).

Meanwhile, having in mind the assurances of Brazilian officials such as that reported in your despatch 6167 of December 31 [84] that they "will eliminate any and everyone you point out as pro-German", are you and Harding [85] in a position to point out specific individuals whose removal would make the present organization of Condor reasonably satisfactory to you? If so it would be helpful to know their names or number and what American or Brazilian personnel might be necessary or advisable to replace them.

The Department feels sure that you will agree that a resumption of flights by Condor prior to the elimination of dangerous German influence might have seriously unfavorable results from a military and naval point of view, to say nothing of the possible use of these planes and personnel in local subversive activities. Consequently the Department believes that the question of licensing gasoline for the use of Condor, which is now on the Proclaimed List, [86] should not, if possible, be brought up until you are satisfied that the Brazilians have taken adequate steps to eliminate the dangerous elements such as pilots. It is, therefore, suggested that, on the basis of information available to you, immediate conversations be initiated with the Brazilians for the purpose particularly of seeing that suspect pilots and airfield operators are immediately eliminated. The Department trusts that these conversations can be carried on in a cooperative manner since it obviously does not desire to make the furnishing of gasoline a *quid pro quo* for this type of action by the Brazilian Government.

Your question regarding purchase of Condor plane by Panair was referred to Army Air Corps today. They have asked us to obtain name and type of plane.

HULL

---

832. 796/767 : Telegram

The Secretary of State to the Ambassador in Brazil (Caffery)

WASHINGTON, February 5, 1942—11 p. m.

290. Your no. 333, February 3, 1942. You may give assurance to Aranha that neither Panair do Brasil nor Pan American Airways will participate in any plan of collaboration that may be worked out between representatives of this Government and the Brazilian authorities in connection with the operations of Condor. It is not the in-

---

[84] Not printed.
[85] William B. Harding, Vice President of the Defense Supplies Corporation, a buying agency of the Federal Loan Agency until February 24, 1942, and thereafter of the Department of Commerce.
[86] For correspondence regarding the application of the Proclaimed List, see pp. 757 ff.

tention of this Government to create any monopoly of Brazilian aviation for Panair. You may state also that in so far as may be desired by the Brazilian authorities this Government is prepared to call upon Pan American Airways to cancel any extensions of service within Brazil that may have been made as a result of the cessation of the Condor flights.

Since it is understood that the Brazilian authorities will probably make a request for the furnishing of gasoline to Condor, it is felt that you should at the earliest moment endeavor to obtain a commitment from them that in order that the company may be regarded as a bona fide national organization the Brazilian Government will be disposed to assume complete control and ownership of Condor and set it up as a wholly Brazilian corporation thus divorcing it from all links with its past corporate set up. While it would appear to be desirable for the name of the company to be changed in order to lend emphasis to the fact that it has been reorganized as a Brazilian national company, Department leaves it to your discretion to decide whether it would be advisable to make a suggestion to this effect to the Brazilian authorities.

It is deemed to be highly important that as a first step action be taken with the view to eliminating from the Condor service all dangerous Axis personnel or persons in sympathy with the Axis powers. It would seem necessary at once to eliminate Hoelen [87] and other key men of his leanings. It is particularly important, in this connection, that all doubtful personnel having anything to do with the operation of radio be removed at the earliest possible moment.

In order that a general survey may be made of the situation as to personnel and equipment, the D. S. C. [88] is sending Tom Hardin [89] to Rio immediately to consult with you in regard to the carrying out of this survey. Hardin with your assistance should be able to suggest names of persons who should be removed from Condor and make recommendations and assist in obtaining United States personnel on a temporary basis pending training of satisfactory Brazilians for the positions vacated. This is considered to be highly desirable in order that we may be in a position to render as much assistance as possible in the way of furnishing temporary substitute personnel as well as equipment. It is thought, in this connection, that if reliable executive personnel could first be provided it would be an important step in the direction of the removal of all Axis influence from the Condor operation.

HULL

---

[87] Presumably this refers to Ernesto Hoelik (also spelled Holck and Hoelck), a German director of Condor.
[88] Defense Supplies Corporation.
[89] Technical aviation expert.

832.796/773 : Telegram

The Secretary of State to the Ambassador in Brazil (Caffery)

WASHINGTON, February 5, 1942—midnight.

292. Your 348, February 4, 8 p. m. You are authorized to make a commitment for the purchase of the Lati planes at a reasonable price upon their being requisitioned by the Brazilian Government, which it is hoped will be done immediately.

The D. S. C. is cabling appropriate authority to Harding to arrange for the purchase of the planes.

HULL

832.796/775 : Telegram

The Ambassador in Brazil (Caffery) to the Secretary of State

RIO DE JANEIRO, February 6, 1942—4 p. m.
[Received 5 : 45 p. m.]

368. Colonel Muricy, the Government's interventor in Condor, has informed the Minister of Air that the statutes of the company have been completely changed and that the total capital stock and the administration is now in the hands of native-born Brazilians. He further informed that "these steps have been taken envisaging the complete reorganization of the company along the lines desired by the Government" and requested permission of the Minister to renew Condor's services. The Minister granted this permission in the following terms "traffic on the lines already authorized may be renewed. A complete list of the company's agents should be presented with the nationality of each indicated".

The Minister also authorized the flight of Condor's *Maipo* from Ceará to Rio for repairs and the *Abaitara* from Buenos Aires to Rio de Janeiro.

CAFFERY

832.796/802 : Telegram

The Secretary of State to the Ambassador in Brazil (Caffery)

WASHINGTON, February 13, 1942—11 p. m.

354. In the course of a discussion between officers of the Defense Supplies Corporation and the Department, the Brazilian Ambassador [90] and the Brazilian Minister of Finance,[91] the Minister was informed that provided Condor was satisfactorily de-Germanized it

---

[90] Carlos Martins.
[91] Arthur de Souza Costa; his presence in Washington was for the purpose of obtaining defense materials from the United States.

might be possible to furnish two or three Lockheed planes and perhaps two or three DC–3's to Condor in the very near future. It was emphasized to Souza Costa that unless a decision was made very promptly these airplanes would not be available since there was a great need for them in the war effort.

Department is advised that this information has been transmitted to the Brazilian Government and that it is probable you will be approached regarding the matter by Condor.

HULL

832.796/805 : Telegram

The Secretary of State to the Ambassador in Brazil (Caffery)

WASHINGTON, February 18, 1942—midnight.

395. For Harding from Weld.[92]

"The purchase of the seven Lati planes and equipment has been approved by Defense Supplies Board for amount of $300,000. If less than all the planes are sold, offer applies pro rata. Ten thousand dollars for expenses in this connection has been allowed by the Board. The certified resolution and a power of attorney are being sent to you. Funds can be made available on short notice for you in Rio bank."

HULL

832.796/787 : Telegram

The Acting Secretary of State to the Ambassador in Brazil (Caffery)

WASHINGTON, February 23, 1942—8 p. m.

439. Further reference is made to your telegram no. 392, February 10, 3 p. m.[93] Colonel Clay[94] who states he saw Harding only 4 days ago, and Colonel Heard of MID,[95] who referred to advices from your Military Attaché reported the following to the Department today:

(1) Condor has resumed flights.
(2) Condor has used FAB gasoline for these flights.
(3) The movement of Brazilian troops to the Natal area has been ordered stopped.
(4) Clandestine radio stations are resuming activity.

Please telegraph urgently whether these reports are correct and whether, particularly if flights have been resumed, they are regular, or special flights for the Brazilian Government.

WELLES

[92] Edward M. Weld, member of the United States Military Mission in Brazil.
[93] Not printed.
[94] Col. Lucius D. Clay, representing the War Department on the Permanent Joint Board for Northeast Brazil.
[95] Presumably Col. R. Townsend Heard, Military Intelligence Division.

832.796/821 : Telegram

The Ambassador in Brazil (Caffery) to the Secretary of State

Rio de Janeiro, March 12, 1942—7 p. m.
[Received 11 p. m.]

829. My 634, February 28, 3 p. m.[96] Eduardo Gomes has given almost enthusiastic approval to the various matters set out in the Department's telegram 428, February 21, 9 p. m.[97] and has given warm promises of cooperation.

At the same time, however, he continues to insist that Condor which he contends now is completely Brazilian should be allowed to resume operations. Standard Oil informs me that they have received instructions from him that the Brazilian Army is requisitioning the remaining stocks of gasoline belonging to Condor, Lati, and Air France.[98] He ordered Standard to deliver immediately 10,000 liters to Corumbá and 15,000 liters to São Luiz do Maranhão. I told Standard to stall for a few days. I shall speak on the subject with Aranha. (As the Department is aware, Gomes is the most popular and most powerful officer in the Brazilian forces and obeys the Minister's instructions only when he want[s] to.)

CAFFERY

832.796/822 : Telegram

The Ambassador in Brazil (Caffery) to the Secretary of State

Rio de Janeiro, March 12, 1942—11 p. m.
[Received March 13—7 : 51 a. m.]

832. For the Acting Secretary. My 829, March 12, 7 p. m. Aranha tells me that President Vargas himself was behind the orders given to Standard Oil. Aranha says that on the one hand President Vargas is cooperating and will continue to cooperate with us in the war business and has only today put out decrees confiscating Axis properties, et cetera et cetera; on the other hand he is convinced that the Washington authorities are all wrong in their attitude to Condor which he considers, especially since the dismissal of so many German employees, a purely Brazilian company and "he is not" says Aranha "disposed to be dictated to by Washington on this".

However, Aranha says he has agreed with the Condor management that they are willing to take on Hardin at once as adviser and follow his advice in the reorganization of the company; they are willing also to change the name but they cannot do that for some months in

[96] Not printed.
[97] *Ante,* p. 648.
[98] One of the pioneer commercial airlines in Brazil.

view of contractual obligations involved. The Lufthansa [99] debt will be taken care of by today's decree.

CAFFERY

832.796/823 : Telegram

The Ambassador in Brazil (Caffery) to the Secretary of State

RIO DE JANEIRO, March 13, 1942—noon.
[Received 5 : 13 p. m.]

837. For the Acting Secretary. My 829, March 12, 7 p. m. On Saturday last, Ribeiro Dantas, Condor president, and Major Muricy went to see President Vargas with a letter Dantas received from Harding when they were both in Buenos Aires recently. The letter contained the following: "I would recommend that the American Government cooperate with Condor if you take the following steps to insure severance of all Axis connections:" Then followed the conditions which in themselves are not objectionable.

However, President Vargas did not like this and had the order issued to Standard Oil.

Aranha says that as much as Vargas wants to cooperate with us in the war against Germany, he is not happy about what he considers attempts on our part to interfere in his domestic concerns.

He feels now apparently about the Proclaimed List as Aranha did a couple of months ago. "He feels likewise", says Aranha, "that he is perfectly competent to decide what activities here are harmful to Brazil and what are not."

Aranha invited pointed attention also to remarks of President Roosevelt in regard to the attitude to be taken to aliens in the United States.

Aranha said moreover that if Standard Oil refused to deliver the 10,000 liters of gasoline at Corumbá and the 15,000 liters at São Luiz the matter would become one for immediate Government action. Under those circumstances I told Standard this morning that it would be the better part of discretion for them to deliver the gasoline; especially as the amounts are small.

I take Hardin to a meeting with Aranha, Dantas and Muricy this afternoon.

CAFFERY

---

[99] Deutsche Lufthansa Aktiengesellschaft Berlin, the chief German commercial aviation company.

832.796/823 : Telegram

The Acting Secretary of State to the Ambassador in Brazil (Caffery)

WASHINGTON, March 14, 1942—7 p. m.

652. Your 829, March 12, 7 p. m., 832, March 12, 11 p. m., and 837, March 13, noon. I am requesting the proper persons interested in this matter to meet on Monday to canvass it anew with a view to sending you a detailed statement of the Department's views. In this connection it would be helpful to have in addition to your report of your conversation yesterday with Aranha your recommendations as to the best way to proceed in this difficult situation.

You, of course, are thoroughly aware that the War Department looks with great concern upon the continued and unrestricted use by Condor of its radio facilities. Reports received from absolutely reliable sources indicate that the Axis is kept fully posted on the movement of all United States military aircraft through Brazil.

From what I know of the situation, it seems that the status of Hardin now becomes almost the crux of the situation because if Condor really follows his advice in effecting the complete reorganization of the company, we would fully attain our objective.

I agree that under the circumstances you took the right course in authorizing the delivery to Condor of the gasoline ordered by the Brazilian Government. I hope, however, that it will be possible to avoid future requests until you are satisfied that the company no longer is a threat.

WELLES

832.796/853a : Telegram

The Acting Secretary of State to the Ambassador in Brazil (Caffery)

WASHINGTON, March 18, 1942—10 p. m.

686. Your recent telegrams on Condor. In view of your references to the requisitioning by the Brazilian Army of the remaining stock of gasoline belonging to Condor, Lati, and Air France the thought arose at an interdepartmental meeting March 16 that this may have been a stratagem adopted by Gomes for the purpose of removing the gasoline in question from the licensing control exercised by this Government. Such a subterfuge obviously would be inconsistent with Aranha's professions contained in your 878 of March 14, 7 p. m.[1] In addition it is felt that in the event of an unsatisfactory reorganization of Condor such a development would seriously complicate the situation. An expression of your views will be appreciated.

---

[1] Not printed.

As you and Hardin and the Brazilian authorities appear to be in agreement regarding the total elimination of German influence, the Department feels that the following conditions should be met before it recommends Condor's removal from the Proclaimed List.

1. All citizens of the Axis powers be removed and only loyal native-born citizens of the American republics be employed in the reorganized Condor. This might be modified on your recommendation in meritorious individual cases.

2. No direct or indirect control over the financial, technical and management functions of the company be exercised except by citizens of the Hemisphere who subscribe to the principles set forth in the Declaration of Lima.[2]

3. An entirely new corporate structure be established as a substitute for that of the present Condor company. This could be substantially accomplished through the separation of Condor's principal assets from its liabilities to Lufthansa. The assets would form the basis of the new company and the liabilities would remain frozen and be removed from the books. Any payments for Condor's assets to be effectively frozen except those accruing to entirely satisfactory persons.

4. Agreement to adopt a new name as soon as possible.

If it would be of immediate assistance in reducing attempts to have Condor delisted; and if you feel steps being taken to de-Germanize Condor warrant such action and would facilitate future negotiations, we would recommend that the Treasury grant licenses for the sale of specific amounts of gasoline approved by you. It should, of course, be clearly understood and agreed to by the Brazilians that the granting of any such licenses is based on the assumption that the complete de-Germanization of Condor is proceeding. We strongly hope, however, that it will be possible to avoid the licensing stage.

As a final step after delisting, an arrangement could be made whereby Condor's successor would obtain such needed equipment as is possible to secure for it provided at least one JU–52 is surrendered for each new airplane furnished, and provided that a sound technical and financial basis is established. In this connection, the Defense Supplies Corporation has a firm commitment from the War Department that the seven DC–3's recently taken away from it by the War Department will be replaced beginning in June or July. You may assure the Brazilians that the Defense Supplies will be able and will-

---

[2] Declaration of the Principles of the Solidarity of America, known as the "Declaration of Lima", approved December 24, 1938, *Report of the Delegation of the United States of America to the Eighth International Conference of American States, Lima, Peru, December 9–27, 1938* (Washington, Government Printing Office, 1941), p. 189.

ing to provide the new company new equipment beginning in June or July provided that the conditions mentioned above are fulfilled by that time.

In other words, there could be three steps; the first to consist of specified and limited licensing of gasoline on the basis of progress already made and satisfactory commitments for the future; second, formal delisting when the points enumerated above have been met; and third, whatever equipment and financial assistance may be needed after the company has operated on the new basis for a few months. It should be understood that step 1 would not be taken unless the Brazilians agreed to take the succeeding measure leading to delisting, and that step 3 (financial assistance and equipment) could only be undertaken on the basis of securing a JU–52 for each new airplane furnished, and on the basis of a reasonably satisfactory financial and technical set-up for Condor's successor.

Your 700, March 5, 2 p. m.[3]

The Department feels that it would be highly desirable if Condor's identity and services were to be completely absorbed by N.A.B.[4] The above is conditioned on the assumption that you and Hardin will consider the above acceptable from your standpoint and the standpoint of the Brazilian Government.

WELLES

832.796/853c : Telegram

The Acting Secretary of State to the Ambassador in Brazil (Caffery)

WASHINGTON, March 26, 1942—10 p. m.

776. Buenos Aires' telegram to you of March 20.[5] It is assumed that the Brazilian Government will sell the expropriated Lati airplanes to this Government and not to the Argentine or to any Argentine company. It is, of course, obvious that Germany and Italy are directly behind attempts of Corporación, Fiat, and other Argentine companies to obtain Lati airplanes.

If you believe it desirable you may reassure the Brazilians that the United States will purchase and pay a reasonable price for the Lati planes.

WELLES

---

[3] Not printed.
[4] Brazilian National Air Force.
[5] See telegram No. 519, March 20, from the Ambassador in Argentina, p. 432. For correspondence on the efforts of the United States to eliminate Axis influence in the operation of commercial air companies in Argentina, see pp. 428 ff.

832.796/823

Memorandum by the Assistant Chief of the Division of the American Republics (Walmsley)[6]

[WASHINGTON,] March 28, 1942.

The gist of Brigadier Gomes' gratuitous remarks on Condor to me last night[7] was:

1. Condor, irrespective of origin or background, did and should still render highly important service to Brazil.

2. Condor has been for some time much more Brazilian than Panair.

3. It is Brazil's prerogative to determine how Condor should be reorganized to make it completely Brazilian.

4. Condor is now making flights which are primarily of a military nature, at his orders. Crews on these flights are by and large Brazilian reserve officers and pilots.

5. There are some sort of contract obligations which make it immediately impossible to change the name; but eventually this should come.

6. Brigadier Gomes expects and wants in due course our assistance in technical aspects of operation and equipment.

W. N. WALMSLEY, JR.

832.796/896a : Telegram

The Secretary of State to the Ambassador in Brazil (Caffery)

WASHINGTON, May 19, 1942—9 p. m.

1275. The Defense Supplies Corporation wishes to make an initial offer of $300,000 for the Lati planes including the spare engines and parts. The Defense Supplies Corporation prefers that you handle the negotiations, aided by McAshan,[8] who has instructions to give you any assistance you may need. McAshan will be authorized to sign any documents on behalf of the Defense Supplies Corporation.

The Department agrees with the Defense Supplies Corporation that the Lati planes should be purchased and removed from Brazil as soon as possible.

HULL

---

[6] Addressed to Philip O. Chalmers, Randolph Harrison, Jr., Philip W. Bonsal, and Livingston Satterthwaite of the Division of the American Republics, and Laurence Duggan, Adviser on Political Relations.
[7] Brig. Eduardo Gomes was on an official visit to the United States at this time.
[8] S. Maurice McAshan, representative of the Defense Supplies Corporation.

832.796/896 : Telegram

The Secretary of State to the Ambassador in Brazil (Caffery)

WASHINGTON, May 22, 1942—5 p. m.

1309. Your 1720, May 20, 9 p. m. and Department's 1242 and 1268.[9] We assume that you will not recommend the deletion of Condor or despatch of technicians until you are satisfied that ties between Condor and Lufthansa have been cut. We are making every effort to hold the technicians, and await your reply.

HULL

832.796/912

The American Ambassador in Brazil (Caffery) to the Brazilian Minister for Foreign Affairs (Aranha)[10]

No. 111   RIO DE JANEIRO, June 1, 1942.

MY DEAR MR. MINISTER: As Your Excellency is aware, I have been endeavoring for some time and am still endeavoring to help Condor. As Your Excellency is also aware, our efforts have been successful to the point of making arrangements at Washington for necessary material and technicians.

However, I must repeat that in my frank opinion, notwithstanding the fact that a number of very useful steps have been taken by the Brazilian Government to cut Condor loose entirely from Lufthansa, all the necessary steps have not yet been taken.

In view of the well known desire of the Brazilian authorities to sever completely all ties between the Deutsche Lufthansa (which is, in effect, the German Government) and the Serviços Aéreos Condor. I venture to make the following suggestions:

1. All outstanding contracts, commitments and agreements between Condor and Lufthansa to be specifically annulled and cancelled by law. (This especially refers to the exchange of letters between Condor and Lufthansa dated December 31, 1941 and the new social contract of Condor dated January 6, 1942. These documents clearly show that just as soon as the war is over, Lufthansa will once more in fact control Condor. See enclosure No. 1.[11])

2. Liquidation of Condor's indebtedness to Lufthansa which is on the books for 54,989 contos. This debt to be completely wiped out. Obviously it is for the Brazilian Government to decide whether it desires to assume this debt or whether it is to be liquidated or cancelled in some other convenient manner.

3. Although Condor has made great strides in the Brazilianization of the line, the financial and corporate structure of the company is

---

[9] None printed.
[10] Copy transmitted to the Department by the Ambassador in his despatch No. 7506, June 2; received June 9.
[11] Not printed.

still very confused. It could be reorganized so that it would possess a solid legal and factual structure, which it lacks today. For example, I cannot believe that the Brazilian Government wishes simply to turn over the very valuable Condor property, which is unquestionably worth many thousands of contos, to the five Brazilian private partners, who have obtained control of it for 100 contos, the total capital!

In view of the very close connections which the present Condor partners maintained with the former Condor–Lufthansa set-up, and the nature of the December 31, 1941 agreement and the contract of January 6, 1942, it is difficult to avoid the conclusion that although these Brazilian partners are nominally in possession of the quotas comprising the 100 contos capital, they might be holding them in trust for the German interests until hostilities have ceased.

Again I venture a suggestion, and that is that the answer to the problem might be in the conversion of Condor into a Sociedade Anonyma. In this manner the properties which are worth, say 40,000 or 50,000 contos, would appear in the form of capital and thus title to the assets of the company would not remain in the hands of the Germans. Furthermore, in accordance with the law of Sociedades Anonymas (Decreto-Lei No. 2627, September 26, 1940) the shares would have to be nominative. However, this of course would be a matter for the Brazilian Government to decide.

4. I venture another suggestion and that is that, in my opinion, an excellent impression would be made if the name "Condor" were changed into, say, a name like "Rondon" for instance.

5. Finally, I venture to invite attention to the fact that Herr Ernest Holck is still a director of the company.

In this connection I enclose the following: Copy of a memorandum of April 6, 1942; Copy of a memorandum of May 29, 1942.[12]

With all good wishes,

Sincerely yours,
JEFFERSON CAFFERY

832.796/912 : Telegram

The Secretary of State to the Ambassador in Brazil (Caffery)

WASHINGTON, June 19, 1942—midnight.

1599. Reference your despatch no. 750 [*7506*], June 2, 1942.[13] Since there are several steps yet to be taken by the Brazilian Government and the Condor organization before that company could be removed from the Proclaimed List, and since there does not seem to be a great likelihood of these steps being taken immediately, the Department and the Defense Supplies Corporation are in agreement that the technicians which Duncan[14] has secured, and Duncan himself, must be released for service with the War Department or other organizations directly connected with the war effort.

---

[12] Neither printed.
[13] See footnote 10, p. 779.
[14] Francis L. Duncan, representative of the Reconstruction Finance Corporation.

We are hopeful, however, that when the Brazilian Government and the Condor organization take steps which would justify removal of that company from the Proclaimed List, it will be possible to find, on reasonably short notice, satisfactory technicians in this country, if they are wanted.

It probably will not be possible to hold the DC–3 airplanes, earmarked for Condor, which will be delivered to the Defense Supplies Corporation in July, but we believe that it will be possible to obtain, in replacement for these, three others from the War Department when and if Condor is removed from the Proclaimed List and it is otherwise considered advisable to sell it this equipment.

In connection with the sale of gasoline to Condor by the Brazilian Government, we cannot lose sight of the fact that a commodity, of which there is a shortage, and which is produced in the United States or abroad by United States companies, and which occupies scarce shipping space, is being diverted by the Brazilian Government to a Proclaimed List firm which we consider to be German in important respects. The Department is confident that both you and Aranha will appreciate the adverse effect of this situation upon the effectiveness of the economic warfare effort of the two Governments.

HULL

832.796/958 : Telegram

The Ambassador in Brazil (Caffery) to the Secretary of State

RIO DE JANEIRO, July 25, 1942—7 p. m.
[Received 10:50 p. m.]

2720. My despatch 7506, June 2. I am sending by air mail tomorrow morning a copy of a letter which I have received from Aranha in which he incloses a copy of the opinion of the legal adviser of his Ministry [15] which he contends satisfactorily answers the questions raised in my letter of June 1.[16]

He told me that the delay in reaching the solution of Condor's status is irritating President Vargas; causing him, Aranha, a variety of difficulties; and impelling General Eduardo Gomes to reprisals. He pleads that something be done to settle the matter.

Aranha asserts that Central Powers already complied with most of our Condor demands; that they have dismissed 200 employees, et cetera, et cetera; that Condor is losing money every day. He says: "Send us some one who can go into Condor and tell them what to do: They

---

[15] Sebastião do Rego Barros; copies of the letter and enclosure transmitted to the Department by the Ambassador in his despatch No. 8033, July 25, 1942, not printed.
[16] *Ante*, p. 779.

will do everything he wants: Holck will be removed as soon as you can give us some one who can really [apparent omission] company."

I said: "What about changing the name?" He said: "That can be done too."

CAFFERY

832.796/958 : Telegram

The Acting Secretary of State to the Ambassador in Brazil (Caffery)

WASHINGTON, August 1, 1942—11 p. m.

2122. The Department believes that prompt decisions are indicated in relation to current aviation problems in Brazil.

(1) Condor. Your telegram 2720 of July 25, 7 p. m. The Department regrets that the letter from Aranha enclosed with your despatch 8033 of July 25 is not accompanied by your specific recommendation whether Condor should or should not be delisted. For your information Defense Supplies Corporation has for some time had seven DC–3 planes on order for Brazil, some of them to be available for Condor. These planes are now about ready but in view of the extreme shortage of equipment it is unthinkable that they be left idle. In view however of the unsatisfactory nature of Aranha's reply to your letter of July [*June*] 1, the Defense Supplies Corporation may be reluctantly forced to allocate these planes elsewhere for their immediate use in the most efficient manner. For example, we hope to use some of them in any case in Brazil for the building up of increased services to and within the Amazon region in connection with the rubber development program.[17]

Although it may be possible to earmark additional planes from future production for Condor, it should be borne in mind that when the conditions for delisting Condor are met it may not be practical to lay hands on planes for it immediately. In this connection please furnish specific details concerning the points which in your opinion remain to be cleared up before delisting can be recommended.

(2) Your airgram A–62 of July 25 [18] which reached the Department on July 30, after the receipt of your telegrams 2759, 2778 and 2779,[19] all of which appear to be favorable replies to our 2030 of July 24,[20] has seriously disturbed this Department, the War Department, the CAB,[21] et cetera. The Brazilian Embassy here furthermore has voiced its distress at the effect of the reduction of the services on the

---

[17] For correspondence on this subject, see pp. 691 ff.
[18] Not printed; it reported the denial of permission to the Pan American Airways to increase its service on the so-called Belém–Barreiras–Rio cutoff (810.-79611 Pan American Airways/3197).
[19] None printed.
[20] Not printed.
[21] Civil Aeronautics Board.

travel of the persons for whom it is seeking urgent priorities, and the Department understands the Brazilian Ambassador has sent a telegram in the premises to the Itamaraty.[22]

(3) It is repeated that the expanded international service on the cut-off was to meet the demands for travel service of the American republics especially Brazil and was operated by Pan American Airways rather than Panair do Brasil to permit the most efficient use of equipment, et cetera in the face of the imperative demands of the armed forces for flying equipment, pilots, et cetera.

There is a crying need for additional air transports in the Caribbean, etc., where the released equipment from the cut-off can be put to efficient use.

Please stress these points to the appropriate Brazilian authorities, whose cooperation is sought in the emergency in the interest of the two countries, not merely of the carrier, and report urgently, submitting your recommendations.

WELLES

832.796/965 : Telegram

The Secretary of State to the Ambassador in Brazil (Caffery)

WASHINGTON, August 14, 1942—5 p. m.

2282. Aranha's compromise suggestion described in your 2816, July 31, 7 p. m.[23] has been found acceptable. The Department hopes to inform you shortly of the proposed personnel.[24]

With respect to Buenos Aires' telegram No. 1532, August 7,[25] and No. 1553, August 11, repeated to you,[25] that Embassy is being instructed to inform Intava [26] that no gasoline supplies should be furnished to Condor under any circumstances, pending further communication from the Department.

It is hoped that a rapid and satisfactory solution to the Condor problem will be found on the return of the Ambassador to Rio de Janeiro. It is essential, however, that the *status quo* be maintained and that detailed conversations be deferred until that time.

HULL

---

[22] The Brazilian Foreign Office.
[23] Not printed.
[24] Alexander B. Royce, a consultant to the Defense Supplies Corporation, was sent to Rio de Janeiro under joint instructions of the Department of State and the Defense Supplies Corporation to study, in consultation with F. W. Duncan of the Supplies Corporation, the situation with respect to Condor.
[25] *Ante*, p. 445.
[26] International Aviation Associates, a marketing agency in Argentina of Standard Oil aviation products.

832.796/1030 : Telegram

The Ambassador in Brazil (Caffery) to the Secretary of State

RIO DE JANEIRO, September 30, 1942—3 p. m.
[Received 4 : 15 p. m.]

3908. The loss of a Panair do Brasil airplane 2 days ago plus the increasing demand for services make it desirable that Panair do Brasil, which can certainly use them, be provided with more airplanes. The loss of the DC–2's without replacement would seriously reduce Panair do Brasil's services.

It is suggested therefore that two of the Defense Supplies' Lockheed Lodestars be sold or leased to Panair as soon as possible. The Air Ministry strongly objects to letting the two DC–2's sold to Pluna [27] leave Brazil. It is believed however that these objections will be overcome if two Lodestars are forthcoming for Panair do Brasil. Obviously definite permission would be obtained to remove the DC–2's from Brazil prior to the sending of the Lodestars. Satterthwaite concurs.

CAFFERY

832.796/1035 : Telegram

The Ambassador in Brazil (Caffery) to the Secretary of State

RIO DE JANEIRO, October 6, 1942—6 p. m.
[Received October 7—1 : 50 a. m.]

4026. For Chalmers from Satterthwaite. Anderson, Standard Oil, has received telegram through Naval Attaché [28] from Michler [29] requesting that I telegraph you my opinion of propriety of delivering fuel and oil to Varig [30] for run Porto Alegre–Montevideo, and to Corporación [31] for proposed Buenos Aires–Rio de Janeiro service.

I recommend that Varig receive reasonable and necessary amounts fuel for Porto Alegre–Montevideo service, but that Corporación not be given any fuel for any extension of its services. Every effort should be made to prevent Corporación from obtaining fuel elsewhere for contemplated run.

Repeated to Buenos Aires. [Satterthwaite.]

CAFFERY

---

[27] Uruguayan airline.
[28] Rear Adm. Augustin T. Beauregard.
[29] G. H. Michler, official of the Standard Oil Company of New York.
[30] S. A. Empresa de Viação Aerea Rio Grandense.
[31] Corporación Sudamericana de Servicios Aéreos, S. A.

832.79635/23 : Telegram

The Acting Secretary of State to the Ambassador in Brazil (Caffery)

WASHINGTON, October 10, 1942—9 p. m.

3032. Your telegram 3782, September 23, 2 p. m.[32] The Department wants to clarify its telegram 2795 of September 22nd, midnight,[33] in the sense that it has no intention of taking any steps to block an international air service desired by the Brazilian Government. The Department does not believe that this Government has any justification to prevent the Brazilian Government from fostering international air services and furthermore believes that any attempt on our part to do so would probably have serious consequences to our general relations with Brazil.

In connection with your expected recommendation for delisting Condor, the Department assumes you are satisfied with your control over Proclaimed List travel and cargo and that you believe censorship is adequate. (Your 4045, October 7, 6 p. m.[32]) This is especially important now that the Buenos Aires service is resumed, as we are not at all satisfied that the local Argentine Condor organization is entirely clean.

In the foregoing connection, reference is made to your A–284 of September 14, 10 p. m. [a. m.],[32] and especially Ambassador Armour's telegram to you of October 7, noon.[32]

WELLES

832.796/1030 : Telegram

The Secretary of State to the Ambassador in Brazil (Caffery)

WASHINGTON, October 21, 1942—10 p. m.

3171. Your 3908, September 30, 3 p. m.

1. The equipment in DSC's pool is intended to be used in the de-Axization program or for the rehabilitation of Latin American air lines to prevent any return of these lines to Axis hands, and in other special situations. The Department understands Panair do Brasil's problem but Defense Supplies states its equipment is not available for the purposes mentioned. If, however, Pan American Airways, on behalf of Panair do Brasil, applies for this extra equipment through the proper channels, which includes approval by the War Department, the Department will be glad to be of assistance.

---

[32] Not printed.
[33] Not printed; in this instruction the Department had disapproved of resumption of flights to Buenos Aires by Condor (832.79635/22a).

2. Defense Supplies equipment is not, it is repeated, intended to fill requirements for the maintenance of existing United States commercial services or for their "normal" expansion.

3. The apparent endeavor to reopen the question of the DC–2's regarding which the Brazilian Government is committed (your telegram 2765 of July 28, 7 p. m.[37]), and the DSC in turn is committed to Pluna, is in our opinion unjustified and unreasonable. The proposed Pluna arrangement on which, we repeat, we are committed, subject to Pluna's fulfillment of prescribed conditions, is also an important part of our aviation program; and the acquisition of the DC–2's for it is entirely unrelated to Panair's problem of extra equipment for "normal" services. The Brazilian Air Ministry will not have forgotten that as part of our efforts to assist Brazilian aviation, two Lodestars have just been delivered to NAB (Department's 1342, May 25, midnight[37]).

The DSC fully concurs in the foregoing.

HULL

832.796/1074 : Telegram

The Secretary of State to the Ambassador in Brazil (Caffery)

WASHINGTON, November 5, 1942—midnight.

3410. Mr. Royce[38] has reported to the Department his recommendations concerning the delisting of Condor, in accordance with his letter to you of October 30, 1942.[37]

The Department is in full agreement with these recommendations and is prepared to recommend deletion to the Interdepartmental Committee as soon as word is received from you that (1) the name will be officially changed, (2) the shares held by Ernesto Hoelck have been transferred to satisfactory persons, and (3) that a satisfactory third director has been named.

Point (3) above, though highly desirable, will not be considered a condition precedent to the delisting of Condor. However, points (1) and (2), as well as your own definite recommendations, are considered essential.

You are informed that the next supplement will be issued as of November 21 and the final meeting of the Committee, preparatory thereto, will take place Thursday, November 12. Therefore, if the delisting of Condor is to appear in the next supplement, it is necessary

---

[37] Not printed.
[38] Alexander B. Royce, consultant for the Defense Supplies Corporation.

that your recommendations be received by the Department not later than the evening of November 11.

Do you think that a special announcement will be desirable?

HULL

832.796/1078 : Telegram

The Ambassador in Brazil (Caffery) to the Secretary of State

RIO DE JANEIRO, November 9, 1942—3 p. m.
[Received 4 : 11 p. m.]

4633. Department's 3410, November 5, midnight. Ribeiro Dantas, president of Condor, reports that he is making every effort to conclude his negotiations covering points 1, 2 and 3 mentioned in the Department's telegram under reference by Wednesday evening. Sampaio promises to give his decision as soon as he can see Air Minister (he hopes) today.[39] Dantas believes and the Embassy concurs, that a special announcement would be desirable.

CAFFERY

832.796/1078 : Telegram

The Secretary of State to the Ambassador in Brazil (Caffery)

WASHINGTON, November 14, 1942—midnight.

3549. Your 4633, November 9, 3 p. m. The Department proposes to announce the deletion of Condor from the Proclaimed List with the following press release: (on which your comments are requested) :

The Government of Brazil has informed the United States Ambassador at Rio de Janeiro that the nationalization of the former German Condor aviation enterprise, begun well over a year ago, has been concluded. The Serviços Aéreos Condor, through agreement between the Brazilian and the United States Governments, has accordingly been removed from the Proclaimed List.

Henceforth the company will be known, the Department has been informed, as (here insert official name of new company).

The ramifications of the former German elements and the legal complications deriving from the former connection between Condor and the German Lufthansa have required a great deal of time and careful investigation.

The United States Government has undertaken to render to the new company all possible assistance which the Brazilian Government may request. This assistance may take the form of technical operating help, equipment, financing and the loan of personnel, all contingent upon their being available during the present war-time shortage.

---

[39] Paulo Sampaio, a shareholder in Condor, was considering the offer of one of the three directorships in the new arrangement.

The Interdepartmental Committee has approved deletion of Condor, effective upon receipt of your recommendation, and subject to the conditions outlined in the Department's 3410, November 5, midnight. Final proofs of the next supplement to the Proclaimed List will be reviewed Thursday forenoon, November 19. If satisfactory telegram is received from you by that time, the deletion will be incorporated in this supplement and the foregoing press release will be issued as of Saturday, November 21, simultaneously with publication of the supplement.

Be sure to give full official new name of Condor.

HULL

832.796/1085 : Telegram

The Secretary of State to the Ambassador in Brazil (Caffery)

WASHINGTON, November 19, 1942—10 p. m.

3607. Your 4809, November 17, 5 p. m.[42] Your recommendation that Serviços Aéreos Condor, Ltd. and Syndicato Condor, Ltd. be removed from the Proclaimed List has been approved. The deletion will appear in the Proclaimed List supplement to be published November 21.[43] Simultaneously, the text of the special announcement, as approved by Aranha, will be issued to the Press.

HULL

810.79611 Pan American Airways/3327 : Telegram

The Secretary of State to the Ambassador in Brazil (Caffery)

WASHINGTON, November 30, 1942—10 p. m.

3750. The Department is in receipt of a letter from the Defense Supplies Corporation [42] calling attention to the fact that the contract between Defense Supplies Corporation and Pan American Airways providing for additional services by Panair do Brasil over routes operated or formerly operated by Condor expires December 31, and, that before December 10, Defense Supplies Corporation must advise Pan American Airways whether it desires this contract renewed. War feels that, in view of the removal of Condor from the Proclaimed List, there is no reason for requiring the continuation of these services. Pan American Airways may, of course, continue to cause them to be operated by Panair after the termination of the contract but we have

---

[42] Not printed.
[43] The company under the new name of Servicos Aéreos Cruzeiro do Sul, Limitada, was removed from the Proclaimed List on November 21, 1942; see Department of State *Bulletin*, November 21, 1942, p. 948.

no assurances that they will do so. If Pan American Airways (or Panair) should cancel some of these strictly replacement services, would this, in your opinion, cause any resentment on the part of the Brazilian Government which might adversely affect favorable solutions of important aviation matters now pending such as the restoration of all Pan American Airways international schedules through the cut-off, the Aerovias Brasil situation etc. etc. [?]

Please expedite reply.[44]

HULL

COOPERATIVE EFFORT BETWEEN THE UNITED STATES AND BRAZIL IN IMPOSING CONTROLS OVER INTERNATIONAL FINANCIAL TRANSACTIONS

811.51/4186a : Circular telegram

The Secretary of State to Diplomatic Representatives in the American Republics

WASHINGTON, May 18, 1942—4 p. m.

Treasury Department is about to amend General Ruling No. 5 under Executive Order No. 8389 by adding the following at the end of that Ruling: "United States and foreign currency imported or otherwise brought into the United States on and after March 19, 1942, shall be deemed to be 'securities or evidences thereof' for the purposes of this general ruling".[45]

This amendment will extend United States control of currency imports beyond that established under General Ruling No. 6A issued on March 13, 1942.[46]

Treasury is also about to issue the following press release:

"The Treasury Department today extended the controls over importation of securities so as to cover the importation of currency. Prior to today's action, controls over the importation of currency have been limited to importations from blocked countries and Proclaimed List nationals. Under this ruling, currency upon importation into this country will be forwarded immediately to a Federal Reserve Bank as fiscal agent of the United States. The Federal Reserve Bank will thereafter hold such currency or deliver it to a domestic bank to be held until such time as the Treasury Department has authorized its release. It was pointed out that just as in the case of the provisions

---

[44] In his telegraphic reply, No. 5099 of December 2, 8 p. m., the Ambassador expressed the belief that Brazil would feel no resentment if Panair do Brasil suspended certain services formerly operated by Condor (810.79611 Pan American Airways/3329).

[45] The amendment took effect on May 19; for text and subsequent amendments of Ruling No. 5, see 5 *Federal Register* 2159, 7 *Federal Register* 3770, and 8 *Federal Register* 12286.

[46] 7 *Federal Register* 2083.

applicable to securities which are subject to similar control, the provisions of the amended general ruling applicable to currency imported from Latin America will be so administered as to prevent interference with legitimate importations of currency from that area, including the bringing in by travelers of reasonable amounts of currency for traveling expenses. Treasury officials suggested that the fact that an importation of currency from Latin America was bona fide could be more easily established if such currency were sent into the United States by and for the account of the central banks (or the equivalent or analogous institutions) of any of the American republics under appropriate assurances from such banks or institutions."

You are instructed to arrange as soon as practicable a meeting with the Minister of Finance or other appropriate officials of the government to which you are accredited and bring the foregoing to their attention. You should assure the Minister of Finance, particularly if substantial amounts of American currency circulate from hand to hand in his country, that every effort will be made to prevent interference with legitimate importations of currency into the United States and further that it is not the intent of this Government to impede the use of United States currency as part of the circulating media of such American republics as have found dollar currency a convenient supplement to their own currency.

You may point out, however, that the Axis countries, particularly Germany, are known to have seized large amounts of American dollar currency and that this currency is being disposed of in part by channels involving persons in neutral countries of Europe and various persons in the American republics. By these means the Germans are able to acquire foreign exchange for their war effort.

It is the hope of this Government that the American republics in keeping with the spirit of Resolution No. V of the Third Meeting of the Foreign Ministers of the American Republics at Rio [47] will cooperate to the best of their ability in defeating the Axis countries in their efforts to derive advantage from looted currency.

To this end it is suggested that the export of dollar currency from countries having central banks be restricted to such banks, which, it is assumed, will make every effort to convince themselves that all dollar currency which they buy from individuals and other banks is not directly or indirectly related to liquidation of currency by the Axis. Pending investigation by the Central Bank as to whether there is a direct or indirect Axis interest in imported currency, the Central Bank might place such currency into blocked accounts.

---

[47] For correspondence concerning this meeting, held January 15–28, 1942, see pp. 6 ff. For text of the Resolutions see the Final Act of the Meeting, Department of State *Bulletin*, February 7, 1942, pp. 117–141; Resolution V recommended that the American Republics cut off commercial and financial intercourse with nations signatory to the Tripartite Pact (League of Nations Treaty Series, vol. CCIV, p. 386).

It should be emphasized that the mere fact that currency has been imported from Europe is regarded by this Government as prima facie evidence that there is beneficial Axis interest in such currency. Moreover, so long as dollar currency moves freely from neutral European countries to the Western Hemisphere, a market for such currency is maintained which is of benefit to the Axis. This Government would view with favor action by the American republics to prohibit further importation of dollar currency from countries outside the Western Hemisphere except reasonable amounts imported by travelers. Such action by the other American republics would be given appropriate weight in the administrative applications of General Ruling No. 5 to currency exported by the central banks of such countries to the United States and would contribute to the protection of their nationals from the risks of loss involved in dealings in currency originating with the Axis.

In the case of countries which do not have a central bank, it is suggested that exports of currency be confined to a similar institution designated by the Government.

Please inform consulates.

HULL

811.51/4188 : Telegram

The Ambassador in Brazil (Caffery) to the Secretary of State

RIO DE JANEIRO, May 20, 1942.
[Received May 20—8 : 25 p. m.]

1707. Department's circular May 18, 4 p. m. Bank of Brazil at the request of Embassy and with approval of Minister of Finance [48] has issued regulations effective immediately and has instructed its agencies to give them wide publicity.

Regulations provide:

(1) Suspend authorization of banking institutions and exchange houses to buy or sell American bank notes.

(2) Designate the Bank of Brazil as sole importer and exporter of American notes. The only exception to this is that persons arriving in Brazil from the United States may within 15 days sell American currency to the Bank of Brazil for milreis up to a total of $100.

(3) Require all holders of American currency to deposit same with Bank of Brazil or its agencies by May 22 if resident in the Federal District, State of Rio de Janeiro or São Paulo, and by May 25 in case of residents elsewhere in Brazil.

(4) Deposit to be accompanied by registration statement of name, address and nationality of owner and years of residence in Brazil, country of origin of notes, name and address of person from whom declarant acquired notes and previous owners to extent known.

---

[48] Arthur de Souza Costa.

(5) Registration statements are to be forwarded by agencies to central office of bank together with a report on veracity, antecedents and political sympathies of declarants.

(6) Central office will subsequently on the basis of decisions in individual cases either (a) reimburse owners in milreis for dollar notes deposited or (b) subject deposit to control under Decree Laws 3911 and 4166 or (c) return to bearer.

The decisions as to point 6 will be made after administrative review with Embassy of the registration statements. Procedure (a) will be followed in cases in which holdings appear to be bona fide with no Axis interests. Procedure (b) will be used in the case of holdings by Axis nationals and procedure (c) will be used in cases of Brazilian[s] or nationals whose connections are dubious or whose explanations of circumstances of holding notes are not satisfactory. Under (c) a record will be made of the serial numbers of the notes before being returned to owner in order to prevent their subsequent sale to the bank through other parties; copies of these records will be forwarded by the Embassy to the Department.

It is believed that this registration will effectively meet the problem inasmuch as offerings of currency subsequent to May 25 will be subjected to the presumption of contraband. It is of course a corollary to this program that the Treasury Department will refuse to license importation of currency from Brazil other than those made for account of Bank of Brazil except shipments which left this country before May 19.

This further evidence of prompt and effective cooperation of the Minister of Finance and the Bank of Brazil merits in my opinion a telegram of appreciation from the Department.

CAFFERY

811.51/4196 : Telegram

The Ambassador in Brazil (Caffery) to the Secretary of State

RIO DE JANEIRO, May 22, 1942—4 p. m.
[Received 8:33 p. m.]

1742. Department's circular telegram of May 18, 4 p. m.; and my 1707. Registration and depositing of note[s] are proceeding as planned. With the following two exceptions only legitimate future importation of bank notes into the United States from Brazil will be for account of Bank of Brazil.

Exceptions:

(1) Travelers leaving Brazil for Western Hemisphere destinations before July 22 may take with them up to a maximum of $400. (This is to take care of persons whose travel plans have been completed and who have already acquired currency from legitimate sources.)

movement of dollar currency can be effectively controlled so as to minimize the ability of the Axis powers to convert their loot. The recording of serial numbers will also be helpful but it is felt that such procedure alone will be too cumbersome to be effective because of the amounts involved. It is suggested that recorded numbers be forwarded to the Department as promptly as possible.

In connection with the other alternatives, you should point out the following to the Bank of Brazil:

(1) reimbursement in milreis will give funds to undesirables at the possible expense of the Bank since, because of the currency's Axis taint, the Bank may encounter difficulty when it subsequently attempts to liquidate the dollar currency thus acquired.

(2) placing milreis in a controlled account will involve the same possibility of loss to the Bank as outlined in (1) to the extent that funds are paid out from such account. Furthermore, the Department agrees with your views as to the general ineffectiveness of such control and hopes that you will be able discreetly to persuade the Bank not to adopt this procedure.

If it is not possible to limit the procedure as outlined above, the Department recommends that you suggest to the Bank of Brazil that deposits of dollar currency by undesirables be placed in controlled dollar accounts and that withdrawals from such accounts be limited to amounts needed for reasonable living expenses and be in the form of dollar currency stamped with a perforated mark in the manner heretofore suggested.

Your telegram indicates that controlled accounts will be used only for Axis nationals. If the procedure is not limited to return of the dollar currency, the Department recommends that the blocked dollar account method be used for all undesirables be they Axis nationals or not in order that the controls be as effective as possible.

It has further been noted that your telegram deals only with deposits by undesirables, although the attachment to your despatch indicates that currency whose origin was deemed unsatisfactory would be returned irrespective of the character of the depositor. It is believed that this change of procedure, if a change has taken place, is predicated upon the feeling that friendly persons who acquired dollar currency in good faith prior to the promulgation of the controls should not be punished. This attitude is probably not objectionable, provided that in the future administration of the controls, any deposits of unstamped dollar currency after May 22 and May 25, respectively, will be presumed to have an Axis taint and be dealt with accordingly, regardless of the character of the person who makes the deposit.

If the Brazilian controls are made internally effective, it is not expected that they will be undermined by markets in other areas which have not adopted measures implementing general ruling no. 5, as Treasury intends to scrutinize dollar imports from such areas with particular care.

With respect to the dollar currency held by the Spanish and French Embassies, it is suggested that you try discreetly to bring the facts to the attention of the appropriate Brazilian authorities with the view to having them make strong protests to the Spanish and French upon the basis that the latter are using their diplomatic immunity to indulge in actions to benefit economically countries unfriendly to the Brazilian Government.

While it is realized that Brazil has gone a long way in cooperating with this Government in the control of currency movements, as well as in other fields, it is hoped that at an opportune moment you will suggest to the appropriate authorities that, in the interests of uniformity with measures already adopted by the United States, Brazil will extend its controls to cover all foreign currency.

HULL

840.51 Frozen Credits/6673 : Telegram

The Ambassador in Brazil (Caffery) to the Secretary of State

RIO DE JANEIRO, June 6, 1942—4 p. m.
[Received 5 : 30 p. m.]

1921. The Bank of Brazil has received a telegraphic request from the Bank of International Settlements, Basel, Switzerland, to transfer to the Banco Central in Buenos Aires the 503 kilos of gold held in the Bank of Brazil for its account.

The Bank of Brazil has replied: "We believe that Brazilian authorities would not permit exportation of the gold during the emergency."

The Director of Exchange [51] says "This is a polite way of saying no."

The gold was imported into Brazil in 1941 and turned over to the Bank of Brazil by the French Embassy here.

CAFFERY

811.51/4243 : Telegram

The Ambassador in Brazil (Caffery) to the Secretary of State

RIO DE JANEIRO, June 10, 1942—9 p. m.
[Received June 11—4 : 15 a. m.]

1975. Department's 1417, June 2, 6 p. m. Bank of Brazil has asked French and Spanish Embassies to indicate bank in United States to which their dollar deposits should be transferred.

---

[51] Francisco Alves dos Santos Filho.

Director of Exchange reports that there is no legal provision permitting perforation or stamping of bank notes.

Following plan has been agreed to by bank:

(A) Deposits of less than $1000. (In Rio 786 of 917 depositors were in this category. Their deposits represented only $128,538 of $1,097,661 total.) Conversion will be made into milreis except in cases concerning which Embassy has adverse information. Objectionable depositors will be given choice of (1) transfer to special account in New York or (2) deposit in controlled dollar account in Bank of Brazil, withdrawals to be permitted only in dollar currency and only with special permit.

(B) Deposits of more than $1000. Each case will be carefully reviewed and placed in one of following categories:

(1) Unobjectionable as to person or source. Conversion into milreis or transfer to account in United States, at depositor's option.

(2) Objectionable. Transfer to account in United States or deposit in special dollar account in Bank of Brazil under Decree Law 3911. Withdrawals only in dollars and only under special permit.

(3) European refugees. Friendly but subject to Axis pressure because of home ties. Transfer to account in the United States or place in the controlled account in Bank of Brazil, withdrawals to be made in dollar currency for living expenses at monthly rate previously agreed to by Embassy. (Most of the deposits are in this category.)

Inasmuch as Bank of Brazil in [is?] acting as our agent in this matter, within legal limitations, Embassy assumes Treasury will license all imports currency made by bank and accompanied by Embassy certificate.

Rio deposits by Axis nationals totaled less than $2,000. Dollar currency is being quoted in black market at 10–12 milreis.

Director of Exchange is sympathetic to plan control other currencies but prefers to discuss details with our Treasury officials during his forthcoming visit to Washington. Director says that he must proceed cautiously with respect to Argentine and Uruguayan currencies.

Please request American shipping companies to arrange to pay off crew members arriving at Brazilian ports in milreis rather than dollars.

CAFFERY

811.51/4243 : Telegram

The Secretary of State to the Ambassador in Brazil (Caffery)

WASHINGTON, June 19, 1942—10 p. m.

1597. Your 1975, June 10, 9 p. m. The following telegram is being sent to all missions in the South American Republics. (See Department's circular telegram of June 19, 1942, 11 p. m.) [52]

Please emphasize to the Finance Minister that this program has been adopted by Treasury because of the necessity for uniformity of treatment by the United States with respect to all importations of currency and because of the existence in other American Republics of conditions which do not exist in Brazil.

You are authorized to state to the Minister of Finance in confidence that the recommendations of the Government of Brazil or of the Bank of Brazil will be given preponderant weight in the determination by Treasury as to whether currency imported from Brazil under this arrangement should be released.

It is expected that certain special arrangements may have to be made for Brazil, but an attempt should be made to have the Bank of Brazil send to the United States as much of the currency already deposited with them as they can on the basis above indicated without violating any undertakings that they have already made with respect to such currency. If Brazil's present regulations do not permit the forwarding of dollar currency on such basis, it is hoped that the regulations can be appropriately altered to permit such disposition of the currency. Please cable at once if this is not possible.

We hope to be able to make special adjustments for Brazil in our own program to provide a smooth working arrangement with the Brazilian authorities.

HULL

811.51/4295 : Telegram

The Ambassador in Brazil (Caffery) to the Secretary of State

RIO DE JANEIRO, June 22, 1942—9 p. m.
[Received June 23—3 : 34 a. m.]

2160. (Section 1) My 1975, June 10; Department's 1597, June 19; circular of June 19, 11 p.m.[53] Program contained in Department's

---

[52] Not printed; the quotation of circular telegram of June 19, 11 p. m., was stricken from this instruction before its transmission and the reference in parentheses substituted. The telegram announced the institution by the Treasury Department of a means of currency control through receiving applications for the release of currency forwarded to the United States by the Central Bank. The application was designed to elicit a variety of facts concerning the source of the currency. (811.51/4186a)

[53] Department's circular telegram of June 19 not printed, but see footnote 52, above.

circular telegram under reference comes at a very late date insofar as Brazil is concerned and places me in embarrassing position before the Brazilian authorities because of their prompt and unqualified cooperation following receipt of the Department's circular telegram May 18, 4 p. m. Aranha,[54] Souza Costa, and the Director of Exchange are responsible for Brazil's collaboration with us in this matter and have frequently pointed to the lack of cooperation of Argentina in controlling the movement of American banknotes. The Bank of Brazil's deposit currency plan of May 21 (see my telegram 1742, May 21 [22]) appeared to be highly satisfactory to the Department of State and Treasury Department as evidenced by Department's congratulatory telegrams 1321, May 21 [23] and 1323, May 23.[55]

(Section 2) Failure to express opposition or criticise in any way details of the plan left me with the impression that the Treasury Department approved and that if it raised any objections in the future that they would not be retroactive.

After an administrative review which included checking of names with the Foreign Office, Bank of Brazil, Proclaimed List Section, Political Section, Military, Naval Attaché, Consulate, and friendly diplomatic missions in regard to their own nationals, Embassy approved 335 deposits totalling $163,973 for liquidation in milreis. Bank of Brazil has purchased the dollars and has paid milreis to the depositors. Conversion of additional deposits of less than $100 each has been approved after consular investigation in cases of recently arrived American tourists, naval and army personnel, merchant seamen, ferry command personnel, this has totaled 10,875.80 in Rio de Janeiro for 150 individuals. There have been many more cases especially in northern Brazil. Is the Embassy correct in assuming that Treasury will automatically license importation of these sums by Bank of Brazil with Embassy certificate?

(Section 3) It is believed that for the following reasons plan adopted in Brazil is more practical than that outlined in Department's circular of June 19 especially in view of tardiness of latter:

1. Brazil plan provided for an immediate and short period of deposit which minimized opportunities for use of cloaks and which automatically created a presumption of Axis origin for any future currency which might be presented.
2. The plan provided on [an] expeditious method of handling small deposits made in many cases by bona fide holders who were in need of prompt settlement of their cases.
3. Brazilian plan has enough elasticity to take care with Embassy or Consulate approval of a multitude of special problems which inevitably arise in bona fide cases having no immediate monetary assets

---

[54] Oswaldo Aranha, Brazilian Minister for Foreign Affairs.
[55] Neither printed.

other than American currency, that is ferry command personnel traveling via Brazil en route to Africa or returning from Africa to the United States; American merchant marine and Allied Nations marine personnel; American naval personnel from the numerous naval vessels calling at Brazilian ports; other American Government personnel; official visitors from other American Republics such as the Chilean Military Mission which has just arrived in Rio with no funds other than American currency. It is pointed out that under Department's plan the Bank of Brazil would not run the risk of converting currency in these cases even with Embassy or Consulate approval.

If the Department so desires Embassy will adopt new plan for the balance of deposits which have not been liquidated. Under existing legislation in Brazil this means giving the depositor the option of having his dollars returned to him or of forwarding by the Bank to the United States on a collection basis as prescribed. It should be recognized however that taking this action appears inconsistent to Brazilian authorities who have cooperated so effectively to date; that it makes no provision for the handling of consular fees and future meritorious cases in which it is in the interest of the United States to request the Bank of Brazil to purchase American currency for milreis; and that the inevitable delays which this centralized procedure entails will create ill will among the many small depositors who acted in good faith in making their deposits. It will be recalled that the original Brazilian plan made provision for forwarding to the United States for deposit in special accounts of dollars held by objectionable depositors.

Please consult with Miller [56] and the Director of Exchange of the Bank of Brazil who are scheduled to arrive in Washington June 23 in regard to this matter. I refer especially to my telegram 2005, June 12, and telegram No. 2069, June 16.[57]

CAFFERY

811.51/4243 : Telegram

The Secretary of State to the Ambassador in Brazil (Caffery)

WASHINGTON, June 25, 1942—10 p. m.

1668. Your 2160, June 22, 9 p. m. The Department is, of course, most anxious to avoid placing you in an embarrassing position with the Brazilian authorities and as previously indicated this Government is most appreciative of the cooperation of the Brazilian Government and intends to do everything possible to minimize possible

---

[56] Edward G. Miller, Jr., of the Department's Foreign Funds Control Division, who had been on a special mission to Brazil and other American Republics.
[57] Neither printed.

difficulties. As was indicated in the latter part of the Department's telegram no. 1597, June 19, 10 p. m., it was recognized that the prior prompt and unqualified cooperation of the Brazilian Government in instituting currency controls would undoubtedly necessitate special arrangements in order to integrate its controls with proposed Treasury program.

The Brazilian authorities should be assured that, if the Treasury's problem were merely that of dealing with currency from Brazil, it would be very easy to solve. However, this Government has the problem of dealing with currency from a large number of countries, including all the American Republics. If a uniform general procedure had not been adopted by the Treasury, it would have been extremely difficult for the United States to place effective controls on those countries refusing to cooperate or whose cooperation was merely nominal. It is believed that the procedure adopted is flexible enough to permit sympathetic cooperation with Brazil.

In line with this approach, and in view of the fact that Brazil has severed diplomatic relations with the Axis powers and has instituted extensive economic and financial controls pursuant to Resolution V,[58] the following procedure has been adopted:

1: Treasury will accept the $163,973 of dollar deposits already liquidated in milreis with the approval of the Embassy.

2: Treasury will accept the $10,875 already liquidated in milreis. In addition, it will accept

(a) Additional and future deposits of less than $100 converted, after investigation by the Bank of Brazil, the Embassy, or the Consulate in such cases as recently arrived American tourists, Army and Navy personnel, merchant seamen, ferry command personnel, et cetera.

(b) All other deposits already made of less than $100 after a similar investigation.

3: With respect to other deposits not yet liquidated, Treasury has suggested that the Treasury procedure be followed and has suggested integrating the Brazilian procedure and the Treasury procedure along the following lines:

(a) If Brazilian regulations do not authorize the Brazilian authorities to forward all United States currency to the United States as contemplated under Treasury procedure, such currency should be placed in a blocked account in Brazil until the owner consents to shipment to the United States through the Bank of Brazil. If this blocking of currency is not possible in all cases under the Brazilian regulations, a strong effort should be made to have the owner voluntarily forward it to the United States under Treasury procedure, advising him that failure to comply

---

[58] See footnote 47, p. 790.

will be a factor which the United States will consider in passing on the currency at any later date, and that the United States has the serial numbers of the currency to enforce observance. The owner should also be cautioned that, as the Treasury procedure indicates, the Treasury expects to refuse applications for the release of currency which is not promptly forwarded to the United States and that consequently, it is to his own interest to act at once.

(b) Wherever it is at all possible under the Brazilian regulations, United States currency should not be released to persons in Brazil even for subsistence purposes. When the Department previously suggested that United States currency might be returned, it was with the thought that it would be perforated by Brazilian authorities and its origin thus clearly indicated. In this connection it should be noted that the return of dollars condones the existence of a black market and is inconsistent with the prohibition which the Department understands exists in the Brazilian law; namely, that all dealings in dollar currency are illegal. Where a person is actually in dire need of funds for subsistence purposes (including a friendly refugee) and such person has complied with all provisions of the Brazilian decree, the Treasury would be prepared to accept the following arrangement: such person should place all his United States currency in a blocked account. The Bank of Brazil might then agree to sell him sufficient milreis for subsistence purposes (holding the amount to a minimum) and accept dollars therefor; provided that in no event would more than 25 percent of such person's currency be permitted to be acquired pursuant to this arrangement. Dollars acquired by the Bank of Brazil under this arrangement would be accepted by the Treasury. Moreover, this procedure would be conditioned upon the person involved promptly authorizing the forwarding of the balance of his currency to the United States under the Treasury procedure.

The Department is discussing the matter with Treasury and would appreciate your telegraphing your views as to whether the above outlined procedure is possible of adoption in Brazil. Should there be any difficulties, political or otherwise, we will attempt to deal with them sympathetically.

With respect to the question which you raised in point 1 of section 3 of your telegram under reference, your attention is called to the fact that the Treasury recommendations for currency controls contemplated the fixing of a particular date for the deposit of dollars in the same manner as Brazil has done. However, problems may arise in connection with deposits made after any such date either by persons entering the country after such date, or by persons in the country having a change of heart with respect to currency in their possession.

HULL

811.51/4327 : Telegram

The Ambassador in Brazil (Caffery) to the Secretary of State

RIO DE JANEIRO, June 27, 1942—3 p. m.
[Received 5 : 50 p. m.]

2260. My 2160, June 21 [*22*], 9 p. m., and Department's 1668, June 25, 10 p. m. I am of the opinion that the plan suggested by the Department's telegram under reference requires some modification in order to meet the actualities of the current situation in Brazil. Of the 1306 depositors throughout Brazil 986 had deposits of less than $500 but these represent less than 20% of money deposited. I am of the opinion that the United States has much more to lose from the standpoint of public relations in Brazil than it could possibly gain in regard to Axis funds by requiring that any of these smaller deposits other than those held by objectionable persons be forwarded to the United States on a basis of collection. The reasons for this conclusion are :

1. That the declaration form stipulated in paragraph 2 of Department's circular of June 19, 11 p. m.[59] is not identical with the form used by the Bank of Brazil and it would be necessary for the 986 depositors to make a new trip to the bank, go through the routine once again and submit to a long period of discussion concerning the advisability of having their funds forwarded to the United States;
2. That the Bank of Brazil does not have the administrative facilities available to enable it to certify whether the facts stated in the application are true;
3. That many of these small deposits are held by Brazilians who acquired them while in the United States or other American Republics on business or pleasure trips, and they naturally will be irritated at the additional red tape and delay;
4. That many of the other small depositors are European refugees of small means who are already panic-stricken over the possibilities of confiscation;
5. That other depositors are nationals of other American Republics who were caught in Brazil on business or pleasure trips and who have borrowed milreis funds on the expectation of a prompt settlement of their cases;
6. That the foregoing factors would create a fertile field for anti-American agitation if the plan is adopted. Furthermore, a study of declaration statements of these small deposits indicates that current Axis interest is confined to exceptional cases which will not, of course, be liquidated in milreis.

I therefore urge the immediate adoption of the following plan :

1. That the Treasury agree to license the importation into the United States of shipments by the Bank of Brazil of all deposits of less than $500 made by unobjectionable depositors;

---

[59] See footnote 52, p. 798.

2. That the Embassy will follow the procedure outlined by the Department for all deposits of more than $500. It is suggested, however, that instead of the 25% limitation on conversion into milreis on these larger deposits, a flat maximum of $500 be established. (This to be used only in cases of necessity and after agreement to send balance as collection to the United States.)

3. It will be necessary in some cases to exceed the $100 limitation for new cases. For instance, the Consulate at Natal has reported that ferry command personnel and travelers en route to the United States from Africa for war purposes are frequently held over in that city for 2 weeks or more. The Embassy has pending at the present time other diplomatic cases of travelers who arrived in Brazil recently with no funds other than American currency.

4. Whether the Bank of Brazil is willing to adopt any alternative other than the return of dollar currency to persons who refuse to have their deposits forwarded to the United States on a collection basis is a question which can only be decided by the Director of Exchange, Doctor [Santos] Filho, who is now in Washington. He is the only Brazilian official in a position of authority in regard to dollar control and it is suggested that the Department and Treasury arrive at a decision with him in regard to the proposal made in section 3 (a) of Department's telegram under reference.

Pending decision on the disposition of the larger deposits, an immediate decision is requested in regard to the Embassy's proposal for deposits of less than $500.

I refer again to Aranha's repeated affirmations in my 2005, June 12, and my telegram No. 2069, June 16.[60]

CAFFERY

811.51/4327 : Telegram

The Secretary of State to the Ambassador in Brazil (Caffery)

WASHINGTON, June 29, 1942—8 p. m.

1718. Your 2220, June 24, 5 p. m.,[61] and your 2260, June 27, 3 p. m. The Brazilian procedure for administering currency controls and the political considerations involved in securing the adoption of the Treasury procedure have been explained to the Treasury Department. As a result the following procedure has been agreed to by Treasury, which the Department and Treasury hope will be satisfactory:

1. Treasury will accept all dollars already deposited, which have been or in the future may be converted into milreis, provided the dollars are accompanied by a certificate from the Embassy or Consulate when shipped to the United States. It is assumed that Treasury will be requested to accept such dollars only with respect to those

---

deposits which have been or may be found to be satisfactory. The deposits by the French and Spanish Embassies should not be liquidated without prior consultation with the Department and Treasury and it is assumed that you will follow a similar procedure with respect to any other unusually large deposits where suspicious circumstances are involved.

2. With respect to deposits objectionable as to person or source and deposits by European refugees who are friendly but subject to Axis pressure because of home ties, it is assumed that the depositor will be given the option of transfer to a special account in the United States or deposit in a special blocked dollar account in the Bank of Brazil as outlined in your 1975, June 10, 9 p. m. Should such deposits be placed in a blocked dollar account in the Bank of Brazil, it is understood that you will permit withdrawals from such accounts only up to the sum of $500, said withdrawals to be in milreis and to be permitted only in cases where funds are necessary for subsistence purposes and only after agreement by the depositor to permit the Bank of Brazil to send the balance to the United States on a collection basis.

3. With respect to future deposits by such persons as recently arrived American tourists, Army and Navy personnel, merchant seamen, ferry command personnel, et cetera, Treasury is prepared to accept reasonable amounts of dollars converted into milreis with the approval of the Embassy or the Consulate.

4. With respect to all other future deposits, it is assumed that there will be no difficulty in following the Treasury procedure of having all such deposits forwarded to the United States on a collection basis in the manner outlined in the Department's 1597, June 10 [*19*], 9 [*10*] p. m.

HULL

832.51/2031b : Telegram

The Secretary of State to the Ambassador in Brazil (Caffery)

WASHINGTON, July 3, 1942—midnight.

1775. The Treasury proposes to sign the stabilization agreement with Brazil on July 6 at which time the following press release will be issued:

"The Secretary of the Treasury, Henry Morgenthau, Jr., and Minister Fernando Lobo, Chargé d'Affaires of the United States of Brazil in Washington, today signed an agreement extending to July 15, 1947 the stabilization agreement [62] entered into 5 years ago.

---

[62] See Treasury Department Press Release No. 10–78, July 15, 1937, *Foreign Relations*, 1938, vol. v, p. 344.

"Under this agreement, as extended today, the United States will make dollar exchange available to the Government of the United States of Brazil for the purpose of stabilizing the Brazilian milreis–United States dollar rate of exchange up to a total amount of $100,-000,000 and will sell gold to the United States of Brazil at such times and in such amounts as the Brazilian Government may request, also to a total amount of $100,000,000. In the agreement as originally drafted these two amounts were $60,000,000.

"The extension of this agreement between the treasuries of the United States of America and the United States of Brazil and the increase in the facilities made available to Brazil under the agreement are a further evidence of the close and friendly relations existing between the two countries and constitute an assurance of continued cooperation between the two treasuries. The friendship and understanding symbolized by this and other agreements with our great sister republic in South America promise much for both a joint attack on the problems of the war and a solution for our common problems in the peace."

The foregoing is sent to you for your information and not for release to the press in Brazil.

HULL

811.51/5110 : Airgram

The Secretary of State to the Ambassador in Brazil (Caffery)

WASHINGTON, September 21, 1942—5 p.m.

A–262. Your despatches nos. 8294, August 27, and 7373, May 20.[63] The Department had assumed from a reading of the instruction of the Bank of Brazil dated May 20, 1942, enclosed with your despatch no. 7373, that the further circulation of dollar currency in Brazil by private persons, banks or exchange houses was prohibited and that the holding of dollar currency by any person or institution other than the Bank of Brazil was also prohibited. It would appear, however, from your despatch no. 8294 that the holding of dollar currency by private persons is not prohibited under existing Brazilian regulations since the Bank of Brazil has made provision for the forwarding of such currency to the United States.

Please clarify the present status of the Brazilian restrictions both with respect to the prohibition against circulation and the prohibition against holding.

HULL

----

[63] Neither printed.

840.51 Frozen Credits/7788 : Telegram

The Ambassador in Brazil (Caffery) to the Secretary of State

RIO DE JANEIRO, September 23, 1942—6 p. m.
[Received 8 : 35 p. m.]

3786. My 1921, June 6, and Department's instruction 3307, September 1.[64] French Financial Attaché has again approached Bank of Brazil requesting shipment of gold to Banco Central, Buenos Aires, for account of Bank of International Settlements. In view of diplomatic nature of case Director of Exchange has found it necessary to refer case to Minister of Finance for decision.

If Department believes that Bank of International Settlements is under Axis control or acting on behalf of Axis interests and that shipment therefore should not be permitted please telegraph so that I can inform Ministry of Foreign Affairs.

CAFFERY

811.51/5116 : Airgram

The Secretary of State to the Ambassador in Brazil (Caffery)

WASHINGTON, September 26, 1942—4 : 30 [p. m.]

A–295. Your 3452, September 11, 5 p. m.[65] The Department and Treasury have found it difficult to arrive at a wholly satisfactory solution concerning the currency deposits by the French Embassy and the Spanish Ambassador,[66] in view of the political questions involved. However, the following plan of procedure is suggested :

1. With respect to the deposit by the French Embassy you will be interested to know that the French have asked Treasury to make arrangements for licensing the use of blocked funds in this country for the support of their Missions in the other American republics. The request of the French was based upon the fact that they were unable to use the currency because of the restrictions imposed by the other American republics. The French have been told that before attention can be given to the problem of licensing the use of blocked funds in this country it will be necessary for them to forward to the United States on a collection basis all currency held directly or indirectly for the account of the French Government in the other American republics. In view of this development it is believed that the matter of the French deposit can be held in abeyance pending an indication from the French as to whether they will comply with the foregoing stipulation. It would seem that the failure of the French to deposit all of their dollar currency constituted a violation of the Brazilian currency controls and that consequently an adequate legal basis may exist for refusing to

[64] Latter not printed.
[65] Not printed.
[66] Raimundo Fernández-Cuesta y Merelo.

return the currency which has been deposited or to convert it into milreis, at least temporarily.

2. With respect to the deposit by the Spanish Ambassador, it is suggested that you make every effort through the Brazilian authorities to persuade him to have the currency forwarded to the United States on a collection basis. In the event that your efforts in this connection are unsuccessful, it would appear that there will be no alternative but to return the currency. Before so doing, however, it is suggested that the Brazilian authorities advise the Spanish Ambassador that this Government has a complete record of the serial numbers. Also it is suggested that you discuss with the Brazilian authorities the possibility of placing some stamp or mark on this currency before returning it to the Spanish Ambassador. It is recognized that in your telegram 1975, June 10, 9 p. m. you reported that there was no legal provision in Brazil permitting this procedure, but it is thought that the fact that Brazil is now at war may afford a basis for reconsidering this possibility.

Please keep the Department advised of all developments.

HULL

811.51/5172 : Airgram

The Ambassador in Brazil (Caffery) to the Secretary of State

RIO DE JANEIRO, October 1, 1942—3 p. m.
[Received October 6—12 : 05 p. m.]

A–390. Reference Department's airgram No. A–262, 5 p. m., September 21, 1942. The instructions of the Bank of Brazil of May 20, 1942, attached as an enclosure to the Embassy's despatch No. 7373 of May 20, 1942,[68] designated the Bank of Brazil as the exclusive forwarder to the United States of American dollar currency destined for exchange into milreis or for deposit to a credit in the United States, and at the same time suspended the authorization for any other banking institution or exchange houses to deal in American dollar currency. However, this instruction by the Bank of Brazil did not prohibit the holding of American dollar currency by any person or institution other than the Bank of Brazil. The regulations adopted by the Bank of Brazil, in accordance with the Embassy's recommendations, to all practical purposes limited the market for American dollar currency to the Bank of Brazil, and as has been reported to the Department, the exchange rate at which American dollar currency was liquidated surreptitiously declined considerably, making it decidedly unprofitable for any legitimate holder of American dollar currency to liquidate this currency other than through the procedure outlined by the Bank of Brazil.

---

[68] Not printed.

Reference is made to the Embassy's despatch No. 8368 of September 9, 1942,[69] titled "Foreign Funds Control—Control of Dollar Currency", wherein the course of the measures adopted by the Bank of Brazil relative to American dollar currency is evaluated. Subsequent measures adopted by the Bank of Brazil for the handling of "new" deposits, as reported in the Embassy's despatch No. 8294 of August 27, 1942 [69] and contained in the circular letter No. 1165 of the Bank of Brazil of August 13, 1942,[70] made provision for the forwarding of these deposits to the United States' Treasury Department on a collection basis, with the exceptions mentioned therein, of all legitimate holders of American dollar currency. The measures adopted therein, in conjunction with Decree Laws No. 3911 and No. 4166, have effectively isolated American dollar currency with Axis connections. As has been reported to the Department substantial quantities of American dollar currency are still in the possession of Axis interests. As developments occur relative to this Axis control of American dollar currency, they shall be reported to the Department.

CAFFERY

840.51 Frozen Credits/7788 : Telegram

The Secretary of State to the Ambassador in Brazil (Caffery)

WASHINGTON, October 1, 1942—8 p. m.

2908. Your 3786, September 23, 6 p. m. Please inform the Minister of Foreign Affairs that this Government is opposed to the contemplated transfer of gold of the Bank of International Settlements to Buenos Aires and that it would view the issuance of a license authorizing the transfer as inconsistent with the objectives underlying Resolution V of the Rio Conference and the Resolutions of the recent Washington Conference.[71] In view of the more adequate freezing controls existing in Brazil, it is believed that a transfer of the gold to Buenos Aires might well result in affording to the Axis powers additional means of acquiring foreign exchange. This possibility appears to be even stronger in view of the interest of the French Financial Attaché in the transaction.

The foregoing view of the transaction is adopted irrespective of

---

[69] Not printed.

[70] Not printed; it was transmitted to the Department by the Ambassador in his despatch No. 8294, August 27, 1942.

[71] For the Resolutions of the Washington Conference held June 30–July 10, 1942, see Pan American Union, Congress and Conference Series No. 39: *Final Act of the Inter-American Conference on Systems of Economic and Financial Control* (Washington, 1942) ; for correspondence concerning the Conference, see *ante*, pp. 58 ff.

whether the Bank of International Settlements is Axis owned or controlled. However, the following factors pertinent to such ownership or control are reported by the Treasury Department:

1. Although the Bank of England and some banking institutions in the United States have an interest in the Bank, the majority ownership is vested in the enemy countries or countries dominated by them. The ultimate voting control of the Bank is in the Axis.

2. Germany is the largest creditor of the Bank.

3. Seventy percent of the total liabilities of the Bank (other than capital and reserves) probably involve German and Italian interests.

4. Germany has a contingent interest in the profits of the Bank in excess of normal earnings.

The Department trusts that in view of the foregoing considerations which indicate that the proposed transfer would not be desirable from the standpoint of the United Nations, it will not be authorized by the Brazilian Government.

Please keep the Department advised of all developments.

HULL

832.515/120 : Telegram

The Acting Secretary of State to the Ambassador in Brazil (Caffery)

WASHINGTON, October 10, 1942—3 p. m.

3024. Your 4027, October 6.[72] Refer to Article 8 of the decree law on currency which provides that the Minister of Finance will establish the conditions under which present coins and bank notes may be exchanged. It is assumed that you have discussed with the appropriate Brazilian authorities the question of utilizing this provision to establish effective freezing controls over coins and bank notes which may have previously been hoarded by undesirable persons, both of enemy and Brazilian nationality, and which will be presented for exchange into new coins and new currency.

Please report to the Department whether this provision will be utilized in this manner.

WELLES

832.51/2092 : Telegram

The Ambassador in Brazil (Caffery) to the Secretary of State

RIO DE JANEIRO, October 20, 1942—11 p.m.
[Received October 21—7 : 15 a. m.]

4299. The Chief of the Economic and Commercial Section of the Ministry of Foreign Affairs[73] today confirmed that the Brazilian

---

[72] Not printed.
[73] Mario Moreira da Silva.

Government is negotiating with the French Embassy here for reinstatement of the payments agreement (see my despatch 7787 of June 29, 1942 [74]) and for the repatriation of franc bonds of the Brazilian funded debt. He stated that the repatriation would be based upon 20% of the nominal value of the bonds or approximately 550 million francs (275,000 contos), the funds to be credited to a special account of the French Embassy here for the exclusive purchase of any foreign products to be warehoused in Brazil until after the war.

I spoke to Aranha about this and expressed disappointment over the decision of the Brazilian Government to resume negotiations with the French Embassy, and pointed out the obvious objections to the proposal. Aranha said that he was not impressed with our arguments but asked me to give them to him in a confidential memorandum.

CAFFERY

811.51/5157 : Airgram

The Secretary of State to the Ambassador in Brazil (Caffery)

WASHINGTON, October 23, 1942—12 : 30 p. m.

A-394. Your despatch no. 8368, September 9.[74] The British Embassy in Washington has reported to the Treasury Department that travelers by air from West Africa to the United States via Brazil have been experiencing difficulty in meeting expenses at Natal and Para through their inability to cash Sterling and West African bank notes. The British Treasury has, therefore, suggested to the West African Governors Conference, (consisting of Nigeria, the Gold Coast, Sierra Leone and Gambia), that to surmount this difficulty all travelers from West Africa by the above route should provide themselves with dollar currency.

The United States Treasury Department would like to cooperate with the British in this matter and to inform them that small amounts of dollar currency will be converted in Brazil for travelers in transit to the United States from West Africa. The maximum amount which each such traveler would be permitted to convert under any such arrangement would be $40 in United States currency.

Please discuss this matter with the appropriate Brazilian authorities and inform the Department whether you believe the above arrangement is satisfactory. You should keep in mind that if some such arrangement as this is not established, it will be practically impossible for travelers from West Africa to provide themselves with the means for settling minor incidental expenses while en route. If

[74] Not printed.

you approve the arrangement, it would, of course, be understood that amounts up to $40 could be liquidated locally by the Bank of Brazil for each such traveler in transit between West Africa and the United States via Brazil and that such currency would be handled in the same manner as currency liquidated locally for United States and Brazilian official personnel in accordance with the Department's 2232, August 11, 8 p. m.[76]

HULL

832.5151/1666 : Airgram

The Secretary of State to the Ambassador in Brazil (Caffery)

WASHINGTON, October 26, 1942—6 : 15 p. m.

A–409. From Treasury.

"Reference your despatch 8571, September 24, 1942.[76]

1. In order to facilitate the negotiation of checks drawn on the Treasurer of the United States the following procedure is suggested.[77]

2. All United States dollar checks drawn on the Treasurer of the United States negotiated by the Banco do Brasil, Rio de Janeiro, are to be delivered to the American Embassy, Rio de Janeiro, accompanied by a list in triplicate with complete description of each check as follows: name of drawer; symbol number; check number; amount; payee's name; date of check.

Consular officer will carefully verify checks against list and advise Treasury by telegram through State Department aggregate amount of checks delivered by bank. Upon receipt of this advice Treasury will effect payment in corresponding amount to the New York correspondent of the Banco do Brasil. Please indicate in first telegram name of correspondent.

Consular officer should instruct bank to use all possible diligence in identification of payee and determining validity of endorsements. Banco do Brasil should endorse checks as follows: 'Pay to the order of the Treasurer of the United States for credit of our account with (name of bank), New York. Signed Banco do Brasil, Rio de Janeiro.' Treasury will look to Banco do Brasil only for usual guarantee under laws applicable in Brazil.

Consular officer should forward checks accompanied by one copy of list to Treasurer of United States, Washington, as promptly as possible by safest means available. Second copy of list should follow by separate carrier at earliest possible date. Third copy should be retained by consular officer.

---

[76] Not printed.
[77] In airgram No. A–717, January 2, 1943, 6 p. m., the Ambassador was instructed that checks drawn on the Secretary of State should be treated by a similar procedure (832.5151/1666).

3. Consular officer should make no arrangements for insurance as shipments of checks will be covered by Government Losses in Shipment Act.[78]

4. The designation of the Banco do Brasil as a depositary of public moneys of the United States is hereby extended to carry out the procedure outlined in this airgram.

5. With reference to the attachment to your despatch No. 8571 please bring to the attention of the Banco do Brasil that this arrangement only covers checks drawn on the Treasurer of the United States negotiated by it.

6. To minimize number of checks drawn on the Treasurer of the United States, suggest you advise disbursing officers that they should cable through their respective departments their local currency requirements. Arrangements will then be made to advance dollar credits to Banco do Brasil, Rio de Janeiro.

7. Please advise Banco do Brasil, Rio de Janeiro, and other United States Government officials of appropriate parts hereof."

The Department approves the foregoing. Any expense incurred in carrying out the instructions contained in this airgram should be included in regular accounts as separate item for billing Treasury in accordance with Sec. V–45, Foreign Service Regulations.

HULL

811.51/5172 : Telegram

The Secretary of State to the Ambassador in Brazil (Caffery)

WASHINGTON, October 30, 1942—8 p. m.

3303. Your 4324, October 21, 11 p. m.; [79] your airgram A–390, October 1, 3 p. m. In view of the increased activity in dollar transactions it is suggested that this might be an appropriate time to take up with the appropriate Brazilian authorities the question of prohibiting the holding of dollar currency in Brazil. The issuance of a new regulation prohibiting the holding of currency would probably stimulate the deposit of substantial quantities of such currency. It is believed that such a prohibition would afford a supplementary method of drying up the dollar market in Brazil and of assisting these authorities in preventing the attempts being made by residents in Brazil to avoid the effects of the new decree requiring the conversion of Brazilian currency. The Department and Treasury have always felt that a prohibition against the holding of dollar currency, together with appropriate penalties for violation of such prohibition, was a necessary part of an effective control over dollar currency.

In issuing any such prohibition Brazilian authorities should, of course, provide that any dollar currency deposited with the Bank of

---

[78] Act of July 8, 1937 ; 50 Stat. 479.
[79] Not printed.

Brazil as a consequence thereof be forwarded to the United States on a collection basis for the account of the depositor.

As far as the difficulties which such a prohibition might create with respect to American and Brazilian traveling official personnel are concerned, it is suggested that an administrative procedure, similar to the one in effect at the present time, might be evolved to permit such personnel to retain reasonable quantities of dollar currency which they might have in their possession.

Please report to the Department the result of any discussions which you may have with the Brazilian authorities on this problem.

HULL

840.51 Frozen Credits/8118 : Airgram

The Secretary of State to the Ambassador in Brazil (Caffery)

WASHINGTON, October 31, 1942—1 : 35 p. m.

A–438. Your despatch no. 8801, October 19.[80] It is assumed that you intend the suggested procedure to be applicable to applications by residents of Brazil whose funds are blocked in the United States (which would include Spaniards, Portuguese, Swiss, et cetera) and not to be limited to applications by residents of Brazil whose funds are blocked under Brazilian law (which presumably would only include Germans, Italians and Japanese). It is not clear, however, from the enclosures to the above despatch whether the Director of Exchange understands that the procedure would be applicable to the broader class of applicants.

Please inform the Department whether you believe the Director of Exchange clearly understands the scope of your proposal. The Department will then attempt to work out the mechanics of the suggested procedure with the Treasury.

HULL

811.51/5303 : Telegram

The Ambassador in Brazil (Caffery) to the Secretary of State

RIO DE JANEIRO, November 18, 1942—8 p. m.
[Received November 19—1 : 34 a. m.]

4841. Department's 3303, October 30, 8 p. m. This matter has been discussed with the Director of Exchange who is of the opinion

---

[80] Not printed; it enclosed correspondence between the Commercial Attaché in Brazil and the Director of Exchange, Bank of Brazil, in which the Embassy recommended that residents of Brazil who had invested capital in meritorious enterprises and whose funds were blocked be granted licenses to transfer the capital from the United States to Brazil provided that an appropriate Brazilian agency would ensure that the funds were used only for purposes mentioned in the application (840.51 Frozen Credits/8118).

that a law prohibiting the holding of dollar currency might have some symbolical importance but would be unenforceable.

The Embassy taking into consideration the troubles Brazil is having in controlling its own currency tends to agree with this viewpoint.

It appears however that steps can be taken to prosecute persons engaging in dollar transactions under a Decree Law enacted on November 27, 1933. The Bank of Brazil has agreed to support the Embassy in the presentation to the police of evidence which it has accumulated in regard to persons dealing in dollar currency.

CAFFERY

AGREEMENTS BETWEEN THE UNITED STATES AND BRAZIL PROVIDING FOR A HEALTH AND SANITATION PROGRAM, SIGNED MARCH 14 AND JULY 17, 1942

[For texts of the agreements of March 14 and July 17, 1942, signed at Rio de Janeiro, see, respectively, Department of State Executive Agreement Series No. 372, or 57 Stat. (pt. 2) 1322, and Executive Agreement Series No. 373, or 57 Stat. (pt. 2) 1325.]

LEND-LEASE AGREEMENT BETWEEN THE UNITED STATES AND BRAZIL, SIGNED MARCH 3, 1942

832.24/3–342

Agreement Between the United States and Brazil Regarding Principles Applying to Mutual Aid in the Prosecution of the War, Signed at Washington, March 3, 1942

WHEREAS the United States of America and the United States of Brazil on the first day of October 1941 concluded an Agreement [81] for the providing of defense articles and defense information by either country to the other country; and

WHEREAS the United States of America and the United States of Brazil are both desirous of modifying the Agreement concluded on the first day of October 1941 to the advantage of both parties; and

WHEREAS the United States of America and the United States of Brazil declare in conformity with the principles set forth in the Final Act of the Third Meeting of Ministers of Foreign Affairs of the American Republics in Rio de Janeiro, approved January 28, 1942,[82] their determination to cooperate jointly for their mutual protection until the

---

[81] For correspondence on the negotiation of Lend-Lease Agreement between the United States and Brazil signed October 1, 1941, and text of the agreement, see *Foreign Relations*, 1941, vol. VI.

[82] For text of the Final Act, see Department of State *Bulletin*, February 7, 1942, p. 117; for correspondence concerning this Meeting, see *ante*, pp. 6 ff.

effects of the present aggression against the Continent have disappeared; and

WHEREAS the President of the United States of America, pursuant to the Act of the Congress of the United States of America of March 11, 1941,[83] and the President of the Republic of the United States of Brazil have determined that the defense of each of the American republics is vital to the defense of all of them;

The undersigned, being duly authorized for that purpose, have agreed as follows:

ARTICLE I

The Agreement concluded by the United States of America and the United States of Brazil on the first day of October 1941 for the providing of defense articles and defense information by either country to the other country, shall cease to have effect upon the signing of the present Agreement. All deliveries of defense materials or defense information by either country to the other country or any payments made by either country to the other country in accordance with the terms of the Agreement concluded by the United States of America and the United States of Brazil on the first day of October 1941 shall be deemed to constitute deliveries or payments in accordance with the terms of the present Agreement.

ARTICLE II

The United States of America proposes to transfer to the United States of Brazil under the terms of this Agreement armaments and munitions of war to a total value of about $200,000,000.

In conformity, however, with the Act of the Congress of the United States of America of March 11, 1941, the United States of America reserves the right at any time to suspend, defer, or stop deliveries whenever, in the opinion of the President of the United States of America, further deliveries are not consistent with the needs of the defense of the United States of America or the Western Hemisphere; and the United States of Brazil similarly reserves the right to suspend, defer, or stop acceptance of deliveries under the present Agreement, when, in the opinion of the President of the Republic of the United States of Brazil, the defense needs of the United States of Brazil or the Western Hemisphere are not served by the continuance of the deliveries.

ARTICLE III

Records shall be kept of all defense articles transferred under this Agreement, and not less than every ninety days schedules of such defense articles shall be exchanged and reviewed.

The Government of the United States of America agrees to accord

---

[83] 55 Stat. 31.

to the Government of the United States of Brazil a reduction of 65 percent in the scheduled cost of the materials delivered in compliance with the stipulations of the present Agreement; and the Government of the United States of Brazil promises to pay in dollars into the Treasury of the United States of America 35 percent of the scheduled cost of the materials delivered. The United States of Brazil shall not be required to pay

> more than a total of $11,666,666.66 before January 1, 1943,
> more than a total of $23,333,333.33 before January 1, 1944,
> more than a total of $35,000,000.00 before January 1, 1945,
> more than a total of $46,666,666.66 before January 1, 1946,
> more than a total of $58,333,333.33 before January 1, 1947, or
> more than a total of $70,000,000.00 before January 1, 1948.

Article IV

The United States of America and the United States of Brazil, recognizing that the measures herein provided for their common defense and united resistance to aggression are taken for the further purpose of laying the bases for a just and enduring peace, agree, since such measures cannot be effective or such a peace flourish under the burden of an excessive debt, that upon the payments above provided all fiscal obligations of the United States of Brazil hereunder shall be discharged; and for the same purpose they further agree, in conformity with the principles and program set forth in Resolution XXV on Economic and Financial Cooperation of the Second Meeting of the Ministers of Foreign Affairs of the American Republics at Habana, July 1940,[84] to cooperate with each other and with other nations to negotiate fair and equitable commodity agreements with respect to the products of either of them and of other nations in which marketing problems exist, and to cooperate with each other and with other nations to relieve the distress and want caused by the war wherever, and as soon as, such relief will be succor to the oppressed and will not aid the aggressor.

Article V

Should circumstances arise in which the United States of America in its own defense or in the defense of the Americas shall require defense articles or defense information which the United States of Brazil is in a position to supply, the United States of Brazil will make such defense articles and defense information available to the United States of America, to the extent possible without harm to its economy and under terms to be agreed upon.

---

[84] For correspondence on this Meeting, see *Foreign Relations*, 1940, vol. v, pp. 180 ff.; for text of Resolution XXV, see Department of State *Bulletin*, August 24, 1940, p. 141.

ARTICLE VI

The United States of Brazil undertakes that it will not, without the consent of the President of the United States of America, transfer title to or possession of any defense article or defense information received under this Agreement, or permit its use by anyone not an officer, employee, or agent of the United States of Brazil.

Similarly, the United States of America undertakes that it will not, without the consent of the President of the Republic of the United States of Brazil, transfer title to or possession of any defense article or defense information received in accordance with Article V of this Agreement, or permit its use by anyone not an officer, employee, or agent of the United States of America.

ARTICLE VII

If, as a result of the transfer to the United States of Brazil of any defense article or defense information, it is necessary for the United States of Brazil to take any action or make any payment in order fully to protect any of the rights of any citizen of the United States of America who has patent rights in and to any such defense article or information, the United States of Brazil will do so, when so requested by the President of the United States of America.

Similarly, if, as a result of the transfer to the United States of America of any defense article or defense information, it is necessary for the United States of America to take any action or make any payment in order fully to protect any of the rights of any citizen of the United States of Brazil who has patent rights in and to any such defense article or information, the United States of America will do so, when so requested by the President of the Republic of the United States of Brazil.

ARTICLE VIII

This Agreement shall continue in force from the date on which it is signed until a date agreed upon between the two Governments.

Signed and sealed in the English and Portuguese languages, in duplicate, at Washington, this third day of March, 1942.

For the United States of America:
SUMNER WELLES
Acting Secretary of State of the
United States of America

For the United States of Brazil:
CARLOS MARTINS PEREIRA E SOUSA
Ambassador Extraordinary and
Plenipotentiary of the United
States of Brazil at Washington

INDEX

INDEX[1]

---

[1] In indexing persons the intention has been to include all references to persons of significance for an understanding of the record, with the following exceptions: (1) The name of the Secretary of State or the Acting Secretary of State appearing as the signer of outgoing instructions unless there is a clear indication of the Secretary's or Acting Secretary's personal interest; (2) the name of an American officer in charge of a mission appearing as the signer of reports to the Department of State, except for personal items; (3) the names of persons to whom documents are addressed.

Persons are not identified by office in the index, but usually where a person is first mentioned in any section a footnote identification is given unless that person is identified in the text.

Brazil—Continued
Hemisphere defense—Continued
Joint Brazil-United States Defense Commission, recommendations of, 668–669, 673–674
Joint Brazil-United States Military Mixed Commission in Rio de Janeiro, 674
Lend-Lease material for Brazil, President Vargas' request for, and information regarding, 634–637, 654, 656, 662–663, 668
Political-military agreement between United States and Brazil, *May 23 and 27*, providing for two Brazilian-American Technical-Military Mixed Commissions, 662
State of war with Axis Powers: Brazil's anticipation of, 634, 656; recognition of existence of state of war with Germany and Italy (*Aug. 22*), 665–666; U. S. reaction, 666–667
United Nations Declaration of *Jan. 1*, Brazil's adherence to, 667, 667n, 670
U. S. Navy vessels, Brazil's consent for operation from Rio de Janeiro and Santos, 643
Inter-American Conference of Police and Judicial Authorities, participation in, 53, 56
International financial transactions, U. S.-Brazilian cooperation in imposing controls over, 789–815
Axis liquidation of American dollar currency, efforts to prevent. *See* Control of currency imports, *infra.*
Bank for International Settlements (Basel, Switzerland), request for transfer of gold deposits to Buenos Aires, 796, 807, 809–810
Coins and bank notes, establishment of controls over exchange of, 477, 810
Control of currency imports:
Development of regulations and procedures for effecting controls, 789–796, 797–805, 811–812
French and Spanish Embassies, dollar currency deposits, question of treatment of, 793–794, 796, 807–808; repatriation of franc bonds of Brazilian funded debt, 810–811
Procedure for checks drawn on U. S. Treasurer or Secretary of State, 812–813
Prohibition against holding of dollar currency in Brazil, question of, 806, 808–809, 813–814, 814–815

Brazil—Continued
International financial transactions, etc.—Continued
Stabilization agreement between United States and Brazil, *July 6*, U. S. press release concerning, 805–806
Transfer of capital from United States to Brazil in certain situations, recommendation concerning, 814
Lend-Lease agreement with United States, *Mar. 3*, text, 815–818
Proclaimed List:
Condor Airline, removal from List, 776, 780–781, 782, 785, 786–788
U. S.-Brazilian discussions concerning application of, 757–765; Brazilian designation of a Consultative Committee, 765–766
Rubber and rubber products, negotiations concerning production, purchase, and distribution of, 691–729
Agreement between Brazil and United States for increasing production of rubber in Brazil, *Mar. 3*, 692
Agreement between Rubber Reserve Co. and Brazil for purchase of Brazilian rubber, signed *Mar. 3:*
Comparison of agreement with proposals made to Bolivia, 560, 562, 565, 566, 567
Negotiations for implementation of. *See specific subject entries, infra.*
Text, 692–693
Air transportation activities for rubber program, 719–720
Buying agent for Rubber Reserve Co., question of, 694–695
Distribution problems. *See* Manufactured products *and* Requirements, etc., *infra.*
Financial matters: Creation by Brazil of Banco de Credito da Borracha, 707; development fund of $5,000,000, 704–706; prices, determination of, 691–692, 693, 694, 697, 702–703, 703–704, 717–718; Reconstruction Finance Corporation credit for purchase of Brazilian rubber, 695–696
Manufactured products and internal consumption (*see also* Tires and tubes, *infra*), 697–702, 703–704; question of redistribution of purchases by United States, 707–714
Recruitment of laborers, agreement between Rubber Reserve Co. and Brazilian organization Semta, 727–729